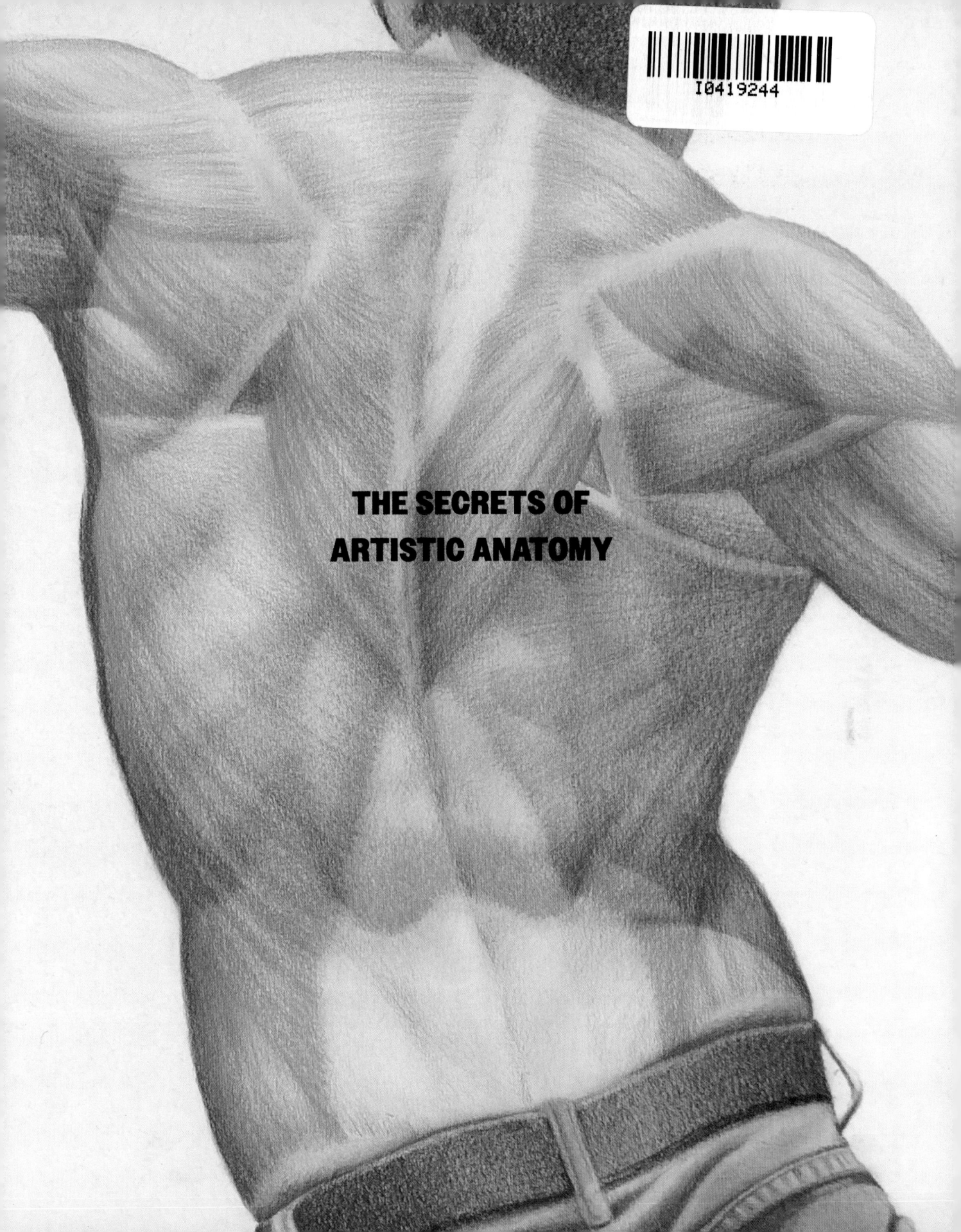

THE SECRETS OF
ARTISTIC ANATOMY

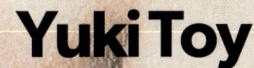

Yuki Toy

THE
SECRETS
of ARTISTIC
ANATOMY

Understanding
the Human Form

The Secrets of Artistic Anatomy:
Understanding the Human Form
Yuki Toy
yukitoy.com

Project editor: Jocelyn Howell
Project manager: Lisa Brazieal
Marketing manager: Koryn Olage
Copyeditor: Jocelyn Howell
Technical editor: Valerie L. Winslow
Interior design: John Calmeyer
Cover design: John Calmeyer
Cover illustration: Yuki Toy

ISBN: 979-8-88814-291-2

1st Edition (1st printing)
© 2026 Yuki Toy
All images © Yuki Toy

Rocky Nook Inc.
1010 B Street, Suite 350
San Rafael, CA 94901
USA
www.rockynook.com
info@rockynook.com
(415) 747-8756

Represented in the E.U. by:
Rheinwerk Verlag GmbH
Rheinwerkallee 4
53227 Bonn
Germany
service@rheinwerk-verlag.de

Distributed in the UK and Europe by Publishers Group UK

Distributed in the U.S. and all other territories by
Publishers Group West

Library of Congress Control Number: 2024952510

ACKNOWLEDGMENTS

I WOULD LIKE to thank Rocky Nook, especially Ted Waitt and Jocelyn Howell for making this book come to light. Special thanks also goes to two of my anatomy heroes: Valerie L. Winslow, who gave a second look on this book, and Rey Bustos, my friend who always oversaw this career path.

This book became a reflection of my love toward anatomical art, figure drawing, and education. I am wholeheartedly grateful for my family, Tim, Ryder, Rachel, and Pop Pop, who have been supporting my practice for many years.

—Yuki Toy

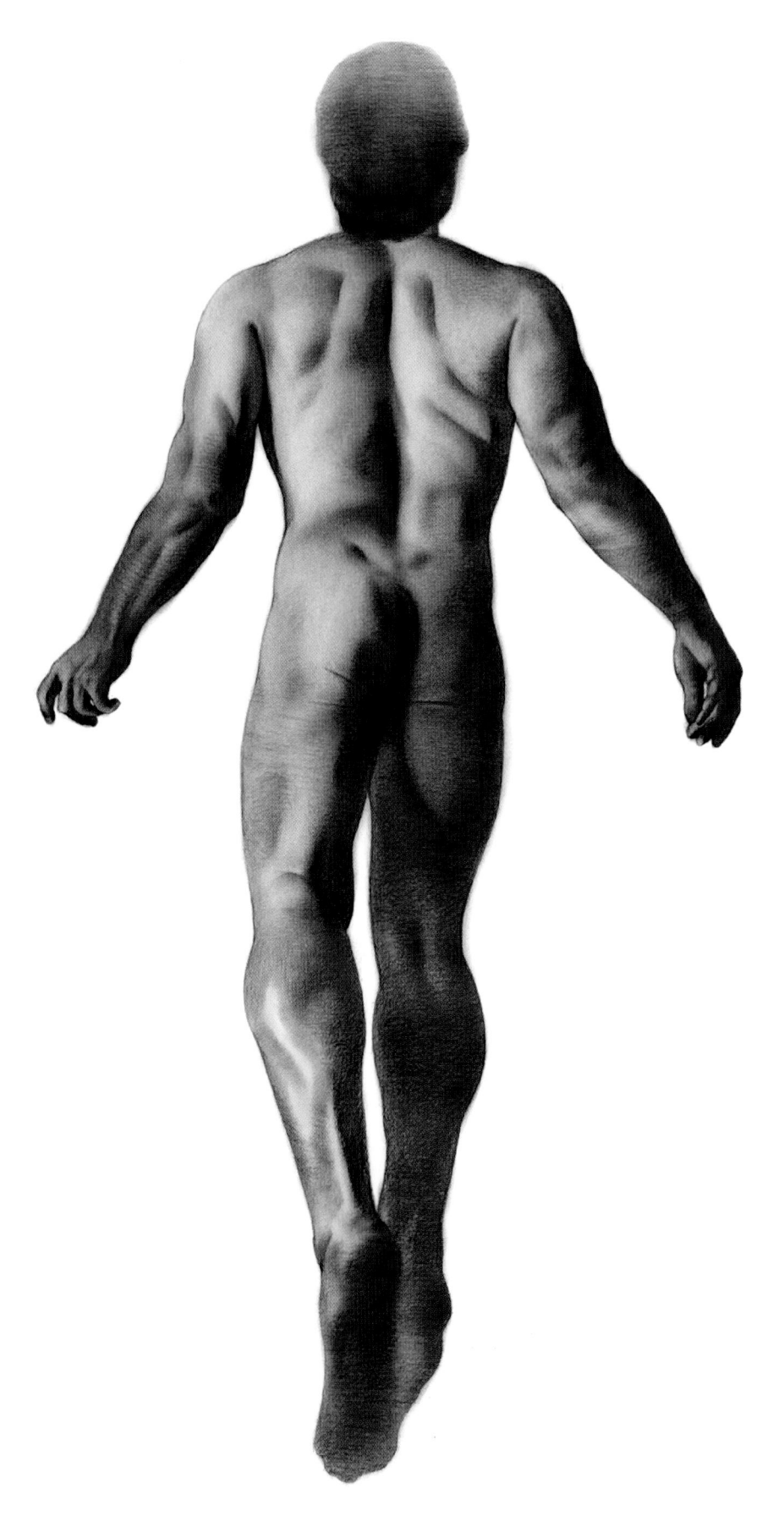

CONTENTS

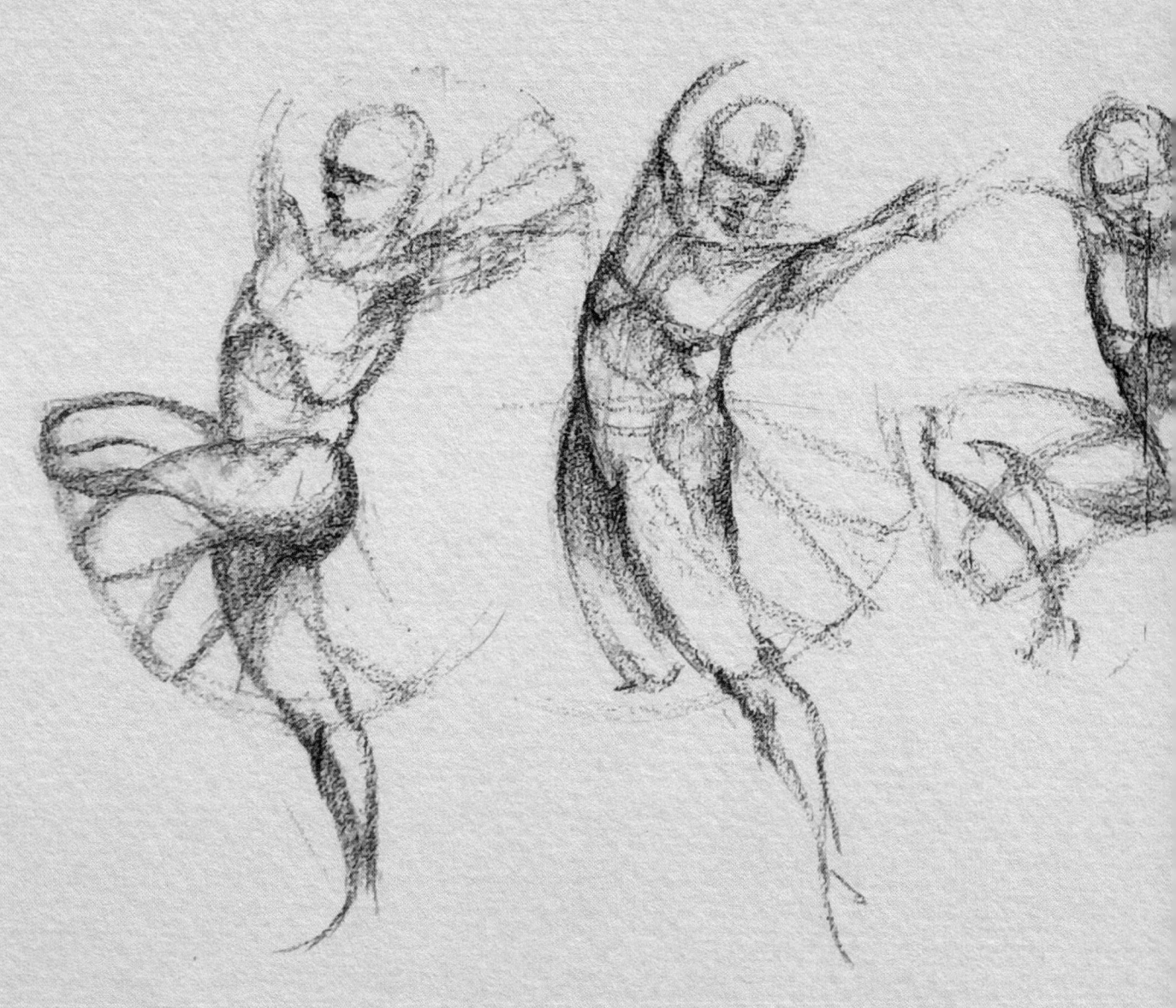

The Skeleton System & Gesture

Anatomical Terms You Should Be Familiar With

There are several anatomical terms that are frequently used when discussing human anatomy for artists. In artistic anatomy, these terms will be used to describe the directions, planes, and movements in the human body.

DIRECTIONAL TERMS

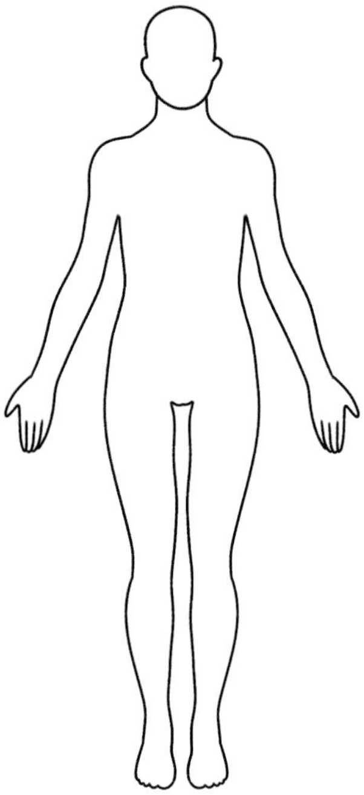

Anterior

Front, Ventral

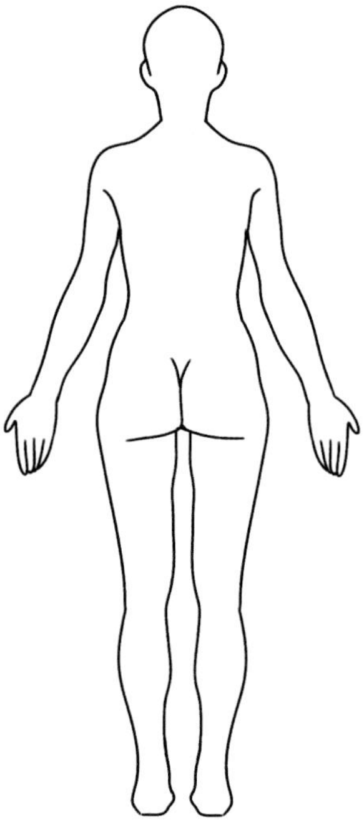

Posterior

Back, Dorsal

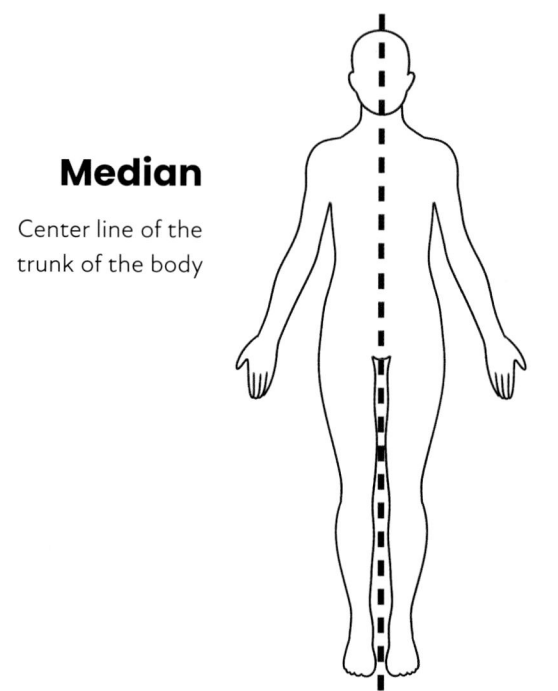

Median

Center line of the trunk of the body

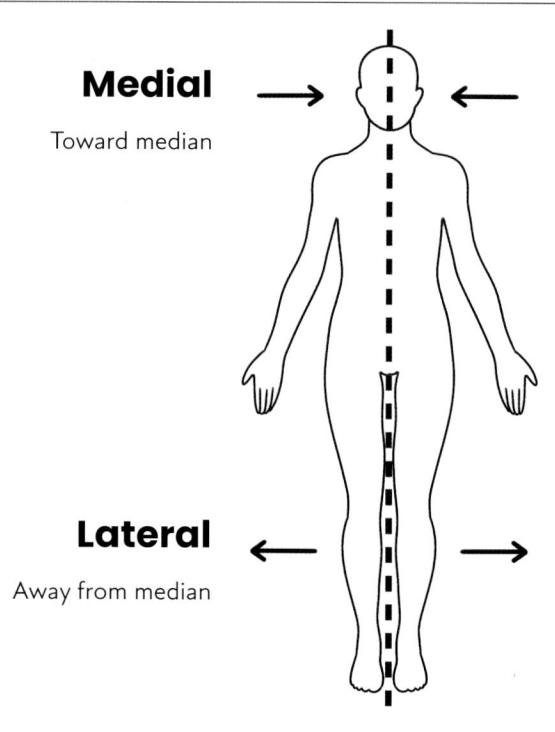

Medial

Toward median

Lateral

Away from median

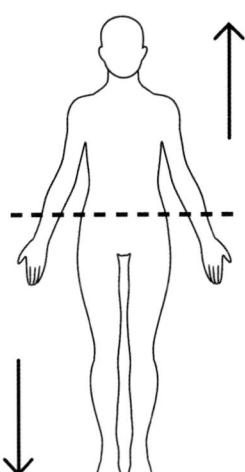

Superior
(Supra)
Upward, or toward the head

Inferior (Infra)
Below, or toward the feet

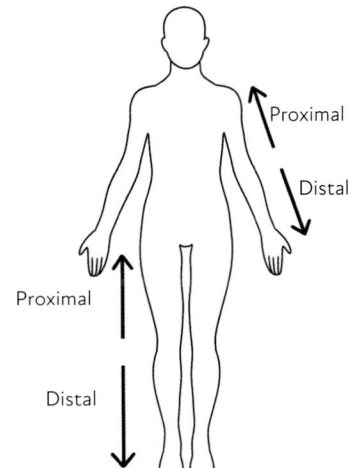

Proximal
Close to the trunk of the body, near the origin

Distal
Far away from the trunk of the body, far from the origin

External
(Superficial)
Surface of the body, or open to the external environment

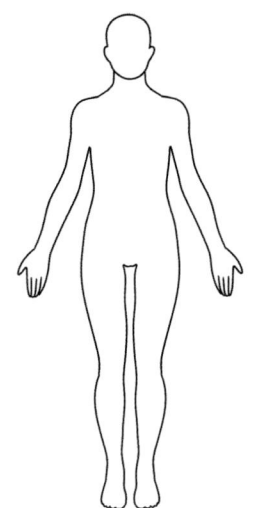

Internal
(Deep)
Away from the body surface, or not open to the external environment

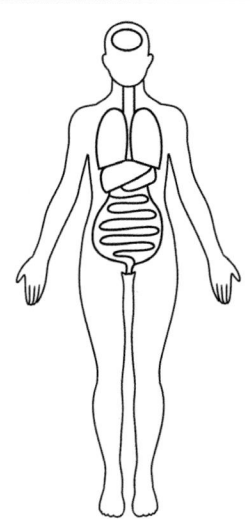

HAND

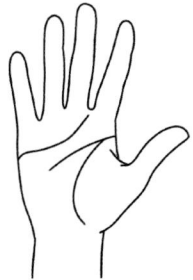 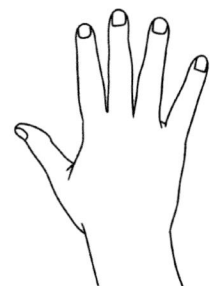

Palmar
Palm of hand

Dorsal
Back of hand

FOOT

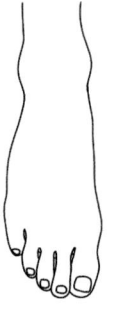 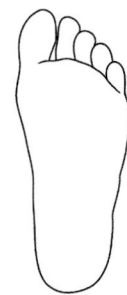

Dorsal
Top of foot

Plantar
Sole of foot

BODY PLANES

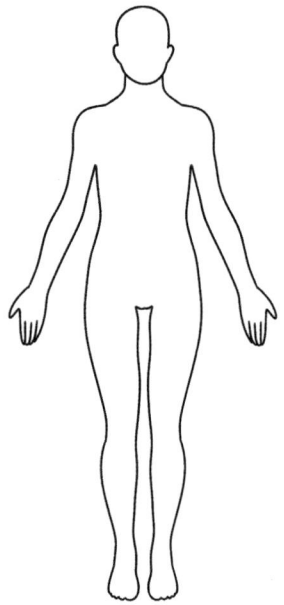

Anatomical Position

Body standing upright, legs parallel to each other, and head, torso, palm of hand, and toes facing forward

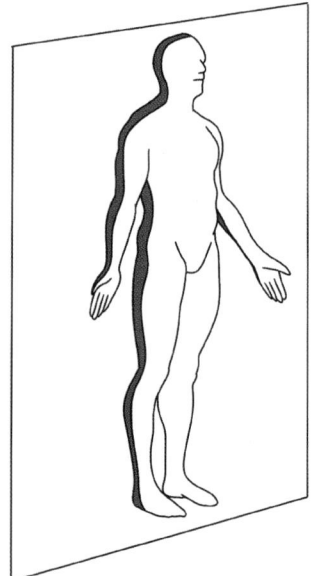

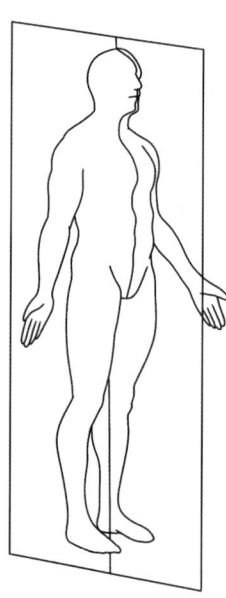

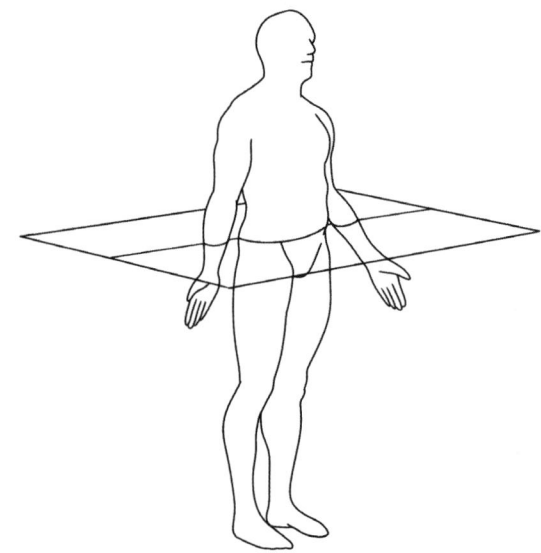

Coronal

Vertical plane that divides the body into anterior and posterior parts

Sagittal

Vertical plane that splits the body into right and left parts

Transverse

Horizontal plane that divides the body into superior and inferior parts

MOVEMENTS

Flexion

Decreasing the angle between two bones

Extension

Increasing the angle between two bones

Hyperextension

Extension movement beyond the anatomical position

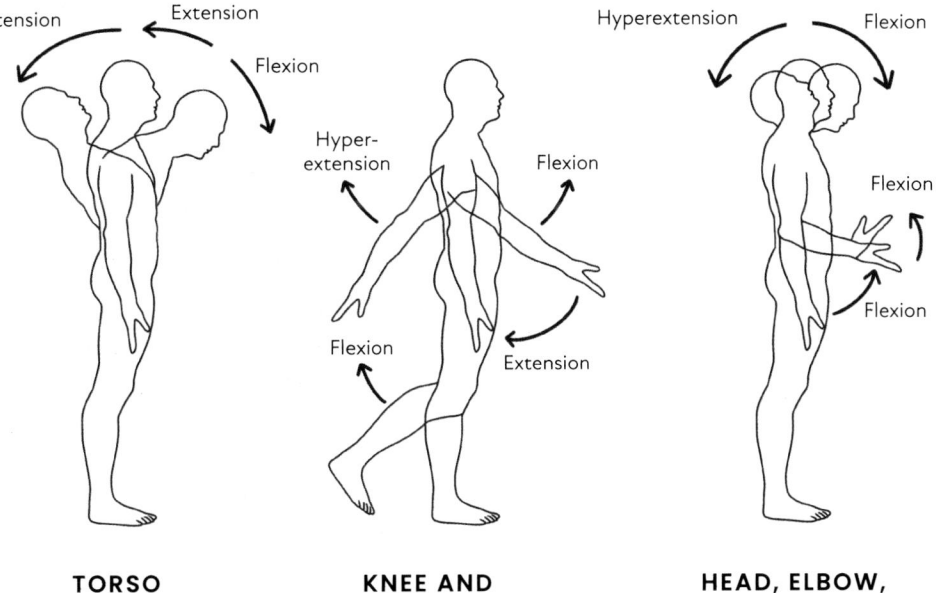

TORSO

KNEE AND SHOULDER

HEAD, ELBOW, WRIST

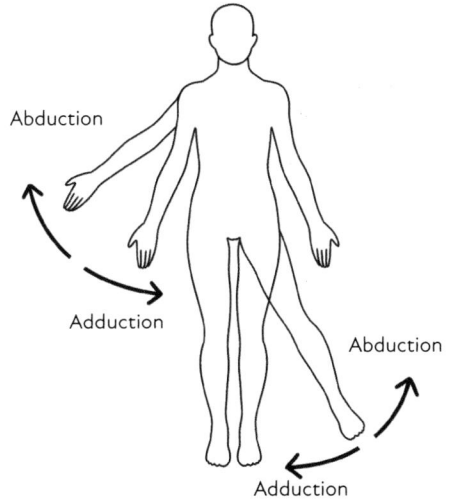

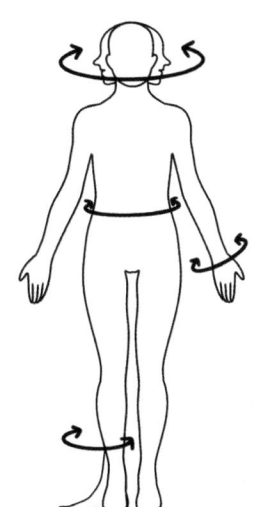

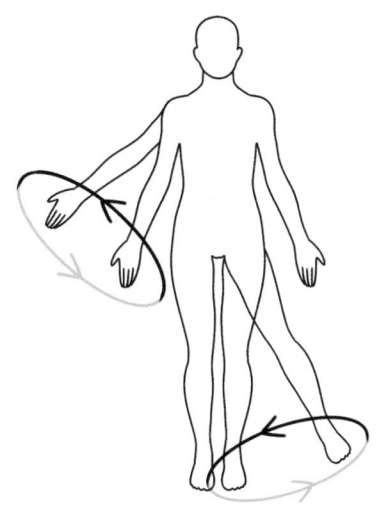

Abduction

Moving away from the median

Adduction

Moving toward the median

Lateral Rotation

Rotation away from the median

Medial Rotation

Rotation toward the median

Circumduction

Circular movement of body parts

MOVEMENTS

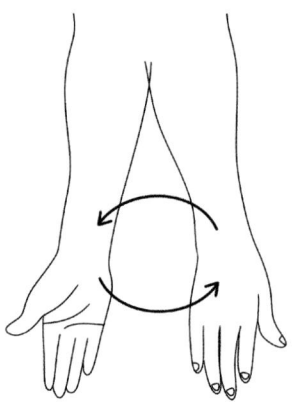

Supination

Palm facing up

Pronation

Palm facing down

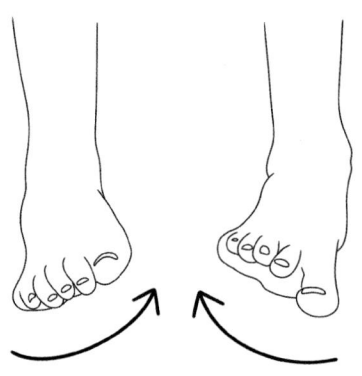

Inversion

Foot rolls inward toward the median

Eversion

Foot rolls outward

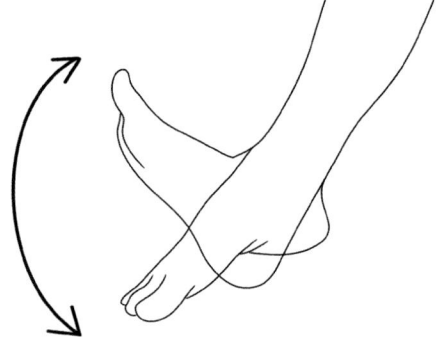

Dorsiflexion

Foot points upward toward the leg

Plantarflexion

Foot points downward

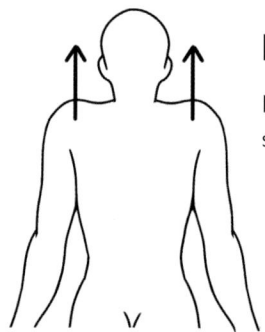

Elevation

Movement in superior direction

Retraction

Movement in posterior direction

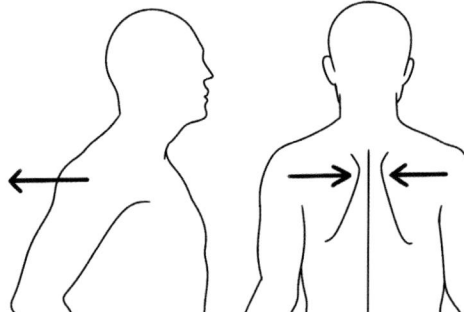

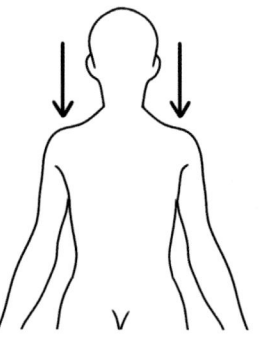

Depression

Movement in inferior direction

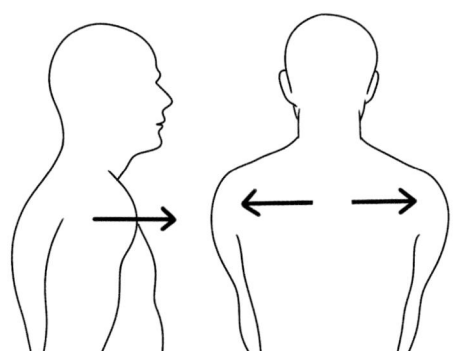

Protraction

Movement in anterior direction

Anatomical Terms You Should Be Familiar With

CONNECTIVE TISSUE (TYPES)

Here are some other anatomical terms for connective tissues and surface features of the bone.

TISSUE

Cartilage (3)
Flexible connective tissue

1. Hyaline Cartilage
2. Fibrocartilage
3. Elastic Cartilage

Ligament (3)
Fibrous connective tissue that connects bone to bone

1. Ligaments of Synovial Joint
2. Inguinal Ligament
3. Nuchal Ligament

Tendon
Fibrous connective tissue that connects bone to muscle

Aponeurosis
Flat sheet tendon

Fascia (2)
Thin, fibrous connective tissue

1. Deep Fascia
2. Superficial Fascia

SURFACE FEATURES OF BONES

Projection

Crest
Ridge that creates a border

Epicondyle
Round projection at the end of a long bone

Process
Projection in general

Spine
Sharp and thin projection

Trochanter
Large projection on femur

Tuberosity
Moderate prominence for the attachment of tendon and muscles

Tubercle
Small round projection

Joint

Condyle
Round projection

Facet
Smooth flat surface

Head
Round prominence at the end of a bone

Trochlea
Pulley-shaped structure

Concavity

Foramen
Opening

Fossa
Depression or hollow

206 Bones in Our Body

A human adult skeleton consists of 206 bones. That sounds crazy because the common skeletal system that we know does not look like it carries that much. There must be many small bones that are hidden, and they probably wouldn't have a visual effect on the surface anatomy. So, what are the most important bones to remember?

Here is the "table of contents" of the human skeleton:

And here are the bones in each section:

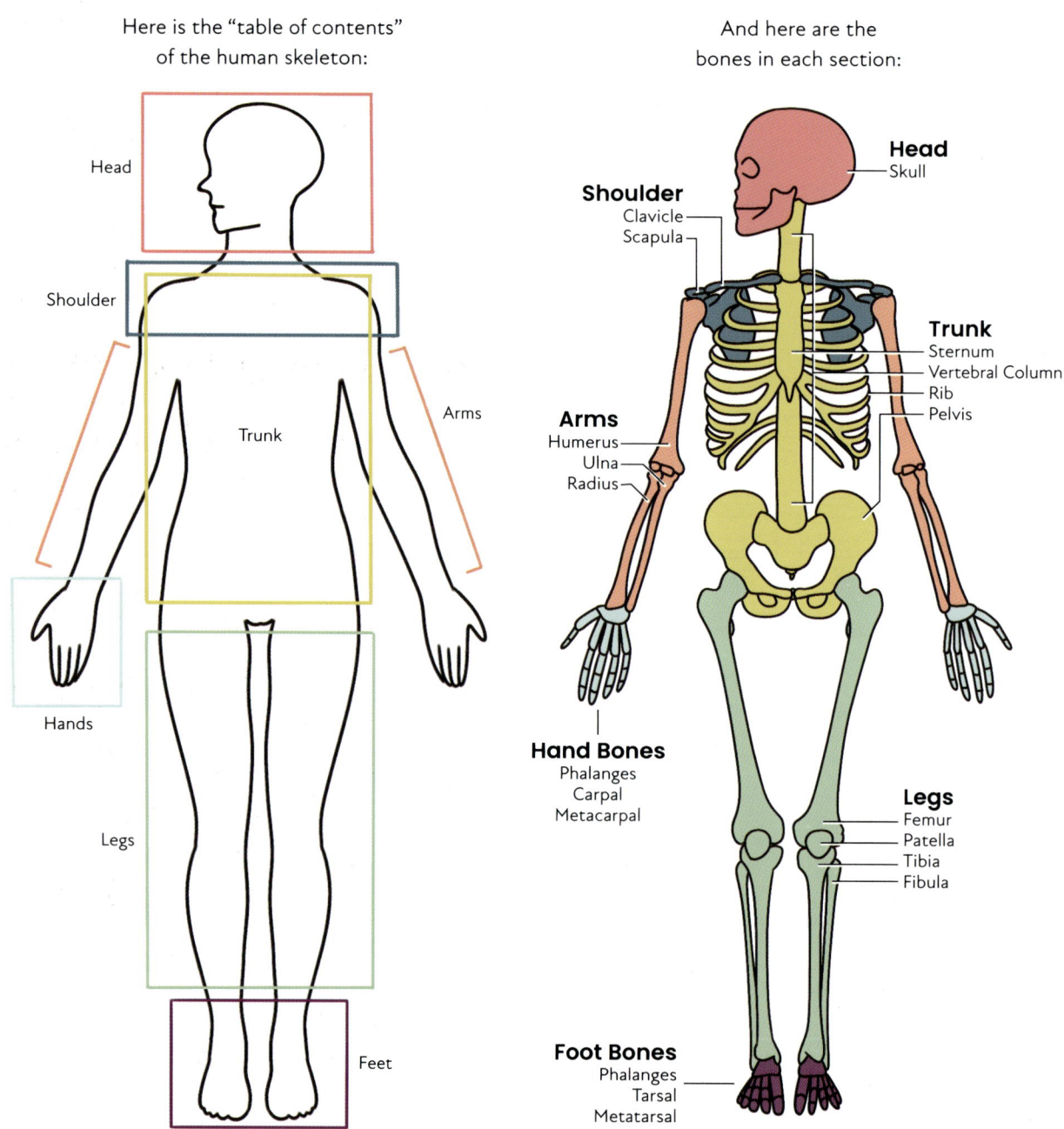

Head

Shoulder

Trunk

Arms

Hands

Legs

Feet

Head
Skull

Shoulder
Clavicle
Scapula

Trunk
Sternum
Vertebral Column
Rib
Pelvis

Arms
Humerus
Ulna
Radius

Hand Bones
Phalanges
Carpal
Metacarpal

Legs
Femur
Patella
Tibia
Fibula

Foot Bones
Phalanges
Tarsal
Metatarsal

This still does not show the math for the total count of the bones. Let's count the bones and take a look at the details of each.

HEAD

Skull

Bone Count: 29

The skull is divided into two major parts, the **Cranium** (head) and the **Mandible** (jaw bone), and the whole is composed of twenty-two major bones. There are some small internal bones in the ear called the Malleus (2), Incus (2), and Stapes (2). There is also a U-shaped bone on the front of the neck called the Hyoid bone (1), which is articulated with muscles and ligaments.

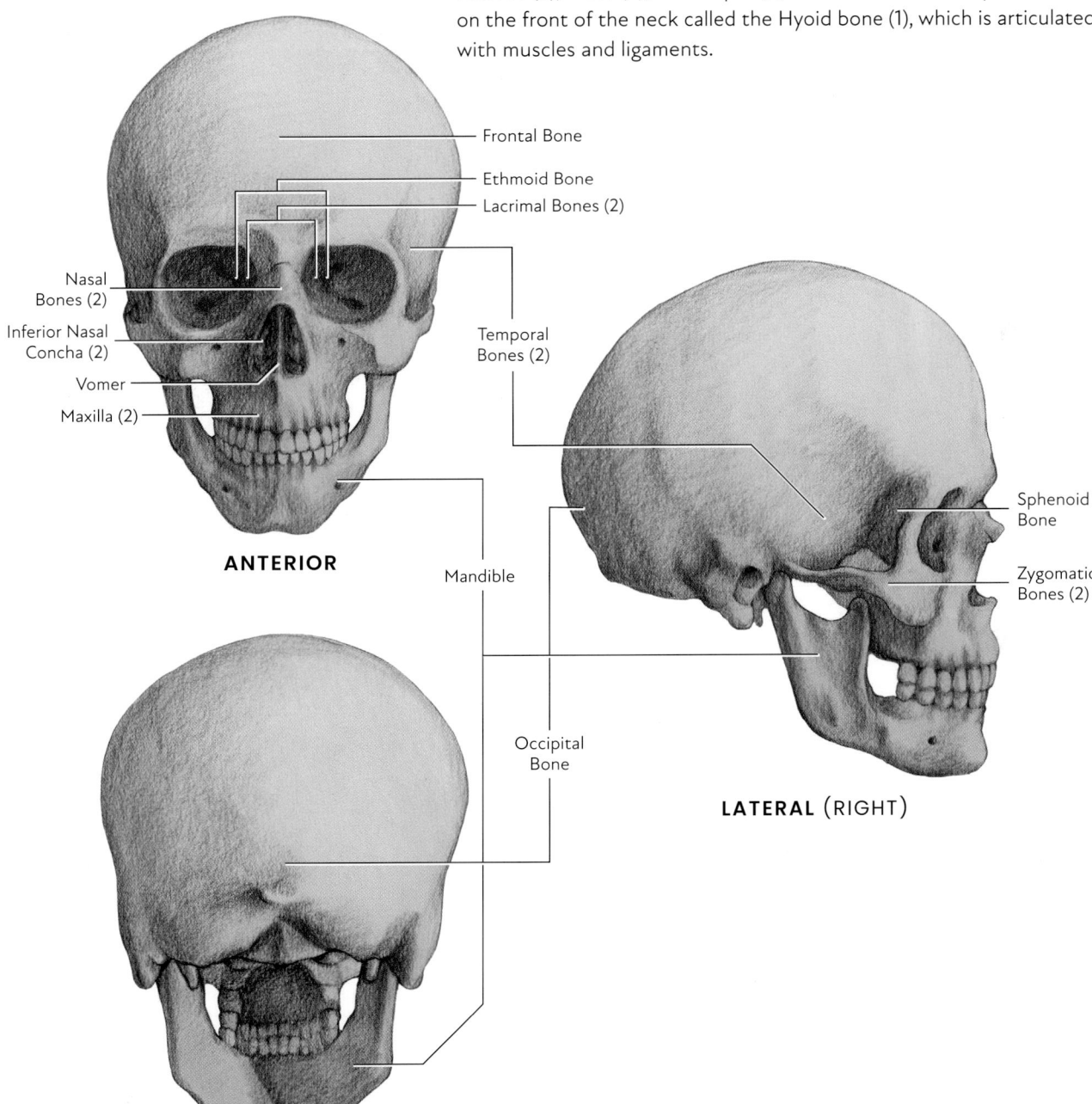

Frontal Bone

Ethmoid Bone

Lacrimal Bones (2)

Nasal Bones (2)

Inferior Nasal Concha (2)

Vomer

Maxilla (2)

Temporal Bones (2)

ANTERIOR

Mandible

Sphenoid Bone

Zygomatic Bones (2)

LATERAL (RIGHT)

Occipital Bone

POSTERIOR

Skull *(cont.)*

Parietal
Bones (2)

P

A

Palatine
Bones (2)

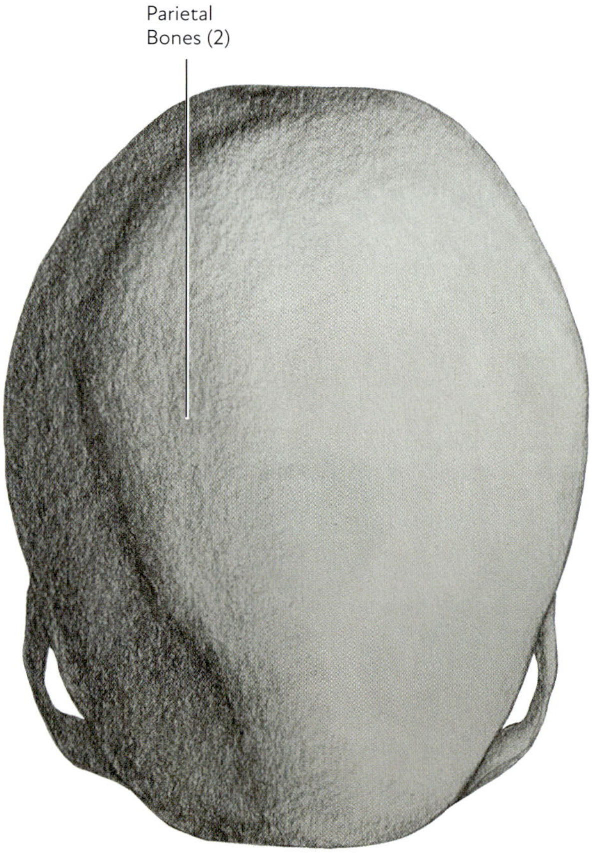

SUPERIOR

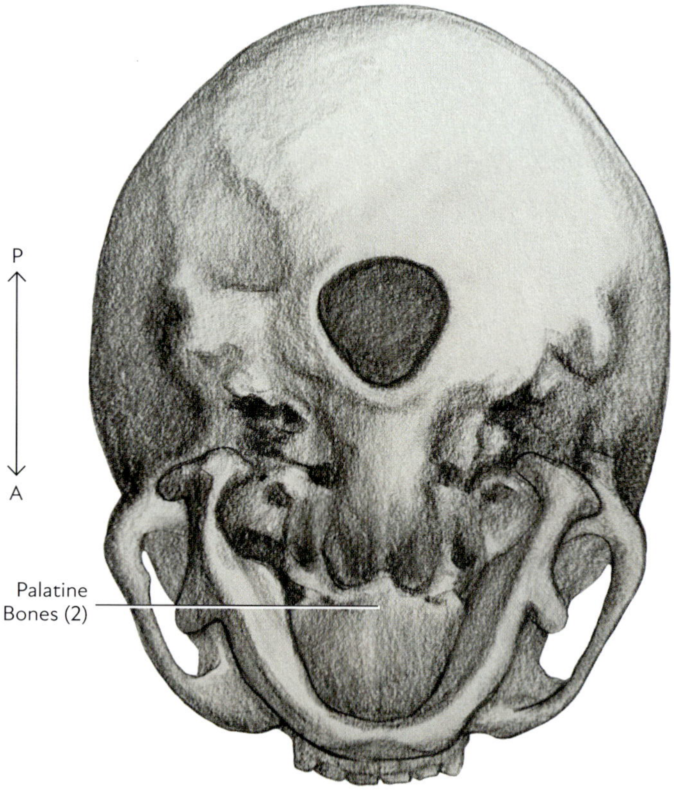

INFERIOR

Teeth

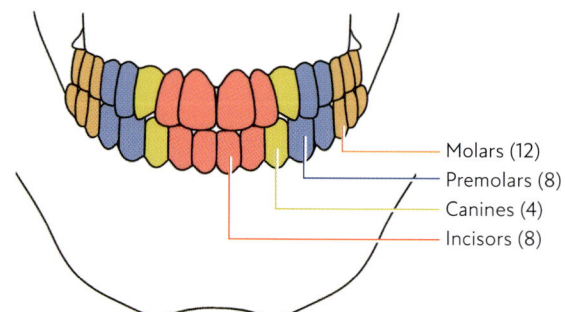

Molars (12)
Premolars (8)
Canines (4)
Incisors (8)

Adult humans have thirty-two teeth, but these are actually not bones. Teeth are composed of a hard tissue called Enamel. This includes the wisdom teeth. If the rear four molars—two on top and two on bottom—bothered you, you may have had these teeth removed.

Rib Cage and Sternum

Bone Count: Rib Cage: 24, Sternum: 1

We have twelve rib bodies on each side of the **Rib Cage**. They are connected to the necktie-shaped frontal bone called the **Sternum**. The Rib Cage is also connected to a part of the spine called the Thoracic Vertebrae.

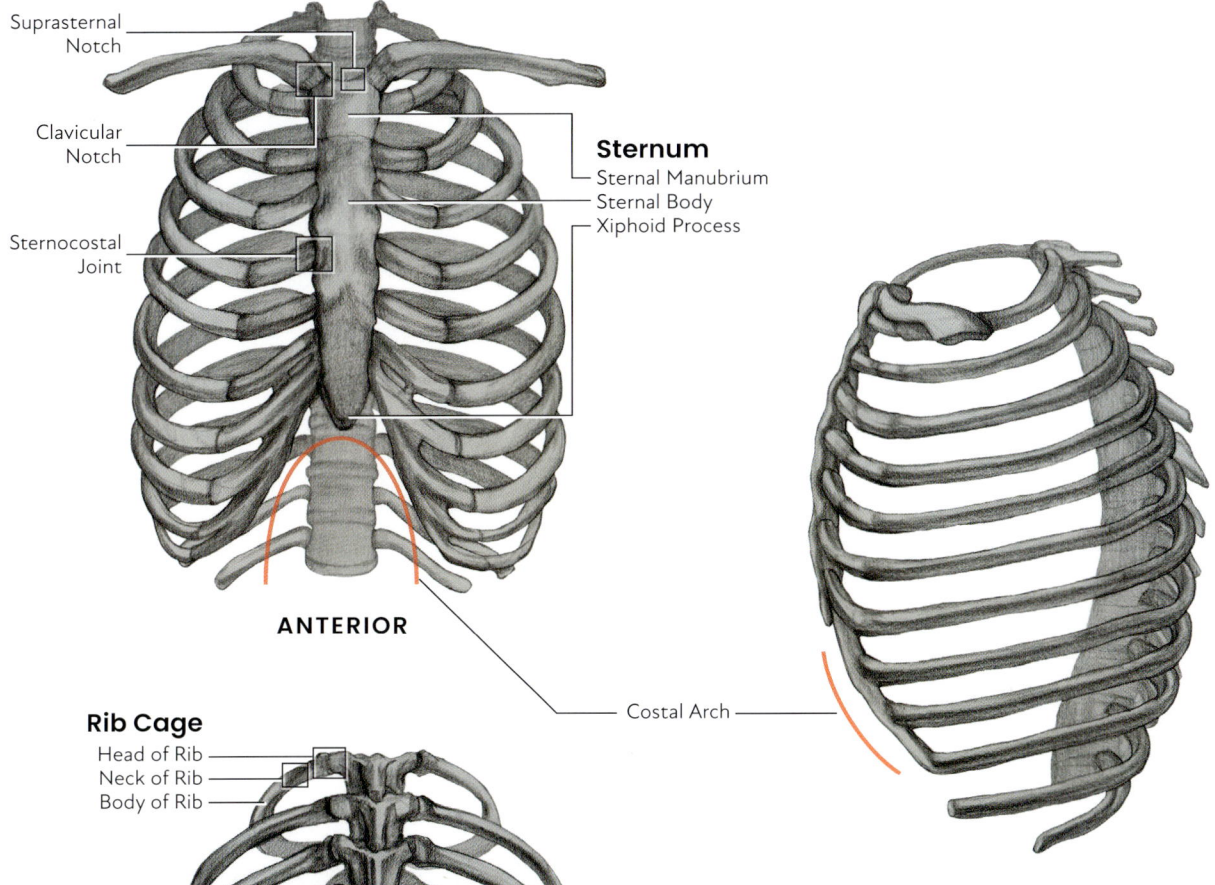

Suprasternal Notch

Clavicular Notch

Sternocostal Joint

Sternum
Sternal Manubrium
Sternal Body
Xiphoid Process

ANTERIOR

Costal Arch

Rib Cage
Head of Rib
Neck of Rib
Body of Rib

POSTERIOR

LATERAL

There are two terms used to differentiate the two groups of rib bodies: True Ribs and False Ribs. The True Ribs are the top seven ribs that are attached to the Sternum. The False Ribs are the lower five ribs, with the eighth rib being the widest from both a front and rear view, and the eleventh and twelfth floating.

The Rib Cage is full of secrets. The angle of the rib bodies and the specific flow of the entire shape are important in artistic anatomy. Paying attention to these forms and getting them right will help you achieve realism in your figure drawing.

Vertebral Column

Bone Count: 26

The **Vertebral Column** is an S-curved back spine that supports the posterior torso in our body. There are seven bones in the neck called the **Cervical**, twelve connected to the ribs called the **Thoracic**, and five large bones that form the lower back called the **Lumbar**.

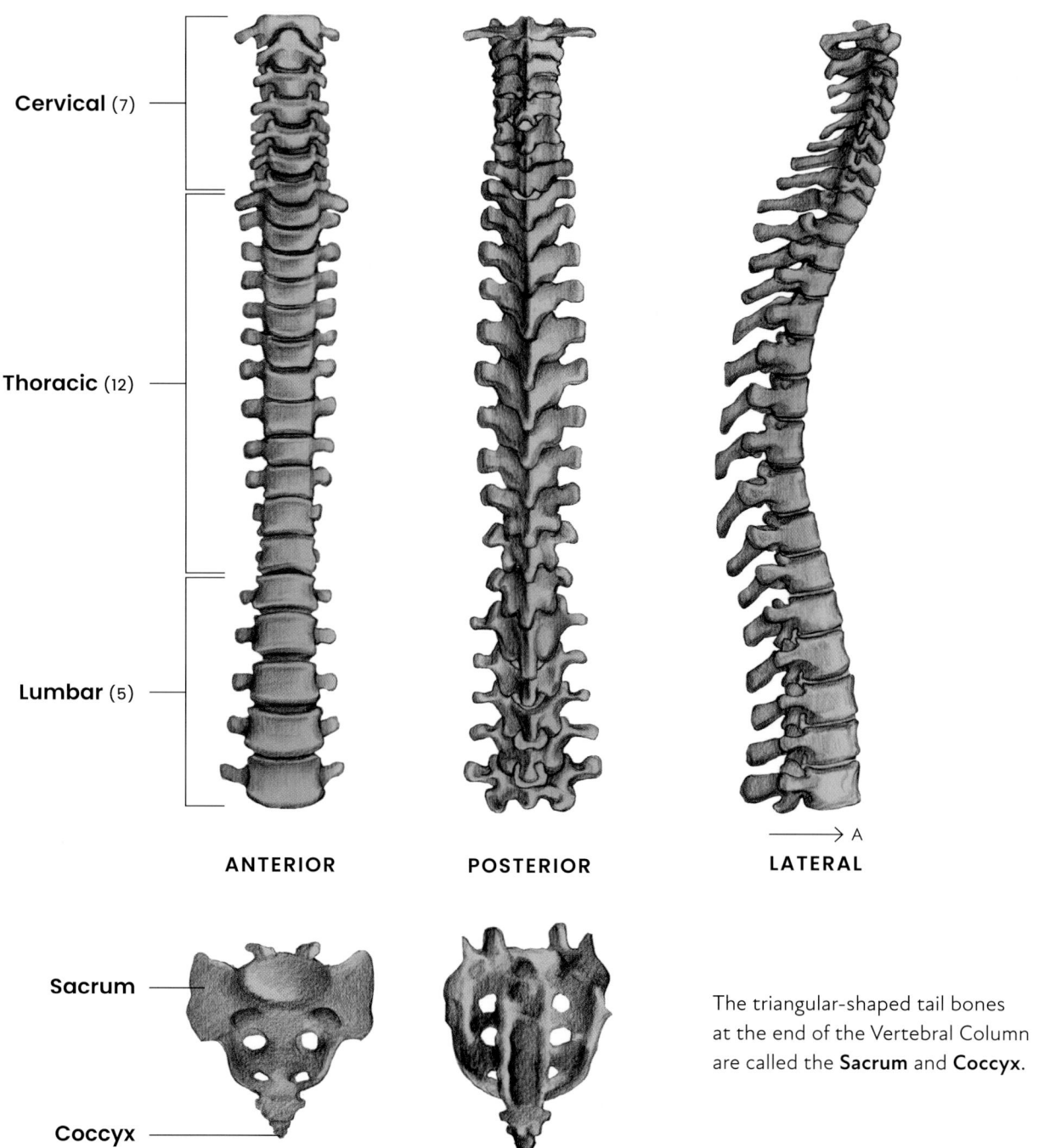

Cervical (7)

Thoracic (12)

Lumbar (5)

ANTERIOR

POSTERIOR

→ A

LATERAL

Sacrum

Coccyx

The triangular-shaped tail bones at the end of the Vertebral Column are called the **Sacrum** and **Coccyx**.

Pelvis

Bone Count: 2

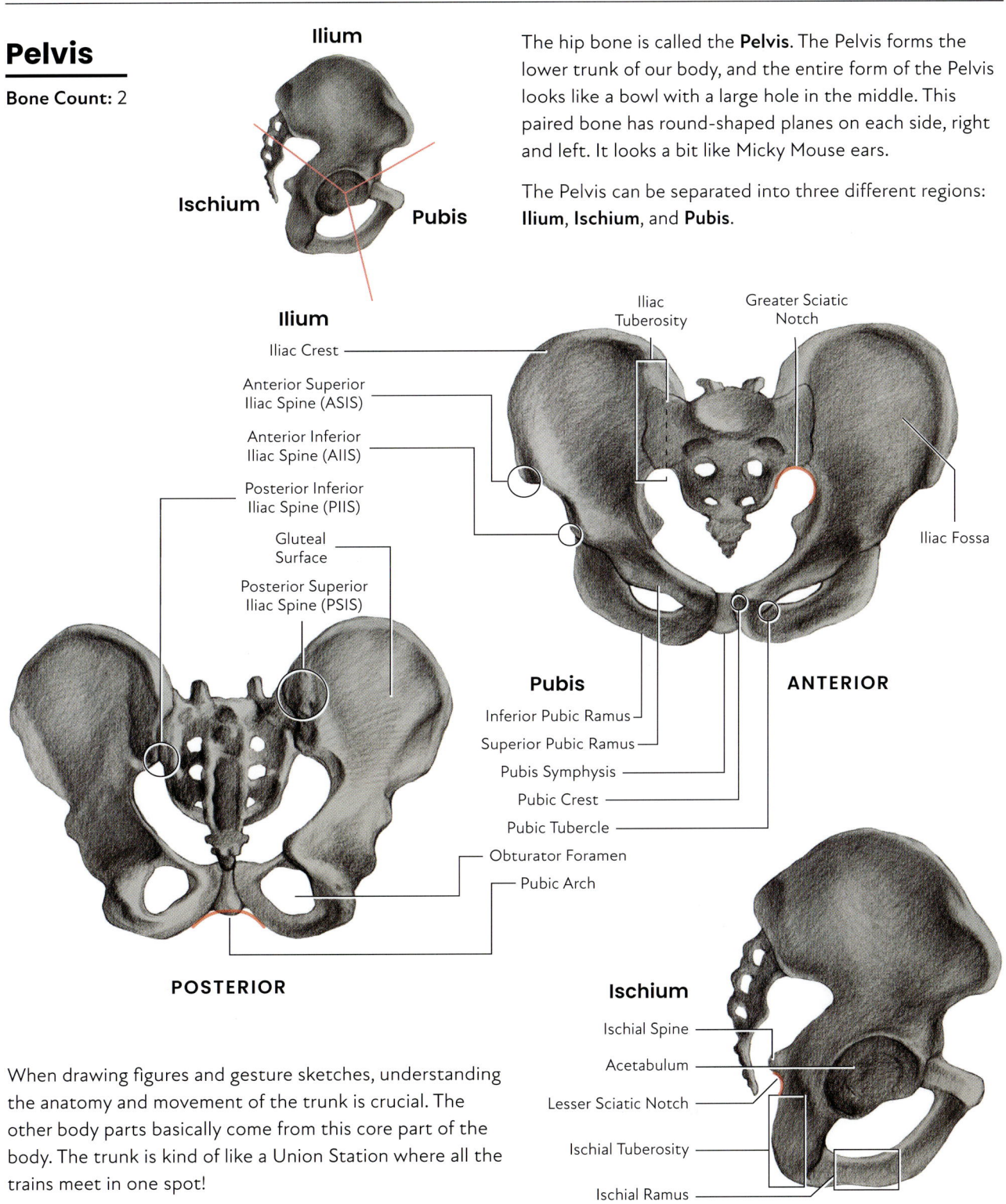

Ilium

Ischium

Pubis

The hip bone is called the **Pelvis**. The Pelvis forms the lower trunk of our body, and the entire form of the Pelvis looks like a bowl with a large hole in the middle. This paired bone has round-shaped planes on each side, right and left. It looks a bit like Micky Mouse ears.

The Pelvis can be separated into three different regions: **Ilium**, **Ischium**, and **Pubis**.

Ilium

Iliac Crest

Anterior Superior
Iliac Spine (ASIS)

Anterior Inferior
Iliac Spine (AIIS)

Posterior Inferior
Iliac Spine (PIIS)

Gluteal
Surface

Posterior Superior
Iliac Spine (PSIS)

Iliac
Tuberosity

Greater Sciatic
Notch

Iliac Fossa

ANTERIOR

Pubis

Inferior Pubic Ramus

Superior Pubic Ramus

Pubis Symphysis

Pubic Crest

Pubic Tubercle

Obturator Foramen

Pubic Arch

POSTERIOR

When drawing figures and gesture sketches, understanding the anatomy and movement of the trunk is crucial. The other body parts basically come from this core part of the body. The trunk is kind of like a Union Station where all the trains meet in one spot!

Ischium

Ischial Spine

Acetabulum

Lesser Sciatic Notch

Ischial Tuberosity

Ischial Ramus

LATERAL

Scapula

Bone Count: 2

The **Scapula**, of which we have two, is the shoulder blade located in the back of the Rib Cage. It has a unique triangular or diamond-like shape with a large spine that lays horizontally on the posterior side. The Scapula lays in between the third and eighth rib bodies.

Pay attention to the form of the **spine of the scapula** and the end of the spine called the **Acromion Process**. These are the key landmarks that many muscles and tendons go around.

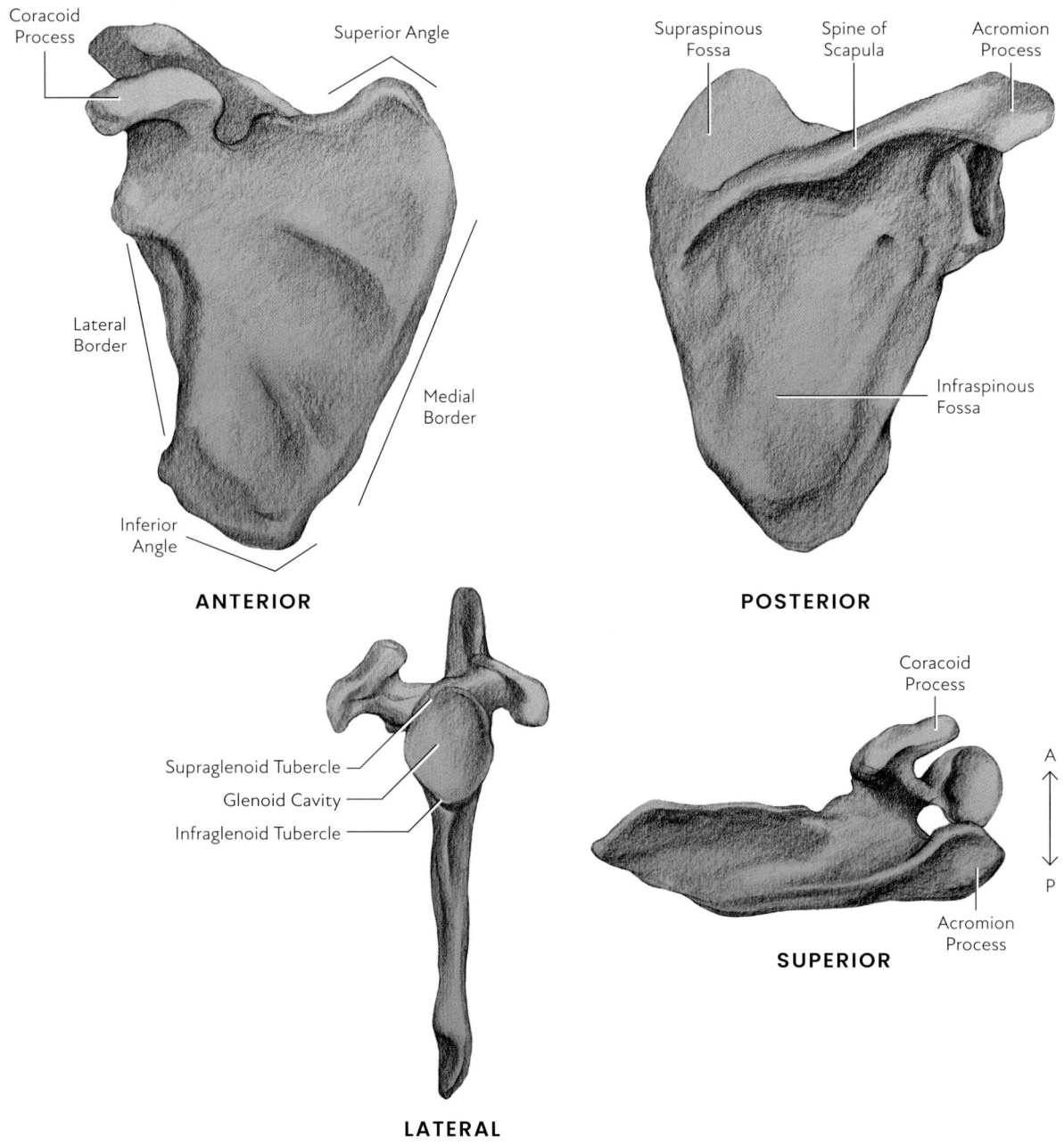

ANTERIOR

POSTERIOR

LATERAL

SUPERIOR

SHOULDER

Clavicle

Bone Count: 2

The **Clavicle** is another bone that is an important landmark on the lower neck. It is also known as the collarbone. There is no muscle or fat directly covering this bone, so you can feel the firmness of it with your fingers.

ANTERIOR

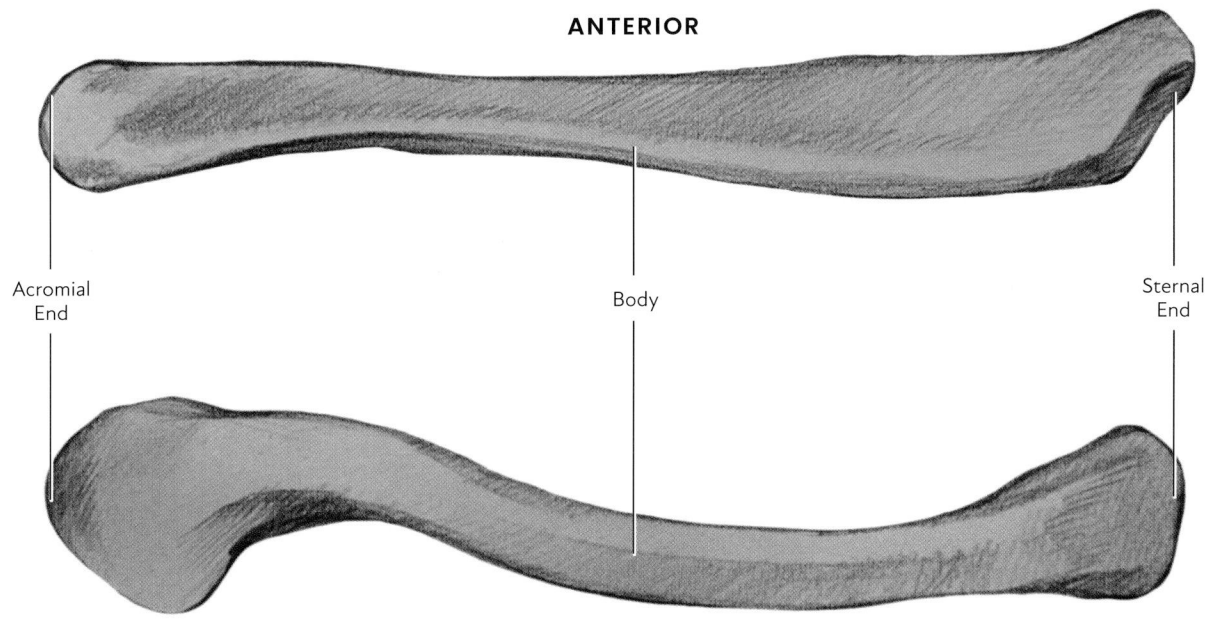

Acromial
End

Body

Sternal
End

SUPERIOR

ARMS

Humerus

Bone Count: 2

The **Humerus** is the bone in the upper arm. The superior head of the Humerus is attached to the Scapula, and this ball-and-socket joint allows you to move your shoulder in a smooth circular motion (circumduction).

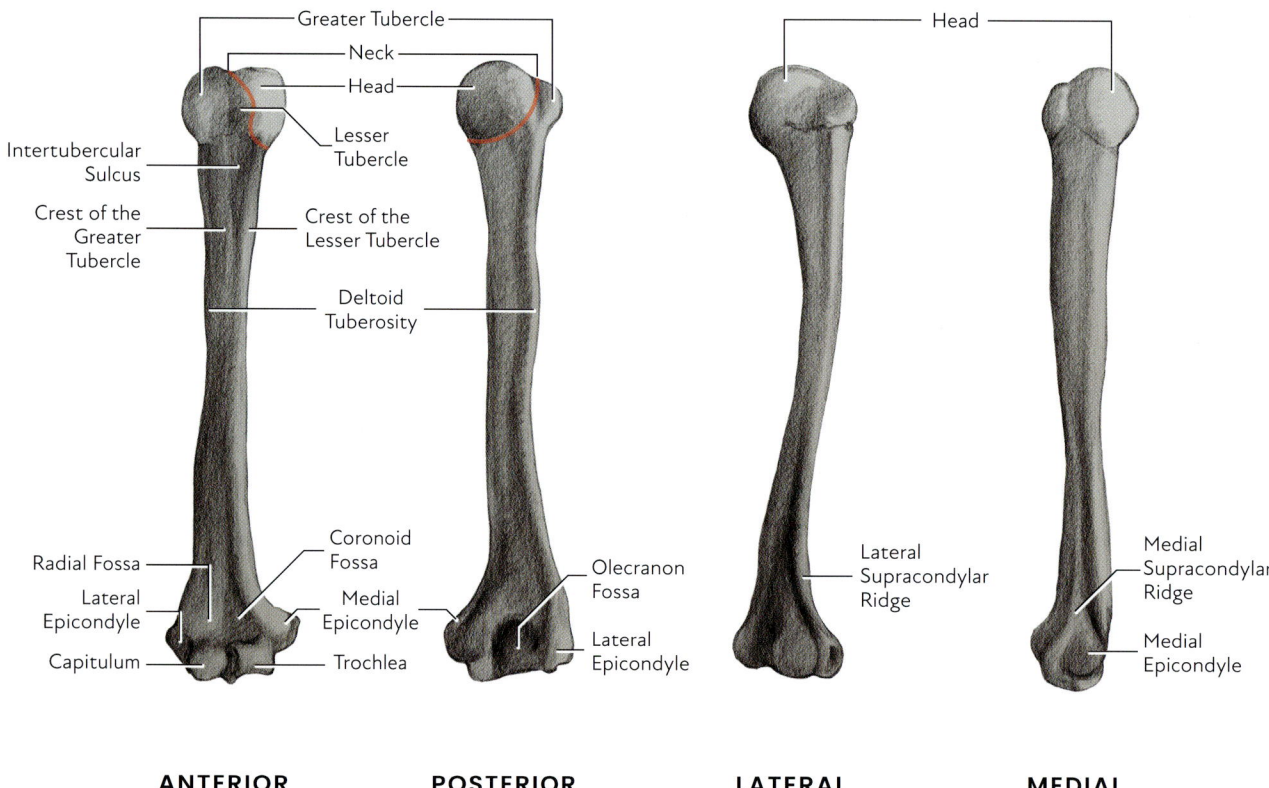

ANTERIOR　　　**POSTERIOR**　　　**LATERAL**　　　**MEDIAL**

ARMS

Radius and Ulna

Bone Count: Radius: 2, Ulna: 2

The **Radius** and **Ulna** are the two bones that are next to each other in the forearm. The superior portion of these bones is connected to the inferior end of the Humerus, which makes the flexion movement possible.

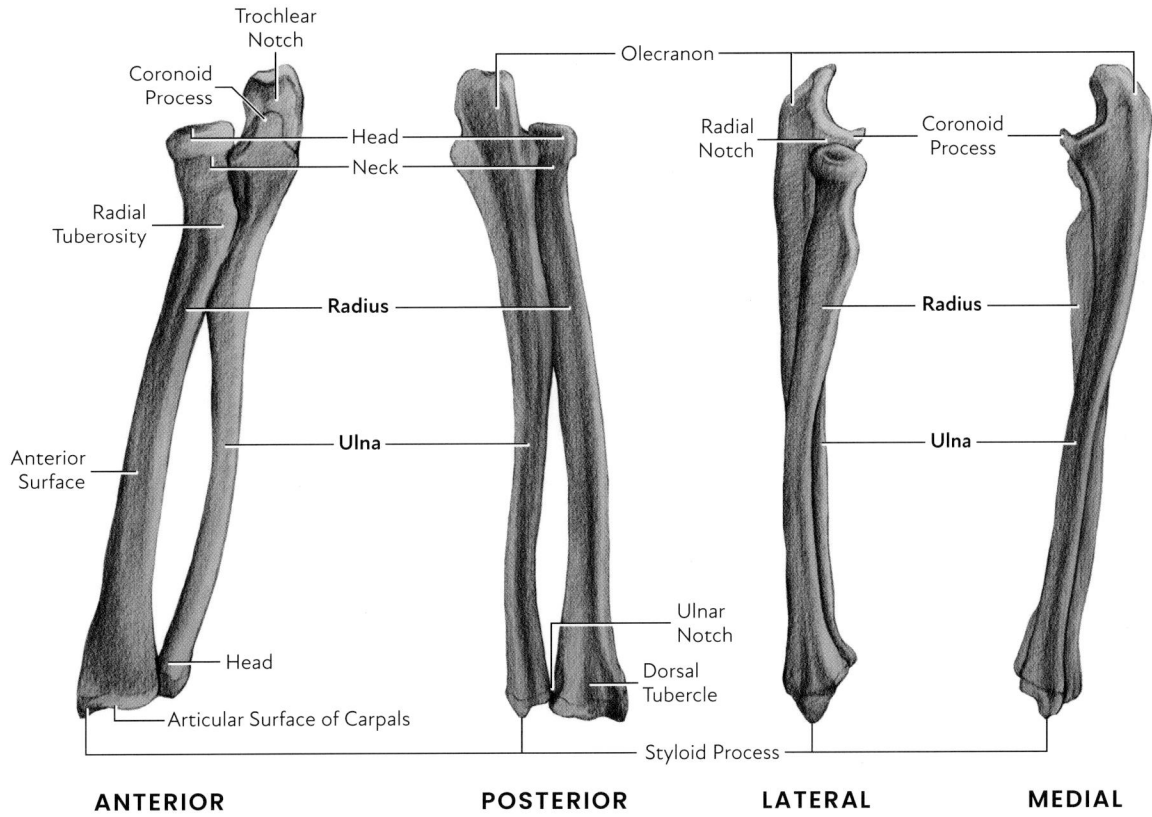

Trochlear Notch

Coronoid Process

Head

Neck

Radial Tuberosity

Radius

Ulna

Anterior Surface

Head

Articular Surface of Carpals

Olecranon

Radial Notch

Coronoid Process

Radius

Ulna

Ulnar Notch

Dorsal Tubercle

Styloid Process

ANTERIOR **POSTERIOR** **LATERAL** **MEDIAL**

HANDS

Hands

Bone Count: 54 (27 each)

The hand bones are broken up into three parts: the **Phalanges** (14) form the fingers, the **Metacarpals** (5) are under each finger, and the **Carpals** (8) are the irregular small rock-like bones in the wrist.

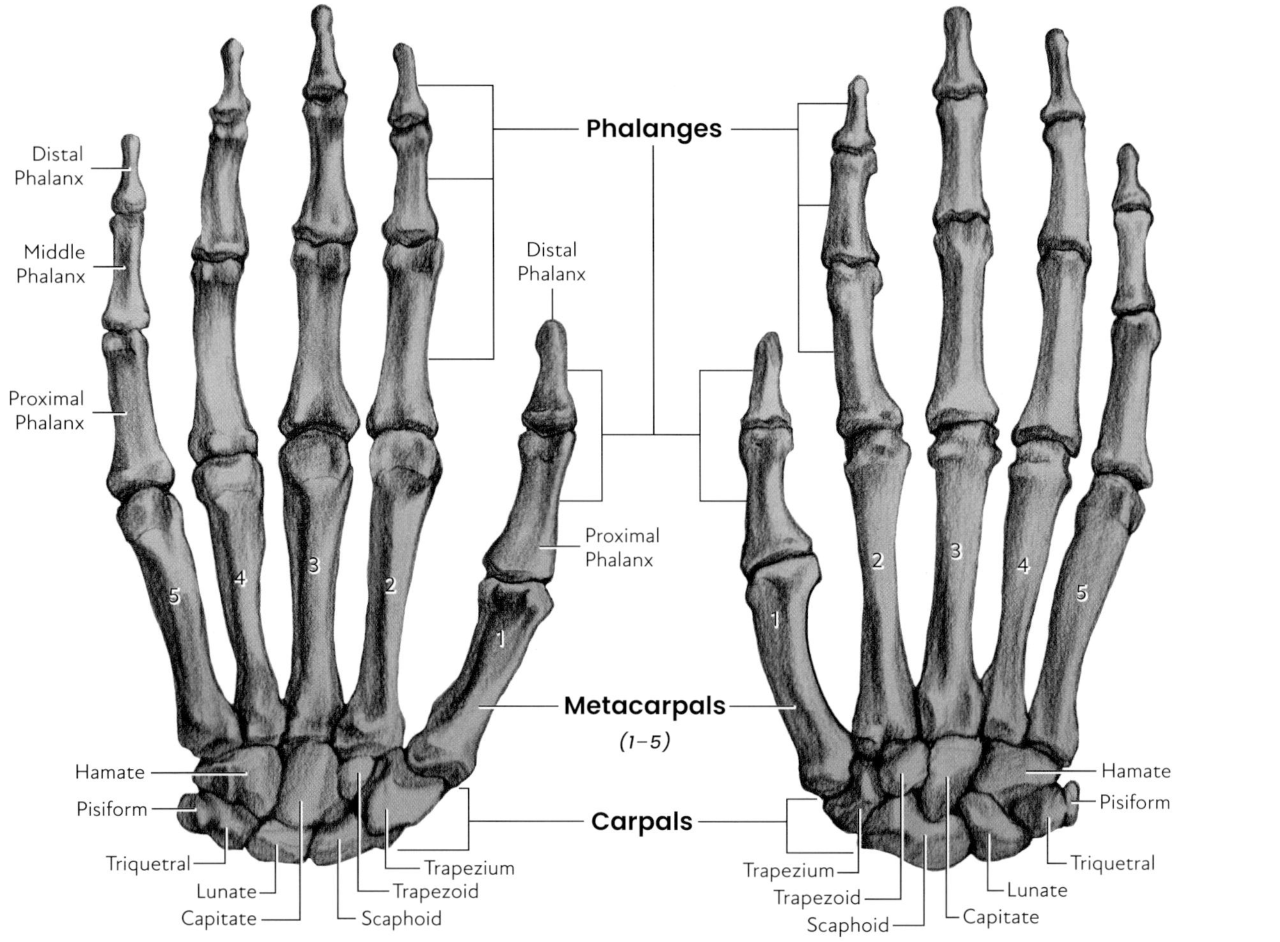

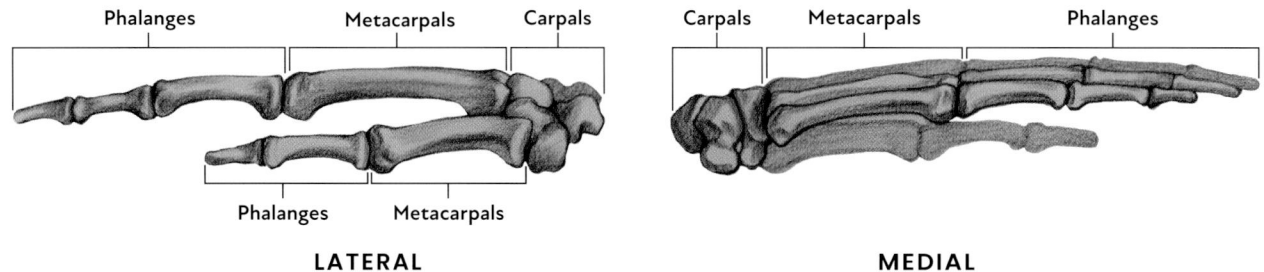

Distal Phalanx

Middle Phalanx

Proximal Phalanx

Phalanges

Distal Phalanx

Proximal Phalanx

5 4 3 2 1

Metacarpals
(1–5)

Hamate
Pisiform
Triquetral
Lunate
Capitate
Trapezium
Trapezoid
Scaphoid

Carpals

PALMAR

Phalanges

1 2 3 4 5

Metacarpals

Trapezium
Trapezoid
Scaphoid
Capitate
Lunate
Hamate
Pisiform
Triquetral

Carpals

DORSAL

Phalanges Metacarpals Carpals

Phalanges Metacarpals

LATERAL

Carpals Metacarpals Phalanges

MEDIAL

LEGS

Femur

Bone Count: 2

The **Femur** is the biggest bone in our body and it is located in the upper leg. The head of the Femur has a ball shape and it goes to the lateral side of the Pelvis as a ball-and-socket joint. You can move your thigh around 360 degrees in the circumduction movement, just like the upper arm.

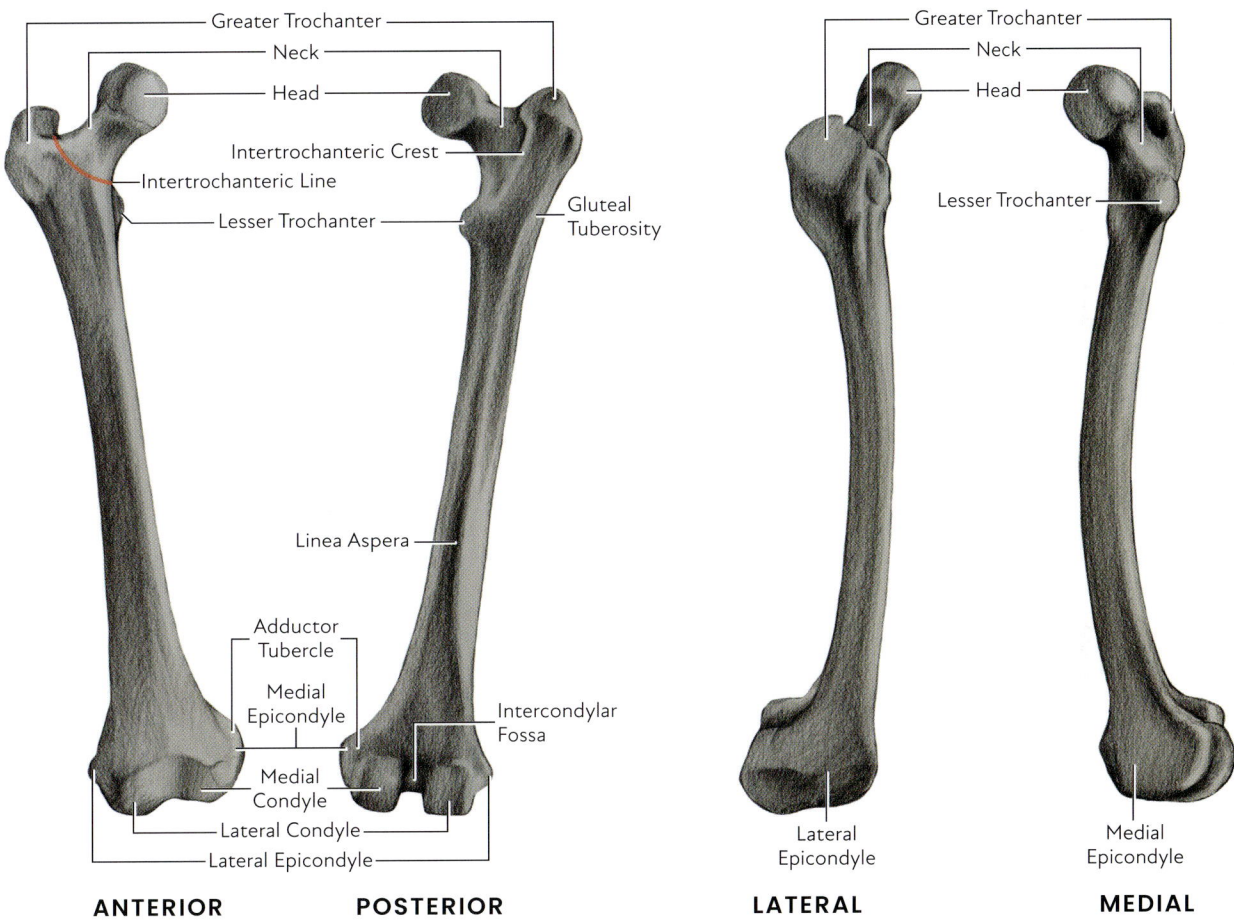

Greater Trochanter
Neck
Head
Intertrochanteric Crest
Intertrochanteric Line
Lesser Trochanter
Gluteal Tuberosity
Linea Aspera
Adductor Tubercle
Medial Epicondyle
Intercondylar Fossa
Medial Condyle
Lateral Condyle
Lateral Epicondyle

Greater Trochanter
Neck
Head
Lesser Trochanter

Lateral Epicondyle

Medial Epicondyle

ANTERIOR   **POSTERIOR**   **LATERAL**   **MEDIAL**

LEGS

Tibia and Fibula

Bone Count: Tibia: 2, Fibula 2

The skeleton of the leg is very similar to that of the arm: one bone in the upper leg and two in the lower leg. The two in the lower leg are called the **Tibia** and **Fibula**. The Tibia, the shin bone, is located on the medial side, and the Fibula is on the lateral side. Notice that the Fibula is slightly lower than the Tibia. This is the reason your ankle has a slanted angle.

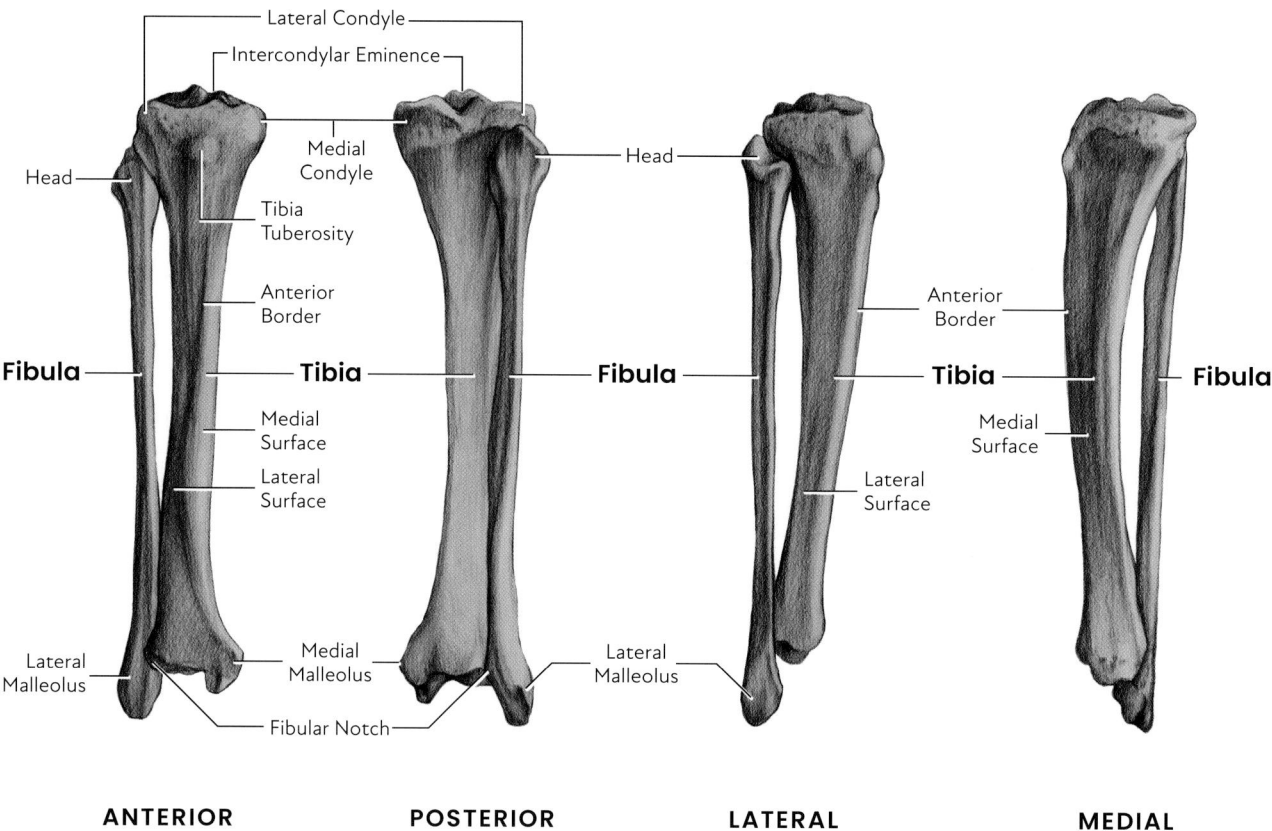

ANTERIOR   POSTERIOR   LATERAL   MEDIAL

Patella

Bone Count: 2

The knee pad bone is called the **Patella**. It is a small plate-like bone. The bottom line of the Patella lies on the anterior side of the bottom border of the Femur. The Patella is strapped with tendons and ligaments and it protects our knee joints.

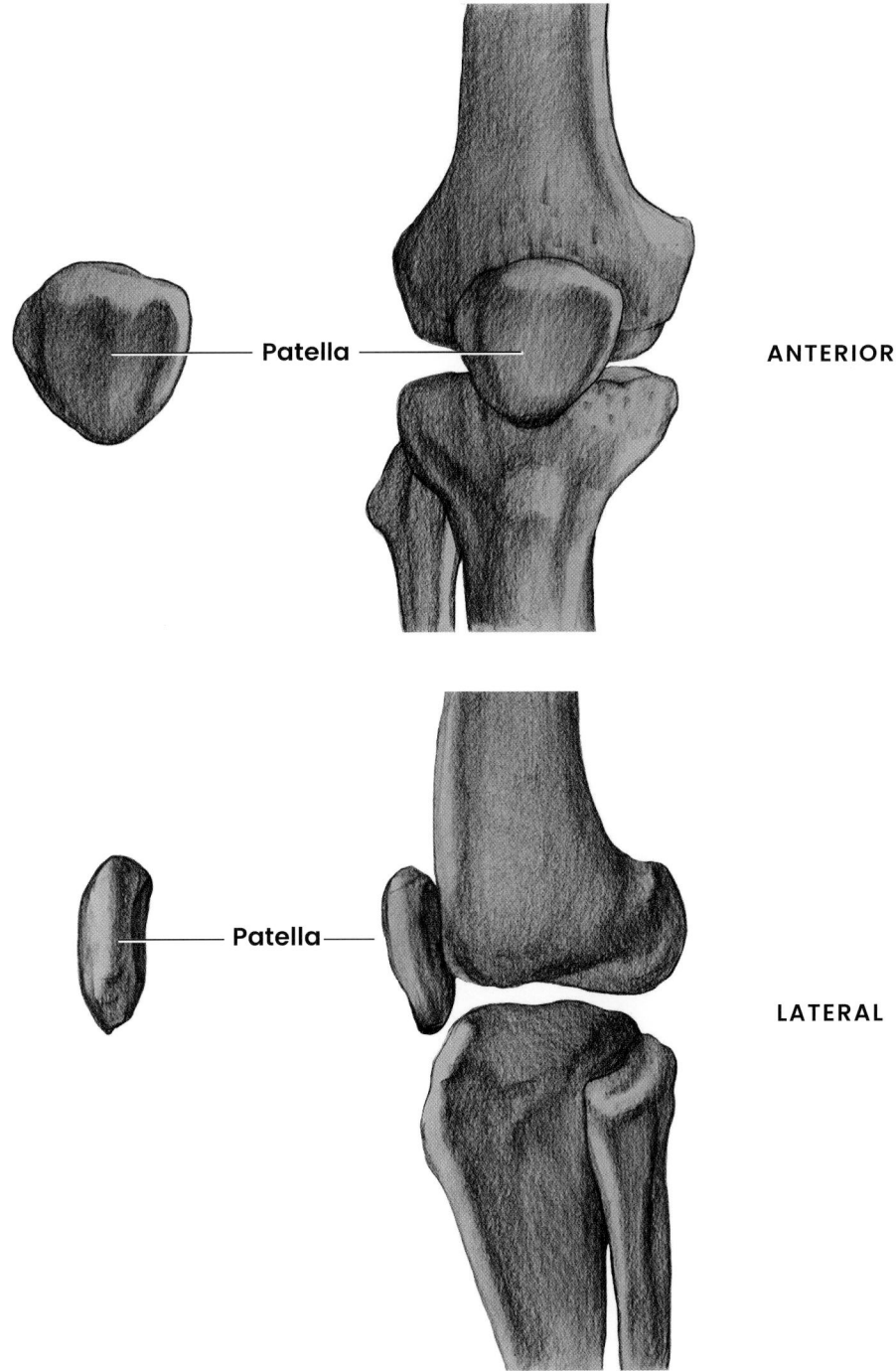

Patella —— Patella

ANTERIOR

Patella ——

LATERAL

F E E T

Feet

Bone Count: 52 (26 each)

Just like the hand bones, the feet bones have three major parts: the **Phalanges** (14) form the toes, the **Metatarsals** (5) form the middle part of the foot, and the irregular block-shaped bones called the **Tarsals** (7) sit under the ankle.

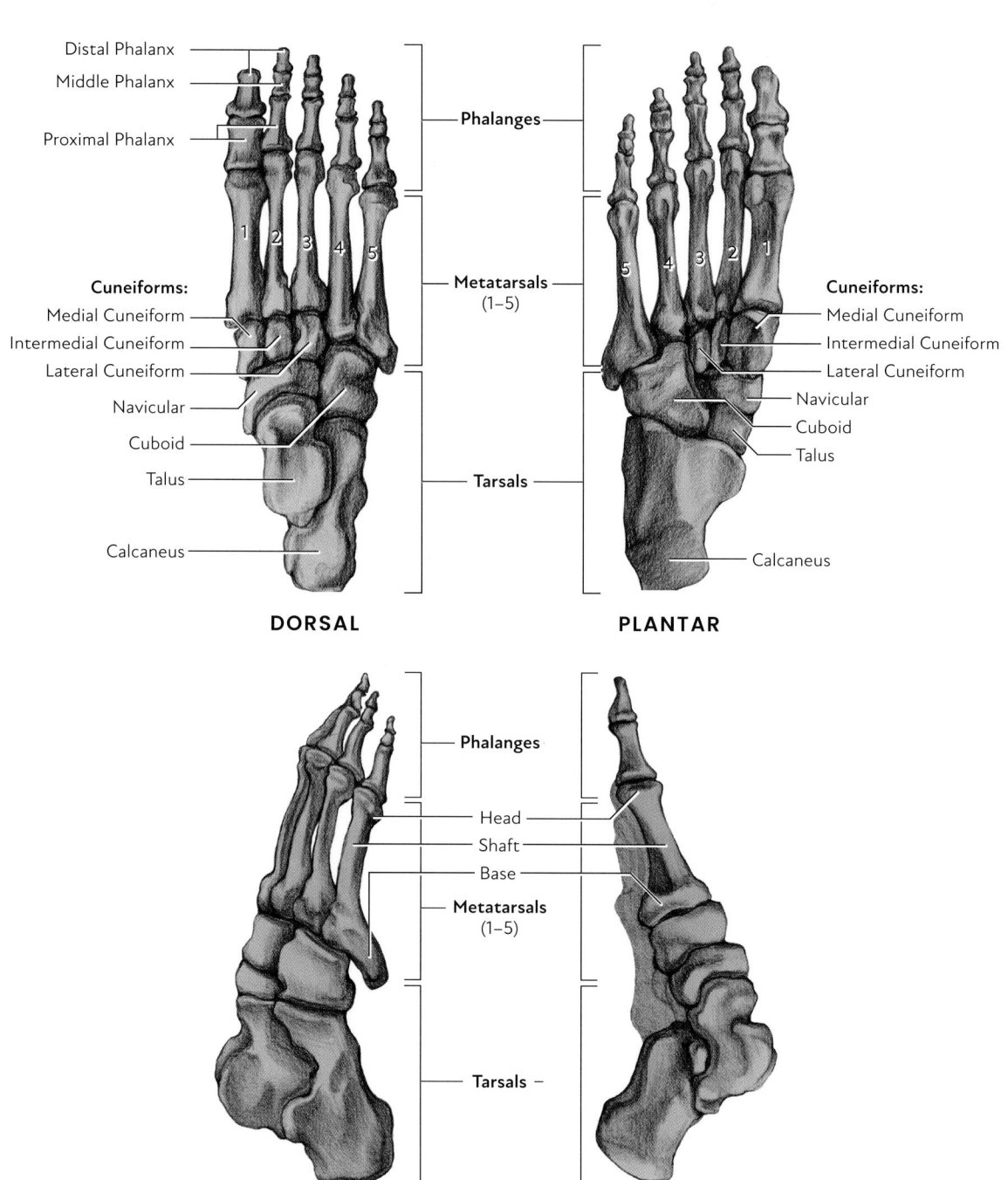

Distal Phalanx
Middle Phalanx
Proximal Phalanx

Phalanges

Cuneiforms:
Medial Cuneiform
Intermedial Cuneiform
Lateral Cuneiform
Navicular
Cuboid
Talus

Metatarsals (1–5)

Calcaneus

Tarsals

DORSAL

Cuneiforms:
Medial Cuneiform
Intermedial Cuneiform
Lateral Cuneiform
Navicular
Cuboid
Talus

Calcaneus

PLANTAR

Phalanges

Head
Shaft
Base

Metatarsals (1–5)

Tarsals

LATERAL

MEDIAL

TOTAL

This brings our total to

Skull 29

Rib 24

Sternum 1

Vertebral Column
(including Sacrum and Coccyx) . 26

Pelvis *(left and right)* 2

Scapula 2

Clavicle 2

Humerus 2

Radius 2

Ulna 2

Hand Bones 54

Femur 2

Patella 2

Tibia 2

Fibula 2

Foot Bones 52

Total **206**

We have 206 bones in our body!

Types of Joints

Get Physical with the Synovial Joints

The most common type of joints in our body are the **Synovial Joints**. These are the joints between our bones and they move against each other. The joints usually have cartilage and fluid in the middle. This makes big movements like running and dancing possible. However, the shape of joint is not always the same. Here are some examples.

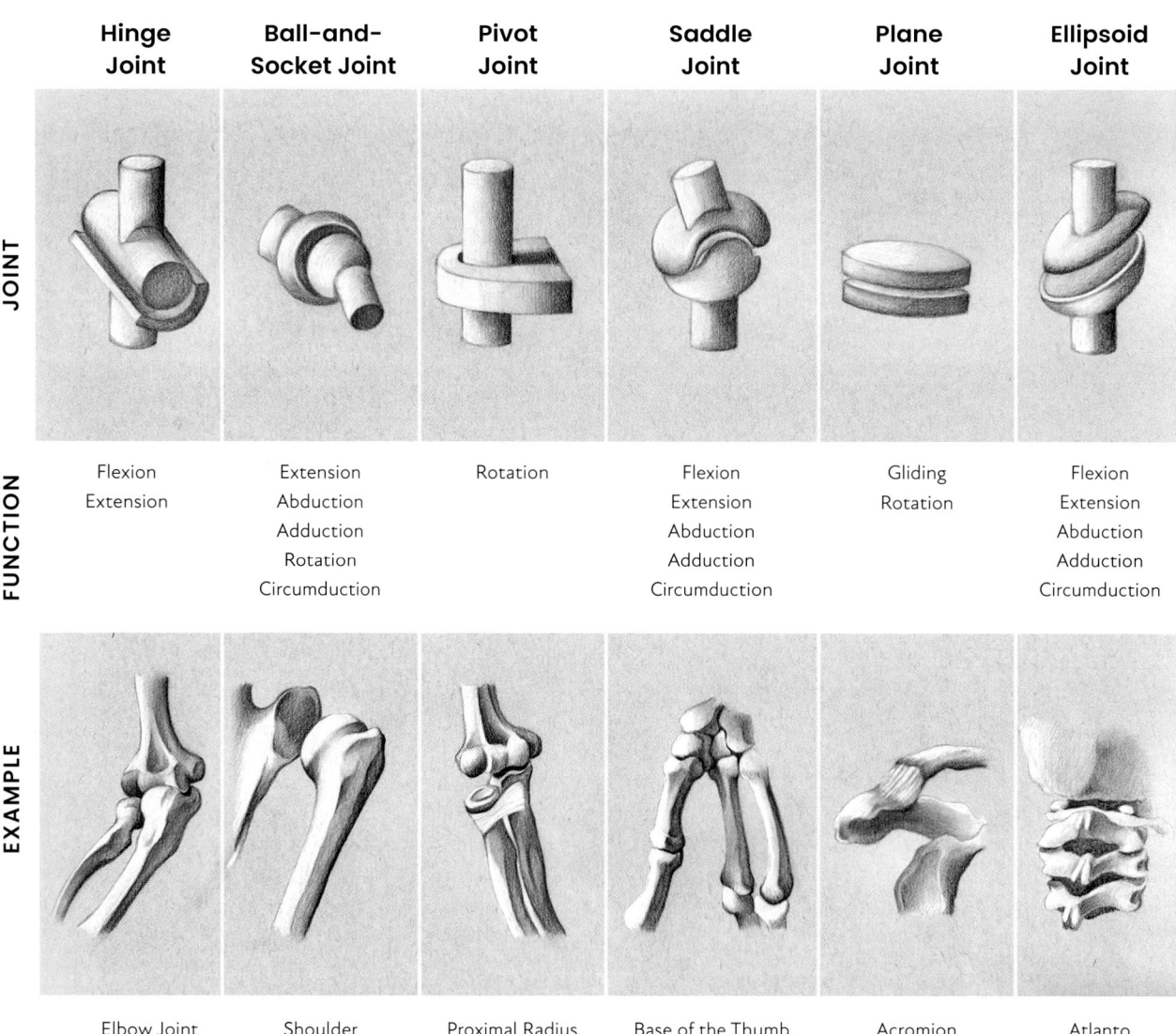

	Hinge Joint	Ball-and-Socket Joint	Pivot Joint	Saddle Joint	Plane Joint	Ellipsoid Joint
JOINT						
FUNCTION	Flexion Extension	Extension Abduction Adduction Rotation Circumduction	Rotation	Flexion Extension Abduction Adduction Circumduction	Gliding Rotation	Flexion Extension Abduction Adduction Circumduction
EXAMPLE	Elbow Joint	Shoulder Joint	Proximal Radius *Ulna Joint*	Base of the Thumb	Acromion *Clavicle Joint*	Atlanto *Occipital Joint*

Types of Muscles

Pump It Up and Draw Your Protein

The muscles are the proteins. They have fibers that run from the muscle's origin to its insertion, not always in one direction. When the muscle is contracted, it could be tightened, shortened, or stretched, depending on the movement. Here are some examples.

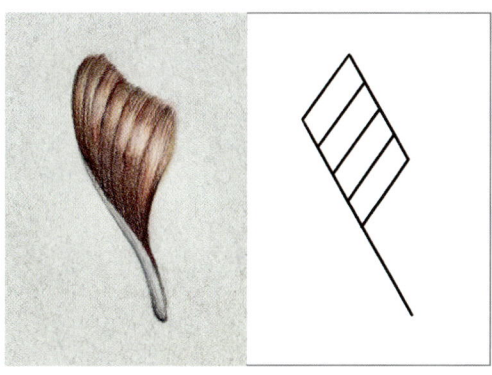

UNIPENNATE

BIPENNATE

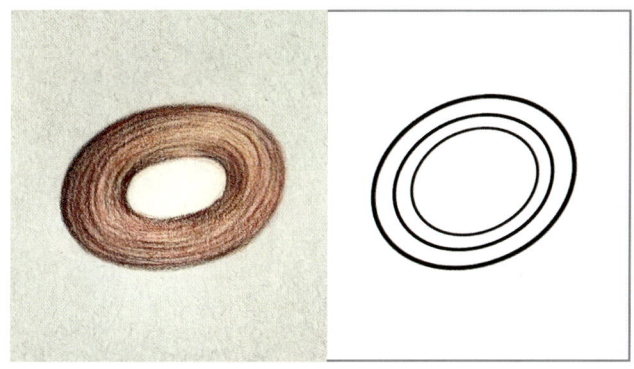
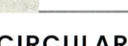

CIRCULAR

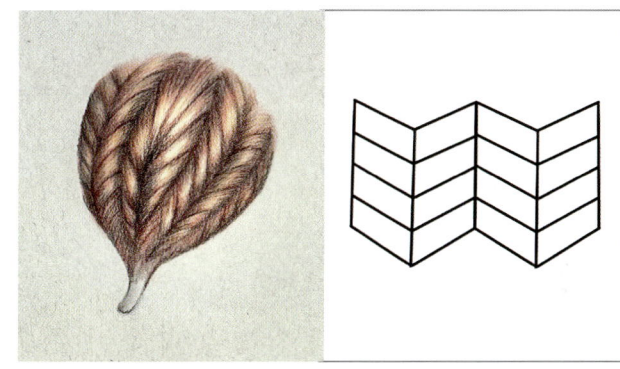

MULTIPENNATE

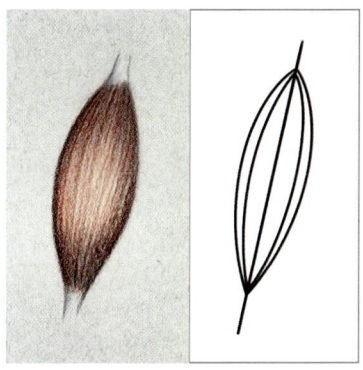
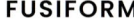

FUSIFORM

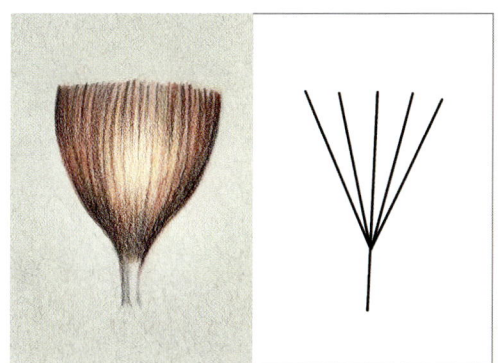

CONVERGENT

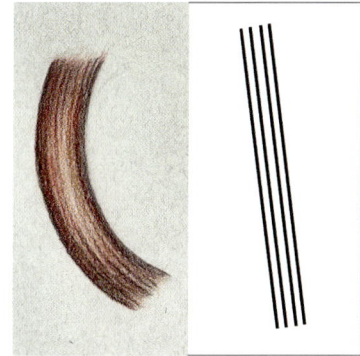

PARALLEL

What the Heck Is Contrapposto?

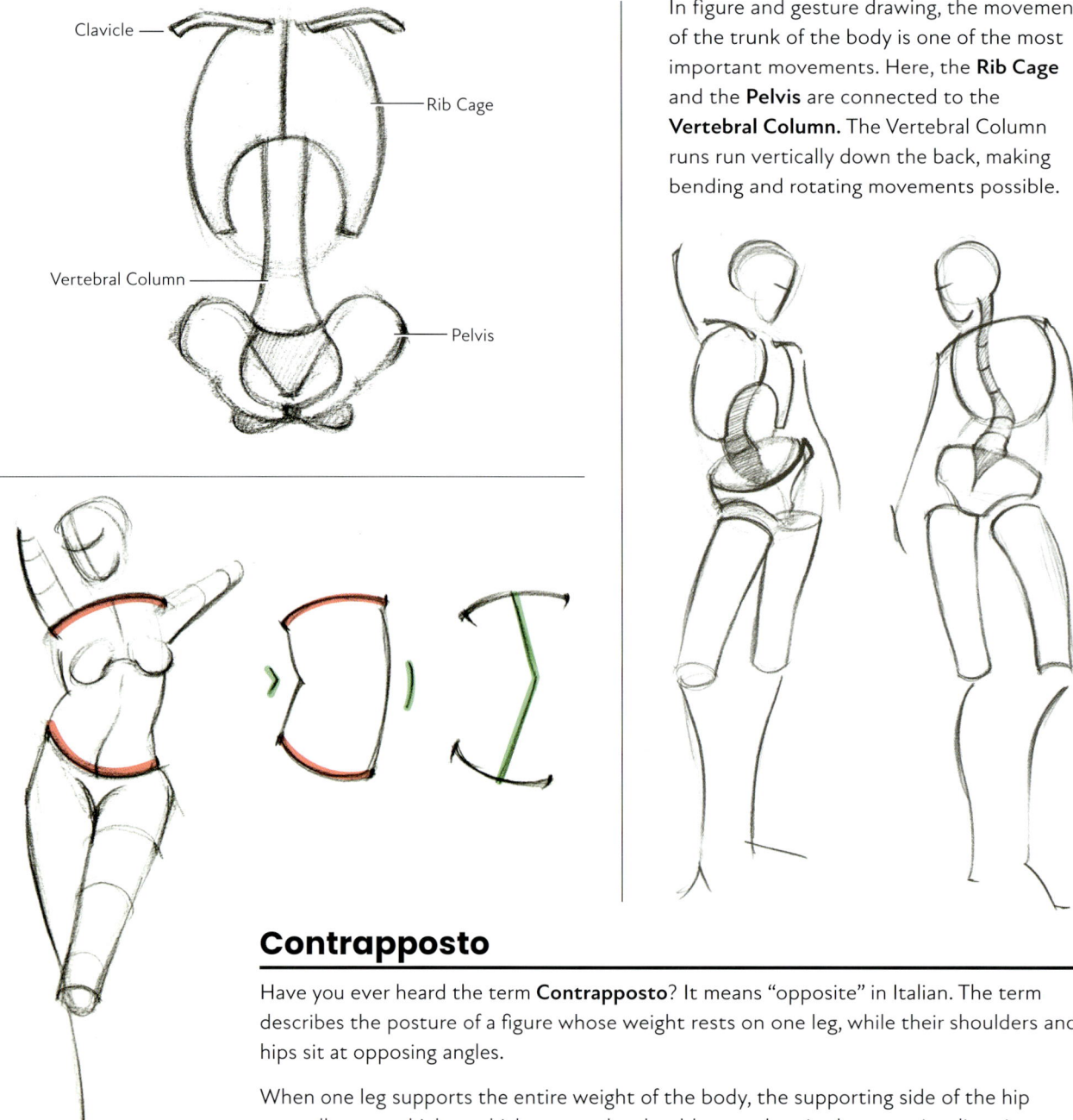

Clavicle

Rib Cage

Vertebral Column

Pelvis

In figure and gesture drawing, the movement of the trunk of the body is one of the most important movements. Here, the **Rib Cage** and the **Pelvis** are connected to the **Vertebral Column.** The Vertebral Column runs run vertically down the back, making bending and rotating movements possible.

Contrapposto

Have you ever heard the term **Contrapposto**? It means "opposite" in Italian. The term describes the posture of a figure whose weight rests on one leg, while their shoulders and hips sit at opposing angles.

When one leg supports the entire weight of the body, the supporting side of the hip naturally moves higher, which causes the shoulders to slant in the opposite direction.

The contrapposto posture makes the figure look much more natural. This stance was first seen in ancient Greek and Roman sculptures, which showed a significant difference from the stiff figure sculptures created in the prior period of Mesopotamia.

So, practice your gestures with the Contrapposto. This will give your figures a flowy and natural look.

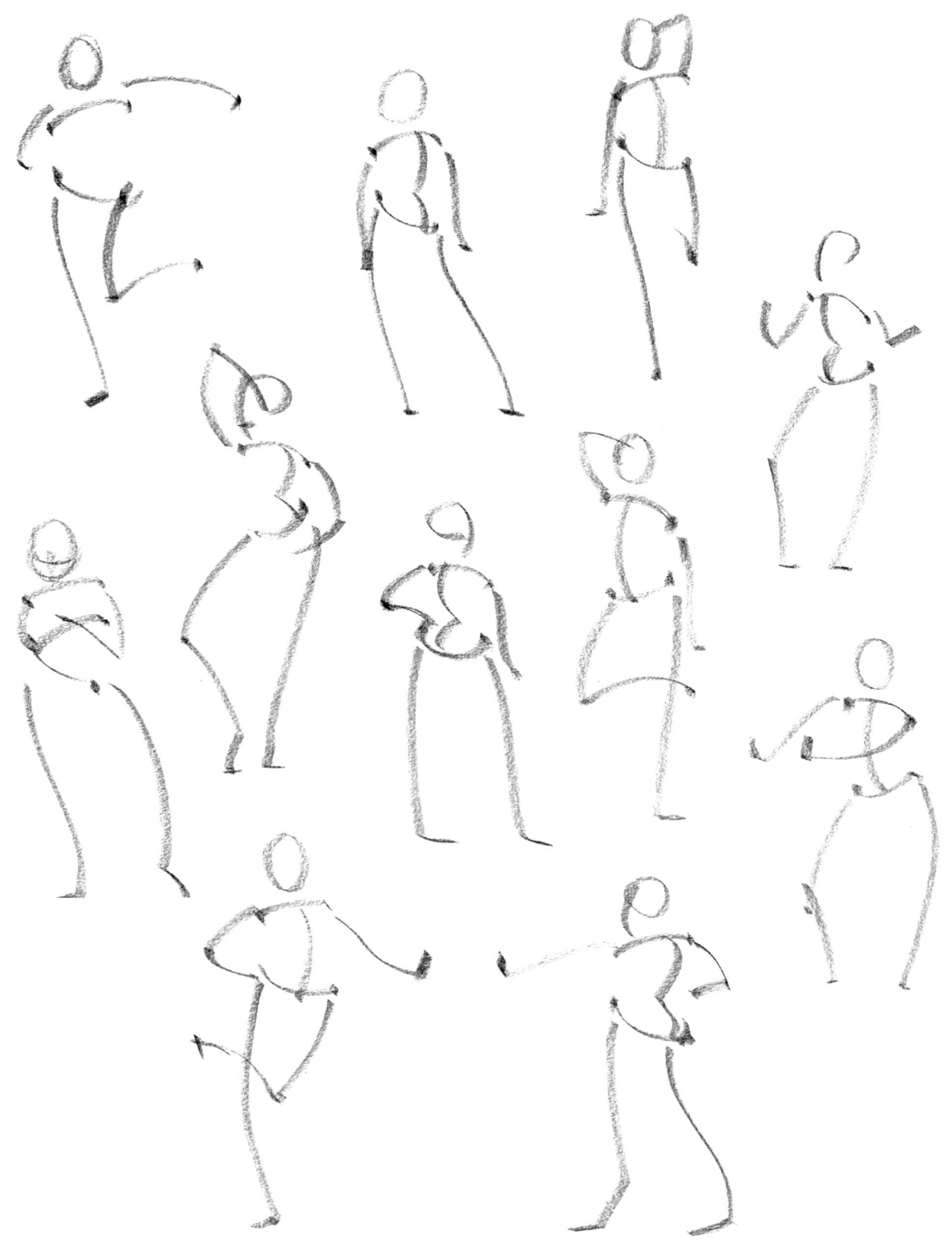

Introducing ASIS and PSIS

So, how do we figure out the Contrapposto? The key to this process can be found in the Pelvis.

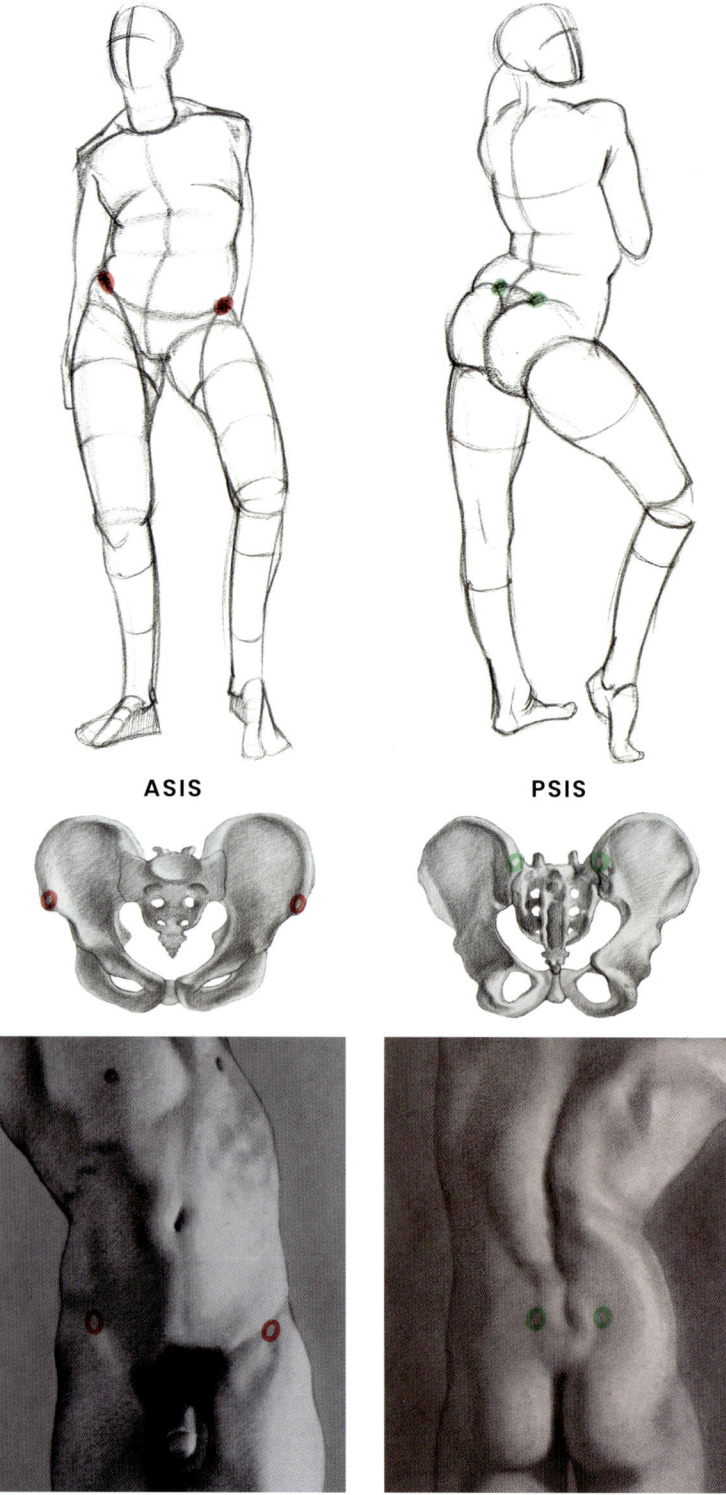

ASIS

PSIS

Finding ASIS and PSIS

ASIS (eh-ee-sis)—**A**nterior **S**uperior **I**liac **S**pine—is the projection of the bone found in the front side of the Iliac Crest of the Pelvis.

ASIS is the landmark of the body that becomes the "central station" for many muscles and tendons. We can often figure out where the ASISs are in the surface anatomy. Because this projection is bony and accurate, you can use the ASIS to find out the natural Contrapposto posture.

On the other side in the back, we have **PSIS** (pee-sis)— **P**osterior **S**uperior **I**liac **S**pine. This is in the back end of the Iliac Crest of the Pelvis.

From the posterior view, we can see that the PSIS lines up with the superior border of the Sacrum, creating the large triangle shape. With the long curved line of the Vertebral Column, the entire spine looks like a downward arrow sign.

Rib Cage and Pelvis   The Practical Torso Movement

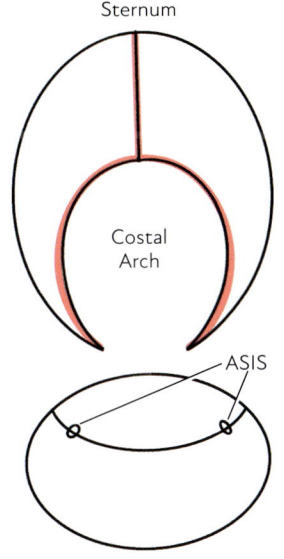

Sternum

Costal
Arch

ASIS

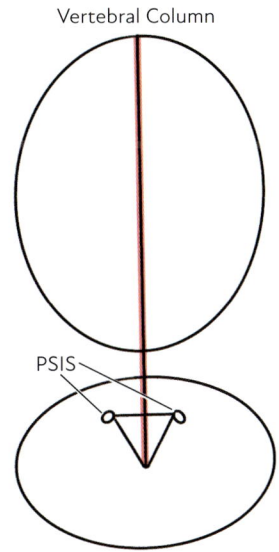

Vertebral Column

PSIS

Now you can use the technique of the Contrapposto to practice the torso movement. Reduce the Rib Cage and Pelvis into simplified geometric shapes. Here, you can see the **Costal Arch** (the opening on the front of the Rib Cage) and the **Sternum** as a small vertical line for the anterior view. The **Vertebral Column** forms a long vertical line for the posterior view. These landmarks will help to control the direction of the torso.

Understanding the cylinder at different angles will help you to create accurate movements. Practice a variety of angles to work on the torso.

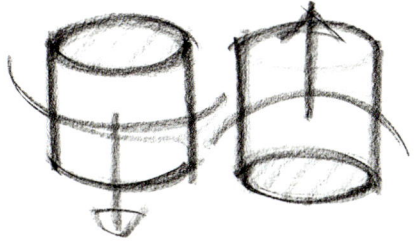

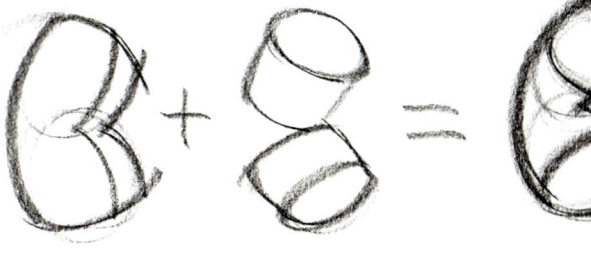

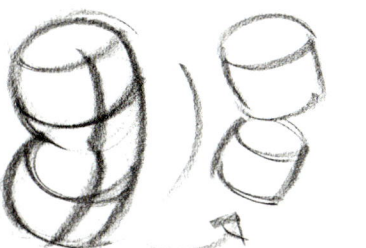

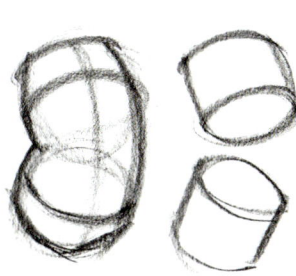

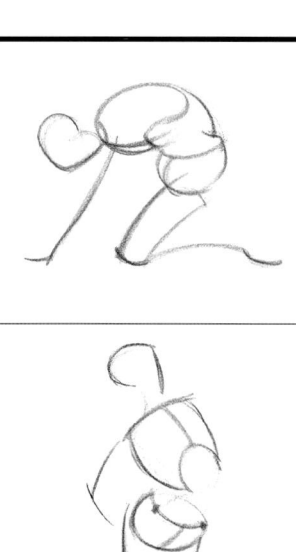
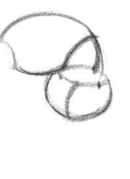
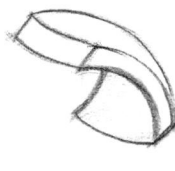

FLEXION

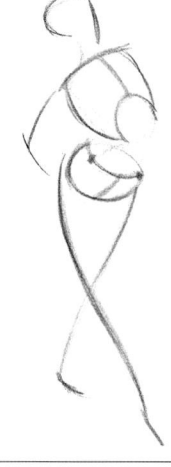
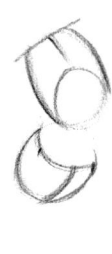
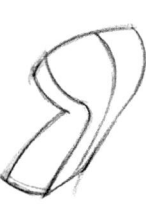

HYPEREXTENSION

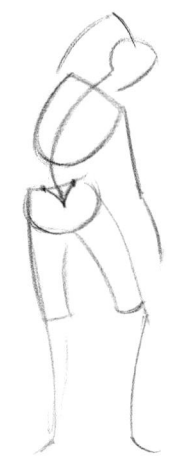
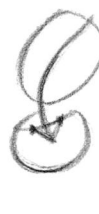
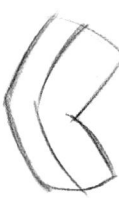

LATERAL FLEXION

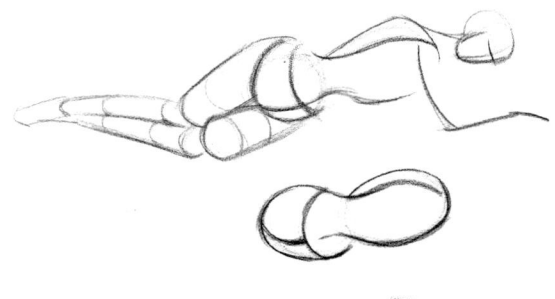
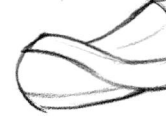

ROTATION

Hybrid

**ROTATION/
LATERAL FLEXION**

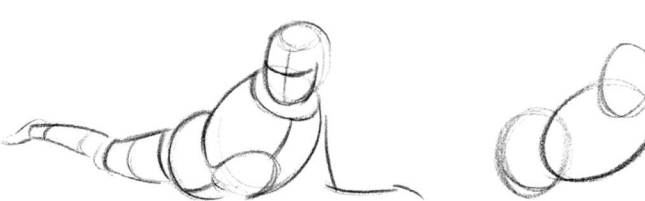

FORESHORTENING

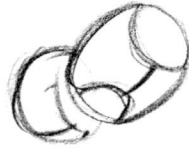 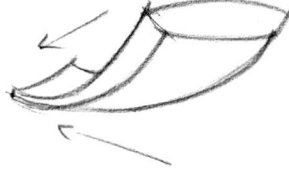

Acetabulum and Its Hip Joint

The "Vinegar Cup" in the Pelvis

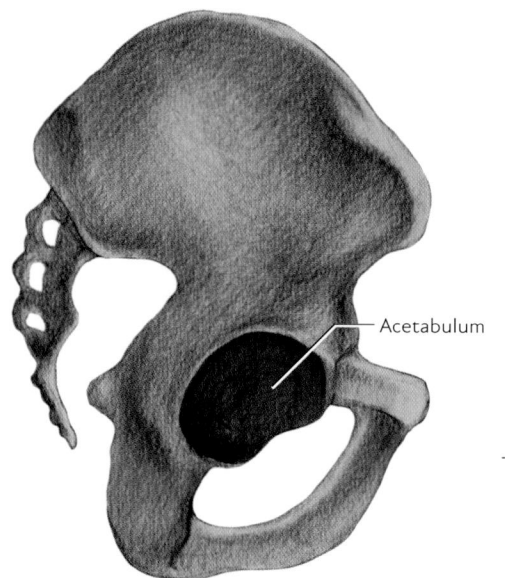

Acetabulum

PELVIS, LATERAL VIEW

Why does vinegar have anything to do with the hip joint? The hip joint is one of the Synovial Joints known as a ball-and-socket joint. The Femur bone goes into a pocket of the Pelvis, and this makes a variety of leg movements possible, including the circumduction movement.

This pocket facing the lateral side of the Pelvis that holds the head of the Femur is called the **Acetabulum**, which meant "vinegar cup" in the ancient Greek and Roman period.

During that time, this palm-sized vinegar cup was used during meals to hold vinegar or a dipping sauce. Apparently, the shape and size of the cup was very similar to the socket of the Pelvis. So, they called it by the same name, and we still use the same term today.

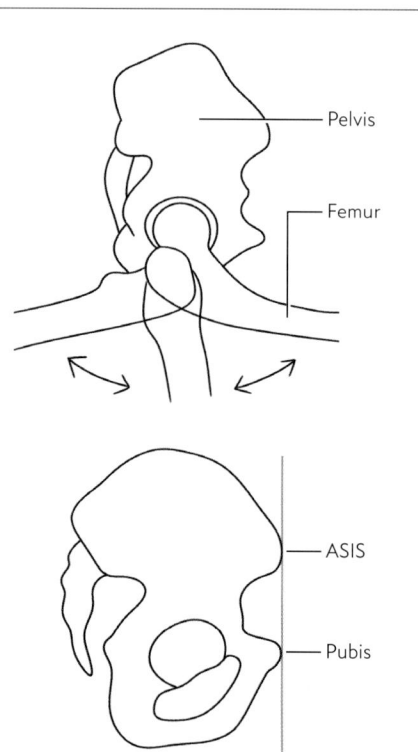

Pelvis

Femur

ASIS

Pubis

ASIS and the anterior surface of the Pubis line up from the lateral view

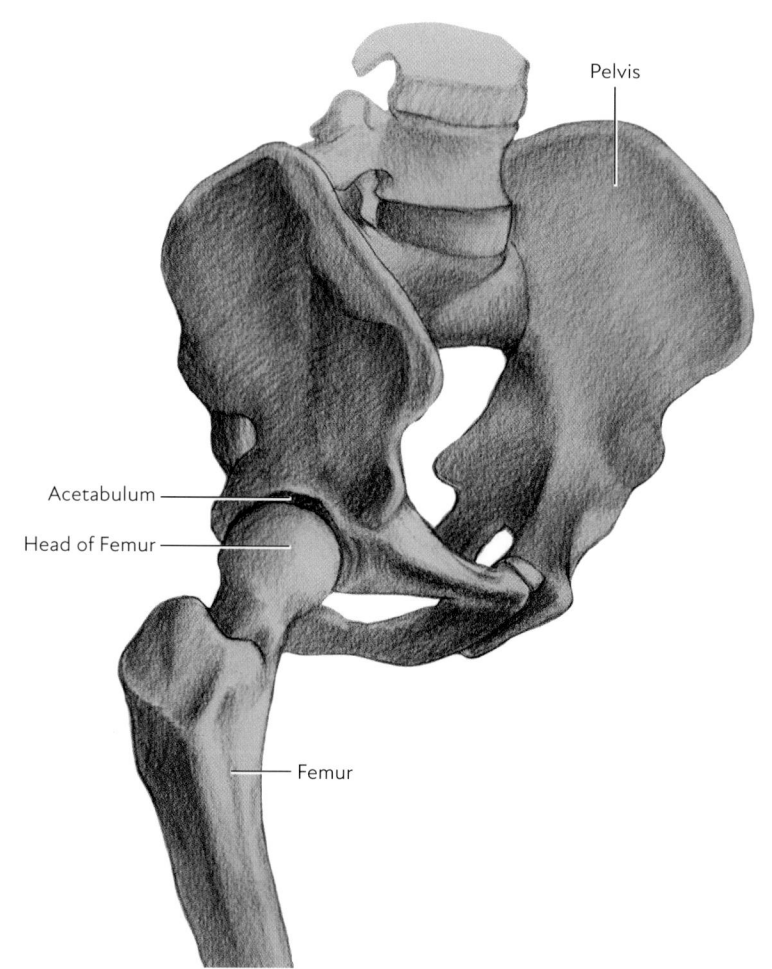

Pelvis

Acetabulum

Head of Femur

Femur

The Femur   The Biggest, Strongest, and Longest Bone

Inside of the Acetabulum is the sphere-shaped head of the **Femur**. The Femur is the thigh bone, and it is the biggest, strongest, and longest bone in our body. Because it is the most powerful bone of the skeleton system, the Femur has many responsibilities within artistic anatomy.

Next to the Head of the Femur is its Neck. Then you can see the curved diagonal form with two bumps at each end. The higher bump is called the **Greater Trochanter** and the one below is called the **Lesser Trochanter.**

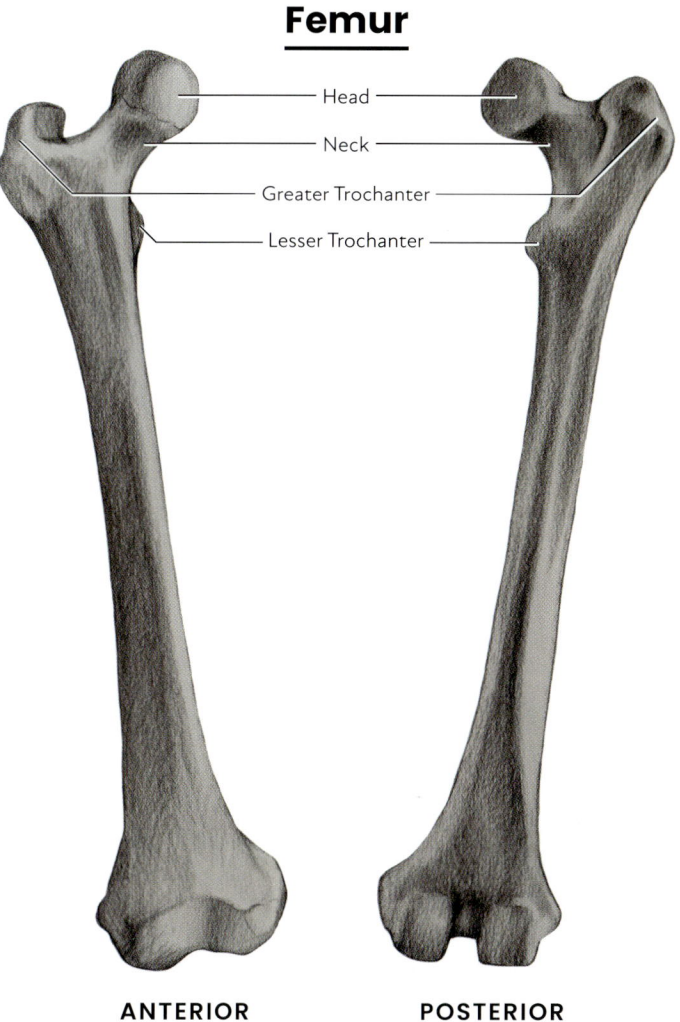

Femur

Head

Neck

Greater Trochanter

Lesser Trochanter

ANTERIOR   **POSTERIOR**

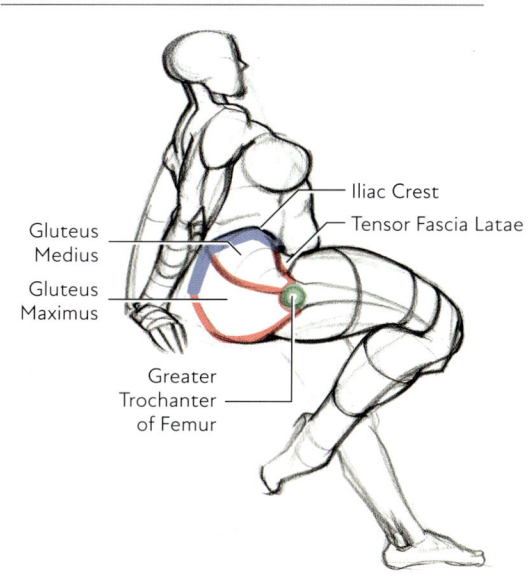

Iliac Crest

Tensor Fascia Latae

Gluteus Medius

Gluteus Maximus

Greater Trochanter of Femur

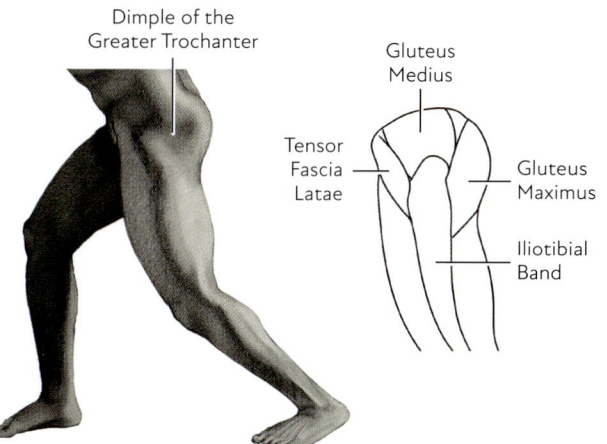

Dimple of the Greater Trochanter

Gluteus Medius

Tensor Fascia Latae

Gluteus Maximus

Iliotibial Band

Greater Trochanter

The Greater Trochanter is a rough and rocky projection of the Femur that faces the lateral side. It is an attachment for the hip muscles, including the Gluteus Medius, Gluteus Maximus, and Tensor Fascia Latae. The biggest characteristic of the Greater Trochanter is that it is quite visible in the surface anatomy. There is no muscle or fat covering this area, so at a certain angle, or depending on the location of the light source, the hollow, shadow, or projection can be seen in this part of the hip.

The Femur *(cont.)*

Lesser Trochanter

The Lesser Trochanter is another projection of the Femur that is located slightly distal to the Greater Trochanter. It is the attachment for two of the interior muscles in the hip (the Psoas Major and the Iliacus) and it goes on the **medial/posterior side** of the Femur. Many animals, including dogs, cats, elephants, and even dinosaurs, have the same structured Femur bone. The Lesser Trochanter on the medial/posterior side is one of the signs biologists and archaeologists use to determine which side of the Femur they are investigating.

Angle of Femur

The anatomical position of the Femur is **diagonal**. With our flesh on, the leg looks like it goes straight down to the ground vertically, but it is only because the medial thigh muscles fill the inner thigh gap.

On the posterior side in the shaft of the Femur, there is a crest that runs vertically called the **Linea Aspera**. This crest is an attachment for most of the **Medial Thigh Muscle Group**.

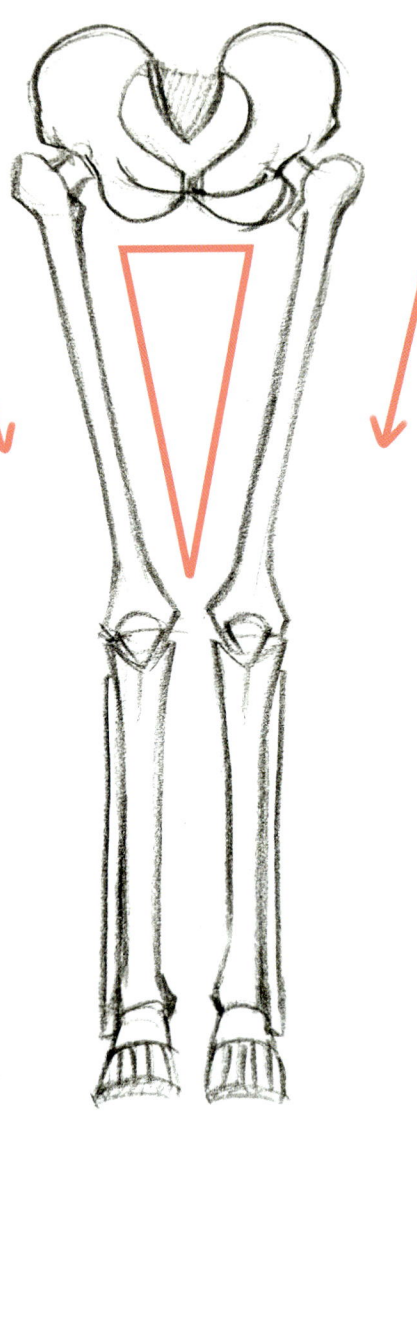

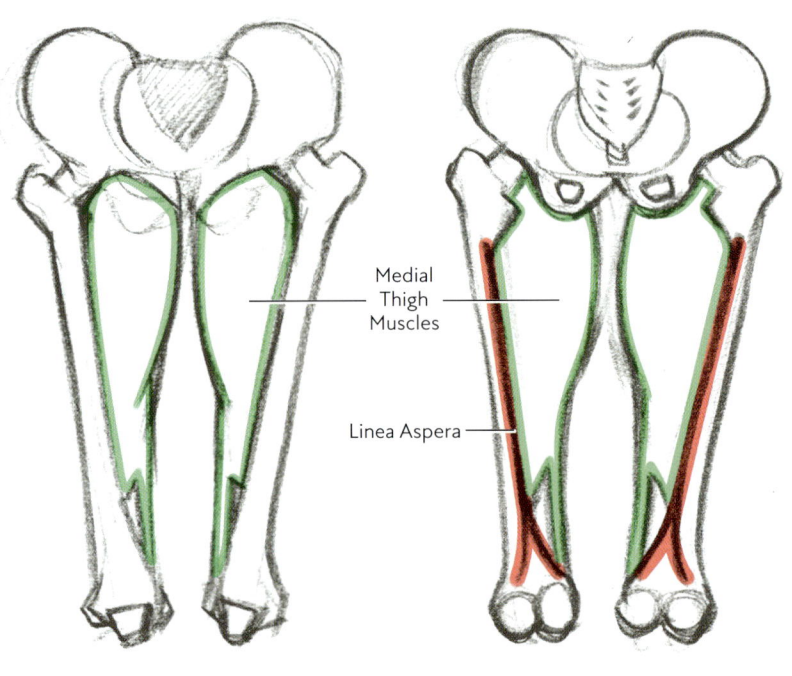

Medial Thigh Muscles

Linea Aspera

ANTERIOR

POSTERIOR

Angles in the Wrist and Ankle

In the skeleton system, the structure of the bones in the arms and legs are similar: one bone for the upper, two for the lower. For the forearm, there are the **Ulna** (medial) and **Radius** (lateral). In the lower leg we have the **Tibia** (medial) and **Fibula** (lateral). The ends of the bones on the lateral side sit lower than the ones on the medial side in both the arms and the legs; therefore, you can see diagonal angles in the wrists and ankles.

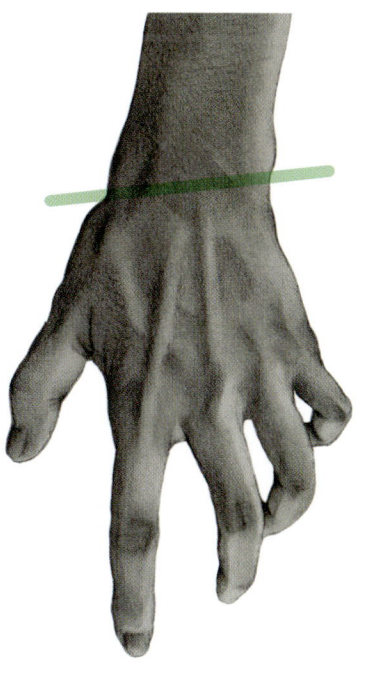

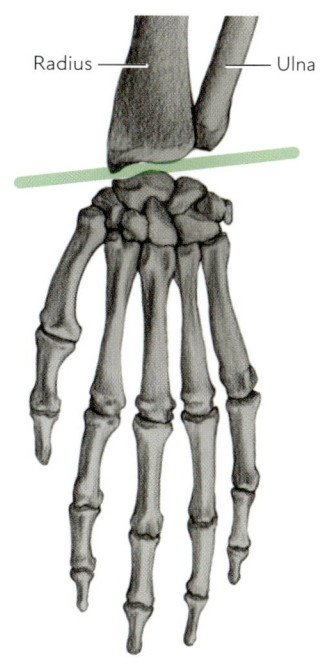

Radius — Ulna

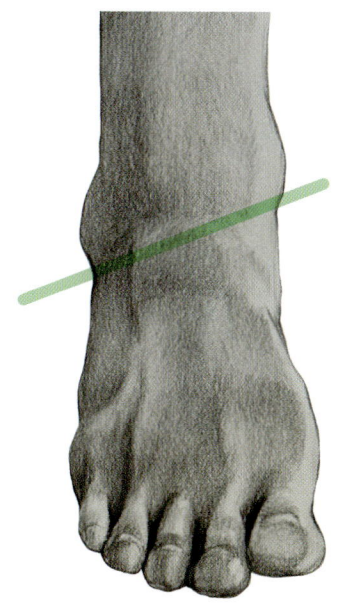

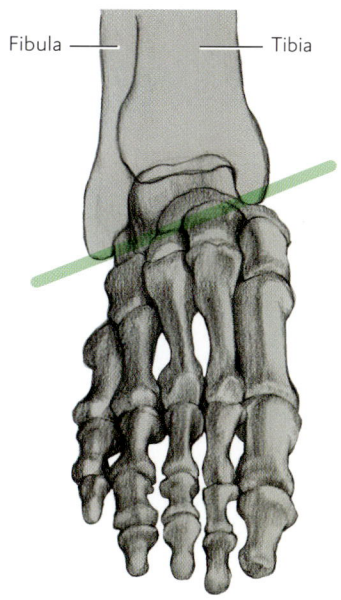

Fibula — Tibia

Proportion and Zig-Zags

The Femur sits in a slanted position, the Contrapposto stance makes the shoulder and hip sit at opposing angles, and we can see a diagonal angle in the wrist and ankle. Does this mean that humans are asymmetrical? Yes, we are. Particularly from the lateral view, you can see a wavy, curved line, and it creates the zig-zagged rhythm in the body.

There is also a generic proportion in the human body. We can define the head as one unit and it can then be used to measure each body part.

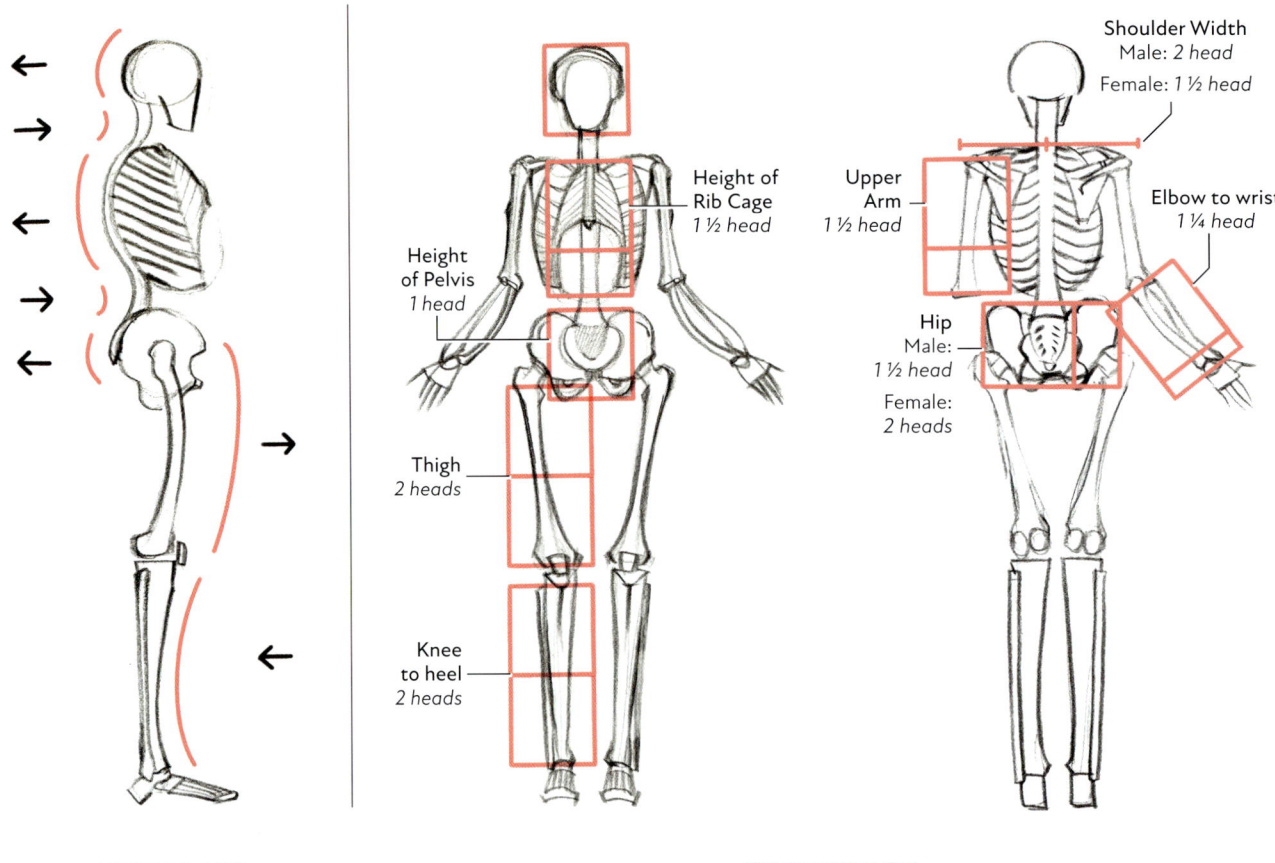

RHYTHM IN LATERAL VIEW

Height of Rib Cage
1 ½ head

Height of Pelvis
1 head

Thigh
2 heads

Knee to heel
2 heads

PROPORTION

Shoulder Width
Male: *2 head*
Female: *1 ½ head*

Upper Arm
1 ½ head

Elbow to wrist
1 ¼ head

Hip
Male: *1 ½ head*
Female: *2 heads*

Baby Fat Follows the Classical Anatomical Order

It is not just random puffs...

You might think that babies are just little chunky soft marshmallow-like adorable creatures, but those plumped limbs and wrinkles between rolls of fat are not just randomly there. Every feature follows the order under the classical anatomical rules.

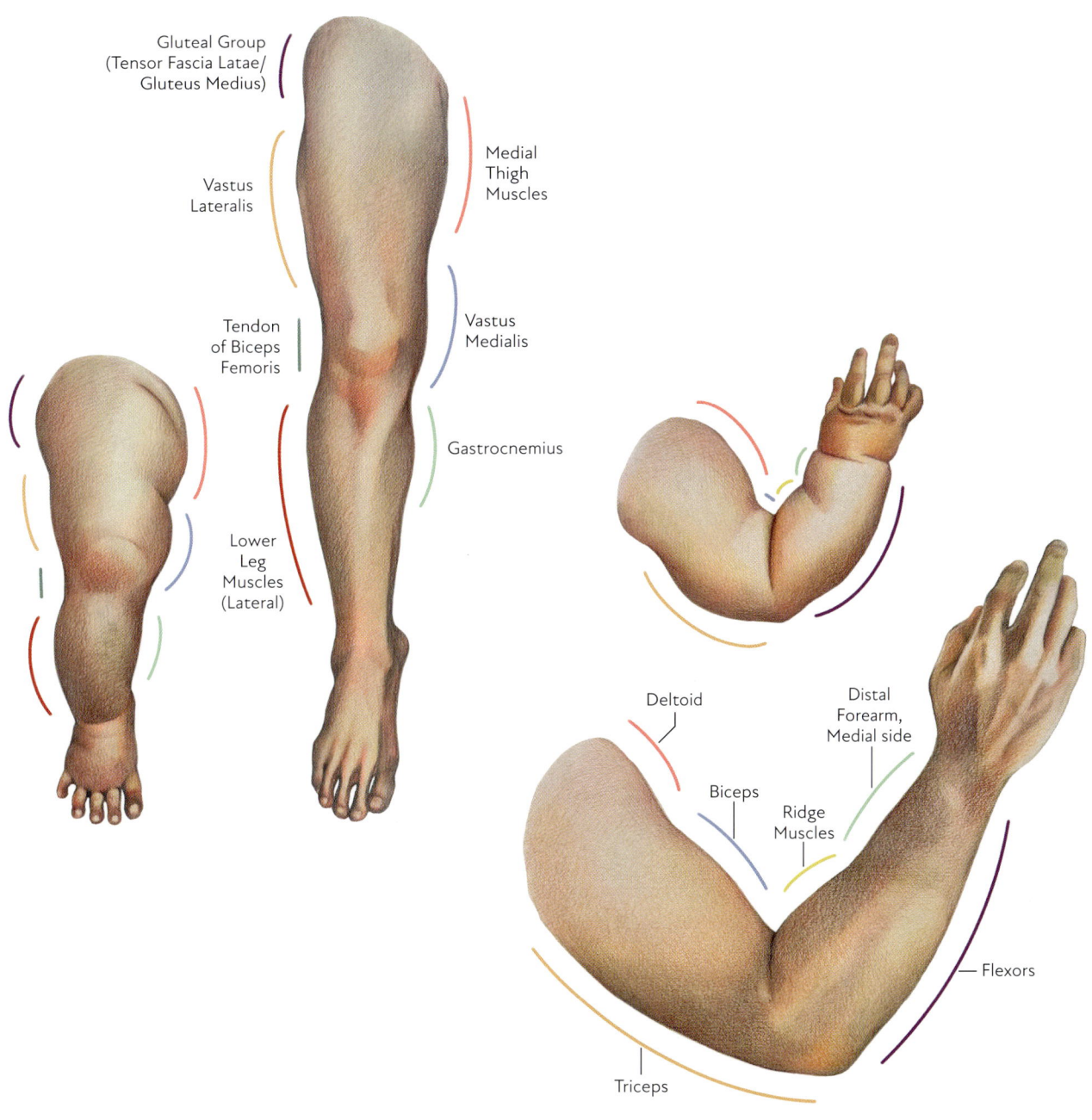

Gluteal Group (Tensor Fascia Latae/ Gluteus Medius)

Vastus Lateralis

Tendon of Biceps Femoris

Medial Thigh Muscles

Vastus Medialis

Gastrocnemius

Lower Leg Muscles (Lateral)

Deltoid

Biceps

Ridge Muscles

Distal Forearm, Medial side

Flexors

Triceps

Give the ACTION to the Figure

Gesture is a core flow of the figure. In order to create a good gesture in your drawing, you need to capture the movement of the body, and not the outline of the body. If you focus only on the outline of figure, you will easily lose the proportion and balance. Create many curved lines in your drawing and try not to use stiff, straight lines.

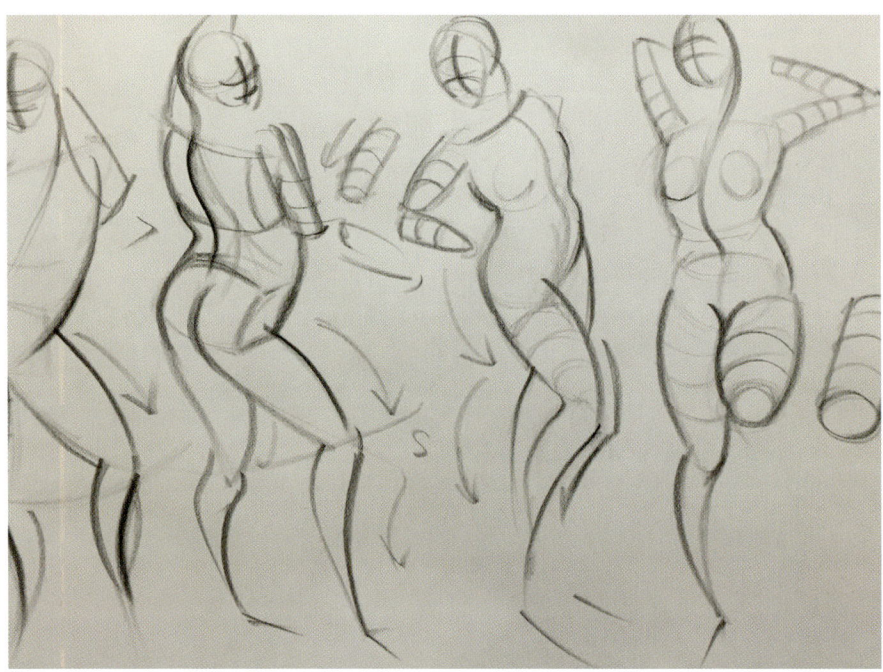

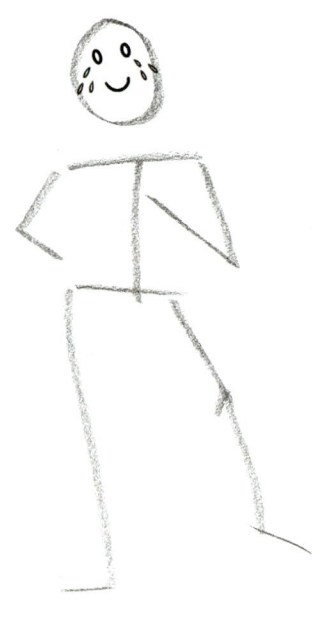

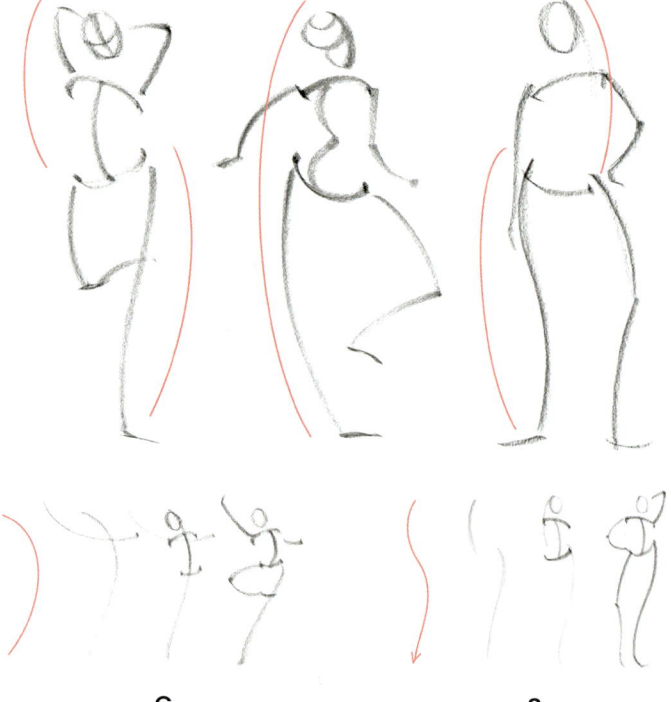

C   S

Action Line

To capture the flow of the figure, the gesture lines need to be soft and smooth. The first line you want to draw will be the connection from head to toe. This can become the core of the entire height of the figure, or arm to arm/arm to leg. This is called the **Action Line**.

The action line should be the longest axes in the body. This line needs to be quick, smooth, and simple. Use a curved line shaped like a C, S, or combination of both.

Track Your G.P.S.

Gesture, Proportion, and Stability

There are different approaches you can use to improve your figure drawing skills. One of the common practices is the use of the **Mannequin Figure**, where you use simple geometric shapes to build a figure. The purpose of the Mannequin Figure process is to understand the human form by using the simplest shapes, and to show accurate planes and volumes of the figure.

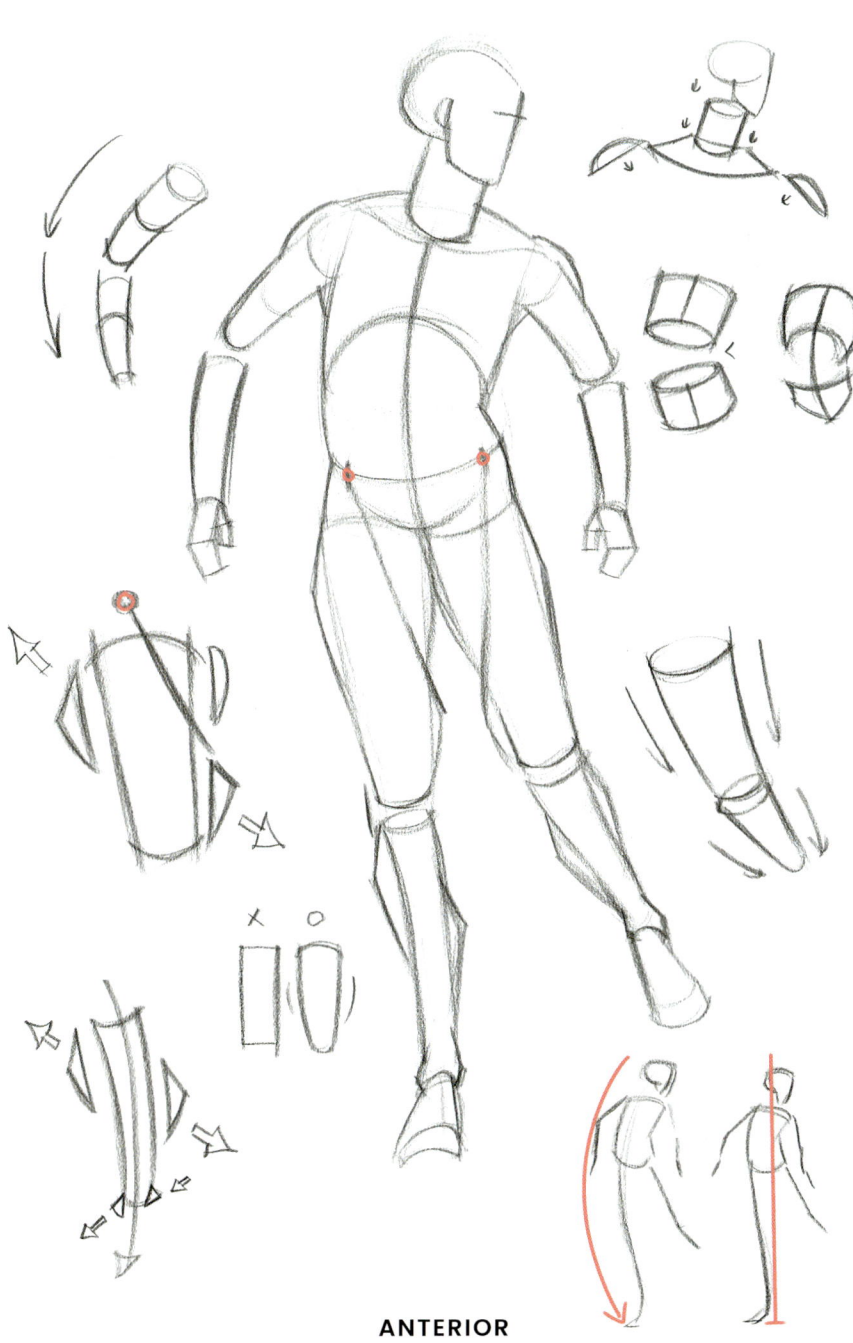

ANTERIOR

You can continue practicing the cylinders, cuboids, and spheres from the different angles and repeat that process many times. You can also use curved lines to practice gestures. The point is to draw the figures realistically, in a **gestural and massive way**. Start with whatever makes you feel good and keep on going. Don't forget about three important elements when practicing:

G.P.S. in Figure Drawing

Gesture – To give action to the figure and to avoid stiffness

Proportion – To achieve accuracy in the human form

Stability – To let the figure stand on the ground on its own and give weight to it

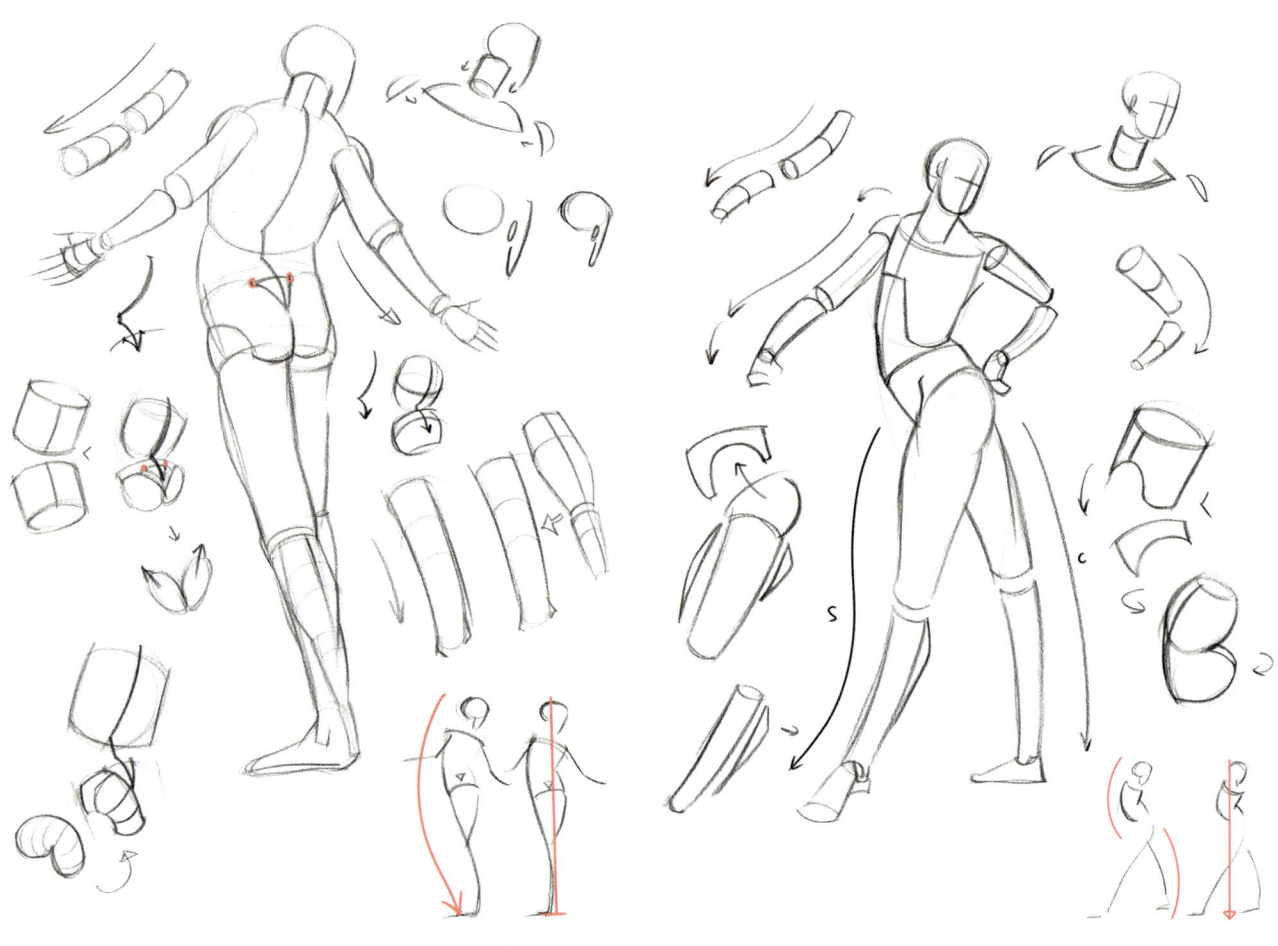

POSTERIOR

LATERAL

Skeleton System Overview

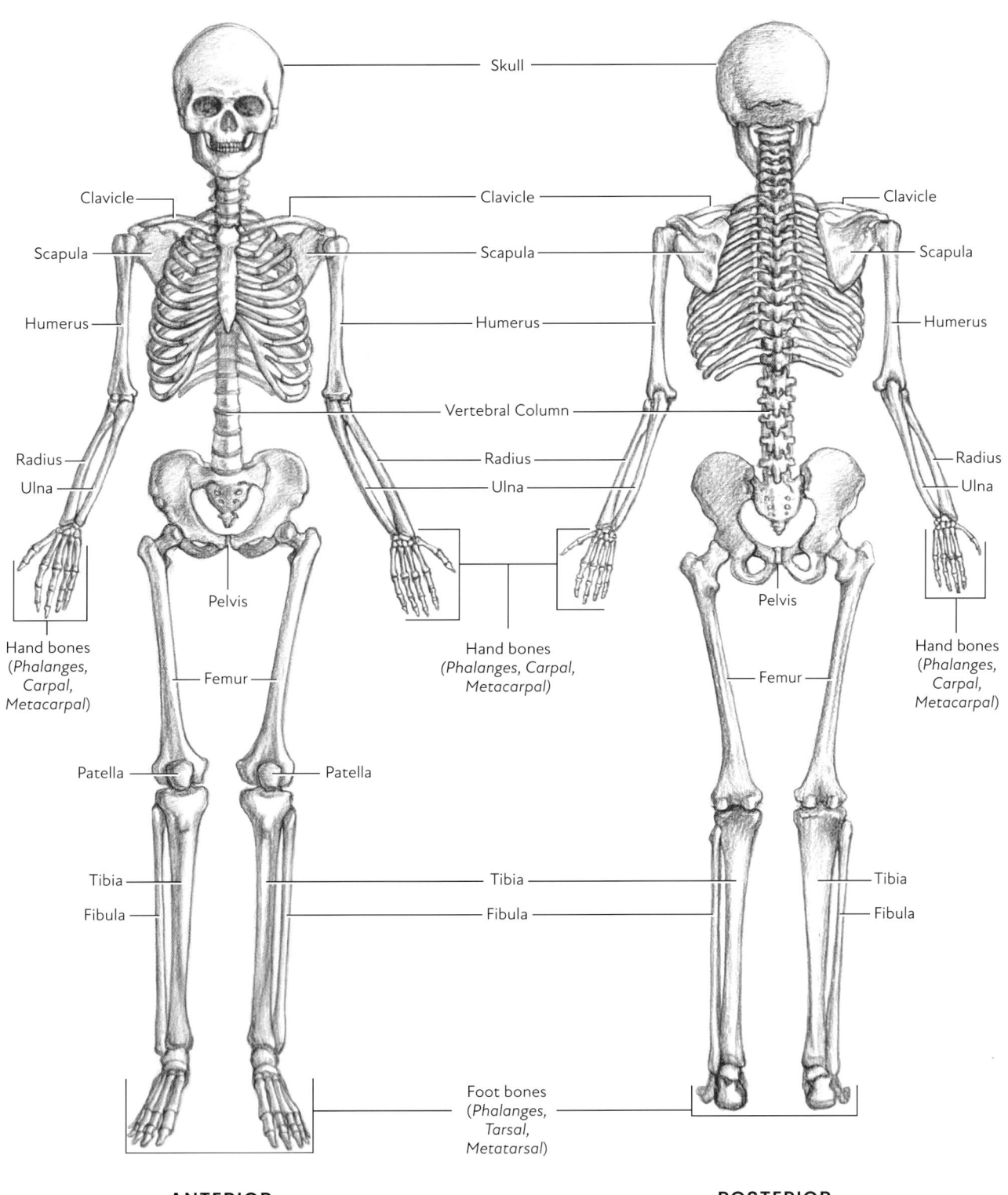

Skull

Clavicle

Scapula

Humerus

Radius

Ulna

Hand bones
(*Phalanges,
Carpal,
Metacarpal*)

Pelvis

Femur

Patella

Tibia

Fibula

Clavicle

Scapula

Humerus

Vertebral Column

Radius

Ulna

Hand bones
(*Phalanges, Carpal,
Metacarpal*)

Patella

Tibia

Fibula

Foot bones
(*Phalanges,
Tarsal,
Metatarsal*)

Clavicle

Scapula

Humerus

Radius

Ulna

Hand bones
(*Phalanges,
Carpal,
Metacarpal*)

Pelvis

Femur

Tibia

Fibula

ANTERIOR

POSTERIOR

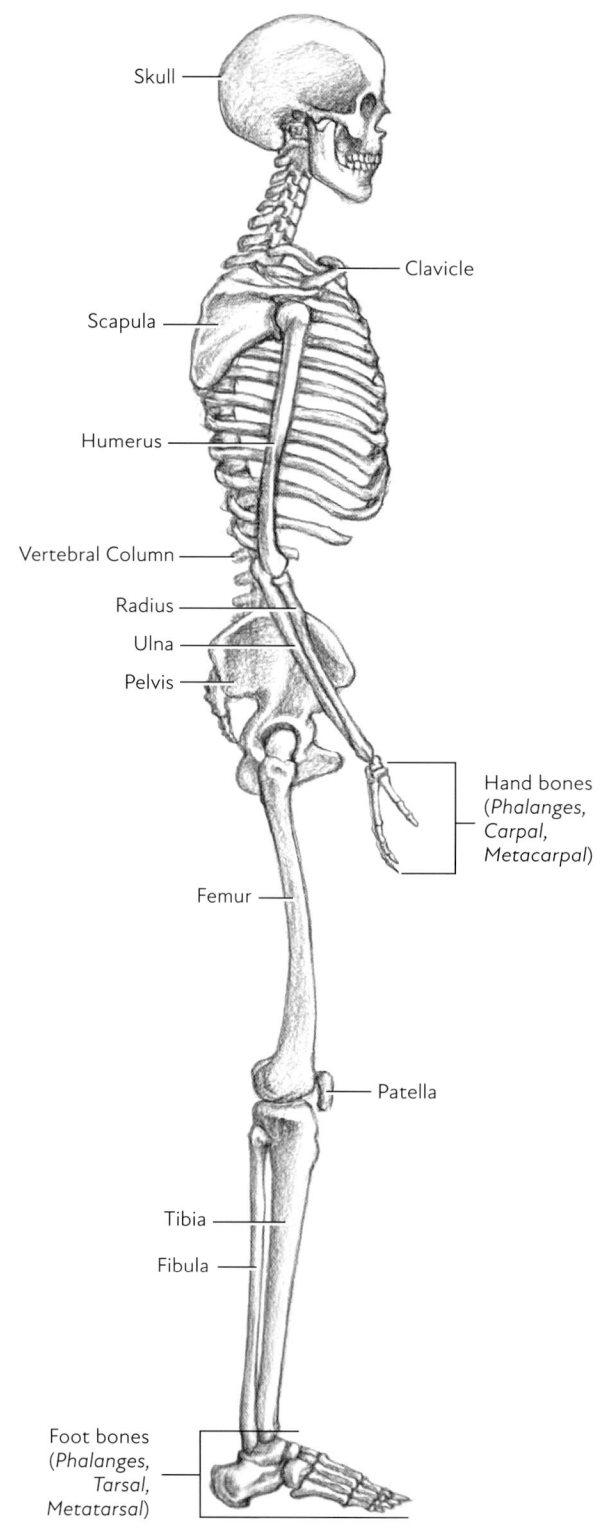

Skull

Clavicle

Scapula

Humerus

Vertebral Column

Radius

Ulna

Pelvis

Hand bones
(*Phalanges,
Carpal,
Metacarpal*)

Femur

Patella

Tibia

Fibula

Foot bones
(*Phalanges,
Tarsal,
Metatarsal*)

LATERAL

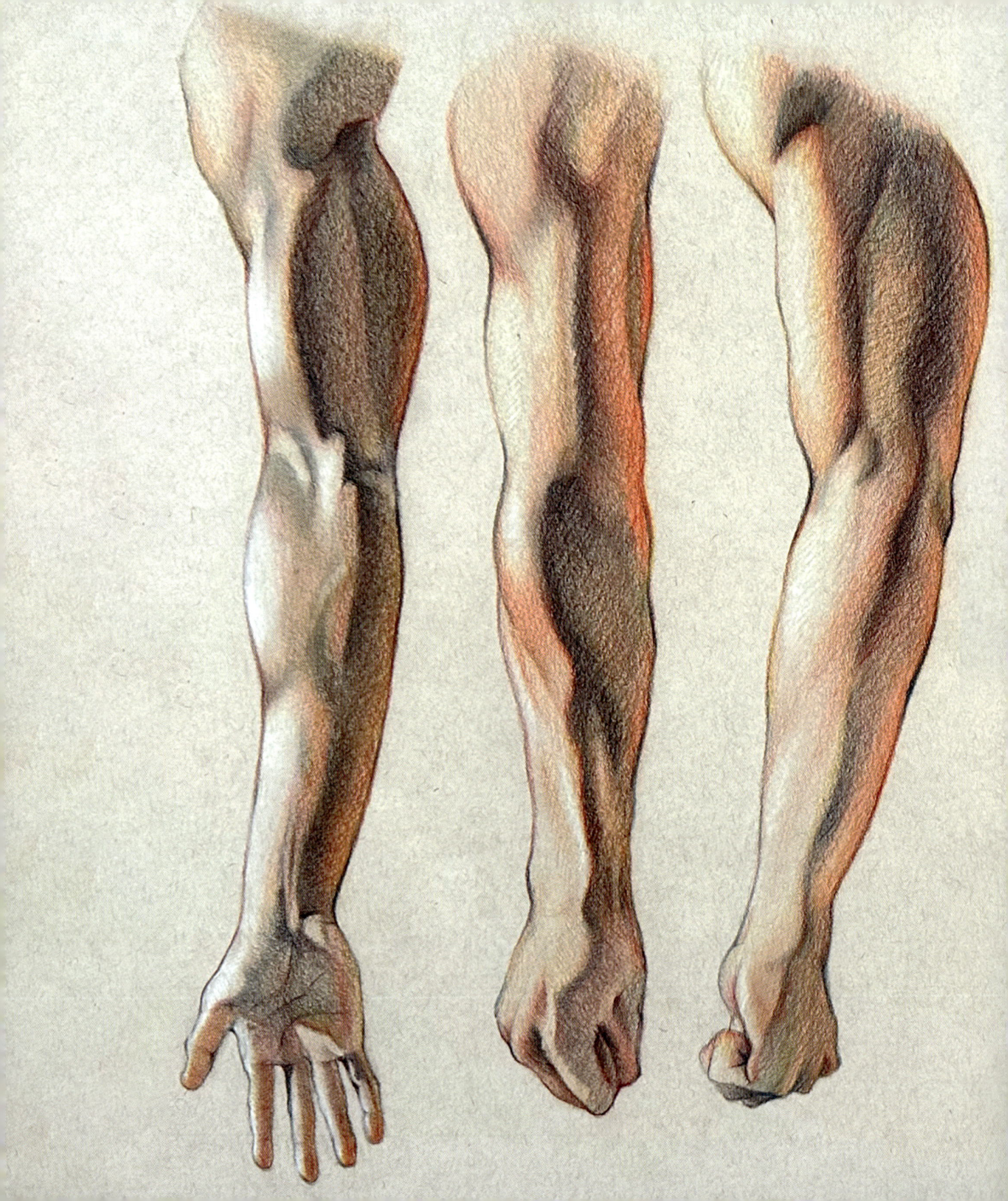

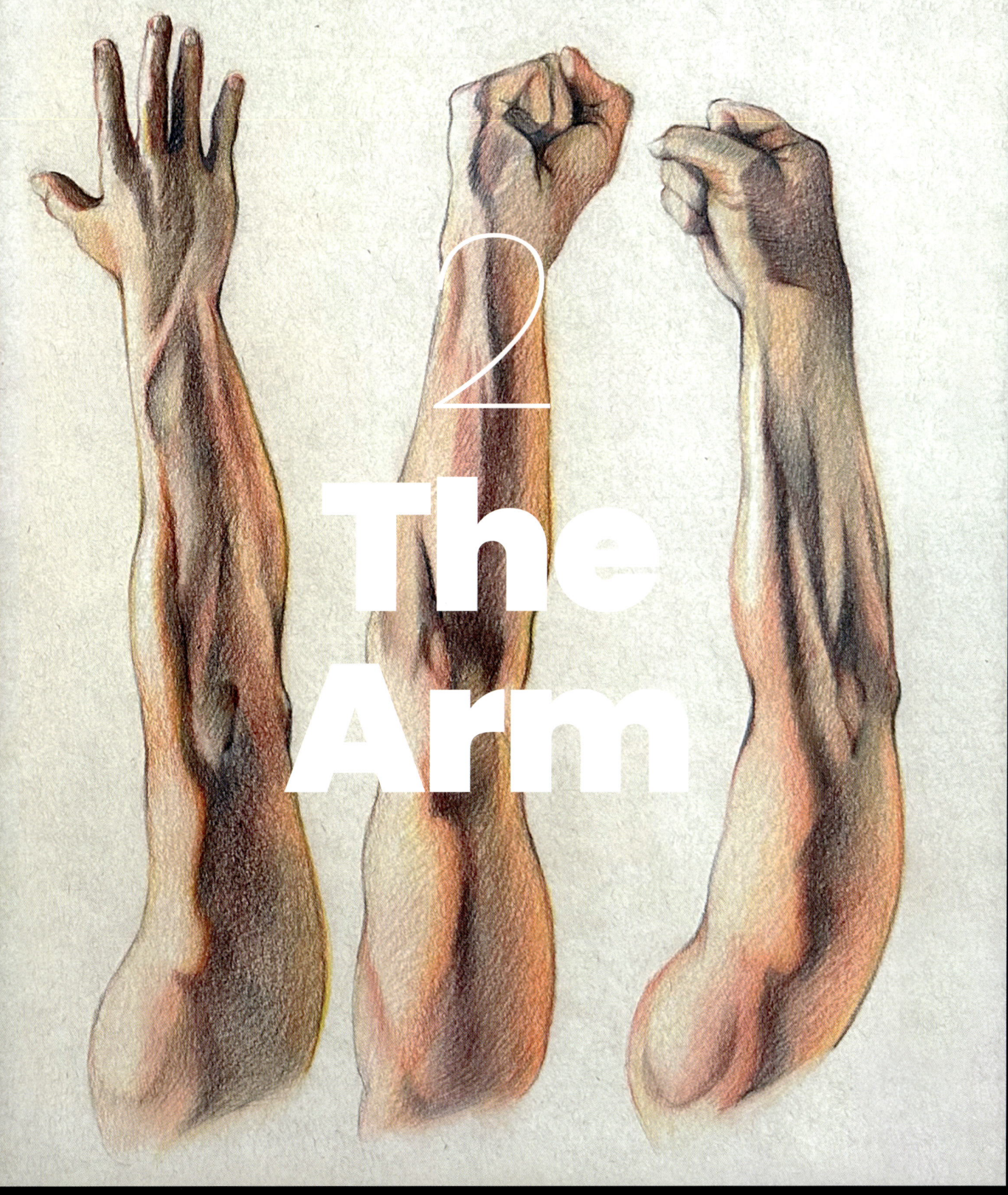

2

The Arm

Major Groups of Muscles You Should Know

The arm muscles can be separated into five distinct groups: **The Sub**, **Ridge Muscles**, **Flexors**, **Extensors**, and **Deep Extensors**.

The Sub

We call the group of upper arm muscles The Sub because two muscles on the front and back, **Biceps Brachii** and **Triceps Brachii**, sandwich the upper arm bone called the **Humerus** and another muscle called the **Brachialis**. It looks like one big submarine sandwich!

Ridge Muscles

The Ridge Muscles are two muscles on the lateral side of the arm: the **Brachioradialis** and the **Extensor Carpi Radialis Longus**. This muscle group extends from the **Lateral Epicondyle of the Humerus** down to the distal part of the Radius.

QUICK NOTE

Pronation

Pronation is a palm-down movement of the arm. With this movement, the two bones in the forearm, the Radius and the Ulna, cross one another. You can often see the volume of the Ridge Muscles following the movement.

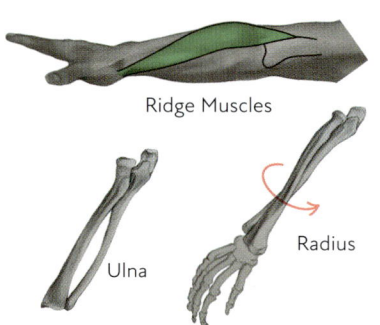

Ridge Muscles

Ulna

Radius

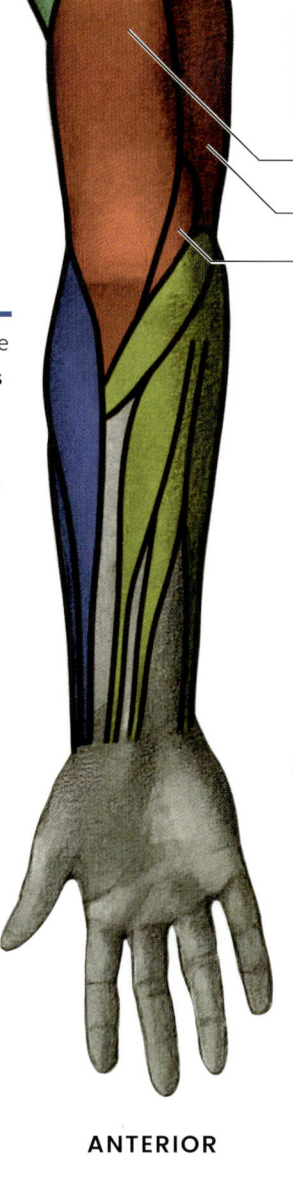

ANTERIOR

The **Brachialis** sits on the distal anterior shaft of the Humerus.

The **Coracobrachialis** is attached from the Scapula to the medial mid-shaft of the Humerus.

The Sub

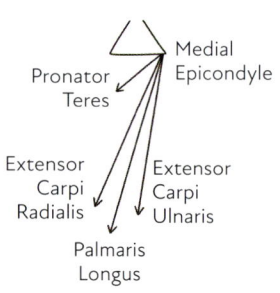

Coracobrachialis —

Biceps Brachii —

Triceps Brachii —

Brachialis —

Flexors

The Flexors are comprised of four muscles: the **Pronator Teres**, **Flexor Carpi Radialis**, **Palmaris Longus**, and **Flexor Carpi Ulnaris**. The origin of all four muscles is the **Medial Epicondyle of the Humerus**.

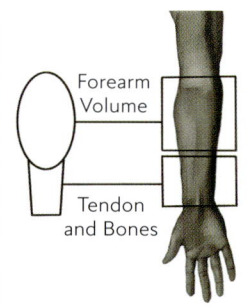

Pronator Teres

Medial Epicondyle

Extensor Carpi Radialis

Extensor Carpi Ulnaris

Palmaris Longus

Forearm Volume

Tendon and Bones

QUICK NOTE

Medial Epicondyle of the Humerus

This projection of the medial distal part of the Humerus is known as the "funny bone." When it is hit, you may feel an electric pain. The Medial Epicondyle of the Humerus can be felt under the skin.

Extensors

The Extensors are comprised of four muscles: the **Anconeus**, **Extensor Carpi Ulnaris**, **Extensor Digitorum**, and **Extensor Digiti Minimi**. The form of the Extensors is similar to the Flexors. However, the origin of the Extensors is the **Lateral Epicondyle of the Humerus** on the posterior side.

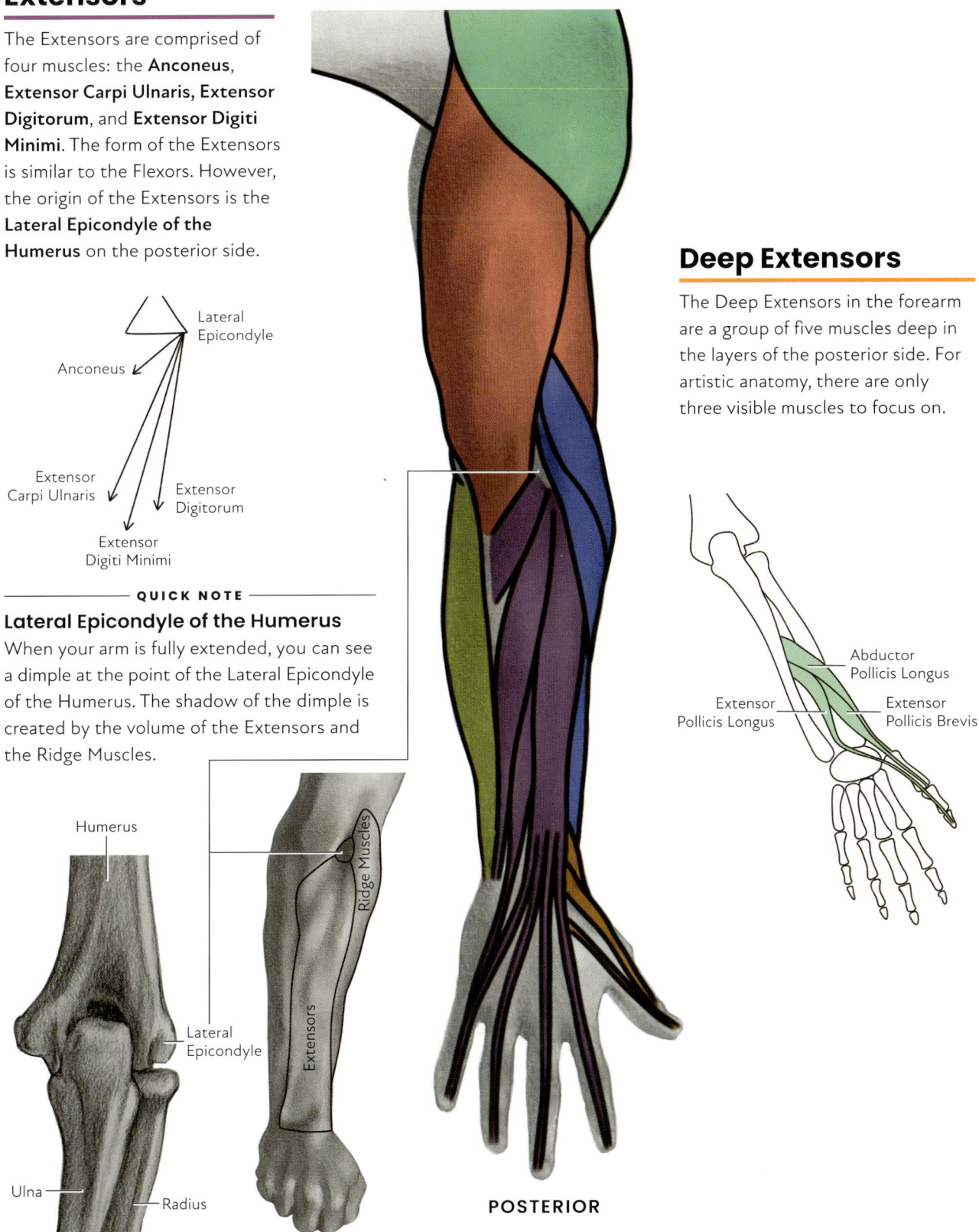

Lateral Epicondyle

Anconeus

Extensor Carpi Ulnaris

Extensor Digitorum

Extensor Digiti Minimi

QUICK NOTE

Lateral Epicondyle of the Humerus

When your arm is fully extended, you can see a dimple at the point of the Lateral Epicondyle of the Humerus. The shadow of the dimple is created by the volume of the Extensors and the Ridge Muscles.

Humerus

Lateral Epicondyle

Ridge Muscles

Extensors

Ulna

Radius

POSTERIOR

Deep Extensors

The Deep Extensors in the forearm are a group of five muscles deep in the layers of the posterior side. For artistic anatomy, there are only three visible muscles to focus on.

Abductor Pollicis Longus

Extensor Pollicis Longus

Extensor Pollicis Brevis

Shape of the Biceps

The **Biceps Brachii** has two heads: the **Long Head** and the **Short Head**.

Biceps Brachii

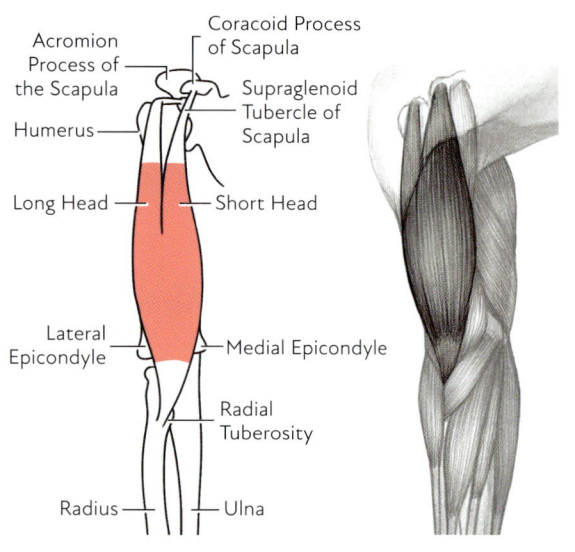

The Long Head sits on the lateral side, and the tendon is stretched vertically. It runs through a groove in the **Humerus**, then it is attached to the **Supraglenoid Tubercle of the Scapula**. On the medial side is the Short Head. The tendon also runs vertically and it is attached to the **Coracoid Process of the Scapula**. Both heads unite and become a large oval-shaped muscle that is attached to a projection called the **Radial Tuberosity**.

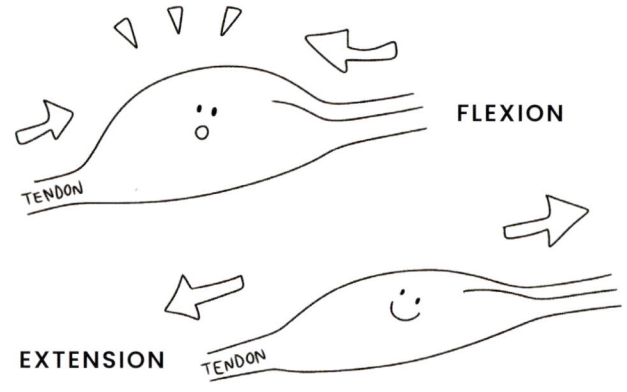

The insertion of the Biceps is squeezed between the **Ridge Muscles** and **Flexors**. You can sometimes see a trianglar-shaped shadow on the inner side of the Elbow.

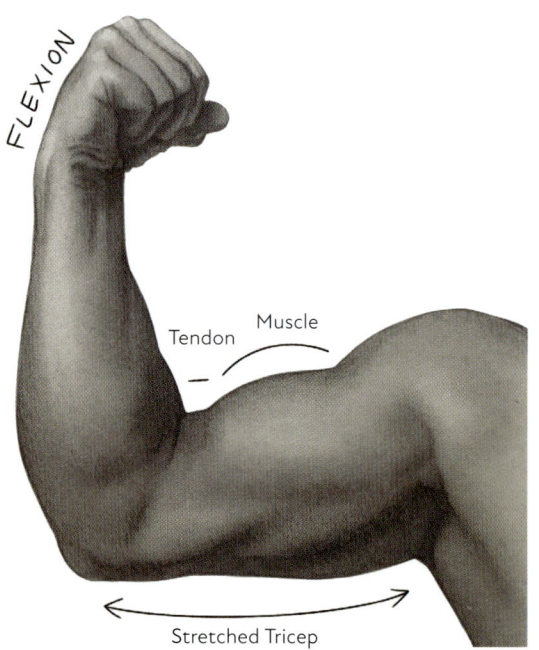

When the arm is flexed, the Biceps muscle bulges while the Tricep is stretched. Even when the Biceps is flexed, you can still see the inferior tendon making a short straight line, compared to the round volume of the muscle.

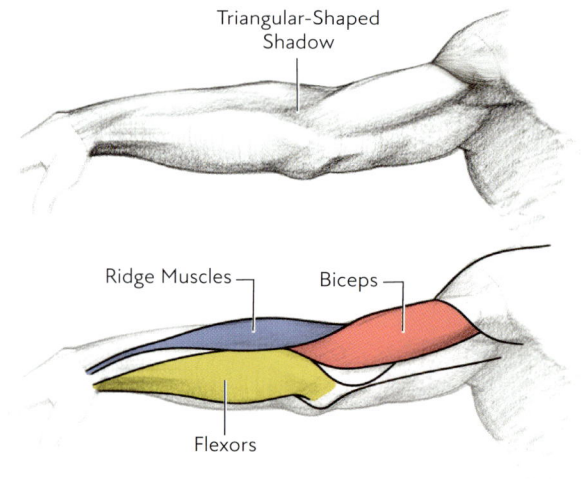

Shape of the Triceps

The **Triceps Brachii** is called the *Triceps* because the muscle has three heads: the **Long Head**, the **Lateral Head**, and the **Medial Head**.

The Long Head sits on the medial posterior side, attached to the **Scapula** (specifically to the **Infraglenoid Tubercle of the Scapula**). The Lateral Head originates on the lateral posterior side of the **Humerus** to the superior part. The Medial Head is overlapped by the other heads, and it also originates from the superior part of the Humerus.

Triceps Brachii

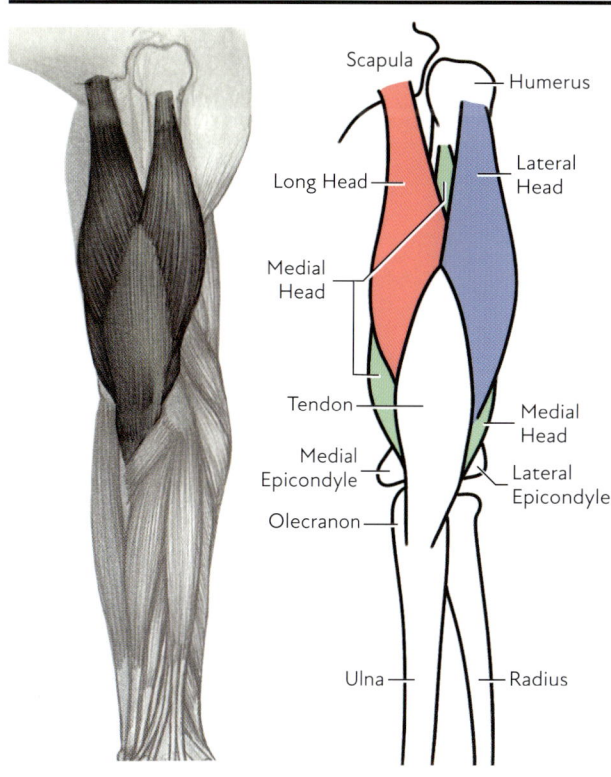

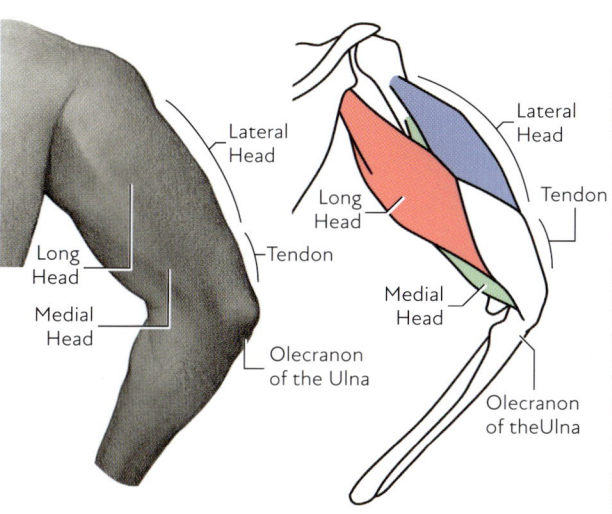

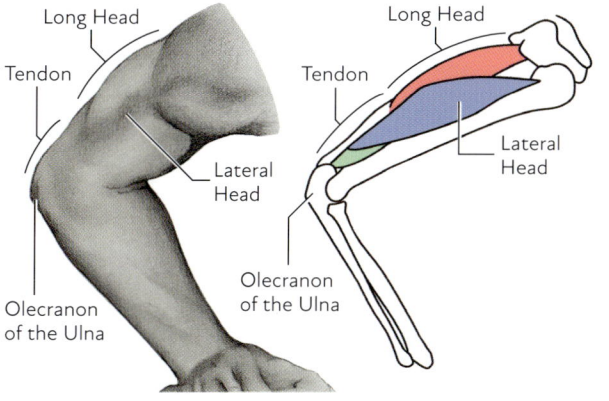

All three heads become the tendon at the insertion of the Triceps, the **Olecranon of the Ulna**. Overall, the Triceps is shaped like a diamond, with the tendon forming another smaller diamond shape within it.

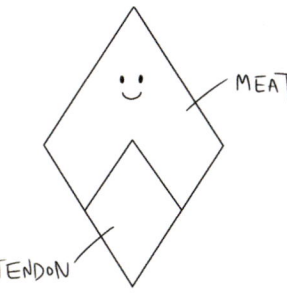

You can see the different and unique curved lines on the Triceps compared to the Biceps. The muscle part and the tendon part of the Triceps usually have their own individual volume. You can emphasize those lines to create a dramatic arm drawing.

The Triangle Shape of the Elbow

Olecranon and Epicondyle

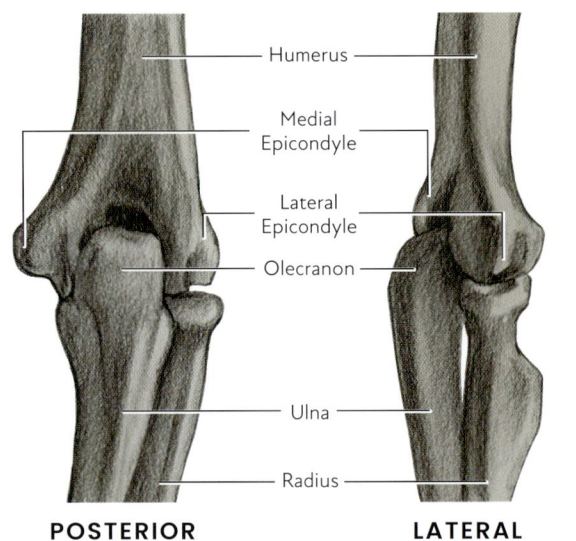

- Humerus
- Medial Epicondyle
- Lateral Epicondyle
- Olecranon
- Ulna
- Radius

POSTERIOR   **LATERAL**

The elbow is formed by the **Humerus** and the **Ulna**. The upper end of the **Ulna**, called the **Olecranon**, hooks into a depression of the lower Humerus called the **Olecranon Fossa**. This hinge joint allows the arm to flex in motion.

On the lateral and medial side of the Humerus next to the Fossa, there are projections called the **Lateral Epicondyle (L.E.)** and the **Medial Epicondyle (M.E.)**.

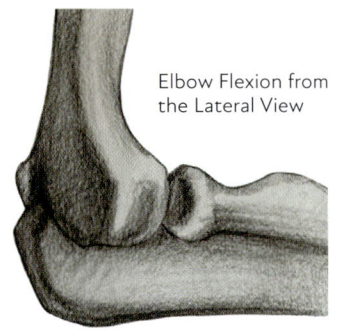

Elbow Flexion from the Lateral View

Extended

When the arm is extended, all three points of the Olecranon and Epicondyles line up.

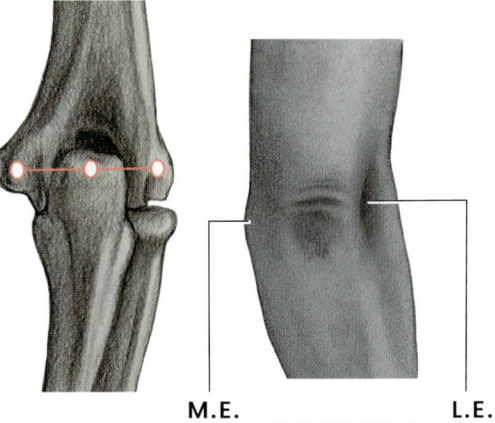

M.E.   L.E.

Flexed

When the arm is flexed, the Olecranon moves lower, and the three points become a triangular shape.

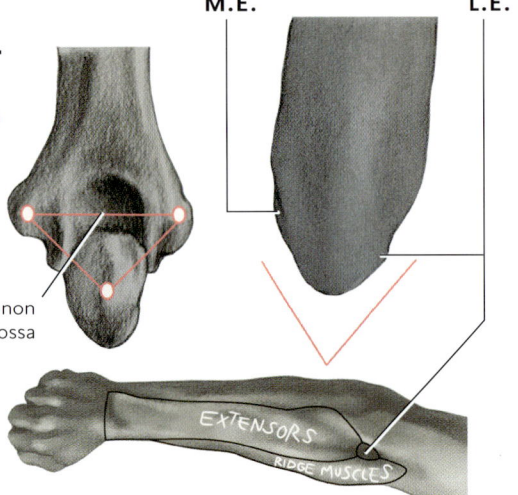

Olecranon Fossa

EXTENSORS

RIDGE MUSCLES

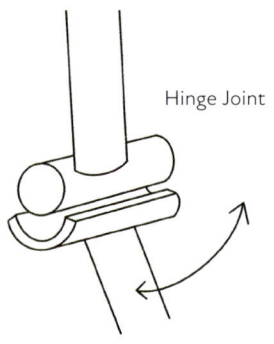

Hinge Joint

Why does hitting your funny bone hurt?

Now we know that the actual anatomical term of the funny bone is the Medial Epicondyle! There

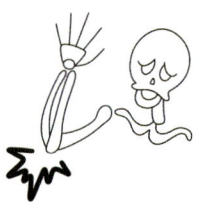

is a nerve system running through the M.E. and Ulna bone that causes the electric-like sharp pain you experience when your funny bone is hit.

Extensor Digiti Minimi

A Secret Muscle in the Forearm

The **Extensor Digiti Minimi** is a cute muscle with a cute name. This muscle is a part of the extensor muscles on the posterior side of the forearm. It peeks out in between the **Extensor Digitorum** and **Extensor Carpi Ulnaris.** The tendon goes down to the fifth digit in the hand, so this muscle may be visible when you wiggle your pinky. If not, that's totally normal too!

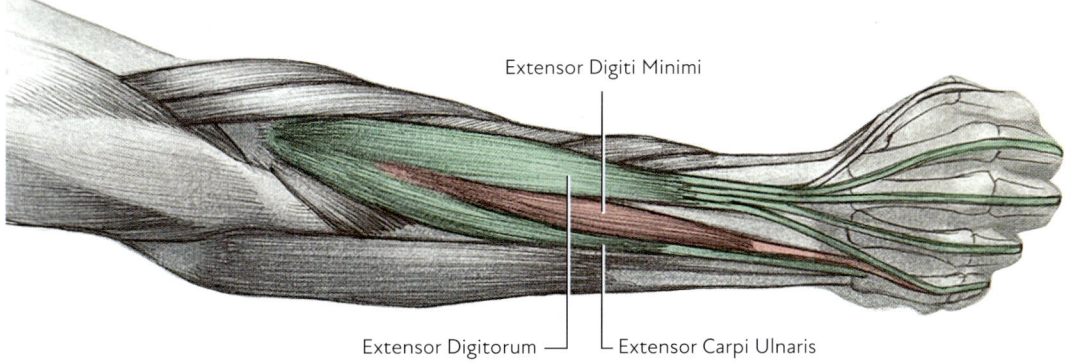

Extensor Digiti Minimi

Extensor Digitorum — └ Extensor Carpi Ulnaris

You can often see this small muscle in the posterior forearms of Michelangelo's sculptures. Michelangelo is known for exaggerating muscles in his artworks. Showing this tiny muscle in his sculptures tells us that he was truly talented and knew the body well.

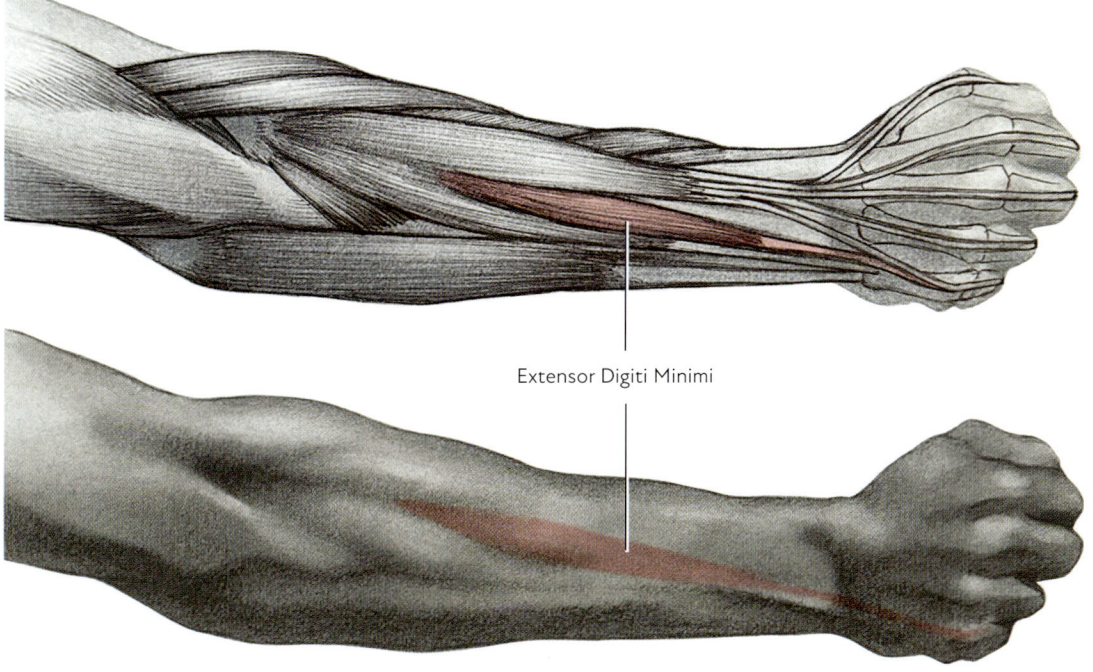

Extensor Digiti Minimi

Are You a Super Evolved Human?

A Story of the Palmaris Longus

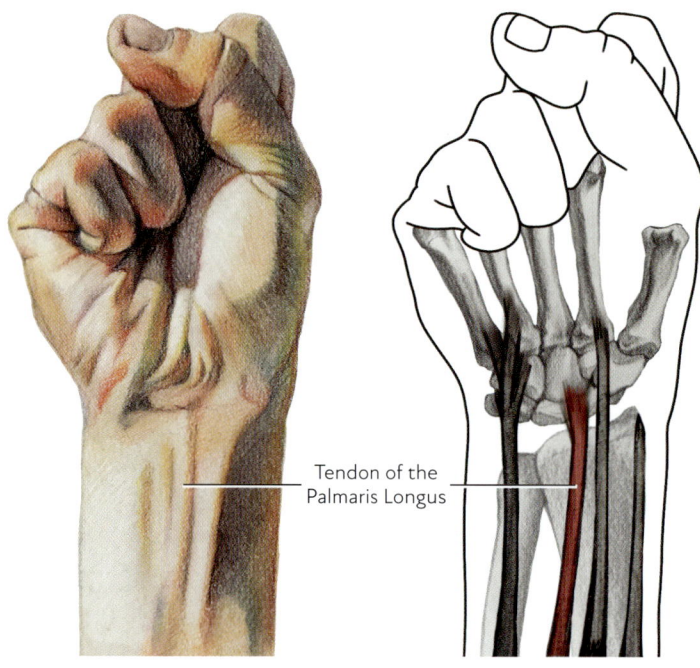

Tendon of the
Palmaris Longus

Do you see a tendon raised under the skin when you make a tight fist and flex your wrist? If you see it, that means that you are looking at the **tendon of the Palmaris Longus**. This tendon can be absent for about 14% of the population because we actually don't have to use this muscle anymore.

The original function of the Palmaris Longus is to stabilize and balance the flexion movement in the wrist. However, it is one of the most random muscles in our body and we don't exactly know how this muscle can be present or absent for some people. Many animal species have well-developed Palmaris Longus tendons to support their weight, but we humans do not walk with our hands, so that ought to tell us something. If you don't see this tendon, maybe you are more developed as a human species than others?

The Palmaris Longus is a part of the flexor muscles in the anterior side of the forearm. It is located in between the **Flexor Carpi Radialis** and the **Flexor Carpi Ulnaris**, and all three originate from the **Medial Epicondyle of the Humerus**. The Palmaris Longus is connected to the triangle-shaped fascia called the Palmar Aponeurosis.

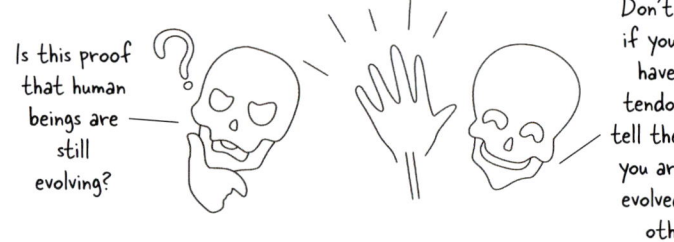

Is this proof that human beings are still evolving?

Don't worry if you don't have this tendon, just tell them that you are more evolved than others!

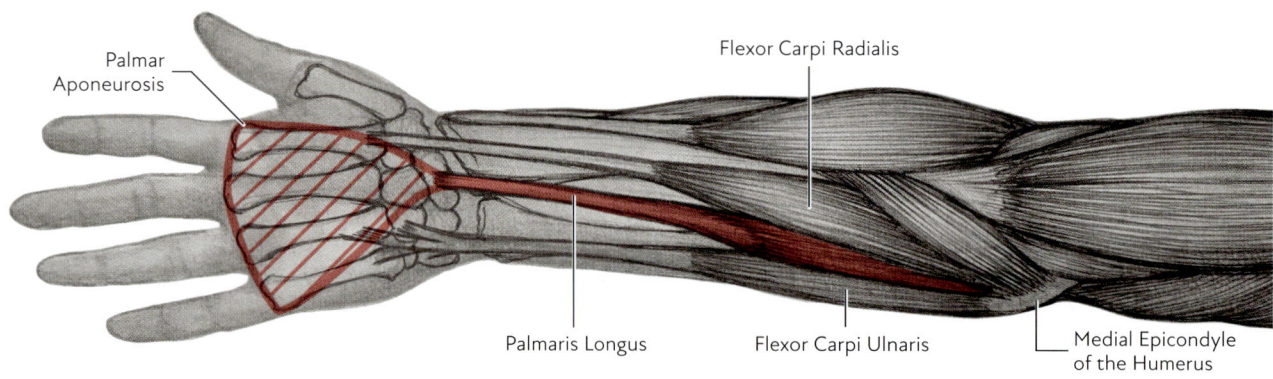

Palmar
Aponeurosis

Flexor Carpi Radialis

Palmaris Longus

Flexor Carpi Ulnaris

Medial Epicondyle
of the Humerus

The Volume Under the Armpit Is Called the Coracobrachialis

Let's talk about why the armpit is a "pit."

The armpit is hollow. In drawings, you would probably add some shading in this area. The reason the armpit is a "pit" and does not receive any light is because there are walls of muscles that make a rooftop above it.

But wait, there is a small, poofy volume in this hollow space. This muscle is called the **Coracobrachialis**. Imagine that there is a small creature sitting under a roof.

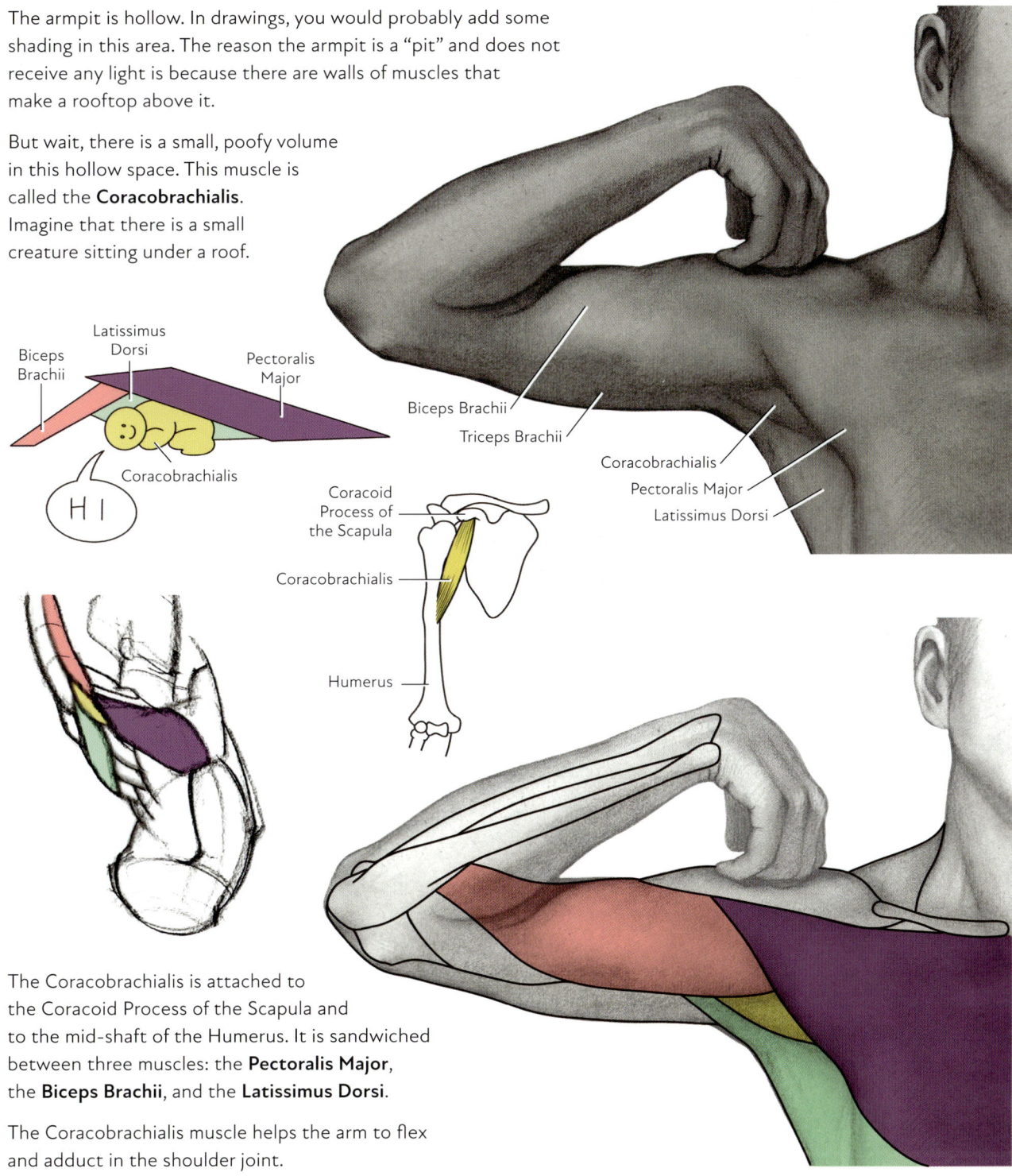

The Coracobrachialis is attached to the Coracoid Process of the Scapula and to the mid-shaft of the Humerus. It is sandwiched between three muscles: the **Pectoralis Major**, the **Biceps Brachii**, and the **Latissimus Dorsi**.

The Coracobrachialis muscle helps the arm to flex and adduct in the shoulder joint.

The Bone-In-Meat Shape of the Forearm

Muscles and Volume of Forearm

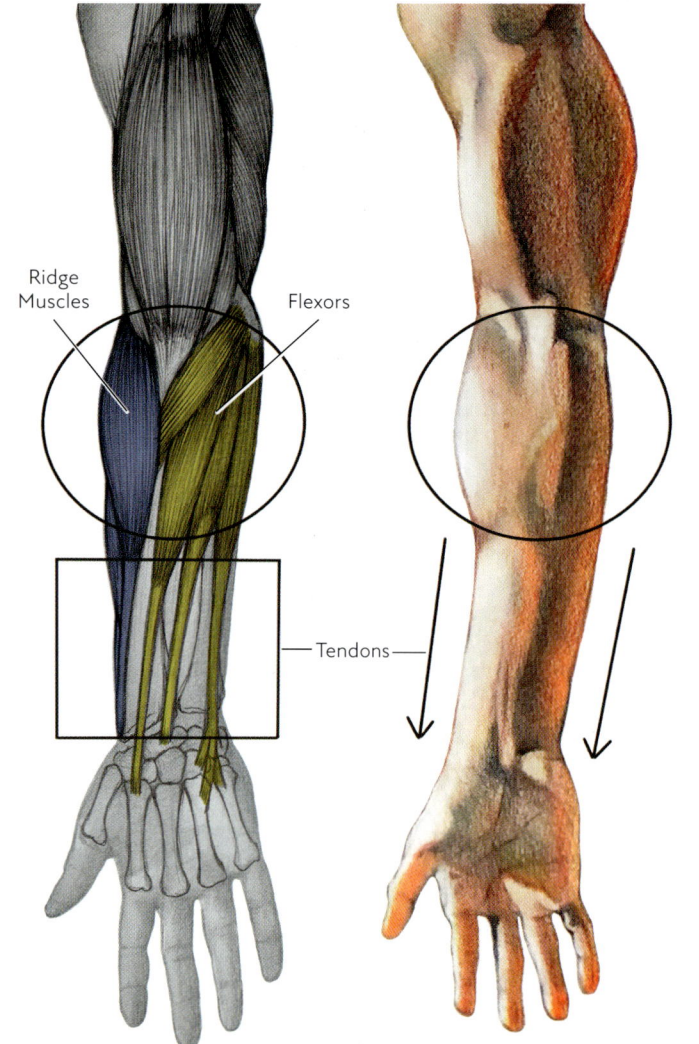

Ridge Muscles

Flexors

Tendons

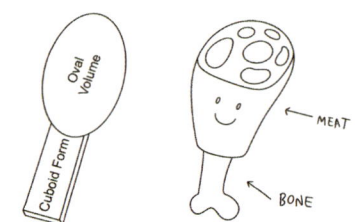

The volume in the forearm appears on the proximal side because that is where the muscles are condensed with the **Ridge Muscles** and **Flexors**.

The distal portion of the forearm is comprised of tendons, resulting in a flat box-like shape, like a cuboid. All together it looks like a cartoon "meat on the bone."

In the pronation position of forearm, the oval and cuboid volumes stay the same. However, the most characteristic part is the movement of the **Ridge Muscles**. Because this muscle group starts on the lateral side of the Humerus and ends on the distal portion of the lateral side of the Radius, it follows the movement of **pronation**, where the Radius and Ulna cross. You can often see the Ridge Muscles bulging.

Another iconic feature you can see in the forearm is the **Flexors**. This muscle group sits on the anterior side, but it can be visible from the posterior view as well.

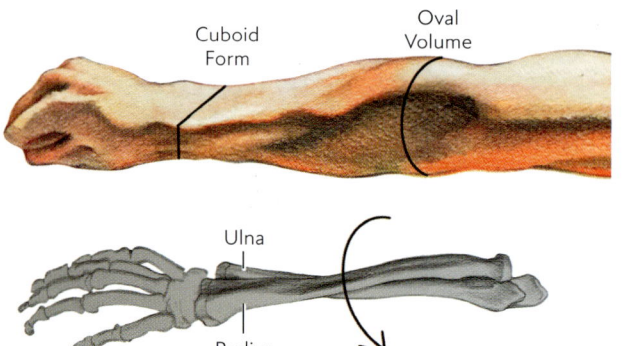

Cuboid Form

Oval Volume

Ulna

Radius

Pronation: The forearm position with the palm facing down. The Radius bone crosses over the Ulna bone and makes an X shape.

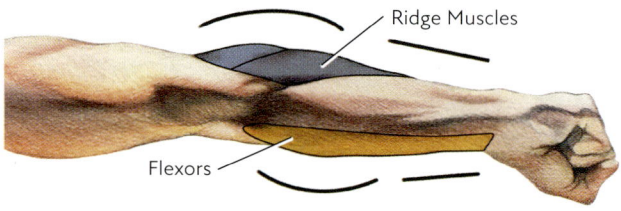

Ridge Muscles

Flexors

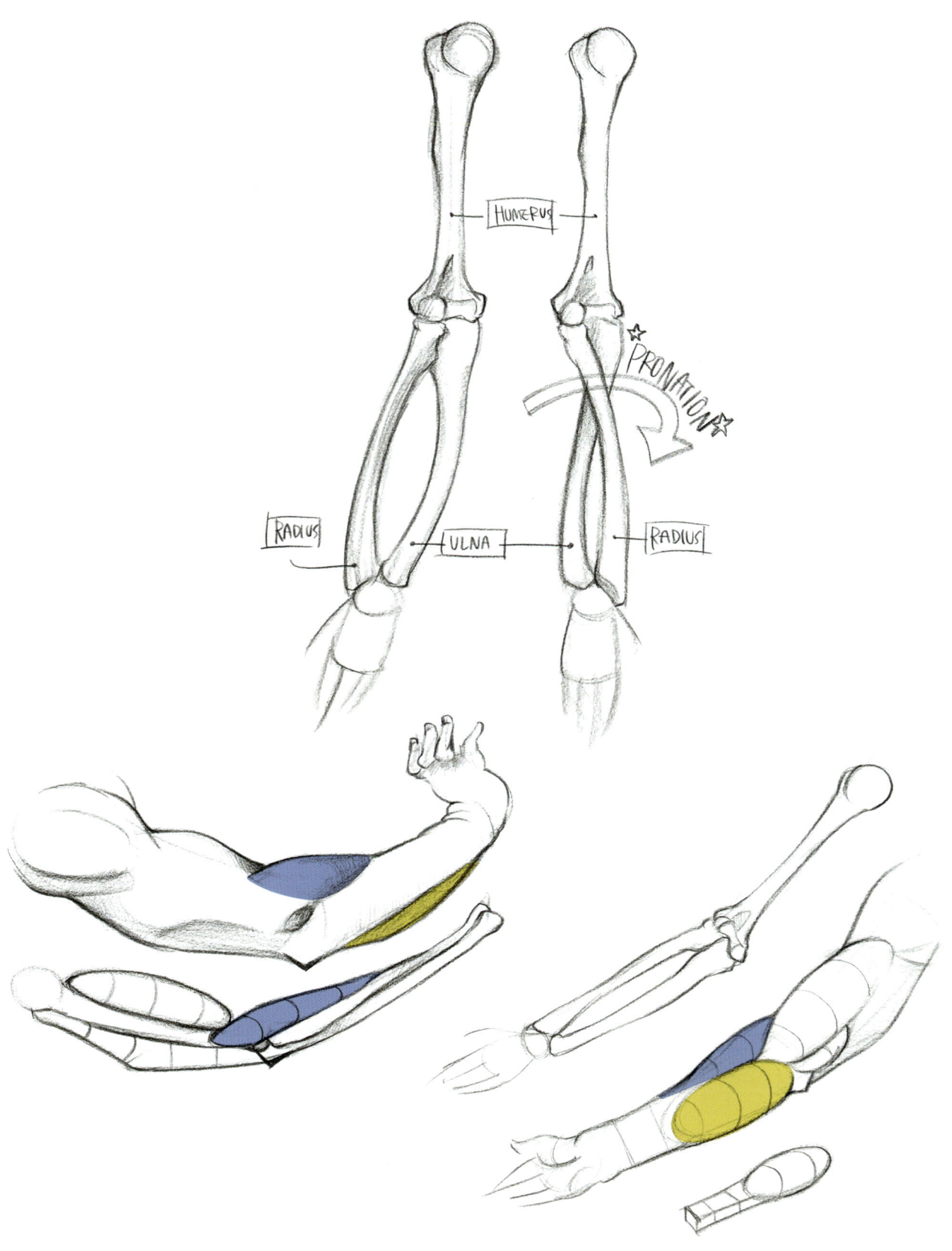

S and C Curves and the Zig-Zag Flow of the Forearm

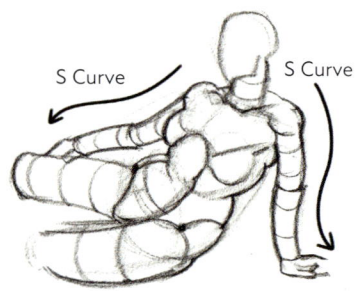

S Curve

S Curve

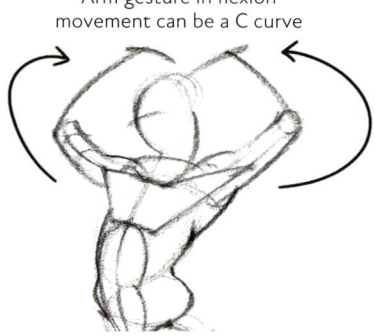

Arm gesture in flexion movement can be a C curve

It is important to understand the overall flow of the arm in a gesture drawing process. You can often go with the **S** curve when the arm is extended, and the **C** curve for the flexion of the arm. This is the easiest and simplest way to capture the shape of the arm. If there is too much symmetry of form, that might come out a bit stiff. There is always a natural flow happening in the human body, and the arm is not an exception.

When you work on your arm sketch, the overall form of the arm should be **asymmetrical**. Imagine that the volume follows the form of a zig-zag. In this posterior view of the arm, you can see the volumes on the lateral and medial sides are uneven. In the shoulder, there is the round form of the **Deltoid**. In the upper arm, there is the volume of the **Triceps Brachii** sitting lower than the Deltoid muscle. Below that, the volume appears back on the lateral side where you see the **Ridge Muscles** bulging. Right under the elbow on the medial side is the **Flexor** volume behind the Ulna bone. There is an angle in the wrist, where the distal part of the Radius sits lower than the Ulna bone. All together the arm volume is asymmetrical and follows a zig-zag pattern.

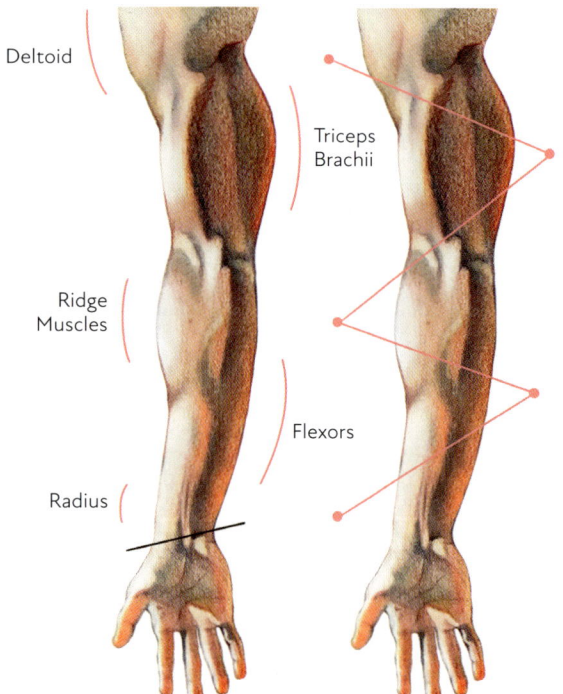

Deltoid

Triceps Brachii

Ridge Muscles

Flexors

Radius

ANTERIOR

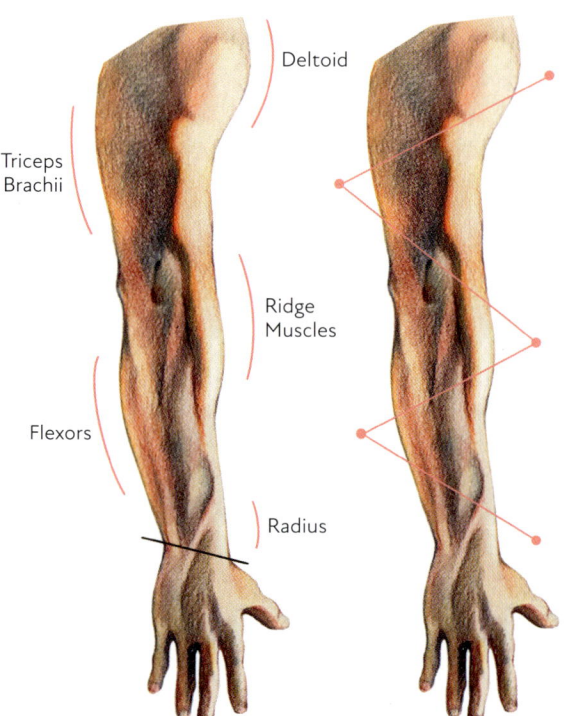

Deltoid

Triceps Brachii

Ridge Muscles

Flexors

Radius

POSTERIOR

Cross Your Arms to See a Common Anatomical Form

When someone crosses their arms, you will see a horizontal line starting at the elbow and running down the forearm, with volume appearing below that line. This line is a line of one of the forearm bones, and the volume under it is one of the flexor muscles being pushed forward.

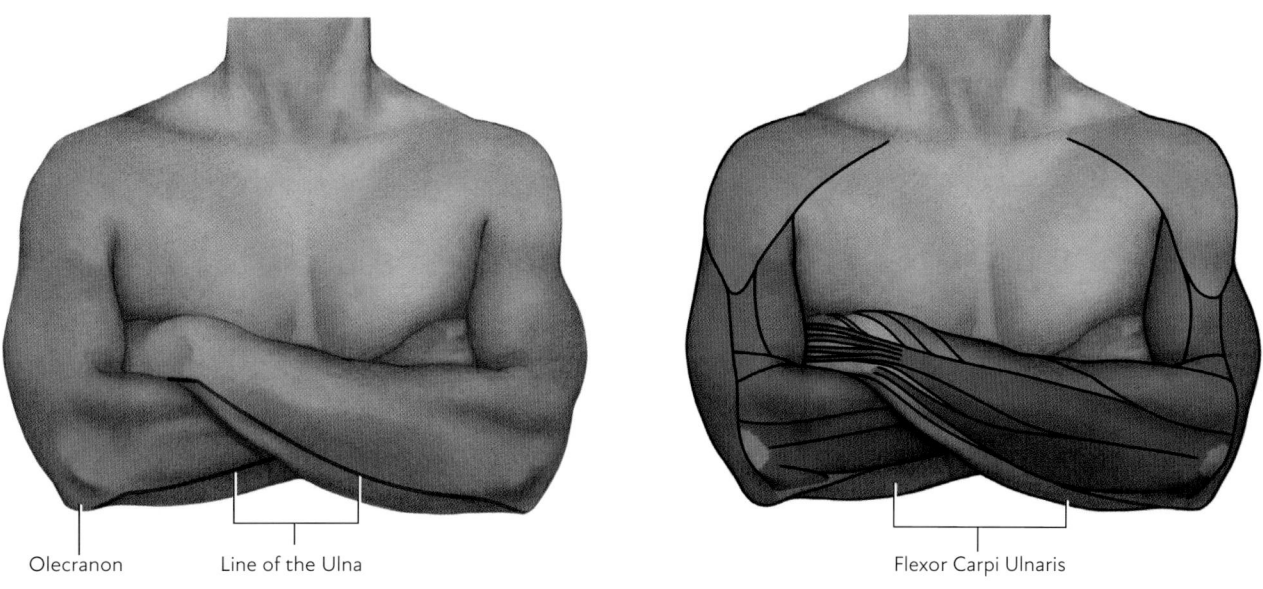

Olecranon   Line of the Ulna

Flexor Carpi Ulnaris

The **Ulna** is a bone that forms your elbow (**Olecranon**) and it goes straight to the wrist on your pinky side. The Ulna is not fully covered by muscles, so depending on the arm position, it may be visible on your arm.

Flexors are the muscles that form on the front side of your forearm. When the arms are crossed, they press against the Ulna, and the volume becomes visible. This flexor muscle is called the **Flexor Carpi Ulnaris.**

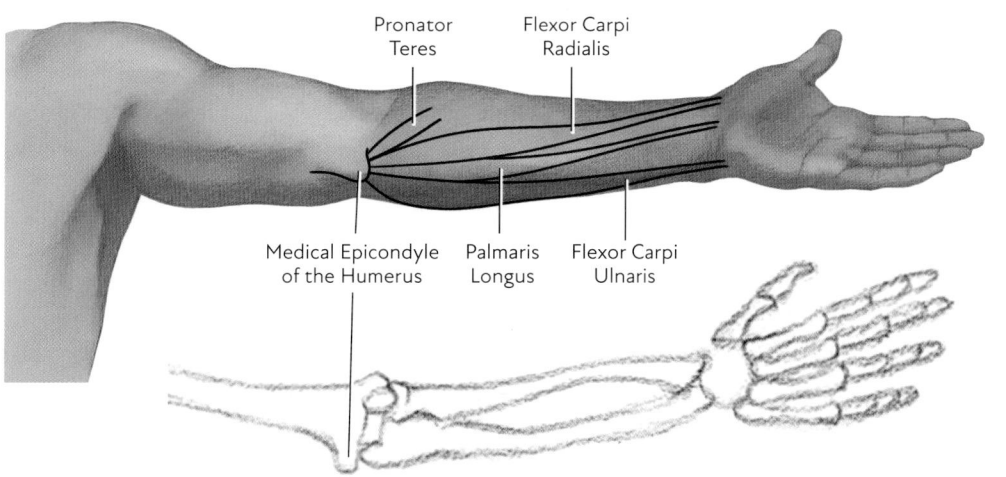

Pronator Teres

Flexor Carpi Radialis

Medical Epicondyle of the Humerus

Palmaris Longus

Flexor Carpi Ulnaris

Flexors in the Forearm

The origin of all four flexor muscles is the **Medial Epicondyle of the Humerus.**

Arm Muscles Overview

Anterior

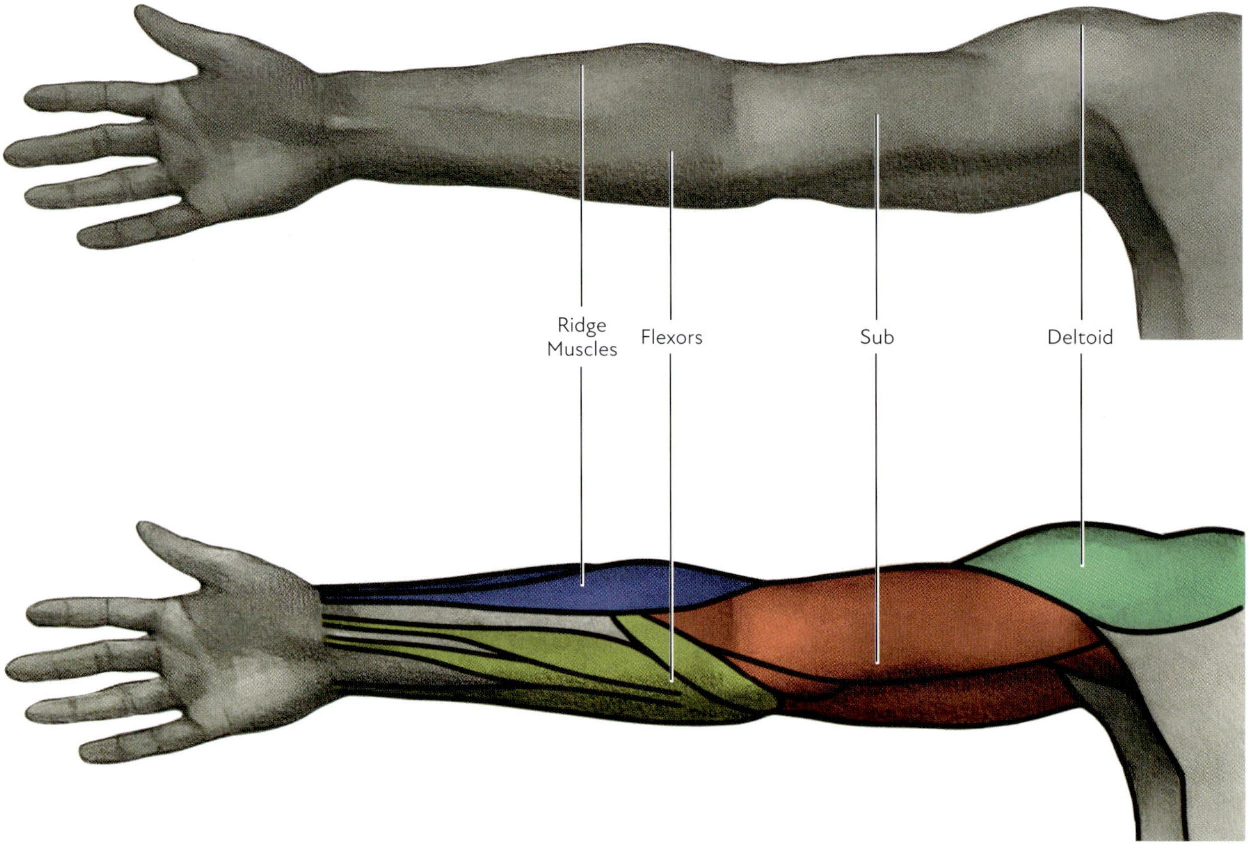

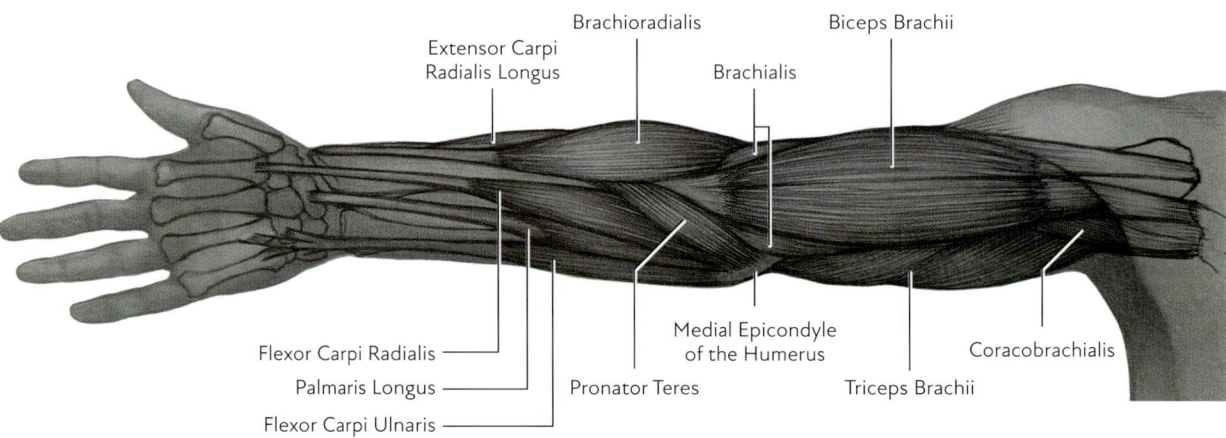

Ridge Muscles   Flexors   Sub   Deltoid

Brachioradialis

Extensor Carpi Radialis Longus

Brachialis

Biceps Brachii

Flexor Carpi Radialis

Palmaris Longus

Flexor Carpi Ulnaris

Pronator Teres

Medial Epicondyle of the Humerus

Triceps Brachii

Coracobrachialis

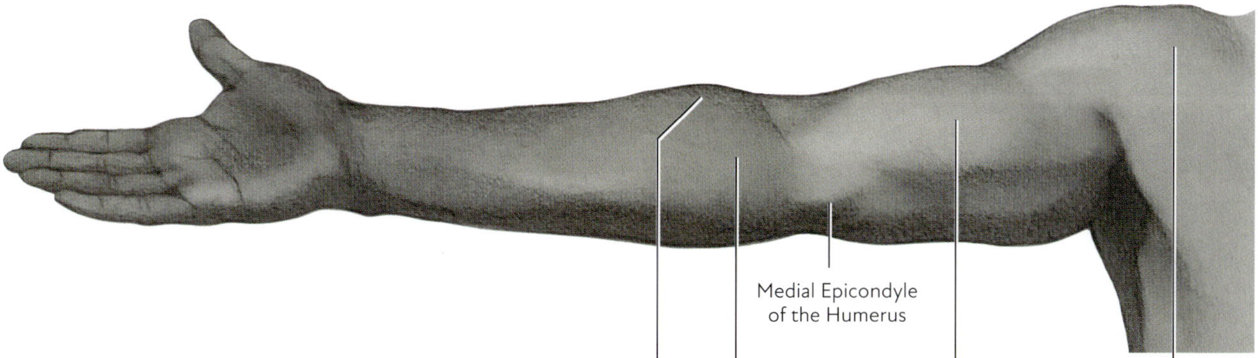

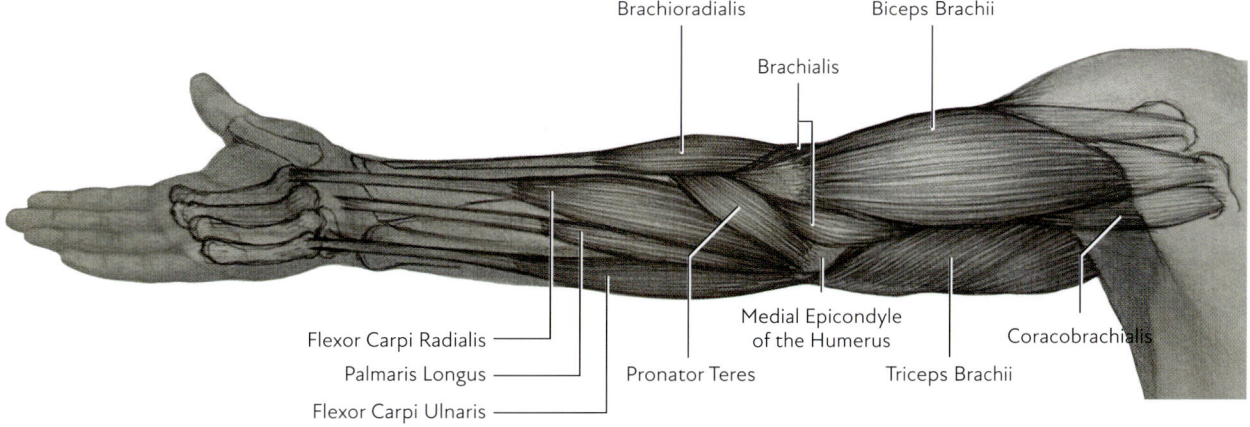

Ridge
Muscles   Flexors

Medial Epicondyle
of the Humerus

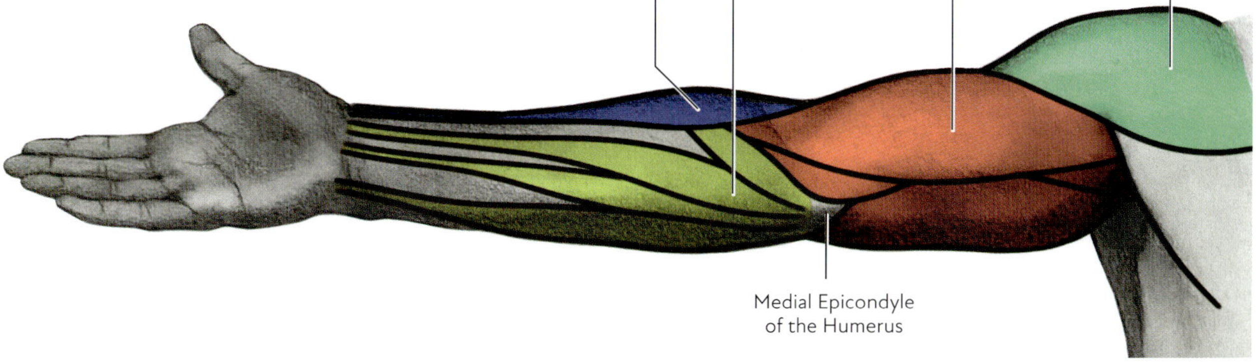

Sub   Deltoid

Medial Epicondyle
of the Humerus

Brachioradialis   Biceps Brachii

Brachialis

Flexor Carpi Radialis

Palmaris Longus

Flexor Carpi Ulnaris

Pronator Teres

Medial Epicondyle
of the Humerus

Triceps Brachii

Coracobrachialis

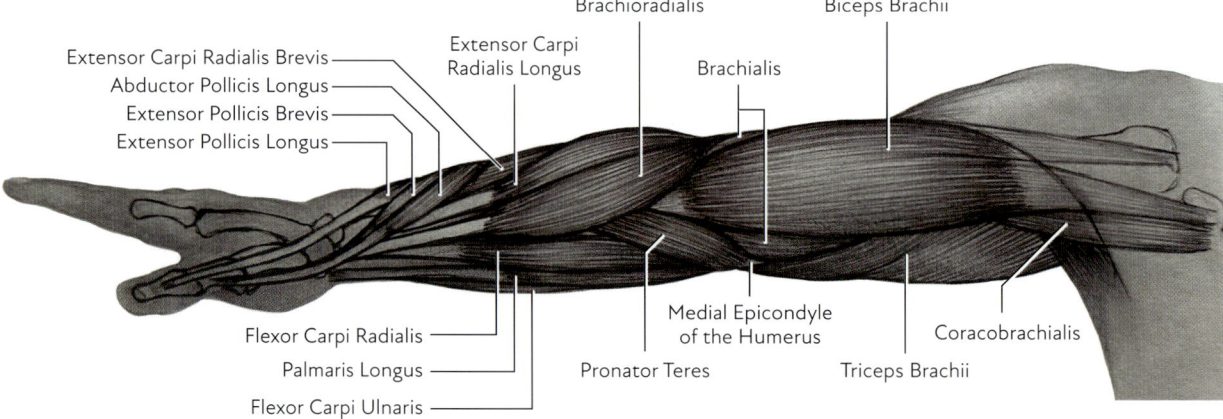

Medial Epicondyle
of the Humerus

Deep
Extensors

Flexors

Ridge
Muscles

Sub

Deltoid

Medial Epicondyle
of the Humerus

Extensor Carpi Radialis Brevis
Abductor Pollicis Longus
Extensor Pollicis Brevis
Extensor Pollicis Longus

Extensor Carpi
Radialis Longus

Brachioradialis

Brachialis

Biceps Brachii

Flexor Carpi Radialis

Palmaris Longus

Flexor Carpi Ulnaris

Pronator Teres

Medial Epicondyle
of the Humerus

Triceps Brachii

Coracobrachialis

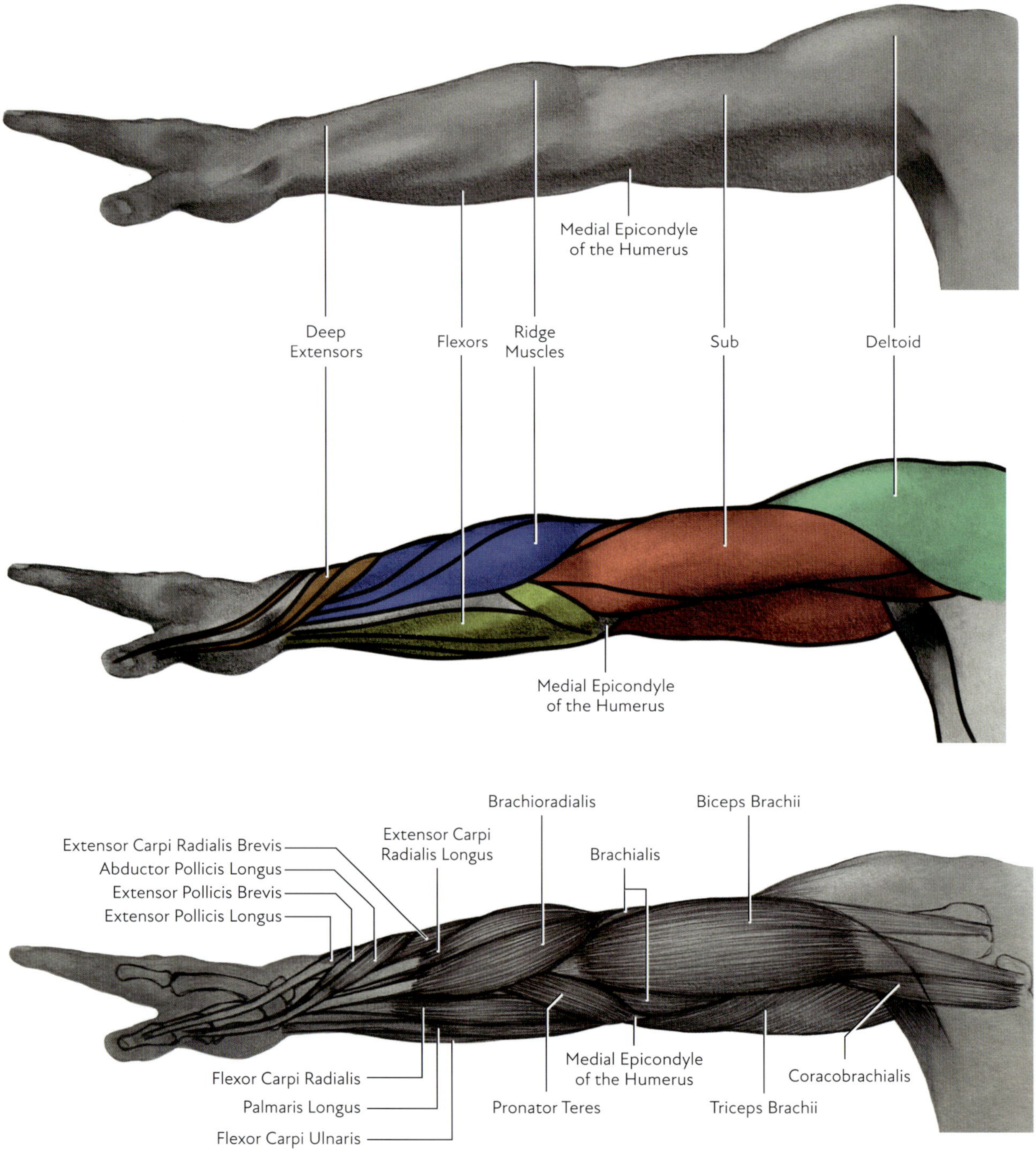

Posterior

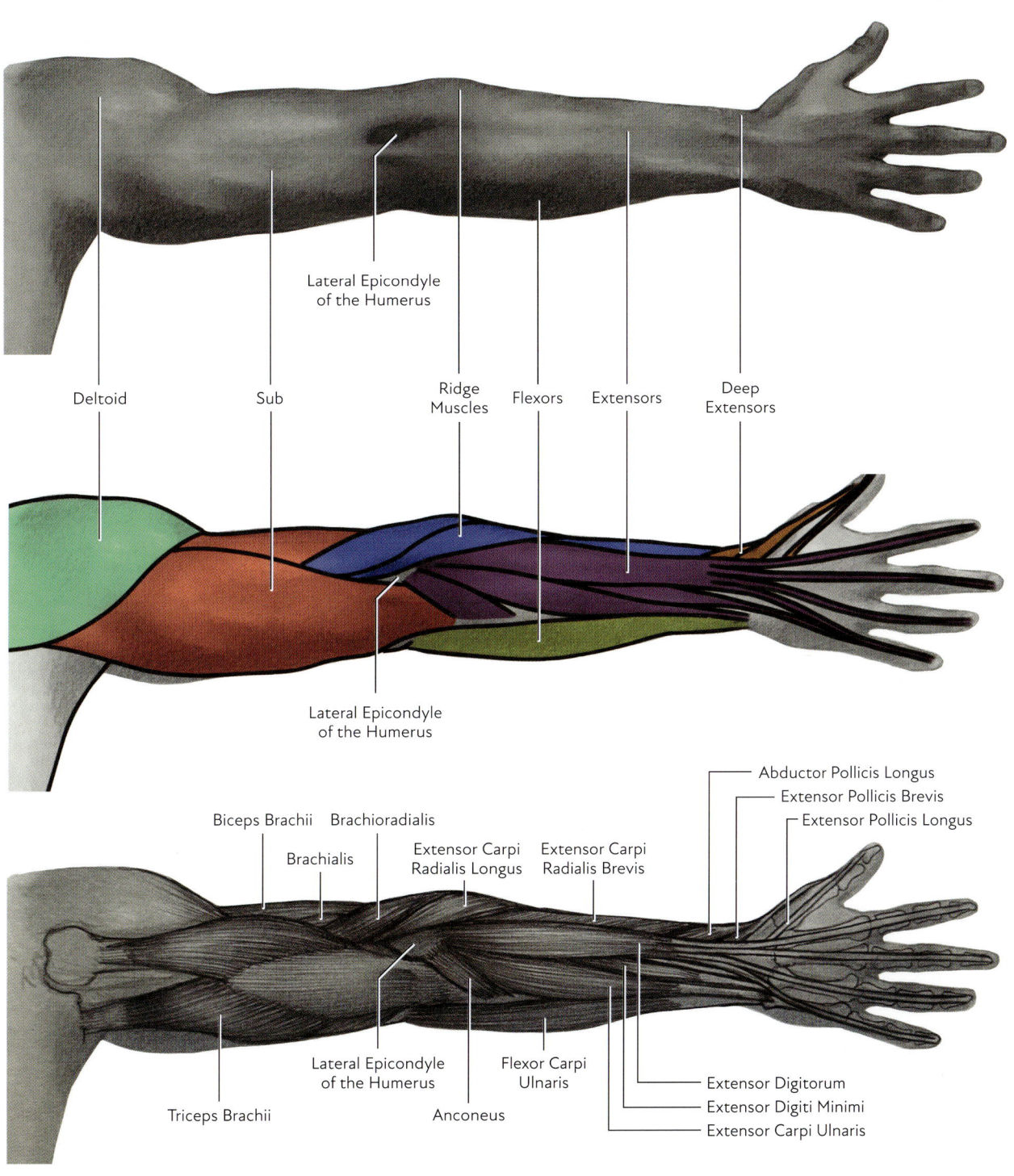

Lateral Epicondyle
of the Humerus

Deltoid   Sub   Ridge   Flexors   Extensors   Deep
                        Muscles   Extensors

Lateral Epicondyle
of the Humerus

Biceps Brachii   Brachioradialis   Abductor Pollicis Longus
                                        Extensor Pollicis Brevis
        Brachialis   Extensor Carpi   Extensor Carpi   Extensor Pollicis Longus
                    Radialis Longus   Radialis Brevis

                Lateral Epicondyle
                of the Humerus   Flexor Carpi
                                    Ulnaris

                                                Extensor Digitorum

Triceps Brachii   Anconeus   Extensor Digiti Minimi

                                            Extensor Carpi Ulnaris

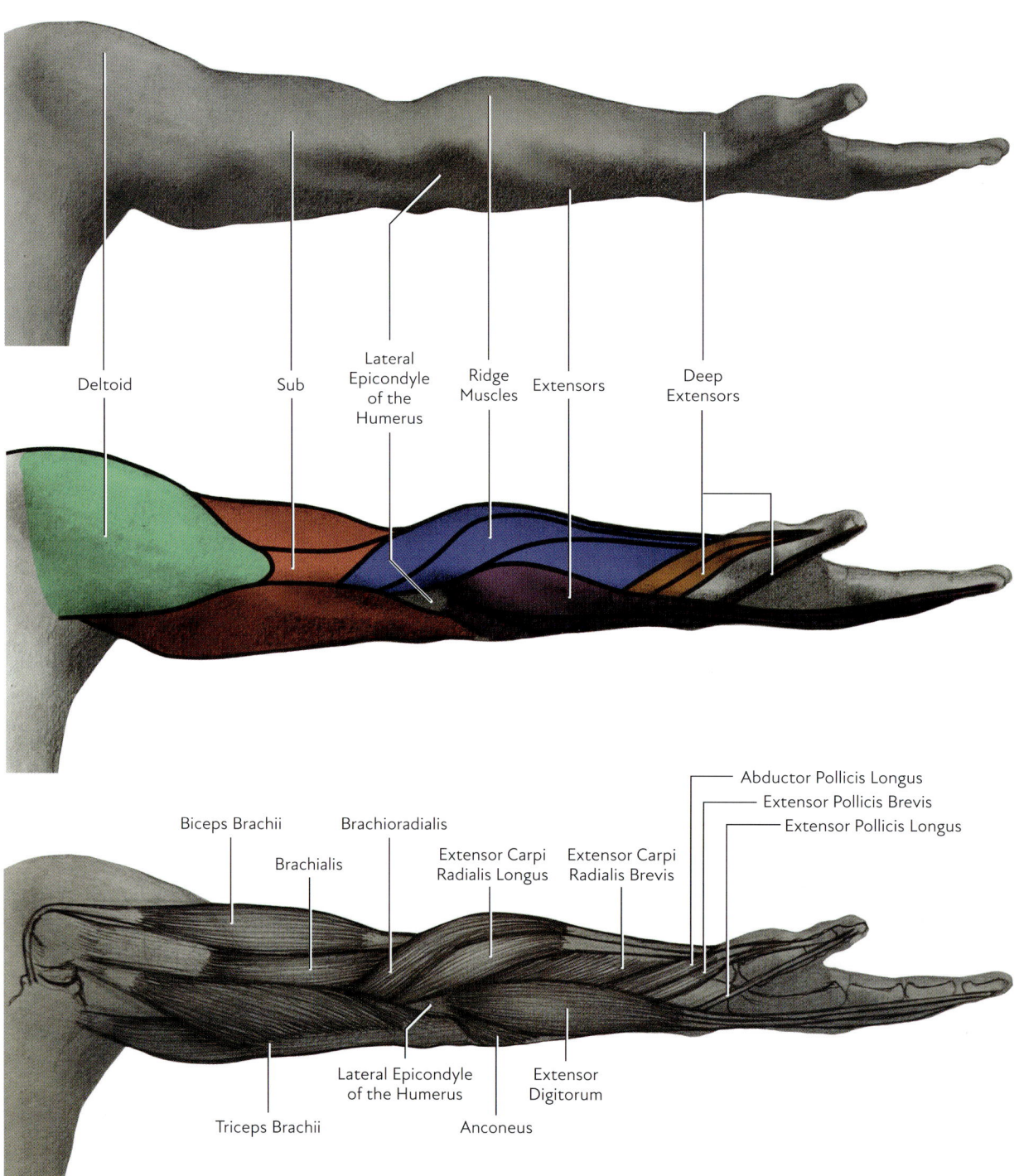

Deltoid

Sub

Lateral Epicondyle of the Humerus

Ridge Muscles

Extensors

Deep Extensors

Biceps Brachii

Brachialis

Brachioradialis

Extensor Carpi Radialis Longus

Extensor Carpi Radialis Brevis

Abductor Pollicis Longus

Extensor Pollicis Brevis

Extensor Pollicis Longus

Triceps Brachii

Lateral Epicondyle of the Humerus

Anconeus

Extensor Digitorum

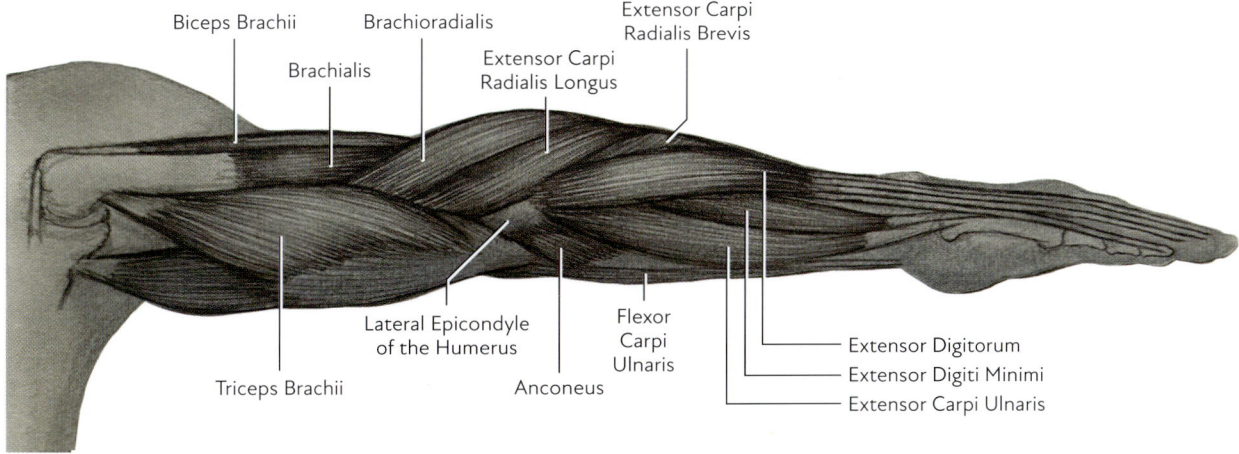

Deltoid

Sub

Lateral Epicondyle of the Humerus

Ridge Muscles

Extensors

Flexors

Biceps Brachii

Brachialis

Brachioradialis

Extensor Carpi Radialis Longus

Extensor Carpi Radialis Brevis

Triceps Brachii

Lateral Epicondyle of the Humerus

Anconeus

Flexor Carpi Ulnaris

Extensor Digitorum

Extensor Digiti Minimi

Extensor Carpi Ulnaris

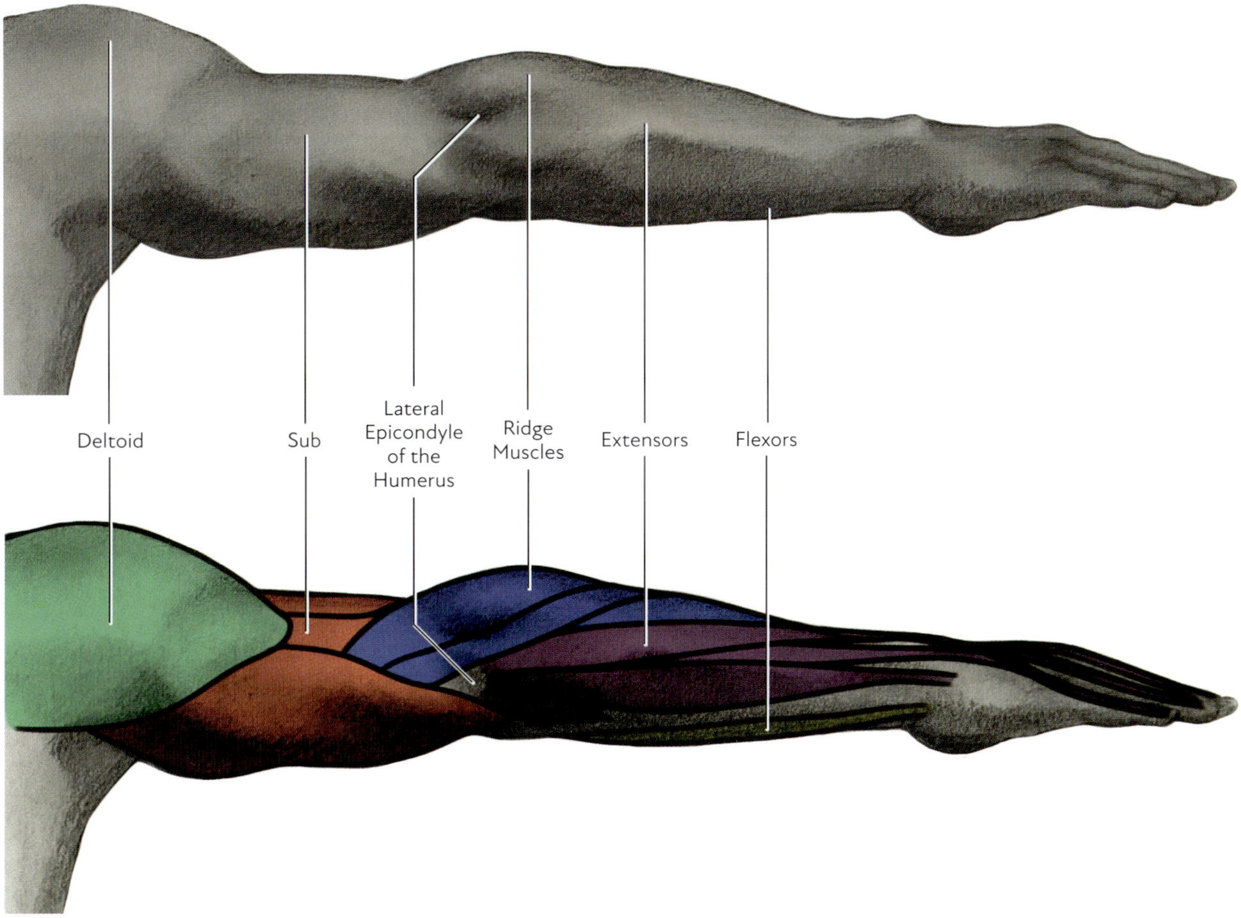

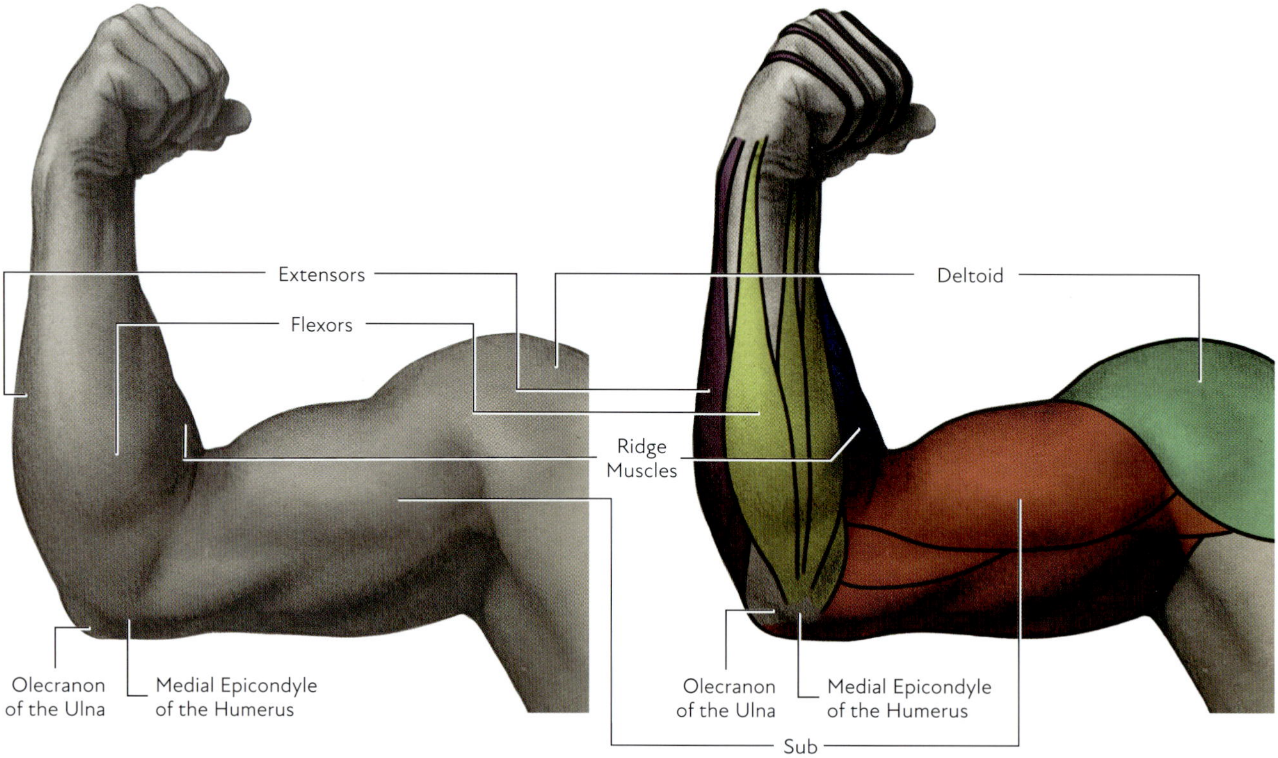

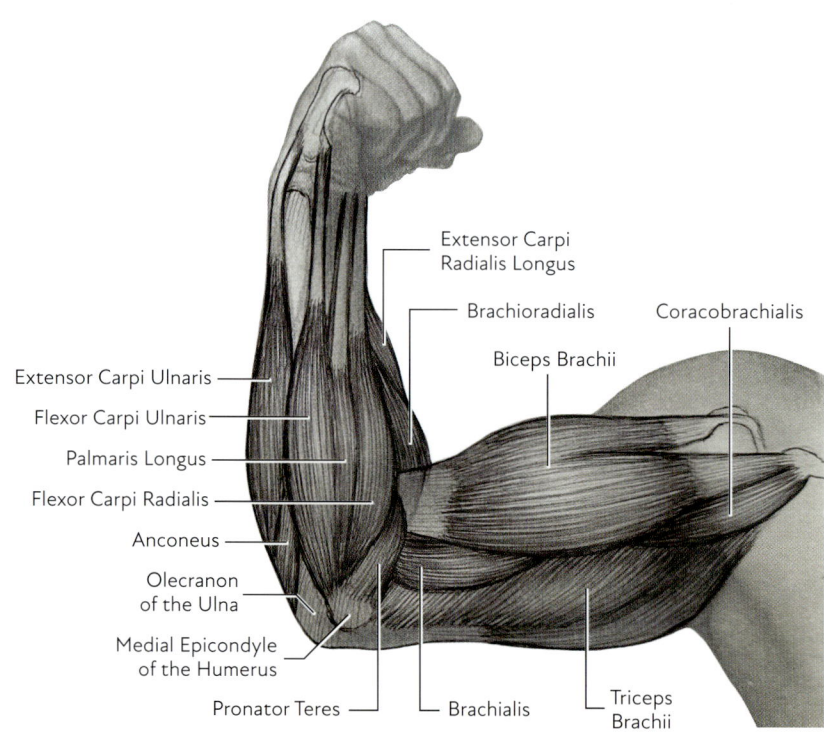

Extensors

Flexors

Deltoid

Ridge
Muscles

Olecranon
of the Ulna

Medial Epicondyle
of the Humerus

Olecranon
of the Ulna

Medial Epicondyle
of the Humerus

Sub

Extensor Carpi
Radialis Longus

Brachioradialis

Coracobrachialis

Biceps Brachii

Extensor Carpi Ulnaris

Flexor Carpi Ulnaris

Palmaris Longus

Flexor Carpi Radialis

Anconeus

Olecranon
of the Ulna

Medial Epicondyle
of the Humerus

Pronator Teres

Brachialis

Triceps
Brachii

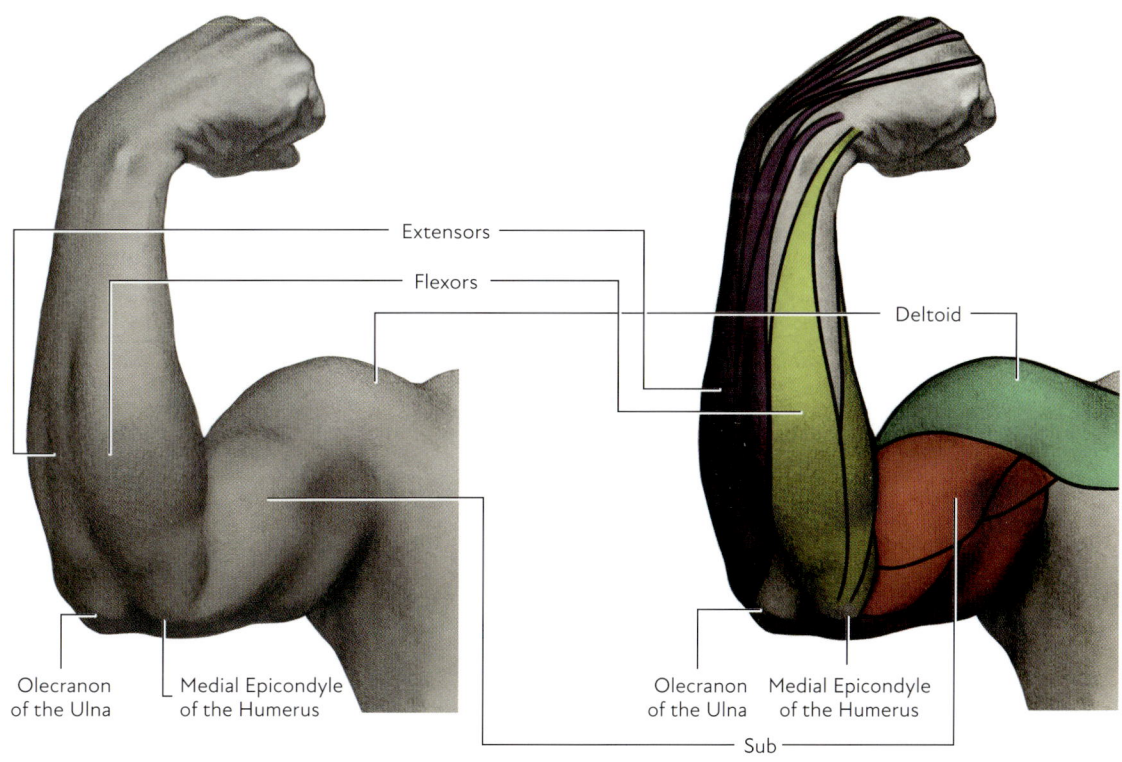

Extensors

Flexors

Deltoid

Olecranon
of the Ulna

Medial Epicondyle
of the Humerus

Olecranon
of the Ulna

Medial Epicondyle
of the Humerus

Sub

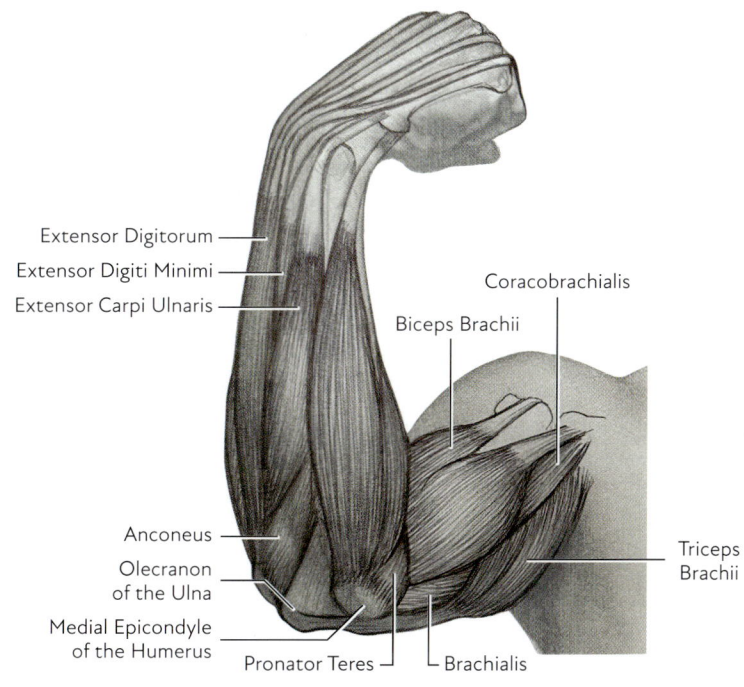

Extensor Digitorum

Extensor Digiti Minimi

Extensor Carpi Ulnaris

Coracobrachialis

Biceps Brachii

Anconeus

Olecranon
of the Ulna

Medial Epicondyle
of the Humerus

Pronator Teres

Brachialis

Triceps
Brachii

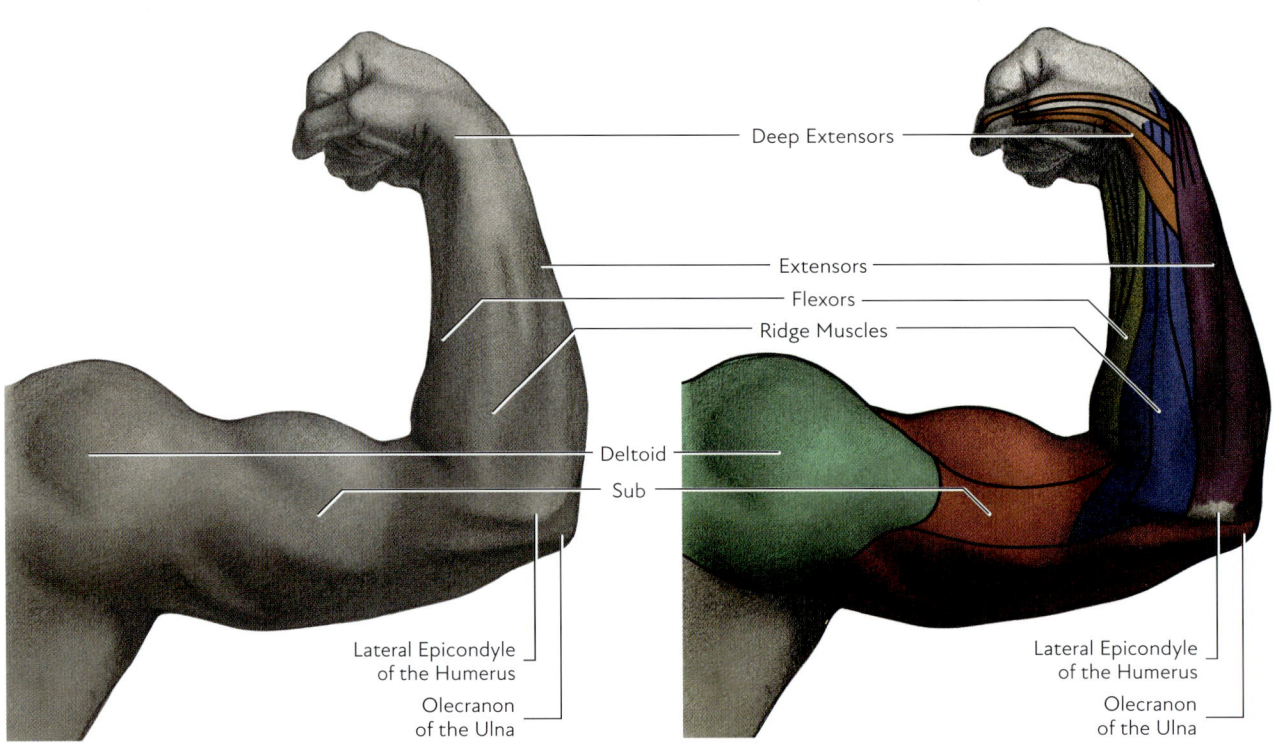

Deep Extensors

Extensors

Flexors

Ridge Muscles

Deltoid

Sub

Lateral Epicondyle
of the Humerus

Olecranon
of the Ulna

Lateral Epicondyle
of the Humerus

Olecranon
of the Ulna

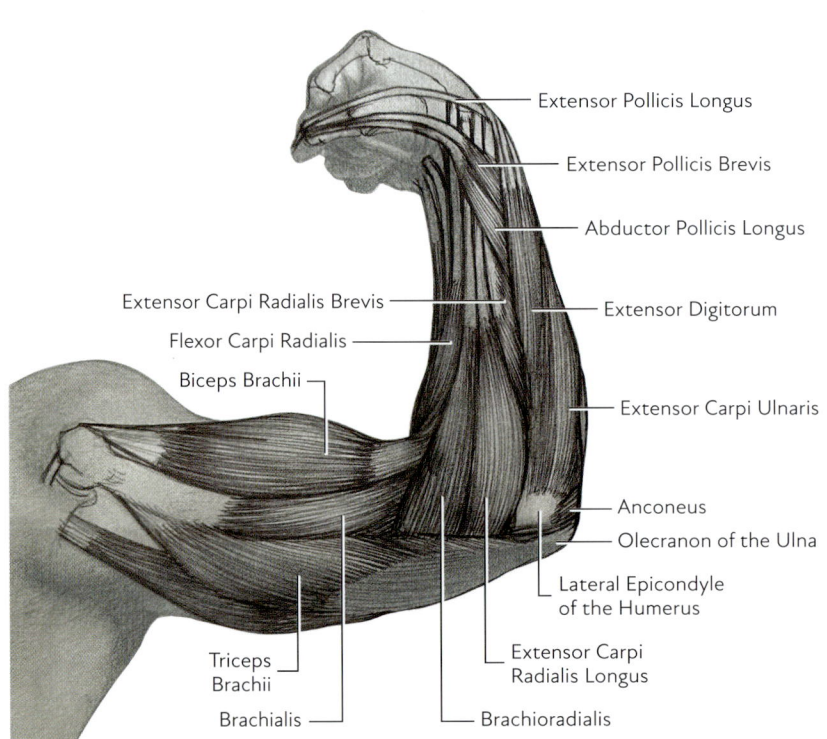

Extensor Pollicis Longus

Extensor Pollicis Brevis

Abductor Pollicis Longus

Extensor Carpi Radialis Brevis

Flexor Carpi Radialis

Biceps Brachii

Extensor Digitorum

Extensor Carpi Ulnaris

Anconeus

Olecranon of the Ulna

Lateral Epicondyle
of the Humerus

Triceps
Brachii

Brachialis

Extensor Carpi
Radialis Longus

Brachioradialis

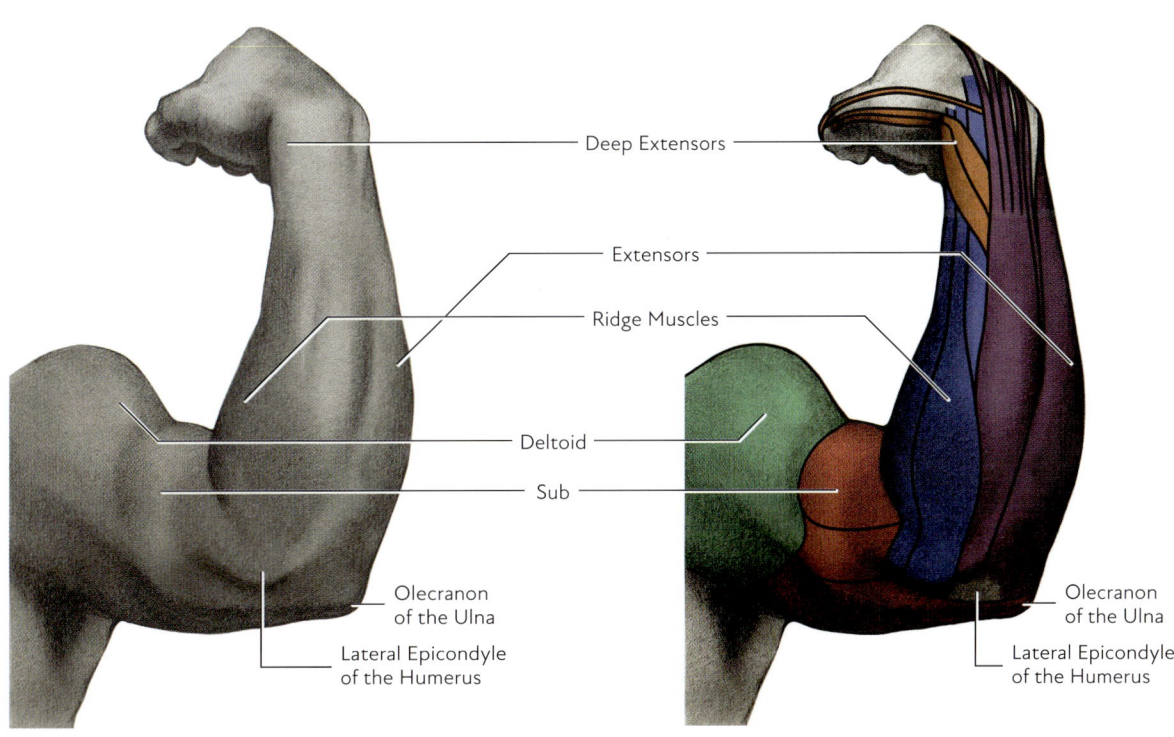

Deep Extensors

Extensors

Ridge Muscles

Deltoid

Sub

Olecranon
of the Ulna

Lateral Epicondyle
of the Humerus

Olecranon
of the Ulna

Lateral Epicondyle
of the Humerus

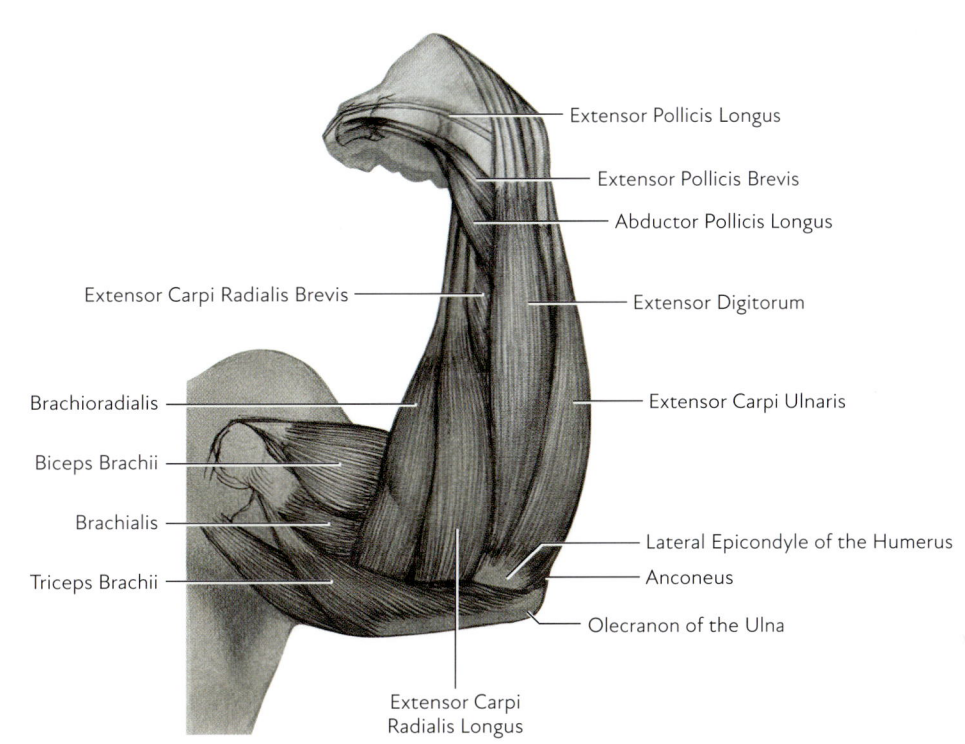

Extensor Pollicis Longus

Extensor Pollicis Brevis

Abductor Pollicis Longus

Extensor Carpi Radialis Brevis

Extensor Digitorum

Brachioradialis

Extensor Carpi Ulnaris

Biceps Brachii

Brachialis

Triceps Brachii

Lateral Epicondyle of the Humerus

Anconeus

Olecranon of the Ulna

Extensor Carpi
Radialis Longus

Crossed Arms

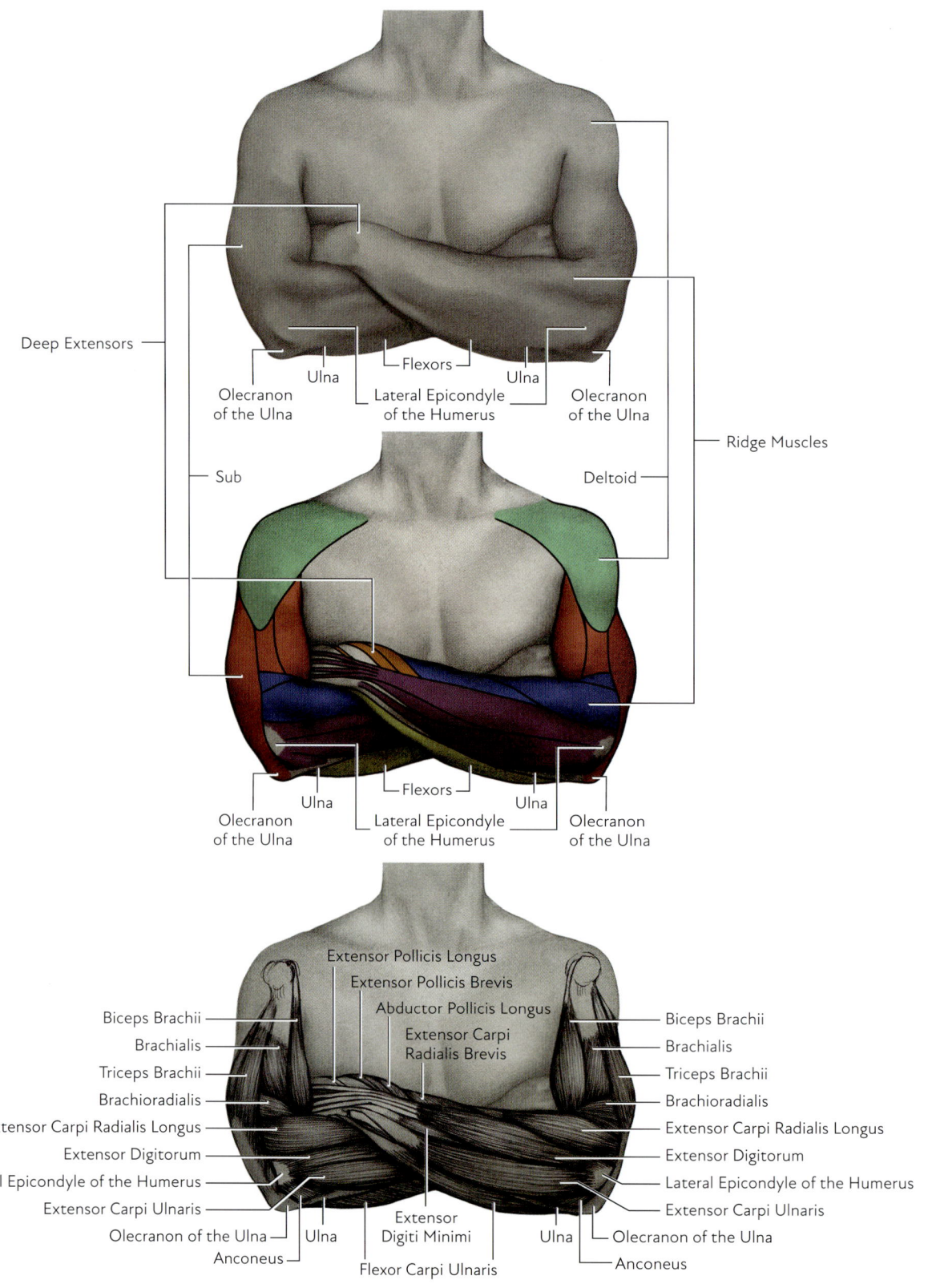

Deep Extensors

Olecranon
of the Ulna

Ulna

Flexors

Lateral Epicondyle
of the Humerus

Ulna

Olecranon
of the Ulna

Ridge Muscles

Sub

Deltoid

Olecranon
of the Ulna

Ulna

Flexors

Lateral Epicondyle
of the Humerus

Ulna

Olecranon
of the Ulna

Extensor Pollicis Longus

Extensor Pollicis Brevis

Abductor Pollicis Longus

Extensor Carpi
Radialis Brevis

Biceps Brachii

Brachialis

Triceps Brachii

Brachioradialis

Extensor Carpi Radialis Longus

Extensor Digitorum

Lateral Epicondyle of the Humerus

Extensor Carpi Ulnaris

Olecranon of the Ulna

Anconeus

Ulna

Extensor
Digiti Minimi

Flexor Carpi Ulnaris

Ulna

Biceps Brachii

Brachialis

Triceps Brachii

Brachioradialis

Extensor Carpi Radialis Longus

Extensor Digitorum

Lateral Epicondyle of the Humerus

Extensor Carpi Ulnaris

Olecranon of the Ulna

Anconeus

Step-by-Step Arm Muscles

Anterior

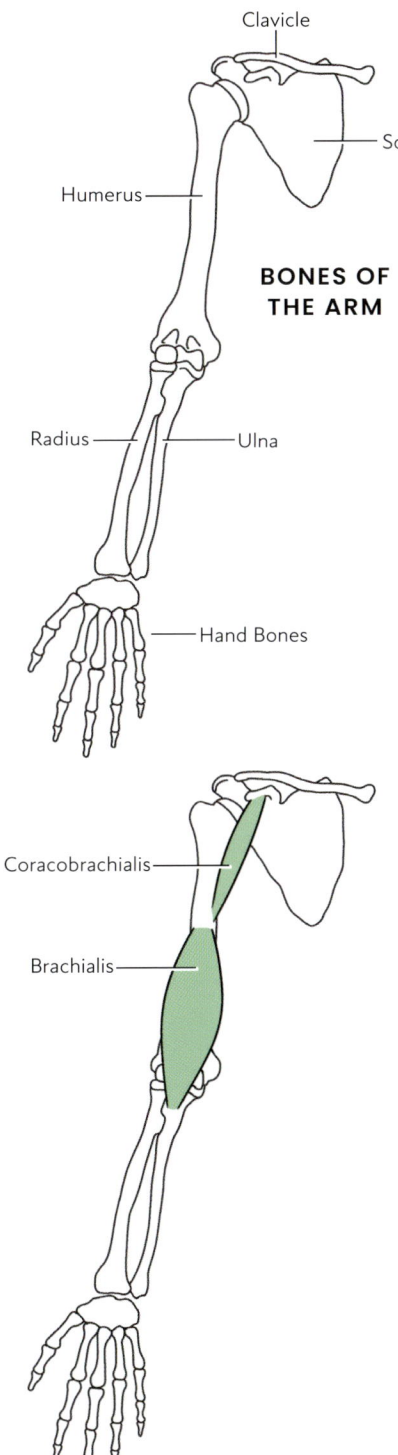

Clavicle

Scapula

Humerus

**BONES OF
THE ARM**

Radius — Ulna

Hand Bones

Coracobrachialis

Brachialis

Coracobrachialis

Origin: Coracoid Process of the Scapula

Insertion: Anterior mid-shaft of the Humerus

Function: Flexion and adduction of the arm

Brachialis

Origin: Anterior surface of the Humerus

Insertion: Coronoid Process of the Ulna

Function: Flexion of forearm

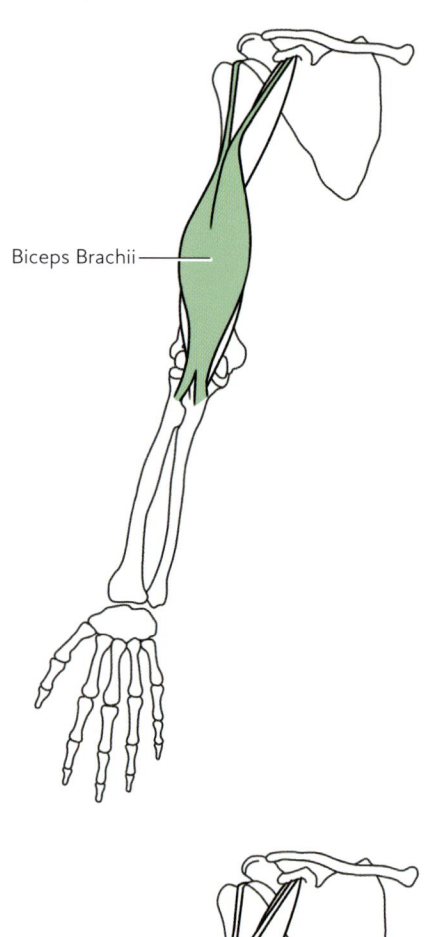

Biceps Brachii

Biceps Brachii

Origin:
• **Short Head:** Coracoid Process of the Scapula
• **Long Head:** Supraglenoid Tubercle of the Scapula

Insertion: Radial Tuberosity of the Radius, deep fascia of the forearm

Function: Flexion and supination of forearm

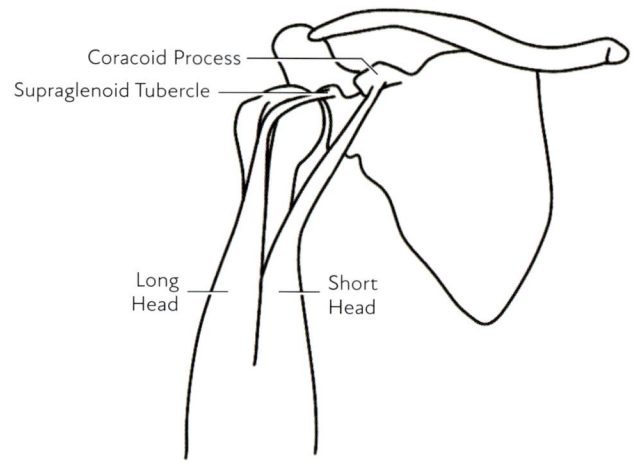

Coracoid Process
Supraglenoid Tubercle
Long Head
Short Head

Flexors (4)

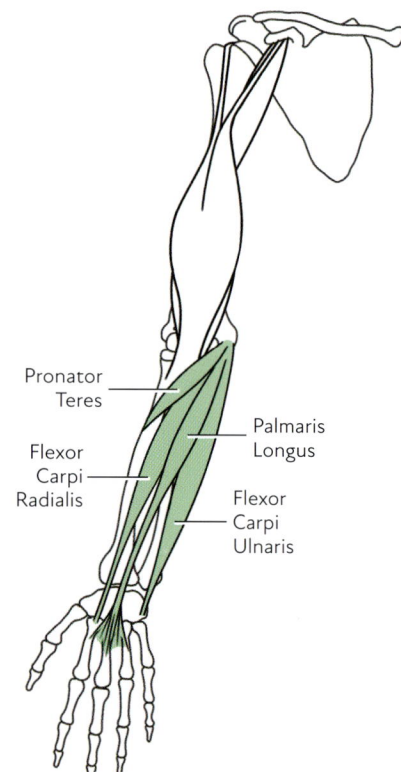

Pronator Teres
Flexor Carpi Radialis
Palmaris Longus
Flexor Carpi Ulnaris

Pronator Teres

Origin: Medial Epicondyle of the Humerus

Insertion: Lateral shaft of the Radius

Function: Pronation and flexion

Palmaris Longus

Origin: Medial Epicondyle of the Humerus

Insertion: Palmar Aponeurosis

Function: Flexion of wrist

Flexor Carpi Radialis

Origin: Medial Epicondyle of the Humerus

Insertion: Base of second and third Metacarpal bone

Function: Flexion and abduction of wrist

Flexor Carpi Ulnaris

Origin: Medial Epicondyle of the Humerus

Insertion: Pisiform bone, Hamate bone, base of fifth Metacarpal bone

Function: Flexion and adduction of wrist

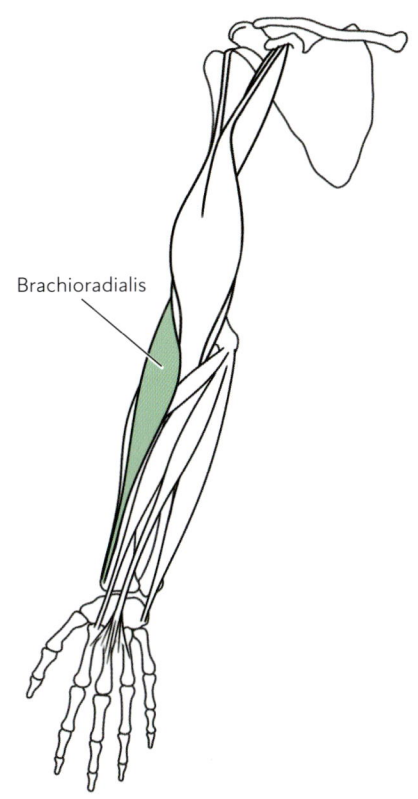

Brachioradialis

Brachioradialis

Origin: Lateral Supracondylar Ridge of the Humerus

Insertion: Styloid Process of the Radius

Function: Flexion of forearm

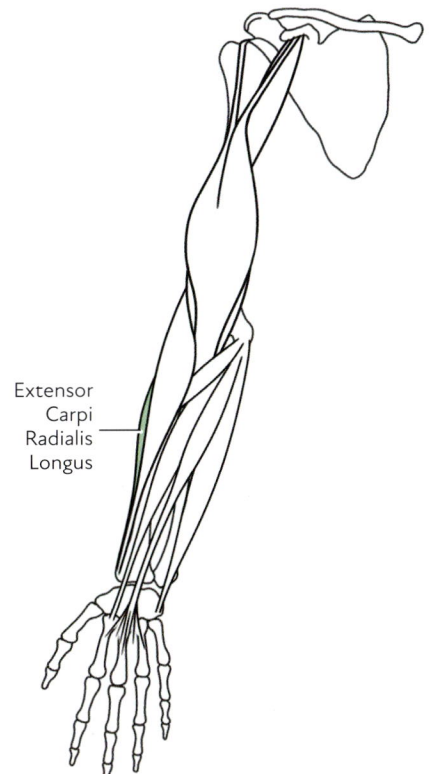

Extensor
Carpi
Radialis
Longus

Extensor Carpi Radialis Longus

Origin: Lateral Supracondylar Ridge of the Humerus

Insertion: Posterior base of the second Metacarpal bone

Function: Hand extension and abduction

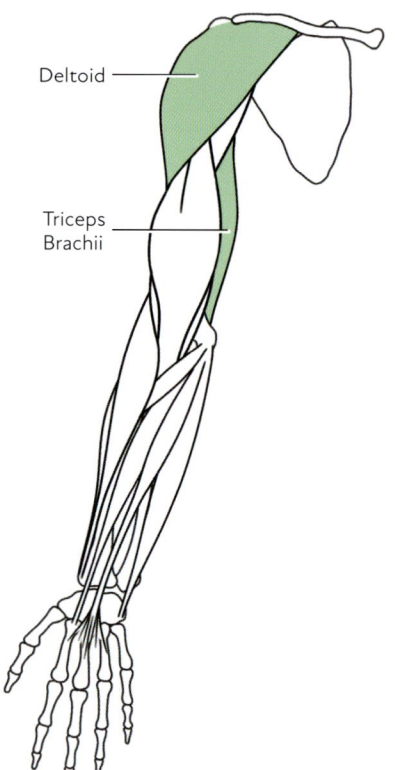

Deltoid

Triceps
Brachii

Deltoid (Anterior, Lateral, Posterior)

Origin: Lateral ⅓ of Clavicle, Acromion Process of the Scapula, Spine of the Scapula

Insertion: Deltoid Tuberosity of the Humerus

Function:
• **Anterior:** Flexion and rotation of the arm
• **Lateral:** Abduction of the arm
• **Posterior:** Extension and rotation of the arm

Triceps Brachii (Posterior)

Origin:
• **Long Head:** Infraglenoid Tubercle of the Scapula
• **Medial Head:** Posterior mid-shaft of the Humerus
• **Lateral Head:** Posterior mid-shaft of the Humerus

Insertion: Olecranon of the Ulna

Function: Extension of forearm, extension and adduction of shoulder

Step-by-Step Arm Muscles

Posterior

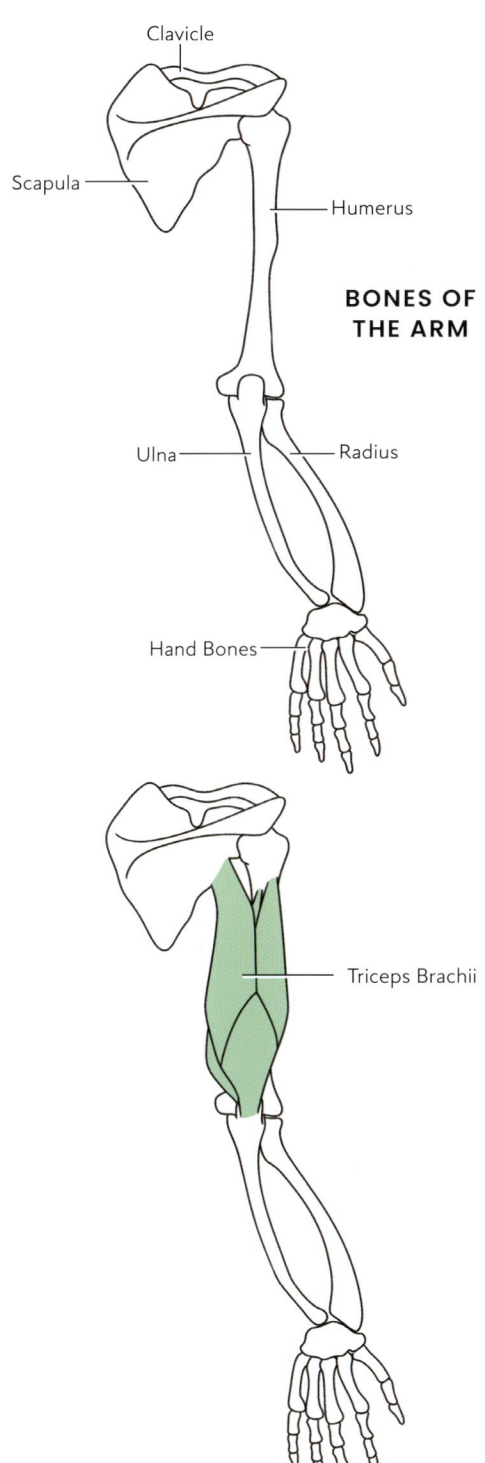

Clavicle

Scapula

Humerus

**BONES OF
THE ARM**

Ulna

Radius

Hand Bones

Triceps Brachii

Triceps Brachii

Origin:
- **Long Head:** Infraglenoid Tubercle of the Scapula
- **Medial Head:** Posterior mid-shaft of the Humerus
- **Lateral Head:** Posterior mid-shaft of the Humerus

Insertion: Olecranon of the Ulna

Function: Extension of forearm, extension and adduction of shoulder

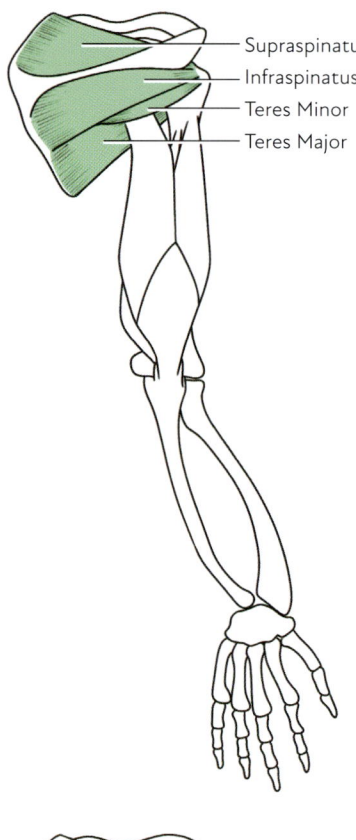

Supraspinatus
Infraspinatus
Teres Minor
Teres Major

Muscles of Scapula (4)

Supraspinatus

Origin: Supraspinous Fossa of the Scapula

Insertion: Greater Tubercle of the Humerus

Function: Abduction of the arm, stabilization of the Humerus head

Teres Minor

Origin: Lateral border of the Scapula

Insertion: Greater Tubercle of the Humerus

Function: Adduction and external rotation of the arm, stabilization of the Humerus head

Infraspinatus

Origin: Infraspinous Fossa of the Scapula

Insertion: Greater Tubercle of the Humerus

Function: External rotation of the arm, stabilization of the Humerus head

Teres Major

Origin: Inferior angle of the Scapula

Insertion: Intertubercular Sulcus of the Humerus (Anterior)

Function: Extension and internal rotation of the Humerus

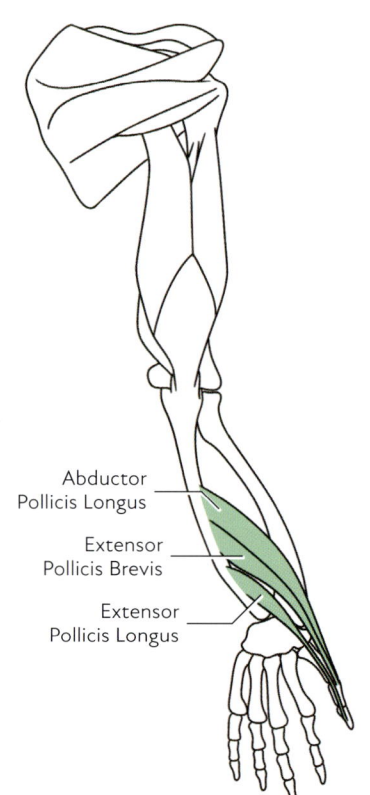

Abductor Pollicis Longus
Extensor Pollicis Brevis
Extensor Pollicis Longus

Deep Extensors (3)

Abductor Pollicis Longus

Origin: Posterior/proximal surface of the Radius, Ulna, and Interosseus Membrane (connective tissue)

Insertion: Base of the first Metacarpal bone

Function: Thumb abduction and extension

Extensor Pollicis Brevis

Origin: Posterior/distal surface of the Radius, Ulna, and Interosseus Membrane (connective tissue)

Insertion: Base of the proximal Phalanx of the thumb

Function: Thumb extension

Extensor Pollicis Longus

Origin: Posterior/proximal surface of the Radius, Ulna, and Interosseus Membrane (connective tissue)

Insertion: Base of the distal Phalanx of the thumb

Function: Weak hand extension and thumb extension

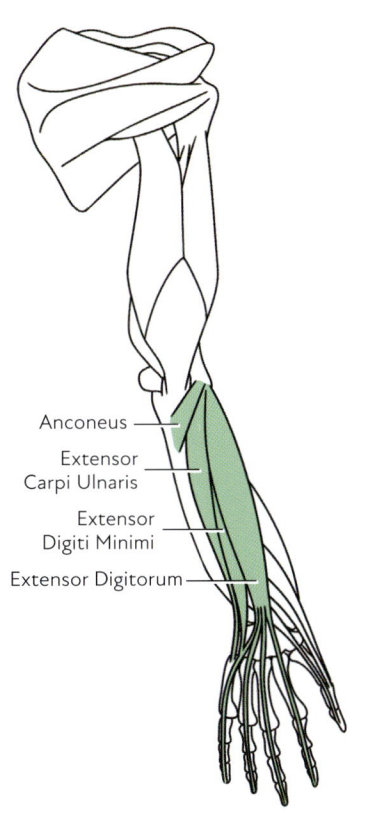

Anconeus —
Extensor
Carpi Ulnaris
Extensor
Digiti Minimi
Extensor Digitorum

Extensors (4)

Anconeus

Origin: Lateral Epicondyle of the Humerus

Insertion: Olecranon of the Ulna

Function: Forearm extension and stabilization of the elbow joint

Extensor Digiti Minimi

Origin: Lateral Epicondyle of the Humerus

Insertion: Dorsal side of Phalanges digit 5

Function: Finger extension of digit 5

Extensor Carpi Ulnaris

Origin: Lateral Epicondyle of the Humerus

Insertion: Base of the fifth Metacarpal bone

Function: Hand extension and adduction

Extensor Digitorum

Origin: Lateral Epicondyle of the Humerus

Insertion: Dorsal side of Phalanges digit 2–5

Function: Finger extension of digit 2–5

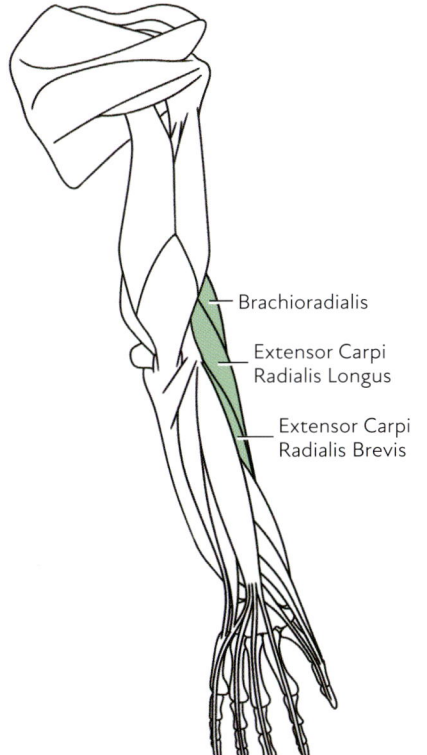

Brachioradialis

Extensor Carpi
Radialis Longus

Extensor Carpi
Radialis Brevis

Ridge Muscles (3)

Brachioradialis

Origin: Lateral Supracondylar Ridge of the Humerus

Insertion: Styloid Process of the Radius

Function: Flexion of forearm

Extensor Carpi Radialis Brevis

Origin: Lateral Epicondyle of the Humerus

Insertion: Posterior base of the third Metacarpal bone

Function: Hand extension and abduction

Extensor Carpi Radialis Longus

Origin: Lateral Supracondylar Ridge of the Humerus

Insertion: Posterior base of the second Metacarpal bone

Function: Hand extension and abduction

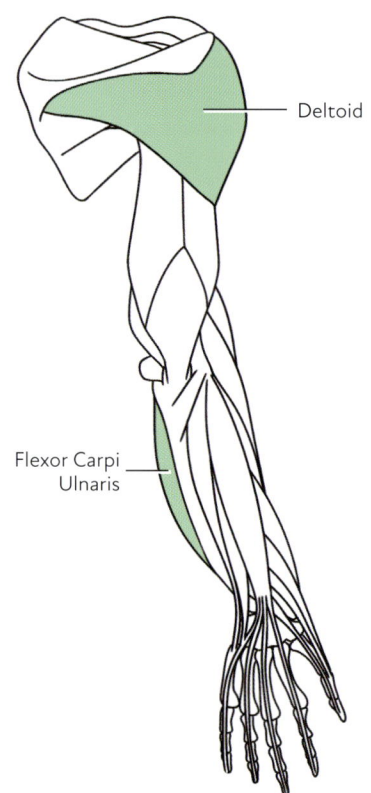

Deltoid

Flexor Carpi
Ulnaris

Deltoid (Anterior, Lateral, Posterior)

Origin: Lateral ⅓ of Clavicle, Acromion Process of the Scapula, Spine of the Scapula

Insertion: Deltoid Tuberosity of the Humerus

Function:
- **Anterior:** Flexion and rotation of the arm
- **Lateral:** Abduction of the arm
- **Posterior:** Extension and rotation of the arm

Flexor Carpi Ulnaris

Origin: Medial Epicondyle of the Humerus

Insertion: Pisiform bone, Hamate bone, base of fifth Metacarpal bone

Function: Flexion and adduction of wrist

Step-by-Step Arm Muscles

Lateral

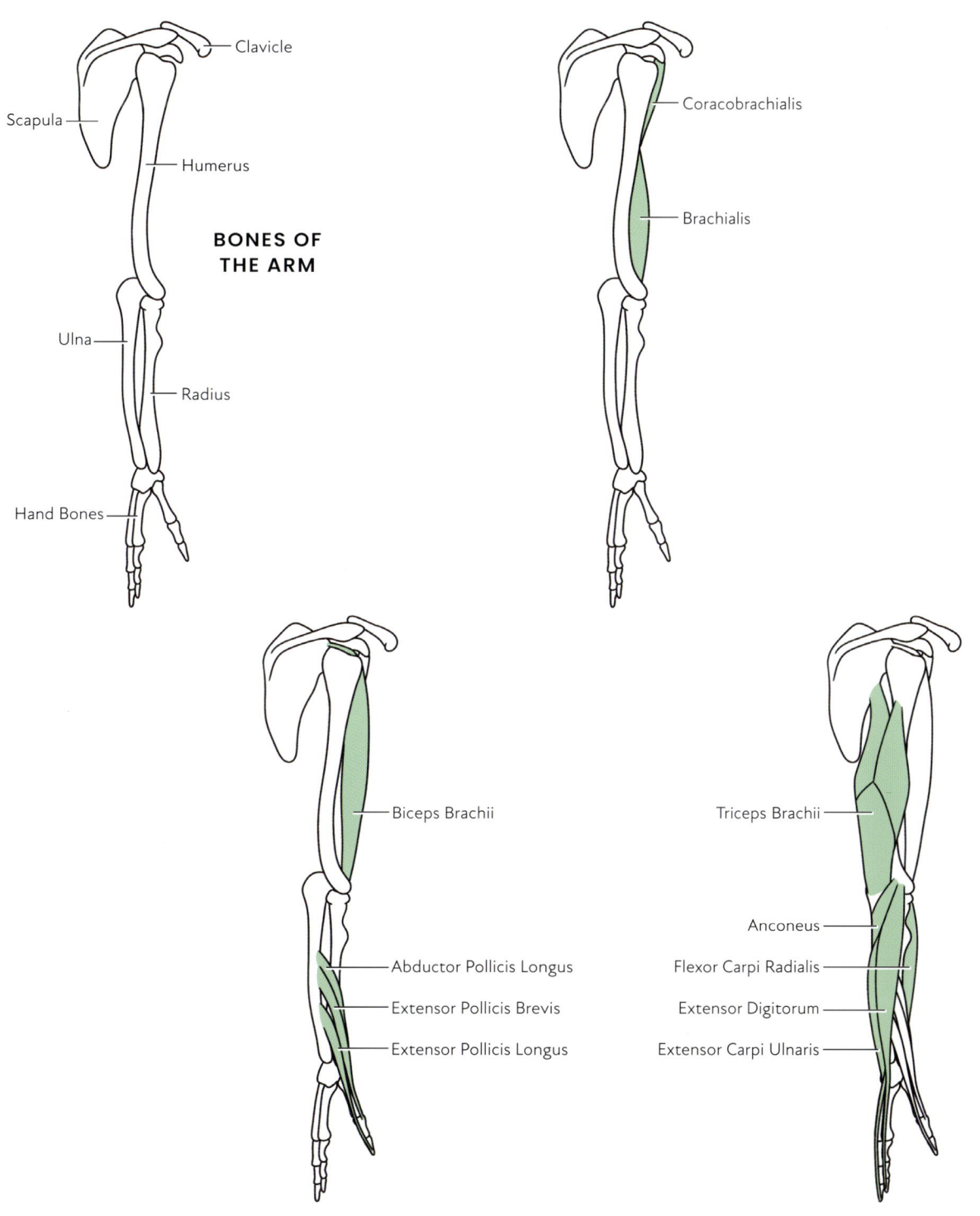

BONES OF THE ARM

Clavicle

Scapula

Humerus

Ulna

Radius

Hand Bones

Coracobrachialis

Brachialis

Biceps Brachii

Abductor Pollicis Longus

Extensor Pollicis Brevis

Extensor Pollicis Longus

Triceps Brachii

Anconeus

Flexor Carpi Radialis

Extensor Digitorum

Extensor Carpi Ulnaris

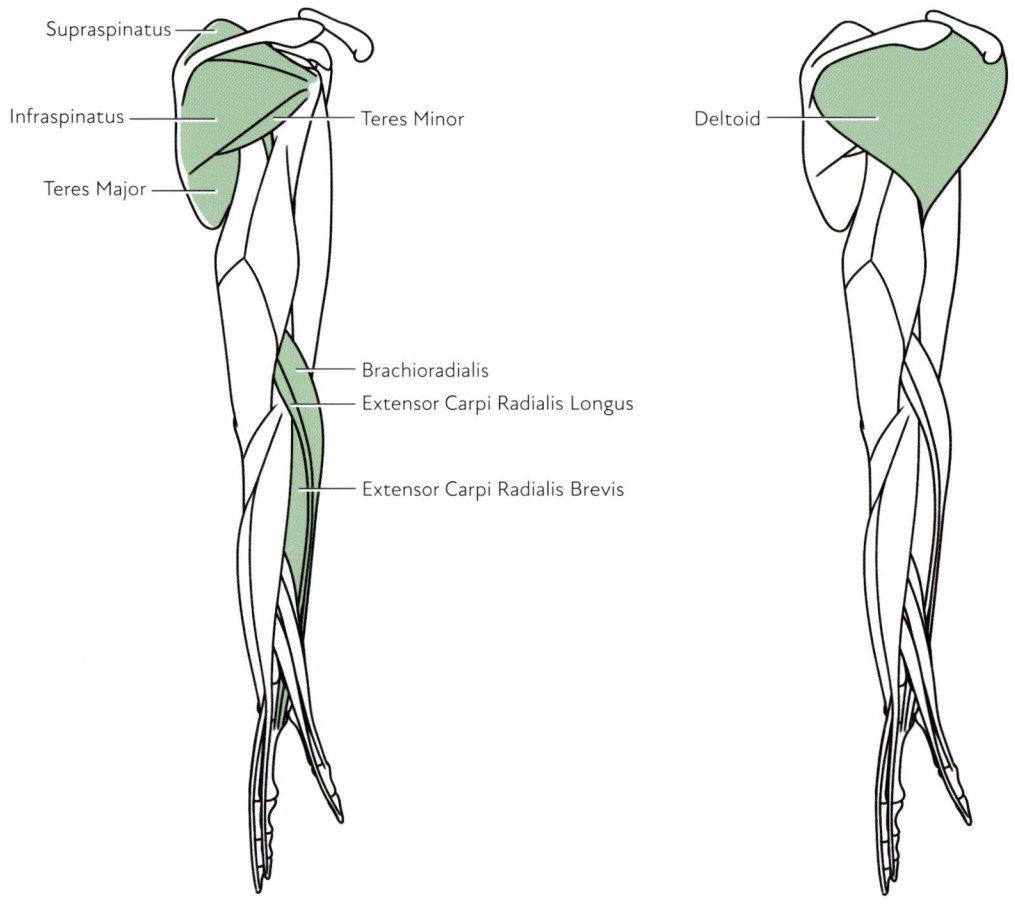

Supraspinatus

Infraspinatus

Teres Minor

Teres Major

Brachioradialis

Extensor Carpi Radialis Longus

Extensor Carpi Radialis Brevis

Deltoid

Step-by-Step Arm Muscles

Medial

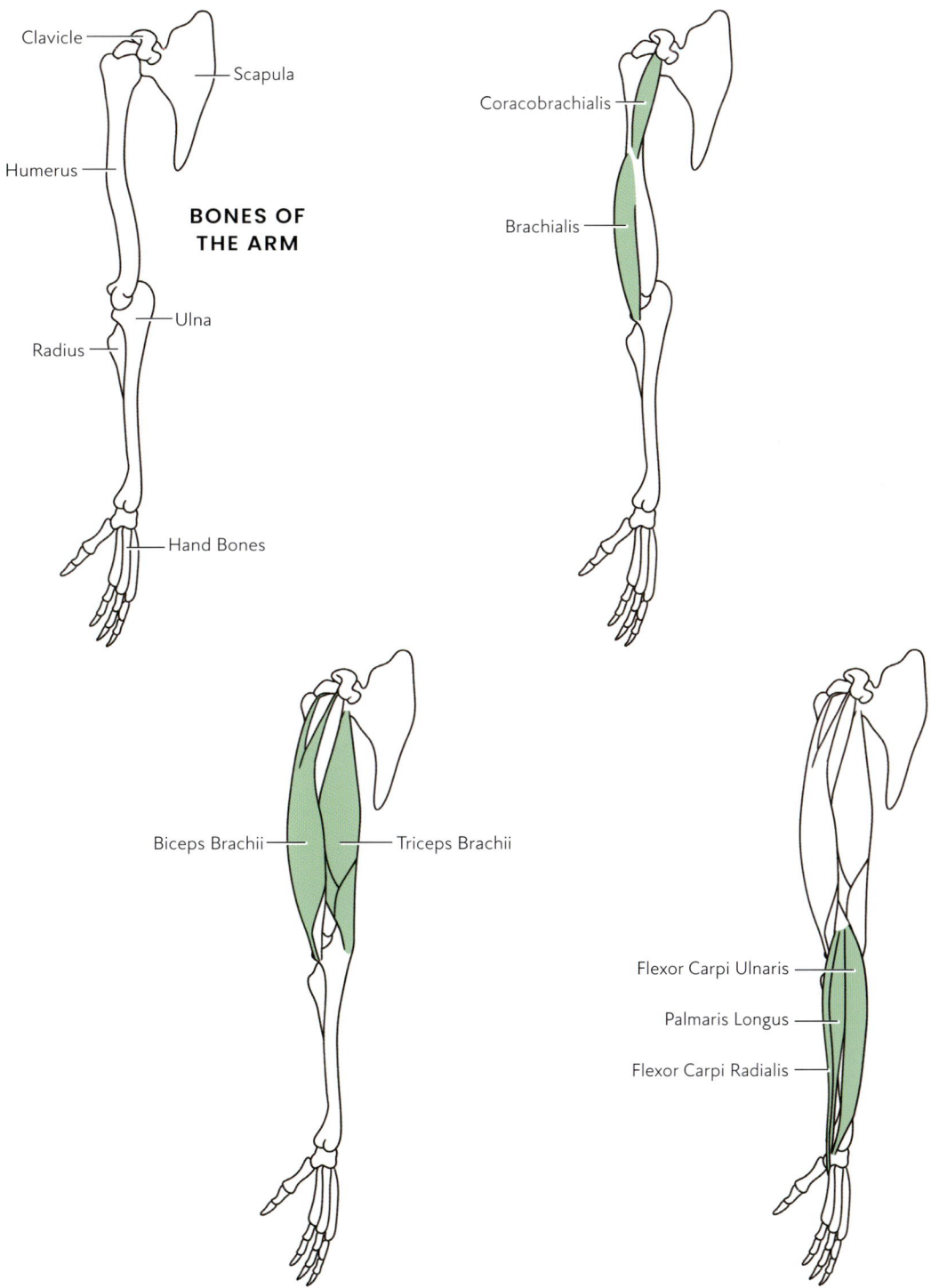

BONES OF THE ARM

Clavicle

Scapula

Humerus

Ulna

Radius

Hand Bones

Coracobrachialis

Brachialis

Biceps Brachii

Triceps Brachii

Flexor Carpi Ulnaris

Palmaris Longus

Flexor Carpi Radialis

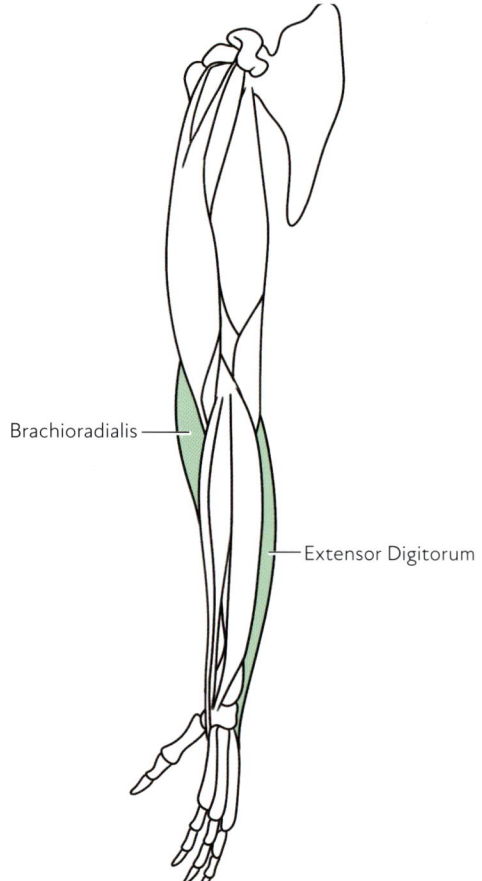

Brachioradialis

Extensor Digitorum

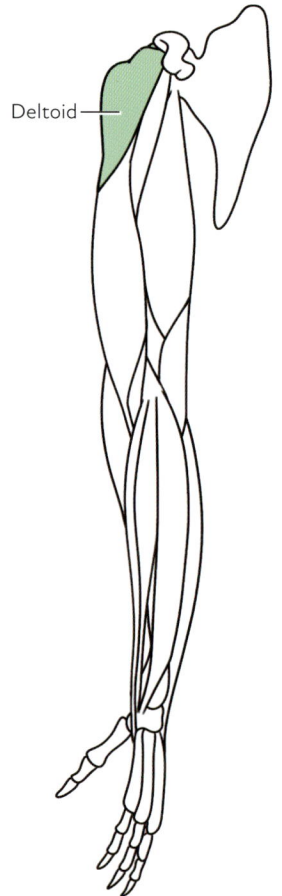

Deltoid

Drawing Arms

Anterior, Pronated

1

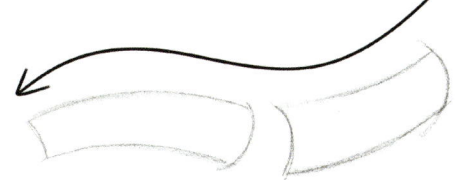

2

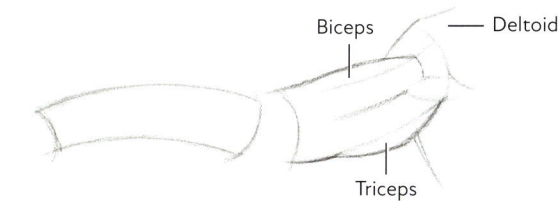

Biceps — Deltoid

Triceps

3

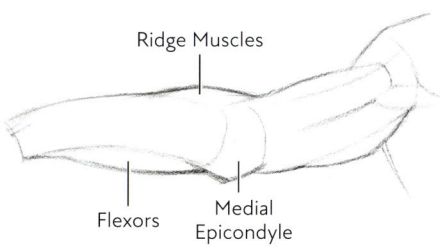

Ridge Muscles

Flexors

Medial Epicondyle

4

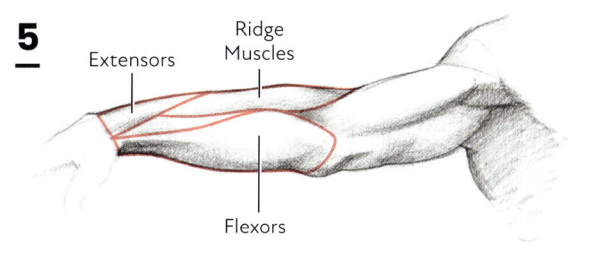

Ridge Muscles *

Palmaris Longus Tendon

Flexors

1. Create the cylinder shapes for the upper and lower arm. In this drawing, the gesture of the arm is an S curve.

2. Sketch in the volumes of the Deltoid, Biceps, and Triceps in the upper arm.

3. Outline the Ridge Muscles, Medial Epicondyle, and Flexors.

4. The distal part of the Biceps has a pointy shape* that sits between the Ridge Muscles and Flexors. The Palmaris Longus tendon is added on the anterior side of the wrist.

5. Develop the volume of the Ridge Muscles, Extensors, and Flexors to add the tone.

6. Use shading to develop the contrast and details.

5

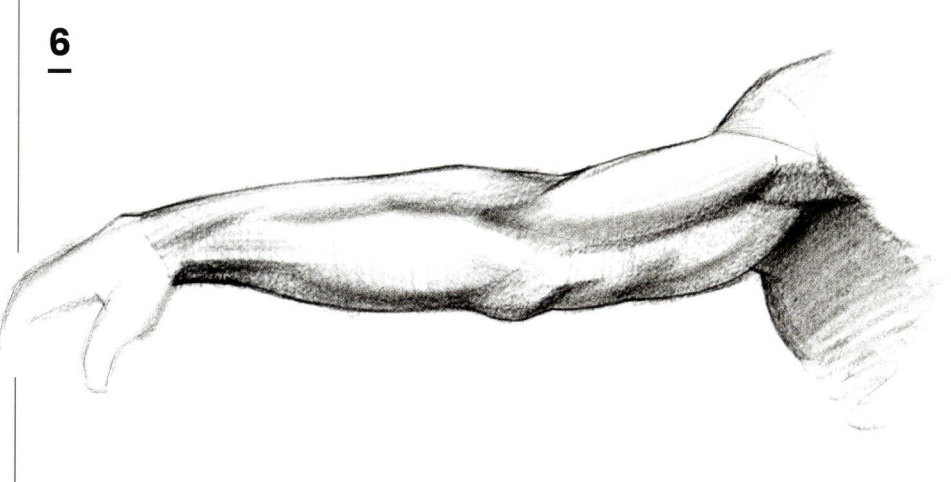

Extensors

Ridge Muscles

Flexors

6

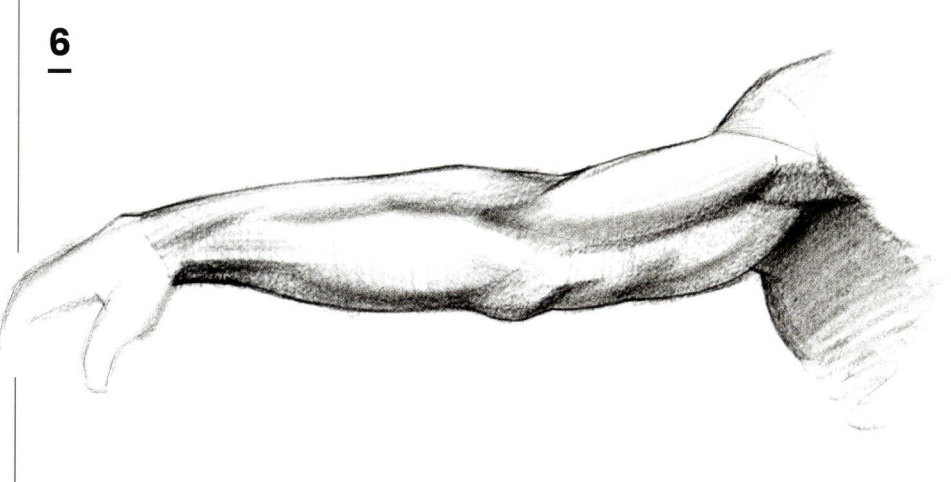

Posterior

1

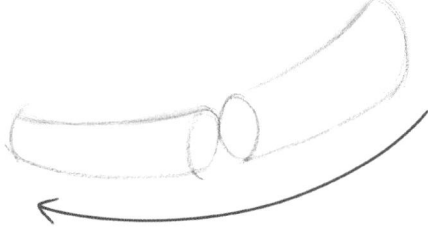

2

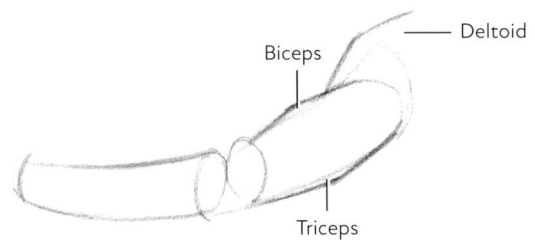

Biceps

Deltoid

Triceps

3

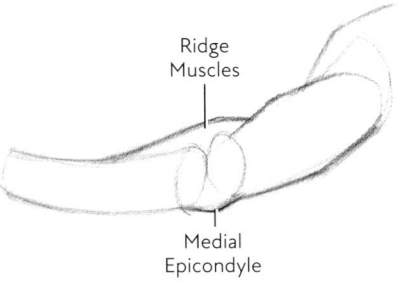

Ridge Muscles

Medial Epicondyle

4

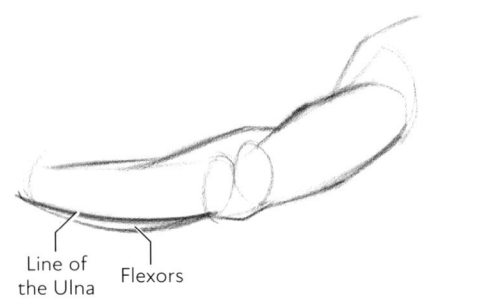

Line of the Ulna

Flexors

1. Draw the cylinder shapes for the upper and lower arm. In this drawing, the gesture of the arm has a C curve.

2. Sketch in the volumes of the Deltoid, Biceps, and Triceps in the upper arm. The Triceps become a part of the elbow, so the line should be longer than the Biceps line.

3. Outline the Ridge Muscles and the Medial Epicondyle.

4. Add the long, downward curved line for the Flexor mass. In this drawing, the bottom line of the cylinder for the forearm can be used as a line of the Ulna.

5. Add the shape of the elbow. Work on the core shadow and even tone in the form shadow area.

6. Use shading to develop the contrast and details.

5

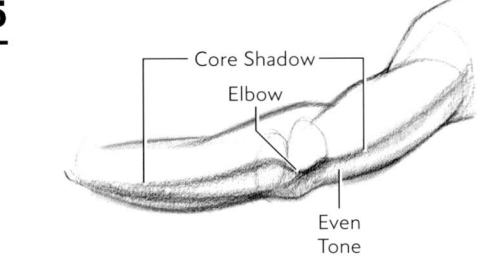

Core Shadow

Elbow

Even Tone

6

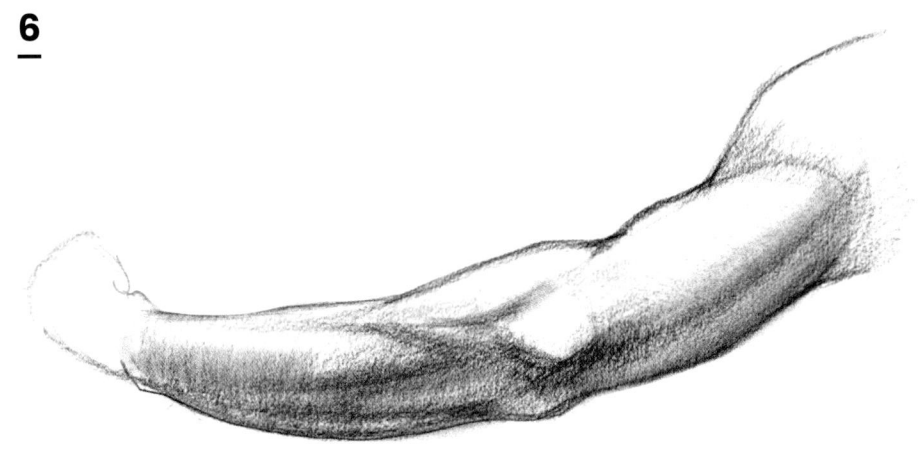

Crossed Arms

1

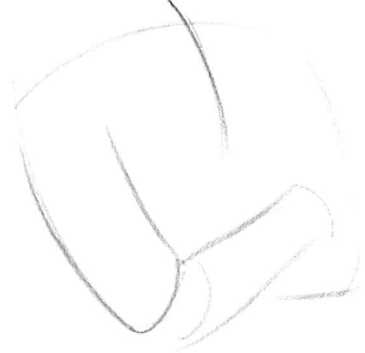

2

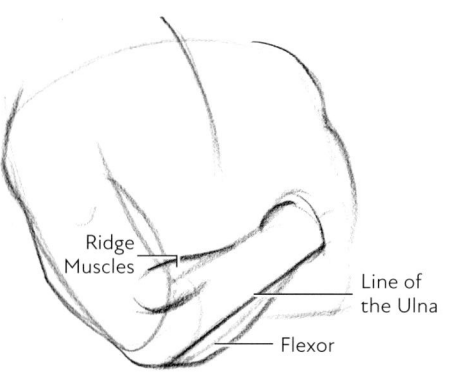

Deltoid

Deltoid

Triceps

Biceps

Triceps

3

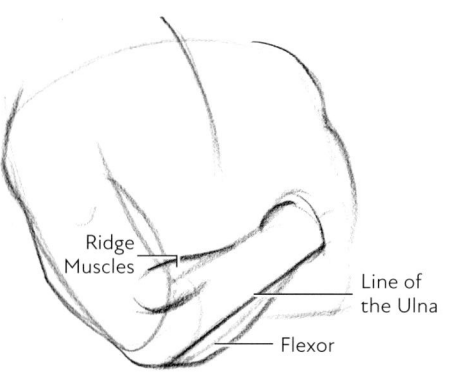

Ridge
Muscles

Line of
the Ulna

Flexor

4

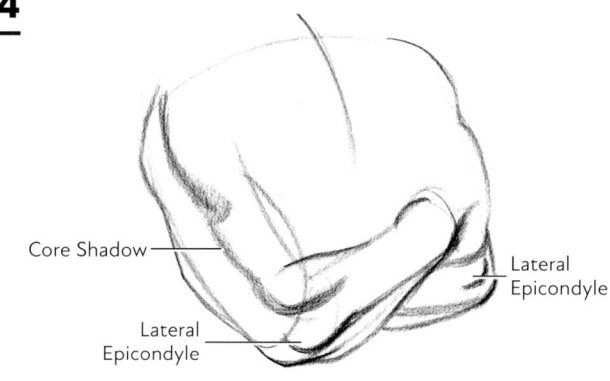

Core Shadow

Lateral
Epicondyle

Lateral
Epicondyle

5

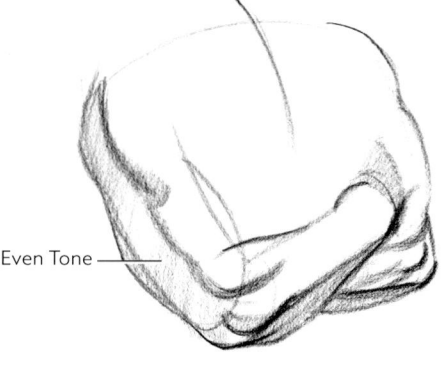

Even Tone

6

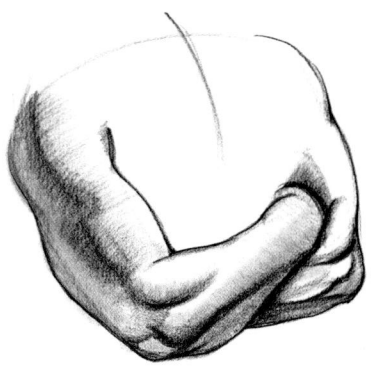

1. Draw a mid-line on the chest to define the direction of the torso. Draw the cylinders for the upper and lower arm.

2. Sketch in the volumes of the Deltoid, Biceps, and Triceps.

3. Add the mass of the Ridge Muscles and the Flexors. Define the Ulna line.

4. Add the volume of the Lateral Epicondyle of the Humerus, and define the core shadow.

5. Develop the even tone.

6. Use shading to develop the contrast and details.

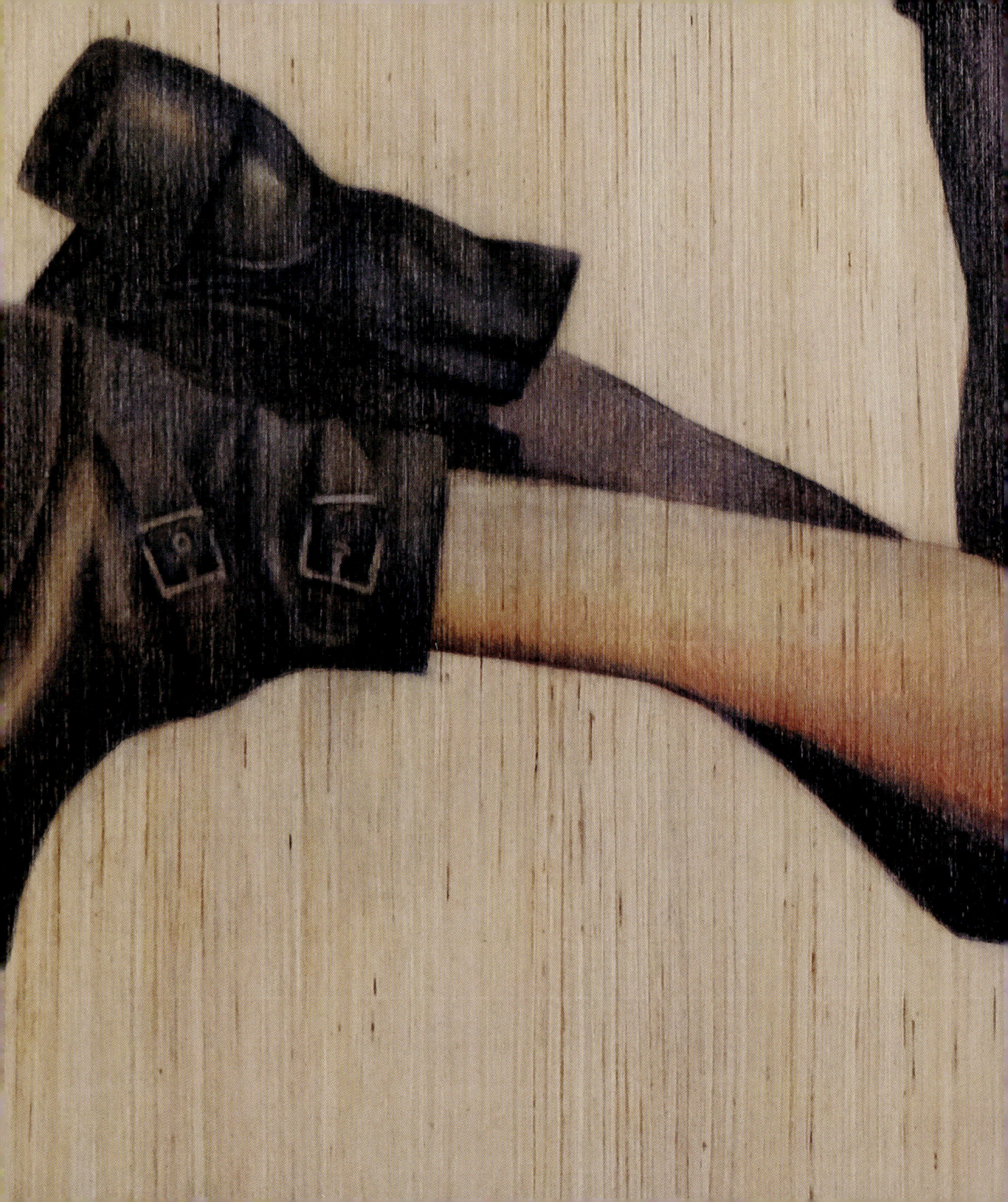

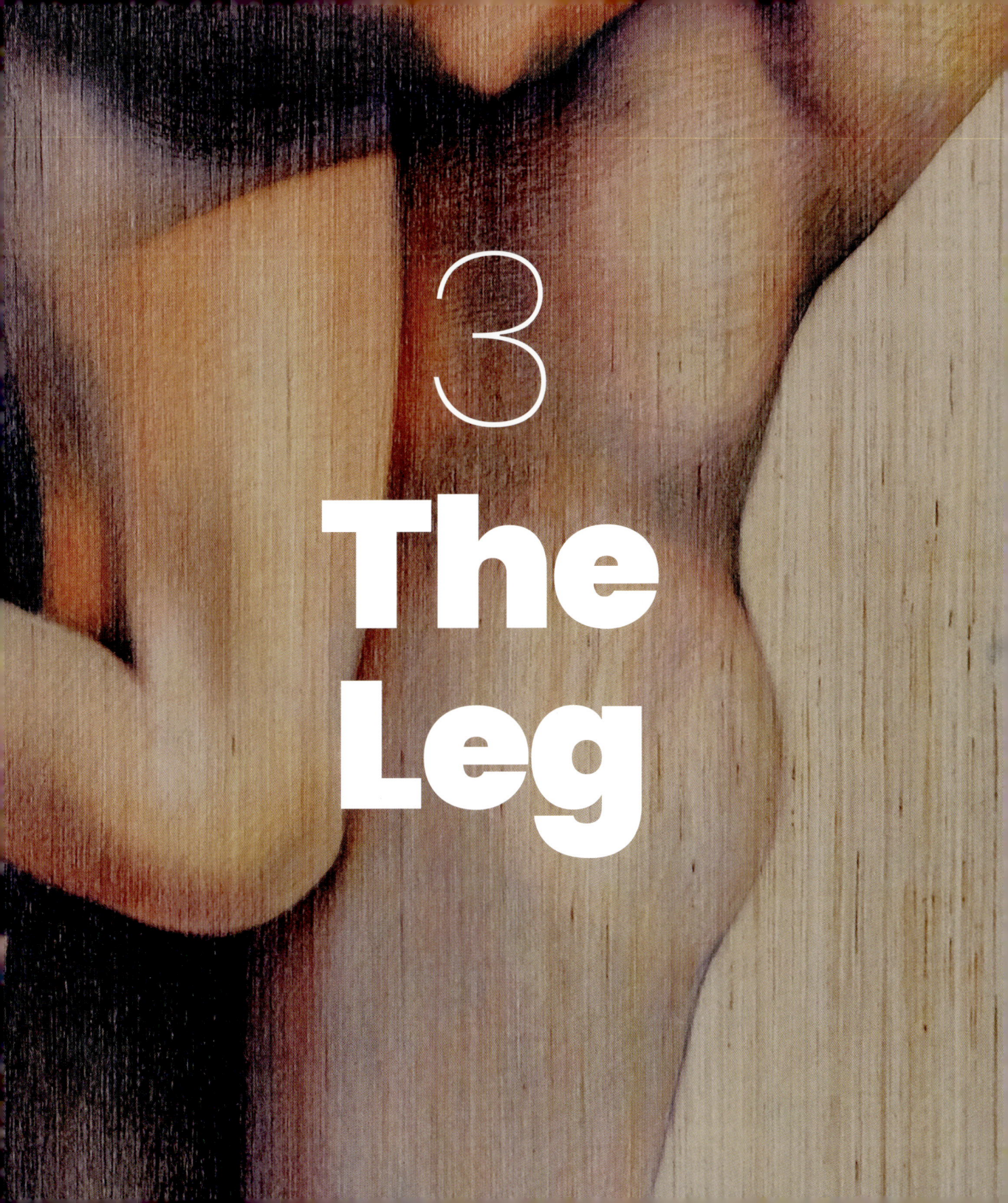

3

The
Leg

Major Groups of Leg Muscles You Should Know

The leg muscles can be separated into six distinct groups: **Medial Thigh Muscles, the Quads, Hamstring Muscles, the Glutes, Lower Leg Muscles (Anterior),** and **Lower Leg Muscles (Posterior)**

The Quads

The Quads are the **Quadriceps Femoris Muscles**, which are a group of four (*quadri*) muscles on the anterior side of the upper leg. For the surface anatomy, we focus on three muscles: the **Vastus Medialis**, the **Vastus Lateralis**, and the **Rectus Femoris**. The Vastus Intermedius lies underneath the Rectus Femoris muscle and is not visible. The Quads follow the slanted angle of the Femur and form a teardrop shape.

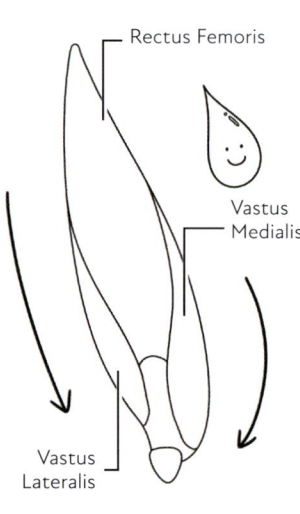

Rectus Femoris

Vastus Medialis

Vastus Lateralis

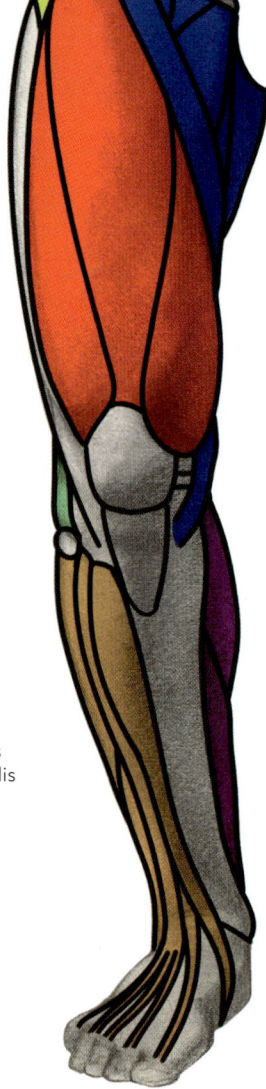

ANTERIOR

Medial Thigh Muscles

The **Medial Thigh Muscles** are the muscles on the medial side of the upper leg. The Femur bone (thigh bone) is slanted at a diagonal angle, and these muscles fill the triangular gap inside. The big muscles in this group are the **Adductor Magnus** and **Adductor Longus/Brevis**. The **Pectineus** muscle joins in the thick tendon near the pubis. The **Gracilis** is a long tape-like muscle on the medial side, and the **Sartorius** is another long muscle that divides the medial thigh muscles and the quads.

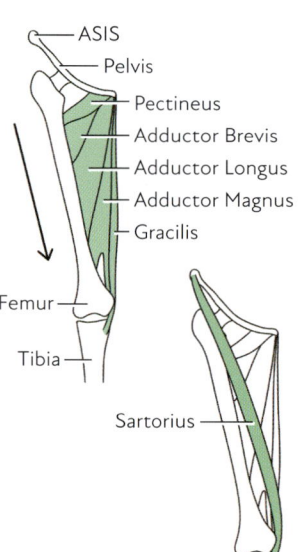

ASIS
Pelvis
Pectineus
Adductor Brevis
Adductor Longus
Adductor Magnus
Gracilis

Femur

Tibia

Sartorius

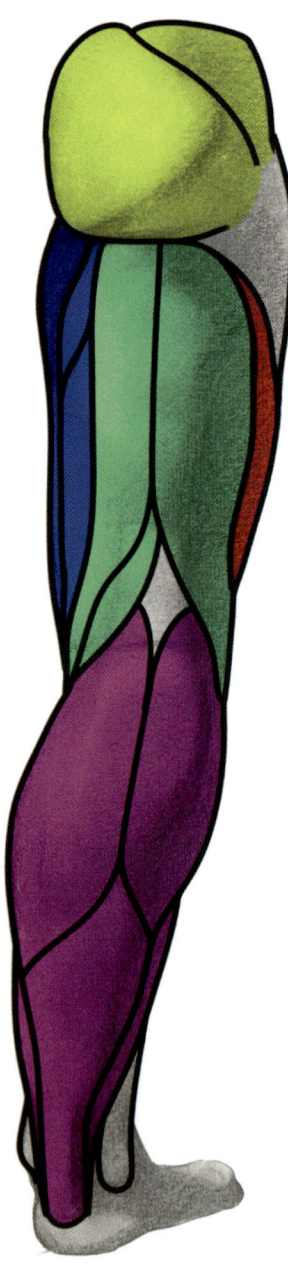

POSTERIOR

The Glutes

The Glutes are the **Gluteal Muscles** that form the hip area. When discussing the surface anatomy, we focus on three muscles. The largest one is the **Gluteal Maximus** on the posterior side, which forms the shape of the butt cheek. It also is the **biggest muscle in our body**. The **Gluteal Medius** is on the lateral side. On the anterior side, there is a palm-sized muscle called the **Tensor Fascia Latae**, which has the muscular volume on top, and then becomes a thin tape tissue called the **Iliotibial Band**.

Hamstring Muscles

The **Hamstring Muscles** are three muscles on the posterior side of the upper leg. The **Semitendinosus** and **Semimembranosus** are the two layered muscles on the medial side, and the **Biceps Femoris** is on the lateral side. They all run vertically in the shape of a parallelogram, and both sides are symmetrical.

Lower Leg Muscles, Posterior

The **Gastrocnemius** is a large muscle that forms the bulk of your calf. Underneath it is the **Soleus** muscle, which looks like a fish. The muscles are layered and become the thickest tendon in our body, the **Achilles Tendon**.

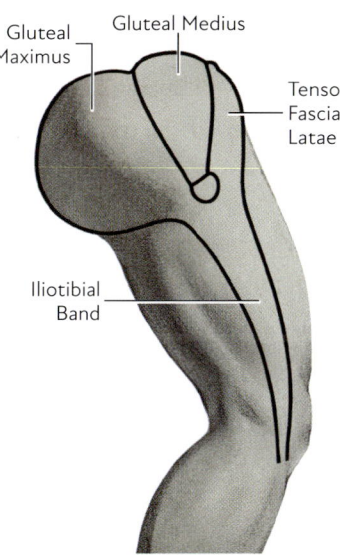

Gluteal Maximus

Gluteal Medius

Tensor Fascia Latae

Iliotibial Band

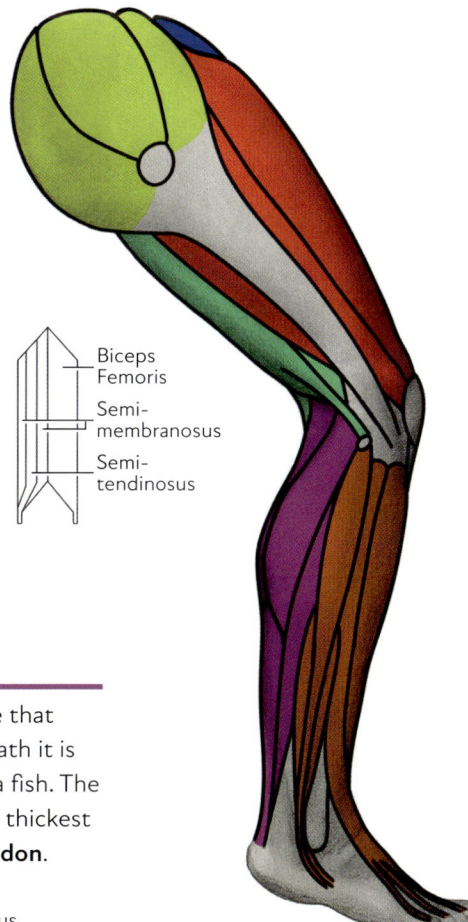

Biceps Femoris

Semi-membranosus

Semi-tendinosus

LATERAL

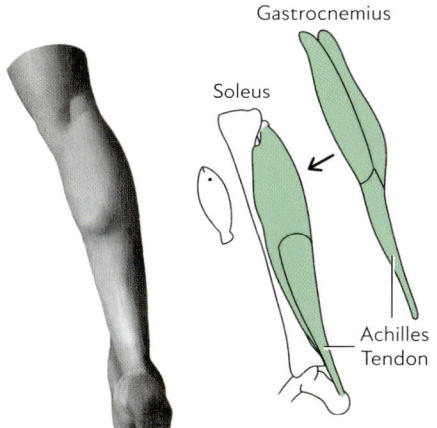

Gastrocnemius

Soleus

Achilles Tendon

Lower Leg Muscles, Anterior

On the anterior side, we will take a look at four muscles that all lay on the **lateral side of the Tibia**. The **Tibialis Anterior** is the muscle on the shin, and the tendon goes diagonally to the plantar of the foot through the medial side. Next to it is the **Extensor Digitorum Longus**. This tendon splits toward the insertion and becomes the visible tendons on toes 2–5. The other two muscles are the **Peroneus Longus** and **Peroneus Brevis**. They are the lateral component of the lower leg muscles attached to the Fibula bone.

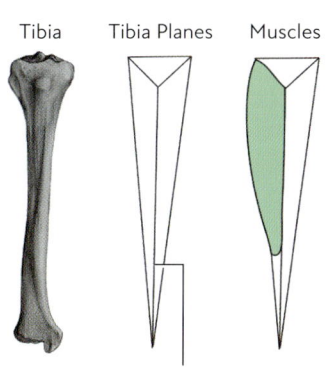

Tibia

Tibia Planes

Muscles

Anterior Crest of the Tibia

QUICK NOTES

Anterior Crest of the Tibia

The shin is called the Anterior Crest of the Tibia. It is a sharp vertical edge, and it divides the Tibia into lateral and medial planes.

The Quads

The Thigh's Teardrop

As mentioned earlier, the Quads (**Quadriceps Femoris**), are a group of four muscles on the anterior side of the upper leg. This muscle group forms your front thigh, and you can focus on its unique shape in artistic anatomy.

Shape of the Quads

The top of the Quads muscle group is pointy by the hip, and more volume can be seen toward the knee, forming a teardrop shape. Since the anatomical position of the Femur bone is in a diagonal line, the Quads naturally follow the angle, and you can see the teardrop shape having a slant.

The Vastus Medialis has a bulge at the bottom. This bulge will form lower than the lateral side. This round volume often can be seen in the leg, and the shape can be visible in your drawing.

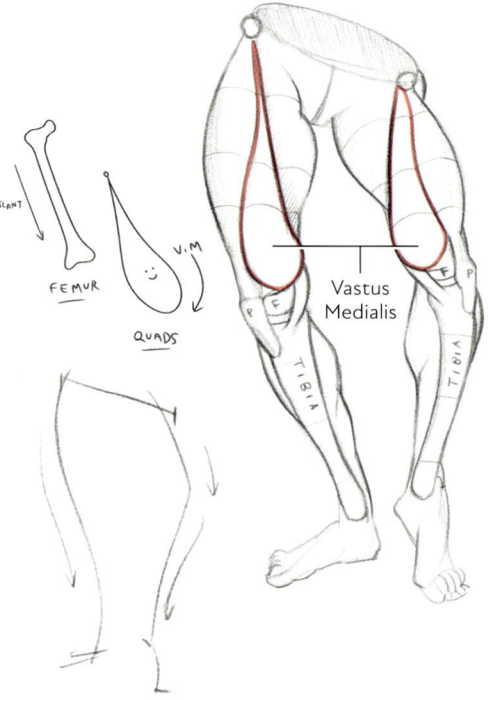

Muscles

Since one of the four muscles—the Vastus Intermedius—is hidden underneath the others, we'll focus on the other three. The muscle on the medial side is called the **Vastus Medialis**, the one on the lateral side is called the **Vastus Lateralis**, and the last one in the middle is the **Rectus Femoris**.

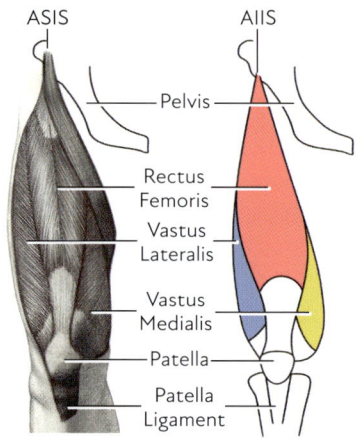

Origin of the Quads

The origin of the teardrop, specifically the origin of the **Rectus Femoris**, is on the **AIIS of the Pelvis**. The AIIS (Anterior Inferior Iliac Spine) is located right below the ASIS (Anterior Superior Iliac Spine).

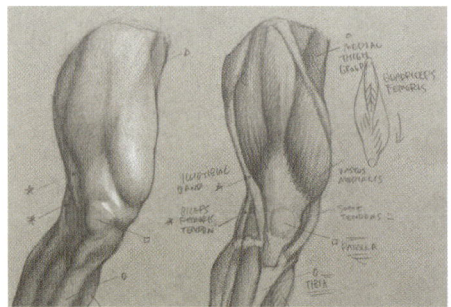

The **ASIS** is an important landmark of the Pelvis. One of the muscles that is attached to the projection is called the Sartorius. It is a long muscle that runs diagonally in the middle of the thigh, and it defines the shape of the Quads and the Medial Thigh Muscles. Make sure to add the Sartorius line to form each volume.

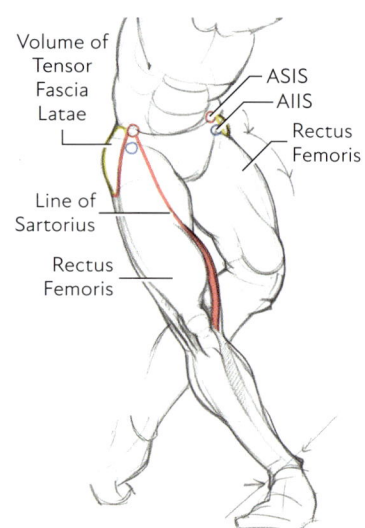

Another muscle that is attached to the ASIS is the **Tensor Fascia Latae**. This is one of the hip muscles and it is located on the lateral side of the ASIS. Both the Sartorius and Tensor Fascia Latae form the upper part of the teardrop shape of the Quads.

The Medial Thigh Muscles

The Triangular Shadow

The **Sartorius** is a lengthy muscle that divides two different muscle groups of the thigh: the Quads and the Medial Thigh Muscles.

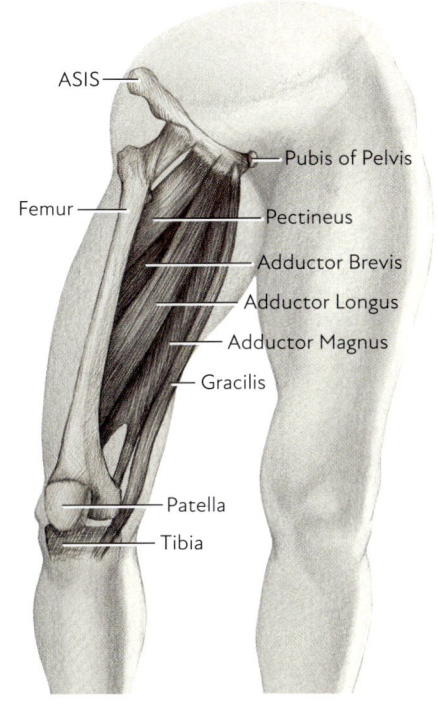

ASIS

Pubis of Pelvis

Femur

Pectineus

Adductor Brevis

Adductor Longus

Adductor Magnus

Gracilis

Patella

Tibia

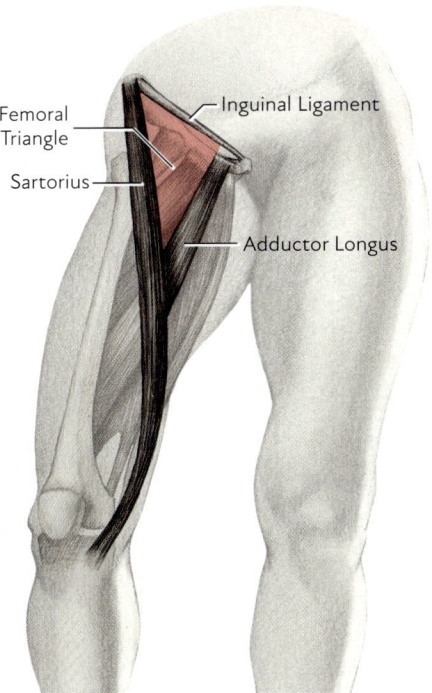

Femoral Triangle

Inguinal Ligament

Sartorius

Adductor Longus

The Medial Thigh Muscles make up the inner thigh volume that is separated from the Sartorius below the genitalia. It has a shape of an isosceles triangle from the anterior view, and the round volume can be seen from posterior view as well.

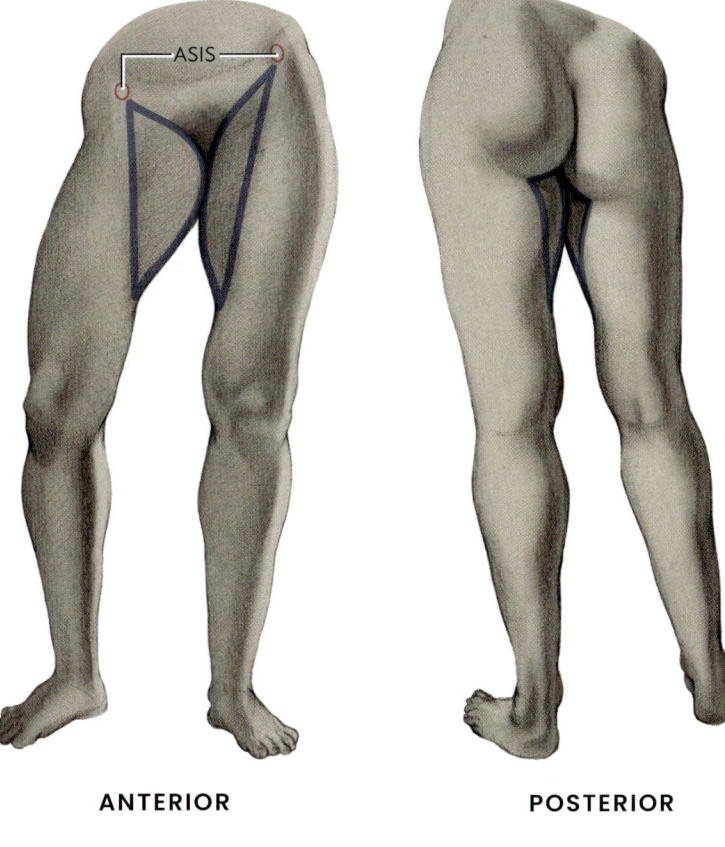

ASIS

ANTERIOR   **POSTERIOR**

Femoral Triangle

The Medial Thigh Muscles hold the subtle smaller triangular depression called the **Femoral Triangle**. The Femoral Triangle is a term that describes the triangular hollow in the upper inner thigh formed by the **Sartorius**, the **Adductor Longus**, and the **Inguinal Ligament** (the "bikini" line).

In the surface anatomy, we can see not only the overall triangular shadow of the Medial Thigh Muscles, but also the smaller triangular depression of the Femoral Triangle.

The *Butterfly* Wheel

Drawing the Hip

Have you ever used two perfect circles to construct a drawing of the hips? The hips aren't exactly circular; in fact, they are closer to ovals.

Instead of the perfect circles, stretch the shapes and make them into ovals. Then tilt the top to the side and open the ovals, as in the shape of butterfly wings. This will make your butt drawing look much more natural.

The **Sacrum**, or the tail bone, has a downward triangle shape as a part of the arrow line of the **Vertebral Column.** The butterfly ovals will sit nicely under the angle of the tail bone like a puzzle piece, giving flexible gestures to your hip drawing.

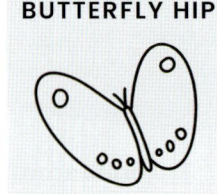

BUTTERFLY HIP

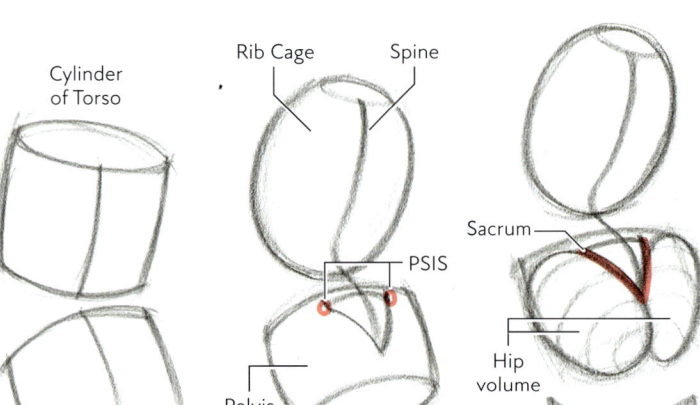

Cylinder of Torso

Rib Cage   Spine

PSIS

Pelvis

Sacrum

Hip volume

POSTERIOR

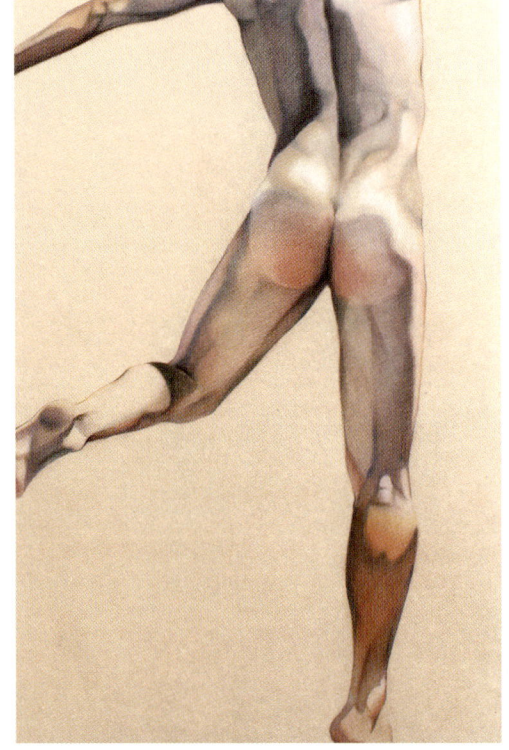

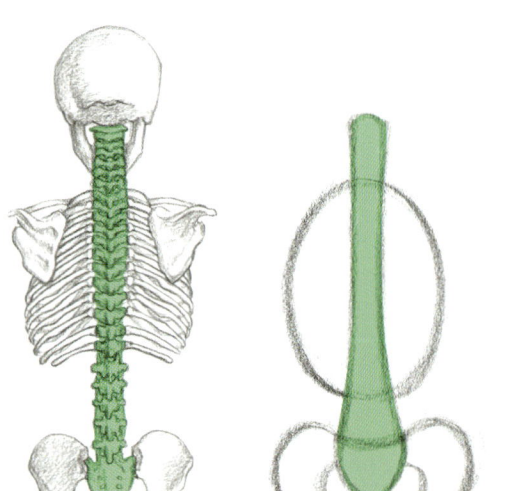

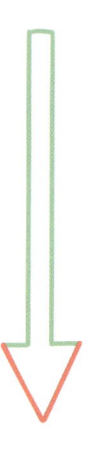

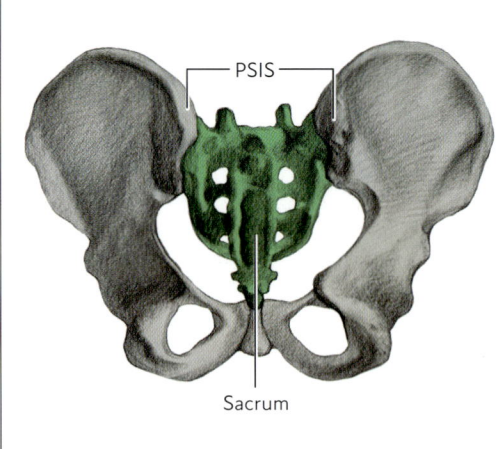

PSIS

Sacrum

PELVIS, POSTERIOR

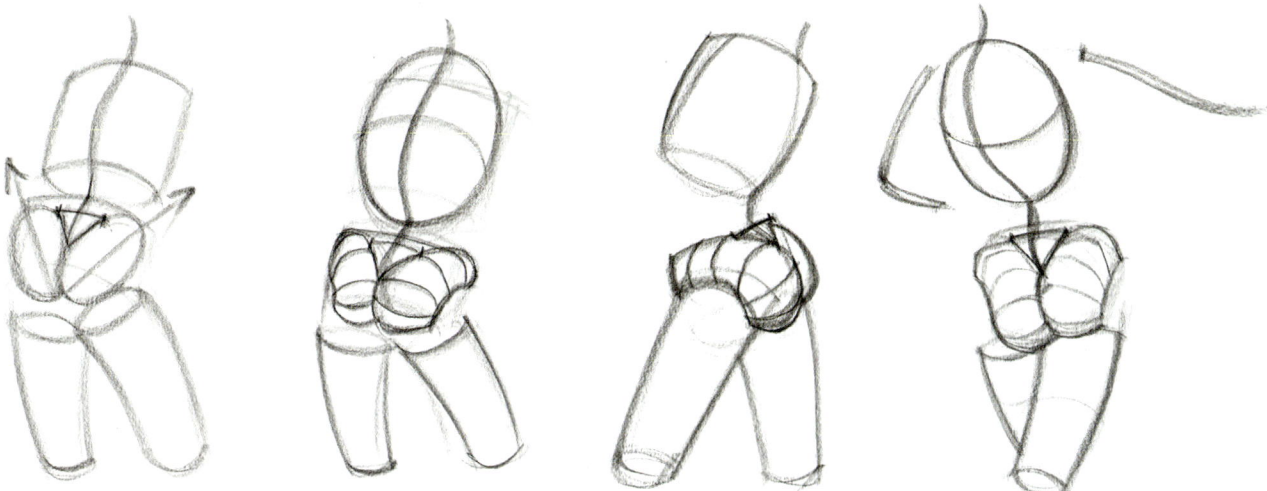

Once you have the butterfly wings in place, add the cross-contour lines to make the shape into a wheel. This technique will give a flat plane to the side of hip. In creating construction drawings for figures, boxes and cuboid shapes are often used to help us understand the accurate planes in the human body. This "butterfly wheel" will allow us to keep the volume of the hip while we design the flatness of the side of the hip.

Why does the butterfly wheel happen?

The lateral side of the Pelvis has an arched crest called the **Iliac Crest**. All the muscles in the **Glutes** group originate alongside this crest and the tail bone, and the wheel-like volume can be seen around the hip area.

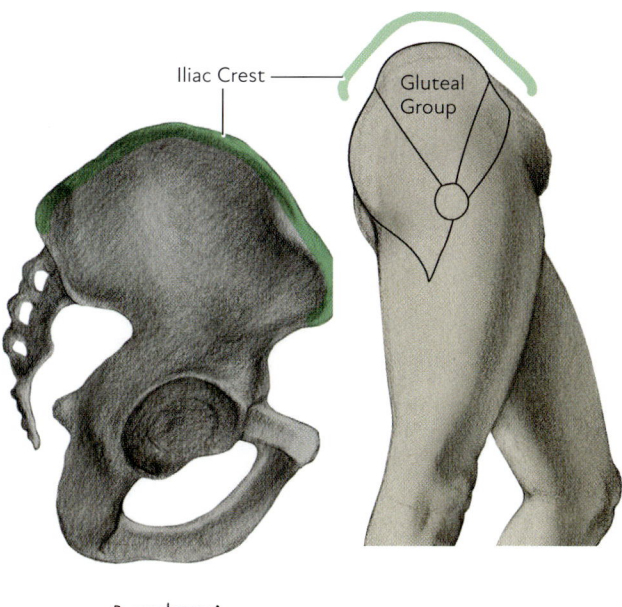

Iliac Crest

Gluteal Group

P ——|—— A

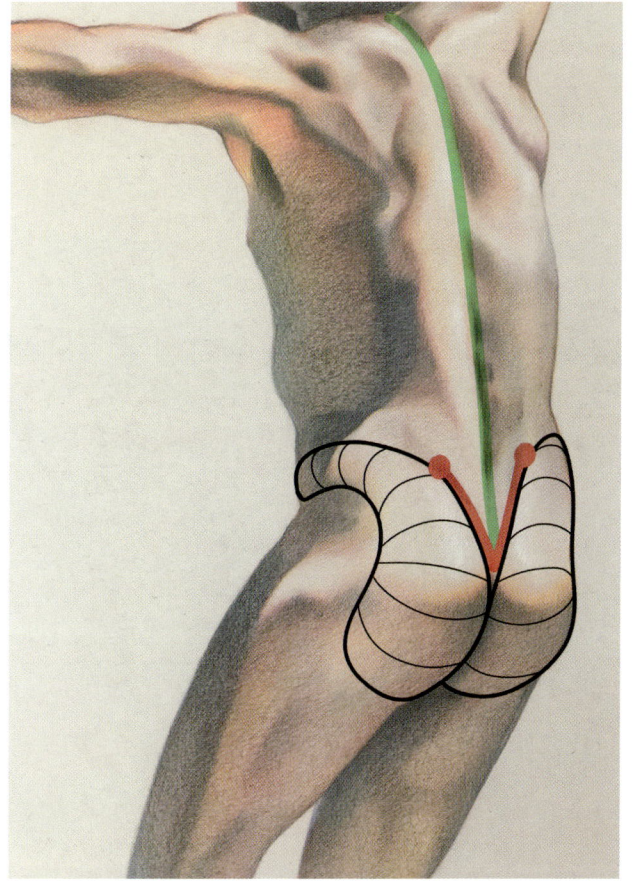

Side of the Hip

Take a look at the lateral view of the hip. Depending on the lighting or angle, you will find a mysterious small projection or depression on the lateral side of the hip.

This is created by a part of the thigh bone called the **Greater Trochanter of the Femur**, which sticks out farther than the Pelvis to the lateral side. It does not have much muscle or fat covering it; therefore, you will see a defined highlight or shadow on the side of the hip.

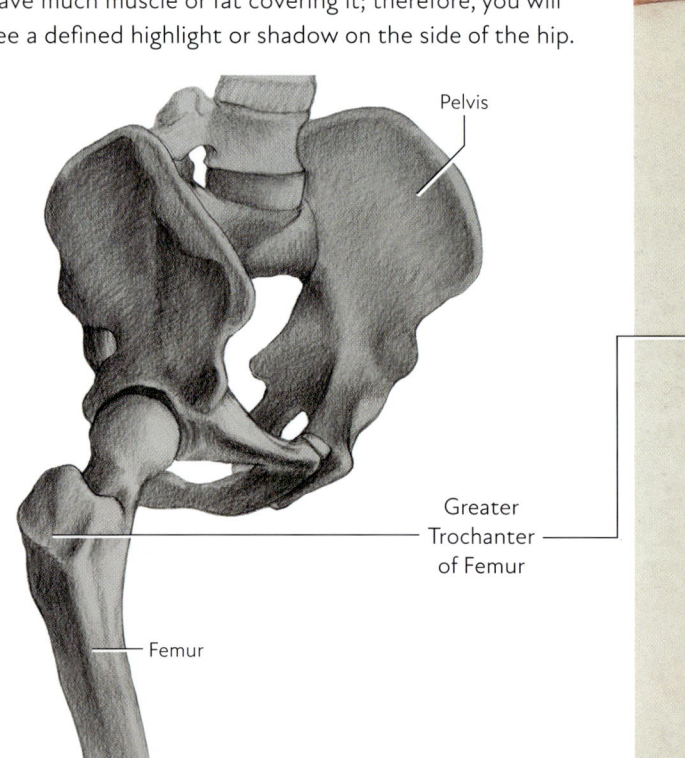

Pelvis

Greater Trochanter of Femur

Femur

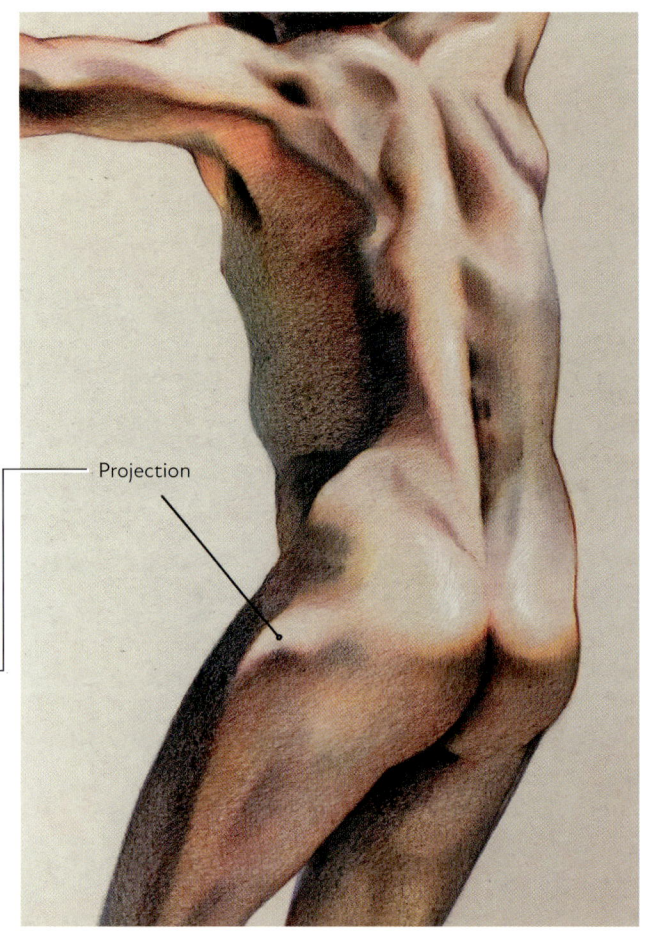

Projection

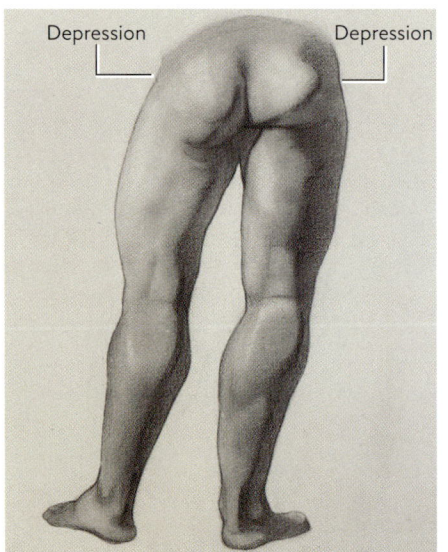

Depression

Depression

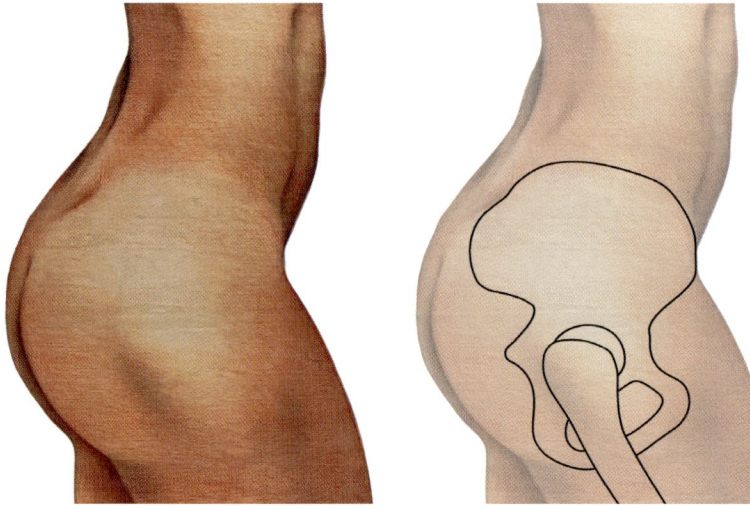

LATERAL VIEW

The Hamstring Muscles   A Parallelogram

Hamstring Muscles

The **Hamstring Muscles** are located on the posterior side of the upper leg. Here we have three muscles: the **Biceps Femoris** on one side, and the **Semitendinosus** and **Semimembranosus** layered together on the other side. They all have a similar shape, which is a vertical parallelogram.

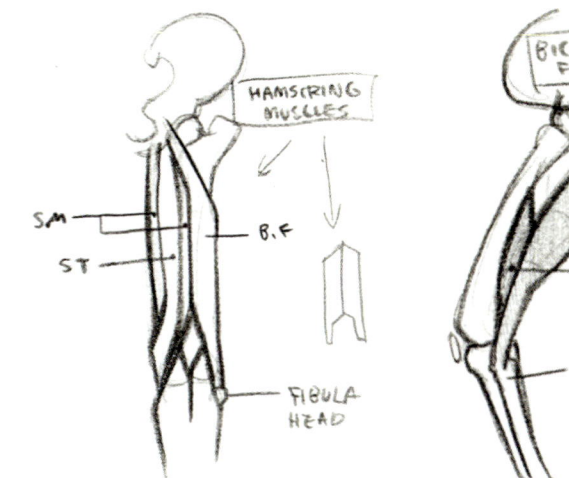

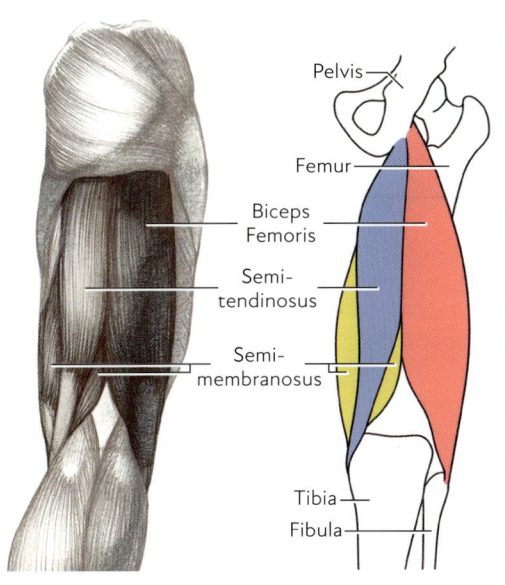

Biceps Femoris

The Biceps Femoris is a *biceps* because it has two heads. Both long and short heads become one tendon, which goes down to the head of the Fibula bone. This tendon is important in surface anatomy. It is visible both when the knee is extended and when it is flexed. When you are sitting down, feel the lateral side of your knee toward the upper leg. You should be able to feel a thick tendon.

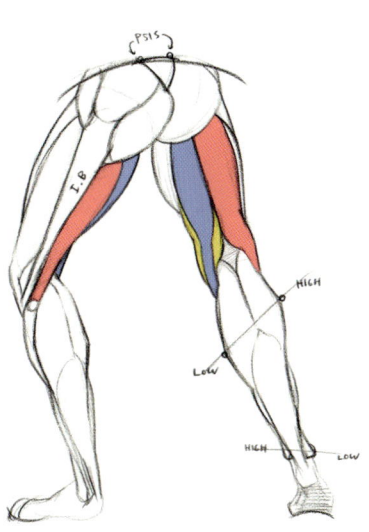

Semimembranosus and Semitendinosus

Mirroring the Biceps Femoris, we see two muscles on the medial side. The larger one is the **Semimembranosus** and the small one that overlaps it is the **Semitendinosus**. These two tendons merge together with other tendons toward the knee, and they go down to the **Medial Condyle of the Tibia**.

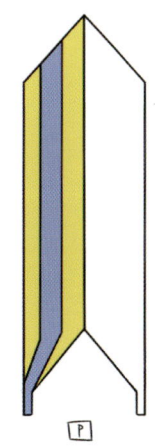

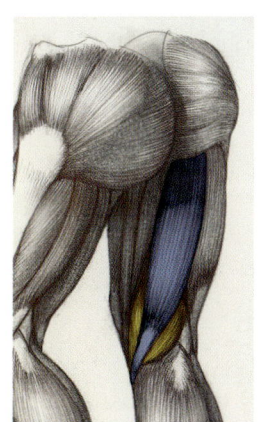

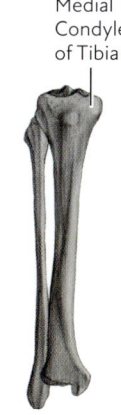

Medial Condyle of Tibia

The Hamstring Muscles *(cont.)*

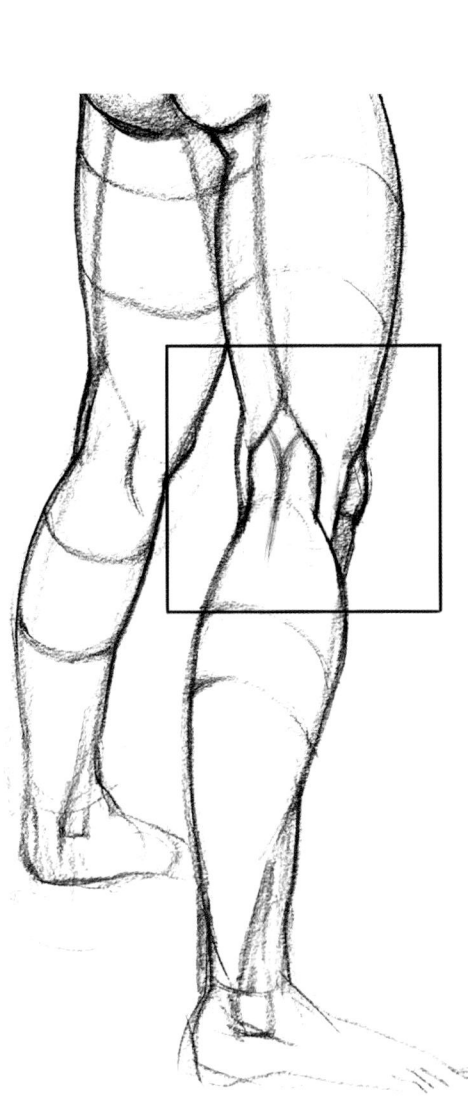

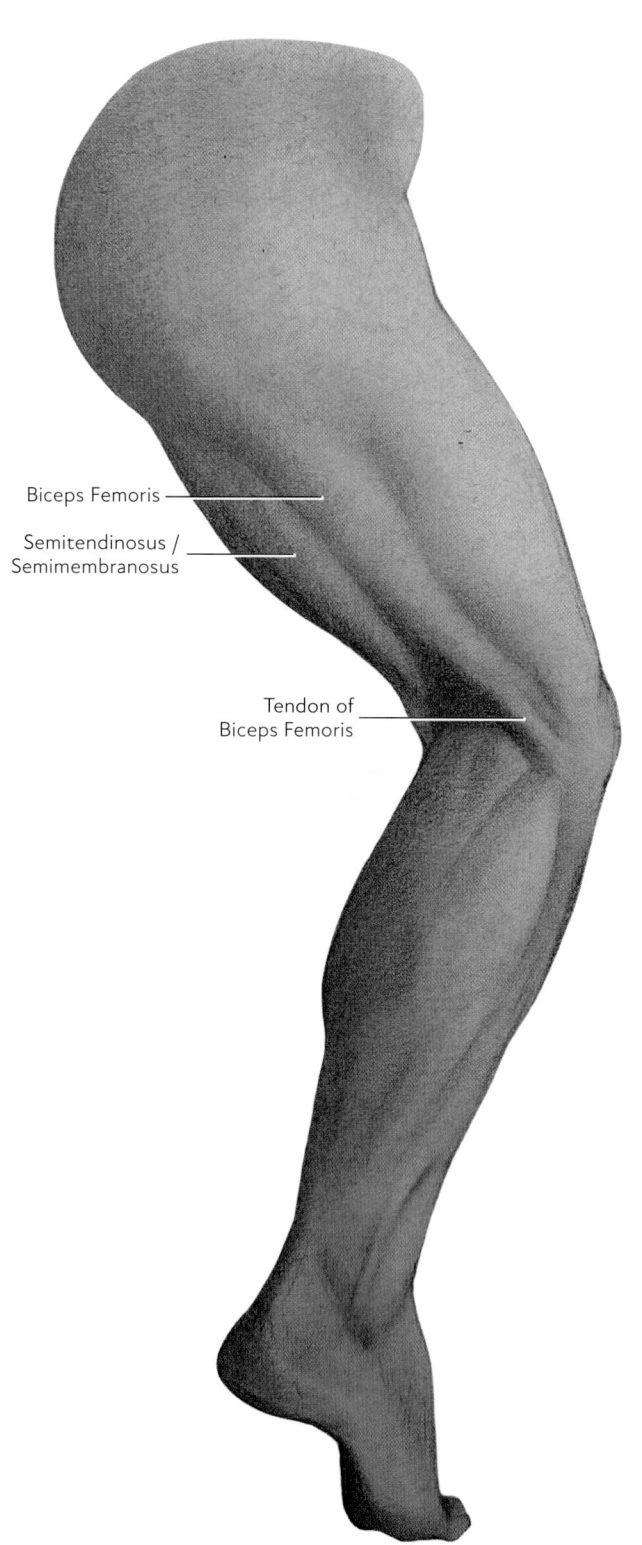

Biceps Femoris

Semitendinosus / Semimembranosus

Tendon of Biceps Femoris

The lines of the Hamstring muscle tendons go down vertically on the sides of the knee. You can see the calf muscle goes through in between.

Mastering the Knees

It is common to struggle with a sketch of the knee. Why is this thing so complicated looking?

Understanding the Knee Joint

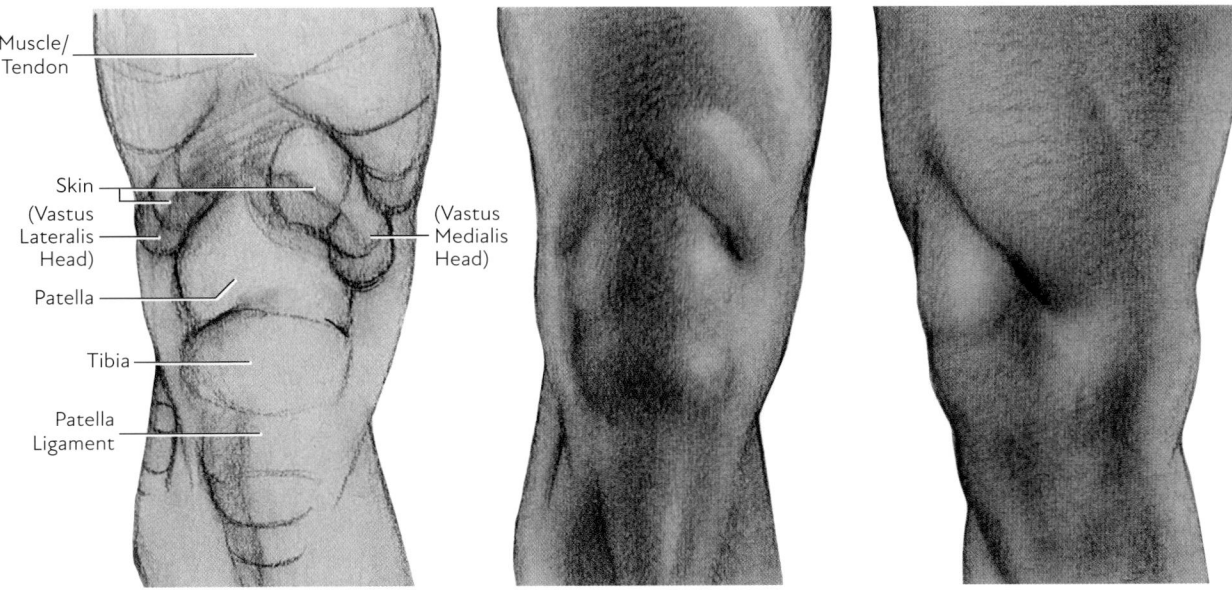

Muscle/Tendon

Skin

(Vastus Lateralis Head)

(Vastus Medialis Head)

Patella

Tibia

Patella Ligament

Tendons of the Knee

Above the Patella bone is a tendon called the **Quadriceps Tendon**, which is in the distal portion of the **Quads**. This tendon can be seen superficially sometimes, but the volume of the Quads and the fat that sits right over the knee pad often covers this tendon partially.

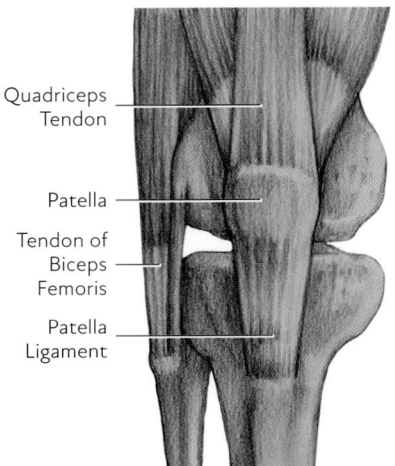

Quadriceps Tendon

Patella

Tendon of Biceps Femoris

Patella Ligament

Skeletal System of the Knee

The main bone of the knee is the **Patella** bone. The Patella works like a knee pad that goes right on the space between the **Femur** and the **Tibia**. This small plate-like bone is floating on the anterior side, and it is anchored with tendons, ligaments, and muscles.

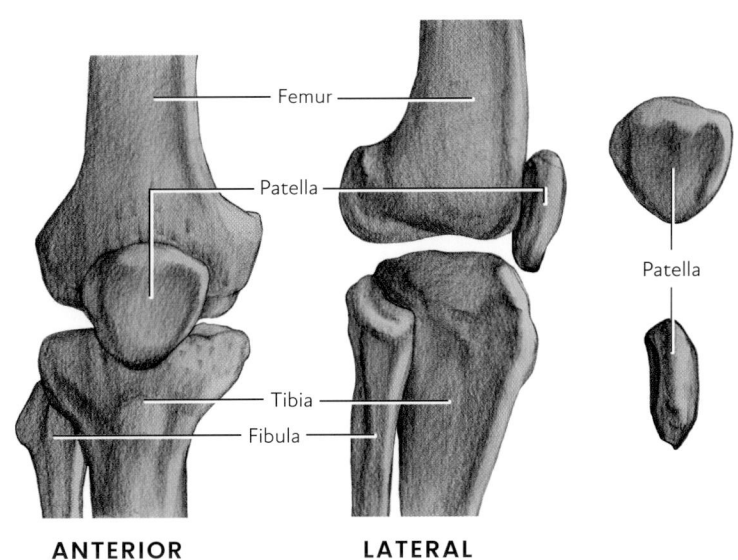

Femur

Patella

Tibia

Fibula

Patella

ANTERIOR   **LATERAL**

Mastering the Knees *(cont.)*

From the lateral side, you can see the **Tendon of the Biceps Femoris.** Also, the **Iliotibial Band** (IT Band) is sometimes visible. The Tendon of the Biceps Femoris goes to the **Fibula**, and the IT Band goes to the anterior side of the Tibia.

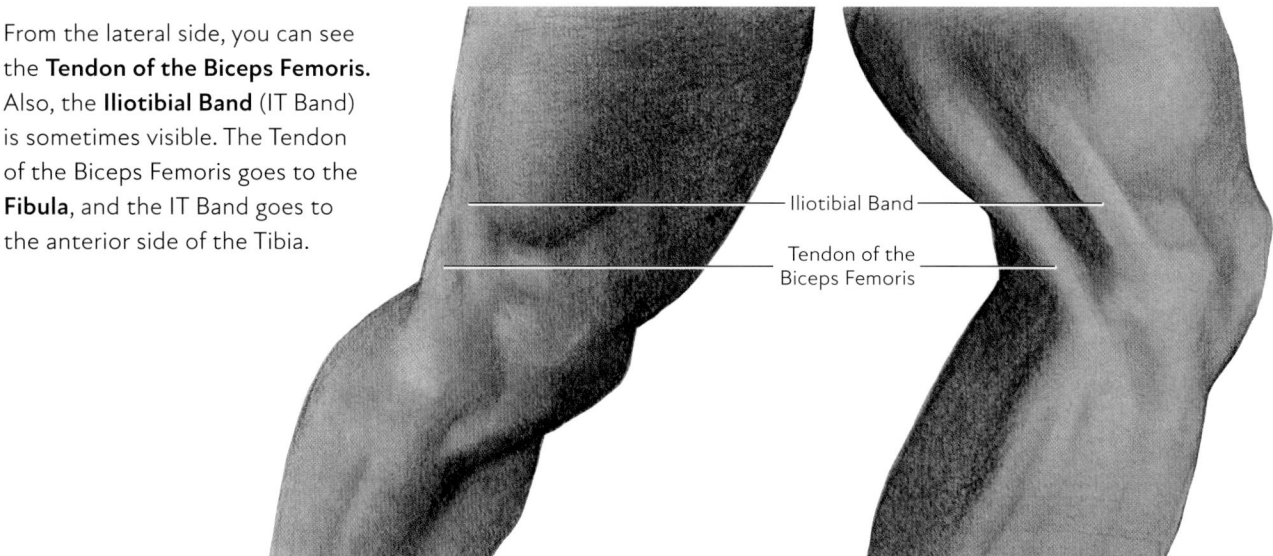

Iliotibial Band

Tendon of the Biceps Femoris

Ligament of the Knee

The **Patella Ligament** is a connective tissue between the Patella and the Tibia. This ligament stretches out from the Patella bone and is attached to a part of the Tibia called the **Tibia Tuberosity**. This structure usually stands out and can be seen as a vertical volume.

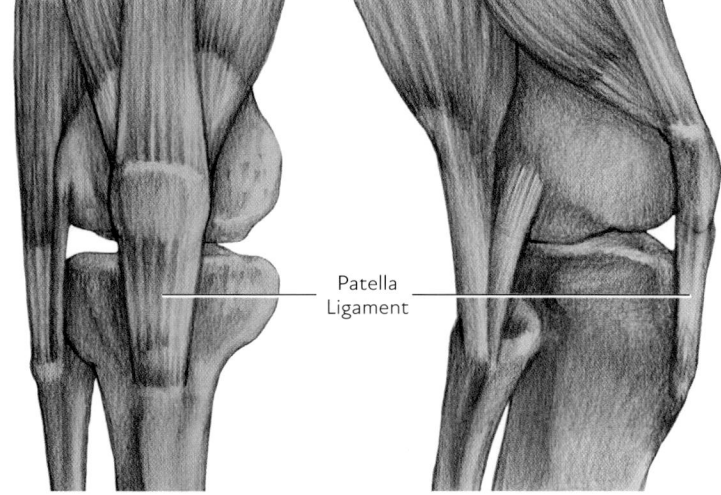

Patella Ligament

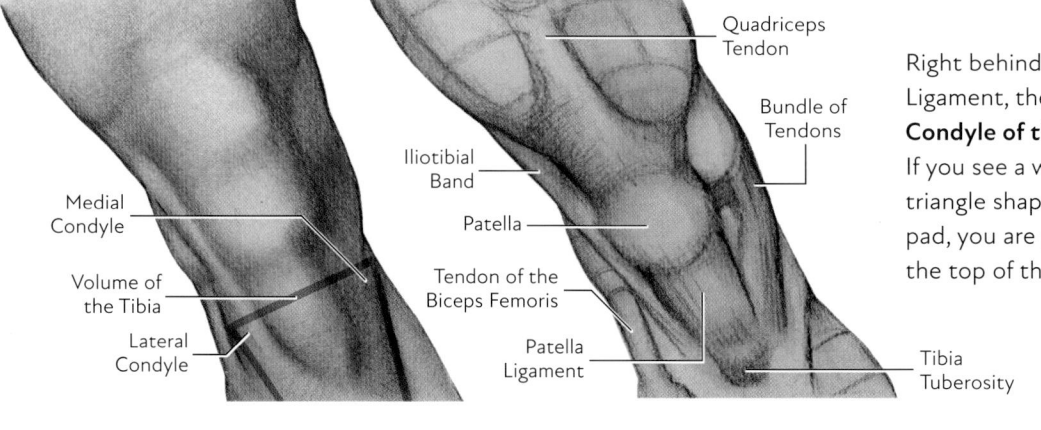

Medial Condyle

Volume of the Tibia

Lateral Condyle

Iliotibial Band

Patella

Tendon of the Biceps Femoris

Patella Ligament

Quadriceps Tendon

Bundle of Tendons

Tibia Tuberosity

Right behind the Patella Ligament, the **Lateral and Medial Condyle of the Tibia** peeks out. If you see a wide, inverted triangle shape under the knee pad, you are probably looking at the top of the Tibia.

Why Does Hitting the Shin Hurt So Bad?

Have you ever experienced hitting your shin against the edge of a table and it feels like it's been struck by lightning? This is so painful because the **Tibia** bone has a sharp crest with an exposed nervous system.

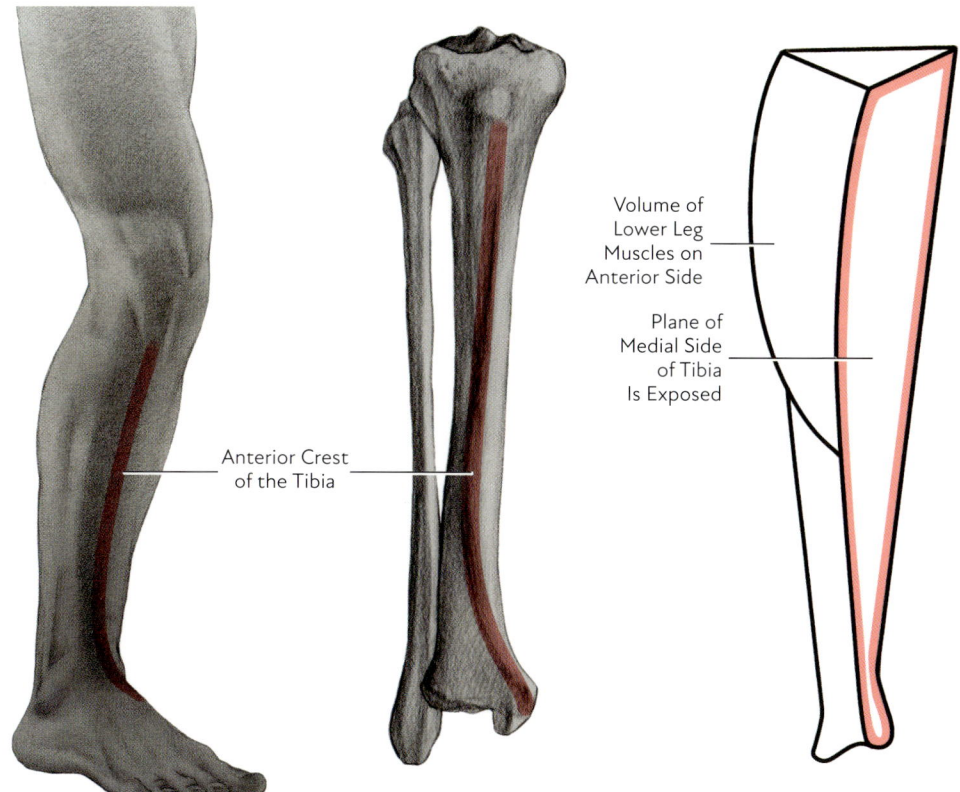

Anterior Crest of the Tibia

Volume of Lower Leg Muscles on Anterior Side

Plane of Medial Side of Tibia Is Exposed

The Tibia is shaped like a tetrahedron that is elongated vertically, and this creates a crest called the **Anterior Crest of the Tibia**. All the lower leg muscles are on the lateral side of the Tibia, and the crest and nervous system are completely exposed without any muscle or fat protecting the area. So, when you hit your shin, it is a direct strike.

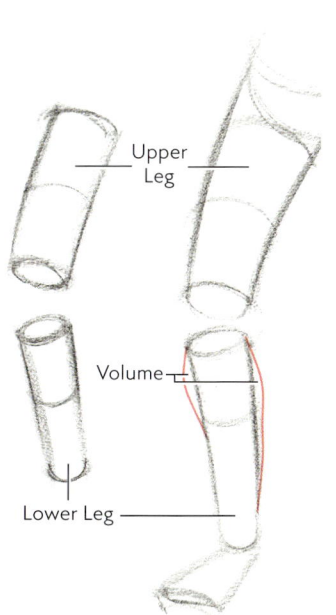

Upper Leg

Volume

Lower Leg

You can take advantage of the shape of the Tibia to create a gestural drawing of the lower leg. The shin has a subtle curve that extends to the dorsal of the foot. You can simply draw a curved cylinder for the shin, and then add the volumes of the anterior and posterior **Lower Leg Muscles**.

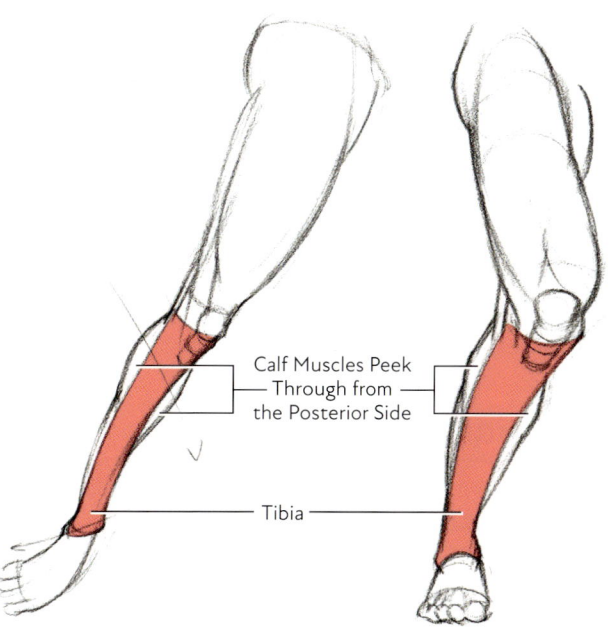

Calf Muscles Peek Through from the Posterior Side

Tibia

Bone-In-Meat Shape of the Lower Leg

Just like the forearm, the lower leg also has a similar bone-in-meat structure. The volume should be added to the proximal portion of the lower leg.

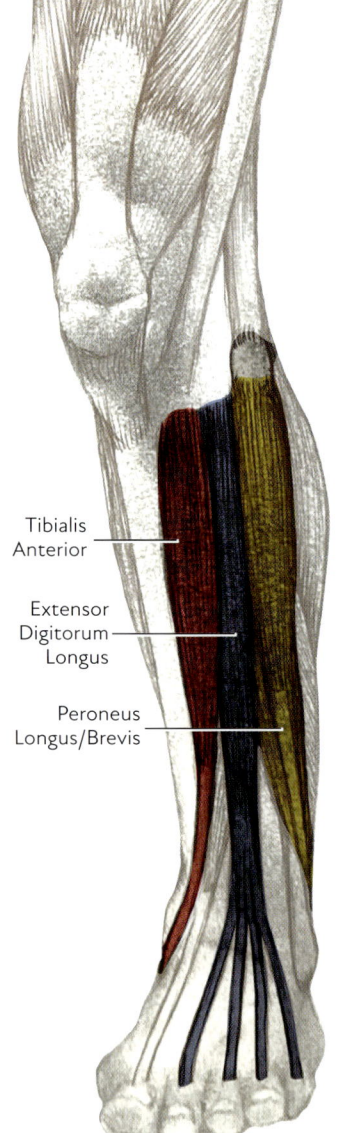

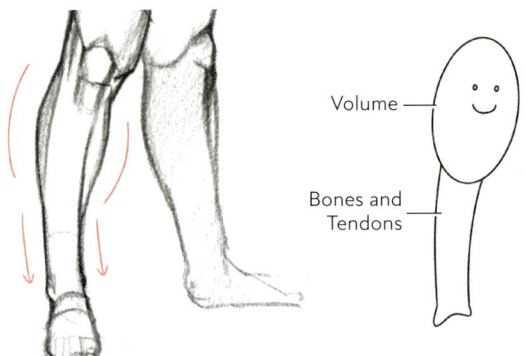

Anterior ← →

On the anterior side are the **Tibialis Anterior** and **Extensor Digitorum Longus** muscles, which are attached to the **Tibia** bone. The muscle volume covers almost half of the superior shaft of the Tibia, and the rest becomes the tendons toward the foot.

Other muscles that are attached to the Fibula bone are the **Peroneus Longus** and **Peroneus Brevis**.

Tibialis Anterior

Extensor Digitorum Longus

Peroneus Longus/Brevis

Volume

Bones and Tendons

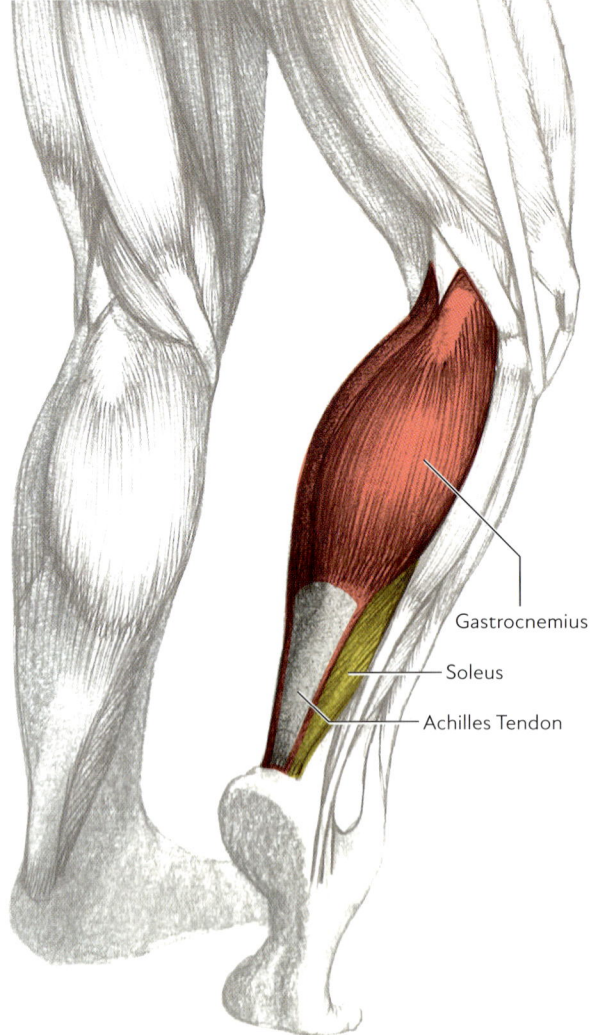

Gastrocnemius

Soleus

Achilles Tendon

Posterior →

You can see two muscles in the posterior view of the lower leg: the **Gastrocnemius** and the **Soleus**. They are layered and together they become a large tendon called the **Achilles Tendon** toward the heel.

The Gastrocnemius has two heads that go into the **Epicondyle of the Femur.** The lateral head is higher than the medial head, and this angle can be spotted from both the anterior and posterior view.

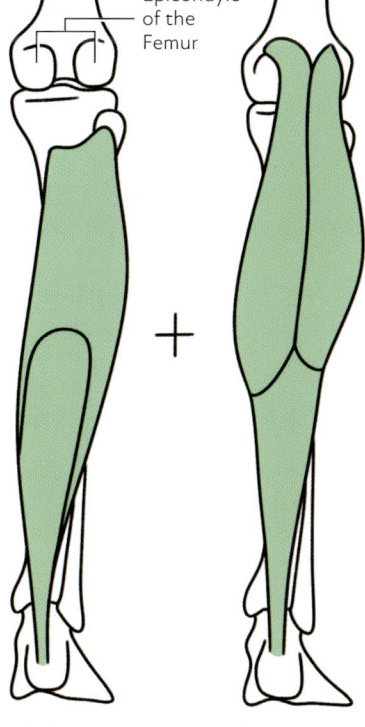

Epicondyle of the Femur

Soleus   Gastrocnemius

The Soleus is a flat fish-shaped muscle that is layered under the Gastrocnemius. It is visible on the surface.

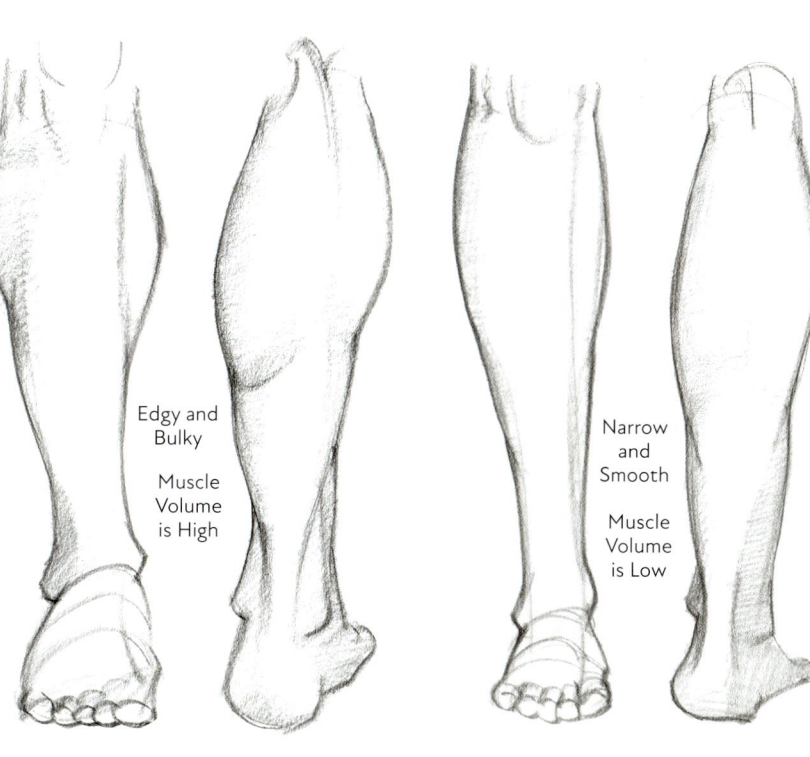

High

Low

High

Soleus

The calf muscle has a different volume in males and females. A male calf can be bulky, and the muscle location is high. If you want to create a female calf, you can make the volume narrower and more elongated.

Edgy and Bulky

Muscle Volume is High

Narrow and Smooth

Muscle Volume is Low

MALE

FEMALE

The Achilles

The Brave Man's Weak Point

The **Achilles Tendon** is the largest tendon in our body. It is thick, firm, and strong, like it could withstand the force of a thousand pounds.

The name Achilles comes from a warrior in Greek mythology. Achilles was considered to be fierce and invincible, but he was killed when he was shot with an arrow that hit his heel.

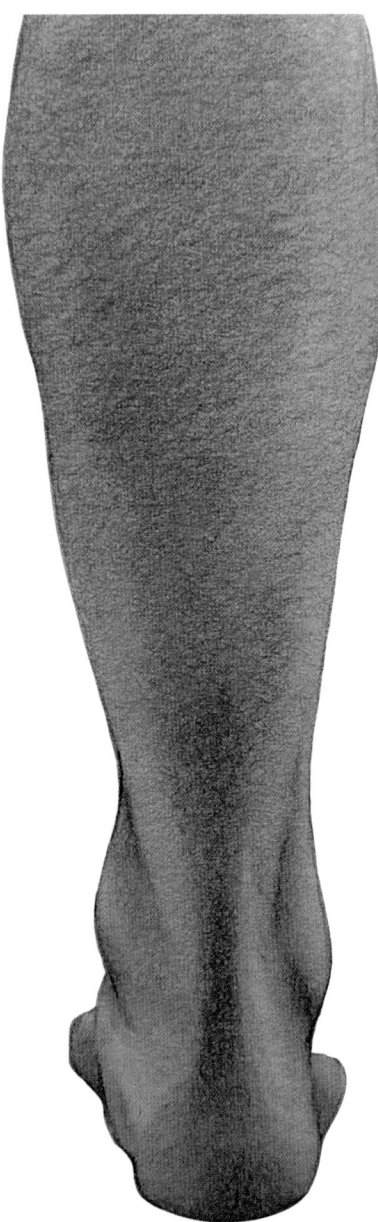

So, in drawing, let's give Achilles a nice firmness. This is the tendon that holds both the **Soleus** and **Gastrocnemius** in the calf, and it is attached to the large bone that forms the heel, which is called the **Calcaneus**. There is a slight gap in between the tendon and the **Tibia/Fibula**. It might work better when you drop a small shadow to separate them.

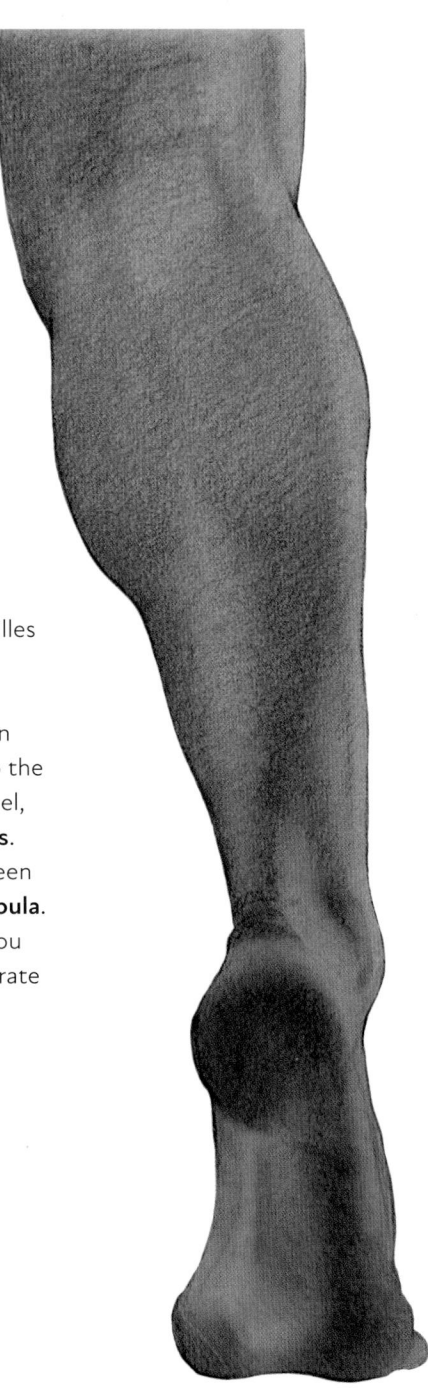

S and C Curves and the Zig-Zag Flow of the Leg

Just like in the gesture of the arm, curves and zig-zags can be found in the rhythm of the legs.

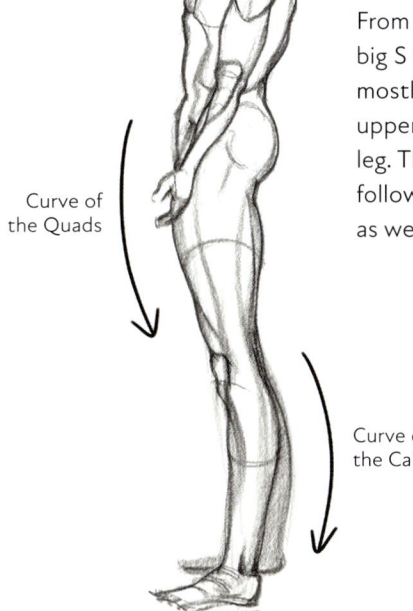

Curve of the Quads

Curve of the Calf

From the lateral view, it is common to use a big S for the general gesture of the leg. It is mostly to focus on the Quad's curve for the upper leg, and the calf's curve for the lower leg. The curves of the Femur and Tibia bones follow the same gesture from the lateral view as well.

After the general gesture sketch of the leg, you can start focusing on the detailed C curves. The curve that you can find in the highest portion of the leg would be that of the Glute on the posterior side. The volume moves down to the Quads on the anterior side, and then a subtle curve for the Hamstrings can be added on the posterior side of the upper leg. The knee would have its own form, a calf volume appears on the posterior side, and then another subtle narrow curve is added for the anterior side of the lower leg.

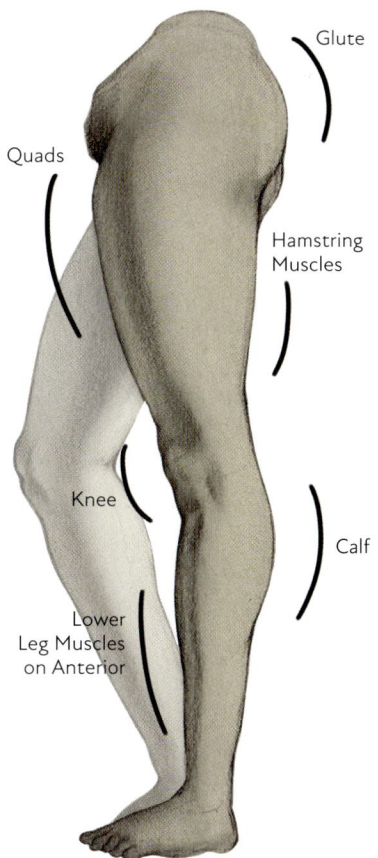

Glute

Quads

Hamstring Muscles

Knee

Calf

Lower Leg Muscles on Anterior

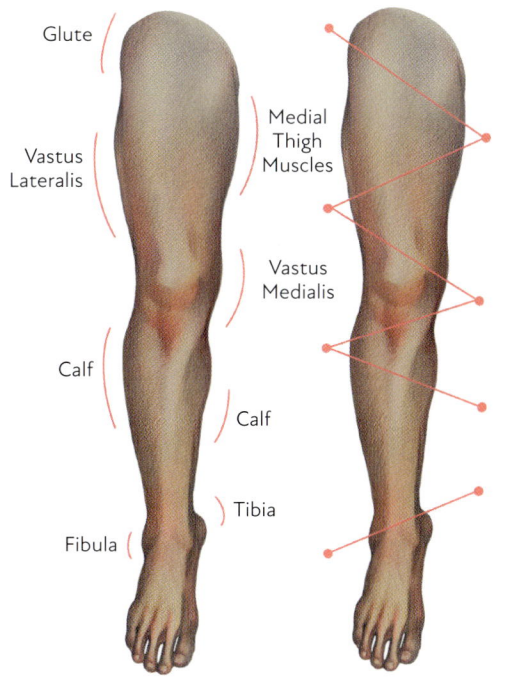

Glute

Vastus Lateralis

Calf

Fibula

Medial Thigh Muscles

Vastus Medialis

Calf

Tibia

The zig-zag rhythm can be distinctive from the anterior/posterior view. On the lateral side at the top is a volume of the Glute. This can be either the Tensor Fascia Latae or the Gluteal Medius depending on the angle. Next are the Medial Thigh Muscles with a soft bulge under the pubis. The curve on the lateral side can be a part of the Quads called the Vastus Lateralis, or simply the line of the Iliotibial Band. The Quads are shaped like a teardrop; therefore, the curve of the Vastus Medialis would be the lower volume on the medial side right by the knee. Moving to the lower leg, the calf volume is higher on the lateral side and lower on the medial side. Lastly, the angle of the ankle has a slant that goes in the opposite direction to the calf. The end of the Fibula is lower than the end of the Tibia.

Leg Muscles Overview

Anterior

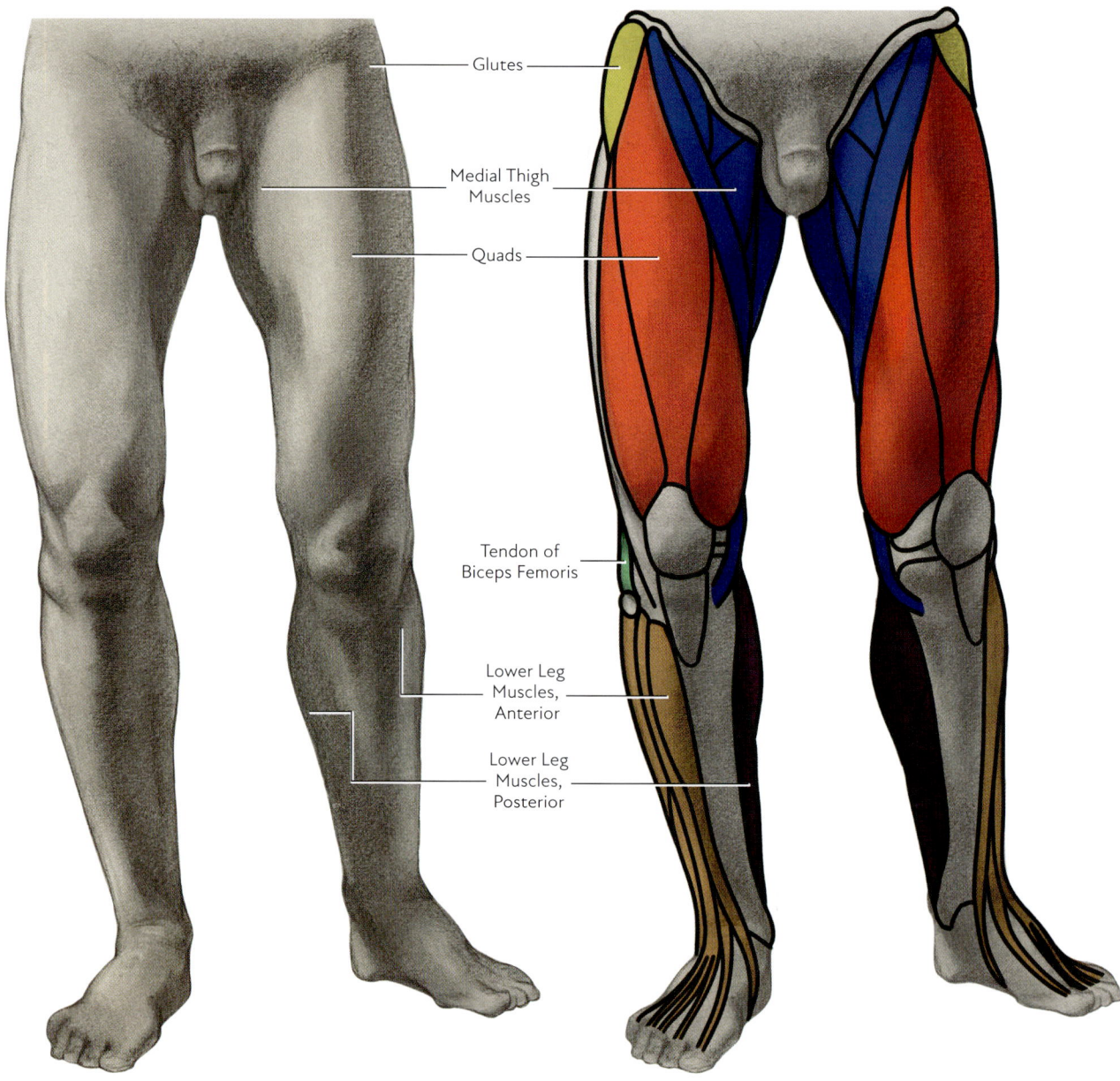

Glutes

Medial Thigh
Muscles

Quads

Tendon of
Biceps Femoris

Lower Leg
Muscles,
Anterior

Lower Leg
Muscles,
Posterior

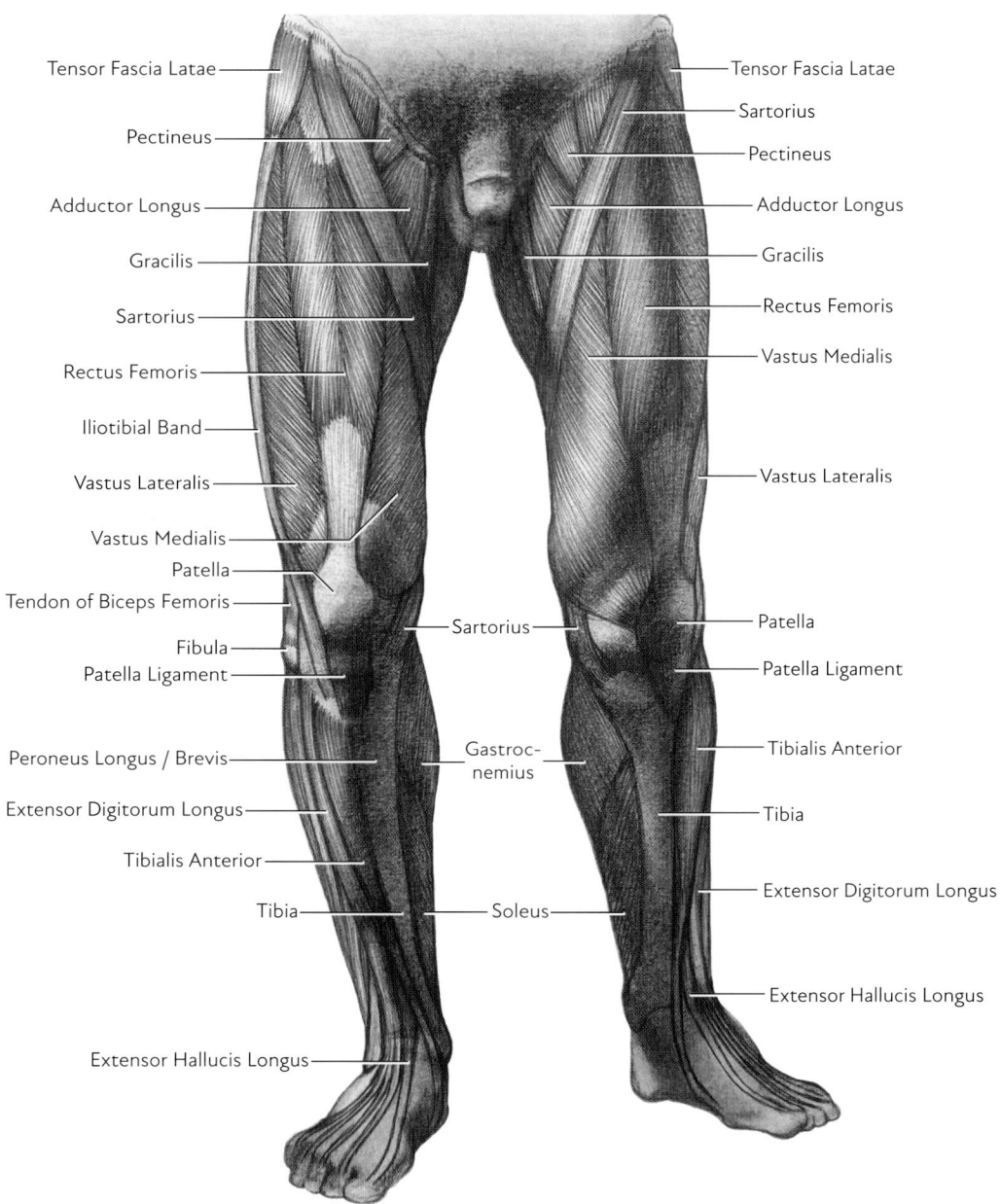

Tensor Fascia Latae

Pectineus

Adductor Longus

Gracilis

Sartorius

Rectus Femoris

Iliotibial Band

Vastus Lateralis

Vastus Medialis

Patella

Tendon of Biceps Femoris

Fibula

Patella Ligament

Peroneus Longus / Brevis

Extensor Digitorum Longus

Tibialis Anterior

Tibia

Tensor Fascia Latae

Sartorius

Pectineus

Adductor Longus

Gracilis

Rectus Femoris

Vastus Medialis

Vastus Lateralis

Patella

Patella Ligament

Tibialis Anterior

Tibia

Extensor Digitorum Longus

Extensor Hallucis Longus

Sartorius

Gastroc-nemius

Soleus

Extensor Hallucis Longus

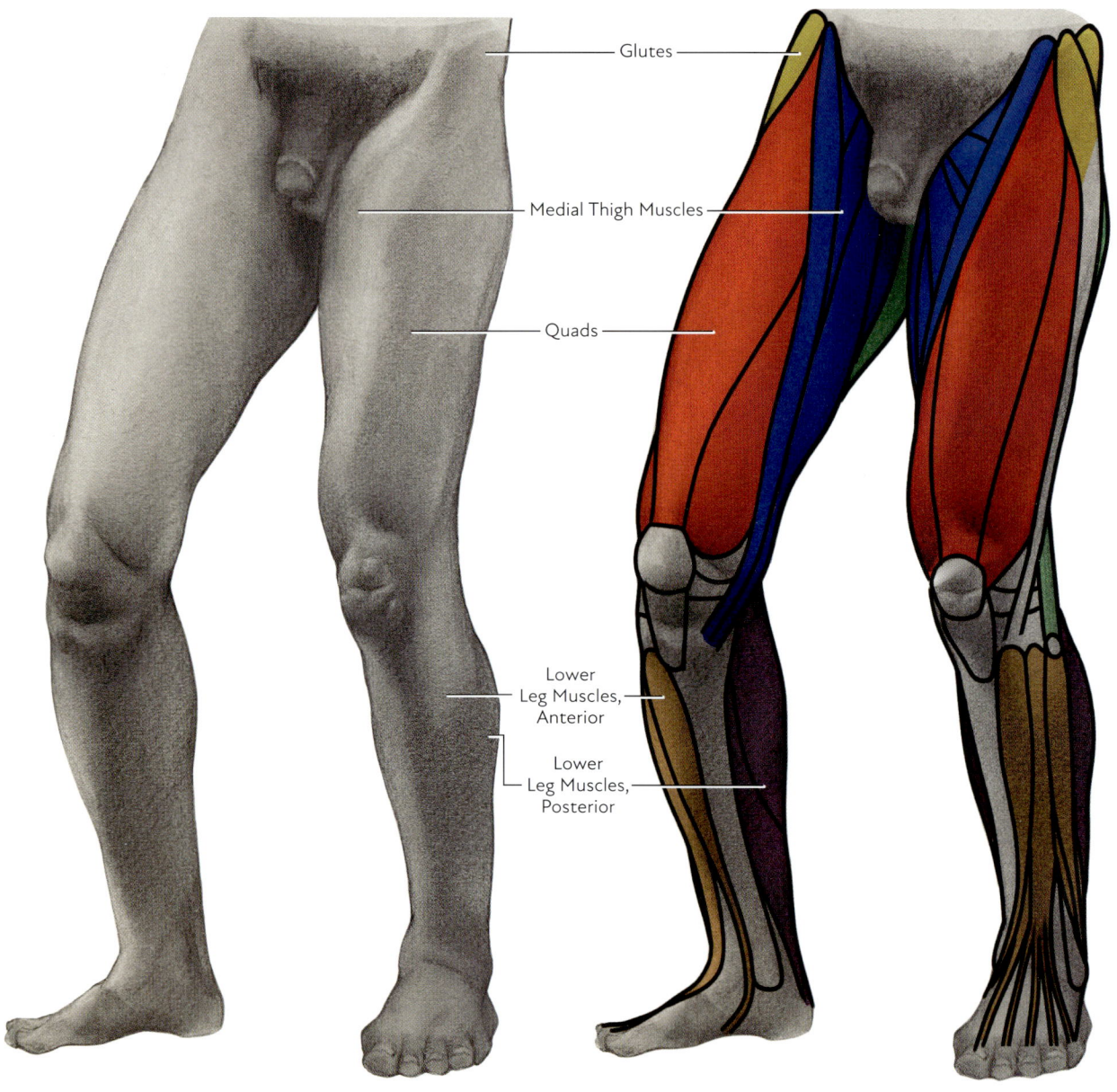

Glutes

Medial Thigh Muscles

Quads

Lower
Leg Muscles,
Anterior

Lower
Leg Muscles,
Posterior

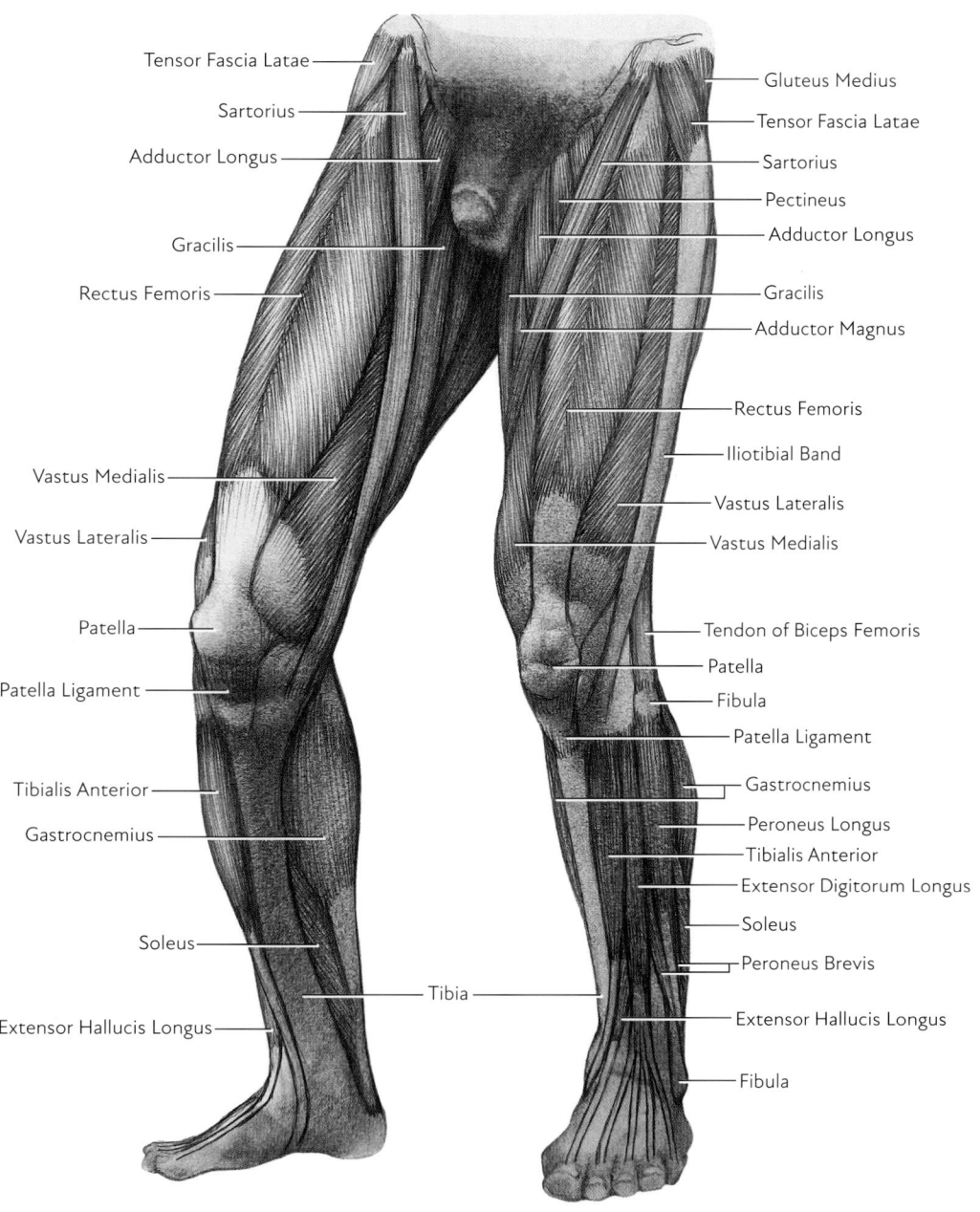

Tensor Fascia Latae

Sartorius

Adductor Longus

Gracilis

Rectus Femoris

Vastus Medialis

Vastus Lateralis

Patella

Patella Ligament

Tibialis Anterior

Gastrocnemius

Soleus

Extensor Hallucis Longus

Gluteus Medius

Tensor Fascia Latae

Sartorius

Pectineus

Adductor Longus

Gracilis

Adductor Magnus

Rectus Femoris

Iliotibial Band

Vastus Lateralis

Vastus Medialis

Tendon of Biceps Femoris

Patella

Fibula

Patella Ligament

Gastrocnemius

Peroneus Longus

Tibialis Anterior

Extensor Digitorum Longus

Soleus

Peroneus Brevis

Extensor Hallucis Longus

Fibula

Tibia

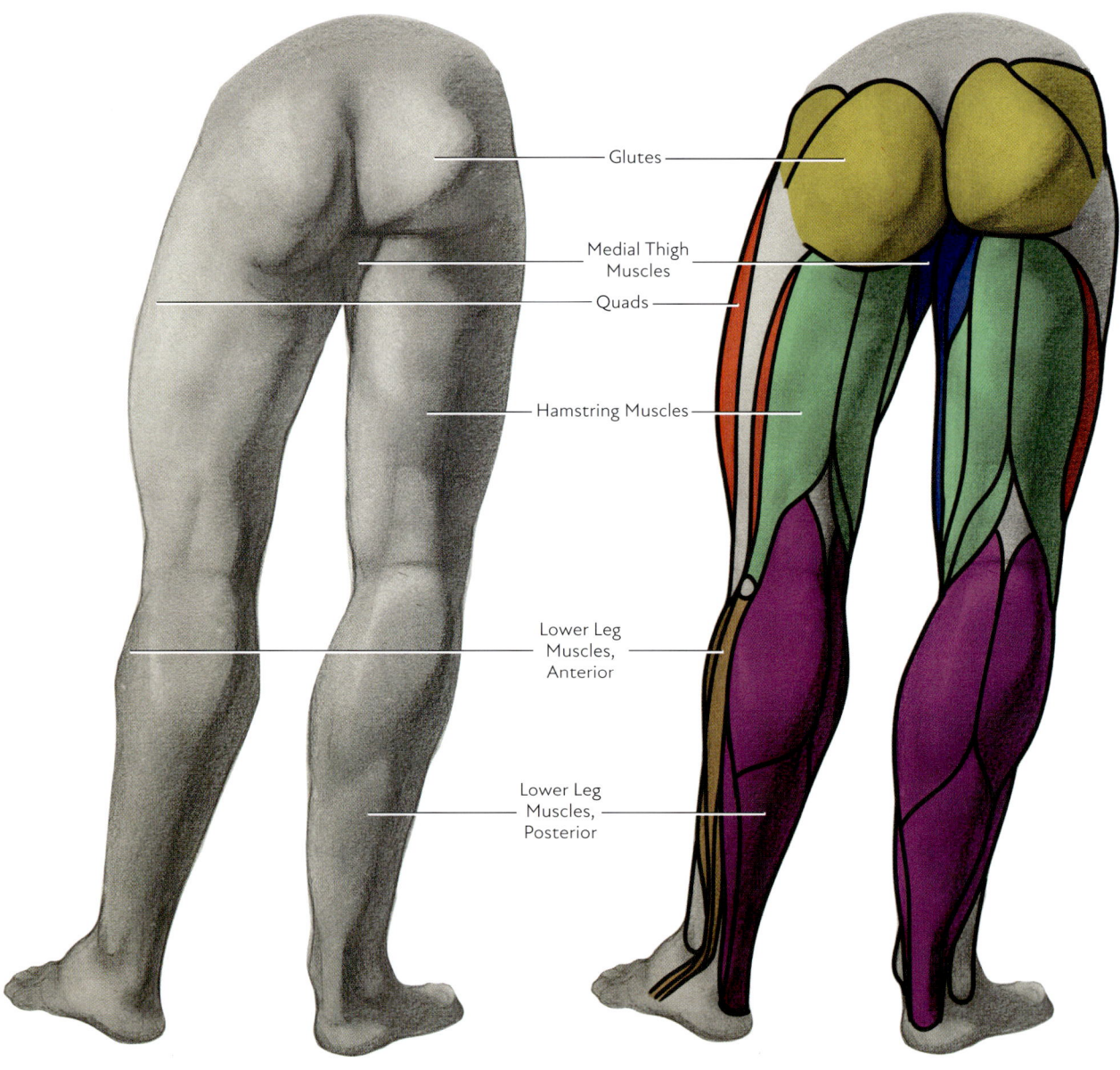

Glutes

Medial Thigh
Muscles

Quads

Hamstring Muscles

Lower Leg
Muscles,
Anterior

Lower Leg
Muscles,
Posterior

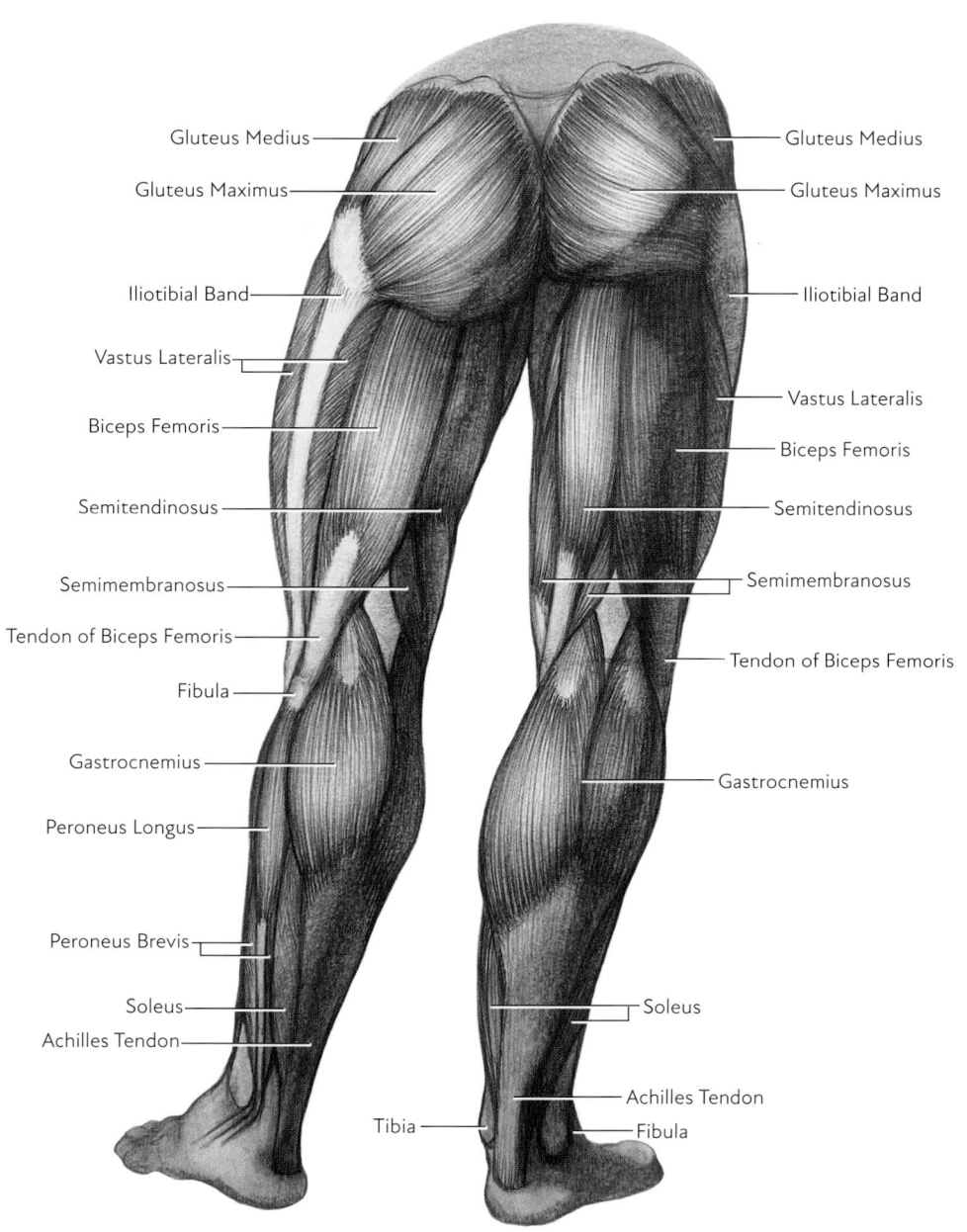

Gluteus Medius

Gluteus Maximus

Iliotibial Band

Vastus Lateralis

Biceps Femoris

Semitendinosus

Semimembranosus

Tendon of Biceps Femoris

Fibula

Gastrocnemius

Peroneus Longus

Peroneus Brevis

Soleus

Achilles Tendon

Gluteus Medius

Gluteus Maximus

Iliotibial Band

Vastus Lateralis

Biceps Femoris

Semitendinosus

Semimembranosus

Tendon of Biceps Femoris

Gastrocnemius

Soleus

Achilles Tendon

Tibia

Fibula

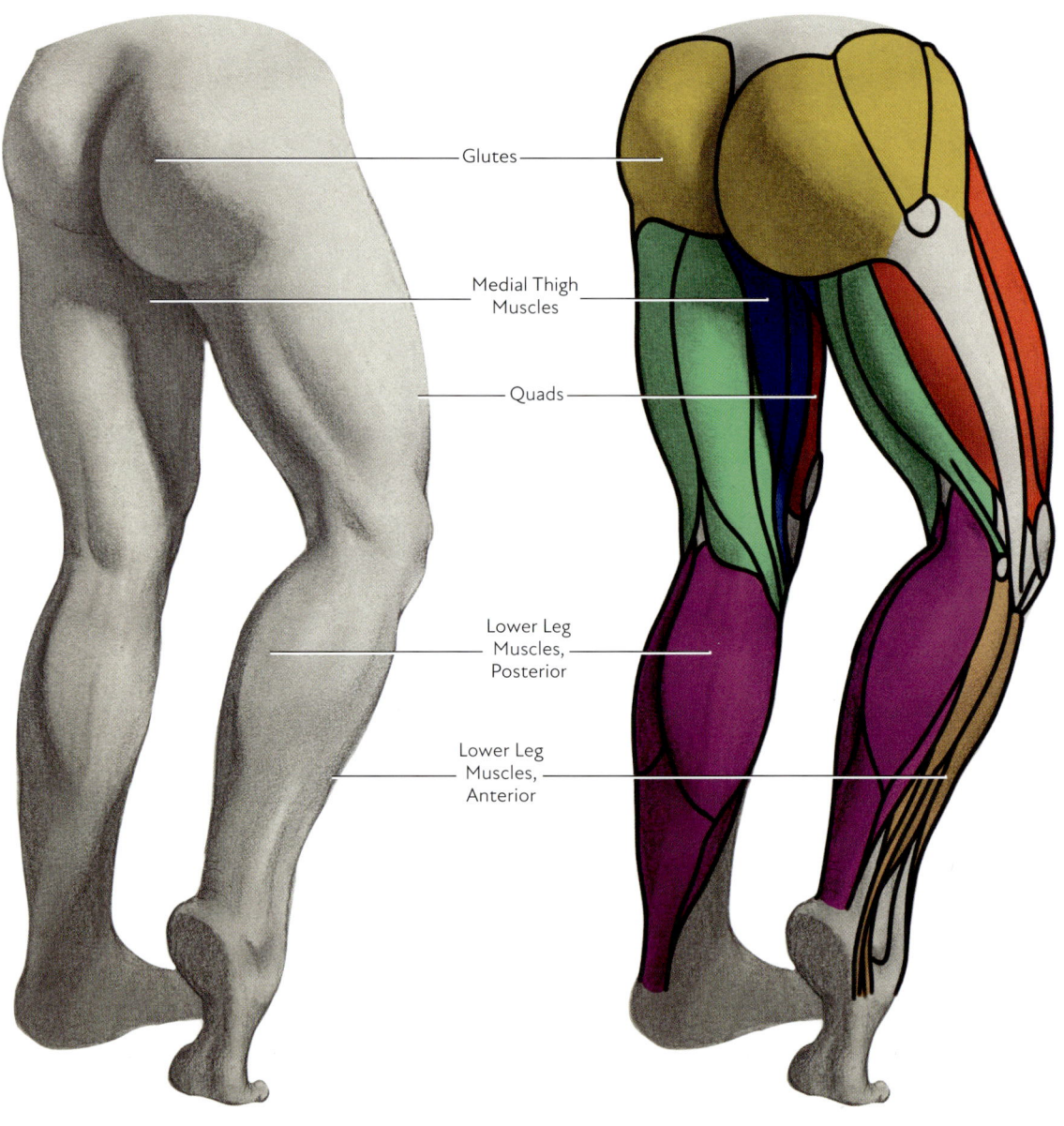

Glutes

Medial Thigh
Muscles

Quads

Lower Leg
Muscles,
Posterior

Lower Leg
Muscles,
Anterior

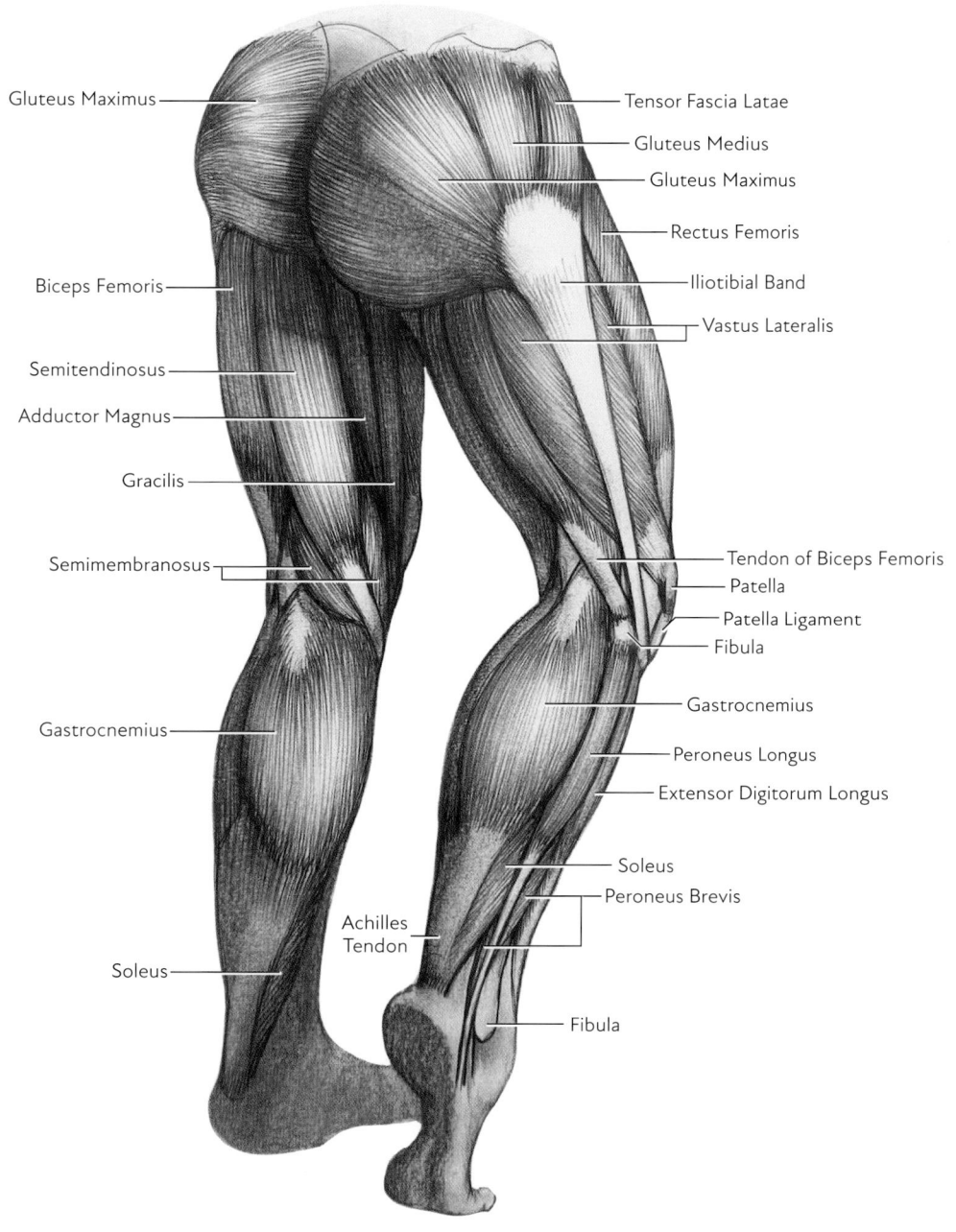

Gluteus Maximus

Biceps Femoris

Semitendinosus

Adductor Magnus

Gracilis

Semimembranosus

Gastrocnemius

Soleus

Achilles
Tendon

Tensor Fascia Latae

Gluteus Medius

Gluteus Maximus

Rectus Femoris

Iliotibial Band

Vastus Lateralis

Tendon of Biceps Femoris

Patella

Patella Ligament

Fibula

Gastrocnemius

Peroneus Longus

Extensor Digitorum Longus

Soleus

Peroneus Brevis

Fibula

Lateral

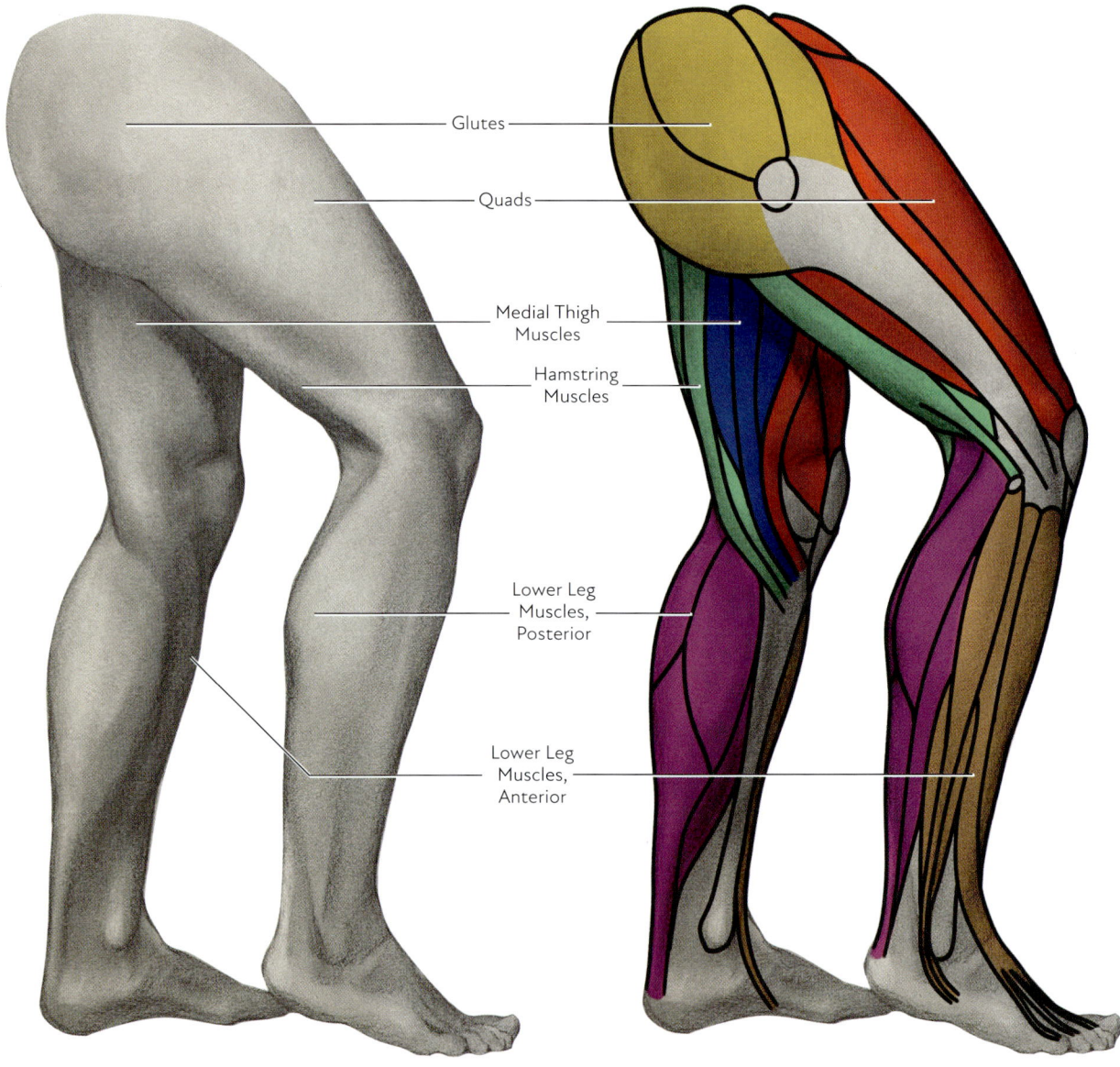

Glutes

Quads

Medial Thigh
Muscles

Hamstring
Muscles

Lower Leg
Muscles,
Posterior

Lower Leg
Muscles,
Anterior

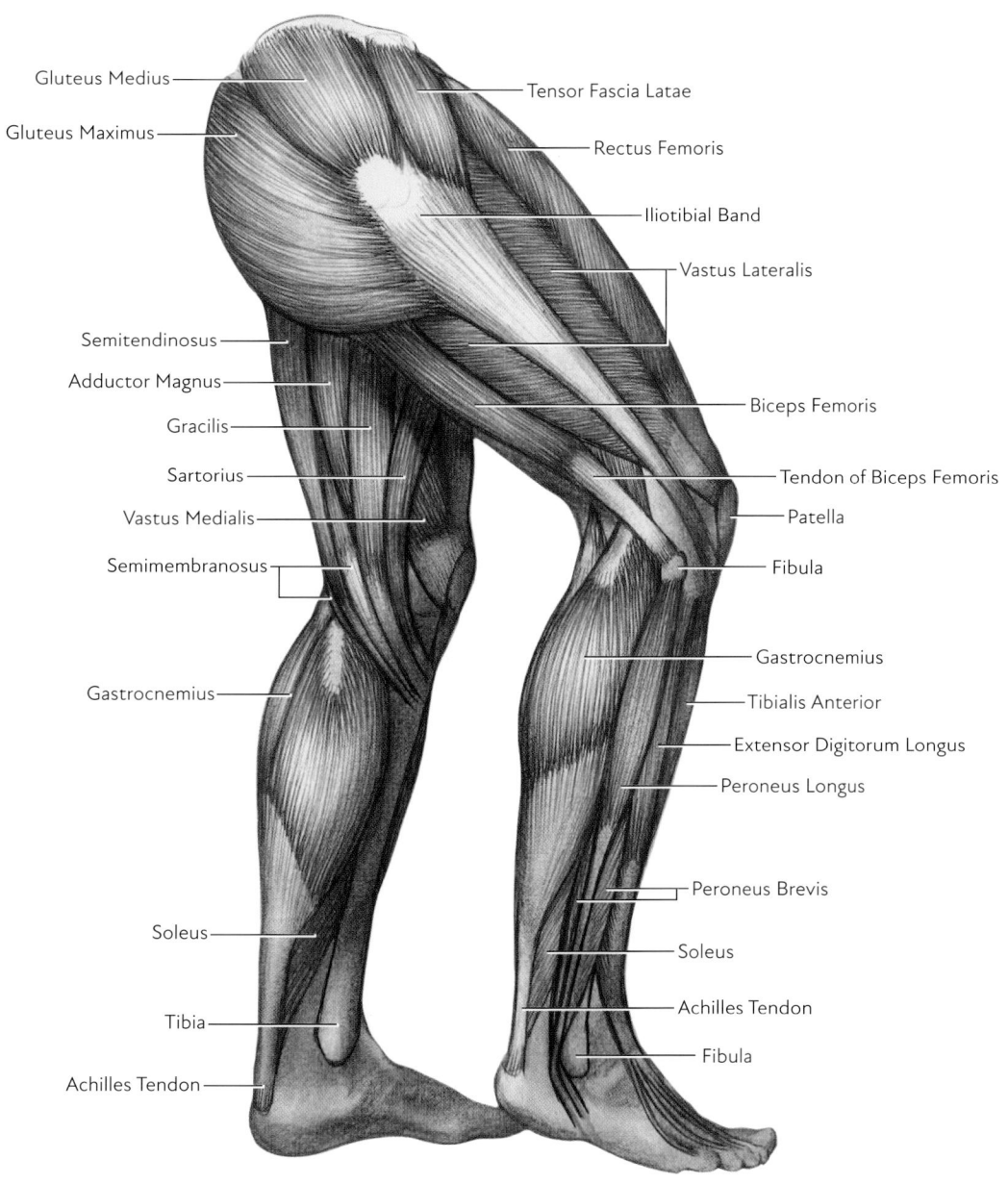

Gluteus Medius

Gluteus Maximus

Semitendinosus

Adductor Magnus

Gracilis

Sartorius

Vastus Medialis

Semimembranosus

Gastrocnemius

Soleus

Tibia

Achilles Tendon

Tensor Fascia Latae

Rectus Femoris

Iliotibial Band

Vastus Lateralis

Biceps Femoris

Tendon of Biceps Femoris

Patella

Fibula

Gastrocnemius

Tibialis Anterior

Extensor Digitorum Longus

Peroneus Longus

Peroneus Brevis

Soleus

Achilles Tendon

Fibula

Step-by-Step Leg Muscles

Anterior

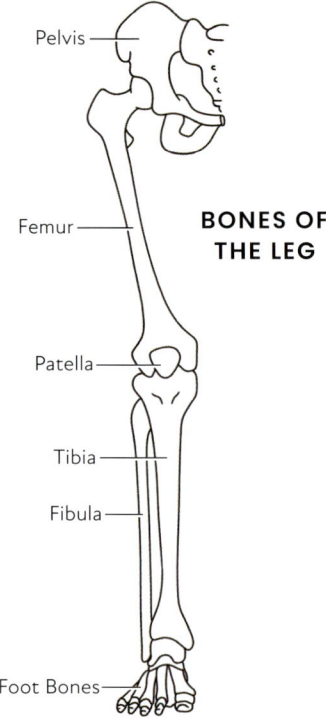

Pelvis

Femur

BONES OF THE LEG

Patella

Tibia

Fibula

Foot Bones

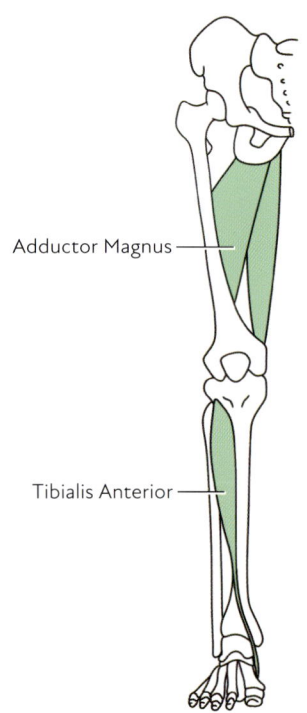

Adductor Magnus

Tibialis Anterior

Adductor Magnus

Origin: Pubic Ramus, Ischial Ramus, Ischial Tuberosity

Insertion: Linea Aspera, Adductor Tubercle of Femur

Function: Flexion, adduction, extension, rotation of the thigh; stabilization of the Pelvis

Tibialis Anterior

Origin: Lateral surface of the Tibia

Insertion: Cuneiform bone, base of Metatarsal bone 1

Function: Dorsiflexion; inversion

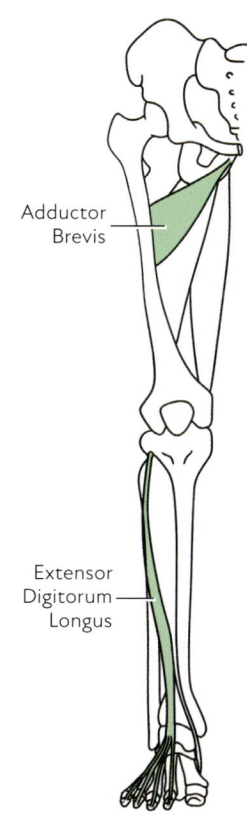

Adductor Brevis

Extensor Digitorum Longus

Adductor Brevis

Origin: Inferior Pubic Ramus

Insertion: Linea Aspera

Function: Flexion, adduction, rotation of the thigh; stabilization of the Pelvis

Extensor Digitorum Longus

Origin: Lateral Condyle of the Tibia, Anterior Surface of the Fibula

Insertion: Distal and middle phalanges digit 2–5

Function: Dorsiflexion; extension of the toes

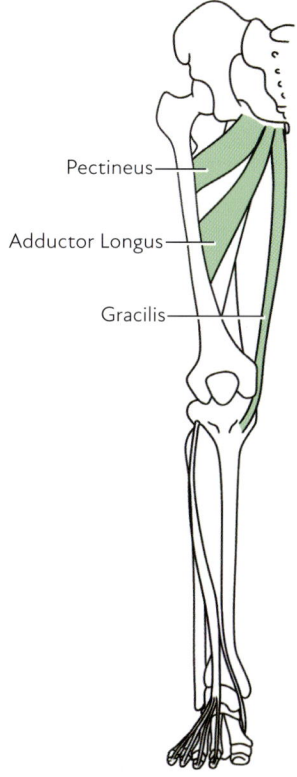

Pectineus

Adductor Longus

Gracilis

Pectineus

Origin: Pubic Ramus

Insertion: Linea Aspera

Function: Flexion, adduction, extension, rotation of the thigh; stabilization of the Pelvis

Adductor Longus

Origin: Pubic Crest

Insertion: Linea Aspera

Function: Flexion, adduction, rotation of the thigh; stabilization of the Pelvis

Gracilis

Origin: Anterior Pubis, Pubic Ramus, Ischial Ramus

Insertion: Proximal surface of medial side of the Tibia

Function: Flexion and adduction of the thigh; flexion and internal rotation of the knee

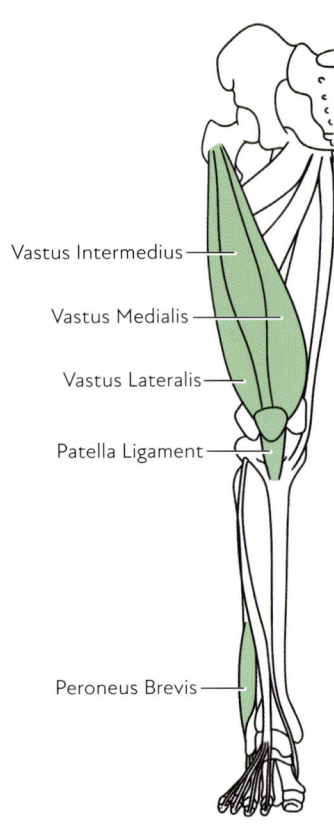

Vastus Intermedius

Vastus Medialis

Vastus Lateralis

Patella Ligament

Peroneus Brevis

Vastus Intermedius

Origin: Anterior surface of the Femur

Insertion: Tibia Tuberosity (through the Patella Ligament)

Function: Flexion of the thigh; extension of the knee

Vastus Lateralis

Origin: Intertrochanteric line, Greater Trochanter, and anterior and side of the Femur

Insertion: Tibia Tuberosity (through the Patella Ligament)

Function: Flexion of the thigh; extension of the knee

Vastus Medialis

Origin: Intertrochanteric line, Linea Aspera, and anterior and medial surface of the Femur

Insertion: Tibia Tuberosity (through the Patella Ligament)

Function: Flexion of the thigh; extension of the knee

Peroneus Brevis

Origin: Distal ⅔ of the surface of the Fibula

Insertion: Metatarsal digit 5

Function: Plantar flexion; eversion

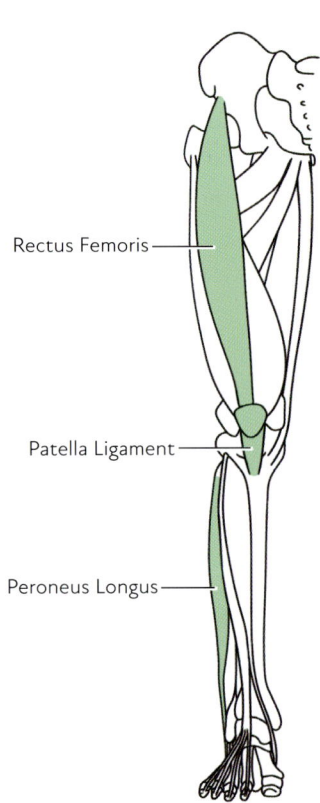

Rectus Femoris

Patella Ligament

Peroneus Longus

Rectus Femoris

Origin: Anterior Inferior Iliac Spine (AIIS) of the Pelvis

Insertion: Tibia Tuberosity (through the Patella Ligament)

Function: Flexion of the thigh; extension of the knee

Peroneus Longus

Origin: Proximal ⅔ of the surface of the Fibula

Insertion: Cuneiform bone, Metatarsal digit 1

Function: Plantar flexion; eversion

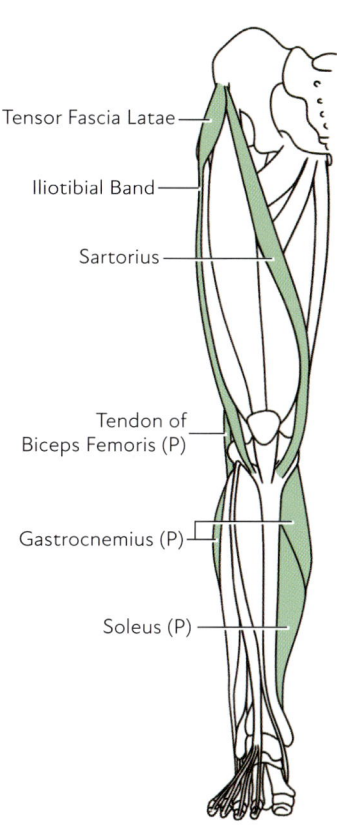

Tensor Fascia Latae

Iliotibial Band

Sartorius

Tendon of
Biceps Femoris (P)

Gastrocnemius (P)

Soleus (P)

Tensor Fascia Latae

Origin: Anterior Superior Iliac Spine (ASIS) of the Pelvis

Insertion: Lateral Condyle of the Tibia (as Iliotibial Band)

Function: Internal rotation of the thigh; stabilization of the hip and knee joints

Sartorius

Origin: Anterior Superior Iliac Spine (ASIS) of the Pelvis

Insertion: Proximal surface of the medial side of the Tibia

Function: Flexion, abduction, external rotation of the thigh; flexion and internal rotation of the knee

Step-by-Step Leg Muscles

Posterior

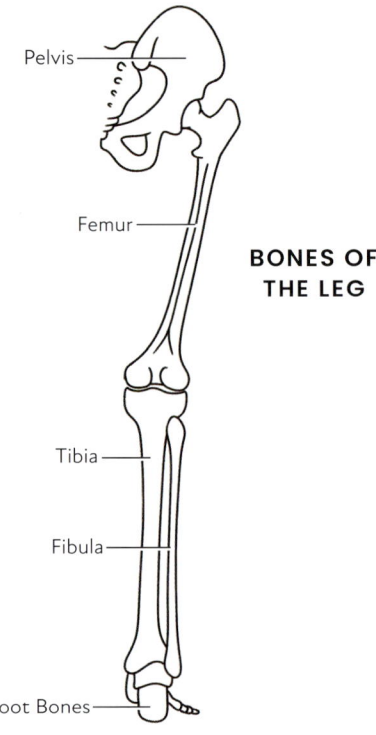

Pelvis

Femur

**BONES OF
THE LEG**

Tibia

Fibula

Foot Bones

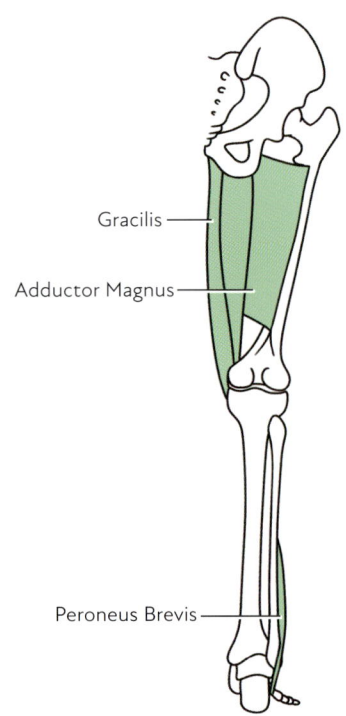

Gracilis

Adductor Magnus

Peroneus Brevis

Gracilis

Origin: Anterior Pubis, Pubic Ramus, Ischial Ramus

Insertion: Proximal surface of medial side of the Tibia

Function: Flexion and adduction of the thigh; flexion and internal rotation of the knee

Adductor Magnus

Origin: Pubic Ramus, Ischial Ramus, Ischial Tuberosity

Insertion: Linea Aspera, Adductor Tubercle of Femur

Function: Flexion, adduction, extension, rotation of the thigh; stabilization of the Pelvis

Peroneus Brevis

Origin: Distal ⅔ of the surface of the Fibula

Insertion: Metatarsal digit 5

Function: Plantar flexion; eversion

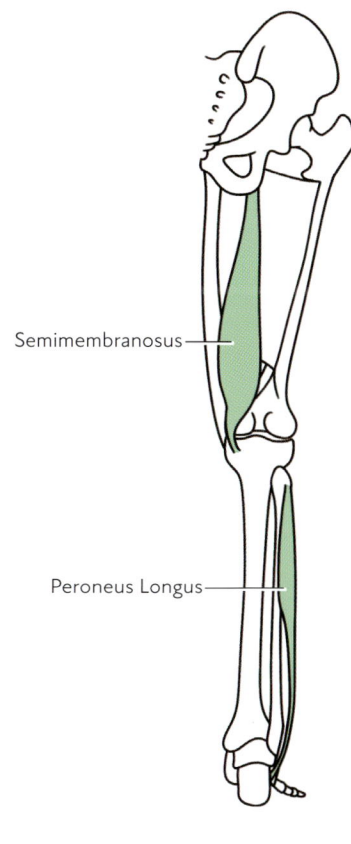

Semimembranosus —

Peroneus Longus —

Semimembranosus

Origin: Ischial Tuberosity

Insertion: Medial Condyle of the Tibia

Function: Extension and internal rotation of the thigh; flexion and internal rotation of the knee; stabilization of the Pelvis

Peroneus Longus

Origin: Proximal ⅔ of the surface of the Fibula

Insertion: Cuneiform bone, Metatarsal digit 1

Function: Plantar flexion; eversion

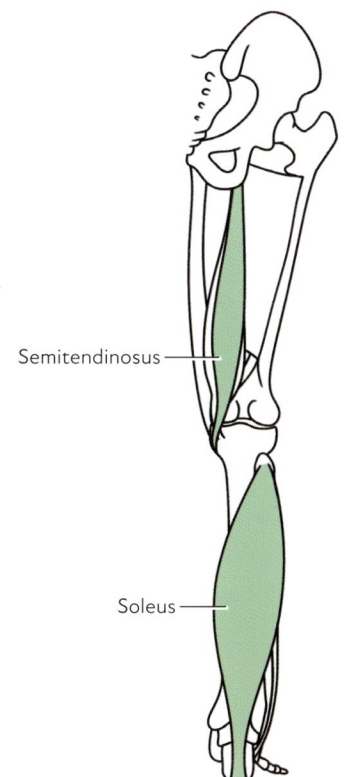

Semitendinosus —

Soleus —

Semitendinosus

Origin: Ischial Tuberosity

Insertion: Medial Condyle of the Tibia

Function: Extension and internal rotation of the thigh; flexion and internal rotation of the knee; and stabilization of the Pelvis

Soleus

Origin: Head and posterior border of the Fibula, medial border of the Tibia

Insertion: Calcaneus (as Achilles Tendon)

Function: Plantar flexion

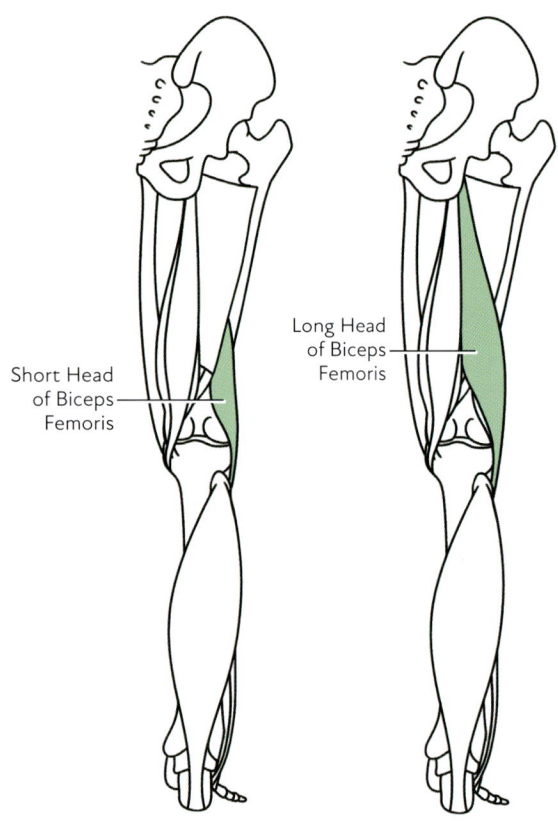

Short Head of Biceps Femoris

Long Head of Biceps Femoris

Biceps Femoris

Origin:
- **Long Head:** Ischium Tuberosity
- **Short Head:** Linea Aspera

Insertion: Head of the Fibula

Function: Extension and external rotation of the thigh; flexion and external rotation of the knee; and stabilization of the Pelvis

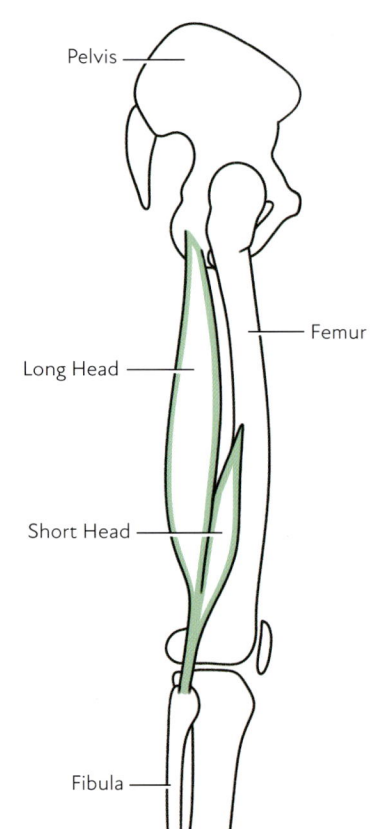

Pelvis

Femur

Long Head

Short Head

Fibula

LATERAL VIEW

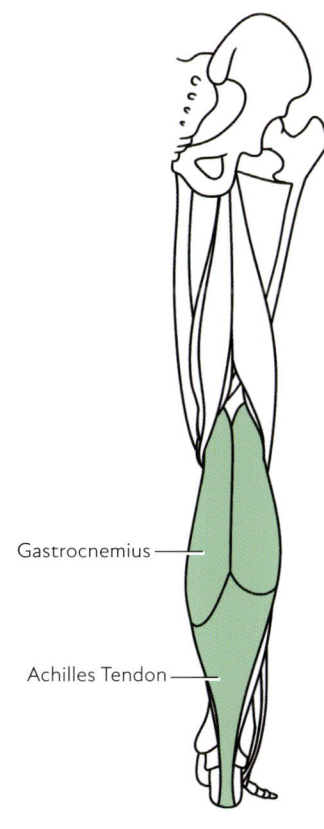

Gastrocnemius

Achilles Tendon

Gastrocnemius

Origin:
• **Lateral Head:** Lateral Condyle of the Femur
• **Medial Head:** Medial Condyle of the Femur

Insertion: Calcaneus (as Achilles Tendon)

Function: Plantar flexion; flexion of the knee

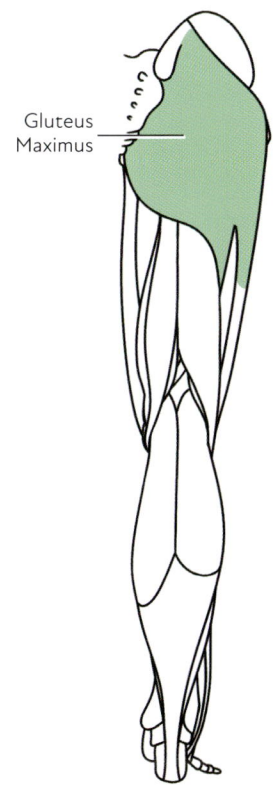

Gluteus Maximus

Gluteus Maximus

Origin: Lateral side of the Sacrum and Coccyx; Gluteal surface of the Ilium

Insertion: Gluteal Tuberosity of the Femur

Function: Extension, external rotation, abduction, and adduction of the thigh

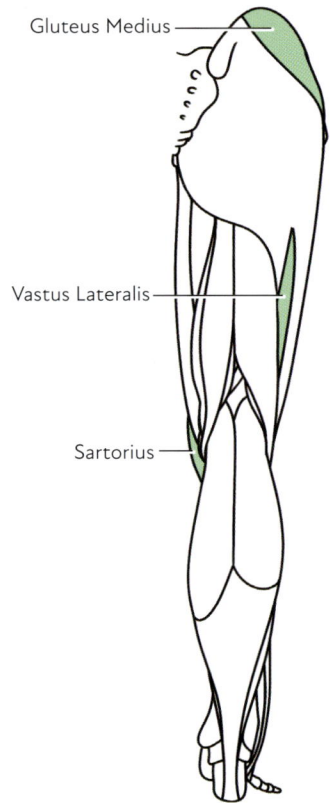

Gluteus Medius

Vastus Lateralis

Sartorius

Gluteus Medius

Origin: Ilium

Insertion: Great Trochanter of the Femur

Function: Adduction and internal rotation of the thigh; stabilization of the Pelvis

Step-by-Step Leg Muscles

Lateral

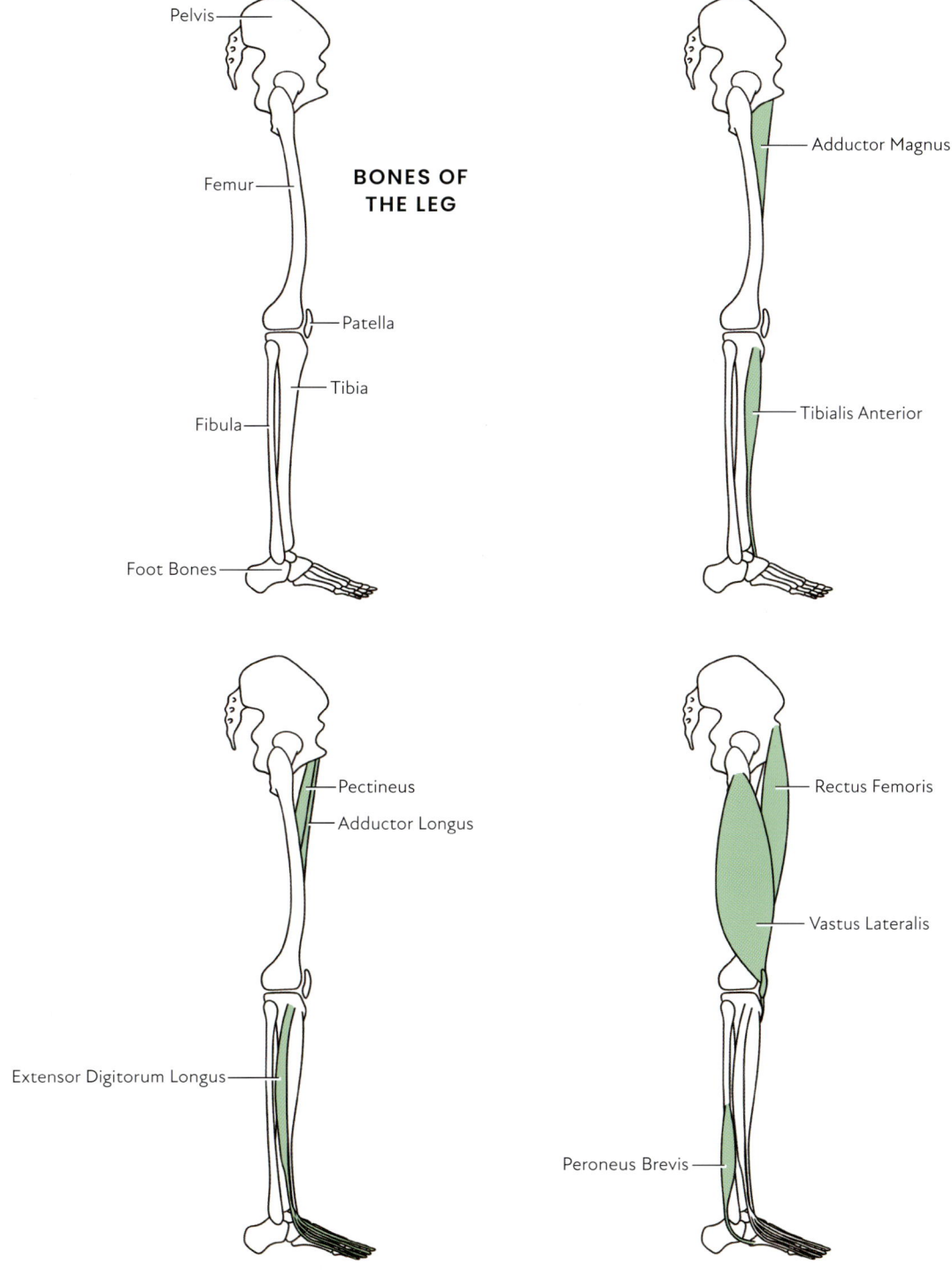

Pelvis

Femur

BONES OF THE LEG

Patella

Tibia

Fibula

Foot Bones

Adductor Magnus

Tibialis Anterior

Pectineus

Adductor Longus

Extensor Digitorum Longus

Rectus Femoris

Vastus Lateralis

Peroneus Brevis

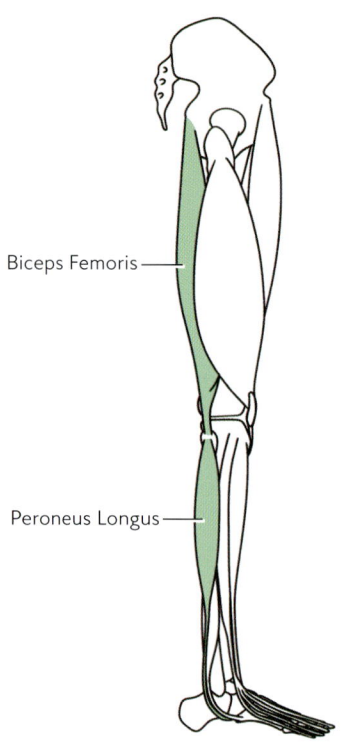

Biceps Femoris

Peroneus Longus

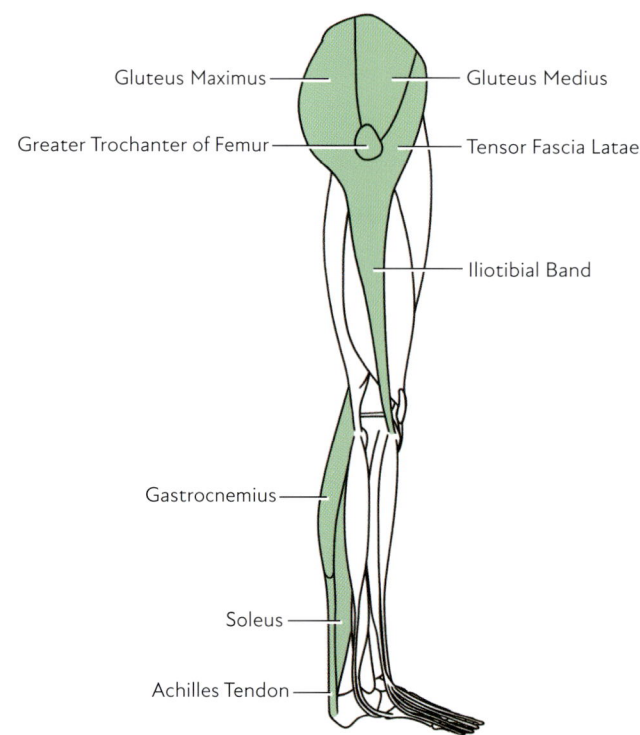

Gluteus Maximus — — Gluteus Medius

Greater Trochanter of Femur — — Tensor Fascia Latae

Iliotibial Band

Gastrocnemius

Soleus

Achilles Tendon

Step-by-Step Leg Muscles

Medial

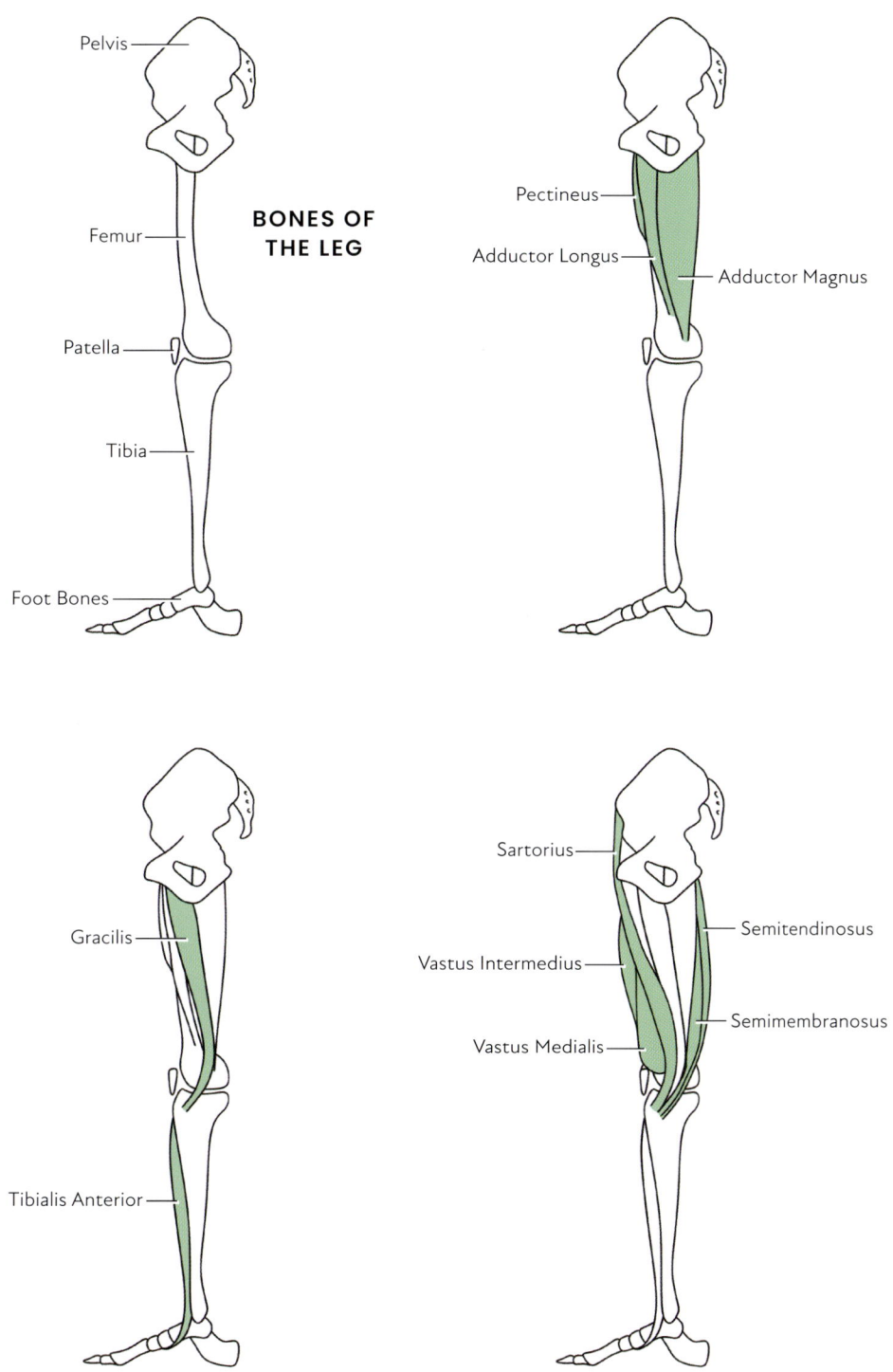

Pelvis
Femur
Patella
Tibia
Foot Bones

BONES OF THE LEG

Pectineus
Adductor Longus
Adductor Magnus

Gracilis
Tibialis Anterior

Sartorius
Vastus Intermedius
Vastus Medialis
Semitendinosus
Semimembranosus

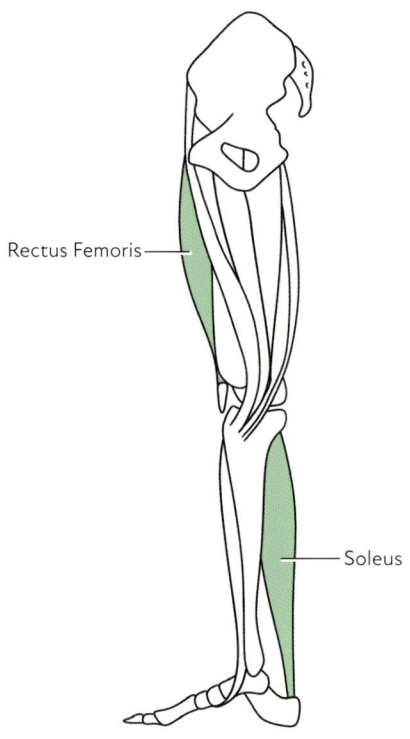

Rectus Femoris

Soleus

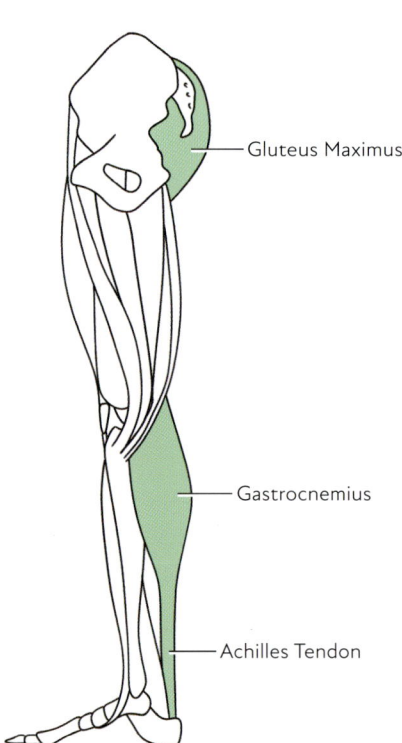

Gluteus Maximus

Gastrocnemius

Achilles Tendon

Drawing Legs

Anterior

1

ASIS

2

Center Line

3
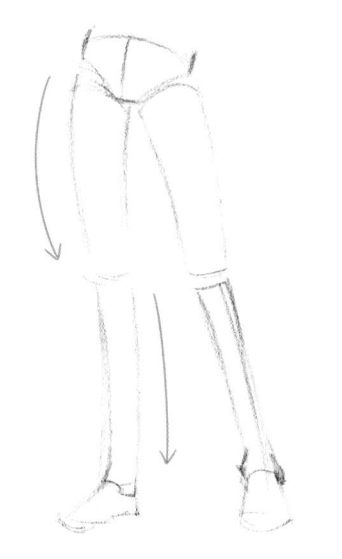

4
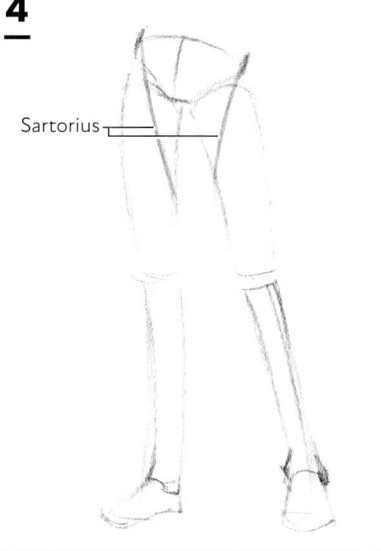
Sartorius

5
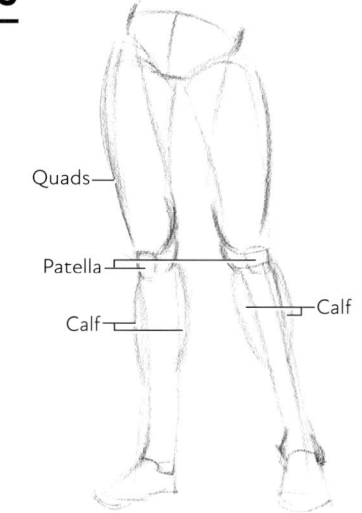
Quads
Patella
Calf
Calf

6
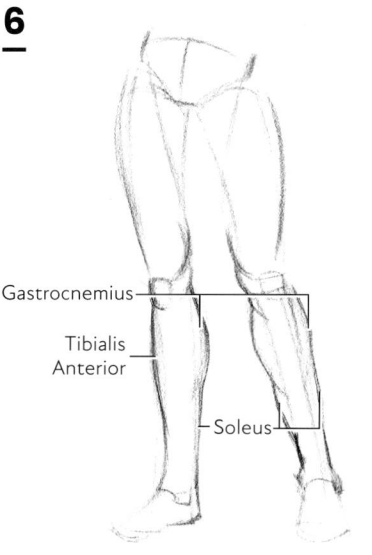
Gastrocnemius
Tibialis Anterior
Soleus

1. Work on the gesture of the leg. Analyze the contrapposto of the figure that you are working on, and mark the ASIS. The knees should be at the midpoint in between the hip and the foot.

2. Create the bikini line for the hip. Adding the center line will help to define the angle of the hip.

3. Create the cylinder shapes for the upper and lower legs. For the upper leg, follow the front curve of the thigh. For the lower leg, focus the curve of the calf.

4. Add the line of the Sartorius to define the Medial Thigh Muscles and the Quads. The line should start from the ASIS and go to the mid/medial–point of the upper leg.

5. Add the volumes for the Quads, Patella, and calves. Use oval shapes for the calves. The volume should be focused on the upper half of the lower leg.

6. Define the outline of the lower leg.

Anterior *(cont.)*

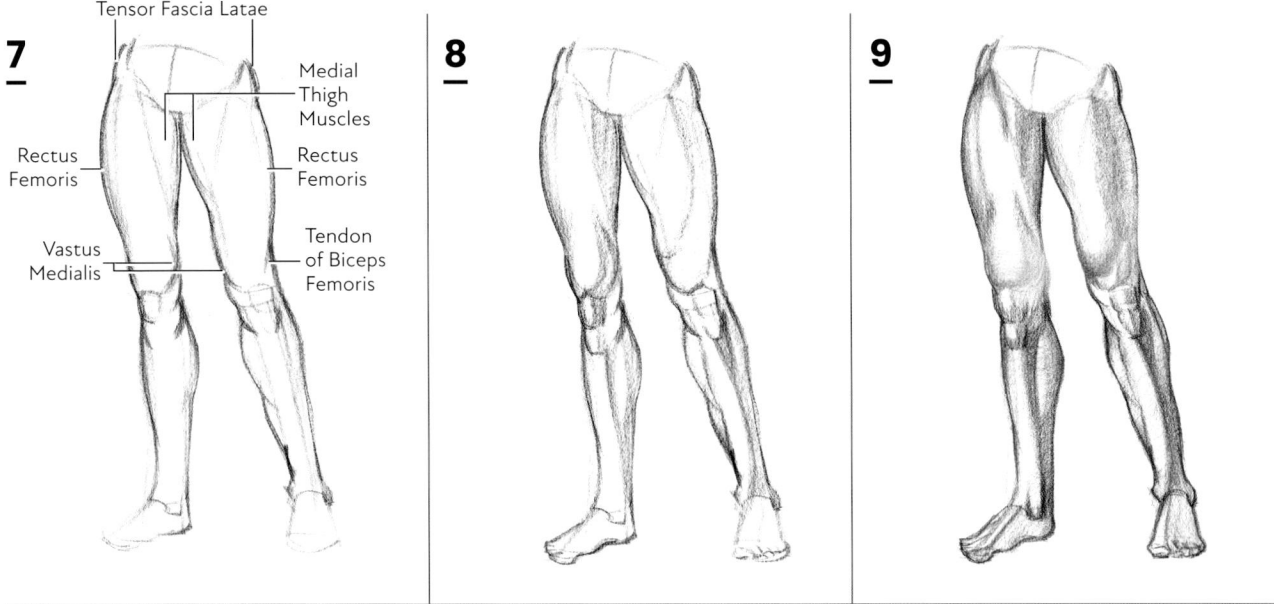

7 Tensor Fascia Latae
Medial Thigh Muscles
Rectus Femoris
Rectus Femoris
Vastus Medialis
Tendon of Biceps Femoris

8

9

7. Define the outline of the upper leg.

8. Follow the volume of each muscle group and create an even tone overall.

9. Use shading to develop the contrast and details.

Posterior

1

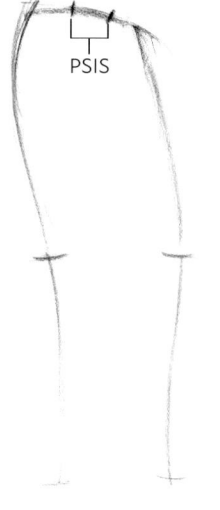

PSIS

2

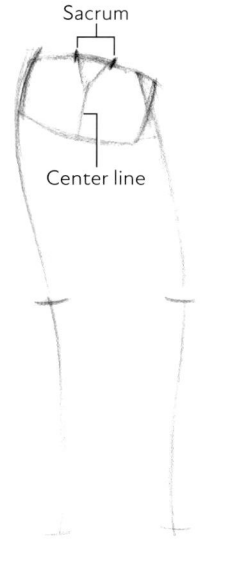

Sacrum

Center line

3

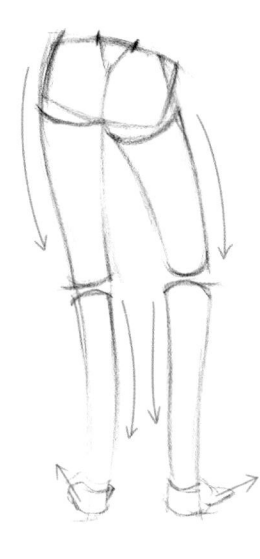

1. Work on the gesture of the leg. Analyze the contrapposto of the figure that you are working on, and mark the PSIS. Mark the back of the knees, which should be at the midpoint between the hip and the foot.

2. Create the box shape for the hips and add the triangle shape of the Sacrum by following the dots of the PSIS. Adding the center line will help to define the angle of the hips.

3. Create the cylinder shapes for the upper and lower legs. For the upper leg, follow the front curve of the thigh. In this image, the curve line is followed by the direction of the toes. For the lower leg, focus the curve of the calf.

Posterior *(cont.)*

4

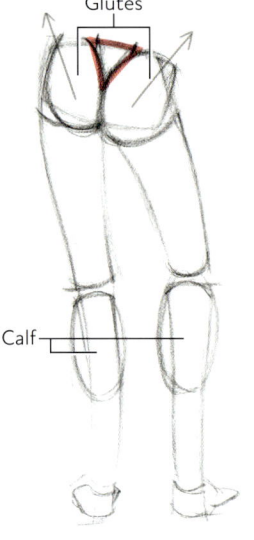

Glutes

Calf

5

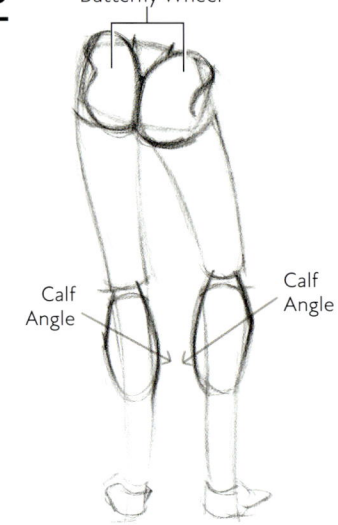

Butterfly Wheel

Calf
Angle

Calf
Angle

6

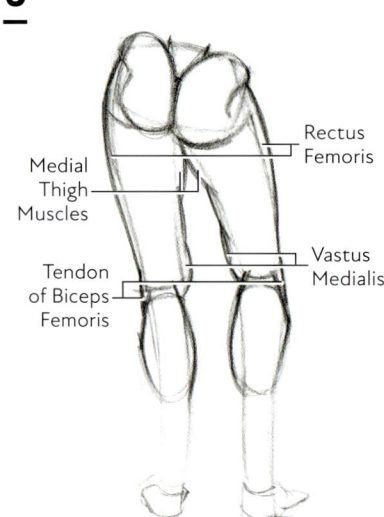

Rectus
Femoris

Medial
Thigh
Muscles

Vastus
Medialis

Tendon
of Biceps
Femoris

7

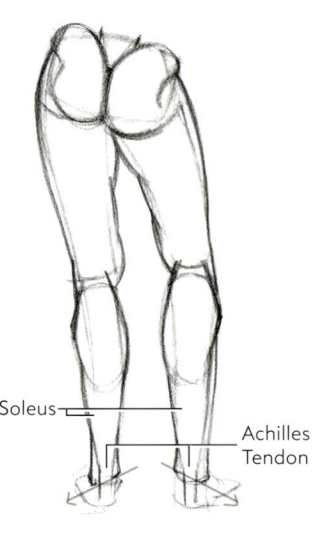

Soleus

Achilles
Tendon

8

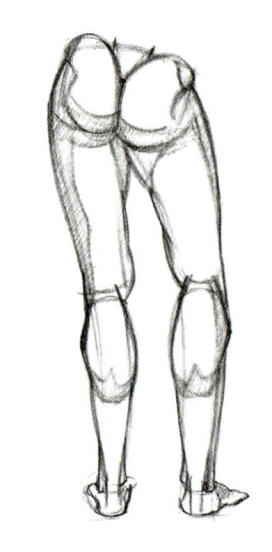

9

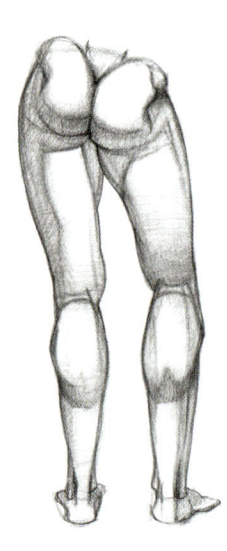

4. Use oval shapes to define the Glutes and the calves. For the Glutes, the top of the ovals should point outward, following the shape of the Sacrum. For the calves, the volume should be focused on the upper half of the lower legs.

5. Define the outline of the Glutes and calves. Use the "butterfly wheel" technique for the Glutes. Focus on the angle for the calves (lateral side – higher; medial side – lower).

6. Define the outline of the upper legs.

7. Define the outline for the rest of lower legs.

8. Follow the volume of each muscle group and create an even tone overall.

9. Use shading to develop the contrast and details.

Lateral

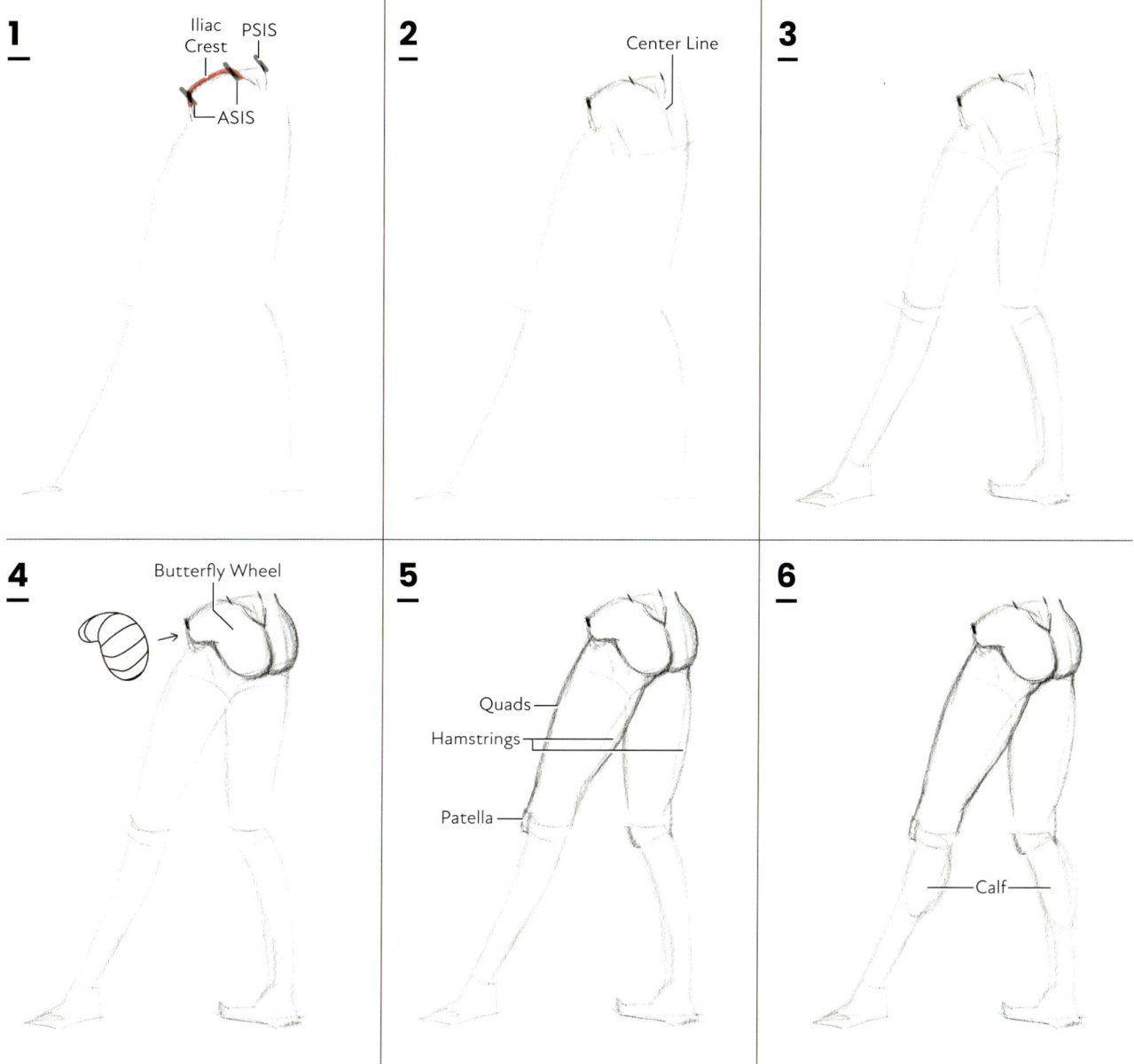

1. Work on the gesture of the leg. If you are able to pinpoint both the ASIS and PSIS in the figure that you are working on, create the marks and connect them together to define the Iliac Crest. The knees should be at the midpoint between the hip and the foot.

2. Create the box shape for the hips. Adding the center line will help to define the angle of the hips.

3. Create the cylinder shapes for the upper and lower legs.

4. Create the "butterfly wheel" of the Glutes.

5. Define the outline of the upper legs.

6. Use oval shapes to define the calves.

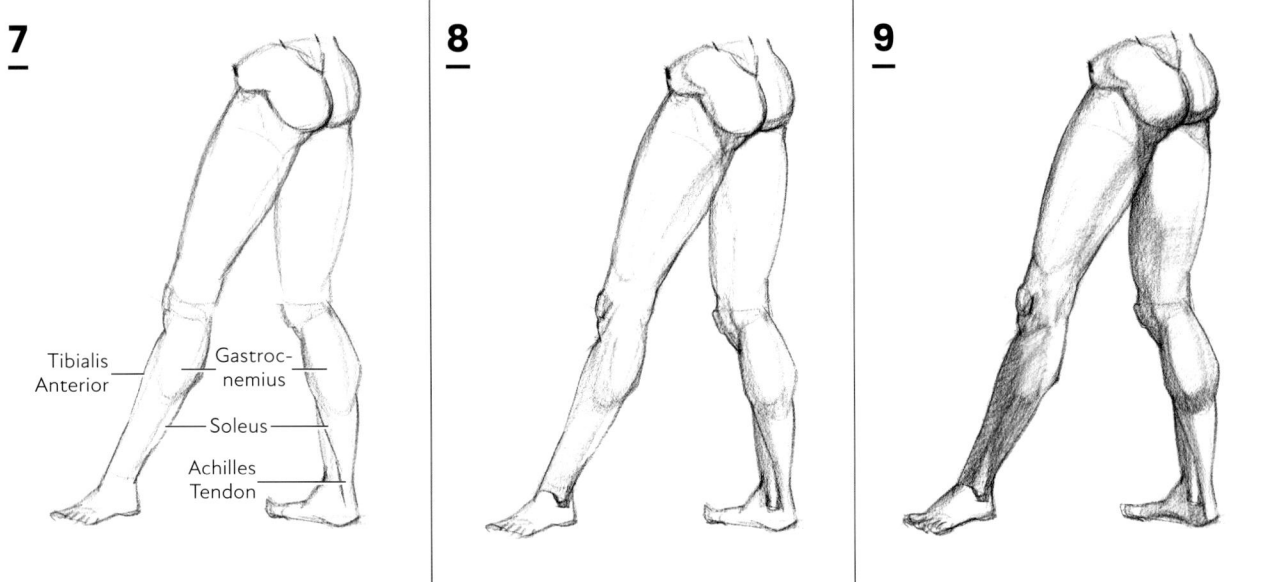

7

Tibialis
Anterior

Gastroc-
nemius

Soleus

Achilles
Tendon

8

9

7. Define the outline of the lower legs.

8. Follow the volume of each muscle group and create an even tone overall.

9. Use shading to develop the contrast and details.

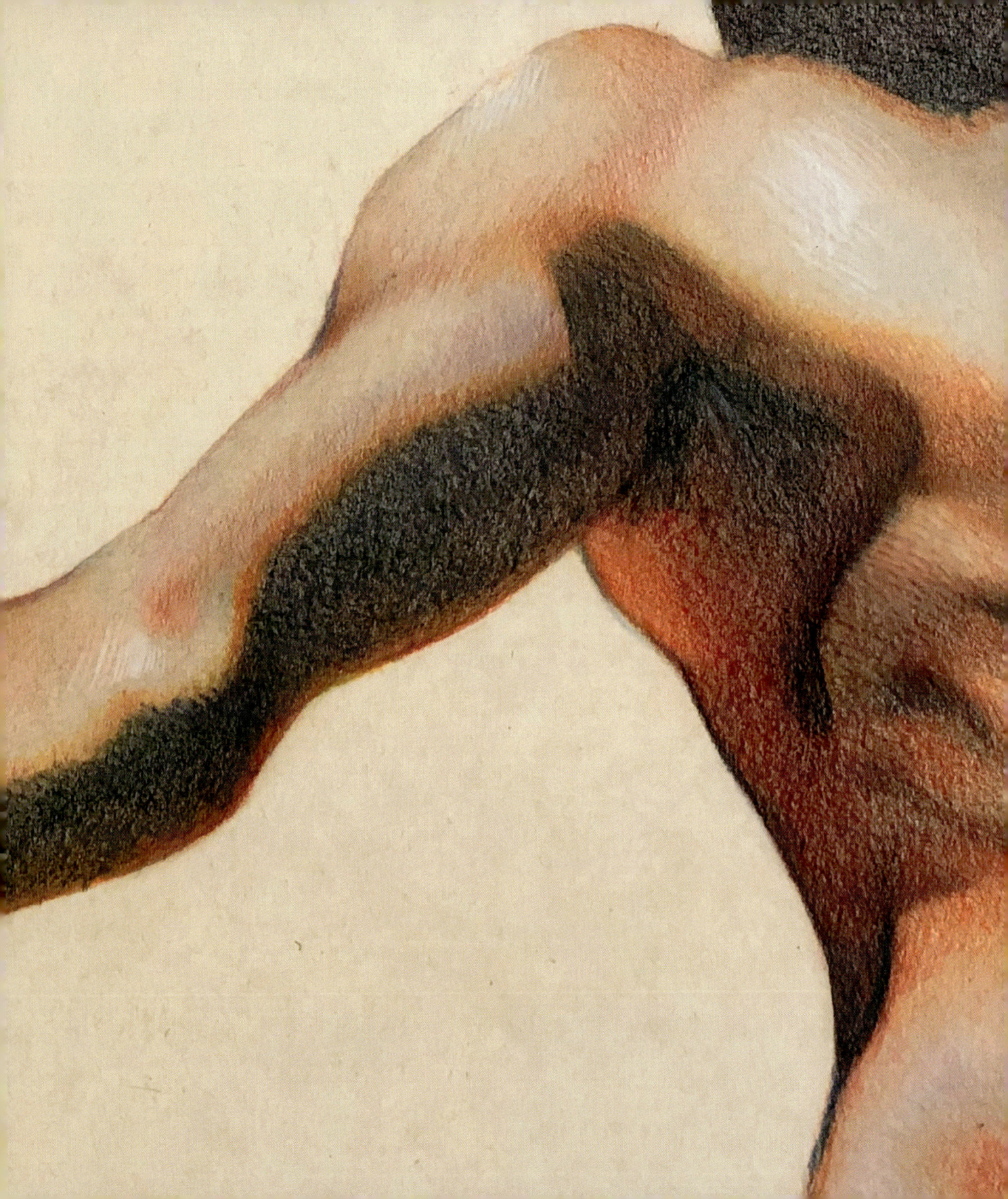

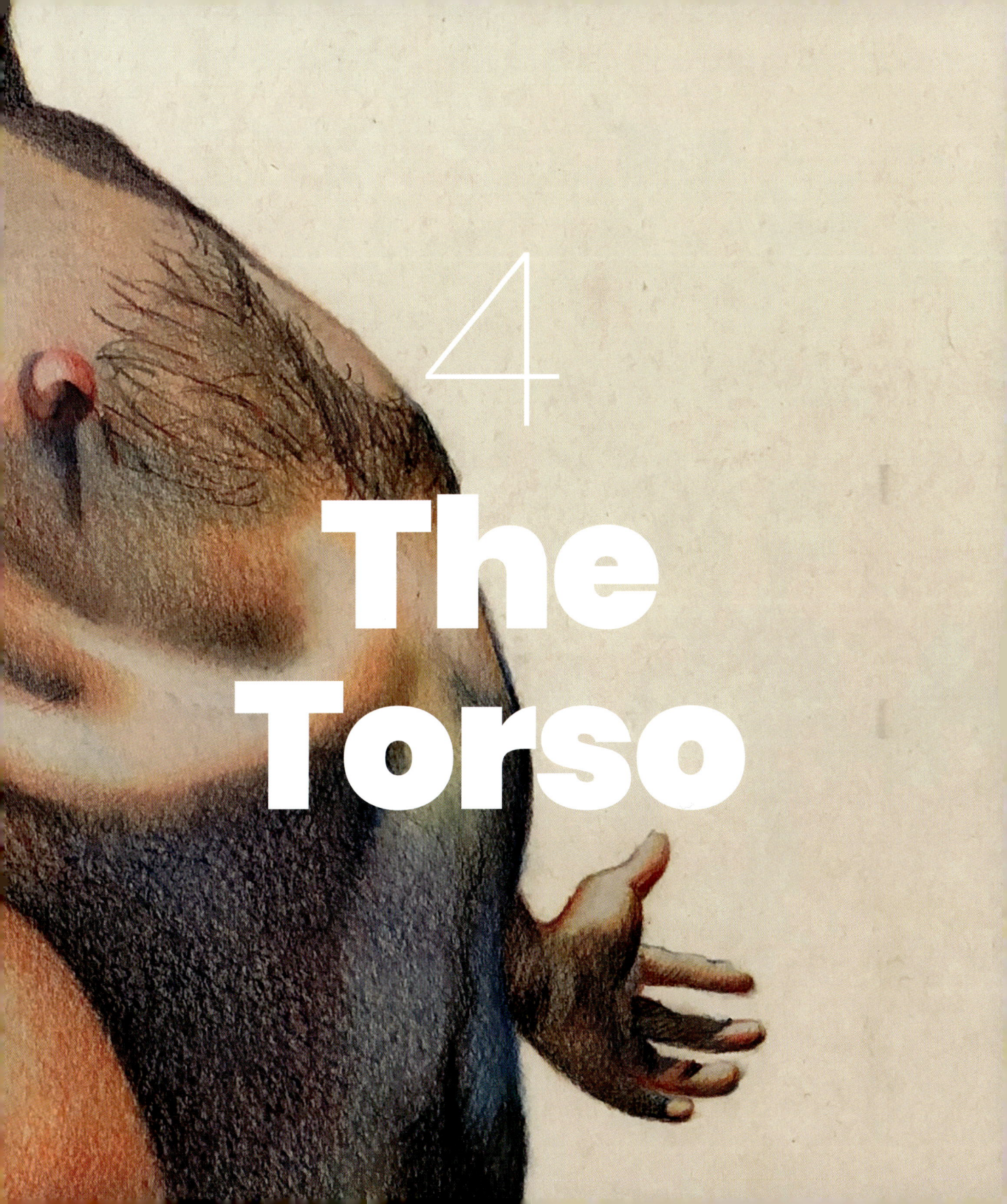

4

The
Torso

Basic Construction Drawing of the Torso

Capturing the movement of the torso accurately is a crucial part of figure drawing. The torso is the core of the body where all the other body parts come from; thus, we need to make sure that the torso is stable and reliable in our drawings. In figure drawing, the **Rib Cage**, **Pelvis**, and **Vertebral Column** are often used as the primary structures for the focal study of gestures.

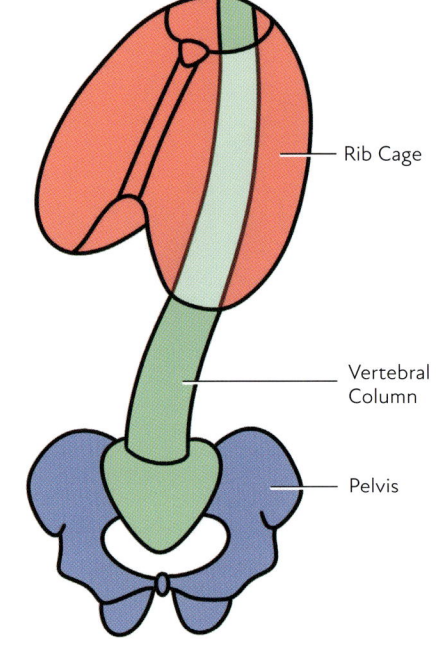

Rib Cage

Vertebral Column

Pelvis

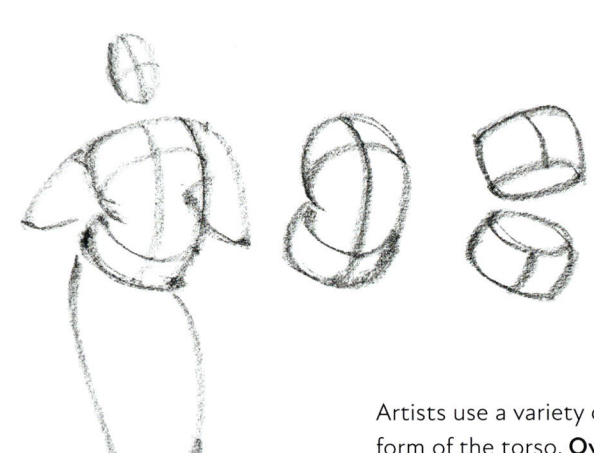

Artists use a variety of geometric shapes to construct the simplified form of the torso. **Ovals**, **cylinders**, and even the uncomplicated shapes of the skeleton are used in the development process. If you think that any of these shapes help you to get the right movement and direction of the torso going, go ahead use them and keep on practicing.

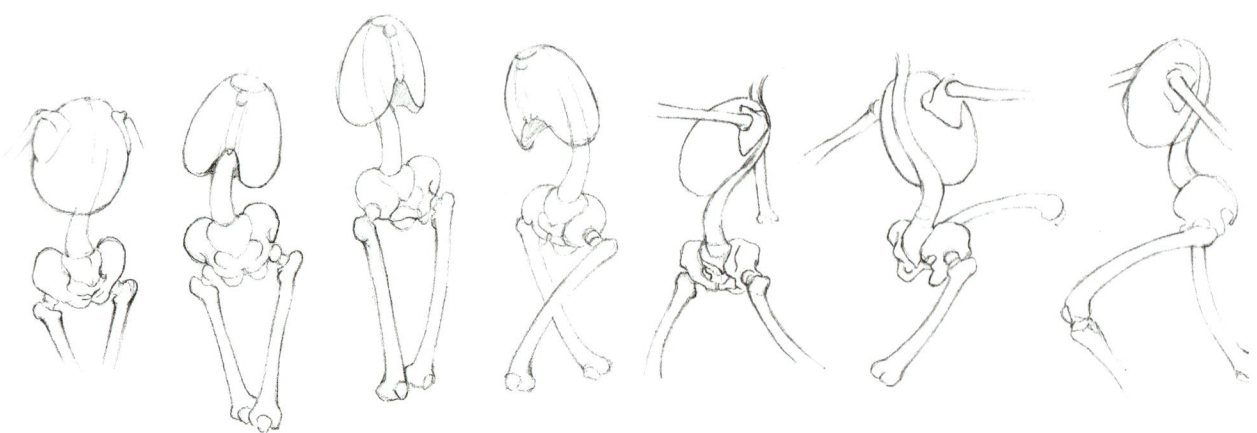

Anatomical Construction Drawing of the Torso

For the anatomical construction drawing of the torso, we can use a set of geometric shapes to work on the detailed muscular structure.

These are four simplified forms of the muscles that appear in the torso. These will work as great puzzle pieces and you will be able to add accurate shading in the figure later on.

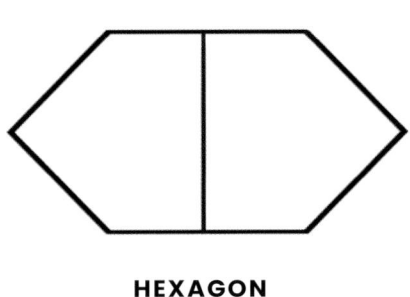

HEXAGON

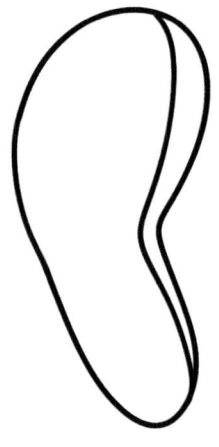

PEANUT

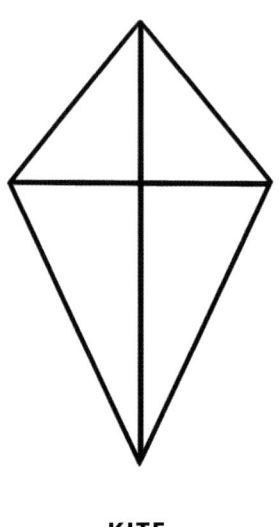

KITE

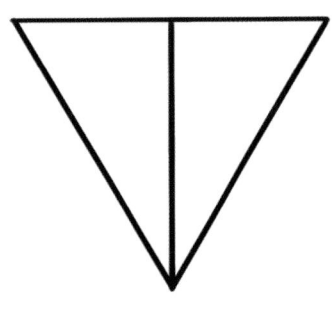

"DORITO"
(a.k.a inverted triangle)

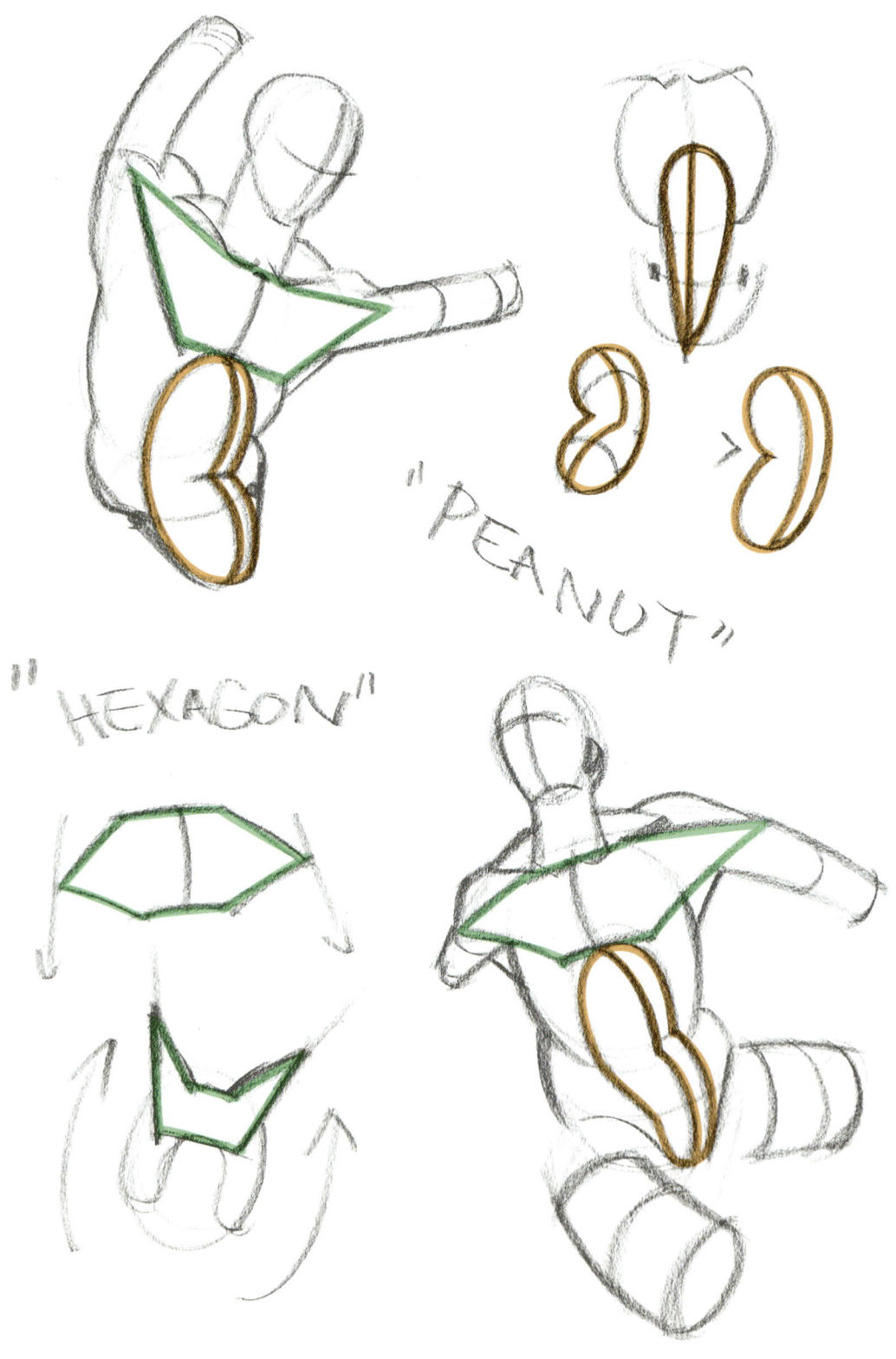

"PEANUT"

"HEXAGON"

Hexagon

The hexagon is a replacement for the chest muscle called the **Pectoralis Major**. This muscle is symmetrical on the left and right sides and it creates the chest wall. At the top of the chest, you'll notice that **the medial region of the Clavicle** becomes the attachment point for this muscle, and this horizontal line creates the top plane of the hexagon. The bottom plane is a horizontal line right above the **Costal Arch of the Rib Cage**. This landmark could be the horizontal line between the **nipples**.

The insertions of the Pectoralis Major are on the left and right, which are on the **proximal anterior side of the Humerus**. These points become the pointy ends of the hexagon. Imagine that this hexagon shape is like a flat, flexible sheet laying on the basic torso construction drawing that you create. You can adjust the shape according to the direction of movement, perspective, and foreshortening in the drawing.

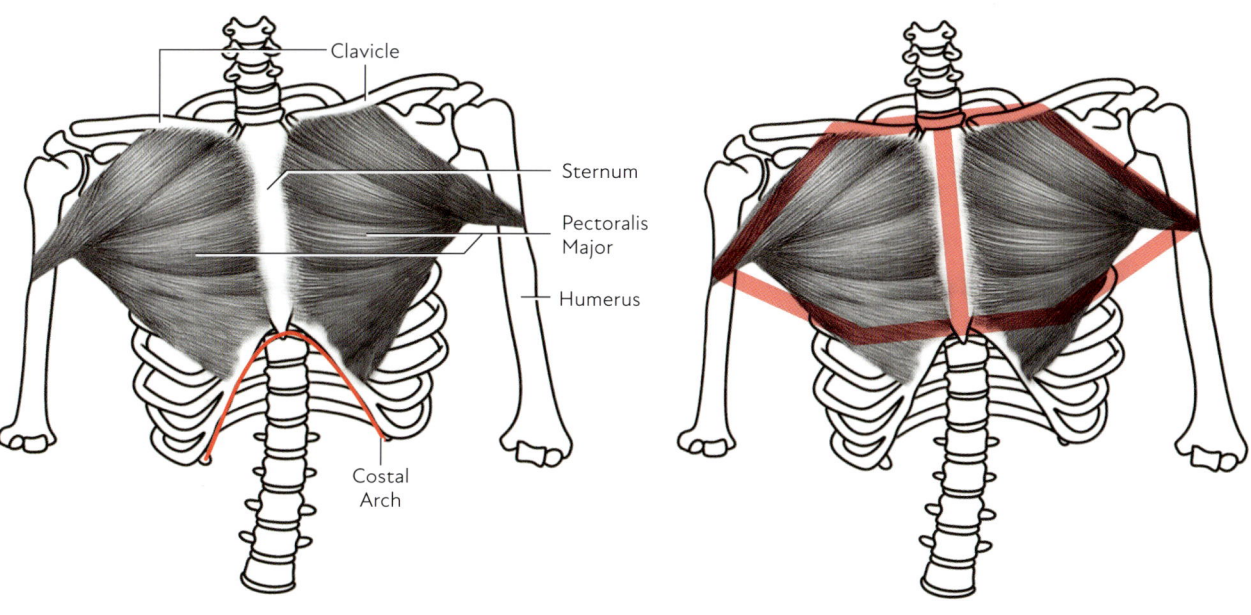

The Hexagon in Arms-Up Position

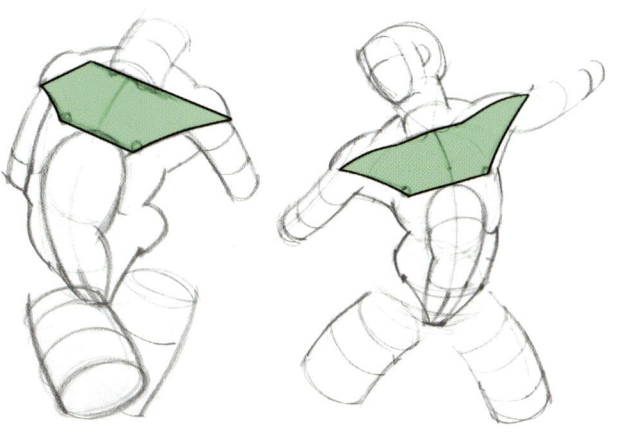

When the figure has raised arms, the hexagon does not keep its shape. If the lateral pointy ends of the shape are connected to the Humerus, it must follow the movement of the upper arms.

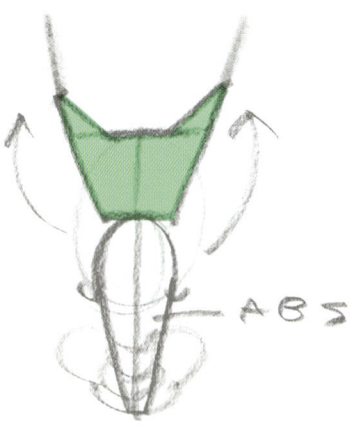

Peanut

A peanut shape can be used for the **Rectus Abdominis** muscle. The abs are located on the anterior surface of the trunk, connected from the **Rib Cage** to the **Pubic Bone**. For people with low body fat, each bump of the abs, the "six pack," can be visible under the skin. The round end of the peanut can be puzzled into the curved line of the **Costal Arch of the Rib Cage**, and then it stretches down to the **Pubic Bone of the Pelvis**. The width of the distal part gets slightly smaller.

Because the mid-point of the peanut is located at the level of the waistline, you can add a little "pinch" on one side depending on the movement of the torso. This will make the belly naturally follow the gesture and give a nice flexibility to the torso.

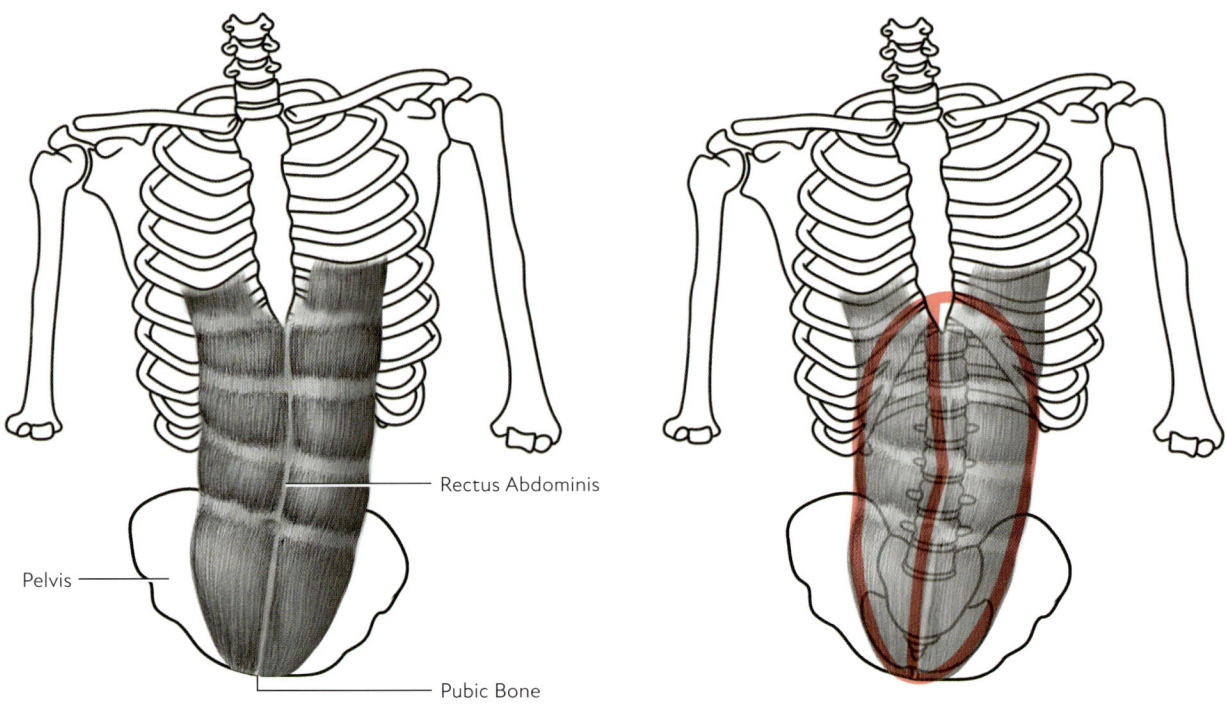

Rectus Abdominis

Pelvis

Pubic Bone

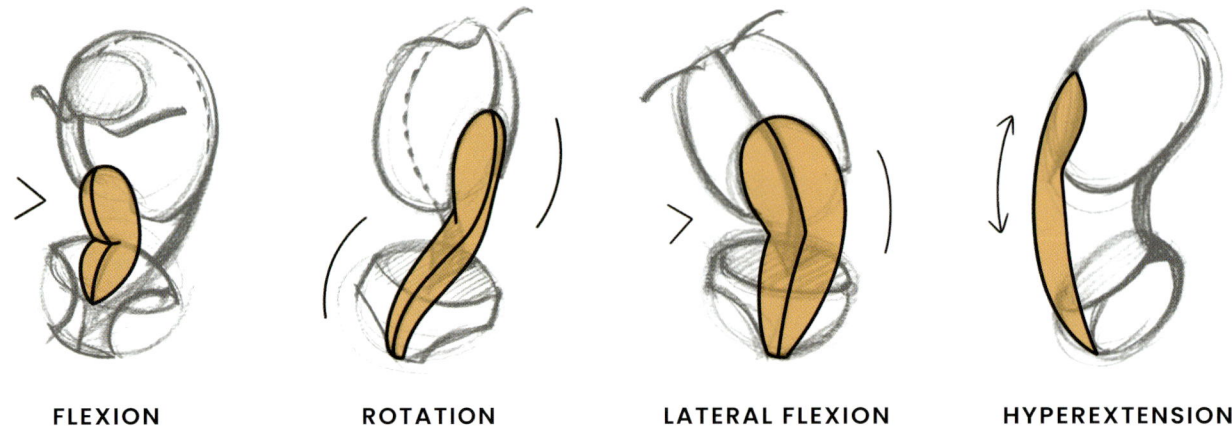

FLEXION   **ROTATION**   **LATERAL FLEXION**   **HYPEREXTENSION**

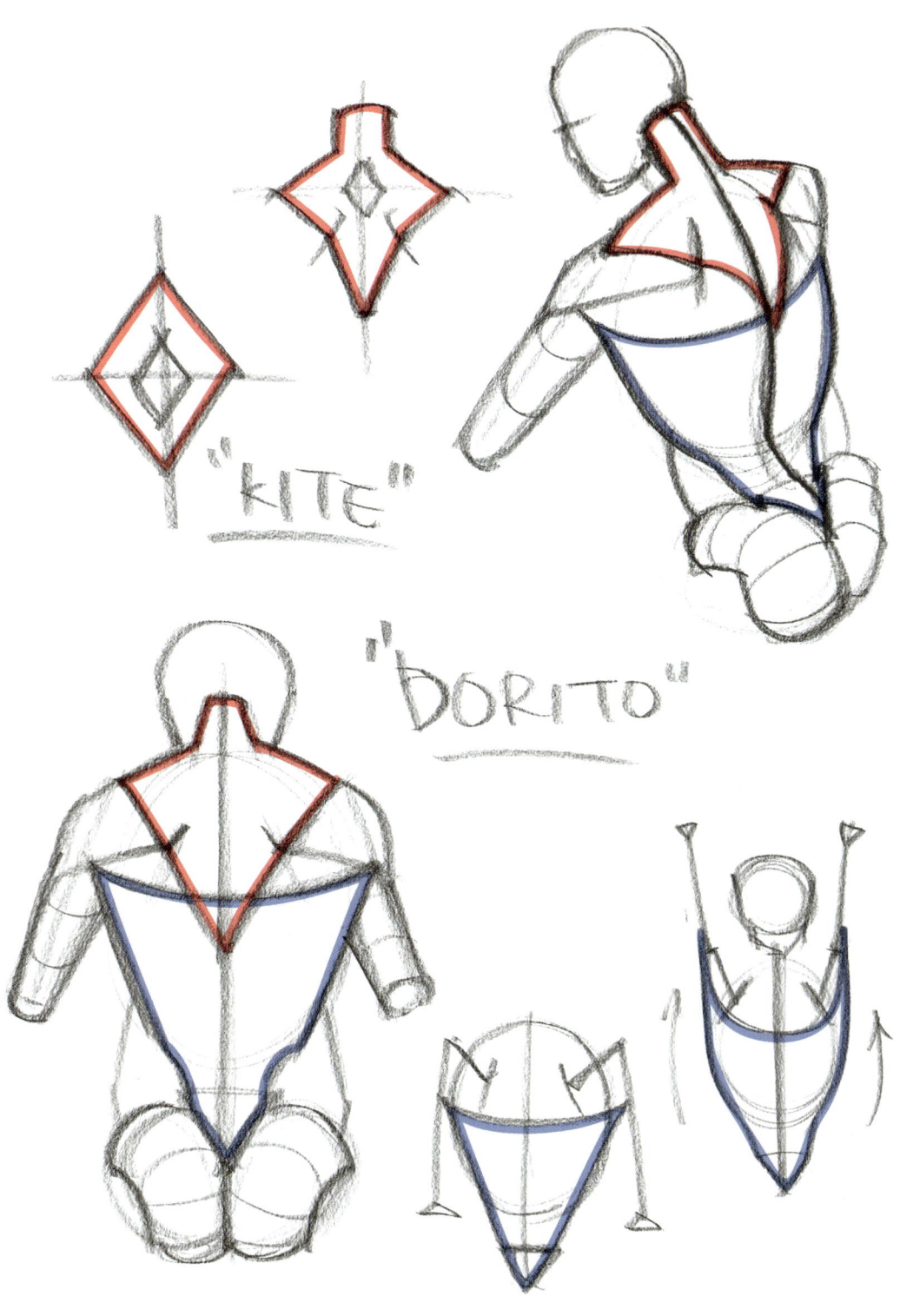

"KITE"

"DORITO"

Kite

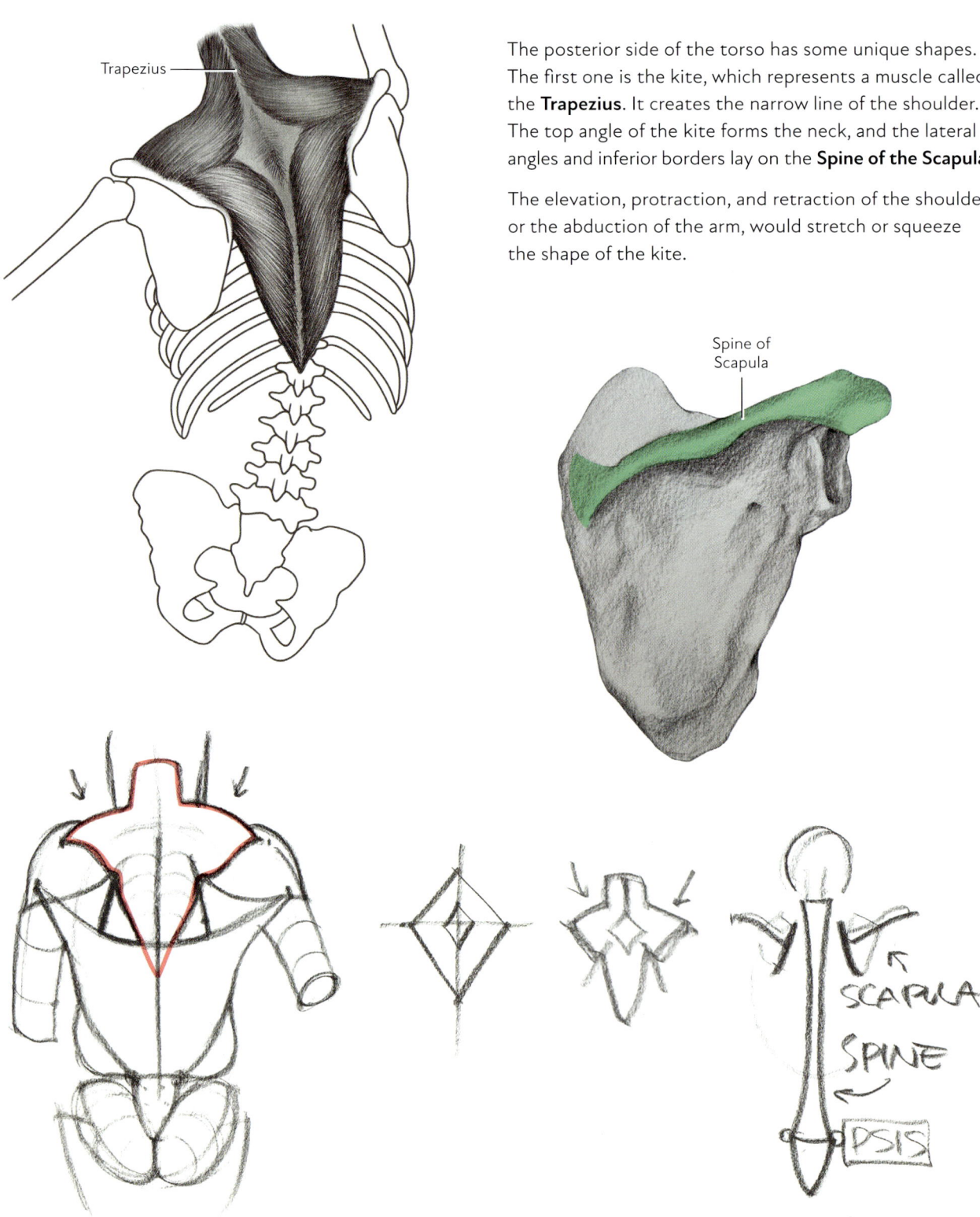

Trapezius

The posterior side of the torso has some unique shapes. The first one is the kite, which represents a muscle called the **Trapezius**. It creates the narrow line of the shoulder. The top angle of the kite forms the neck, and the lateral angles and inferior borders lay on the **Spine of the Scapula**.

The elevation, protraction, and retraction of the shoulder, or the abduction of the arm, would stretch or squeeze the shape of the kite.

Spine of Scapula

SCAPULA

SPINE

PSIS

"Dorito"

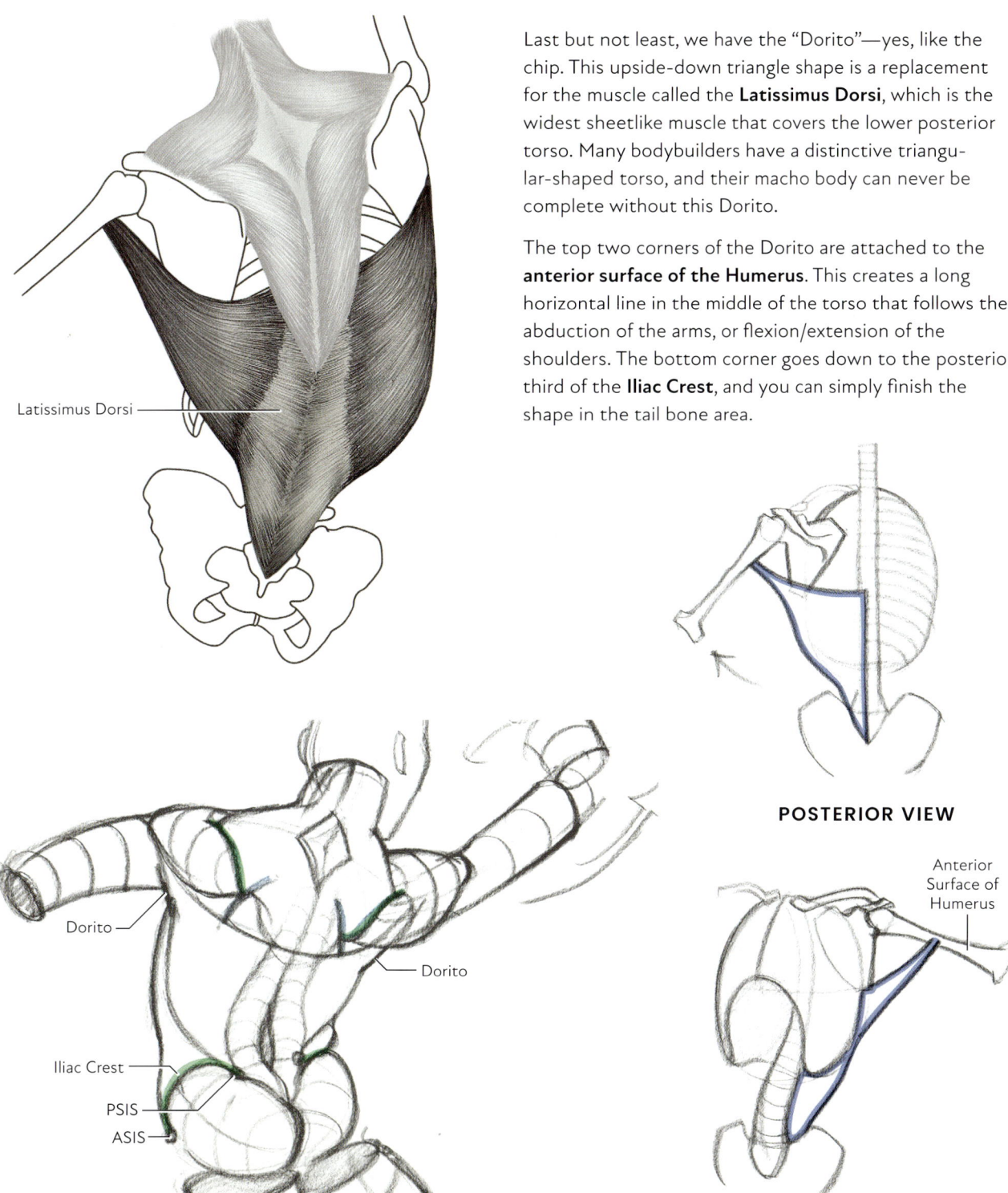

Last but not least, we have the "Dorito"—yes, like the chip. This upside-down triangle shape is a replacement for the muscle called the **Latissimus Dorsi**, which is the widest sheetlike muscle that covers the lower posterior torso. Many bodybuilders have a distinctive triangular-shaped torso, and their macho body can never be complete without this Dorito.

The top two corners of the Dorito are attached to the **anterior surface of the Humerus**. This creates a long horizontal line in the middle of the torso that follows the abduction of the arms, or flexion/extension of the shoulders. The bottom corner goes down to the posterior third of the **Iliac Crest**, and you can simply finish the shape in the tail bone area.

Latissimus Dorsi

Dorito

Dorito

Iliac Crest

PSIS

ASIS

POSTERIOR VIEW

Anterior Surface of Humerus

ANTERIOR VIEW

Drawing the Chest Muscles

The Pectoralis Major

The hexagon, a.k.a. the **Pectoralis Major**, can be transformed into different shapes in the construction drawing process. To draw accurate chest muscles, it is important to understand the movement of the arms, the attachment of the muscles, and the flow of the muscle fibers.

Movement

The shoulder is a ball-and-socket joint with the Humerus and the Scapula, which means that the arm can make many motions, including flexion/extension, abduction/adduction, rotation, and circumduction. We need to analyze what the shoulder is doing and where the arm is located in the movement in order to determine the correct shape of the pecs.

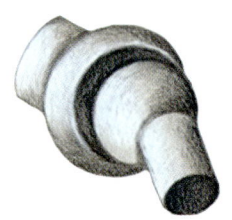

Ball-and-Socket Joint

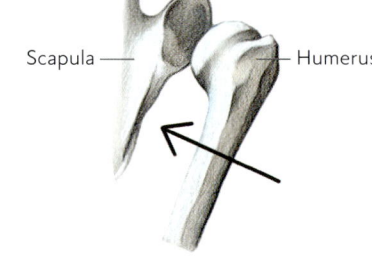

Scapula — Humerus

Attachment

The origin of the pecs is on the median line of the hexagon, which is the medial side of the **Clavicle**, the entire **Sternum**, and the **tendon of Rectus Abdominis**. These represent the vertical center line and the top and bottom borders of the hexagon, and they do not move around. However, the lateral angle of the hexagon can change depending on the movement of the upper arm/shoulder.

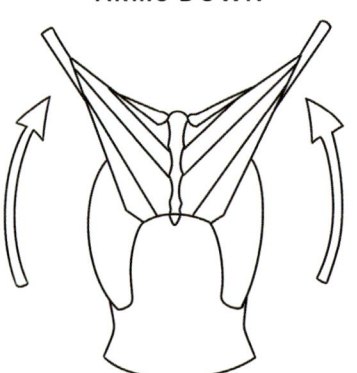

Clavicle

Sternum

Humerus

ARMS DOWN

ARMS RAISED

Pectoralis Major

Rectus Abdominis

Muscle Fibers

The pecs muscles have two sections: the **Sternocostal Head** and the **Clavicular Head**. The fibers of the pecs follow this shape like a fan, and the lines of fibers get dense when they go into the insertion on the Humerus. The Clavicular Head goes over the Sternocostal Head. You can simply separate these two in the construction process.

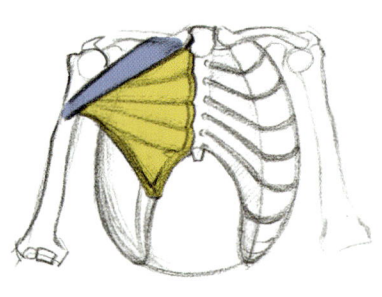

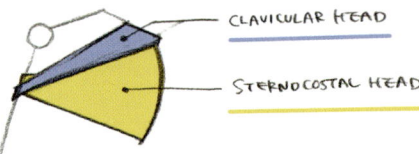

CLAVICULAR HEAD

STERNOCOSTAL HEAD

Drawing the "Six Pack"

Rectus Abdominis

If you want six-pack abs, why not draw them?

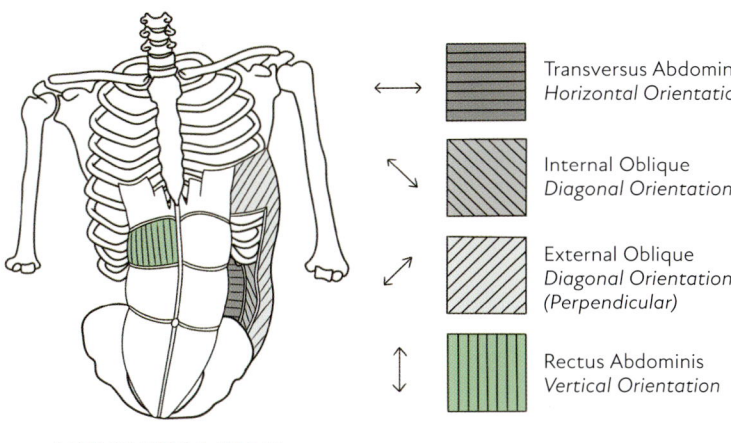

Transversus Abdominis	*Horizontal Orientation*
Internal Oblique	*Diagonal Orientation*
External Oblique	*Diagonal Orientation (Perpendicular)*
Rectus Abdominis	*Vertical Orientation*

ABDOMINAL WALL

The abs are symmetrical on the left and right, and you can see a long vertical connective tissue line called the **Linea Alba** in the middle. In figure drawing, artists often use this line to capture the accurate direction and movement of the torso.

The superior part of the abs is attached to the anterior medial side of the **5**th, **6**th, and **7**th **rib bodies** and the **Xiphoid Process**. It is layered under the **Pectoralis Major**, and the muscle width becomes slimmer toward the Pubic Bone. Because of the location and the size, a peanut shape can be used for the simplified anterior torso construction drawing.

The horizontal lines that divide each volume of the abs are called the **Tendinous Intersections**. As you can see based on the number of sections in the abs, it can technically be called an "eight pack." The lower volume of the abs is the longest, and its superior border is where the belly button is located.

The **Rectus Abdominis** muscle is attached from below the chest on the **Rib Cage** to the **Pubic Bone**. It is one of the four layers of belly muscles. This specific layer is external, and the fiber is oriented vertically.

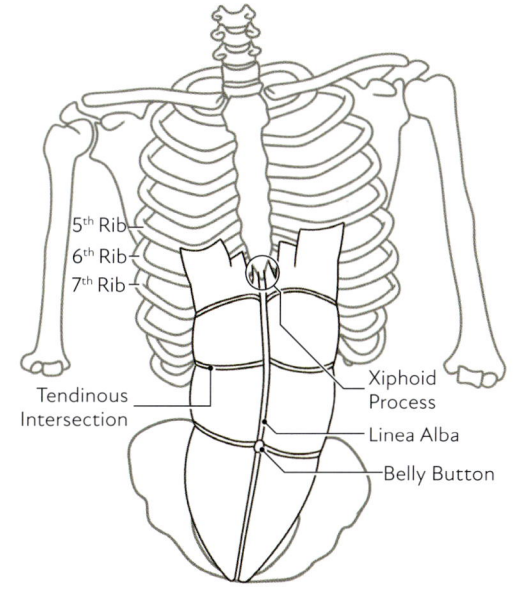

5th Rib
6th Rib
7th Rib
Tendinous Intersection
Xiphoid Process
Linea Alba
Belly Button

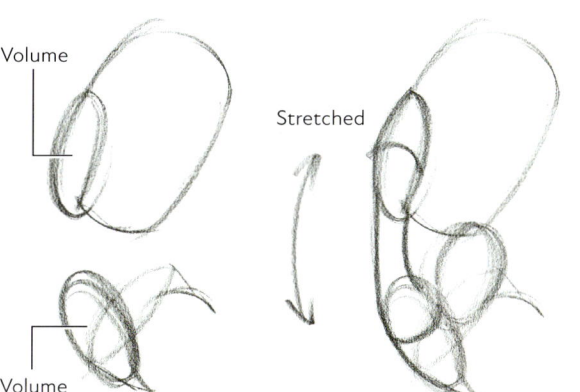

Volume

Stretched

Volume

— **QUICK NOTE** —

Bean Volume of the Abdominis

To be more advanced with the peanut shape, you can try focusing on the volume in the costal cartilage and lower abdominis, and connect them together.

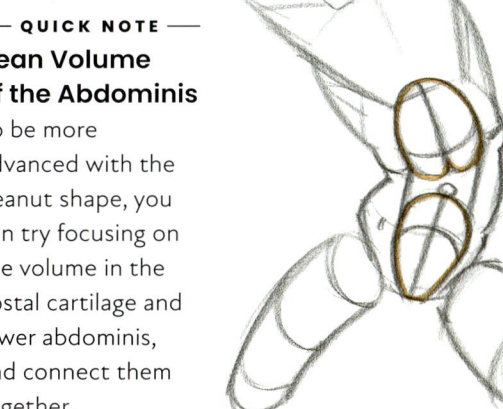

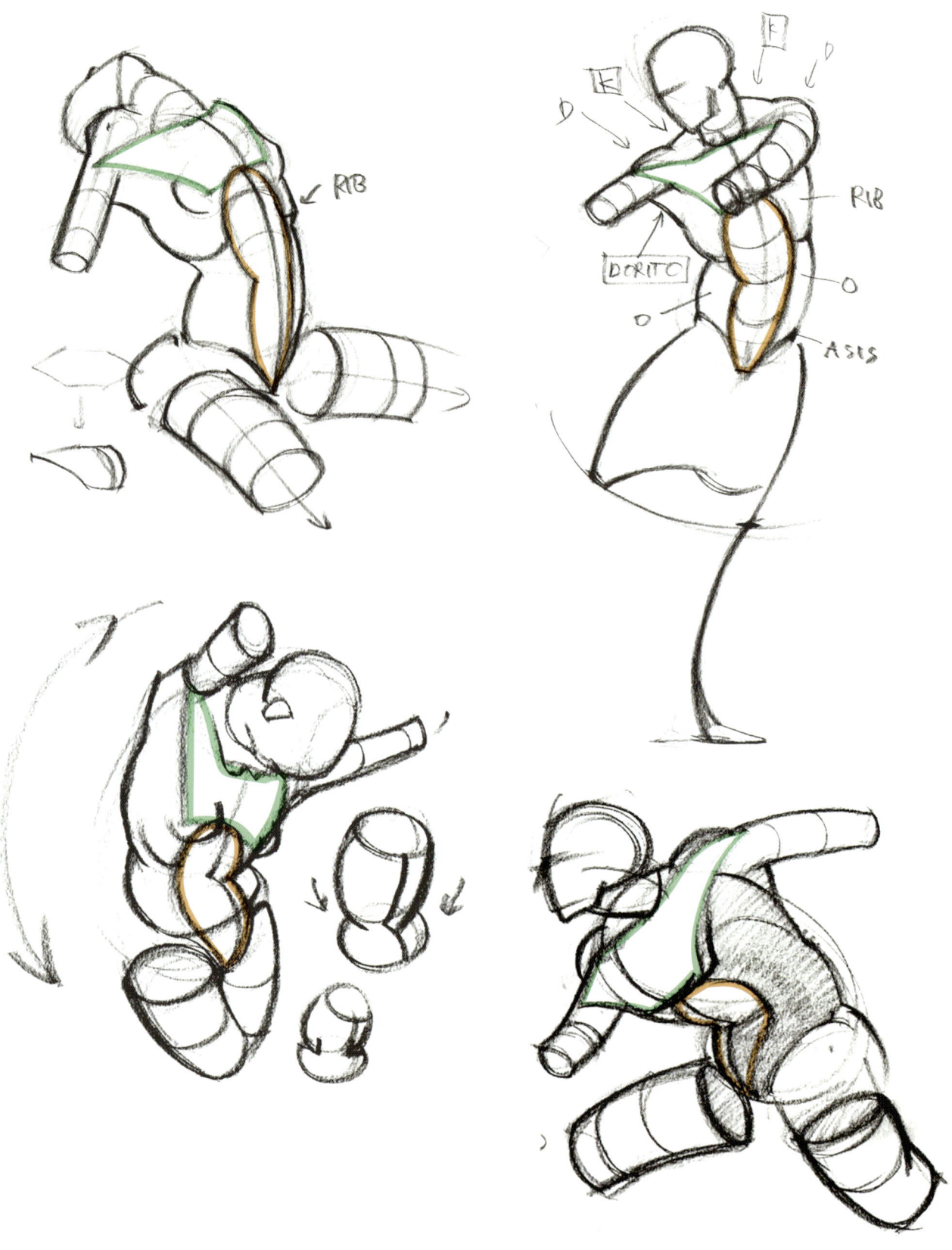

The Zig-Zags

Serratus Anterior and External Oblique

You might notice mysterious diagonal lines appearing on the side of the torso. This is a muscle called the **Serratus Anterior**. It lies between the Scapula and Rib Cage on the posterior side, and the muscles wing out like a fan toward the rib bodies on the lateral side.

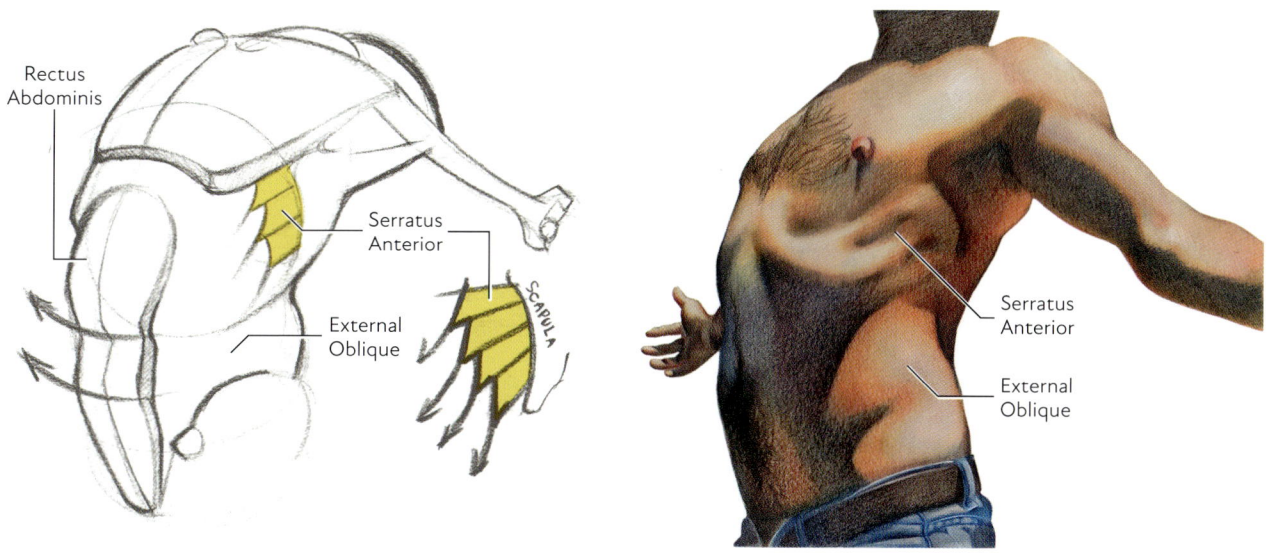

The Serratus Anterior muscle originates on **Ribs #1–9**. This means that each muscle in the upper portion follows an upward angle, and each muscle in the lower portion follows a downward angle, just like a fan that is splayed out sideways. On the other hand, the fibers of the External Oblique only go downward toward the waistline. The origin of the External Oblique muscle is on **Ribs #5–12**, which is lower than the Serratus Anterior. Imagine that the gears are meshing perfectly on the side of torso.

The diagonal lines you see aren't formed only by the Serratus Anterior, but also by its relationship with another muscle that sits underneath it called the **External Oblique**. In the diagram below, you can see that the end of the Serratus Anterior interlocks with the superior part of the External Oblique.

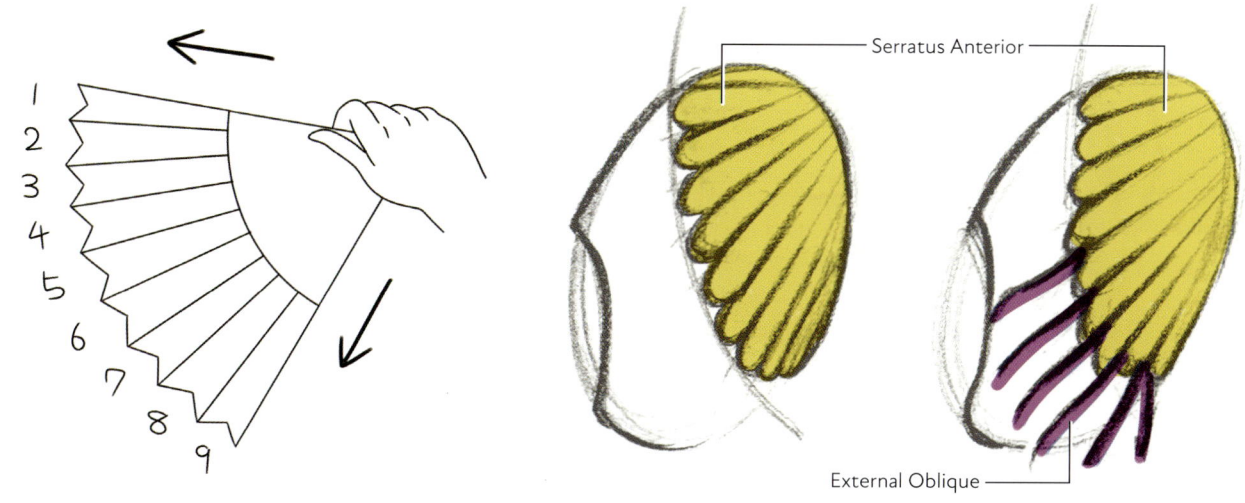

The Oblique | The "Love Handles"

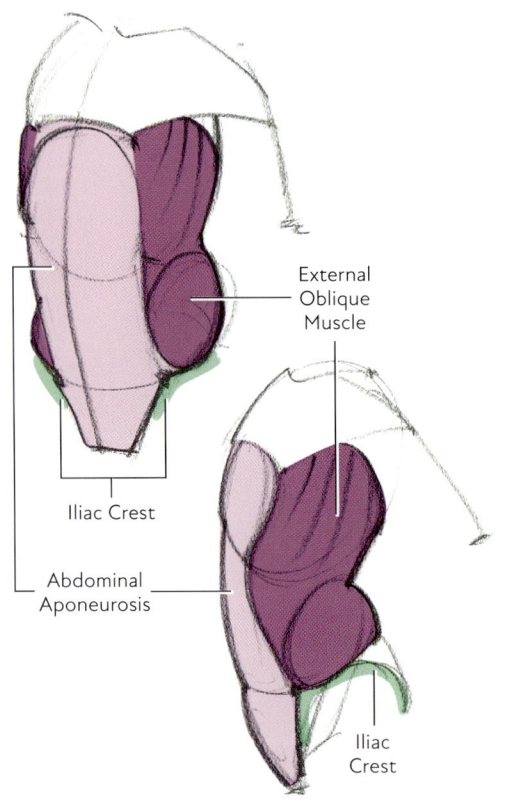

External
Oblique
Muscle

Iliac Crest

Abdominal
Aponeurosis

Iliac
Crest

Now we know that the connection between the **Serratus Anterior** and the **External Oblique** makes the zig-zag volume on the lateral side of the torso. The External Oblique, often known as the "love handles," has a rich bulbous shape, and is an important landmark for many artists.

The origin of the External Oblique muscle is on rib bodies #5–12 on the lateral side, and the insertion is the anterior half of the **Iliac Crest**. That means that this muscle pretty much covers the entire lateral side of the torso.

The official name of this muscle is the External Abdominal Oblique. Yes, it is "abdominals" like the Rectus Abdominis. The abdominal muscles have four layers in the belly, but only two muscles—the External Oblique and the Rectus Abs—appear on the surface anatomy.

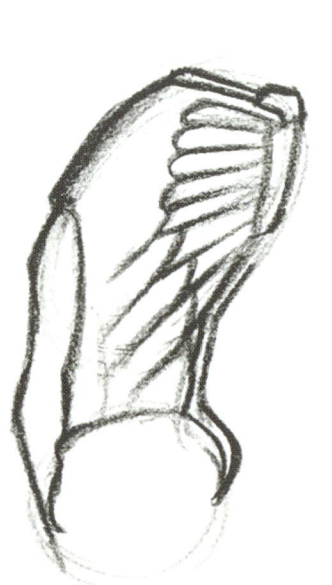

Note: The Abdominal Muscles include: the External Oblique, the Internal Oblique, the Rectus Abdominis, and the Transversus Abdominis.

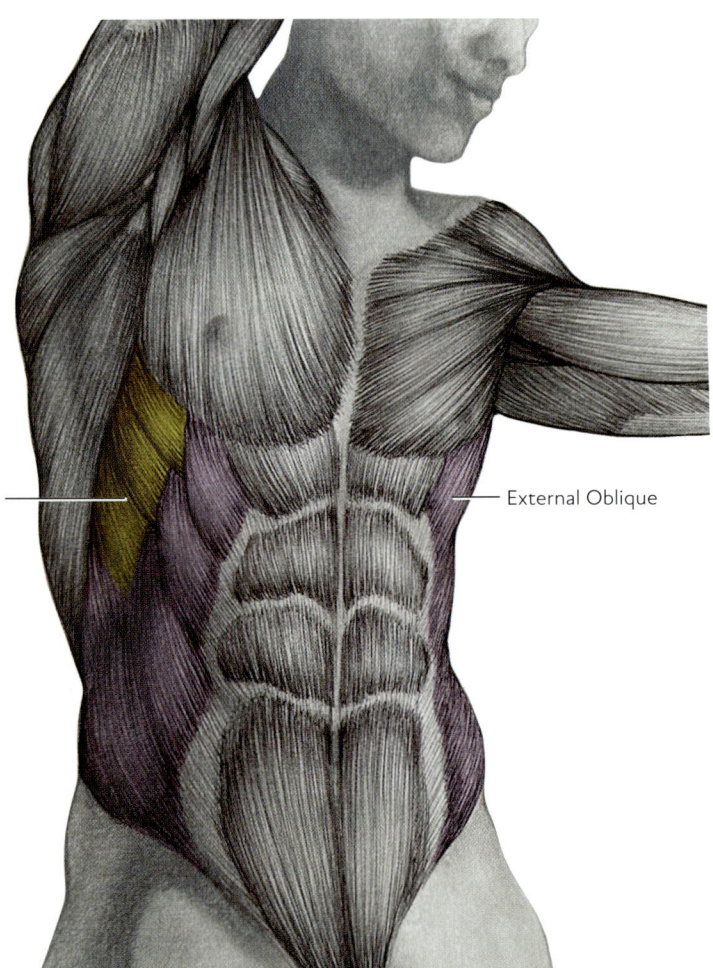

Serratus
Anterior

External Oblique

The Bond Between the Deltoid and the Trapezius

The **Deltoid** is the shoulder muscle and it wraps around your shoulder from front to back. There are two origins for the Deltoid muscle: the anterior lateral third of the **Clavicle**, and the **inferior border of the Spine of the Scapula**, including the **Acromion Process** (A.P.) on the posterior side. Because this muscle covers the entire shoulder, the form looks like shoulder pads in a football uniform. The insertion of the Deltoid is the **Deltoid Tuberosity**, which is located on the lateral side of the **Humerus**.

The Deltoid

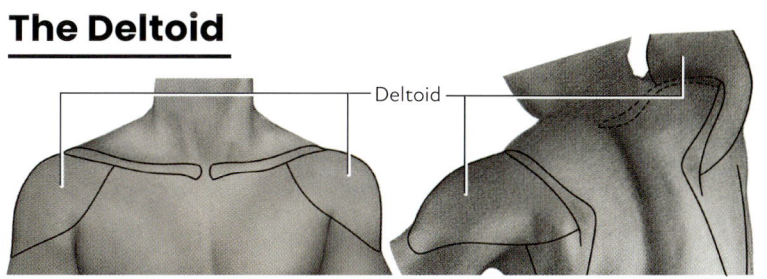

Showing accurate landmarks helps in drawing the shoulder. Make sure to show the **Clavicle line** from the anterior view. For the posterior view, you can focus on the **medial border of the Scapula** and the **Spine of the Scapula** to work on the form of the Deltoid.

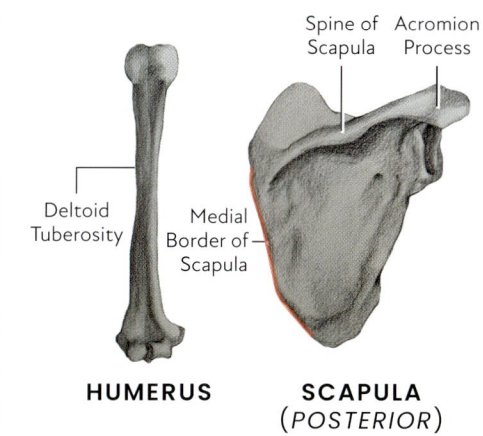

HUMERUS

SCAPULA (*POSTERIOR*)

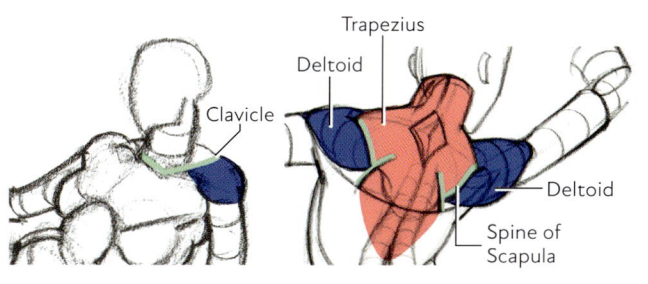

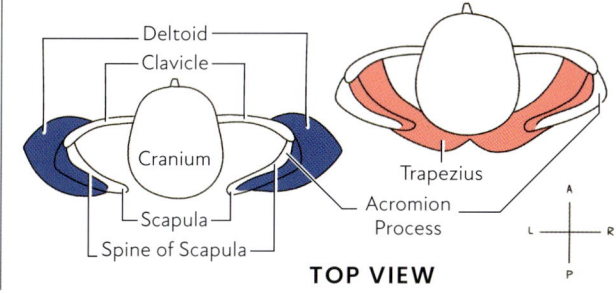

TOP VIEW

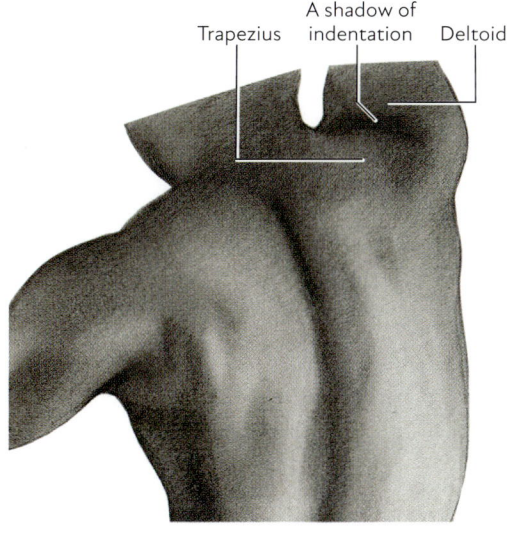

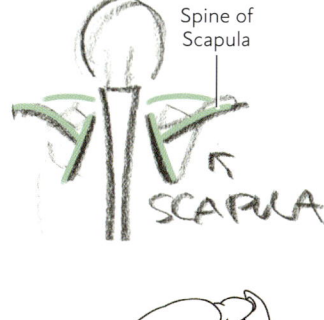

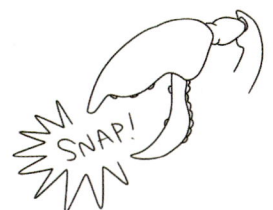

The "Lobster Claw"

When the arm rises, the Deltoid follows the movement of the upper arm. This movement creates an indentation between the Deltoid and the lateral corner of the Trapezius, and a hollow shadow appears on top of the shoulder in between these two muscles. When these muscles "latch," the anatomical construction form of the Deltoid looks like a large lobster claw.

The Trapezius

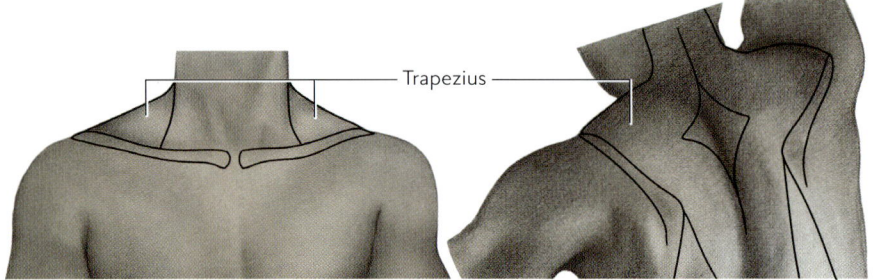

Trapezius

The top angle of the Kite forms the posterior neck and shoulder mass, and the bottom half of the Kite sits on the **superior border of the Spine of the Scapula** and points down to the Vertebral Column.

The **Trapezius** forms the neck and upper back. It has a symmetrical diamond shape, like a kite.

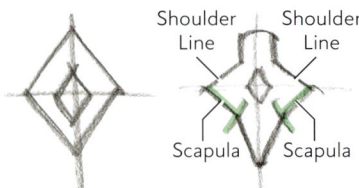

Shoulder Line   Shoulder Line

Scapula   Scapula

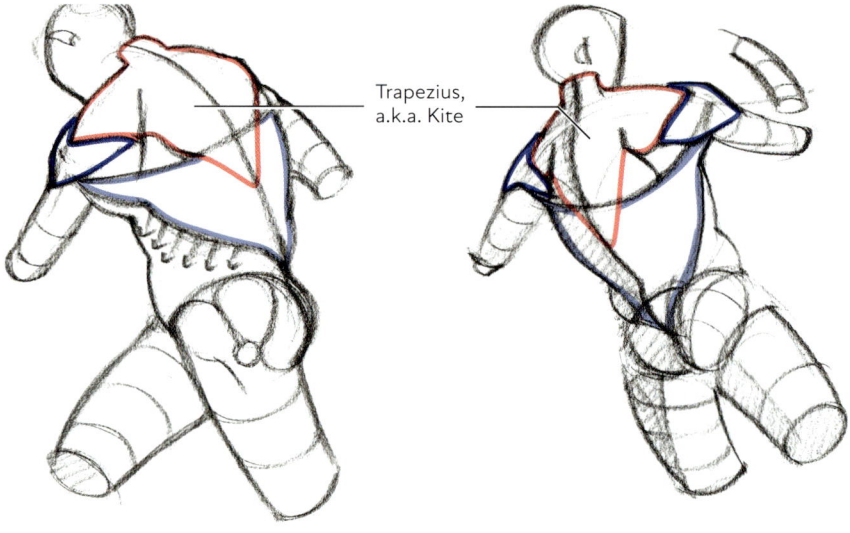

Trapezius, a.k.a. Kite

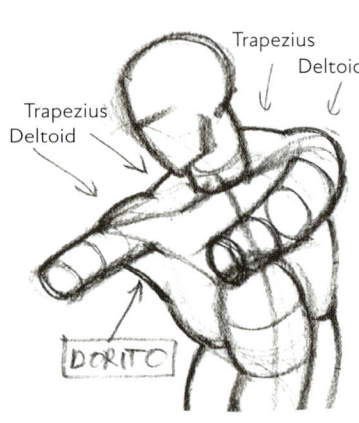

Trapezius
Deltoid

Trapezius
Deltoid

DORITO

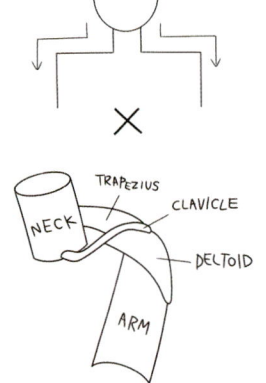

TRAPEZIUS
NECK   CLAVICLE
DELTOID
ARM

The Detail of the Shoulder

The transition from the neck to the shoulder is not a straight edge, nor is there a consistent downward curve. Focus on the following details when drawing the shoulder:

- Use a cylinder to create the volume of the neck.

- Draw a subtle upward curve to create the superior line of the Trapezius.

- Add a small bump to create the lateral end of the Clavicle (or it could be the Acromion Process; they are connected).

- Lastly, draw a downward curve to form the Deltoid.

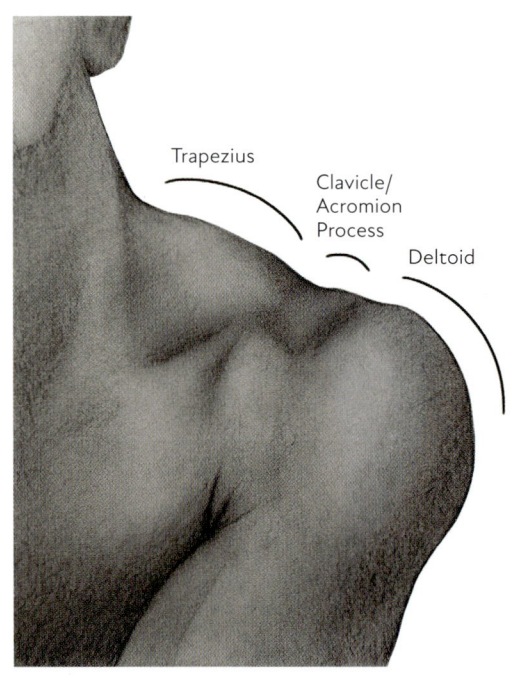

Trapezius

Clavicle/
Acromion
Process

Deltoid

The Raised-Arm Pose

There is a lot going on in the artistic anatomy of the armpit. The armpit is a hollow area created by multiple muscular walls in the torso. Some of the posterior muscles are attached to the anterior plane of an arm bone, which makes many insertions under the armpit look complicated.

So, in an effort to keep you from getting lost in this pit, I've outlined some of the important rules that you should know.

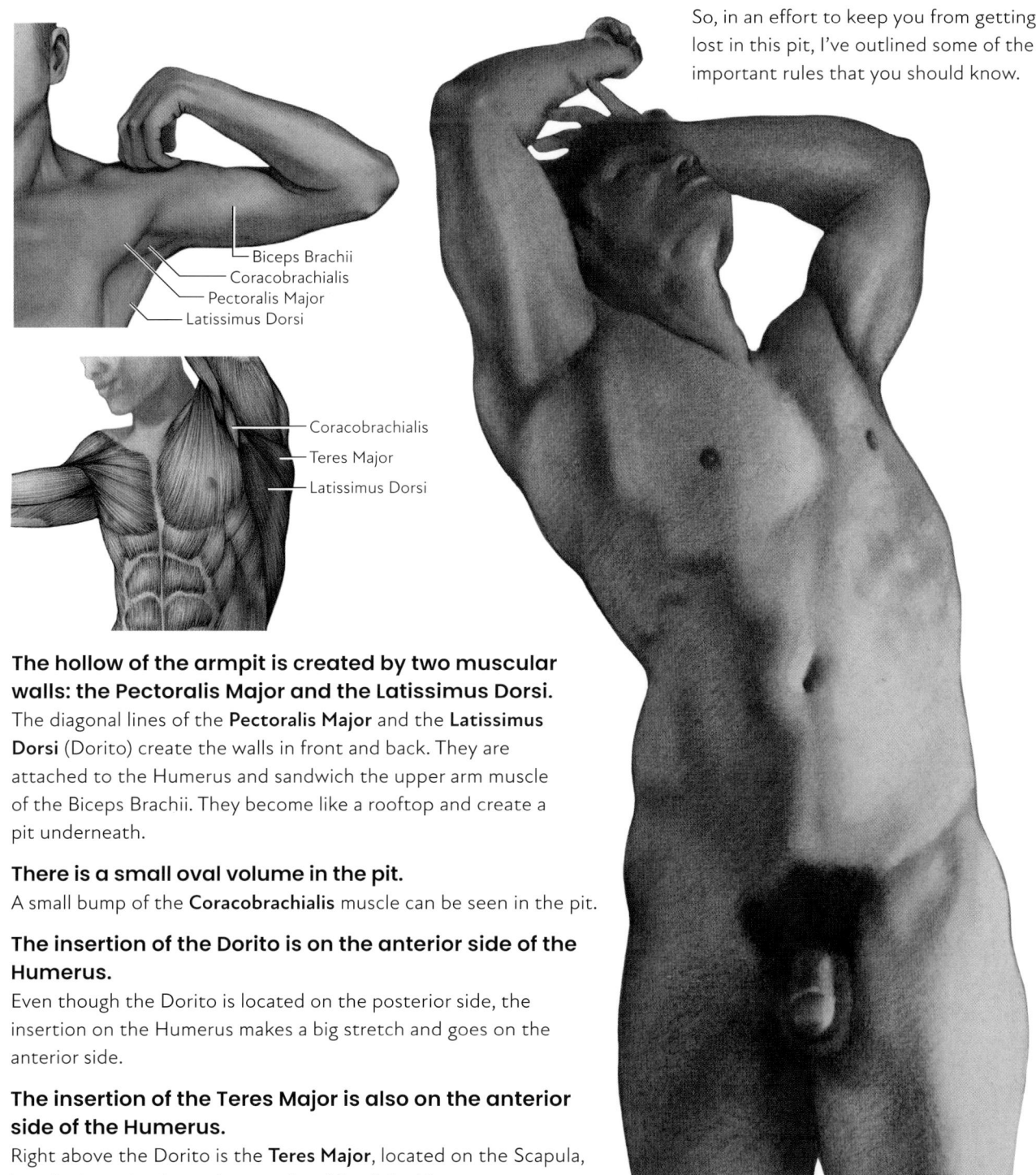

- Biceps Brachii
- Coracobrachialis
- Pectoralis Major
- Latissimus Dorsi

- Coracobrachialis
- Teres Major
- Latissimus Dorsi

The hollow of the armpit is created by two muscular walls: the Pectoralis Major and the Latissimus Dorsi.

The diagonal lines of the **Pectoralis Major** and the **Latissimus Dorsi** (Dorito) create the walls in front and back. They are attached to the Humerus and sandwich the upper arm muscle of the Biceps Brachii. They become like a rooftop and create a pit underneath.

There is a small oval volume in the pit.

A small bump of the **Coracobrachialis** muscle can be seen in the pit.

The insertion of the Dorito is on the anterior side of the Humerus.

Even though the Dorito is located on the posterior side, the insertion on the Humerus makes a big stretch and goes on the anterior side.

The insertion of the Teres Major is also on the anterior side of the Humerus.

Right above the Dorito is the **Teres Major**, located on the Scapula, but the insertion is on the **anterior side of the Humerus**.

Seeking the Teres Major

The Rotator Cuff Muscles

The **Rotator Cuff** muscles are a group of muscles located on the posterior side of the **Scapula** that support the stability and movement of the shoulder. There are four muscles in the Rotator Cuff structure: Supraspinatus, Infraspinatus, Subscapularis, and Teres Minor. They all are attached to the **Greater Tuberosity of the Humerus**. In the surface anatomy, the **Infraspinatus** and **Teres Minor** can be visible on the back of shoulder.

However, the star muscle of the Scapula in figure drawing would be the **Teres Major**. This muscle is thick and visible on most people. It stretches out to the **anterior side of the Humerus**, which is the same insertion as the Latissimus Dorsi muscle. The Teres Major is located on the **inferior angle of the Scapula**, right above the horizontal line of the Latissimus Dorsi, and it is even more visible when the arm is raised.

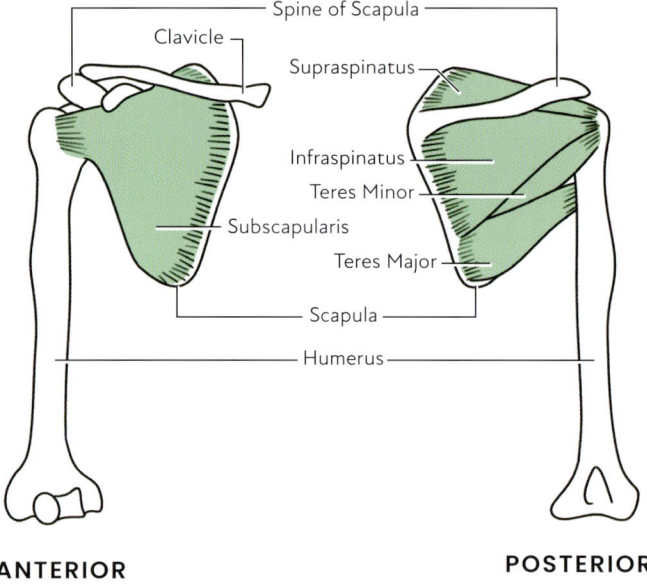

ANTERIOR　　　　　**POSTERIOR**

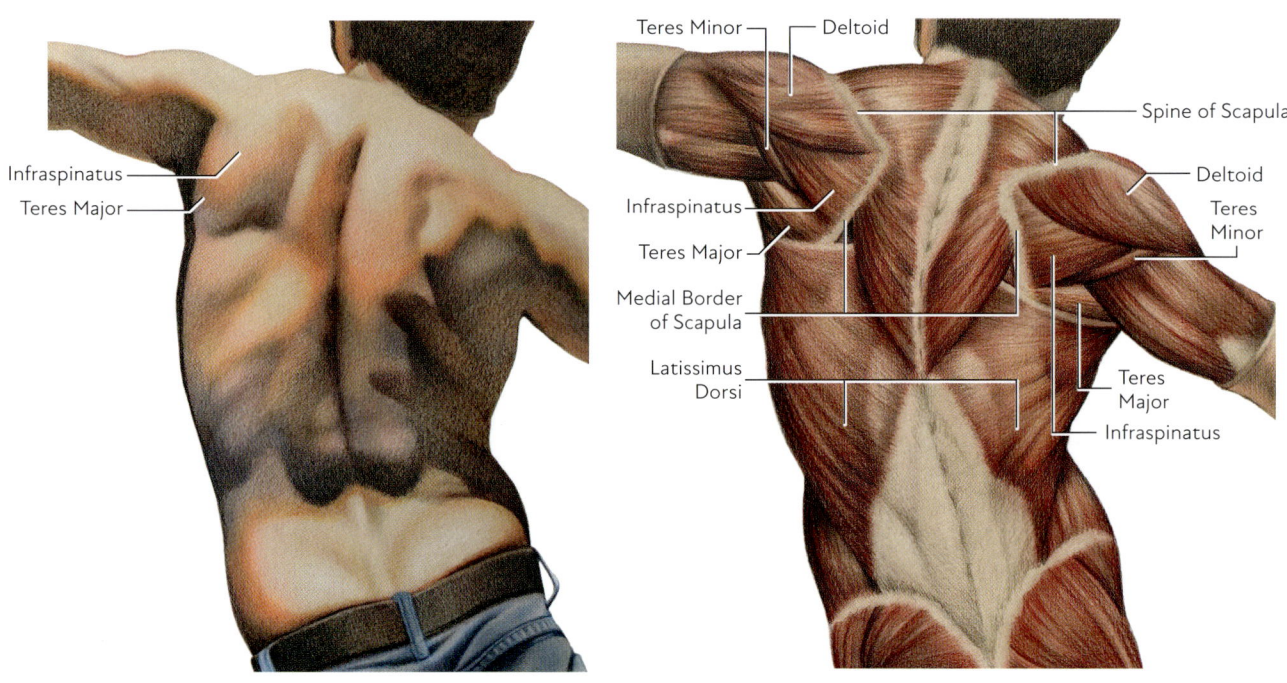

The Triangle of Auscultation

Now we get the structure of the torso muscles in the posterior view. But wait, what is this triangular indentation that we see in the middle?

This is called the **Triangle of Auscultation**. The three borders that create this mystery triangle are the **inferior border of the Trapezius**, the **superior border of the Latissimus Dorsi**, and the **medial border of the Scapula**. This triangle can be more visible when the torso is flexed and the arms are folded toward the chest.

There is a muscle that sits inside of this triangular hole called the **Rhomboid Major**. In very rare cases, we might be able to see the Rhomboid Major puffing up inside the triangle.

When you go to the doctor, they use a stethoscope to listen to the inside of your torso. This triangle shows where they put the instrument to check your lung from the posterior side.

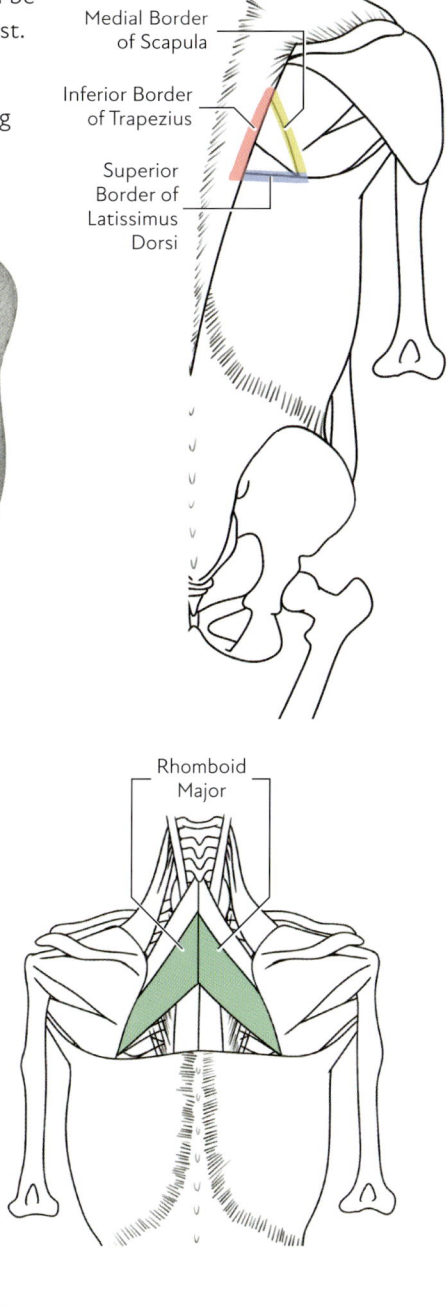

Medial Border of Scapula

Inferior Border of Trapezius

Superior Border of Latissimus Dorsi

Rhomboid Major

The Erector Spinae Group

The Back Tube

The **Erector Spinae Group** is a group of three muscles (with more parts in each) that runs vertically on the spine in the posterior torso. This is not an external muscle, but you can see the large tube-like volume underneath the Latissimus Dorsi.

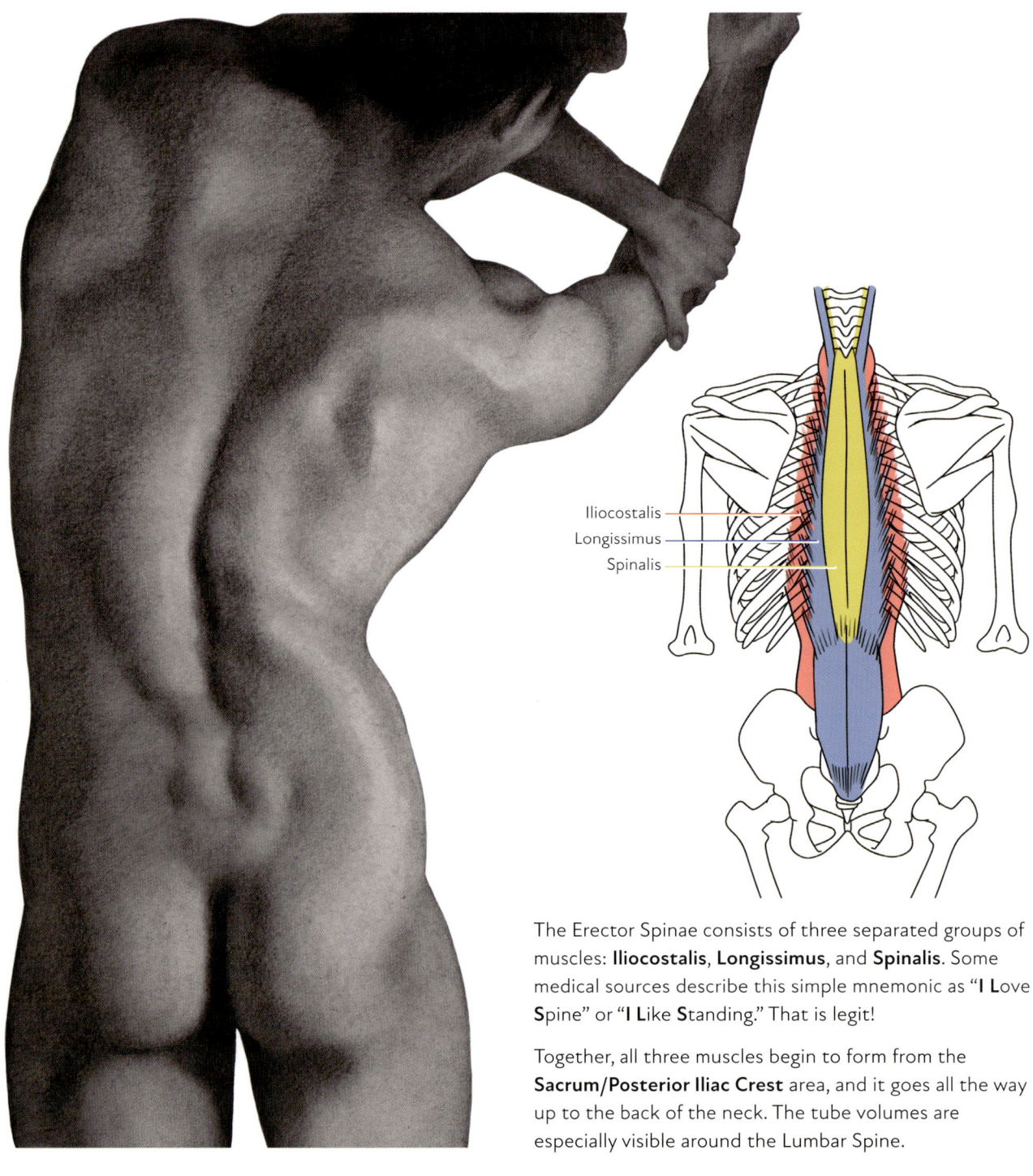

Iliocostalis
Longissimus
Spinalis

The Erector Spinae consists of three separated groups of muscles: **Iliocostalis**, **Longissimus**, and **Spinalis**. Some medical sources describe this simple mnemonic as "**I L**ove **S**pine" or "**I L**ike **S**tanding." That is legit!

Together, all three muscles begin to form from the **Sacrum/Posterior Iliac Crest** area, and it goes all the way up to the back of the neck. The tube volumes are especially visible around the Lumbar Spine.

Torso Muscles Overview

Anterior

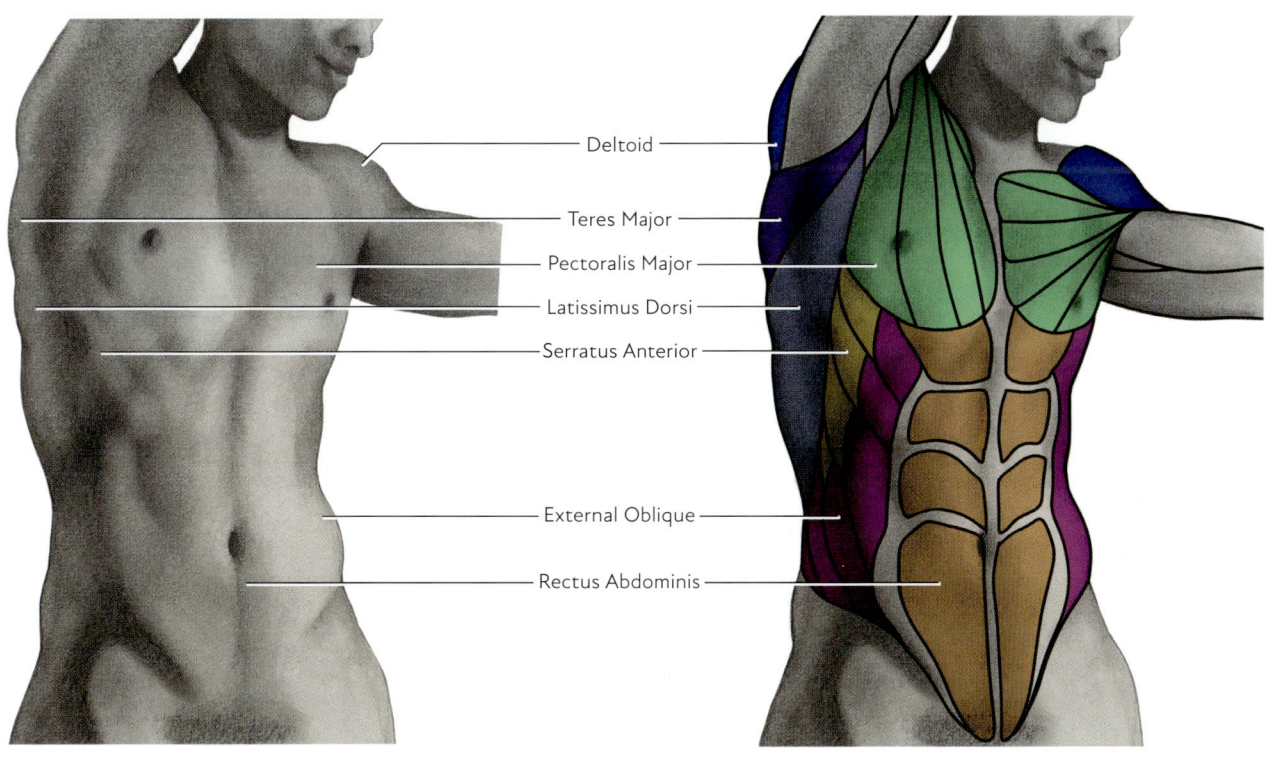

Deltoid

Teres Major

Pectoralis Major

Latissimus Dorsi

Serratus Anterior

External Oblique

Rectus Abdominis

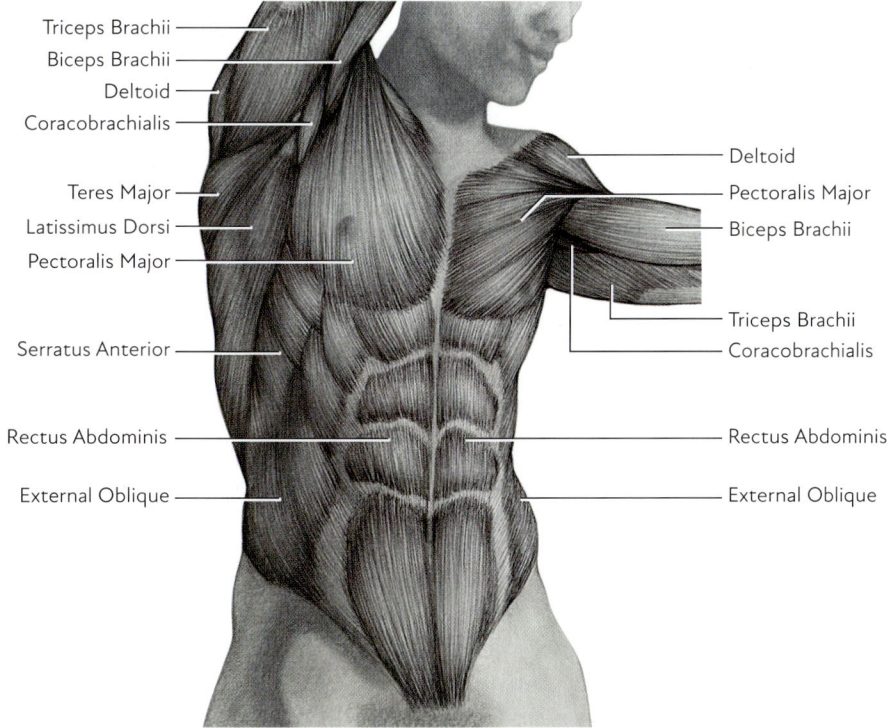

Triceps Brachii

Biceps Brachii

Deltoid

Coracobrachialis

Teres Major

Latissimus Dorsi

Pectoralis Major

Serratus Anterior

Rectus Abdominis

External Oblique

Deltoid

Pectoralis Major

Biceps Brachii

Triceps Brachii

Coracobrachialis

Rectus Abdominis

External Oblique

Posterior

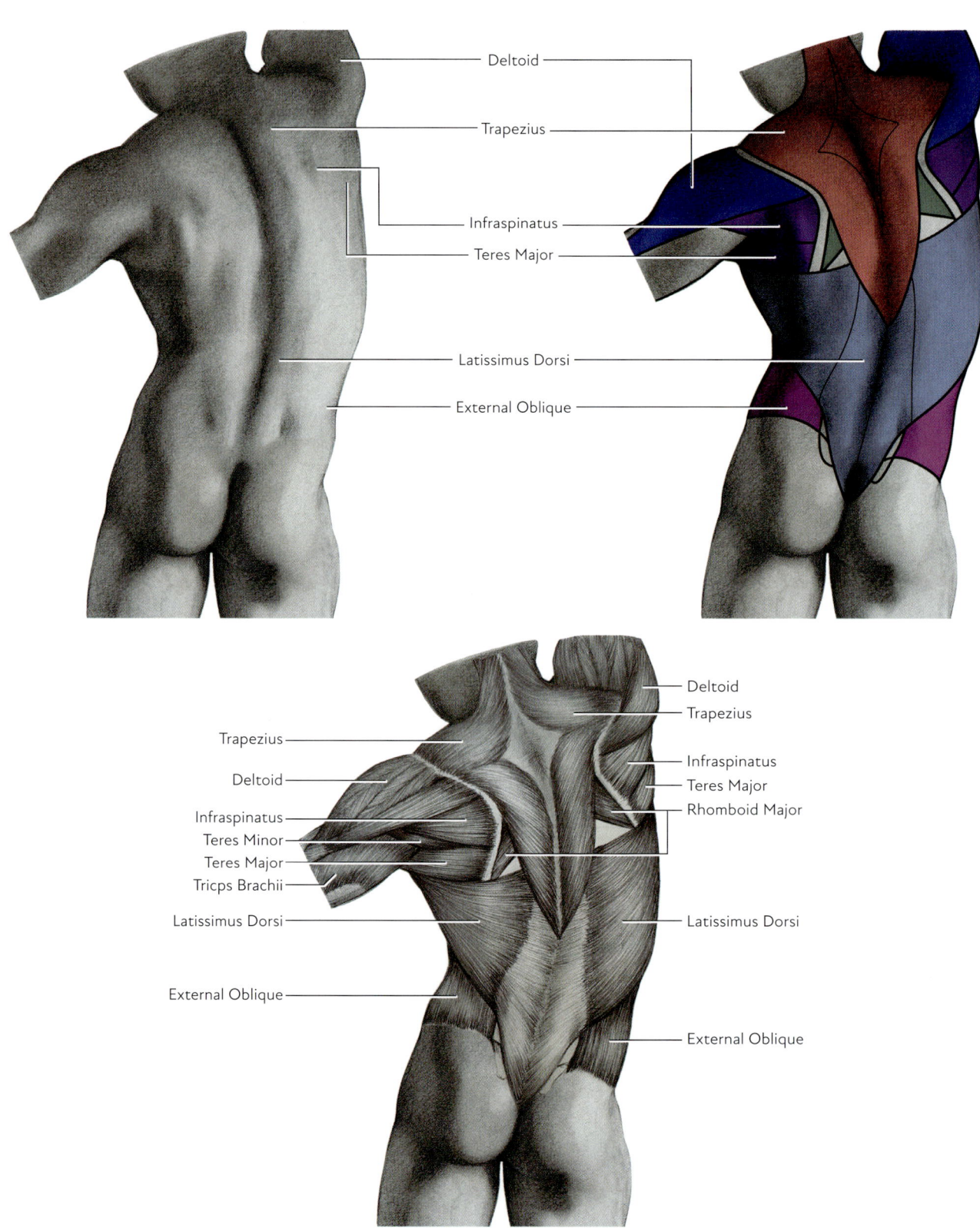

Deltoid

Trapezius

Infraspinatus

Teres Major

Latissimus Dorsi

External Oblique

Trapezius

Deltoid

Infraspinatus

Teres Minor

Teres Major

Tricps Brachii

Latissimus Dorsi

External Oblique

Deltoid

Trapezius

Infraspinatus

Teres Major

Rhomboid Major

Latissimus Dorsi

External Oblique

Lateral

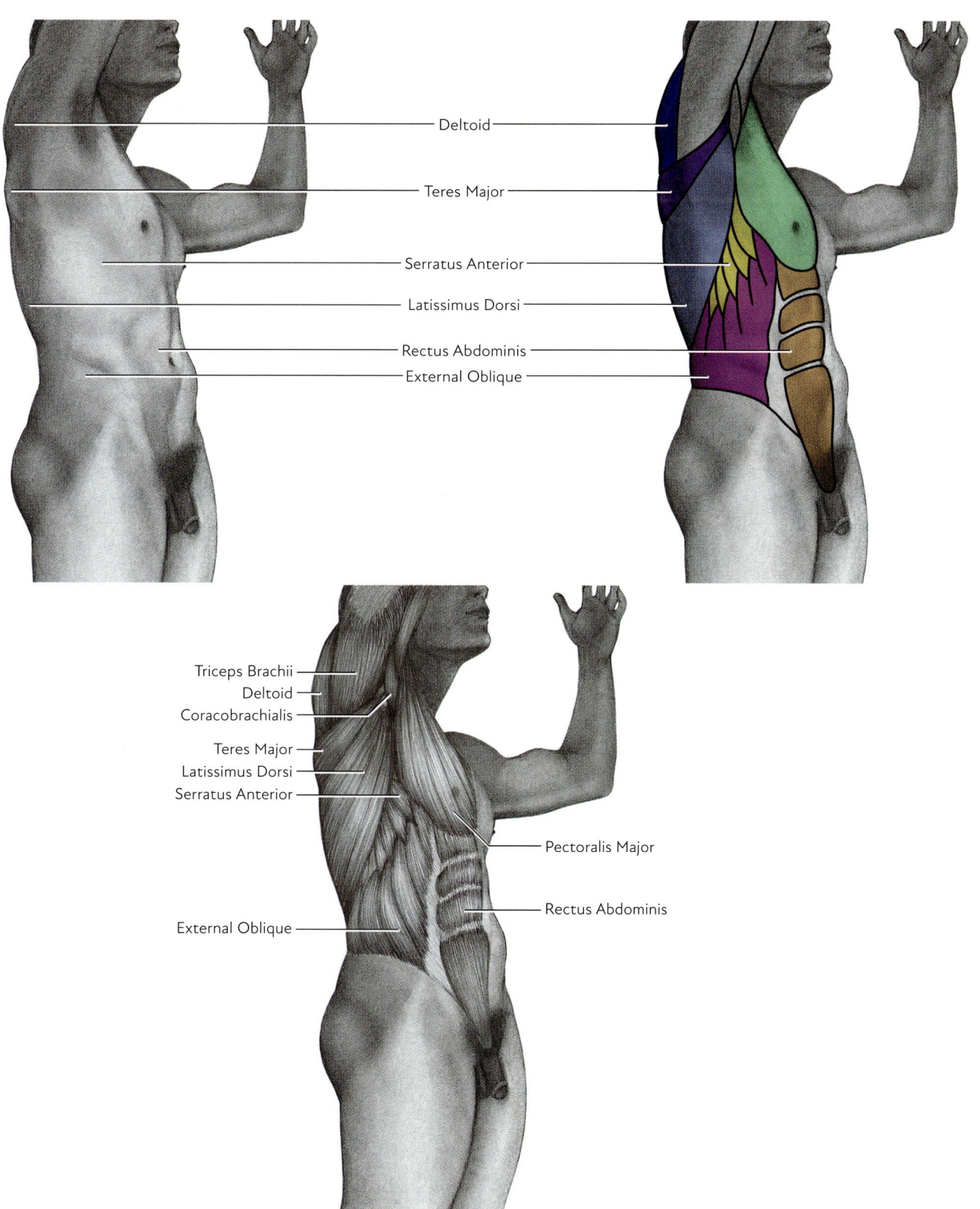

Deltoid

Teres Major

Serratus Anterior

Latissimus Dorsi

Rectus Abdominis

External Oblique

Triceps Brachii

Deltoid

Coracobrachialis

Teres Major

Latissimus Dorsi

Serratus Anterior

External Oblique

Pectoralis Major

Rectus Abdominis

Step-by-Step Torso Muscles

Anterior

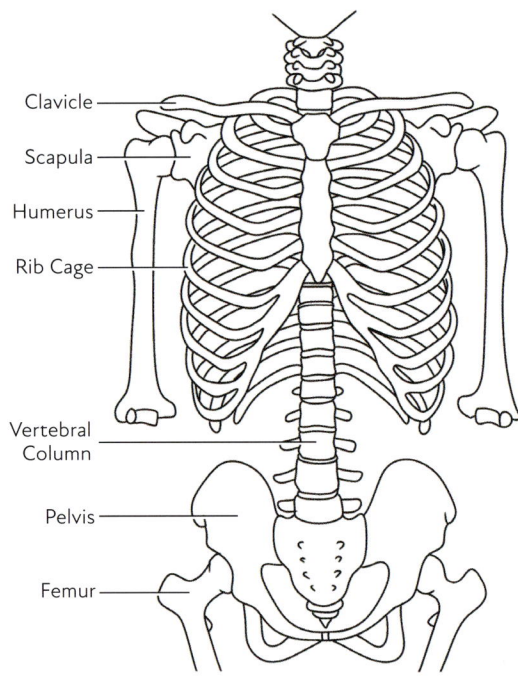

Clavicle

Scapula

Humerus

Rib Cage

Vertebral
Column

Pelvis

Femur

BONES OF TORSO

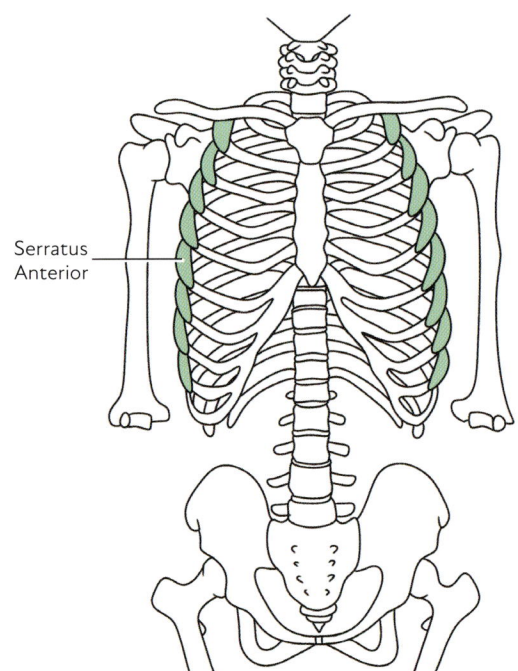

Serratus
Anterior

Serratus Anterior

Origin: Ribs #1–9

Insertion: Anterior surface of Scapula

Function: Suspension and rotation
of the Scapula

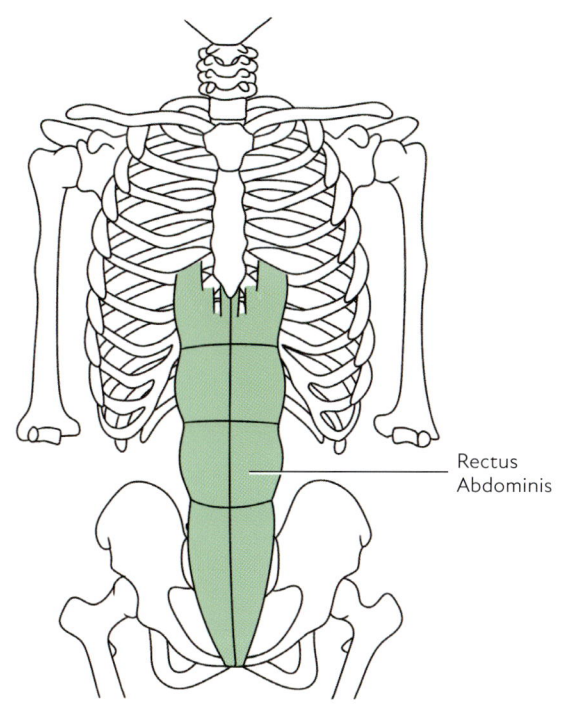

Rectus
Abdominis

Rectus Abdominis

Origin: Pubic Symphysis, Pubic Crest

Insertion: Xyphoid Process, Costal
Cartilage of Ribs #5–7

Function: Flexion of Torso

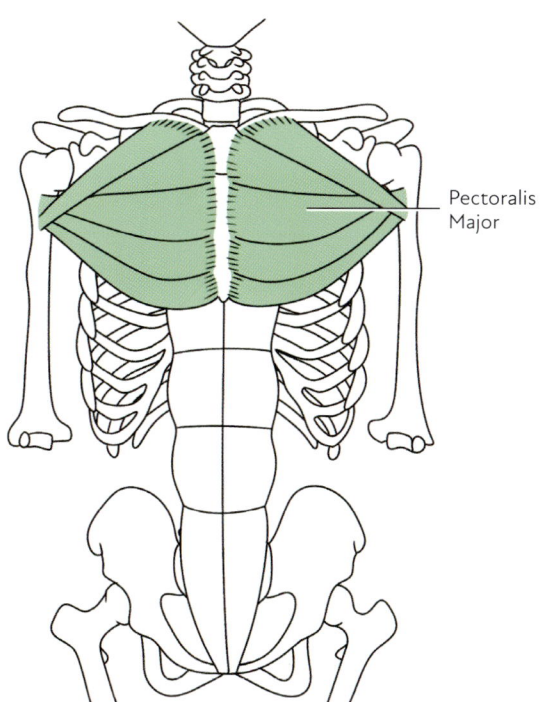

Pectoralis
Major

Pectoralis Major

Origin: Medial half of Clavicle,
Sternum, Rectus Sheath

Insertion: Crest of Greater Tubercle
of Humerus

Function: Adduction, internal
rotation, flexion, extension of arm

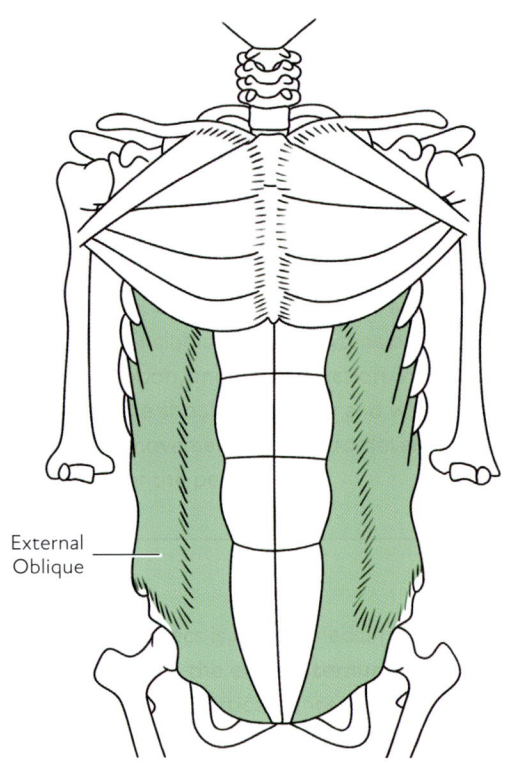

External
Oblique

External Oblique

Origin: Ribs #5–12

Insertion: Linea Alba, Pubic Tubercle,
anterior half of Iliac Crest

Function: Flexion, lateral flexion,
and rotation of Torso

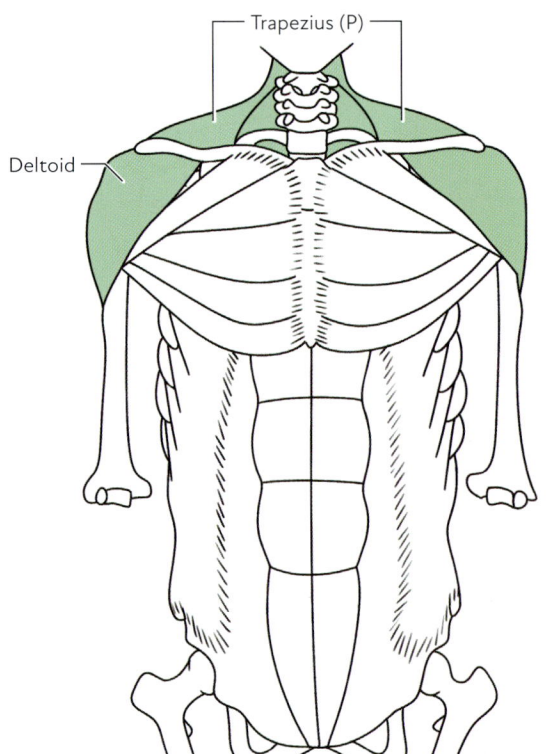

Trapezius (P)

Deltoid

Deltoid
(Anterior, Lateral, Posterior)

Origin: Lateral third of Clavicle, Acromion
Process of Scapula, Spine of Scapula

Insertion: Deltoid Tuberosity of Humerus

Function:
• **Anterior:** Flexion and rotation of arm
• **Lateral:** Abduction of arm
• **Posterior:** Extension and rotation of arm

Trapezius

Origin: Vertebrae T1–T12, Vertebrae C1–C7

Insertion: Lateral third of Clavicle, Spine of
Scapula, Acromion Process of Scapula

Function: Stabilization of Scapula

Step-by-Step Torso Muscles

Posterior

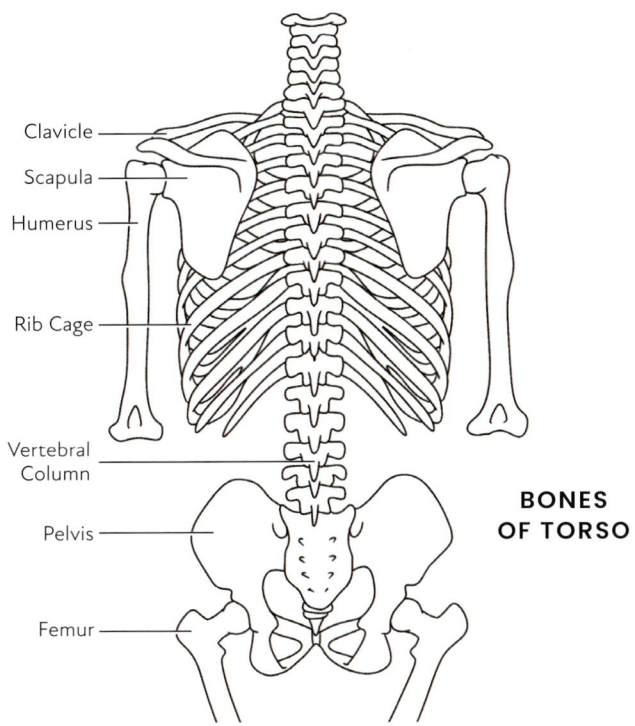

Clavicle

Scapula

Humerus

Rib Cage

Vertebral
Column

Pelvis

Femur

**BONES
OF TORSO**

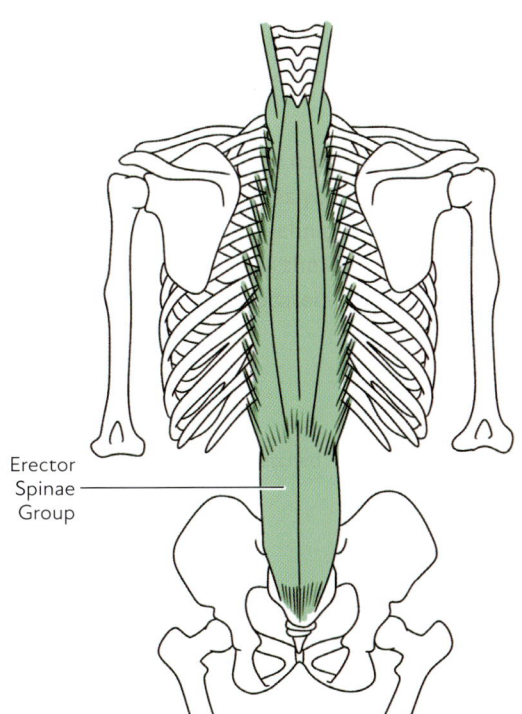

Erector
Spinae
Group

Erector Spinae Group

Attachments: Three deep muscles
(Iliocostalis, Longissimus, Spinalis) located
on the Vertebral Column in between Cranium
and Pelvis

Function: Lateral flexion and extension of
the spine

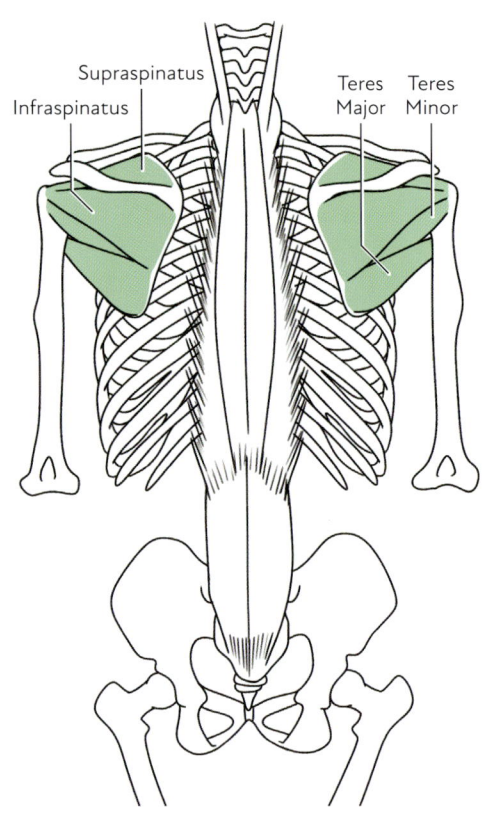

Muscles of Scapula

Infraspinatus

Origin: Infraspinous Fossa of Scapula

Insertion: Greater Tubercle of Humerus

Function: External rotation of arm, stabilization of Humerus head

Teres Major

Origin: Inferior angle of Scapula

Insertion: Intertubercular Sulcus of Humerus (anterior)

Function: Extension, adduction, and internal rotation of Humerus

Supraspinatus

Origin: Supraspinous Fossa of Scapula

Insertion: Greater Tubercle of Humerus

Function: Abduction of arm, stabilization of Humerus head

Teres Minor

Origin: Lateral border of Scapula

Insertion: Greater Tubercle of Humerus

Function: Adduction and external rotation of arm, stabilization of Humerus head

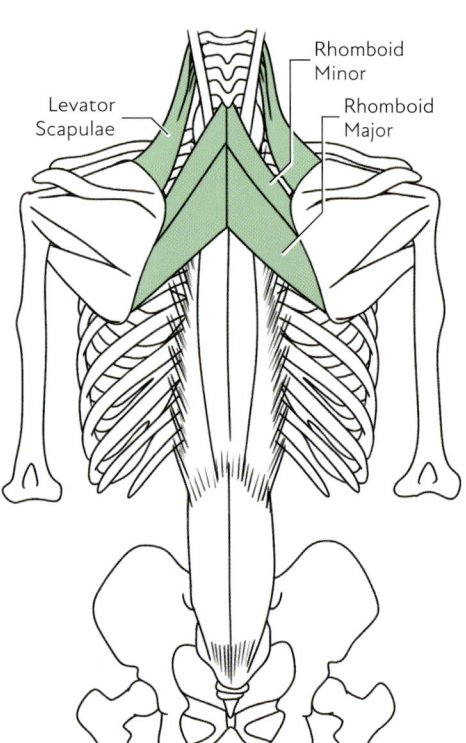

Levator Scapulae

Origin: Vertebrae C1–C4

Insertion: Medial/superior border of Scapula

Function: Lateral flexion and extension of neck; elevation of the Scapula

Rhomboid Minor

Origin: Vertebrae C7–T1

Insertion: Medial end of Spine of Scapula

Function: Stabilization of Scapula

Rhomboid Major

Origin: Vertebrae T2–T5

Insertion: Medial border of Scapula

Function: Stabilization of Scapula

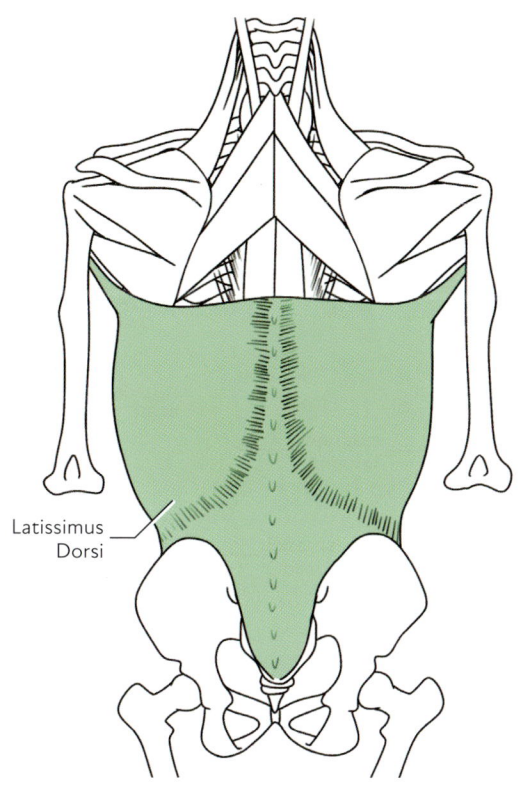

Latissimus Dorsi

Latissimus Dorsi

Origin: Posterior third of the Iliac Crest, Ribs #9–12, T1–T12, Vertebrae L1–L5, Sacrum, inferior angle of Scapula

Insertion: Intertubercular Sulcus of Humerus (anterior)

Function: Adduction, internal rotation, extension of arm

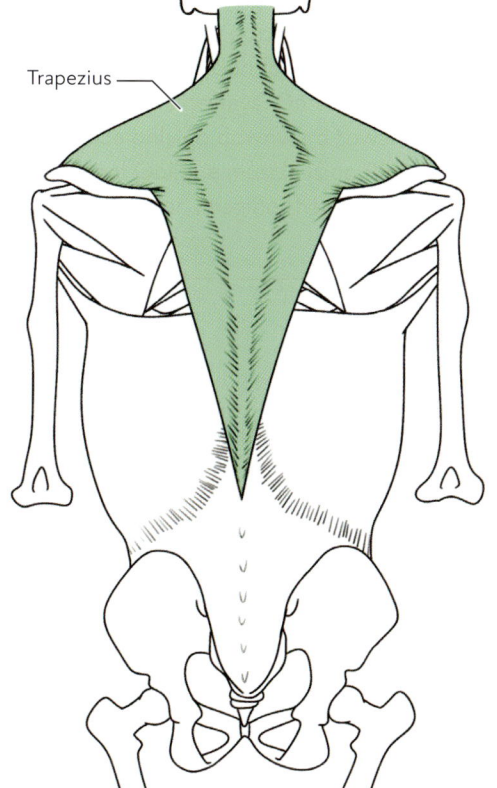

Trapezius

Trapezius

Origin: Vertebrae T1–T12, Vertebrae C1–C7

Insertion: Lateral third of Clavicle, Spine of Scapula, Acromion Process of Scapula

Function: Stabilization of Scapula

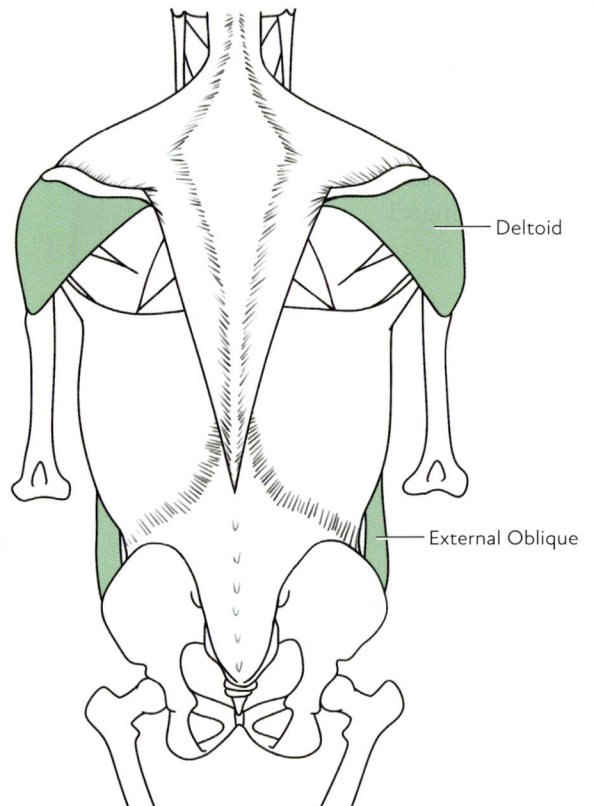

Deltoid

External Oblique

Deltoid

Origin: Lateral third of Clavicle, Acromion Process of Scapula, Spine of Scapula

Insertion: Deltoid Tuberosity of Humerus

Function:
- **Anterior:** Flexion and rotation of arm
- **Lateral:** Abduction of arm
- **Posterior:** Extension and rotation of arm

External Oblique

Origin: Ribs #5–12

Insertion: Linea Alba, Pubic Tubercle, anterior half of Iliac Crest

Function: Flexion, lateral flexion, and rotation of Torso

Step-By-Step Torso Muscles

Lateral

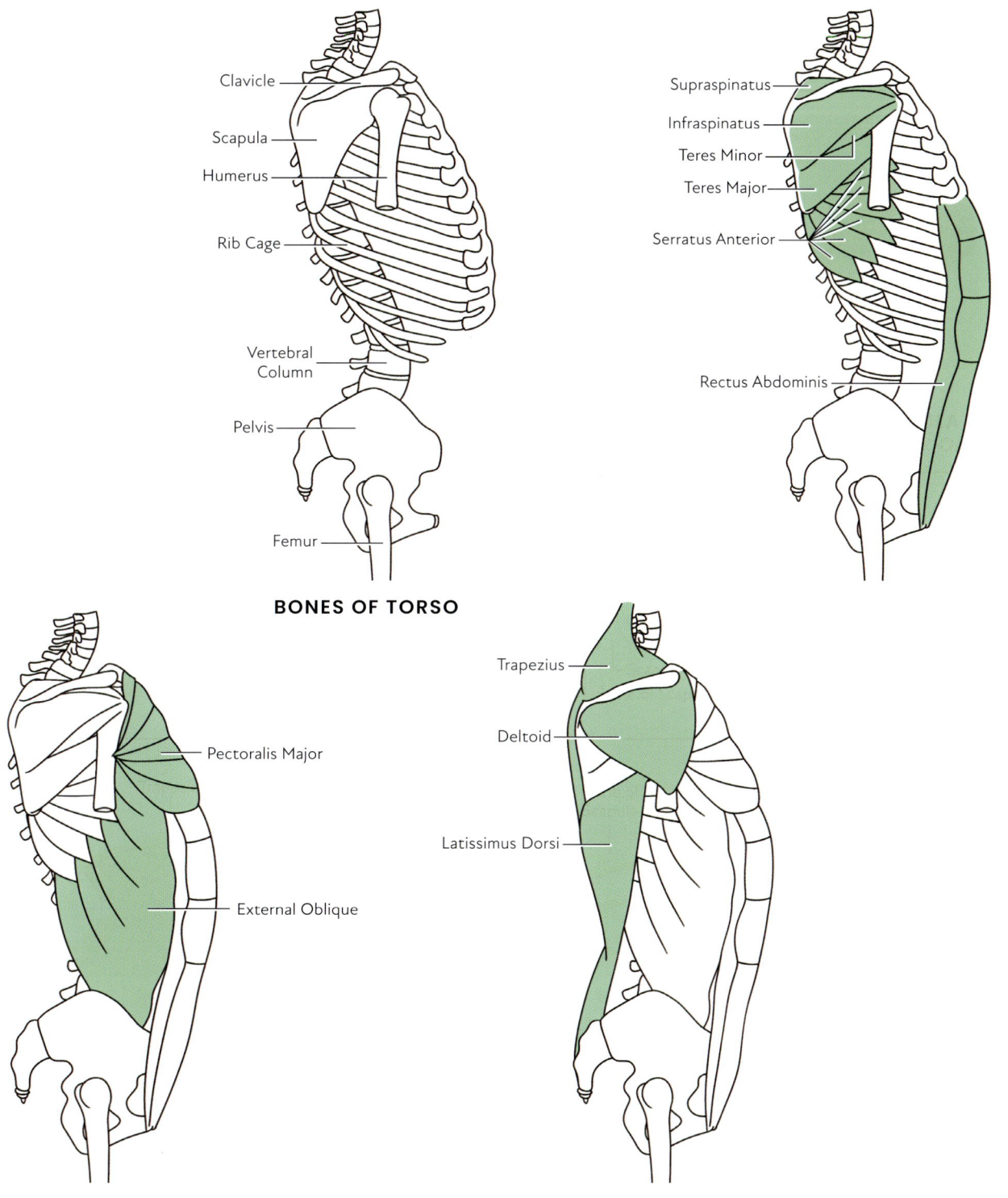

BONES OF TORSO

Clavicle

Scapula

Humerus

Rib Cage

Vertebral Column

Pelvis

Femur

Supraspinatus

Infraspinatus

Teres Minor

Teres Major

Serratus Anterior

Rectus Abdominis

Pectoralis Major

External Oblique

Trapezius

Deltoid

Latissimus Dorsi

Step-by-Step Torso Muscles

Arm Raised

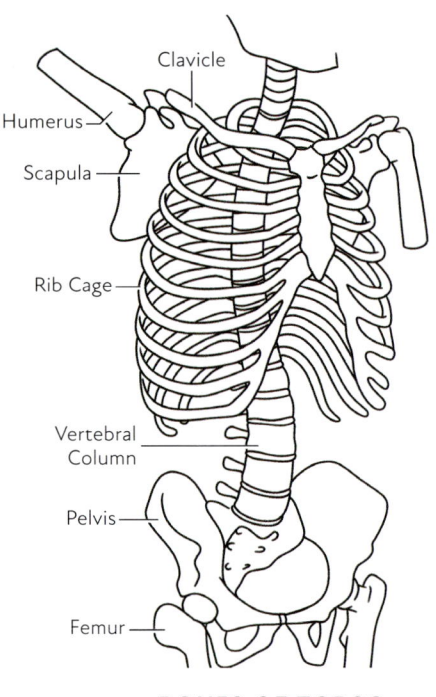

BONES OF TORSO

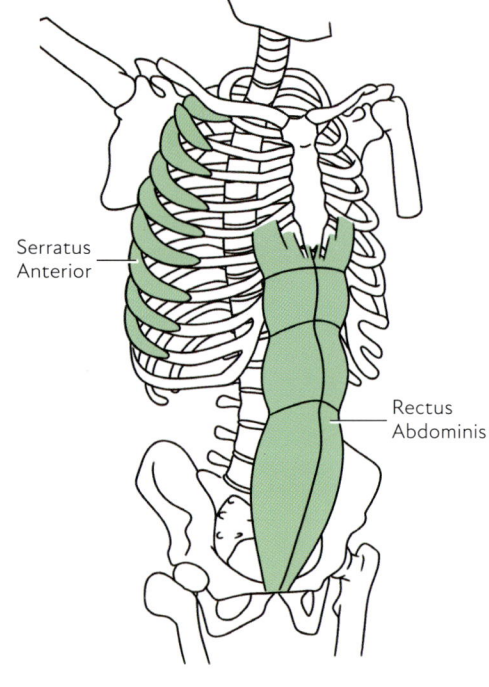

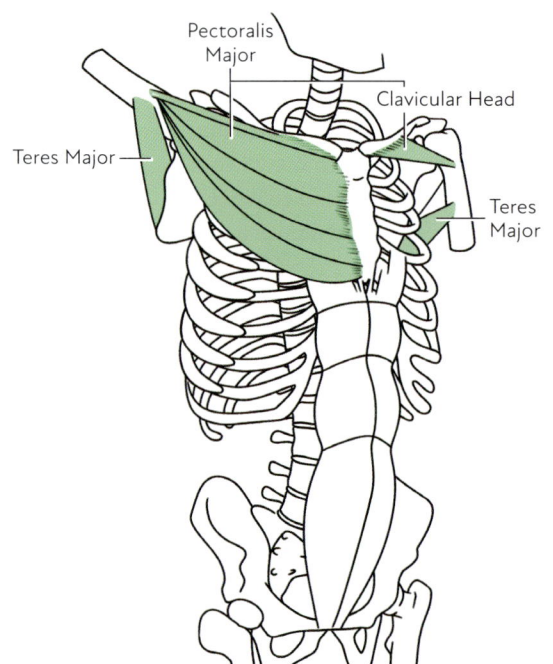

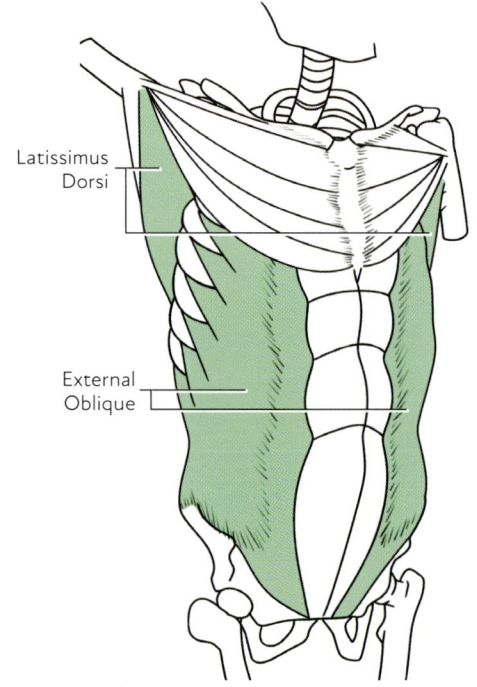

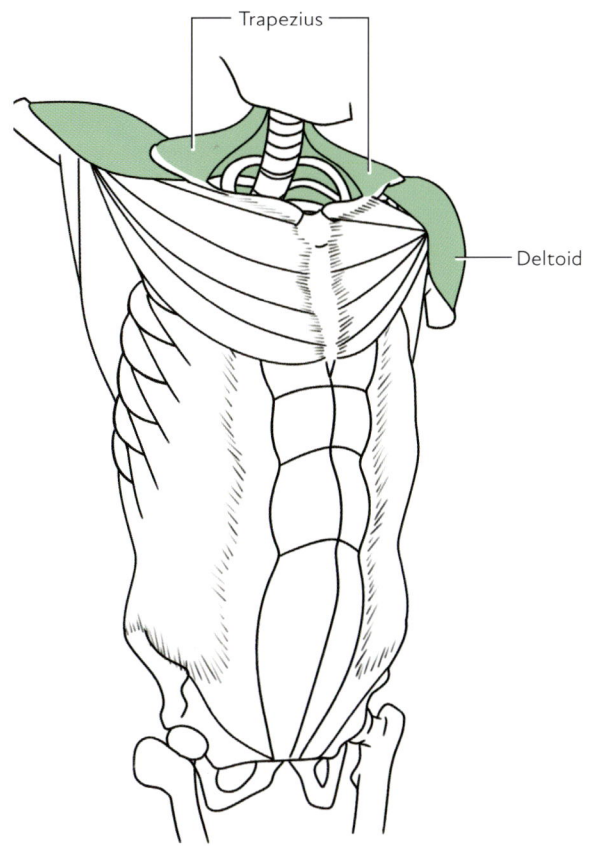

Trapezius

Deltoid

Drawing the Torso

Anterior

1

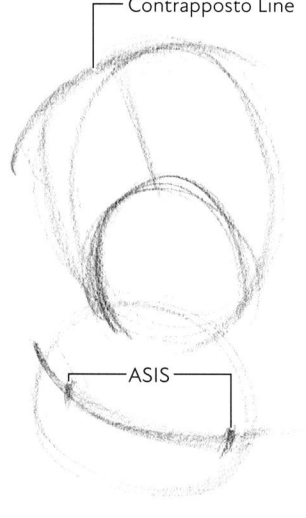

Contrapposto Line

ASIS

2

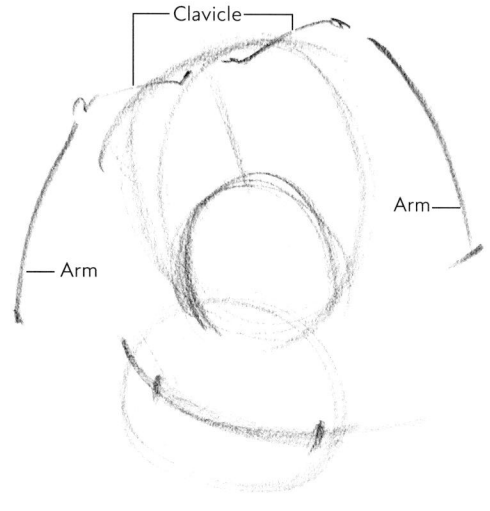

Clavicle

Arm

Arm

3

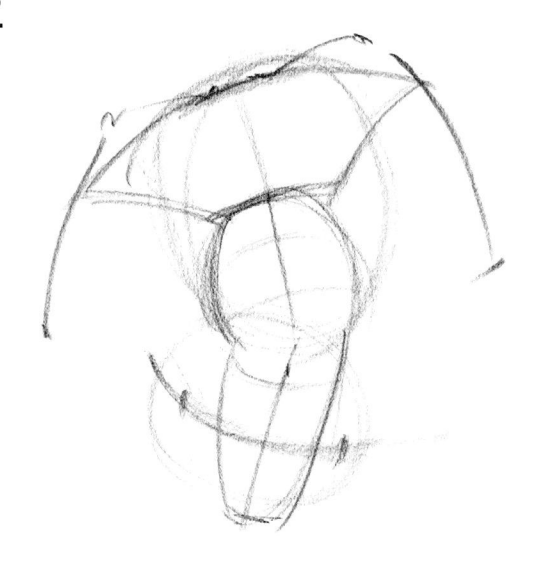

4

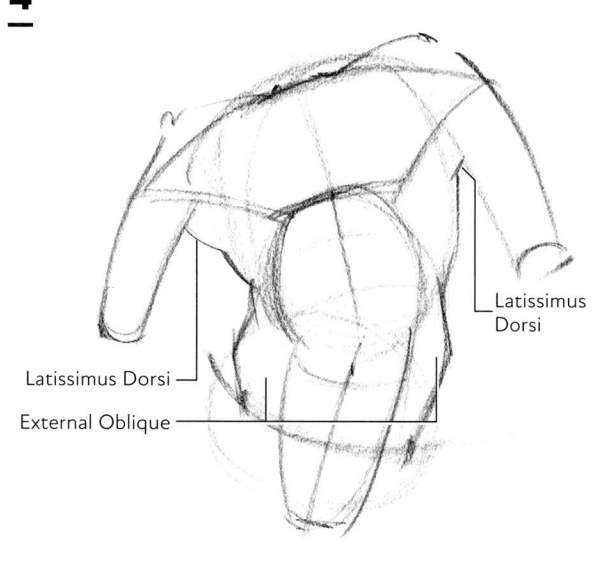

Latissimus Dorsi

Latissimus Dorsi

External Oblique

1. Start with the simplified torso skeleton. Focus on the contrapposto within the oval shapes for the Rib Cage and Pelvis. Define the ASIS.

2. Add the Clavicle line and lines for the upper arms.

3. Add a hexagon shape for the Pectoralis Major, and a peanut shape for the Rectus Abdominis.

4. Work on the side of the torso: define the External Oblique and Latissimus Dorsi. Add cylinder shapes for the arms.

5

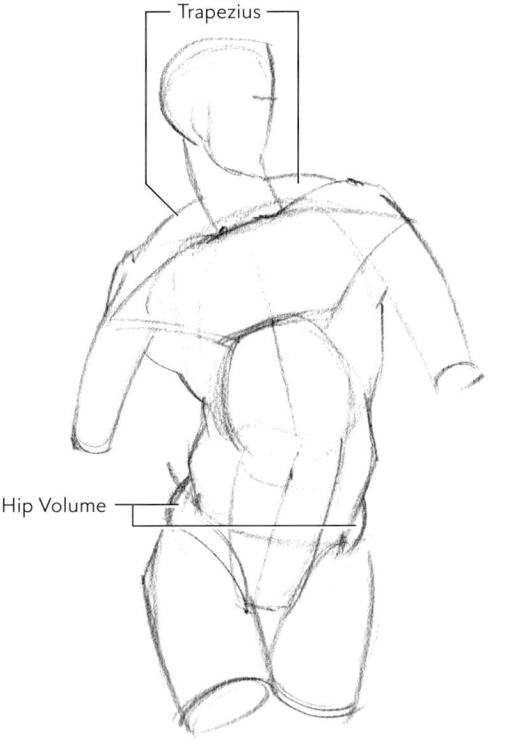

Trapezius

Hip Volume

6

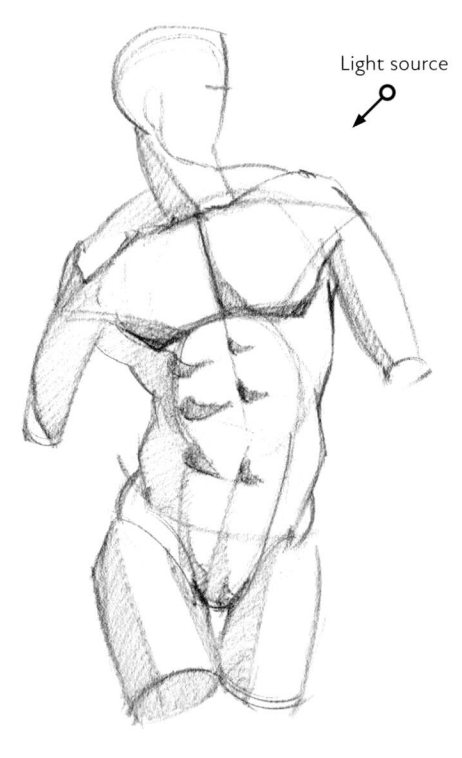

Light source

7

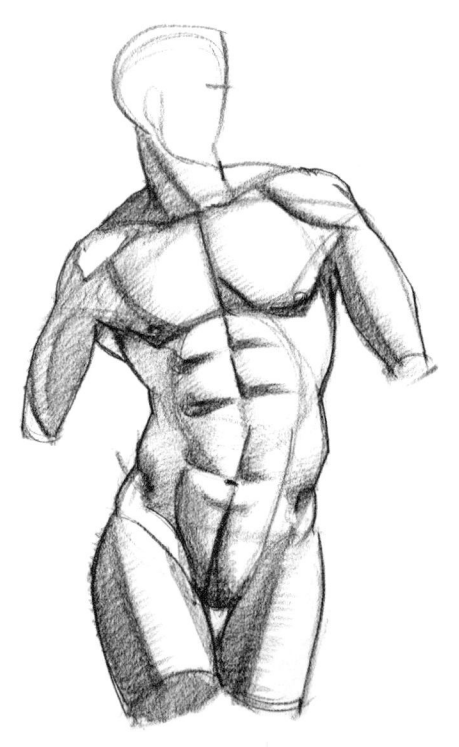

5. Add the head, neck, and legs to balance the gesture and proportions. The Trapezius peeks out in between the neck and the shoulder. Add the hip volume between the love handles and the legs.

6. Analyze the light source. Follow the geometric muscular form and use shading to create an even tone.

7. Continue developing the details and contrast.

1

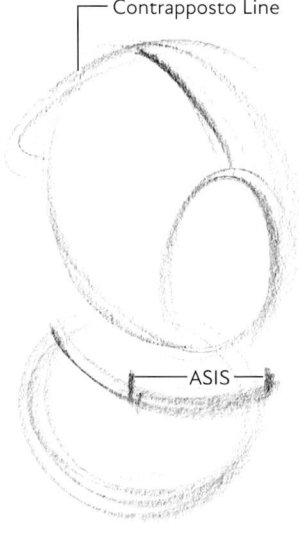

Contrapposto Line

ASIS

2

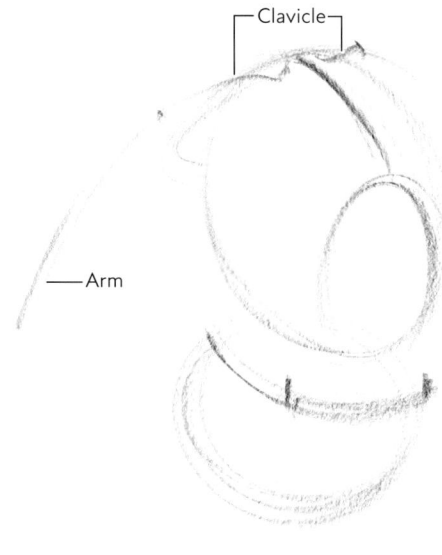

Clavicle

Arm

3

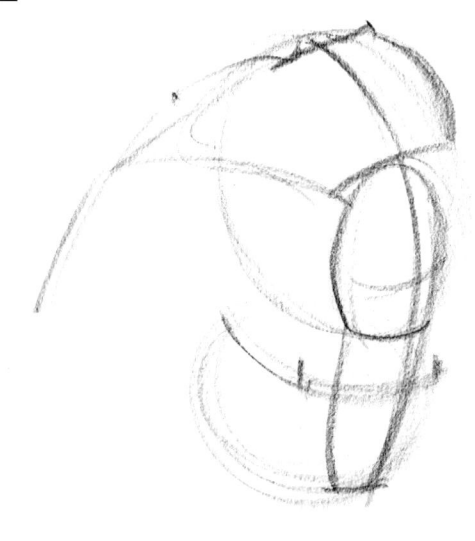

4

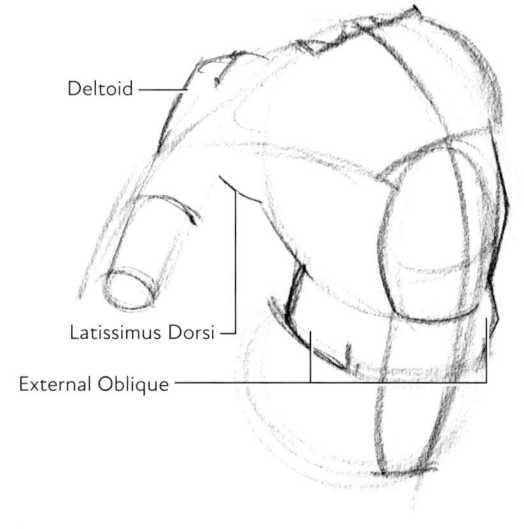

Deltoid

Latissimus Dorsi

External Oblique

1. Start with the simplified torso skeleton. Focus on the contrapposto within the oval shapes for the Rib Cage and Pelvis. Define the ASIS.

2. Add the Clavicle line and the upper arm.

3. Add a hexagon shape for the Pectoralis Major, and a peanut shape for the Rectus Abdominis. At this angle, the hexagon will not be a full shape.

4. Work on the side of the torso: define the External Oblique and Latissimus Dorsi. Add a cylinder shape for the arm, and then define the Deltoid.

5

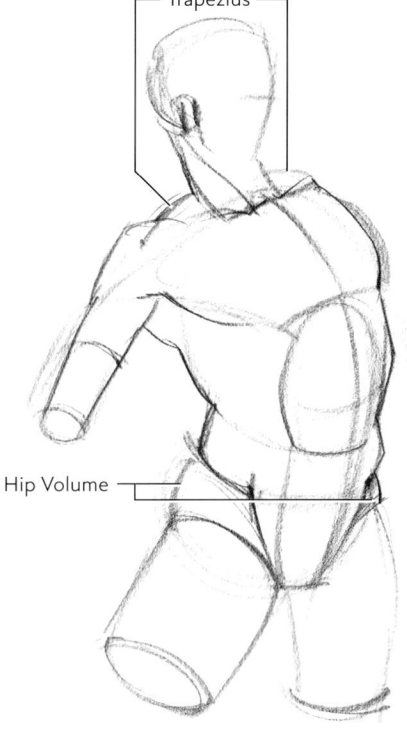

Trapezius

Hip Volume

6

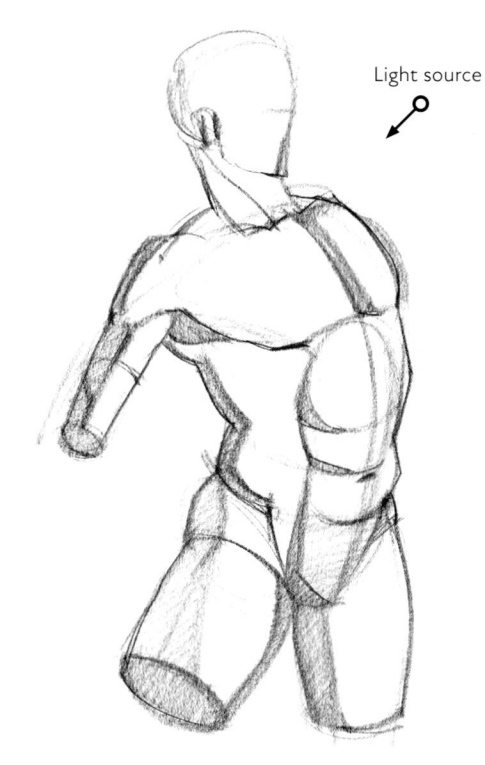

Light source

7

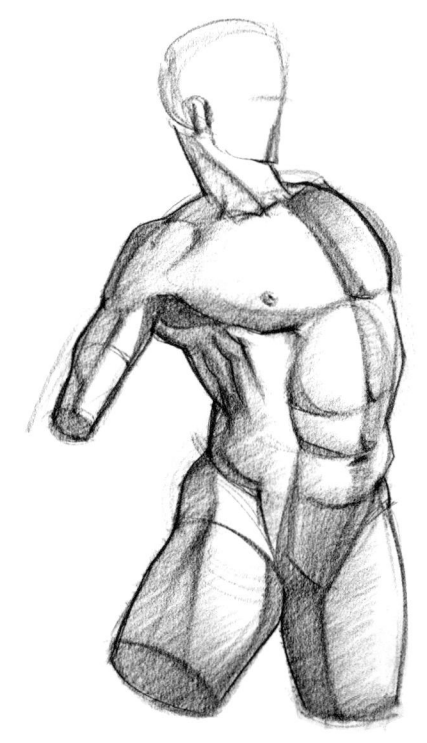

5. Add the head, neck, and legs to balance the gesture and proportions. The Trapezius peeks out in between the neck and the shoulder. Add the hip volume between the love handles and the legs.

6. Analyze the light source. Follow the geometric muscular form and use shading to create an even tone.

7. Continue developing the details and contrast.

Anterior | Arms Up

1

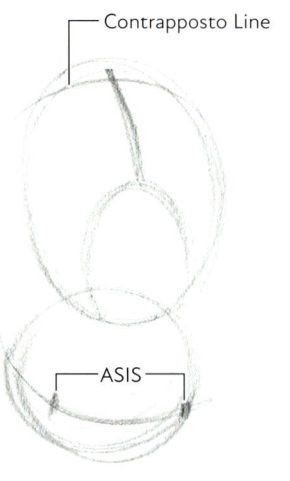

Contrapposto Line

ASIS

2

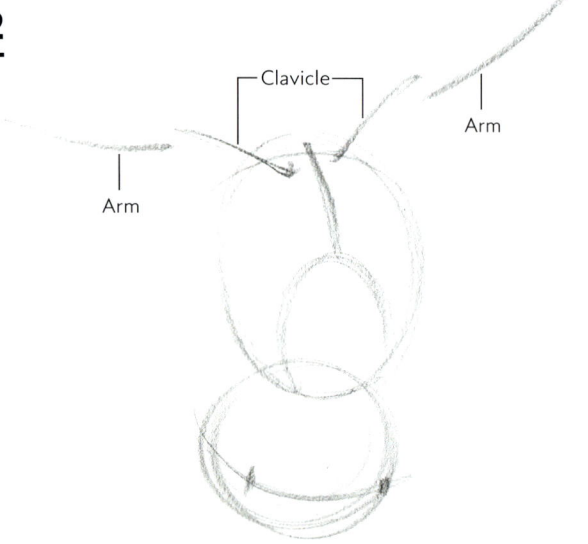

Clavicle

Arm

Arm

3

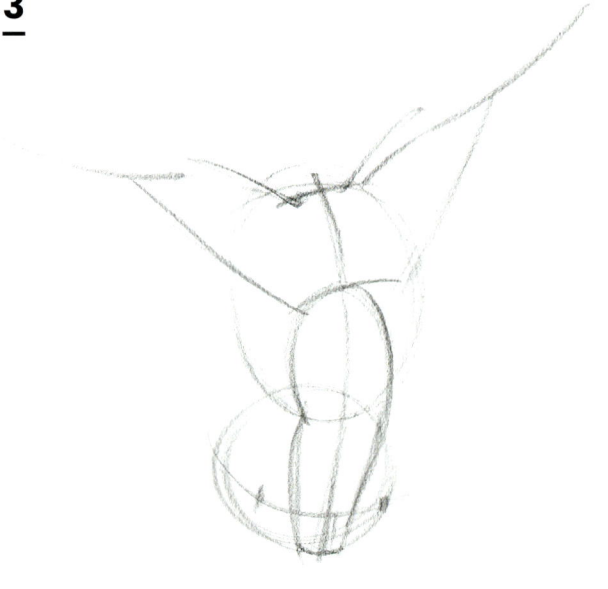

4

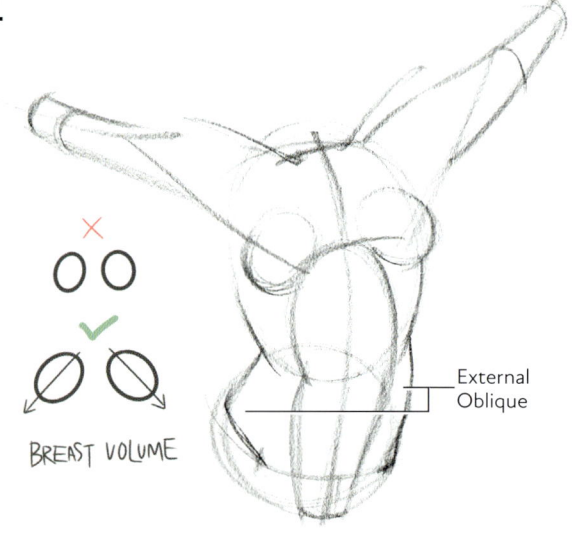

BREAST VOLUME

External Oblique

1. Start with the simplified torso skeleton. Focus on the contrapposto within the oval shapes for the Rib Cage and Pelvis. Define the ASIS.

2. Add the Clavicle line and the upper arms. In this pose, the arms are abducted, and the lateral end of the Clavicle follows the movement of the arm.

3. Add a hexagon shape for the Pectoralis Major, and a peanut shape for the Rectus Abdominis. At this angle, the lateral angle of the hexagon will follow the movement of the arm.

4. Work on the side of the torso and define the External Oblique. Add a cylinder shape for each arm. The breast volume should be drawn on the inferior angle of the hexagon.

5

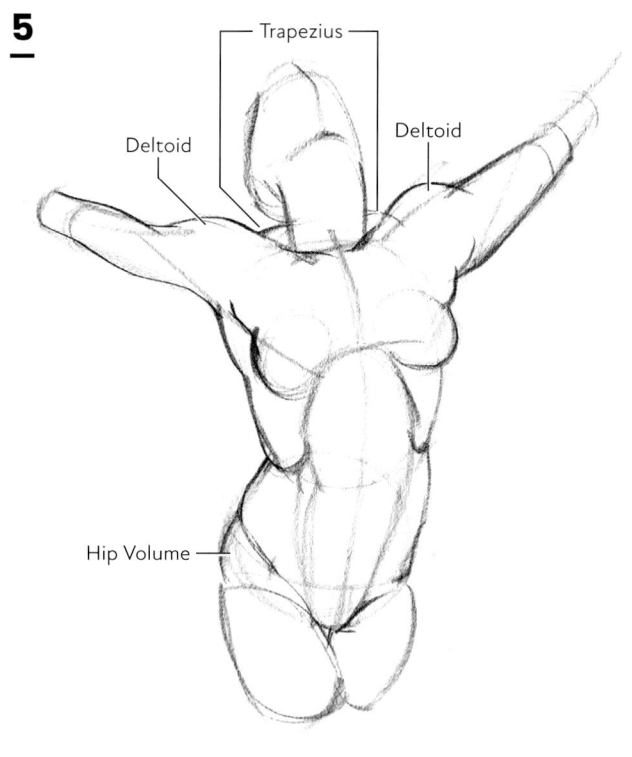

Trapezius

Deltoid

Deltoid

Hip Volume

6

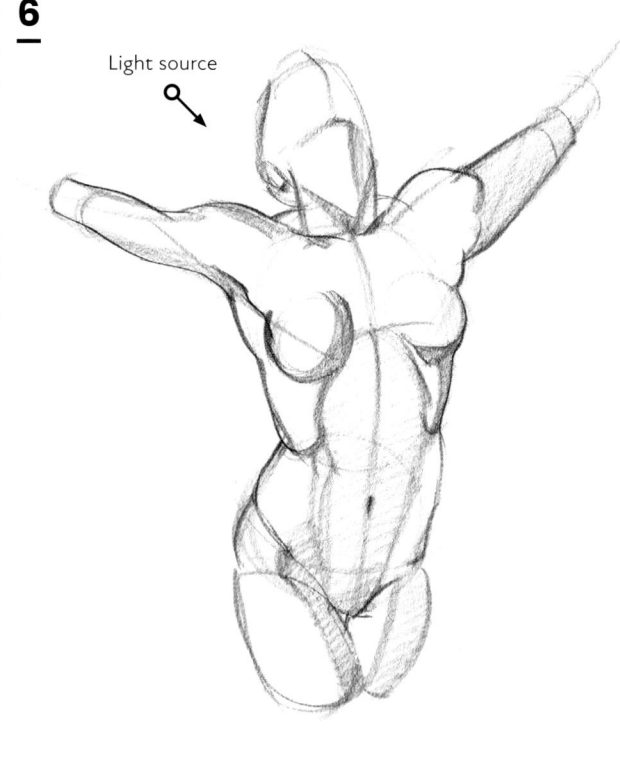

Light source

7

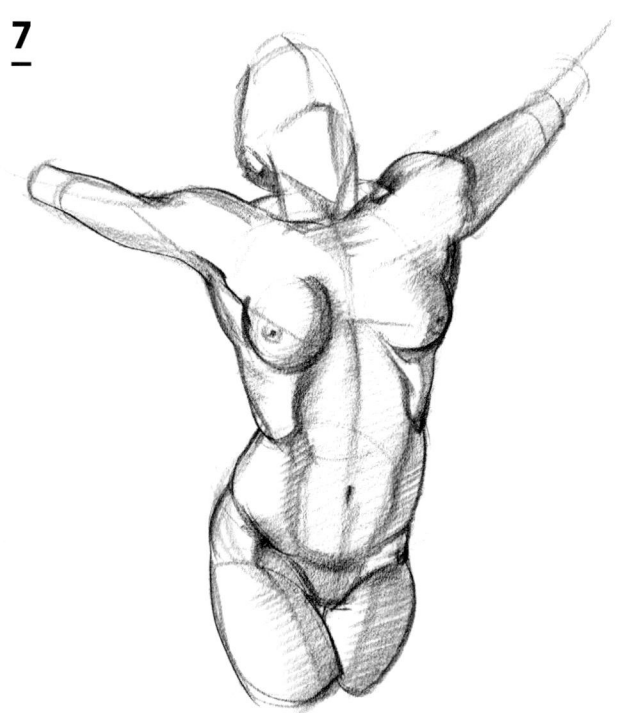

5. Add the head, neck, and legs to balance the gesture and proportions. The Trapezius peeks out in between the neck and the shoulder. Add the hip volume between the love handles and the legs.

6. Analyze the light source. Follow the geometric muscular form and use shading to create an even tone.

7. Continue developing the details and contrast.

Posterior

1

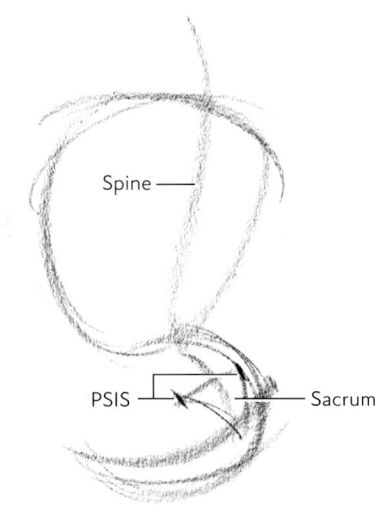

Spine

PSIS — Sacrum

2

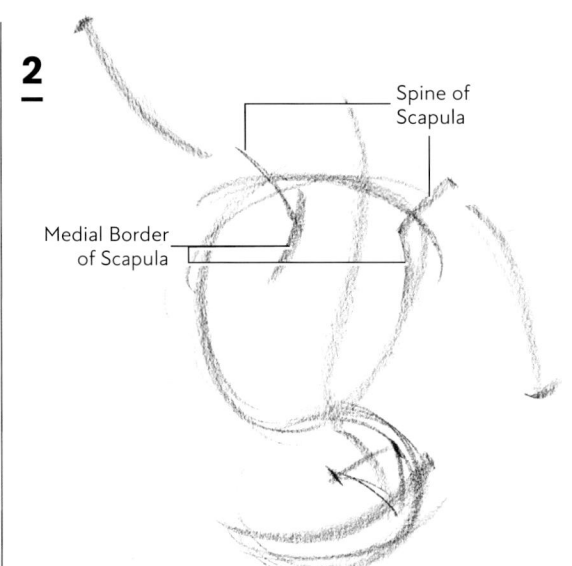

Spine of Scapula

Medial Border of Scapula

3

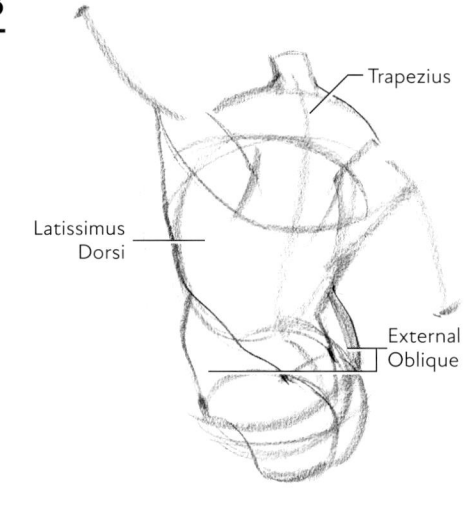

Trapezius

Latissimus Dorsi

External Oblique

4

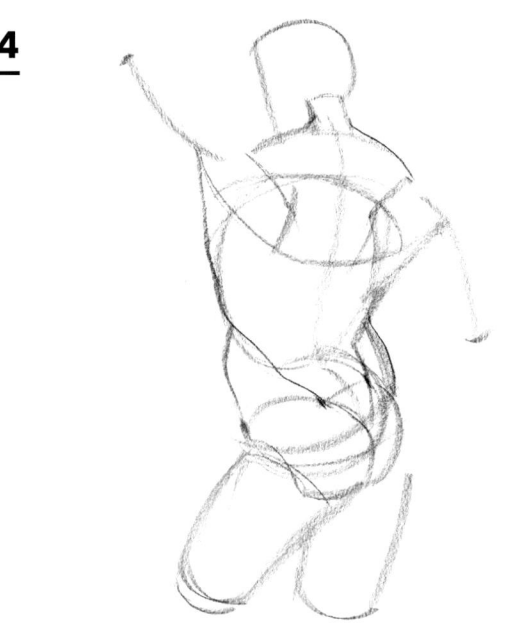

1. Start with the simplified torso skeleton. Analyze the direction of the torso and draw the line of the spine. The lower part of the line will be connected to the triangular shape of the PSIS/Sacrum.

2. Add the Scapula (medial border and spine) and the gesture of the arm.

3. Create the Trapezius, Latissimus Dorsi, and External Oblique following the landmarks. Add the volume of the hip under the PSIS/ Sacrum.

4. Add the head and legs to balance the gesture and proportions.

5

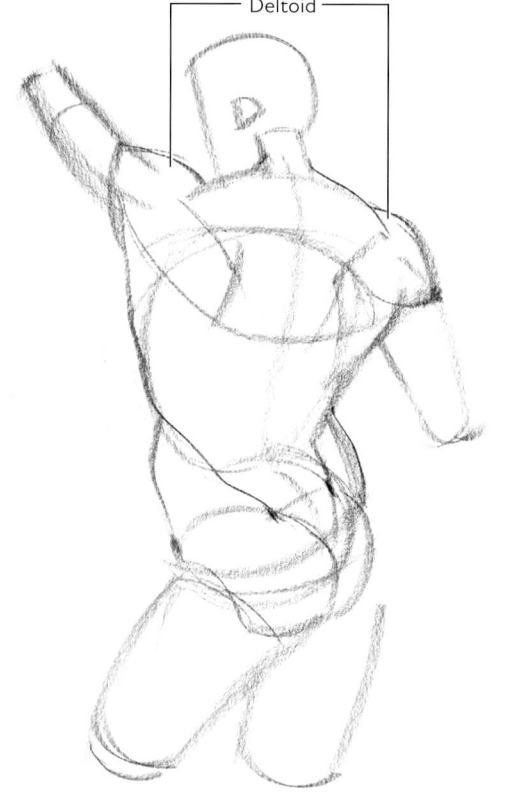

Deltoid

6

Light source

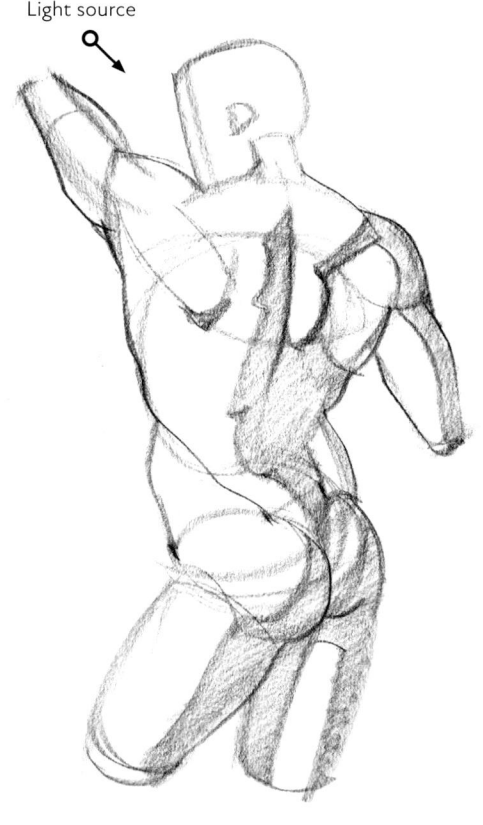

7

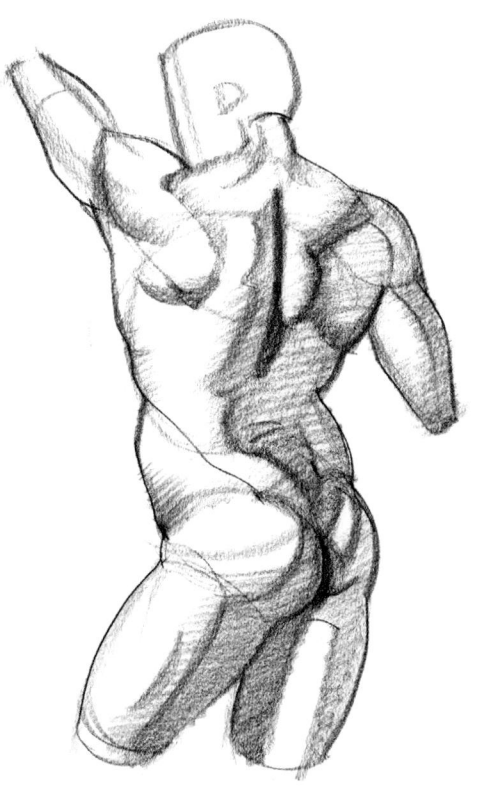

5. Add cylinders for the arms and place the Deltoids on top. The Deltoid muscle sits on both the anterior and posterior side. The construction of the Deltoid should wrap the lateral end of the Trapezius.

6. Analyze the light source. Follow the geometric muscular form and use shading to create an even tone.

7. Continue developing the details and contrast.

Posterior/Lateral

1

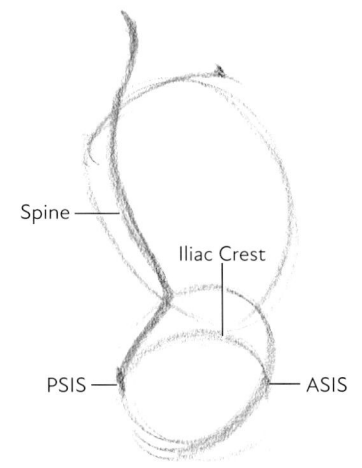

Spine

Iliac Crest

PSIS

ASIS

2

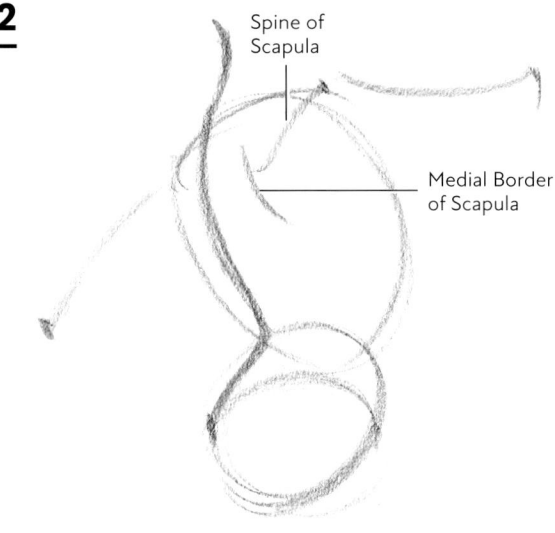

Spine of Scapula

Medial Border of Scapula

3

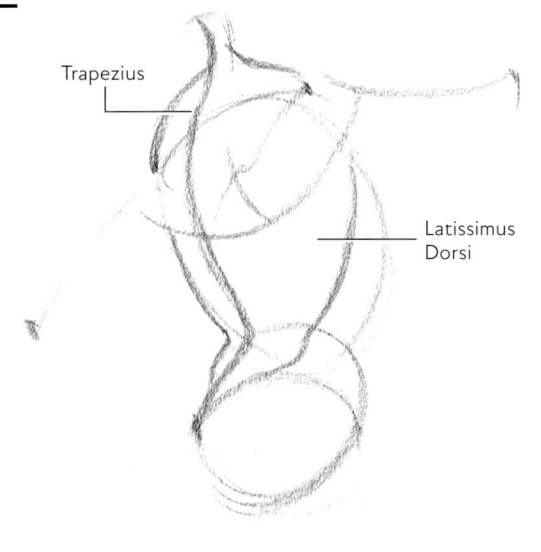

Trapezius

Latissimus Dorsi

4

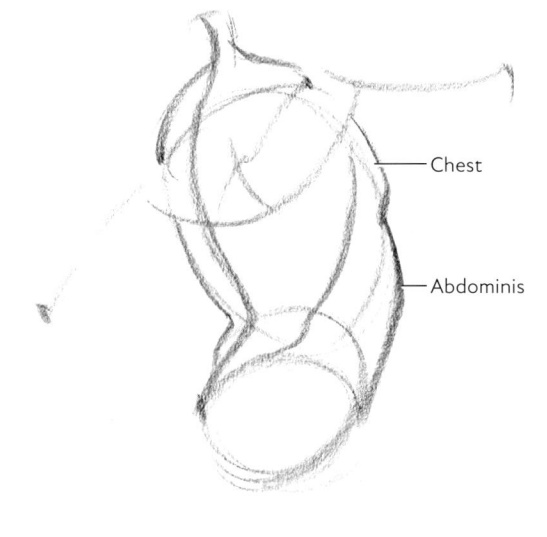

Chest

Abdominis

1. Start with the simplified torso skeleton. Analyze the direction of the torso and draw the line of the spine. From the lateral view, the landmarks of ASIS and PSIS can be applied. Connect them with an arch, which represents the Iliac Crest.

2. Add the Scapula (medial border and spine) and the gesture of the arm.

3. Create the Trapezius and Latissimus Dorsi following the landmarks.

4. Work on the side of torso: Add the shape of the chest and the Rectus Abdominis line, which goes down to the ASIS.

5. Add the head and legs to balance the gesture and proportions.

5

6

Deltoid

7 Light source

8

6. Add cylinders for the arms and position the Deltoids on top. The Deltoid muscle sits on both the anterior and posterior side. The construction of the Deltoid should wrap the lateral end of the Trapezius.

7. Analyze the light source. Follow the geometric muscular form and use shading to create and even tone.

8. Continue developing the details and contrast.

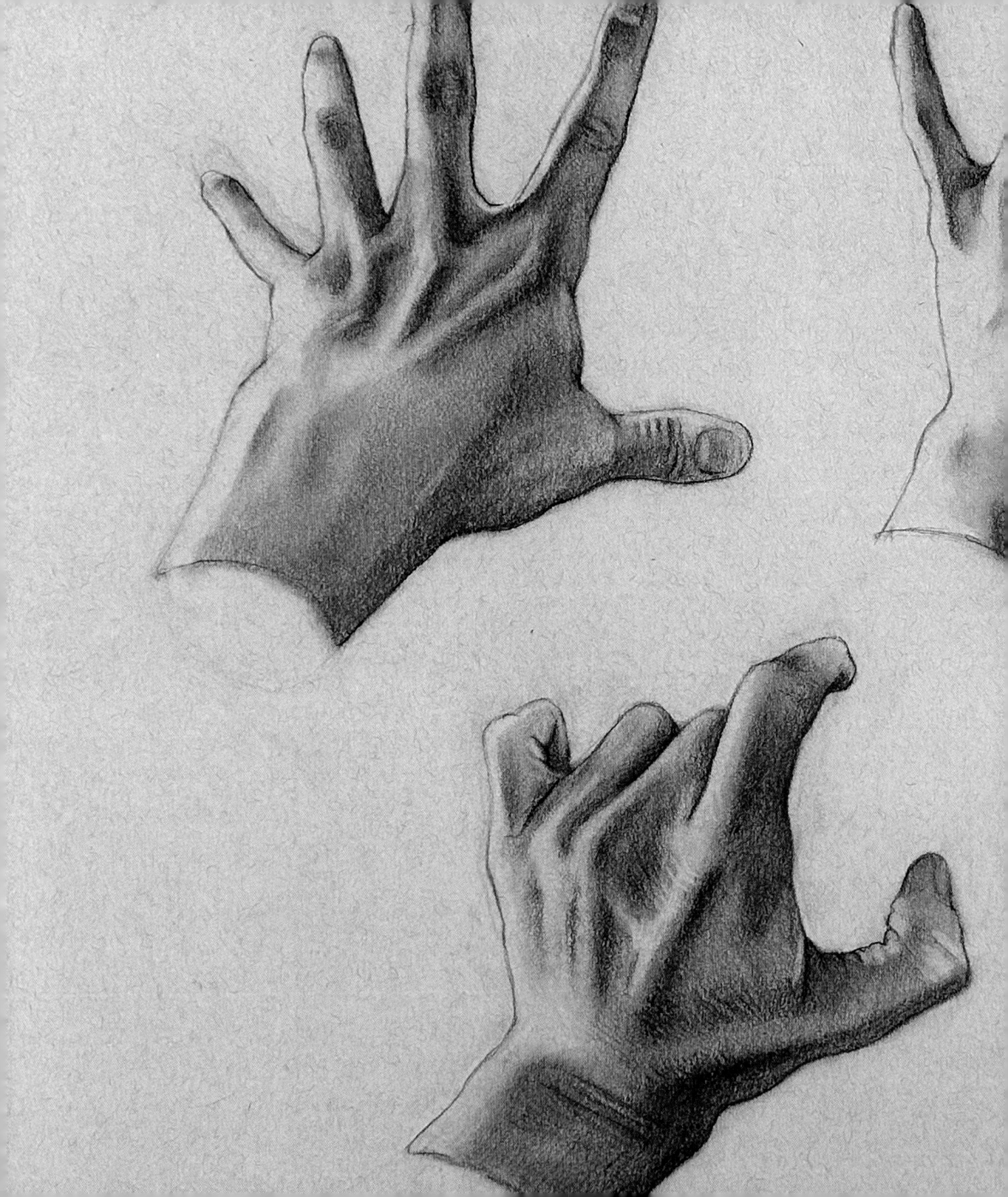

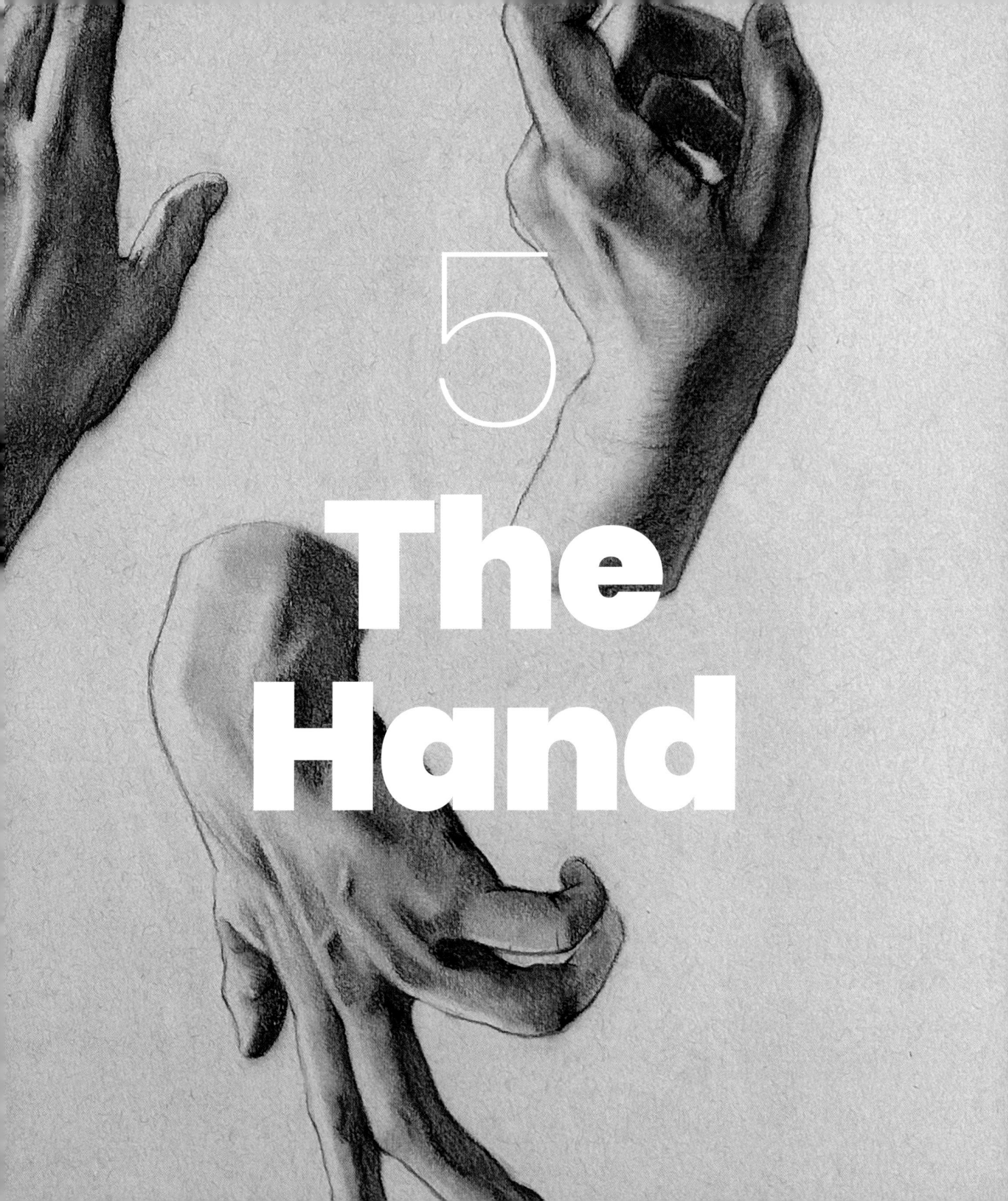

5

The
Hand

Why Is Drawing Hands So Challenging?

Artists often struggle with drawing hands compared to other parts of the body. We all use hands, look at hands, do everything with our hands every day. We are familiar with them, but why is it so challenging to draw hands?

Perspective

You might think of your hand as being flat without having any angles, but often the planes of the hand and/or fingers are foreshortened. So you will have to analyze and adjust the subtle size/angle differences more than you think.

Gestures of the Fingers

Each finger moves like it has a mind of its own. Drawing one hand is like drawing five models at the same time!

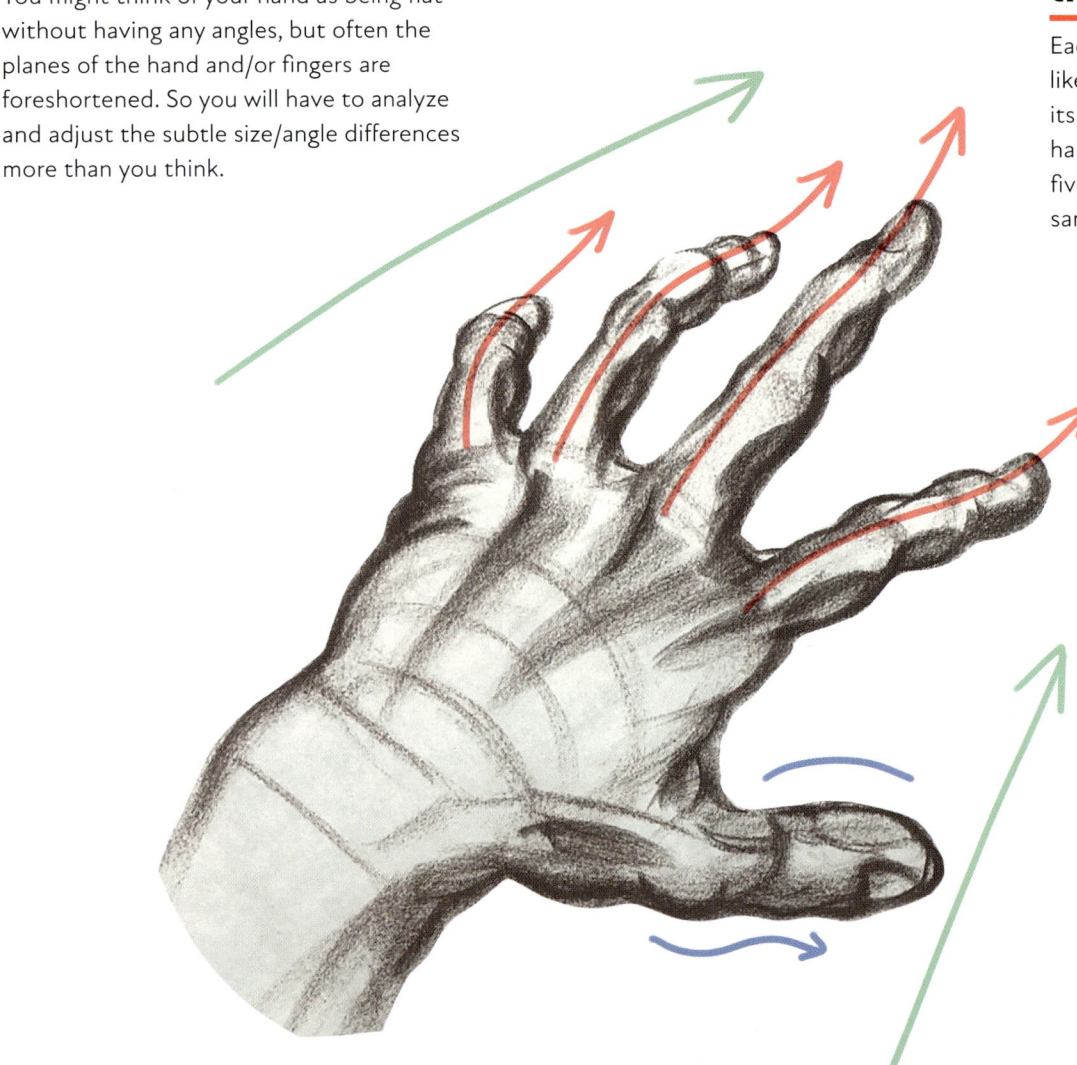

The Asymmetrical Curve Between the Knuckles

When you look at your fingers from the side, you can see a small, outward curve between each knuckle. We have fourteen Phalanges in one hand, so that ought to tell you something.

So where do we start? Let's take a look at the skeletal system of the hands.

Bones of the Hand

We have fifty-four bones in our hands. To improve your hand drawings, it's more helpful to understand the skeletal structure than the muscular structure.

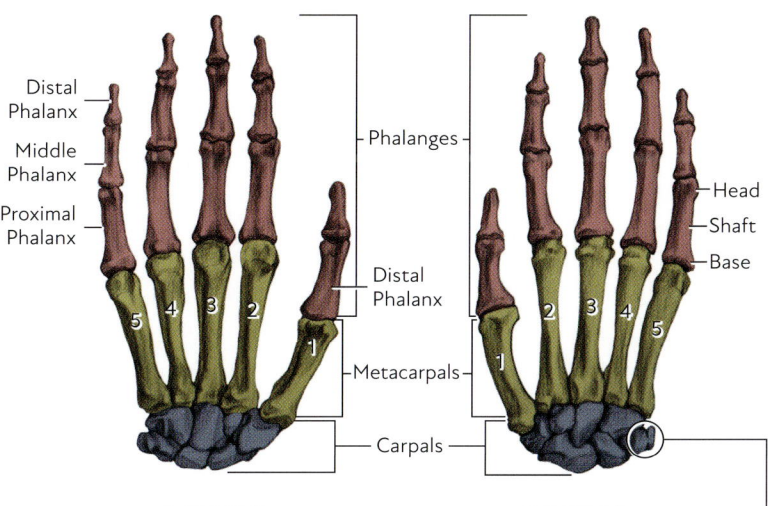

Distal Phalanx
Middle Phalanx
Proximal Phalanx

5 4 3 2 1

Phalanges

Distal Phalanx

Metacarpals

Carpals

PALMAR

Head
Shaft
Base

1 2 3 4 5

DORSAL

The skeleton of the hand can be divided into three major sections: **Phalanges**, **Carpals**, and **Metacarpals**.

Phalanges

The Phalanges are the finger bones. Fingers 2–5 hold three Phalanges each, and finger 1 (the thumb) holds only two Phalanges. This is the opposable thumb that allows us to flex, adduct, and abduct to hold things in our hand.

Metacarpals

The Metacarpals are the palm bones. There are five of these bones in one hand. The Metacarpal region can be used to create the block of the palm in the construction drawing for the hand. It kind of looks like a slice of sandwich bread, and this will be an important base structure of the hand.

Carpals

The Carpals are the group of small, irregular, rock-shaped bones in the wrist. There are eight of them sitting all together in the wrist region. Carpals are not visible in the surface anatomy, but this part will be considered as the proximal end of the hand.

Joints of the Fingers

DIP
PIP
MCP

The joints of the Phalanges make a motion of flexion and extension. The joint that is next to the Metacarpals is called the Metacarpophalangeal (**MCP**) joint. The joint that is in between the first (proximal) and second (middle) Phalanx is called the Proximal Interphalangeal (**PIP**) joint, and the one that is in between the second and third (distal) Phalanx is called the Distal Interphalangeal (**DIP**) joint.

A Built-In Drawing Compass in Your Wrist!

Can you draw a perfect circle without using a compass tool? The **Pisiform** is one of the eight Carpals, and it is located on the medial/anterior side of the wrist. In Latin, pisiform means a "pea," and this small, firm projection can be felt under the skin. You can actually use this projection like the needle of a compass to draw a circle.

Place the pisiform bump on a piece of paper as you hold a pencil. Stabilize your hand, and spin the paper with other hand. You can make a good-looking circle without using a special tool!

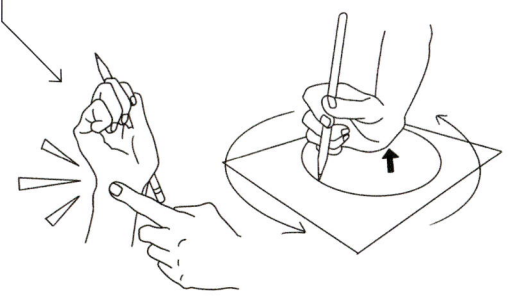

Basic Construction Drawing for a Hand

The Mitten

First, we will take a look at the basic ratio of the hand. To make it easy, let's start with a vertical oval shape. When you draw a curved horizontal line in the middle, the top half of the oval will be the Phalanges area, and the bottom half will be the Carpal/Metacarpal area. This means that the base knuckles of the hand (MCP) are going to be the mid-point of the entire hand.

Continue the curved horizontal line out of the oval on one side and angle it slightly downward. Then draw another curved line up from the bottom of the oval and connect it with the horizontal line to create a triangular form on the side of the oval. Add a small line to represent the opposable thumb. This additional shape will make the entire form looking like a mitten.

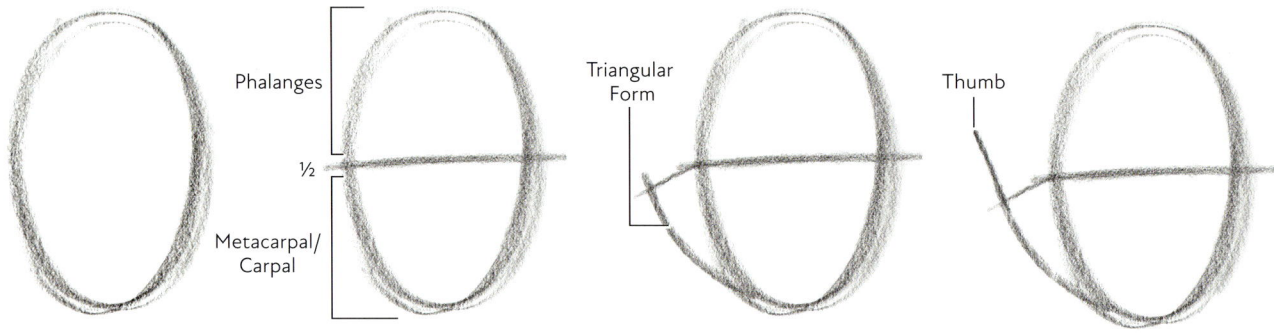

Wire Fingers

To add the other fingers, draw some simple lines, like wires. The fingers are not rigid, but should be softly curved in a relaxed-hand position.

Take a look at your hand; spread your fingers and bring them back again. You'll notice that fingers 1, 2, 4, and 5 make an abduction movement, but finger 3, the middle finger, stays in the center.

The middle finger is the midline of the hand. When the hand is relaxed, fingers 2, 4, and 5 will curve toward the center line. The thumb is the exception, and it usually curves outward, away from the middle finger.

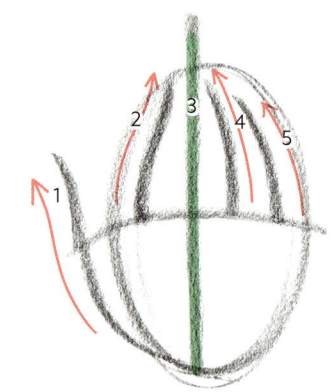

CENTER

Asymmetrical Curve on the Knuckles

To work on fingers 2–5, we must establish the location of the knuckles first. To do so, we will add more horizontal curved lines across the finger lines. Finger 3 (the middle finger) is the tallest, and the peak of each curve will be at finger 3. Fingers 2 (index finger) and 4 (ring finger) are the second tallest, and their heights can be similar. Finger 5 (pinky) will be the shortest of all. Use the curved lines to mark the joints on each finger. These lines should be asymmetrical curves over all the fingers.

The placement of the tip of the thumb can be found by extending the line marking the location of the PIP knuckle.

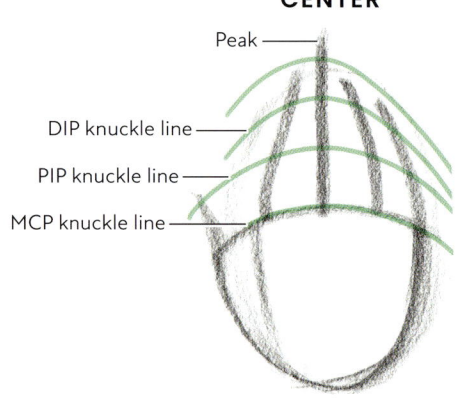

Rules of the Fingers

Fingers and Fat Pad

Fingers are bony structures, but we have some fat with them. Each Phalanx is is shaped like an iconic dog bone. The distal Phalanx with a nail is the exception, as it has a pointy end. When you look at the Phalanges from the side view, the shape of the bone looks like an old school phone with the round volume on each end. The fat pad sits right in between those volumes, and it makes the palm side of the fingers soft and squishy.

Ratio of the Fingers

Fingers 2–5 have three Phalanges each. The proximal Phalanx is the longest, and the distal Phalanx the shortest. The Phalanges decrease in size by approximately 25% from proximal to middle to distal. This number is very similar to the golden ratio.

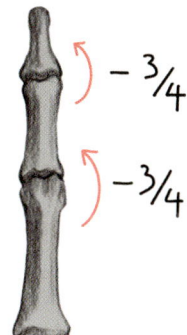

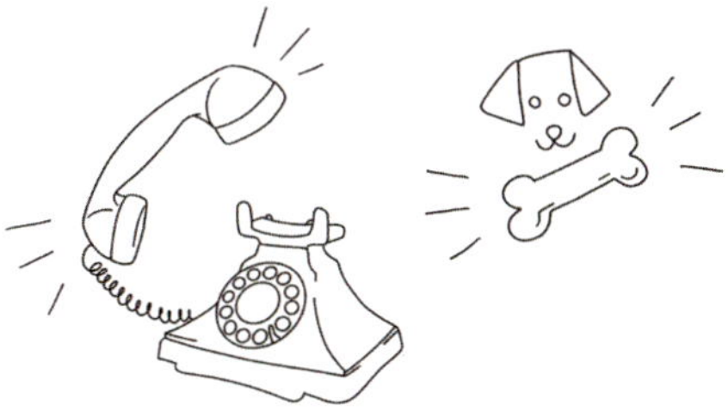

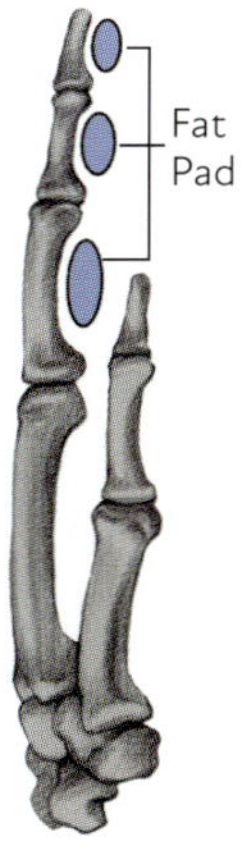

Fat Pad

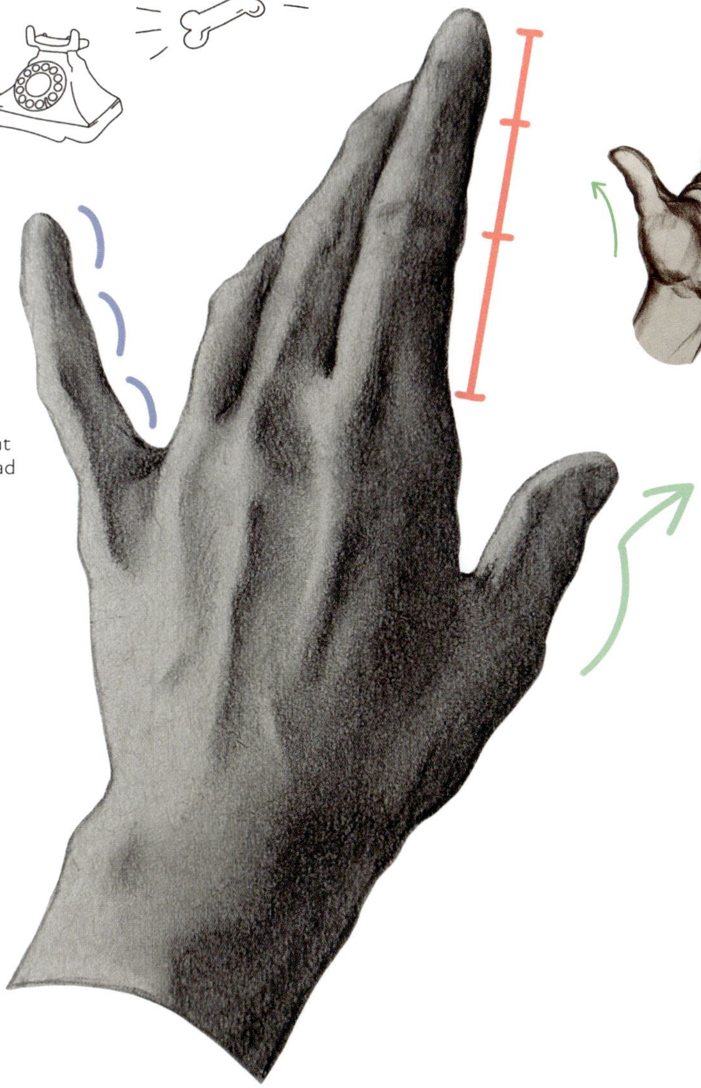

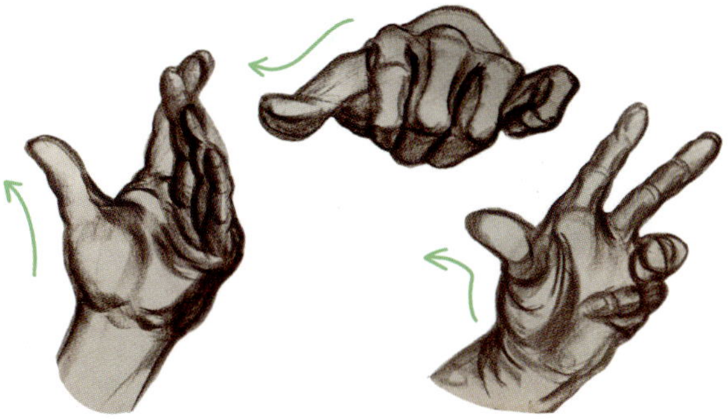

Shape of the Thumb

The finger that has only two Phalanges is the thumb. The thumb has its own unique shape that is different from the other four fingers, but it also has a knuckle that stands out in the flexion motion just like others. It has more of a slanted angle from the distal knuckle to the beginning of the nail. The thumb tip points upward compared to the other fingertips.

Flexion of the Fingers

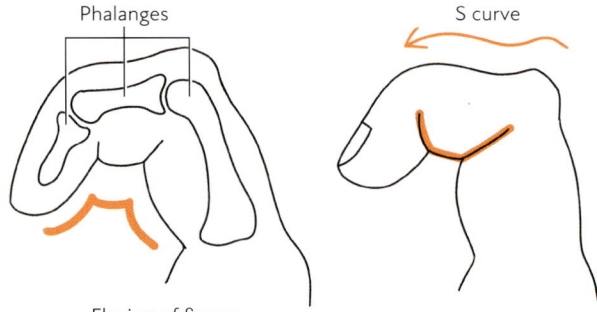

Phalanges

Flexion of finger

S curve

Flex your finger and take a look at it from the side. The finger fat gets compressed when the finger is flexed, and this motion creates the lines in between the fat pads. The knuckles stand out and become firm, which makes the skin tighten and leaves fewer wrinkles. There is a subtle S curve spotted on the dorsal side of the fingers from the toned knuckles.

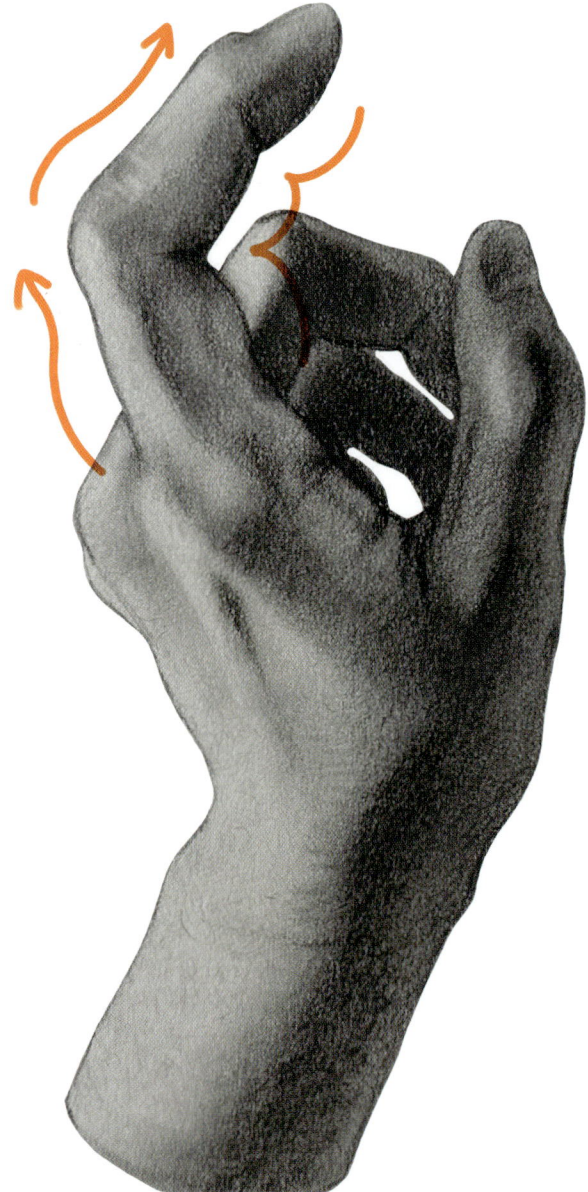

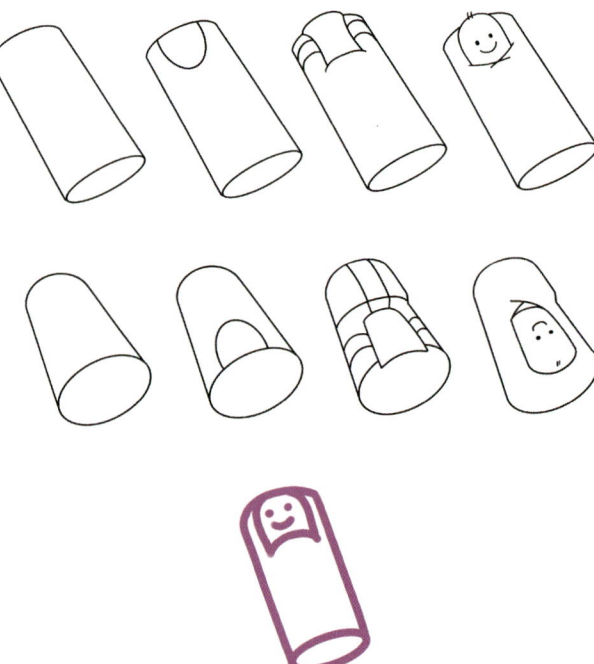

Fingernails: A Baby in the Cradle

Now let's take a look at the distal Phalanx with a nail. Usually, the DIP joint bulges out the most compared to the other finger joints. The nail is like a small sheet of paper that wraps onto the cylindrical volume of the finger. There is a small level difference between the DIP and the nail. This reminds us of a swaddled baby in a cradle.

Tendons of the Hand

On the back of the hand, you can see superficial tendons covered by the thin skin. These tendons often come out on the surface when you hyperextend your wrist and tighten fingers like claws.

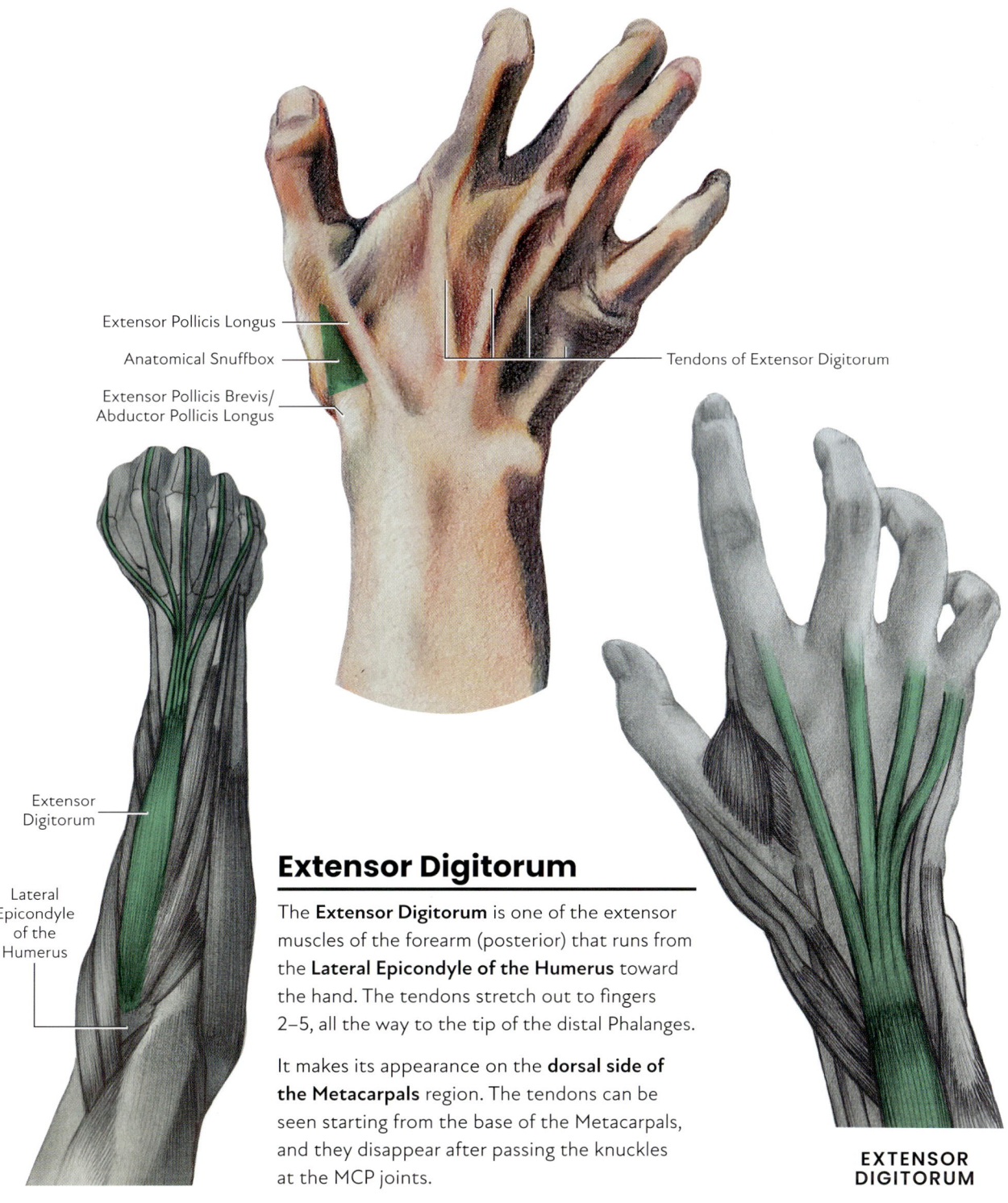

Extensor Pollicis Longus

Anatomical Snuffbox

Extensor Pollicis Brevis/ Abductor Pollicis Longus

Tendons of Extensor Digitorum

Extensor Digitorum

Lateral Epicondyle of the Humerus

Extensor Digitorum

The **Extensor Digitorum** is one of the extensor muscles of the forearm (posterior) that runs from the **Lateral Epicondyle of the Humerus** toward the hand. The tendons stretch out to fingers 2–5, all the way to the tip of the distal Phalanges.

It makes its appearance on the **dorsal side of the Metacarpals** region. The tendons can be seen starting from the base of the Metacarpals, and they disappear after passing the knuckles at the MCP joints.

EXTENSOR DIGITORUM

Veins

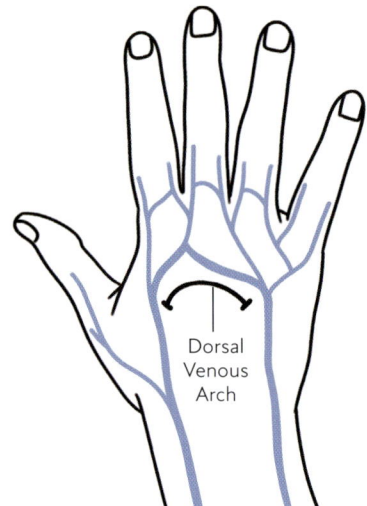

Dorsal Venous Arch

If you have low body fat, you might see some random veins crossing the tendons of your hand. The common dorsal vein is the Dorsal Venous Arch, which is an arched vein that crosses horizontally on the dorsal side of hand. It might not be a perfect arch, but could randomly pop up.

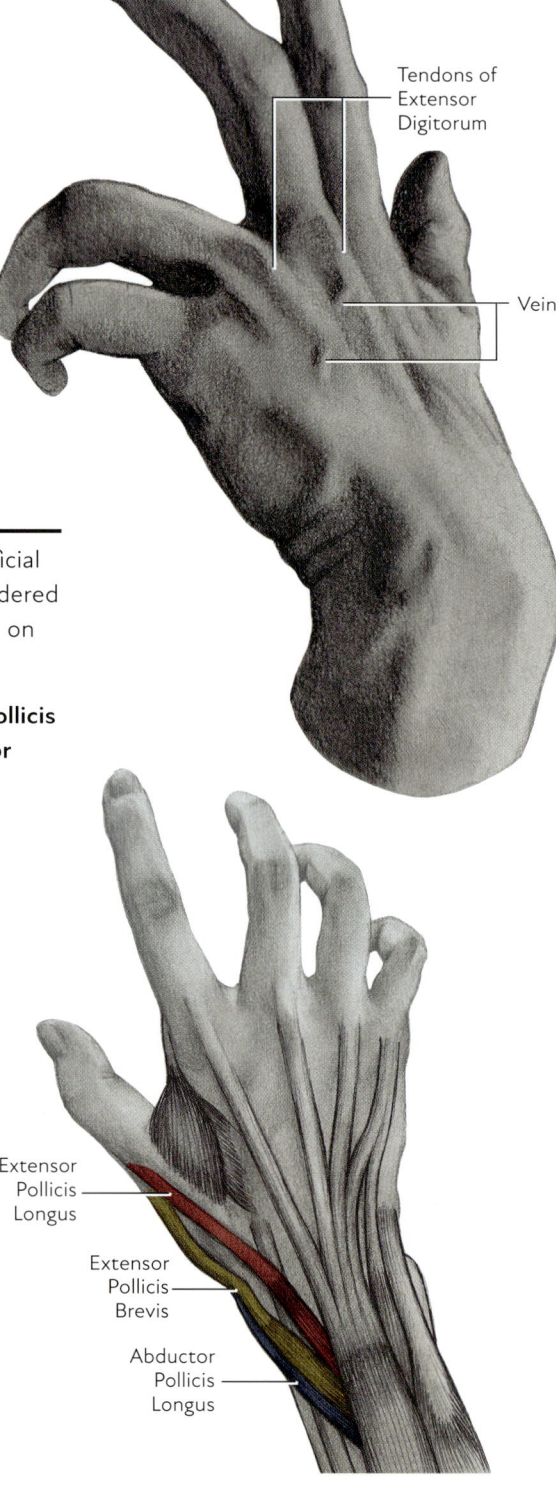

Tendons of Extensor Digitorum

Vein

Anatomical Snuffbox

You might think this term is some kind of a joke, but it is the official name. The **Anatomical Snuffbox** is a triangular space that is bordered by the **Deep Extensor** (posterior) tendons. This space is located on the lateral side of the hand between the thumb and the wrist.

The medial border of the Anatomical Snuffbox is the **Extensor Pollicis Longus**. The lateral border has two muscle tendons: the **Extensor Pollicis Brevis** and the **Abductor Pollicis Longus.**

The origin of the name is from centuries ago when people used to put drugs in this space and sniff them through their nose!

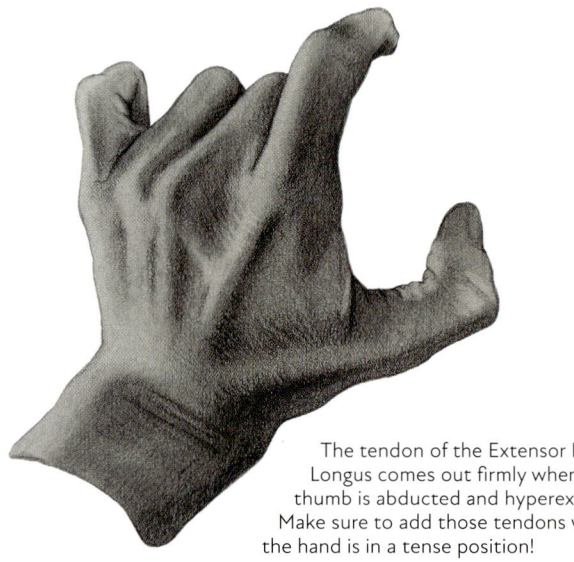

The tendon of the Extensor Pollicis Longus comes out firmly when the thumb is abducted and hyperextended. Make sure to add those tendons when the hand is in a tense position!

Extensor Pollicis Longus

Extensor Pollicis Brevis

Abductor Pollicis Longus

Knuckles and Fist

As we have learned in the basic construction drawing of the hand, the knuckles create the asymmetrical arch. The horizontal line in the knuckles of the MCP is the midpoint of the hand, and the middle finger (3) is the tallest and becomes the center of the hand.

Knuckles

In the lateral view of a finger, we notice that the dorsal side of the finger is much bonier than the other side. The dorsal side creates the unnatural S curve, where the knuckles make the harsh projection and the surface of the Phalanges make a soft curve.

On the palmar surface, the finger has fat pads. When the finger is flexed, those fat pads are compressed together and the side becomes much softer and squishier.

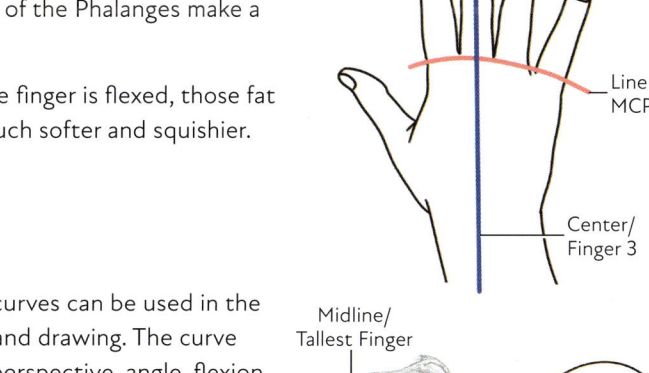

Line of MCP

Center/ Finger 3

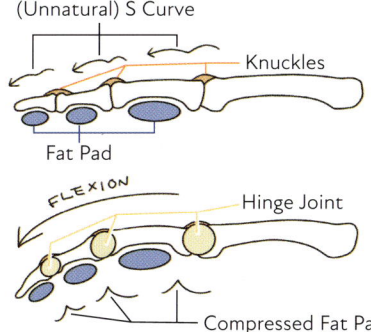

(Unnatural) S Curve

Knuckles

Fat Pad

FLEXION

Hinge Joint

Compressed Fat Pad

The asymmetrical curves can be used in the draft sketch of a hand drawing. The curve should follow the perspective, angle, flexion, and/or gesture of the hand. Imagine that the hand is like a slinky as a whole. The cross-contour lines of the slinky could be the curve lines of the knuckles.

Midline/ Tallest Finger

Think about the differences between the dorsal and palmar sides of the fingers when creating the outlines of the fingers. Analyze the angles of the fingers and figure out where you can see the joint/bone structure or fat pads.

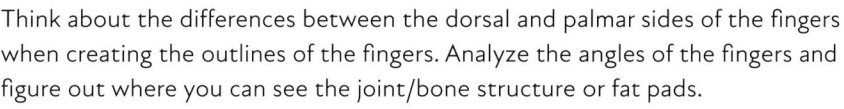

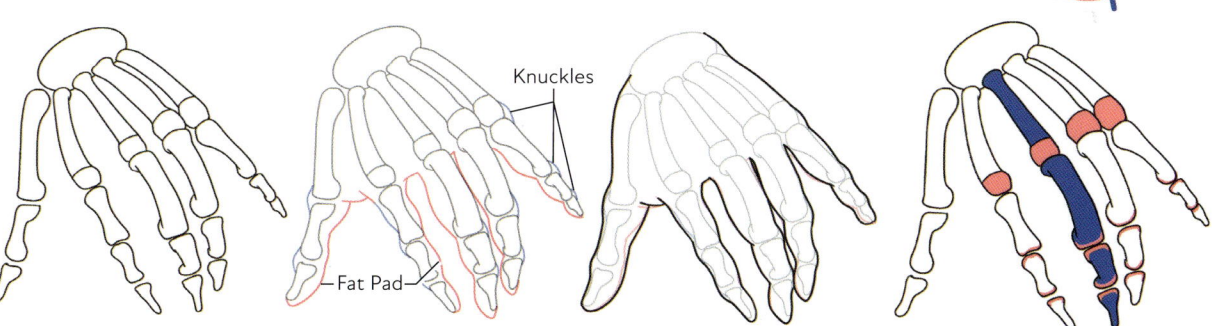

Knuckles

Fat Pad

Knuckles in a Baby's Hand

Babies' knuckles are the opposite of the bony projections in an adult's hand. Because of their extra fat, small dimples can be found where the MCP knuckles are located. Each finger is also covered in fat. Therefore, the dorsal side of the finger has a much softer S curve compared to the adult's finger.

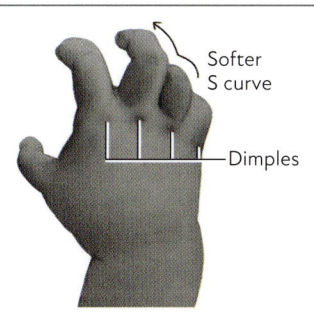

Softer S curve

Dimples

Fist

The fist as a symbol usually represents power and strength. You can easily exaggerate those curves and knuckles to create a mighty fist in your drawing.

Overall Gesture

When the fist is soft, it looks like a simple rectangular box shape. It is symmetrical and there is no stress added. When the fist is tightened, the rectangular shape becomes asymmetrical. The sides start closing toward the bottom, and knuckles 4 and 5 slant down lower.

Fingers

The direction of the fingers also follows the overall gesture of the fist. While the fingers in the soft fist go straight down vertically, the tightened fist shows stronger rhythm. Fingers 4 and 5 tend to lean toward the middle finger. However, finger 2 does not face the middle finger because of the bulged muscles under the thumb.

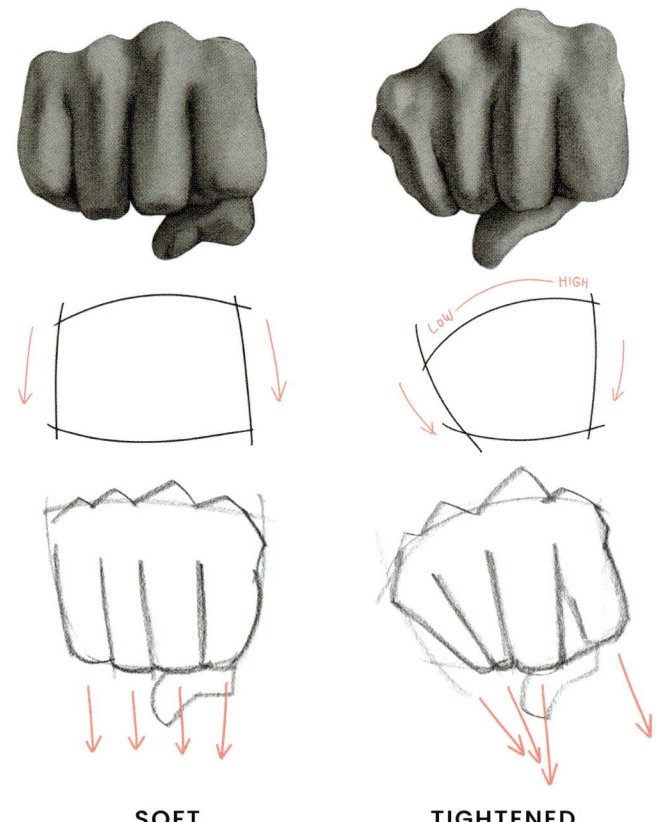

SOFT   **TIGHTENED**

Folded Skin

Bulge of Muscle

Distal Palmar Crease

Skin

There is a specific fold of skin you can see in the tightened fist. It starts appearing by the lateral side of finger 5. This fold is created from the line of the Distal Palmar Crease, which is a horizontal line you can see on the palmar side of the hand. When the fist is tightened, the fold becomes a small triangular shape and peeks out on the lateral side.

Muscles of the Hand

Three Almond-Shaped Volumes That You Can See in the Hand

Most of the markers we use to draw the hand come from the skeletal system, but there are a few muscular volumes in the hand that you can focus on as well: two on the palmar side, and one on the dorsal side. They all have an almond-like shape.

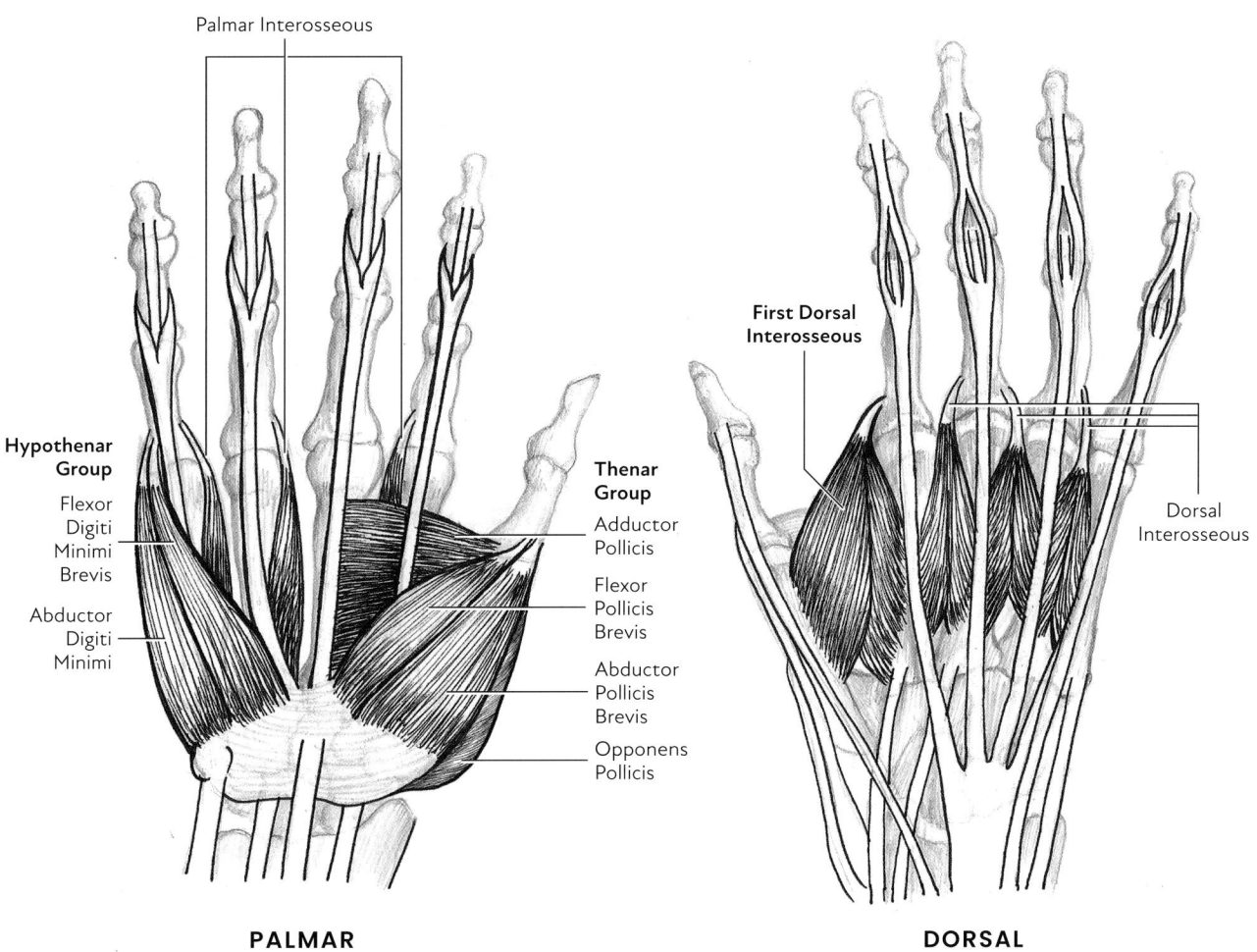

Palmar Interosseous

Hypothenar Group

Flexor Digiti Minimi Brevis

Abductor Digiti Minimi

Thenar Group

Adductor Pollicis

Flexor Pollicis Brevis

Abductor Pollicis Brevis

Opponens Pollicis

First Dorsal Interosseous

Dorsal Interosseous

PALMAR

DORSAL

Trivia: The Lizard-Like Muscle that Vanishes Before Birth

Did you know that the human embryo has a small muscle in the hand that can only be found in reptiles like lizards? This muscle is called the Dorsometacarpales and it disappears before the baby is born!

Palmar

Thenar Group

One of the most important puffing volumes that you can see in the hand is in the palmar side by the thumb. This group of muscles is called the **Thenar Group**. It has four muscles: the **Flexor Pollicis Brevis**, **Abductor Pollicis Brevis**, **Opponens Pollicis**, and **Adductor Pollicis** (deep layer muscle). These muscles support the movement of the thumb.

The Thenar Group starts from the Carpal area, and it is attached to the bones of the thumb. You can see an almond-shaped volume by the thumb that is visible in both opened and closed motion of the hand.

Hypothenar Group

Moving on to the lateral side of the palm, the **Hypothenar Group** has two muscles below the pinky: the **Flexor Digiti Minimi Brevis** and the **Abductor Digiti Minimi**. This group is not as big as the Thenar Group, but it is longer and skinnier.

Dorsal

First Dorsal Interosseous

The muscle on the dorsal side that creates a nice visible volume is called the **First Dorsal Interosseous**. It is located in between the first and second Metacarpal bones. You can see an almond-shaped volume especially when you adduct your thumb.

You can also see the volume being sandwiched in between the Extensor Digitorum tendon on finger 2 and the medial border of the Anatomical Snuffbox. When you extend your thumb, the skin will follow the movement and it contours the shape of this muscle even more.

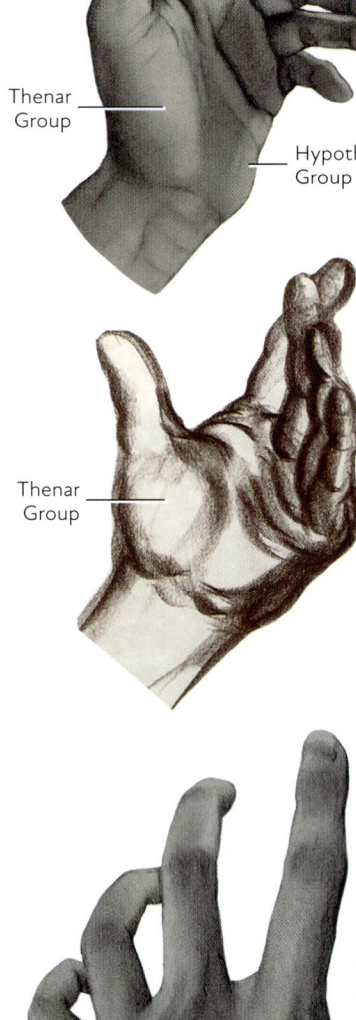

Thenar Group

Hypothenar Group

Thenar Group

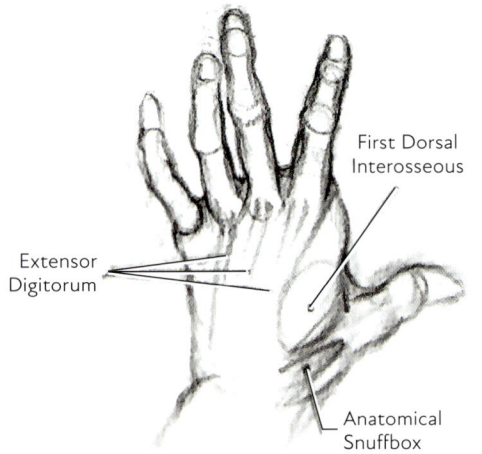

Extensor Digitorum

First Dorsal Interosseous

Anatomical Snuffbox

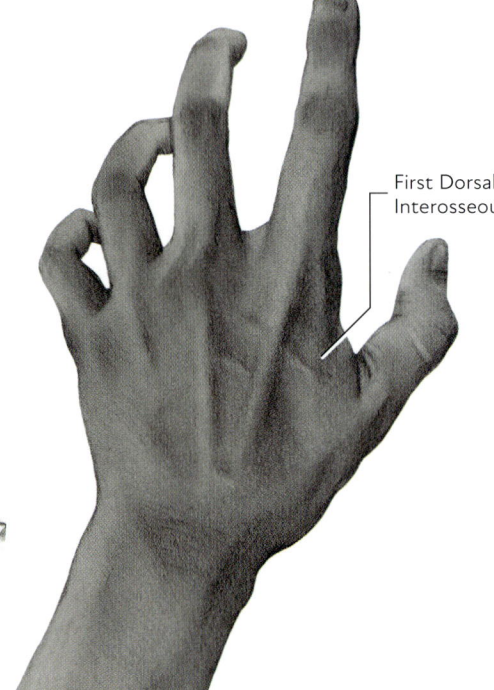

First Dorsal Interosseous

Drawing the Hand

Dorsal

1

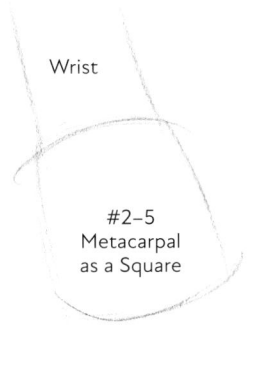

Wrist

#2–5
Metacarpal
as a Square

2

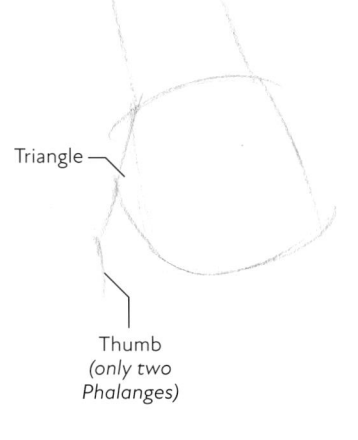

Triangle —

Thumb
*(only two
Phalanges)*

3

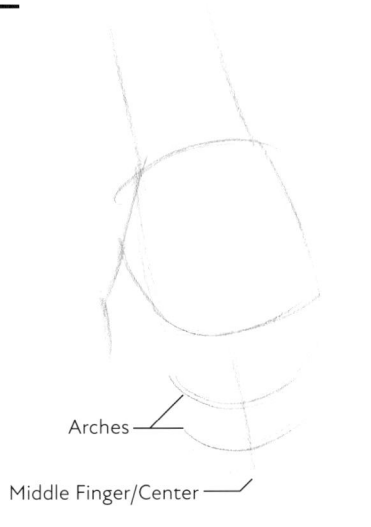

Arches —

Middle Finger/Center —

4

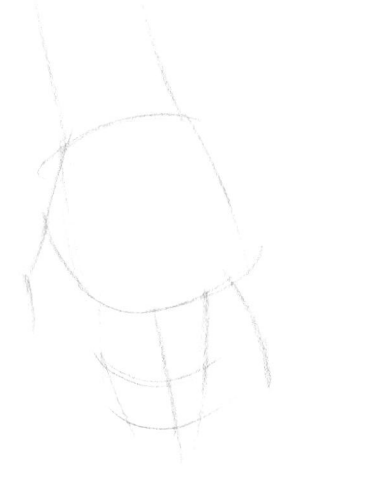

5

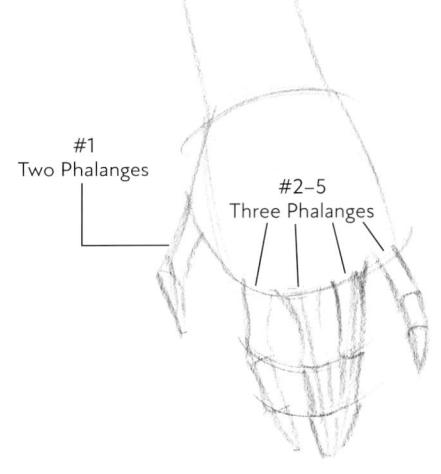

#1
Two Phalanges

#2–5
Three Phalanges

1. Create a square shape for the Metacarpal region of the hand. Outline the wrist.

2. Add on the triangular shape as a connection to the first Metacarpal. Create a wire-thumb with a gesture.

3. Create the arches for the knuckles. Draw a line for the middle finger in the center.

4. Work on the wire fingers. Think about the gestures of each finger.

5. Work on the individual Phalanges. You can use simple cylinders or bone shapes.

Dorsal *(cont.)*

6

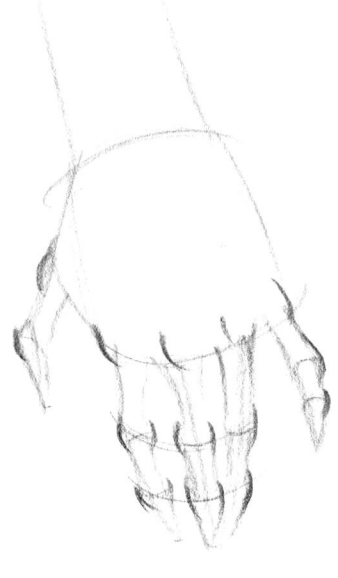

7

8

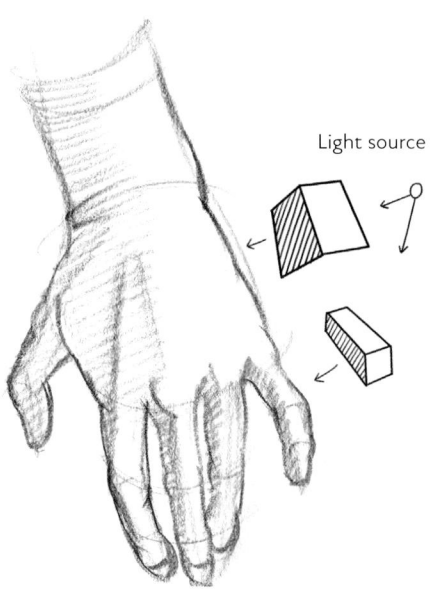

Light source

9

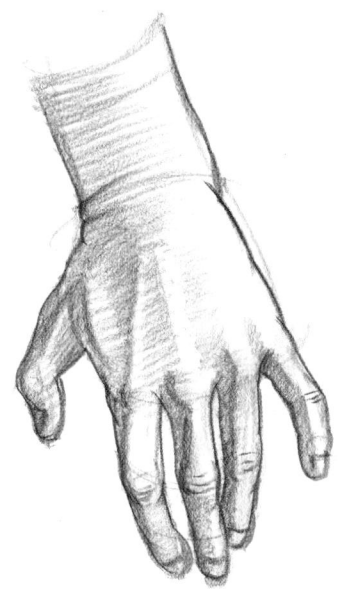

6. Emphasize the knuckles.

7. Work on the outlines. Think about the perspective on each finger and pay attention to the size and length of the fingers.

8. Analyze the light source and work on creating an even tone.

9. Use shading to develop the contrast and details in the image.

Palmar

1

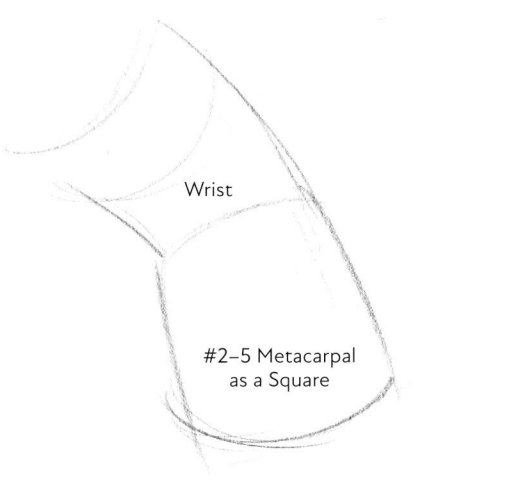

Wrist

#2–5 Metacarpal as a Square

2

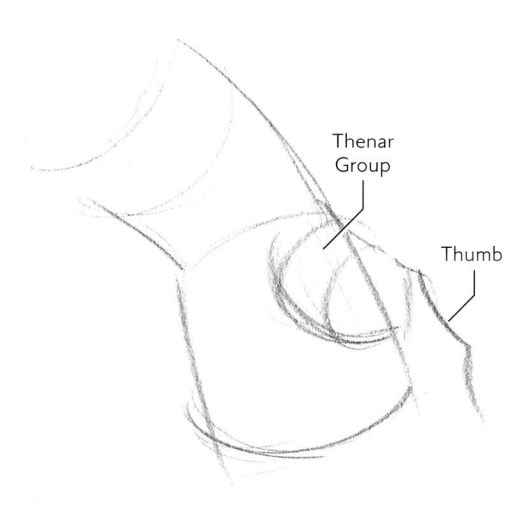

Thenar Group

Thumb

3

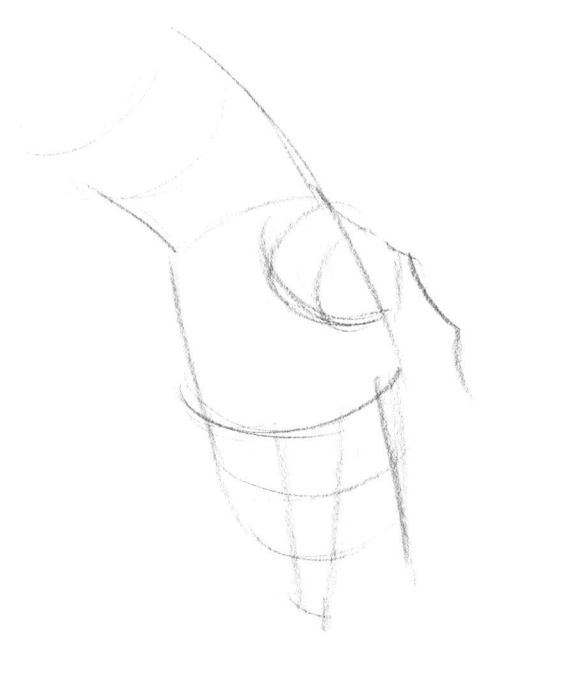

4

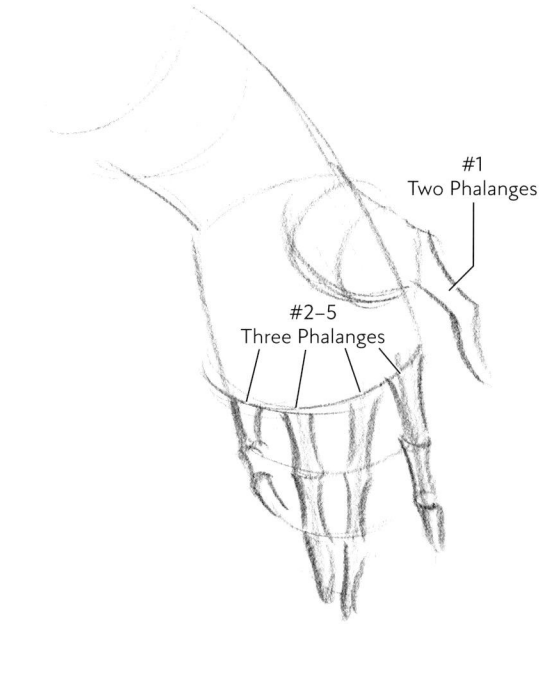

#1 Two Phalanges

#2–5 Three Phalanges

1. Create a square shape for the Metacarpal region of the hand. Outline the wrist.

2. Create an oval volume to represent the Thenar group of the hand. Add a wire thumb with a gesture.

3. Create the arches for the knuckles and work on the rest of the wire fingers. Pay attention to the gestures of each finger.

4. Work on the individual Phalanges. You can use simple cylinders or bone shapes.

5

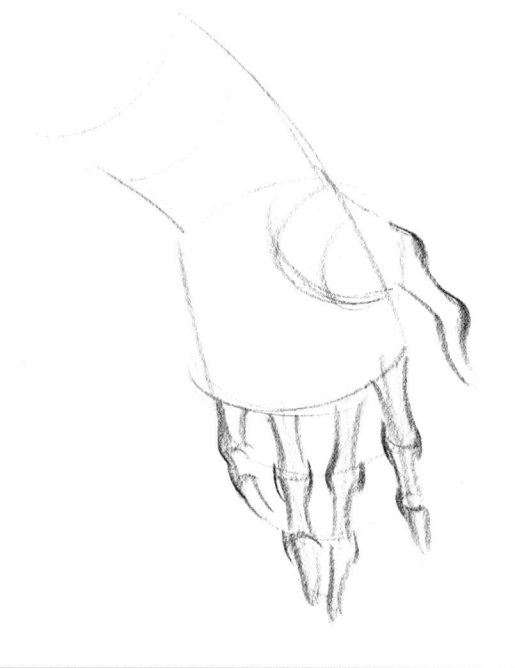

6

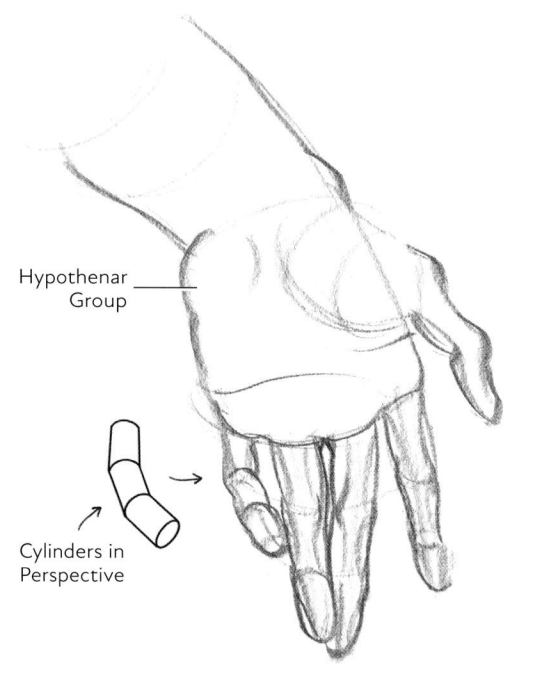

Hypothenar Group

Cylinders in Perspective

7

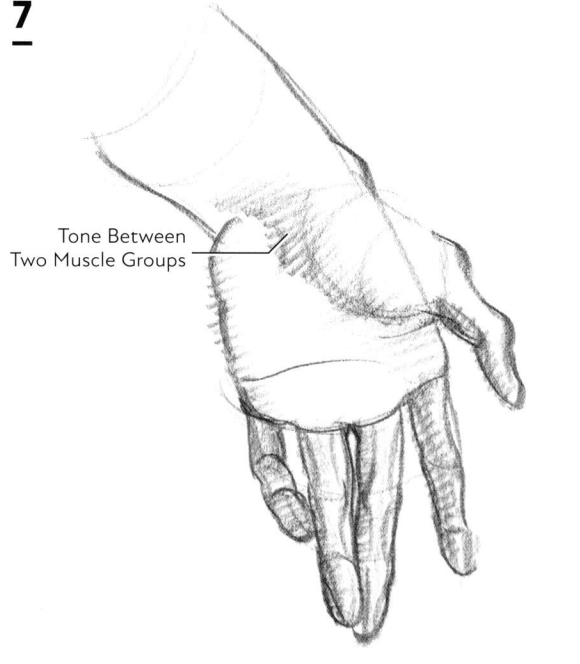

Tone Between Two Muscle Groups

8

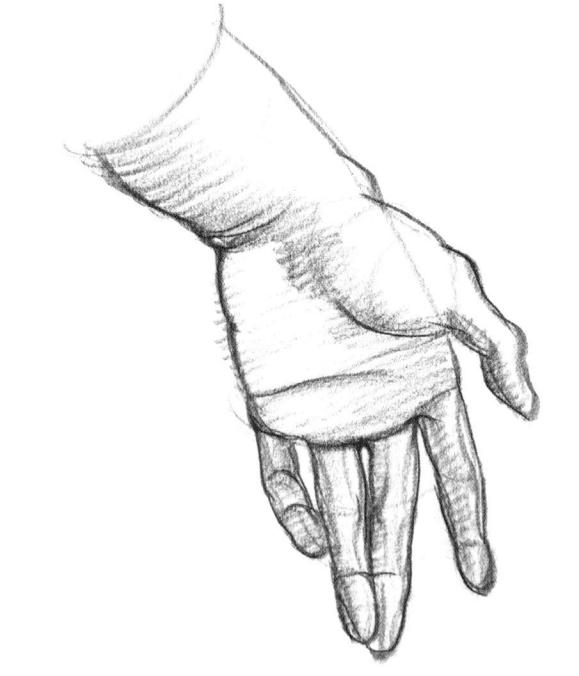

5. Emphasize the knuckles.

6. Work on the outlines and sketch in the wrinkles of the hand. Add a light line to represent the Hypothenar group.

7. Work on creating an even tone.

8. Use shading to develop the contrast and details in the image.

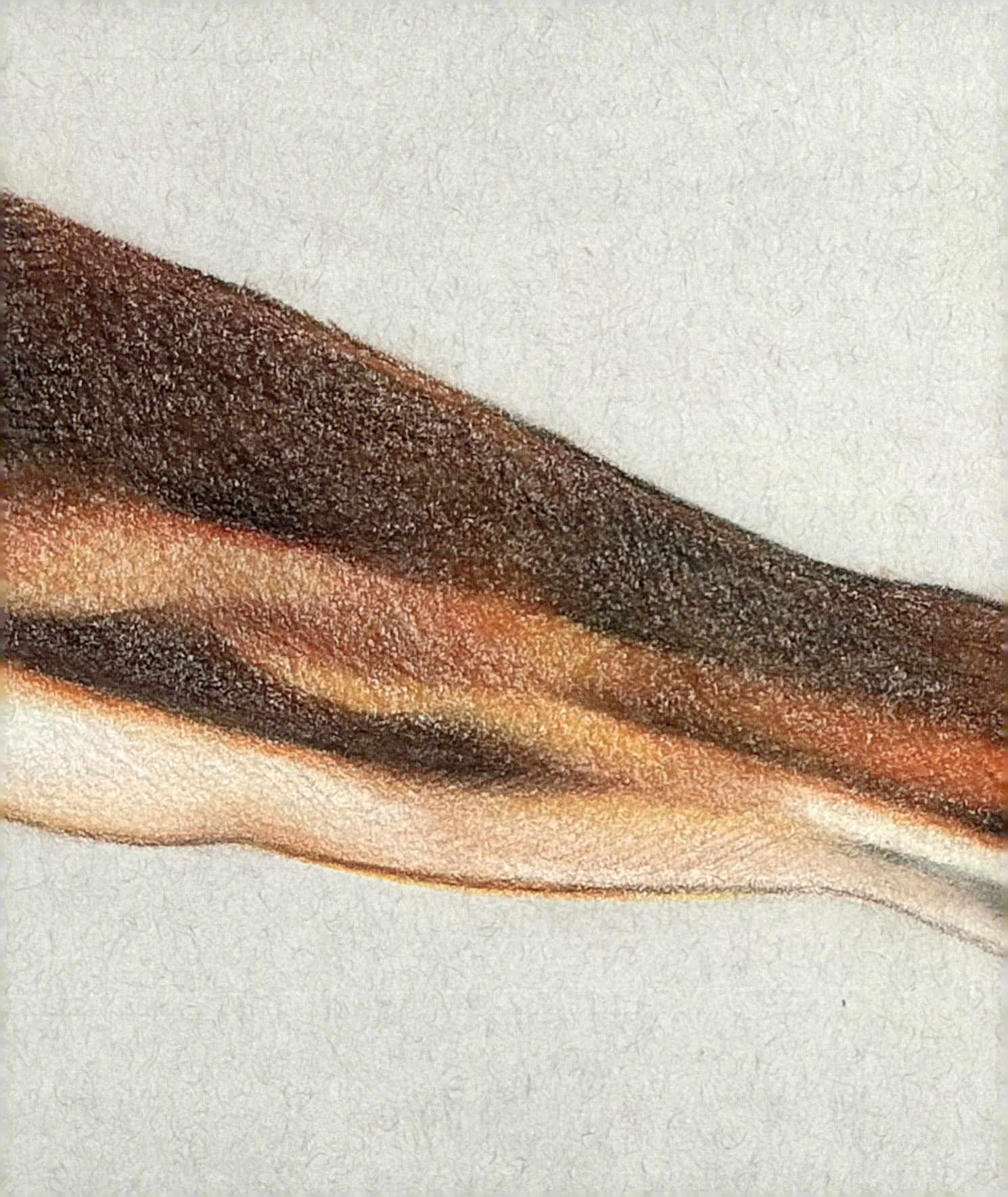

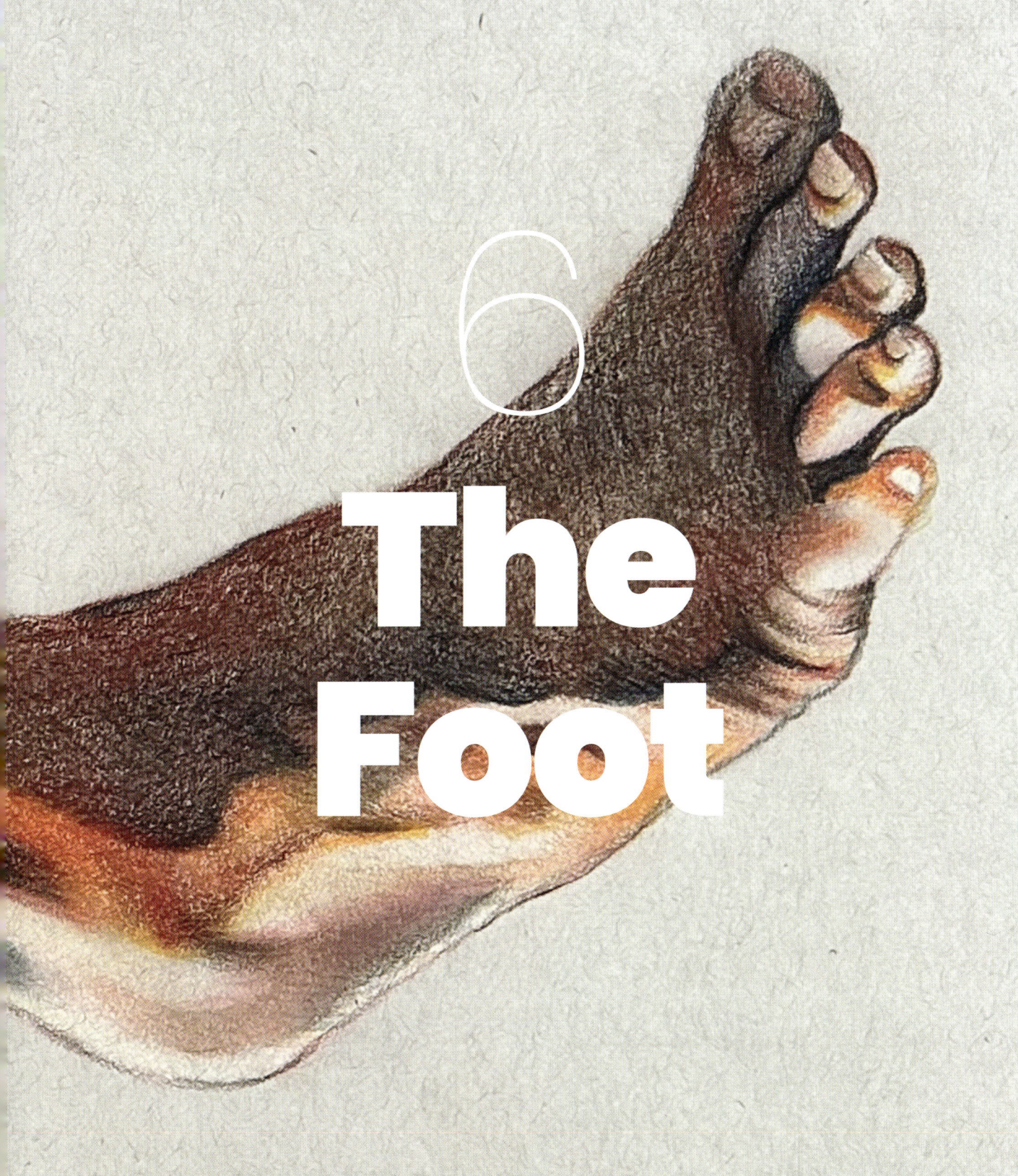

6

The Foot

What Is Your Toe Type?

When you go places where bare feet are the norm, like a pool or yoga studio, you may look down and realize that people have completely different feet. Do I have funny-looking feet, or do they? Well, we all have different-shaped feet, just like we all have different faces and body shapes.

The genetics and origins of foot shape can be traced back to ancient populations. Today, some people even read personality types based off toe alignment. There is no scientific evidence behind this, but it is true that we all have different-shaped feet and toes. Here are some of the major toe types you'll see.

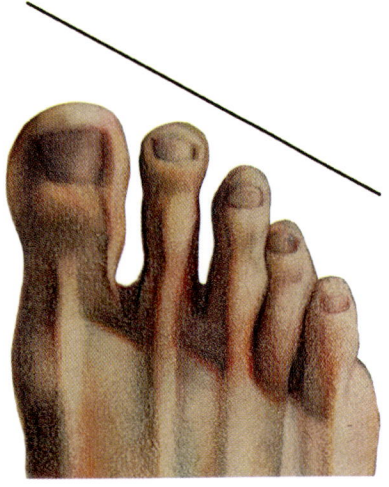

EGYPTIAN
The first toe is the tallest and the rest get progressively smaller toward the fifth toe. This is the most common type of toes.

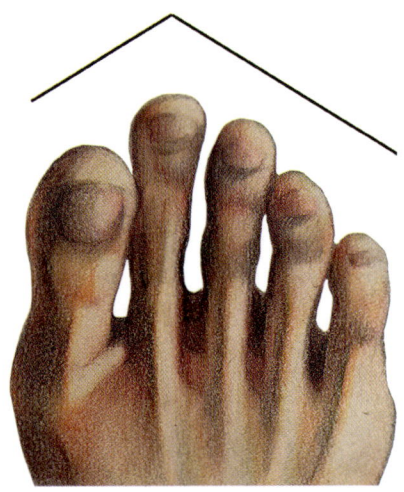

GREEK
The second toe is the tallest. This type of toe is often seen on Greek sculptures.

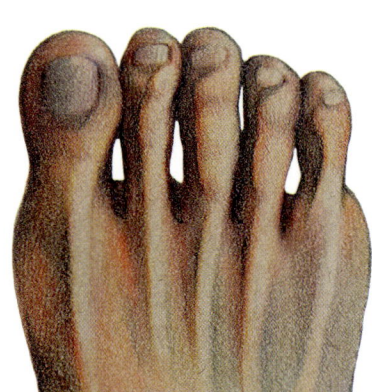

ROMAN
All the toes, or toes 1–3, are the same length. This type of toe is often found in Roman art.

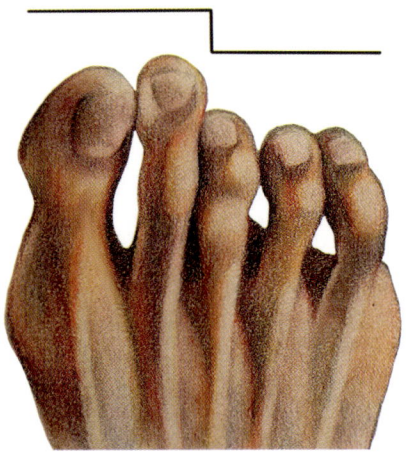

CELTIC
The second toe is the tallest, like with the Greek toes, but the rest of the toes (3–5) make a square-like shape.

Bones of the Foot

The feet are amazing. Think about it, these little bones can hold your entire body weight! We are able to walk, run, jump, and do all kinds of athletic stuff with them. Let's take a look at the skeletal system of the foot to learn its structure.

The structure of the foot bones is similar to that of the bones in the hand. There are three major sections in the foot bones: **Phalanges**, **Tarsals**, and **Metatarsals**.

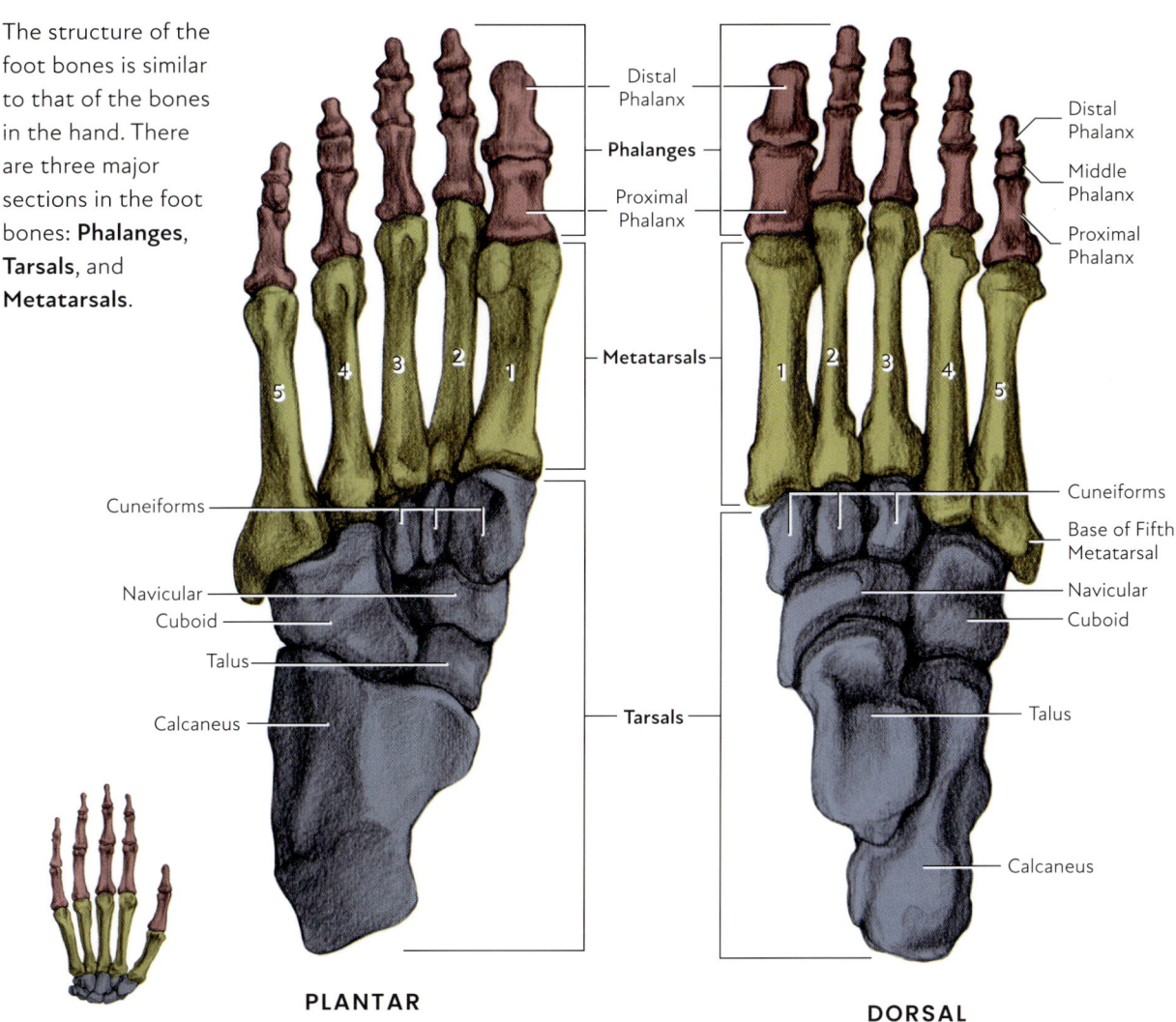

HAND BONES

PLANTAR

DORSAL

Phalanges

The **Phalanges** are the toe bones. The Phalanges have the same number of bones as those in the hand: two in toe 1 (the big toe), and three each in toes 2–5.

Tarsals

The **Tarsals** are a group of seven bones that form under the ankle. Unlike the invisible Carpal bones of the hand, the Tarsals create the heel and show its structure around the ankle.

Metatarsals

The **Metatarsals** are the bridges between the Phalanges and the Tarsals. Similar to the Metacarpals of the hand, they are long and make up the body of the foot. All the Metatarsal bones are similar in shape, except the first Metatarsal, which is shorter and thicker than the others. From the lateral view, the **base of the fifth Metatarsal** sticks out, and it is the midpoint in between the baby toe and the heel.

Basic Construction Drawing of the Foot

The simplified construction drawing of the foot looks like the foot of a robot. Here are some of the key points for making an accurate draft of the foot.

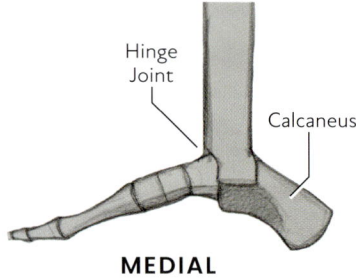

MEDIAL

Hinge Joint
Calcaneus

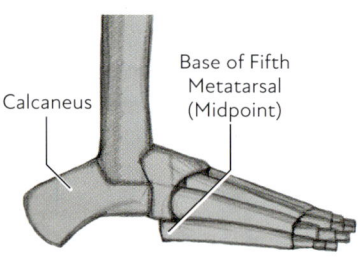

LATERAL

Calcaneus
Base of Fifth Metatarsal (Midpoint)

Ankle Joint

The ankle is formed with the lower leg bones of the **Tibia** and **Fibula**. It becomes a hinge joint that latches onto one of the Tarsal bones called the **Talus**. The ankle joint allows you to make the dorsiflexion/plantarflexion movement and the inversion/eversion movement, in which the sole of the foot faces inward/outward.

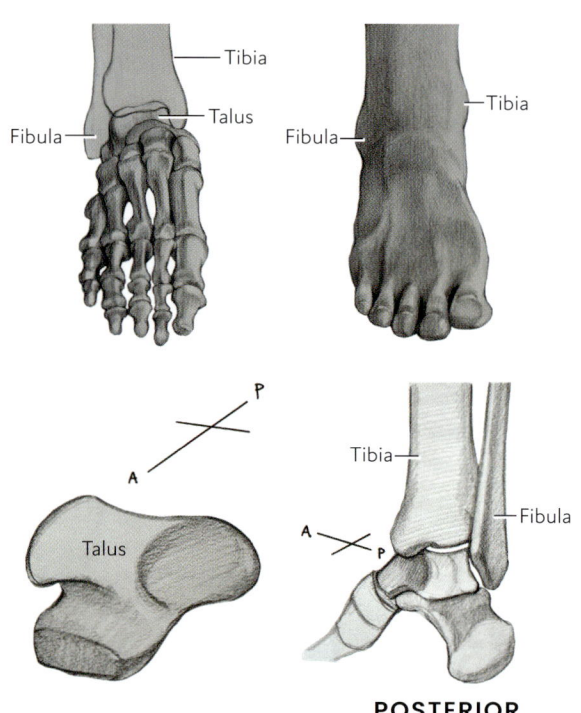

Tibia
Talus
Fibula

Tibia
Fibula

Talus

Tibia
Fibula

POSTERIOR

The Heel Bone

There is one large blocky bone that forms the heel called the **Calcaneus**. The Calcaneus is a part of the Tarsal bones, and it is the largest bone of the foot. It projects posterior to the Tibia and Fibula, and the bone becomes the attachment of the Achilles Tendon from the calf muscles.

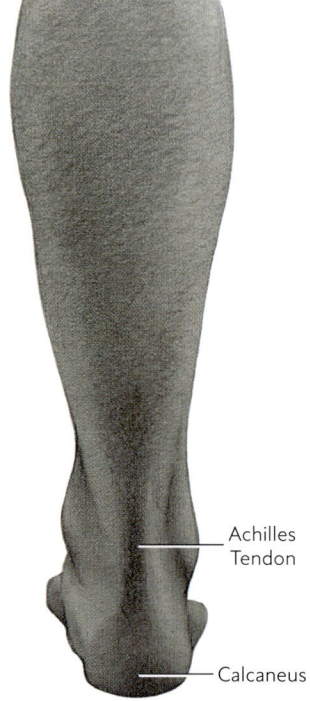

Achilles Tendon
Calcaneus

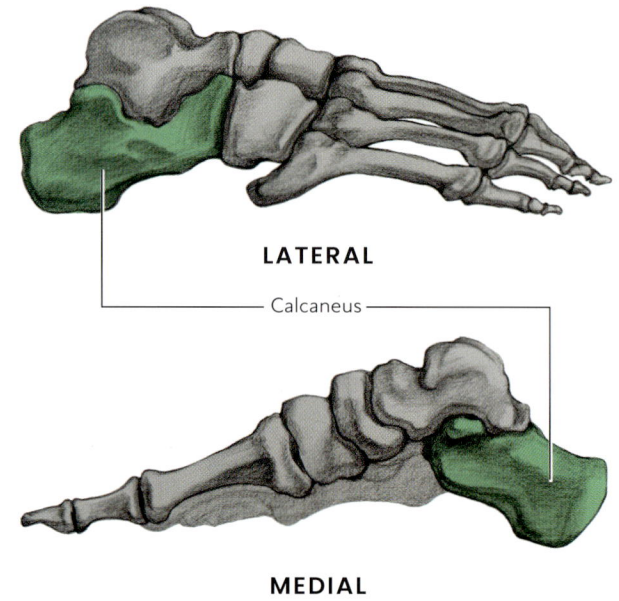

LATERAL

Calcaneus

MEDIAL

Arches of the Foot

The three arches—the **Medial Arch**, **Lateral Arch**, and **Transverse Arch**—make the foot flexible and strong. They work to absorb the shock under the foot in motion.

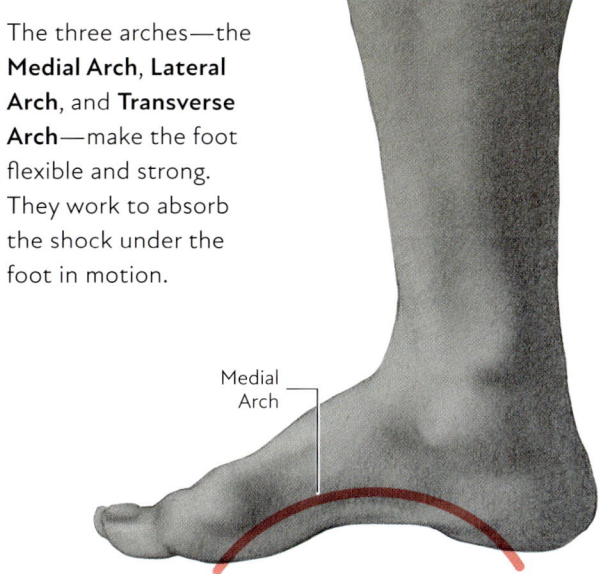

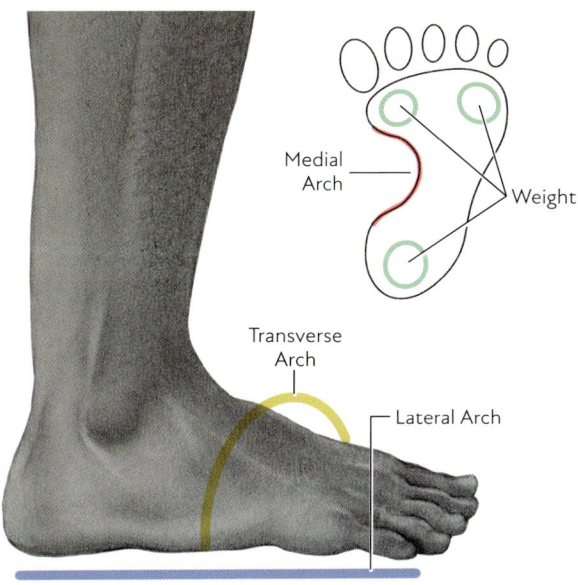

Medial Arch
The **Medial Arch** is the arch found on the medial side of the foot. The body weight is held on three points in the sole. The iconic footprint image shows where the medial side is. The curved line of the footprint is formed because the medial arch does not touch the ground.

Lateral Arch
The **Lateral Arch** is not quite as curved as the Medial Arch. It is flatter and touches the ground when you're standing.

Transverse Arch
The **Transverse Arch** is the dorsal arch of the foot. The arch is asymmetrical, with its peak on the line in between **the first and second toes**. From this peak, the curved line slants down toward the lateral side of the foot. The arch is taller near the Tarsal bones, and it gets flatter near the Phalanges.

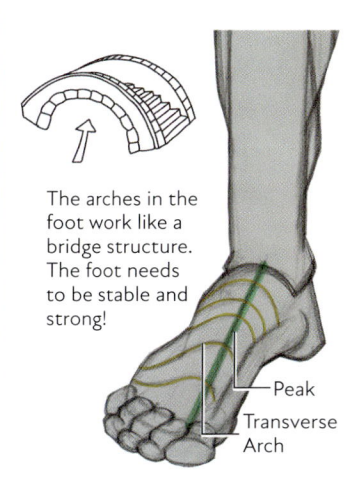

The arches in the foot work like a bridge structure. The foot needs to be stable and strong!

Overview of the Foot

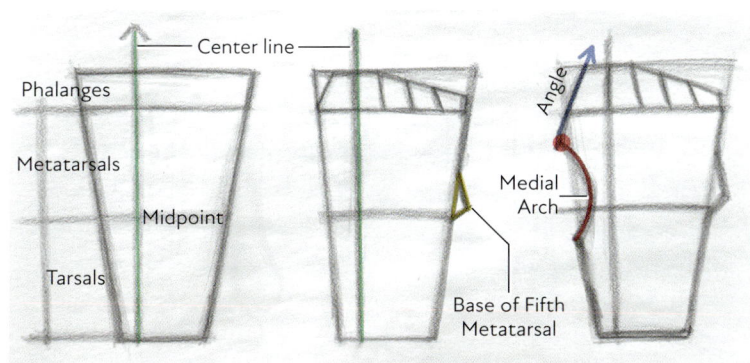

The midpoint of the foot bones in the Tarsal and Metatarsal region is on the base of the fifth Metatarsal bone.

The center line (peak) of the Transverse Arch is in between the first and second toes.

The base of the fifth Metatarsal sticks out from the overall form of the foot.

The Medial Arch emphasizes the projection of the head of the first Metatarsal, making a slanted angle toward the big toe.

Rules of the Toes

There are different types of toes, but there are certain anatomical rules that fit the majority of people.

Dorsal

The construction drawing of the toes is comprised of small cylindrical shapes. Because the feet are on the ground most of the time, it's easy to use a foreshortening technique with the geometric shapes. For the nails, imagine small square pieces of paper wrapped onto the cylinders.

Toes 2–4 have a staircase shape. The "step" on the proximal and middle Phalanges is a bit taller, and the distal Phalanx levels down and looks like it is gripping onto the ground.

Toe 5 looks like a small bean that curves inward.

The big toe is similar to the thumb of the hand, and the tip of it goes upward.

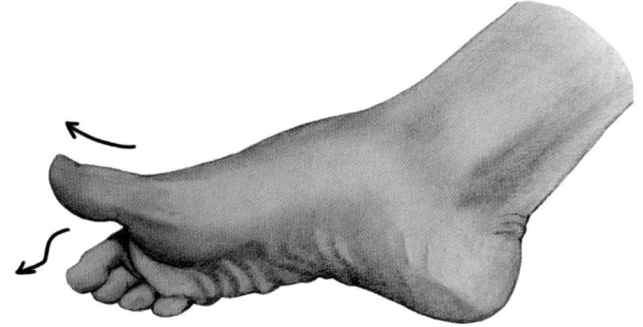

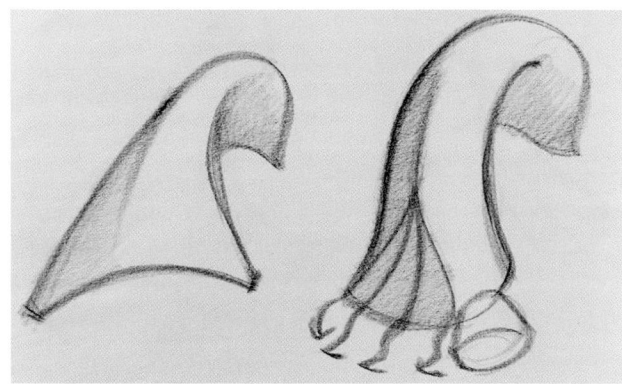

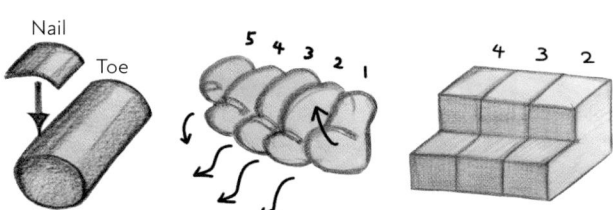

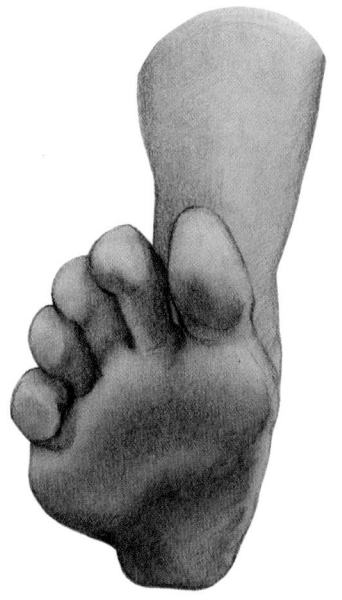

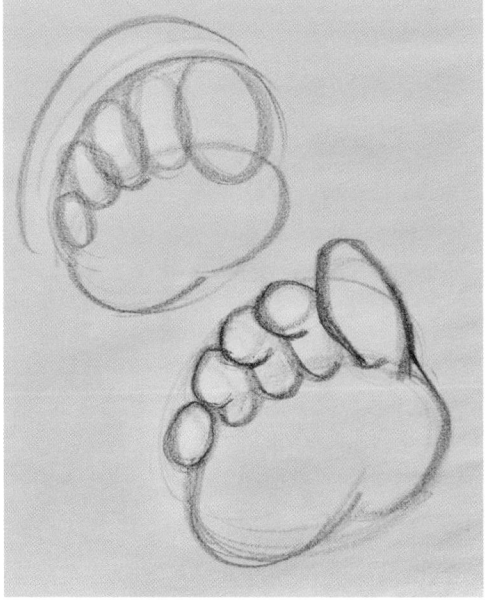

Plantar

The top of the toes creates an arch, and the toes get progressively smaller from toe 1 down to 5. The big toe (1) has a diamond shape, toes 2–4 are shaped like small mushrooms or ear pods, and toe 5 is shaped like a bean.

The Footprint

Plantar of the Foot

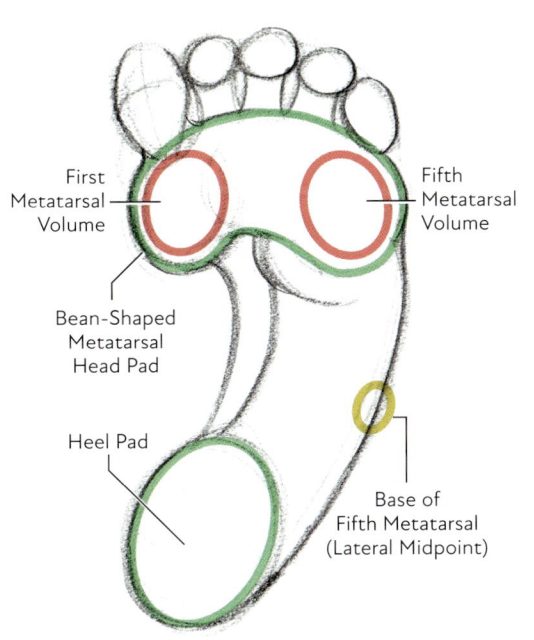

First Metatarsal Volume

Fifth Metatarsal Volume

Bean-Shaped Metatarsal Head Pad

Heel Pad

Base of Fifth Metatarsal (Lateral Midpoint)

Just like the iconic footprint images out there, we have a specific volume on the plantar of the foot. It has three points that support the bodyweight like a tripod in a standing position. One is on the heel with the Calcaneus bone. The heel mark is an oval volume. The second and third points are under the toes, where the weight sits on Metatarsal heads. There are two circle-shaped volumes under toe 1 and toe 5, and the region under all the toes becomes a bean-shaped volume.

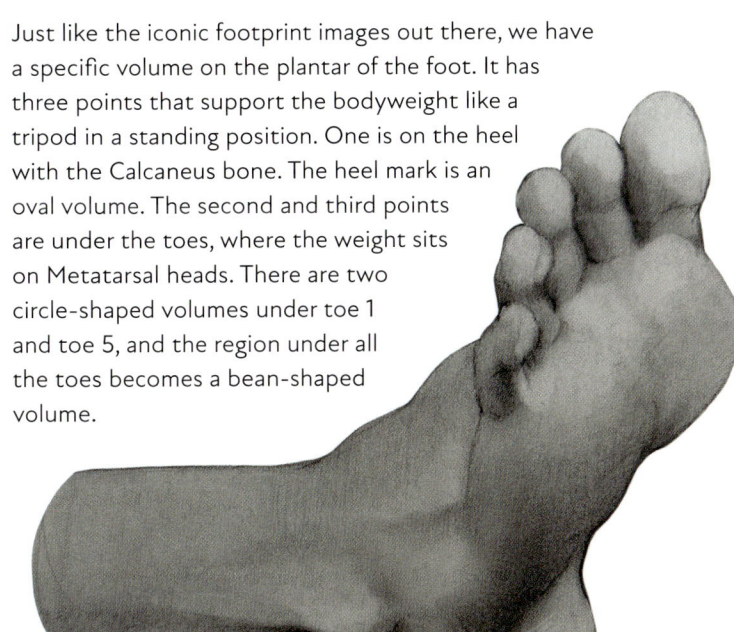

Along the lateral side of the foot is a long cylindrical volume, which is comprised of the muscle group called the **Lateral Plantar Muscles**. There are different layers in the plantar of the foot, but here we have one major muscle that forms the lateral volume along with the fat pad—the **Abductor Digiti Minimi.**

Sound familiar? We talked about muscles with the same name in the arm and hand chapters. The words Digiti Minimi mean "small finger." Every time you hear this phrase, you can assume that it has something to do with the little finger or toe. The Abductor Digiti Minimi in the foot runs from the Calcaneus bone to the base of the proximal fifth Phalanx.

Because the lateral arch of foot is flatter, it appears as a tube-like volume.

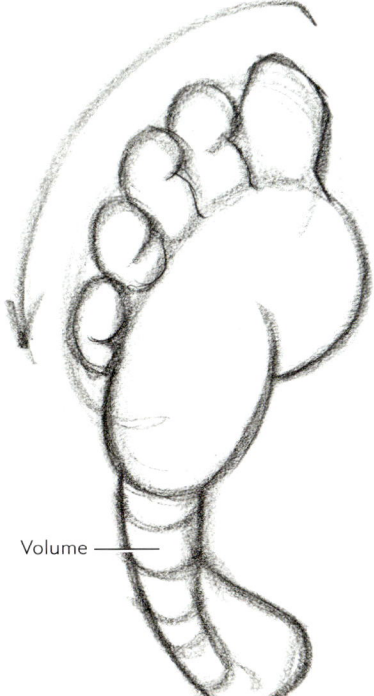

Volume

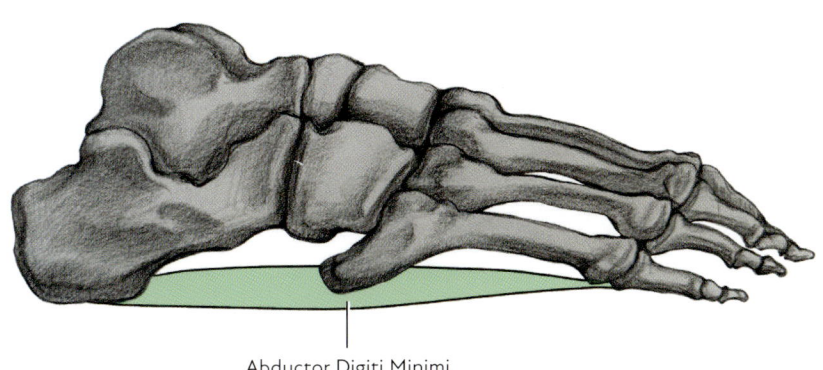

Abductor Digiti Minimi

Tendons of the Foot

The dorsal side of the foot has the superficial tendons that are visible in artistic anatomy.

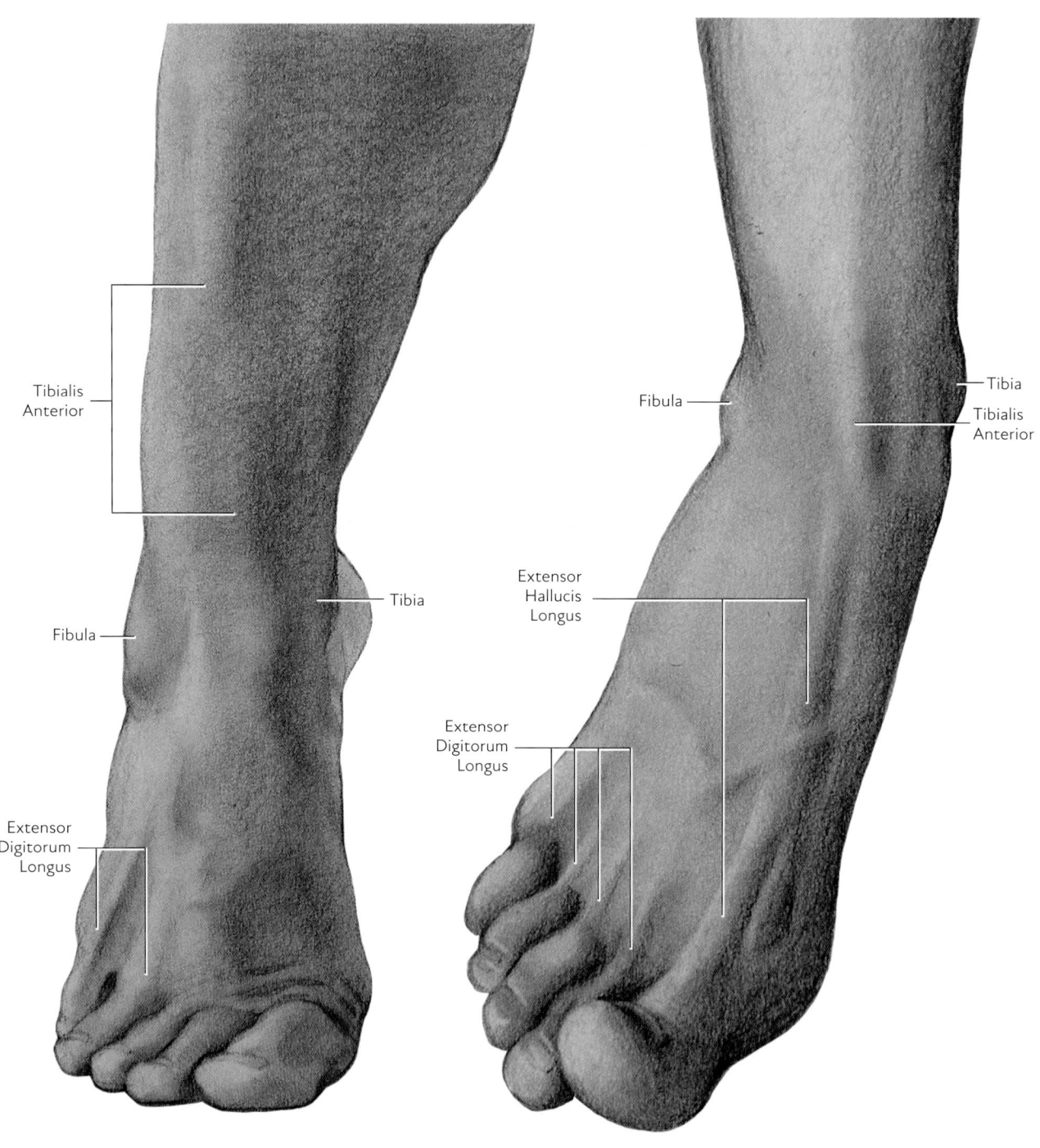

Tibialis Anterior

Fibula

Tibia

Extensor Digitorum Longus

Fibula

Tibia

Tibialis Anterior

Extensor Hallucis Longus

Extensor Digitorum Longus

Extensor Digitorum Longus

Similar to the Extensor Digitorum in the forearm, the **Extensor Digitorum Longus** is a muscle in the anterior lower leg. The tendons spread out toward toes 2–5 on the dorsal side of the foot, which are the same digits the Extensor Digitorum tendons spread toward in the hand. Some people can see the tendons in the relaxed position, but they become more visible when you extend your toes.

The tendons start appearing above the Tarsal region. They are most visible on the distal part of the Metatarsal region and start disappearing toward the toes.

Extensor Hallucis Longus

The **Extensor Hallucis Longus** is a thin, small muscle, but its tendon makes a firm tube-like appearance on the dorsal side of the foot. The muscle is attached to the mid-shaft of the Fibula bone. It runs diagonally and the tendon stretches out to the big toe. This tendon is much thicker compared to the tendons of the Extensor Digitorum Longus. It acts to extend the big toe.

Tibialis Anterior

You might notice that there is another tendon that runs right above the Extensor Hallucis Longus tendon. This is a tendon of the **Tibialis Anterior**. The Tibialis Anterior is a muscle located on the anterior of the lower leg, lateral to the Tibia. You can see the volume of the muscle as well as the tendon that runs into the sole of the foot from the medial side.

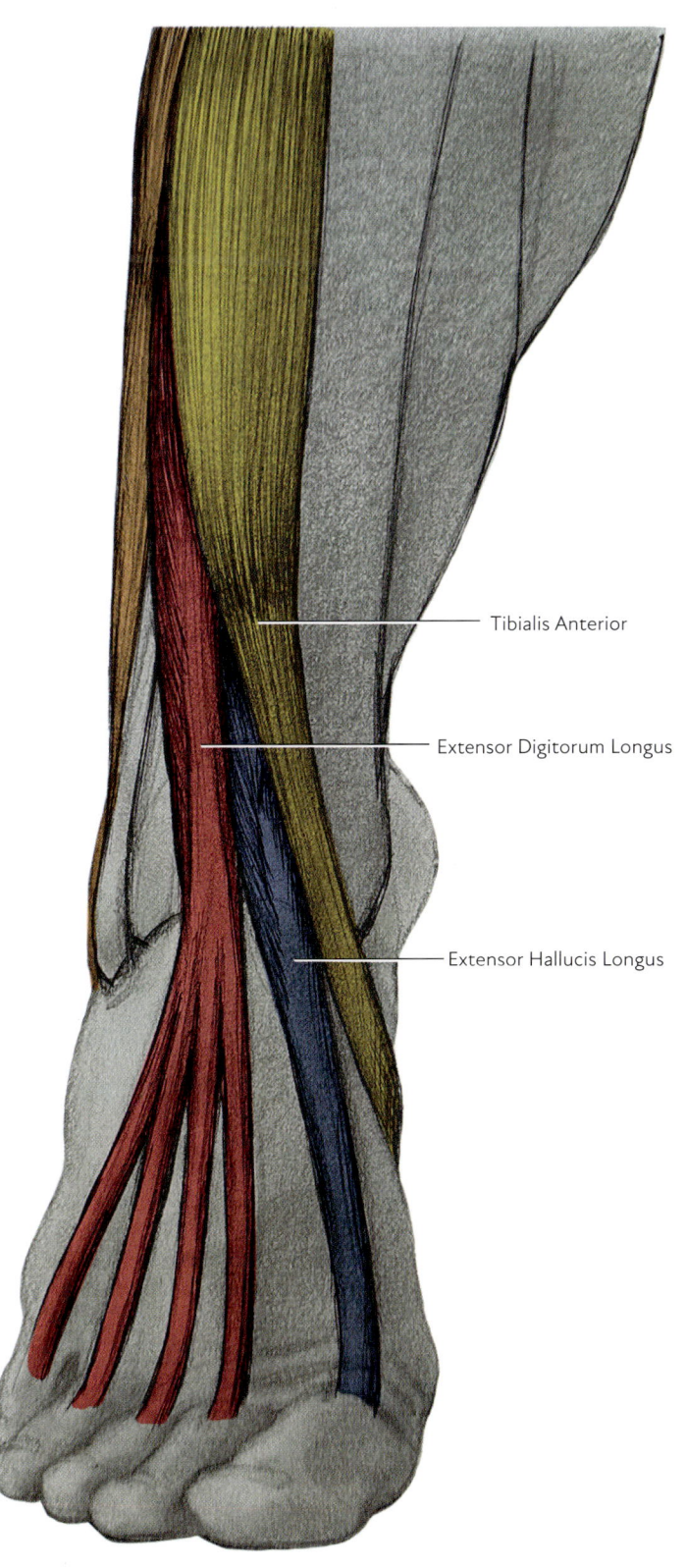

Tibialis Anterior

Extensor Digitorum Longus

Extensor Hallucis Longus

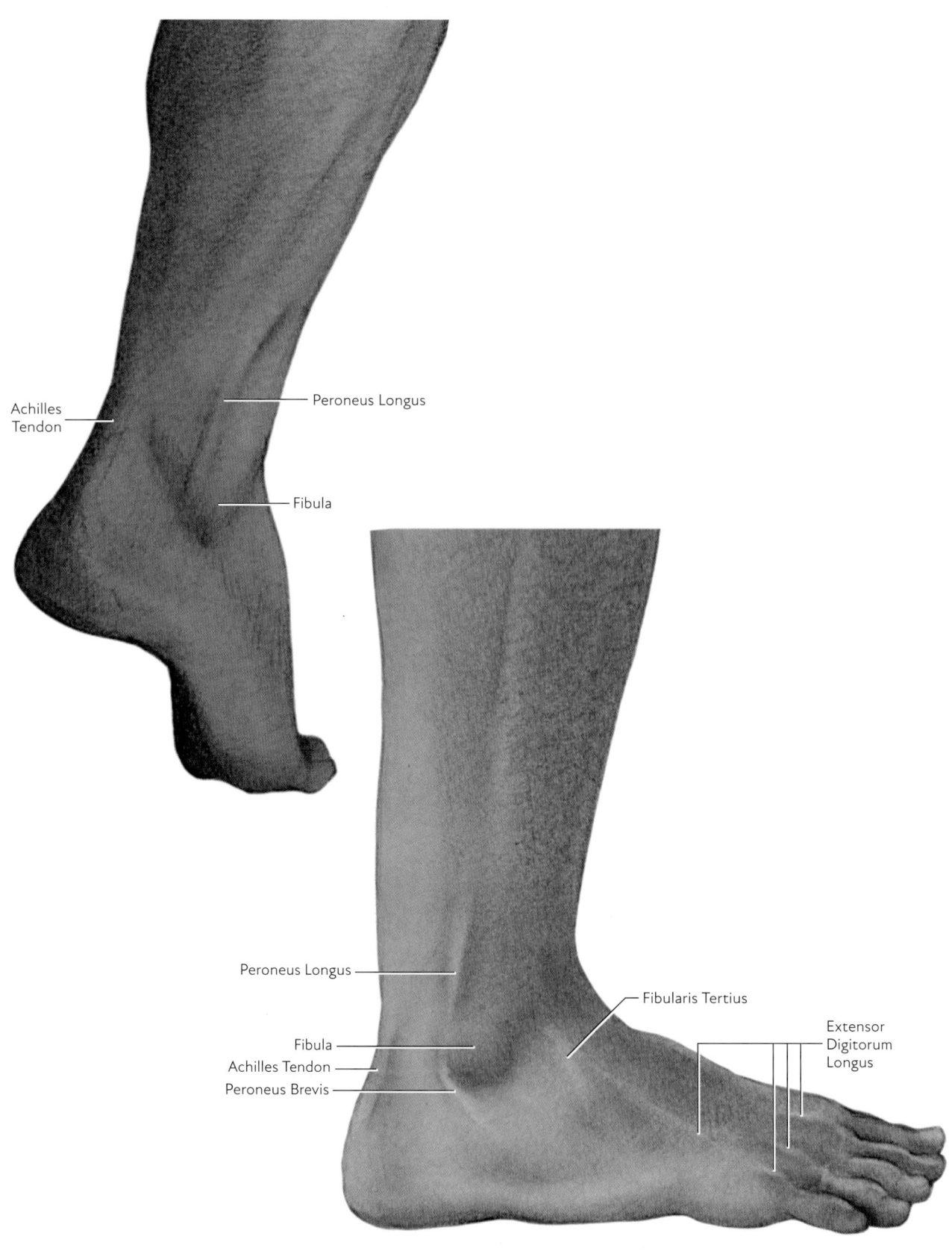

Achilles
Tendon

Peroneus Longus

Fibula

Peroneus Longus

Fibularis Tertius

Extensor
Digitorum
Longus

Fibula

Achilles Tendon

Peroneus Brevis

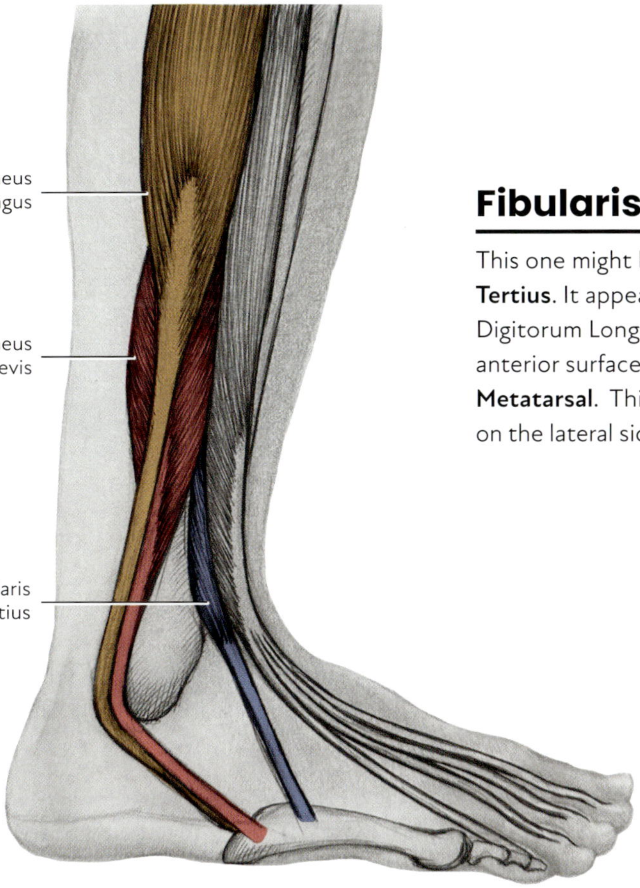

Fibularis Tertius

This one might be easy to miss, but this is the tendon of the **Fibularis Tertius**. It appears on the lateral side of the tendon of the Extensor Digitorum Longus. The Fibularis Tertius muscle starts from the lower anterior surface of the Fibula, and the tendon is attached to **the fifth Metatarsal**. This means that if a tendon appears above the midpoint on the lateral side, you are looking at the tendon of the Fibularis Tertius.

Peroneus Longus

Peroneus Brevis

Fibularis Tertius

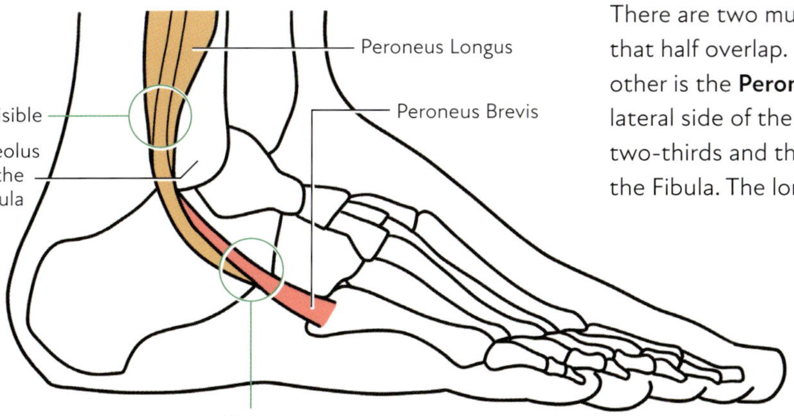

Peroneal Tendons

Tendons of the Ankle – Are They Tangled?!

There are two muscles on the lateral side of the lower leg that half overlap. One is the **Peroneus Longus** and the other is the **Peroneus Brevis**. Both are attached to the lateral side of the Fibula bone. The brevis takes the distal two-thirds and the longus takes the proximal two-thirds of the Fibula. The longus lays over the brevis.

Both tendons go down together and run through the posterior side of the **Malleolus of the Fibula**. Even though the longus overlaps the brevis, the tendons start crossing as they pass through the ankle, and finally, the brevis tendon comes to the surface.

Peroneus Longus

Visible

Malleolus of the Fibula

Peroneus Brevis

Visible

Note: If you spot a tendon above the ankle, you are looking at the Peroneus Longus. If you see a short, diagonal tendon below the ankle, that would be the Peroneus Brevis.

Plantar Aponeurosis

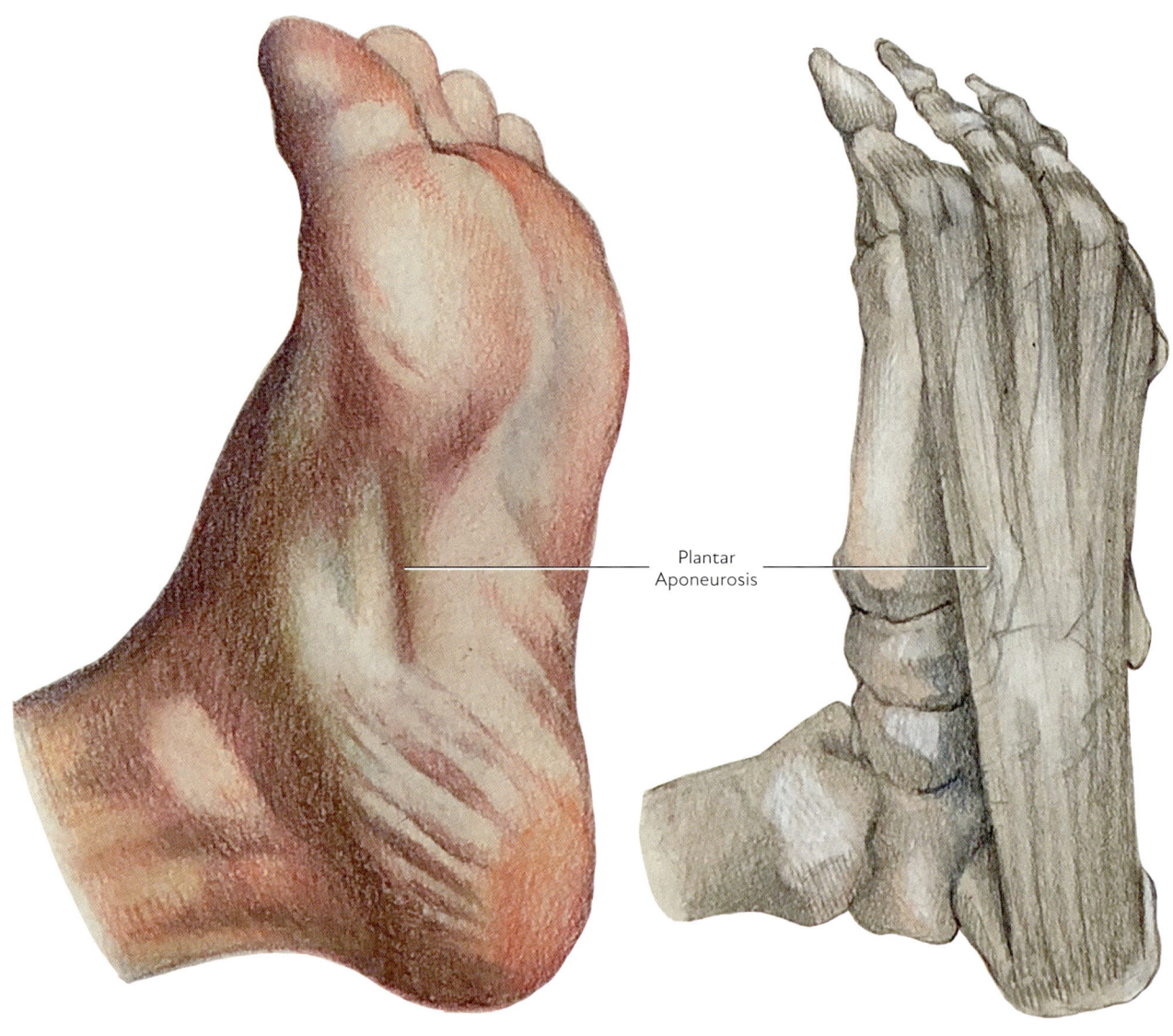

Plantar
Aponeurosis

The plantar of the foot has one recognizable tendon-like tissue called the **Plantar Aponeurosis** (also called the Plantar Fascia). It is a thick tissue that connects from the heel to the toes. Because the medial arch creates open space, the medial side of the fascia stands out and you will be able to see a firm vertical volume on the medial surface when you flex your ankle.

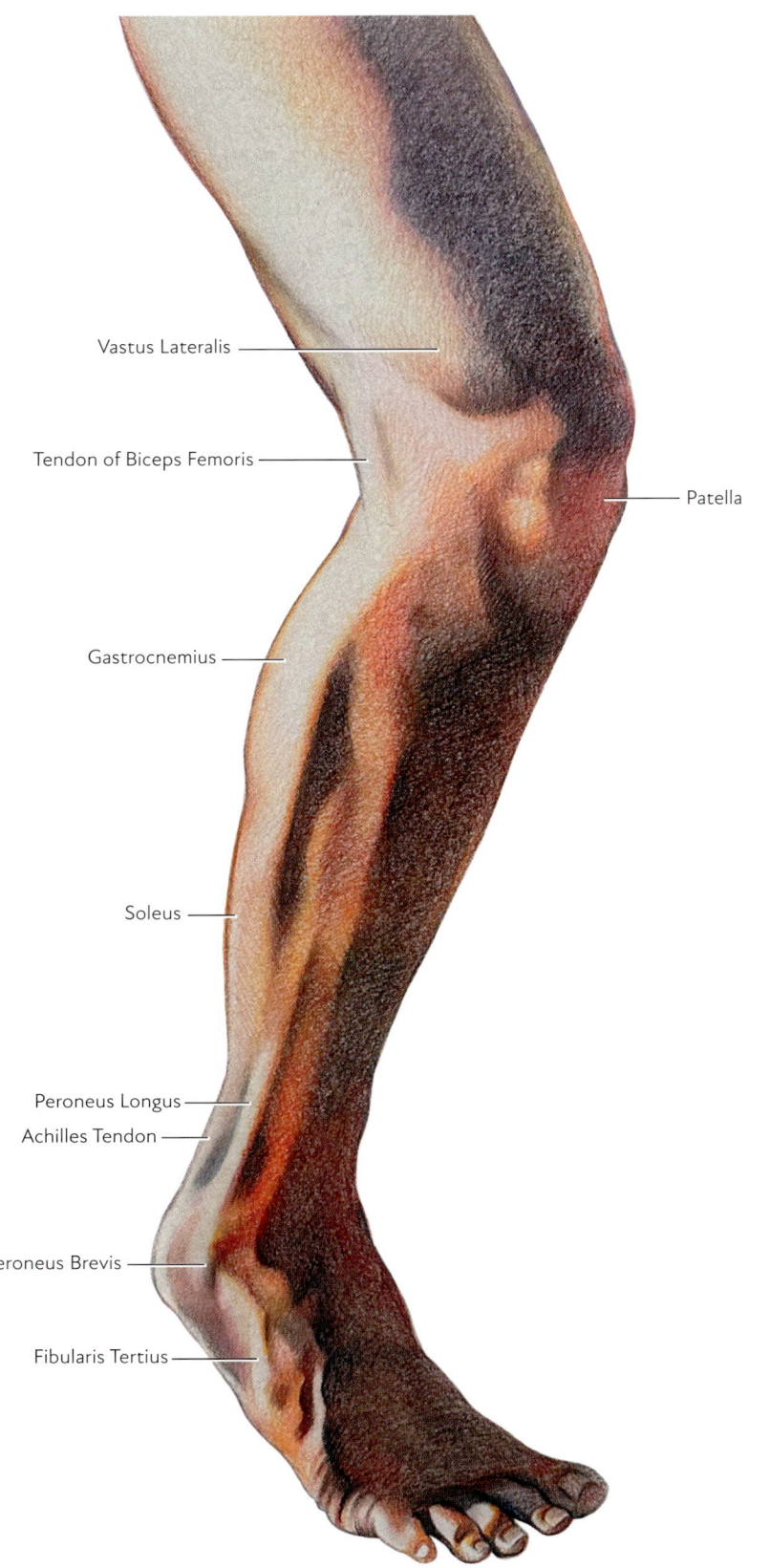

Vastus Lateralis

Tendon of Biceps Femoris

Patella

Gastrocnemius

Soleus

Peroneus Longus

Achilles Tendon

Peroneus Brevis

Fibularis Tertius

Drawing the Foot

Medial

1

Lower Leg

Heel

Dorsal Plane

Peak of Transverse Arch

Toes

2

3

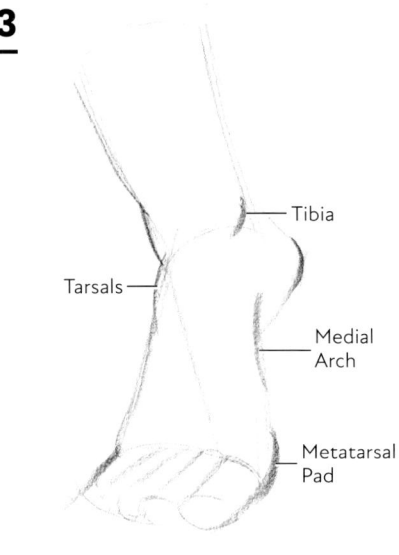

Tibia

Tarsals

Medial Arch

Metatarsal Pad

4

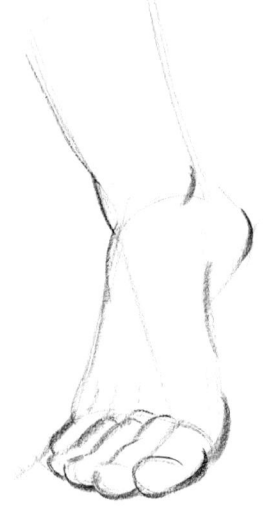

5

Light Source

Peak of Transverse Arch

6

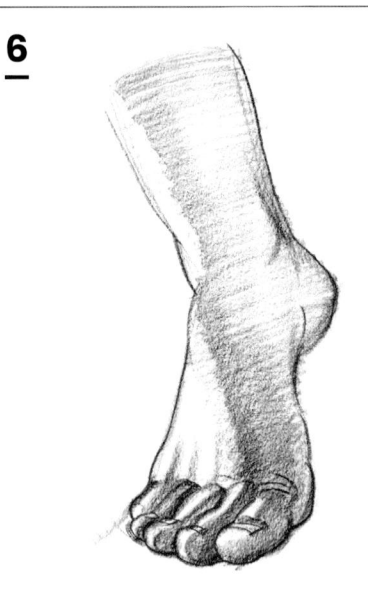

1. Use simplified geometric shapes to define the shape of the foot.

2. Create small cylinders for the toes.

3. Emphasize the landmarks.

4. Add the details of each toe.

5. Analyze the direction of the light source and work on creating an even tone. In this image, the peak line of the transverse arch becomes the transition between light and shadow.

6. Use shading to develop the contrast and details.

Lateral

1

Lower Leg

Heel

Dorsal Plane

Toes

2

Bean shape for the little toe

3

Fibula

Hinge Joint (Tibia)

Dorsal Plane

Lateral Plane

Metatarsal Pad

4

Lateral Plantar Muscle Volume

5

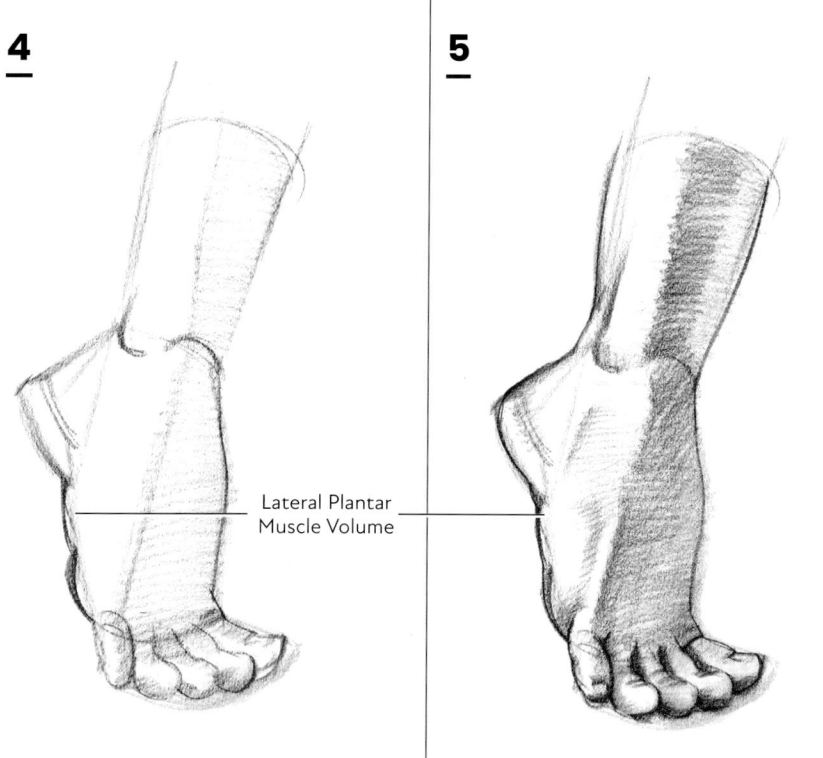

1. Use simplified geometric shapes to define the shape of the foot.

2. Create small cylinders for the toes.

3. Emphasize the landmarks. Add the line to separate the dorsal plane and the lateral plane of the foot.

4. Analyze the direction of the light source and work on creating an even tone.

5. Use shading to develop the contrast and details.

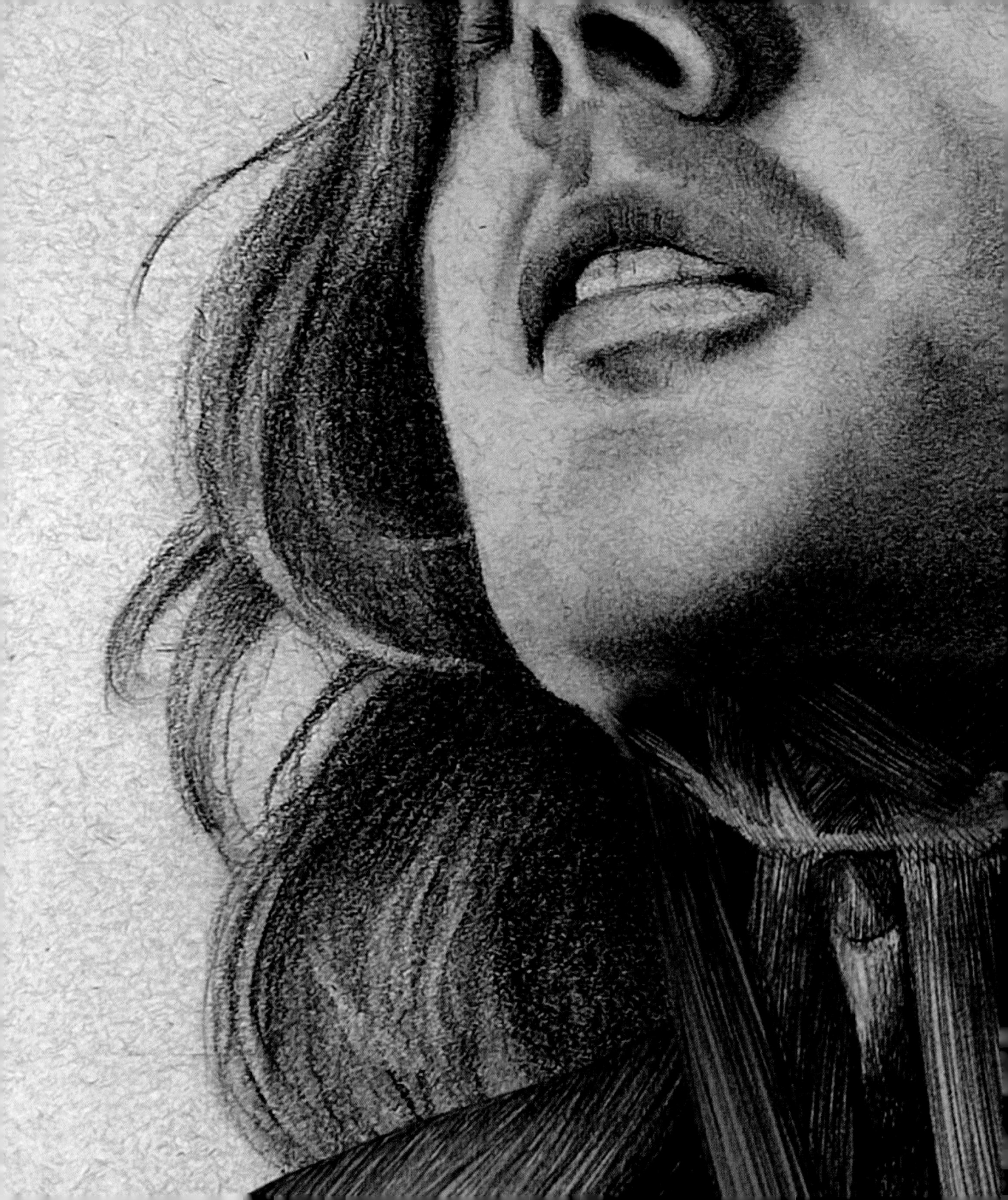

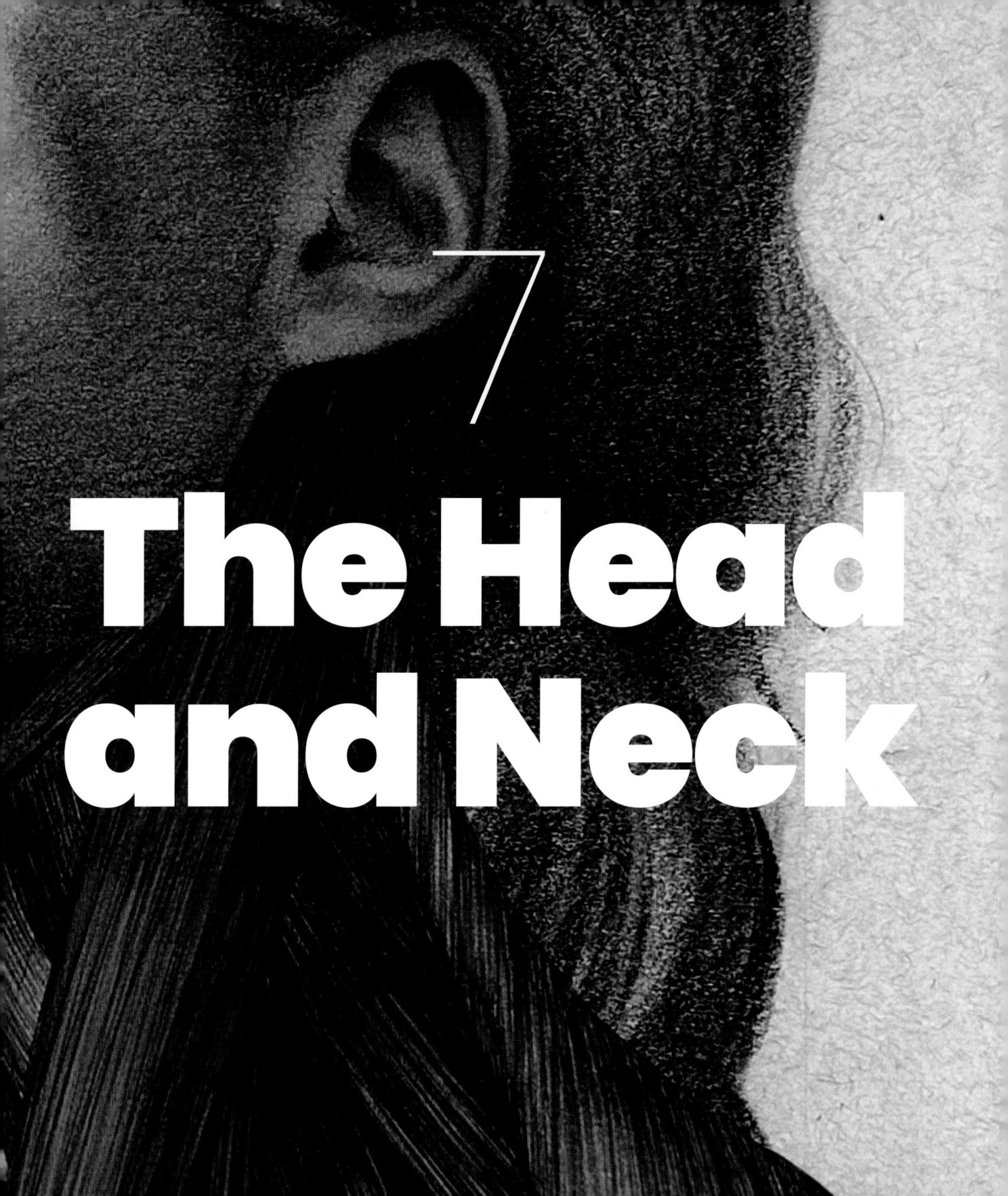

7

The Head and Neck

The Shape of the Head and Facial Planes

Basic Form of the Head

Many beginner artists draw the head in the shape of a sphere, but it is more like a rectangular box. We can think of the plane with the facial features as the frontal plane, and the side planes are the surfaces where the ears are attached.

Creating a boxy head will help you to see angles accurately, and you will be able to control the light and shadow properly.

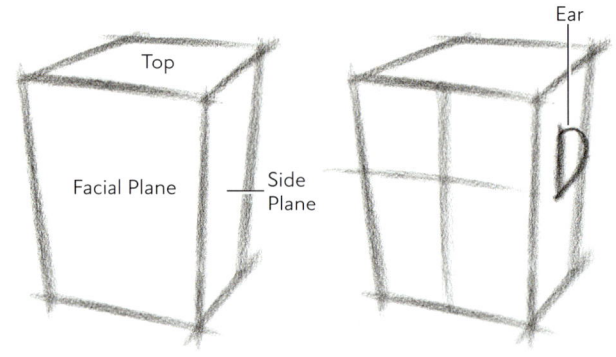

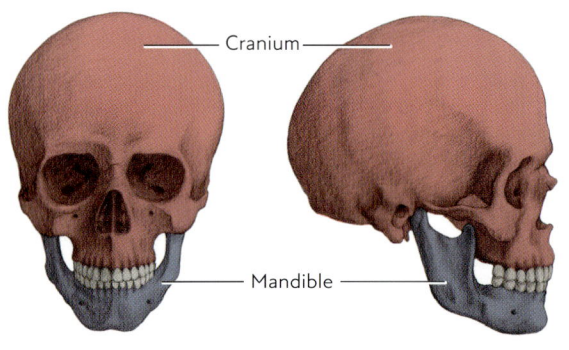

Basic Form of the Skull

The skull has roughly two different bone structures: the **Cranium** and the **Mandible**. The Cranium is the top half of the head that holds the brain and eyeballs. The Mandible is the jawbone that forms the lower half of the face.

On the sides of the Cranium, we have the **Temporal** bones. These are plate-like bones that make the sides of the head flat. From the front view, we can see the top of the Cranium forming a smooth arched line, which then slants down toward the sides of the head.

From the lateral view, the Mandible is shaped like a slanted letter L. The jawline ends on the side of the head under the ear, which is at the center of the Cranium.

In a quick gesture-drawing process, think of the head as being separated into two shapes: an oval for the Cranium, and a rectangle for the facial plane.

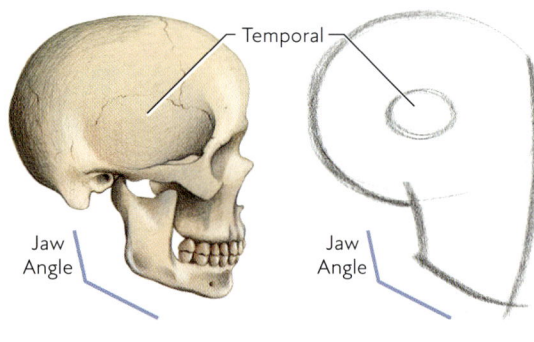

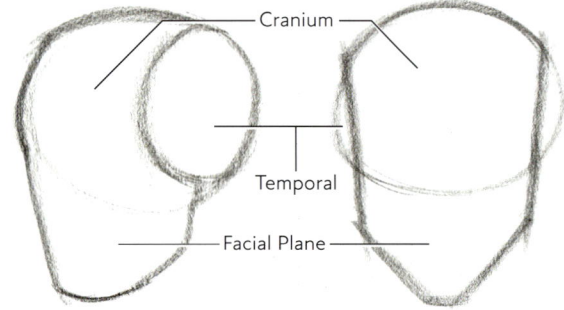

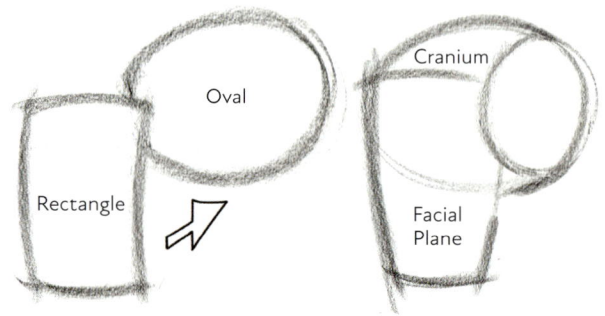

Ratio of the Head and Facial Features

Just like human beings have different body types, there are a variety of facial structures in the human head as well. Learning the generic rules of the head will help you to improve your portrait work.

Head

In the form of a two-bone structured head, the Cranium accounts for the upper two-thirds, and the jaw occupies the lower one-third. The ratio is the same from the lateral side.

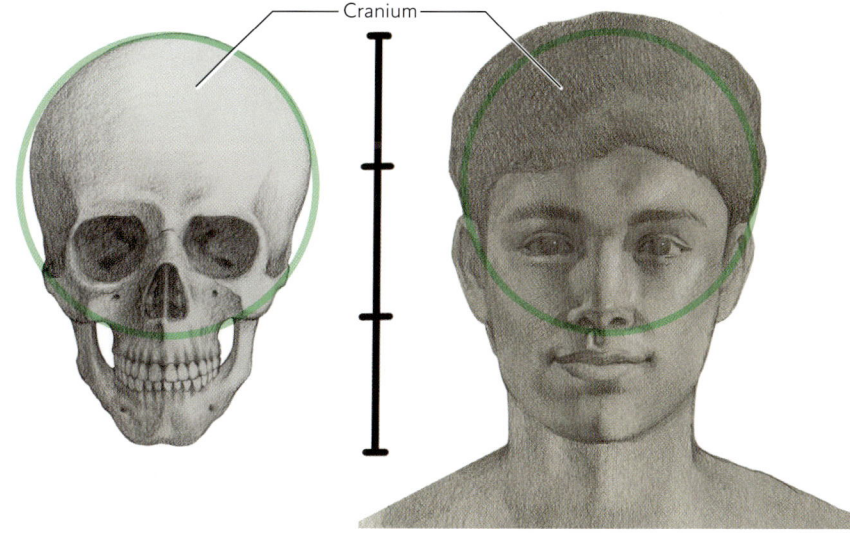

Cranium

Facial Features

Now let's examine the general ratio of facial features.

Rule of Thirds

The face can be divided into three roughly equal sections: from the hair line to the brow line, the brow line to the bottom of the nose, and the bottom of the nose to the chin. The space from the hair line to the top of the skull can be added to this ratio. Many beginner artists often miss the top and back volume of the Cranium, which makes their portrait work less sophisticated.

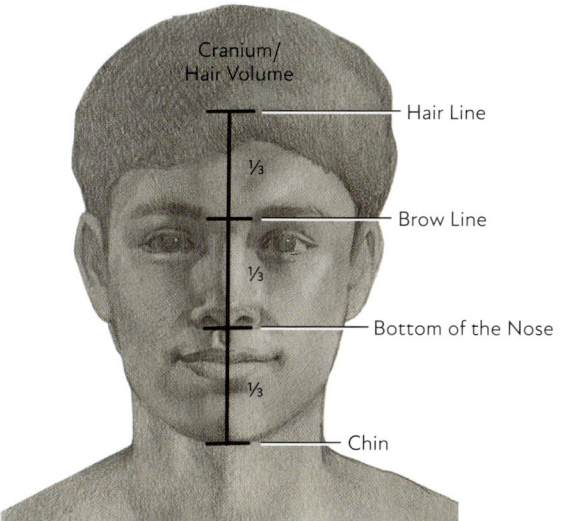

Cranium/
Hair Volume

Hair Line

⅓

Brow Line

⅓

Bottom of the Nose

⅓

Chin

Location of the Ears

The ears are generally located in between the brow line and the bottom of the nose on the lateral side of the head. In the gesture-drawing process, you can use the concept of facial thirds to help you place the ears. This will help you to show the head accurately from any angle.

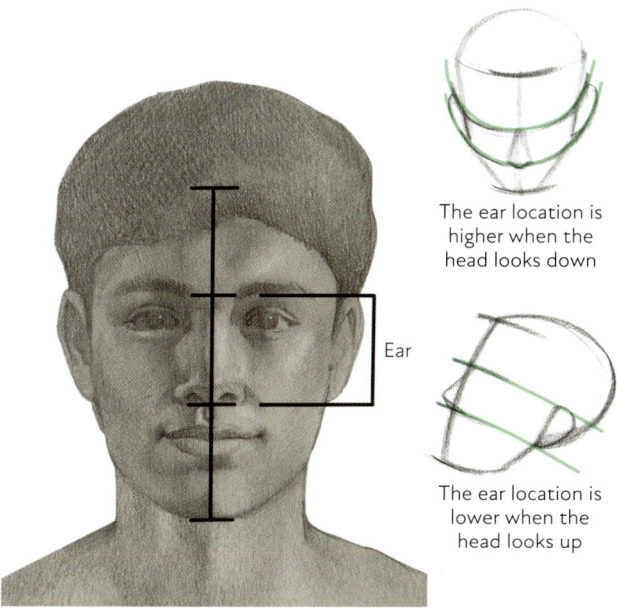

Ear

The ear location is higher when the head looks down

The ear location is lower when the head looks up

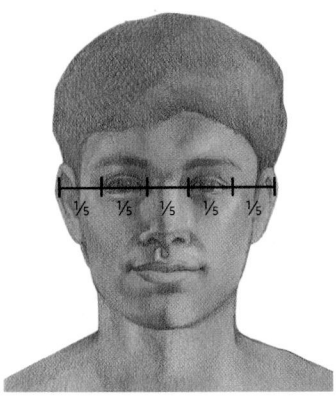

Rule of Fifths

The width of the head can be divided into five equal sections. Working at the eyeline, the area from one side of the head (including the ear) to the outside corner of the nearest eye is one-fifth. From the outside corner of the eye to the tear duct—the width of the eye—is another unit. The nasal space from the tear duct of one eye to the tear duct of the other is another unit.

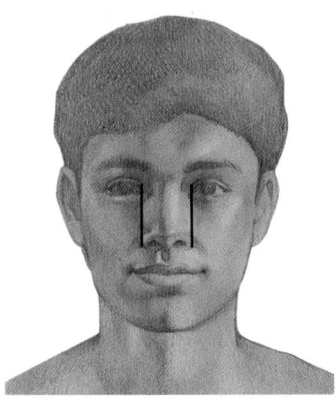

Wing of the Nose

Once you have established the placement of the eyes, you can figure out the size of the lower part of the nose by aligning the wing of the nose with the tear duct above it. This means that the more space there is between the tear ducts, the more width you will see in the wings of the nose, and the same for the other way around. Simply draw a vertical line down from each tear duct to find the location of the wings of the nose. This technique will help you avoid making the nose too large or too small.

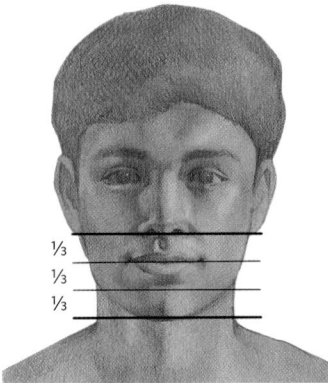

Location of the Lips

The lips are located in the lower third of the face, which is the area between the bottom of the nose and the chin. The line where the top and bottom lips meet usually lines up around the top third of that area.

The corners of the lips line up with the **inner edges of the irises.** When a smile forms, the corners of the lips could line up with the **pupils,** or the **outer edges of the irises.**

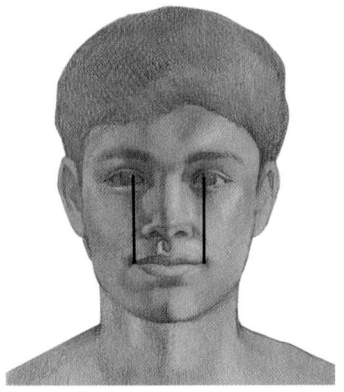

Basic Construction Drawing of the Head

Now that we know the basic measurements of the head, we are ready to start constructing a drawing. Just like with the drawings of the hands and feet, understanding the bone structure is more important than the muscular structure when creating a good portrait.

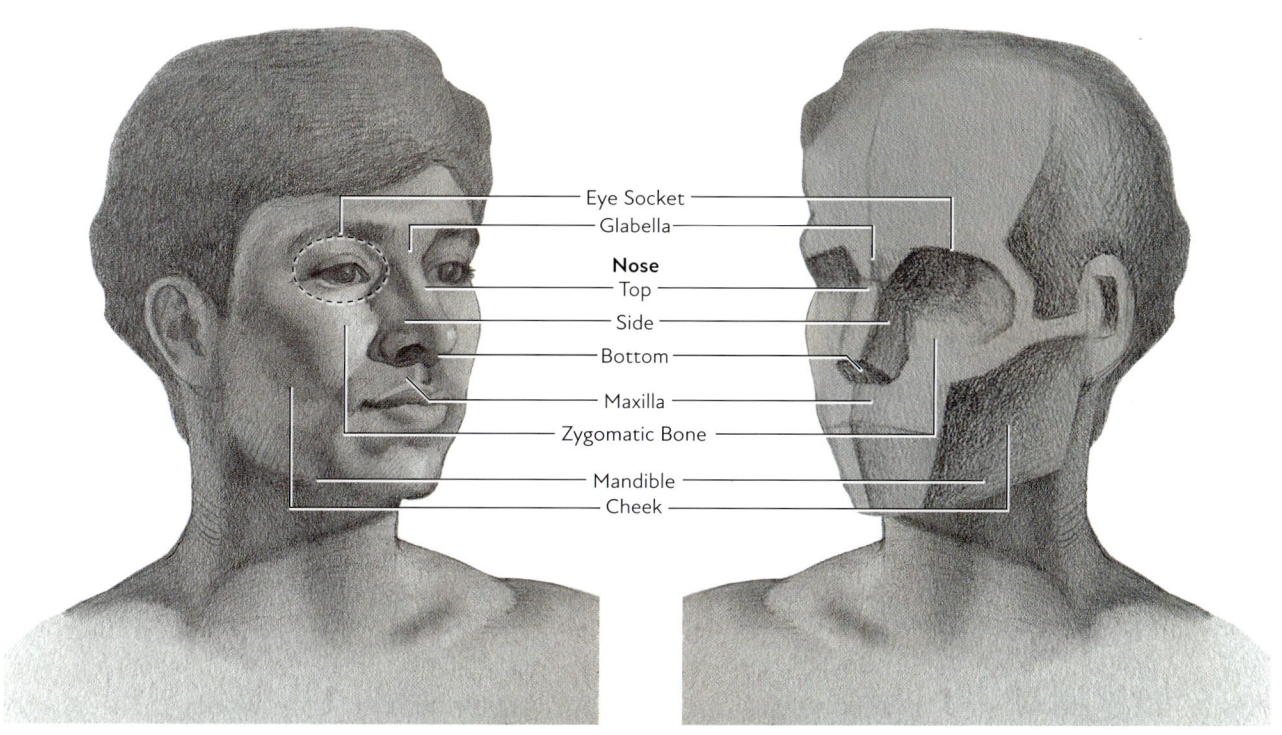

Eye Socket
Glabella
Nose
Top
Side
Bottom
Maxilla
Zygomatic Bone
Mandible
Cheek

Glabella

The **Glabella** is a small space in between the brows. It becomes the true center of the entire head from the anterior view. Establishing the Glabella in the drawing is important because many facial parts—including the eyes, brows, and nasal bone—surround this small area.

From the lateral view, you can see that the plane of the Glabella faces downward. Therefore, this space can be darkened slightly in the shading process since it does not receive as much light from the light source in a standard environment.

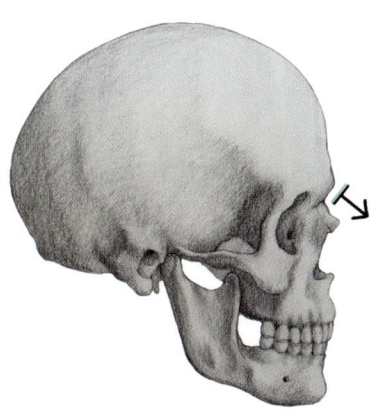

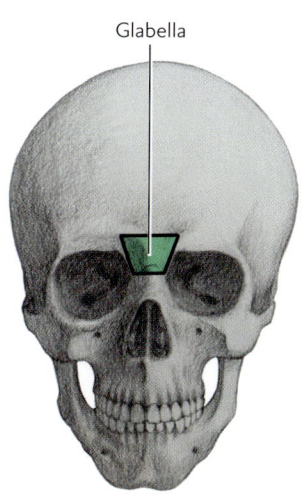

Glabella

Nose

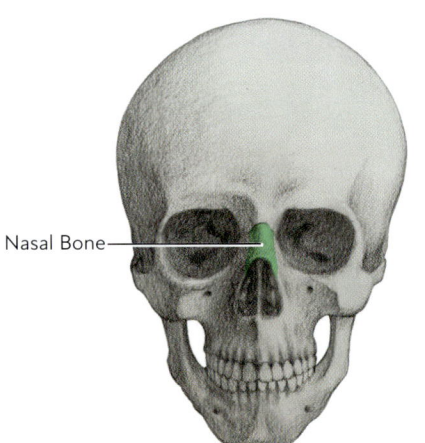

Nasal Bone

The nose is one of the facial parts that sticks far out from the head plane. In the construction drawing of the nose, make sure to focus on four planes: top, sides (two), and bottom. This structure will be located under the Glabella.

The top plane represents the bridge of the nose. It is firm and usually receives the most light from the light source.

There are two side planes. Depending on the environment, one side could be lighter and the other could be darker.

The bottom of the nose is the only plane that faces down, and it receives the least amount of light in a standard environment. In comic book art, artists often emphasize the shadow of the bottom plane and leave the other planes completely blank. This creates the illusion of the nose existing on the facial surface. The same system can be applied for the lips as well.

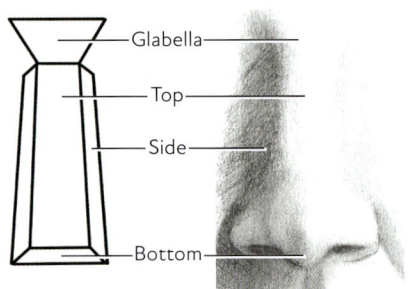

Glabella
Top
Side
Bottom

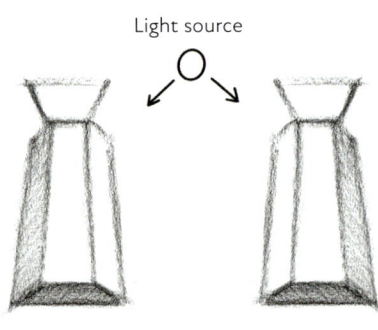

Light source

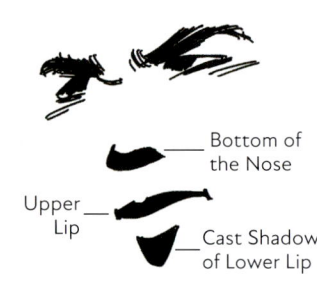

Bottom of the Nose
Upper Lip
Cast Shadow of Lower Lip

Zygomatic Bone

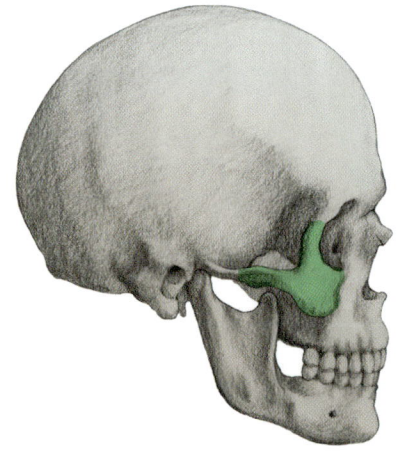

Zygomatic Bone

The **Zygomatic bone** is a cheek bone. It is different from the lower cheek because the bone is firmly projected. The cheek of the Zygomatic bone shows a different tone compared to the soft part of the cheek.

When you touch the cheek bone area under the eyes, you can feel the firmness of the bone, which travels horizontally toward the ear. The space in between the cheek bone and the jaw line is mostly just the soft fat, and it faces laterally.

The term "apple cheek" comes from the Zygomatic bone reflecting a large amount of light. This area is a round volume with a strong highlight.

Eyeballs

The eyes are not just two-dimensional almond shapes; they are spheres sitting under the thin skin of the eyelids. Always remember to think of the eyes as three-dimensional geometric forms like balls. This will help you to create the accurate angle and shape of the eyes in portrait work.

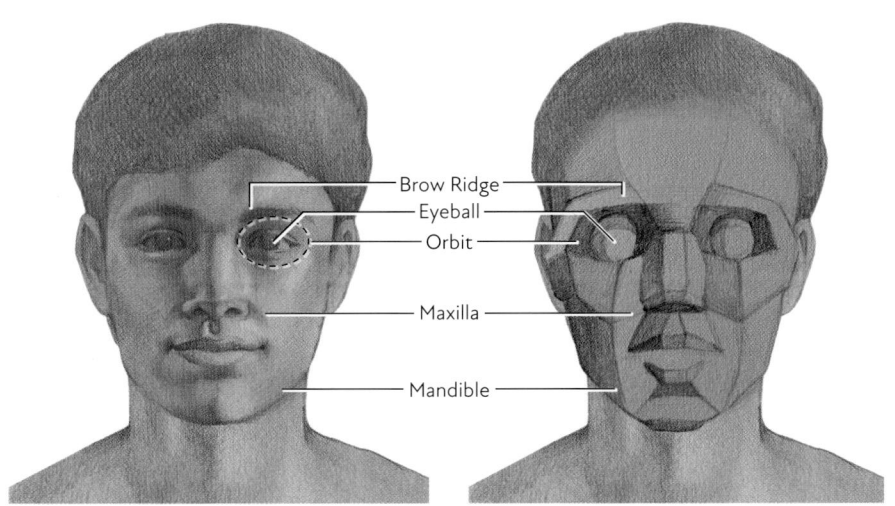

Brow Ridge
Eyeball
Orbit
Maxilla
Mandible

Brow Ridge and Eye Socket

Next to the Glabella is the brow ridge. It sticks out slightly farther than the frontal surface of the forehead, creating a large cave around the eye socket (or **Orbit**).

You might be able to see a shadow cast by the ridge on the top surface of the eyelid, or the actual silhouette of the socket, depending on the facial type and the location of the light source.

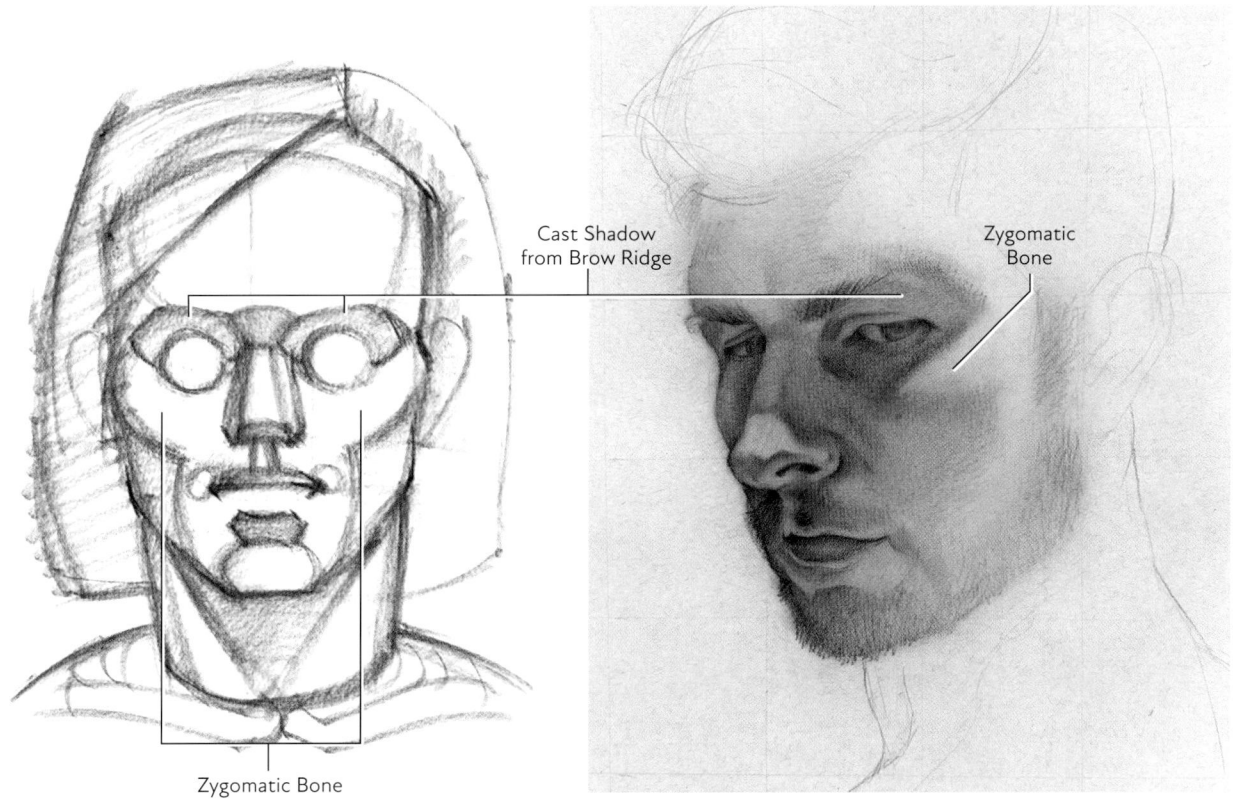

Cast Shadow from Brow Ridge

Zygomatic Bone

Zygomatic Bone

Maxilla and Teeth

The **Maxilla** is a part of the Cranium that forms the upper jaw. It is located on the medial side of the Zygomatic bone around the nose, and it holds the upper teeth. Just like the U-curve of the teeth structure, the Maxilla also follows the same arch line. In the construction drawing process of the head, the Maxilla/teeth can be projected from the front plane while the cheek plane forms the lateral plane.

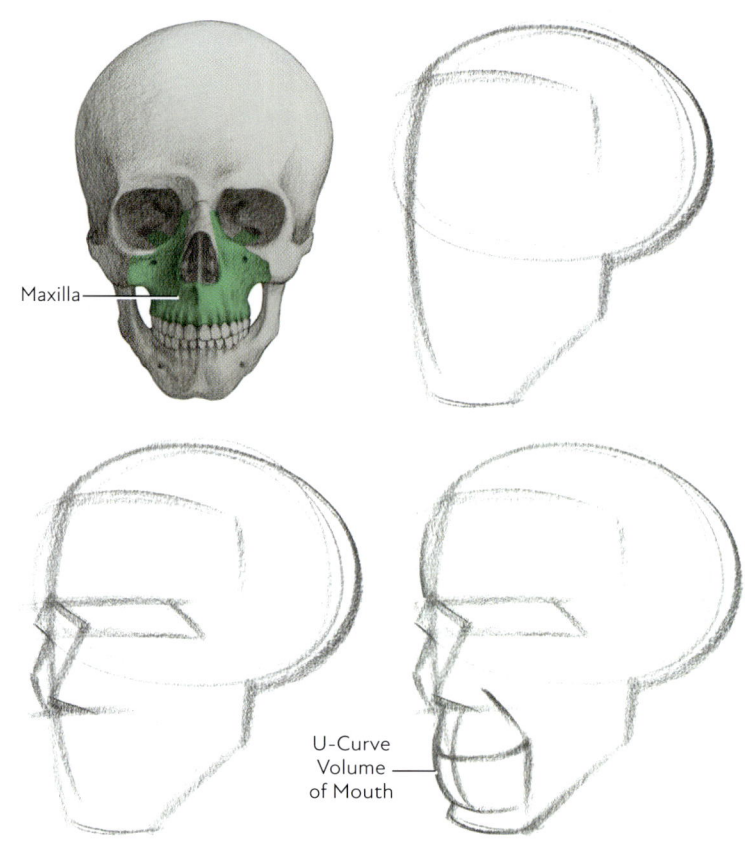

Maxilla

U-Curve Volume of Mouth

Mandible

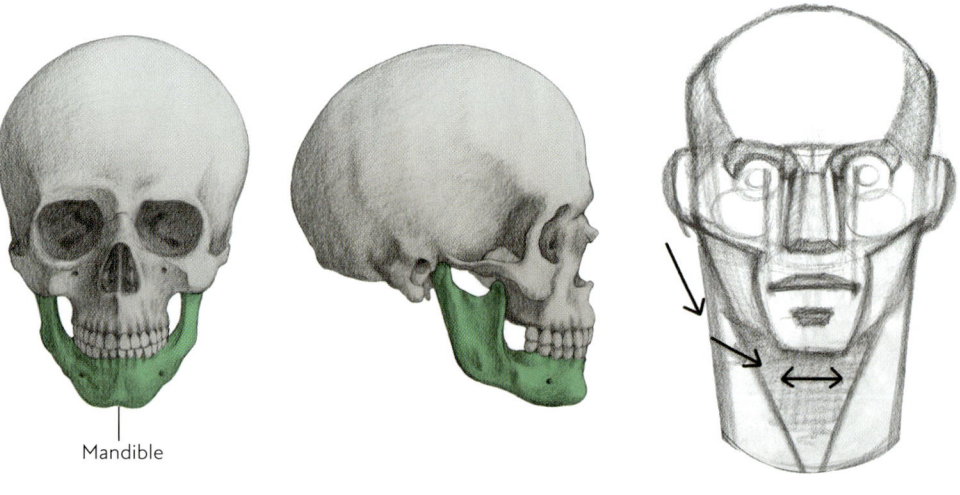

Mandible

The **Mandible** is the jawbone that creates the lower half of the facial line. The Mandible line has a specific angle. From the anterior view, you can see that the bottom of the chin becomes flat. From there, the jawline goes up diagonally, then the angle turns again and it goes back behind the ear.

Step-by-Step Robot Head

Let's construct the head in a simplified form. I call this a "robot head."

Anterior

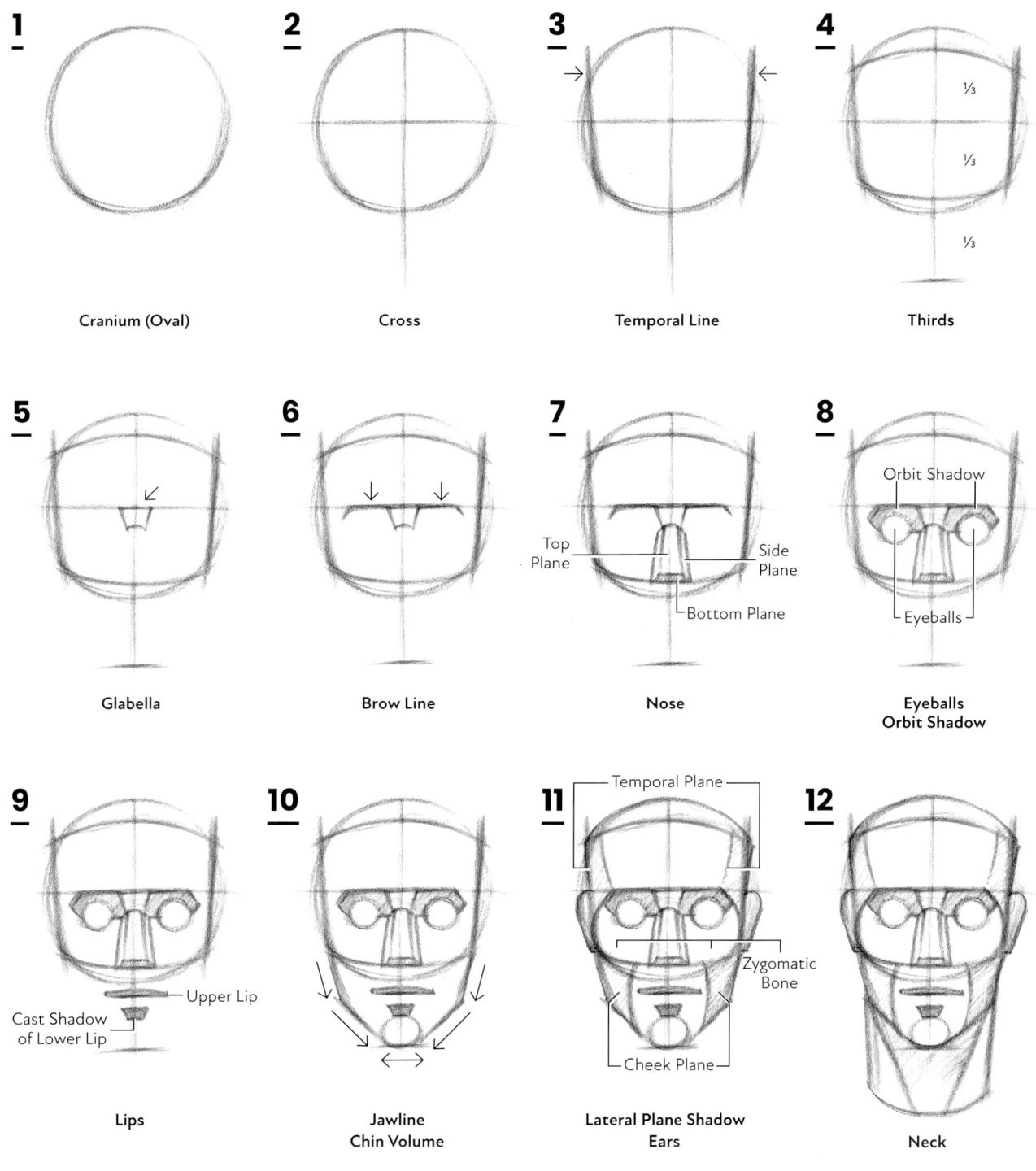

1 Cranium (Oval)

2 Cross

3 Temporal Line

4 Thirds — ⅓ ⅓ ⅓

5 Glabella

6 Brow Line

7 Nose — Top Plane, Side Plane, Bottom Plane

8 Eyeballs Orbit Shadow — Orbit Shadow, Eyeballs

9 Lips — Upper Lip, Cast Shadow of Lower Lip

10 Jawline Chin Volume

11 Lateral Plane Shadow Ears — Temporal Plane, Zygomatic Bone, Cheek Plane

12 Neck

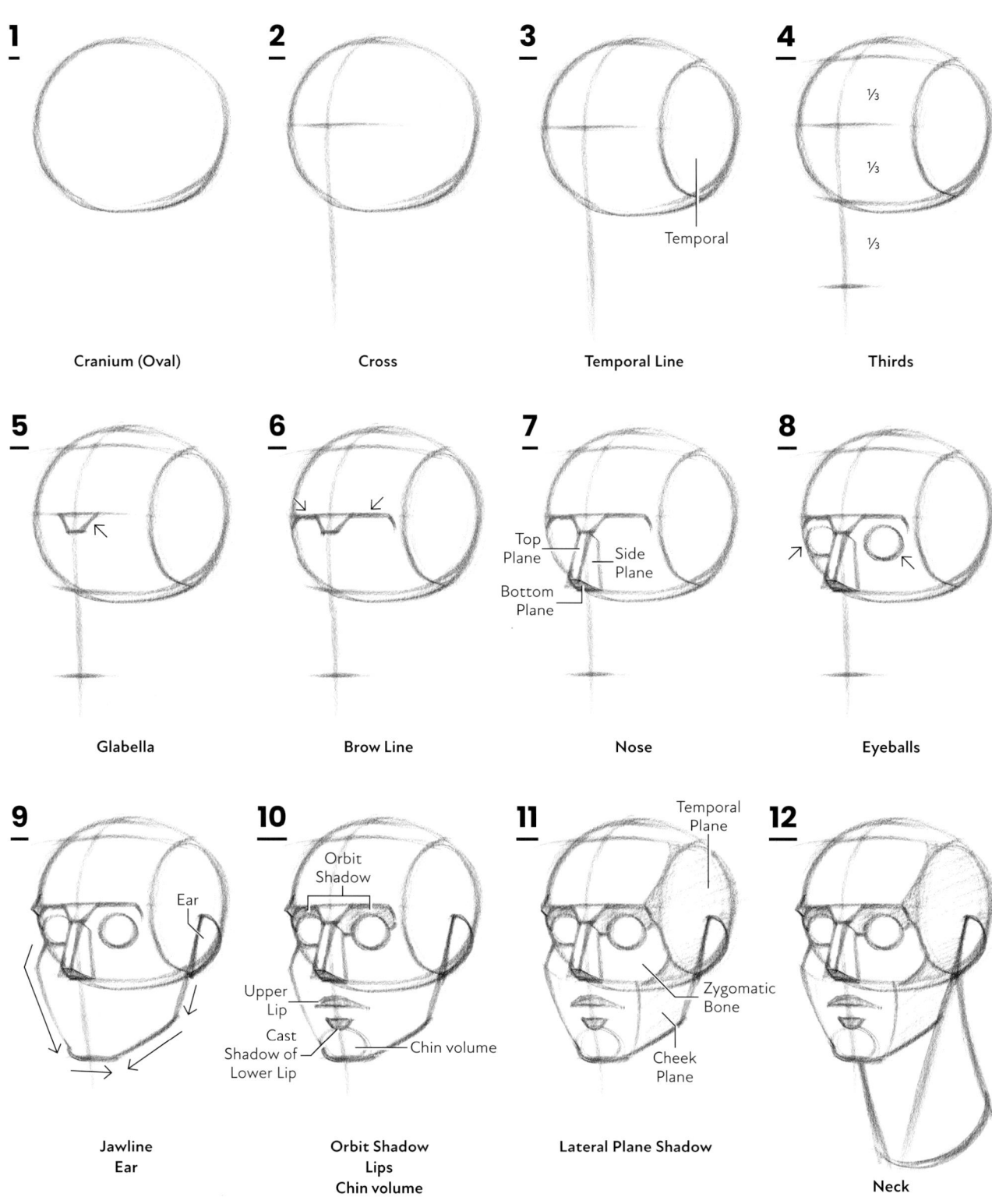

1 Cranium (Oval)

2 Cross

3 Temporal Line
Temporal

4 Thirds
⅓
⅓
⅓

5 Glabella

6 Brow Line

7 Nose
Top Plane
Side Plane
Bottom Plane

8 Eyeballs

9 Jawline Ear
Ear

10 Orbit Shadow Lips Chin volume
Orbit Shadow
Upper Lip
Cast Shadow of Lower Lip
Chin volume

11 Lateral Plane Shadow
Temporal Plane
Zygomatic Bone
Cheek Plane

12 Neck

Lateral

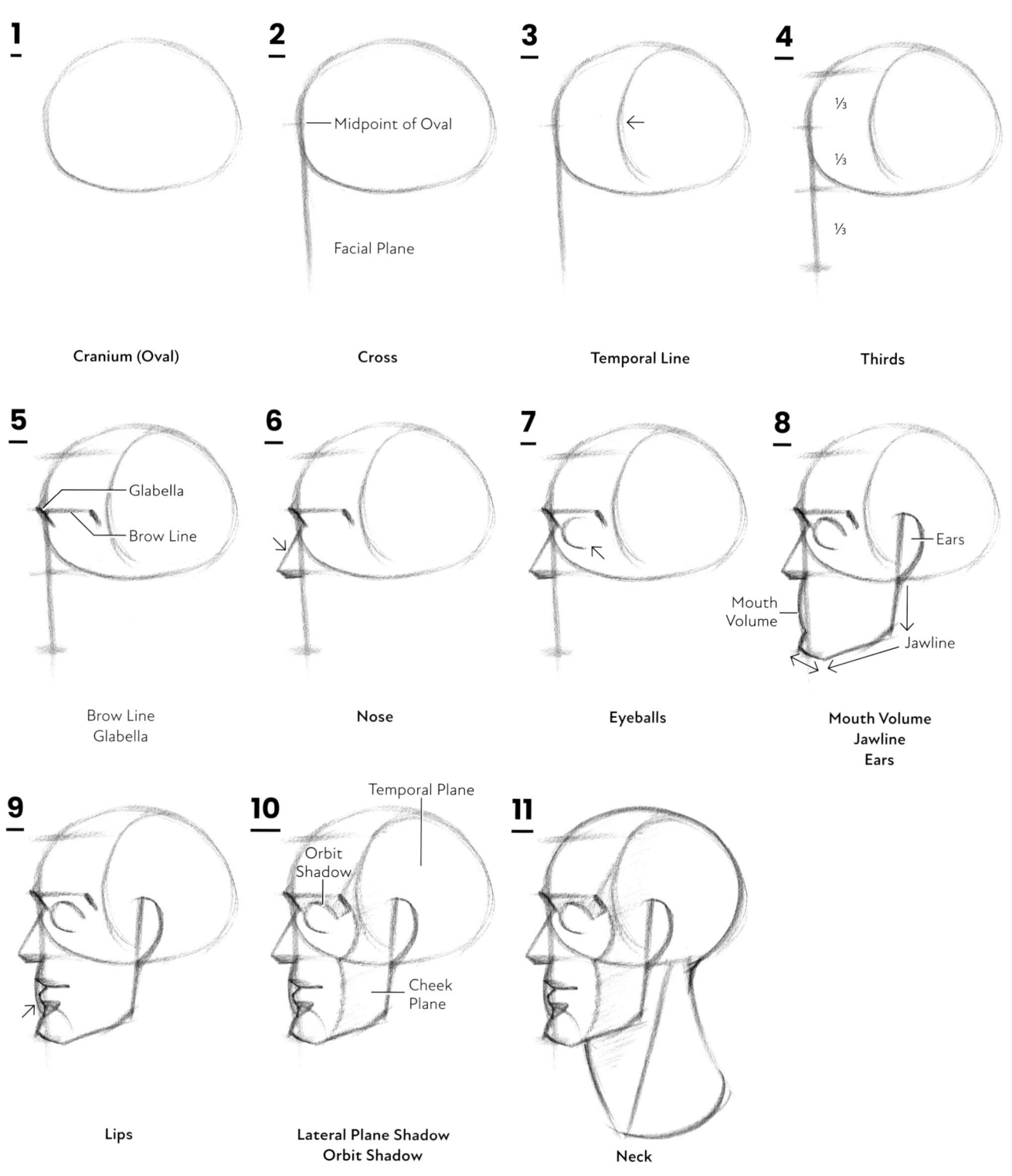

1
Cranium (Oval)

2
Midpoint of Oval

Facial Plane

Cross

3
Temporal Line

4
⅓
⅓
⅓

Thirds

5
Glabella
Brow Line

Brow Line
Glabella

6

Nose

7

Eyeballs

8
Ears
Mouth Volume
Jawline

Mouth Volume
Jawline
Ears

9

Lips

10
Temporal Plane
Orbit Shadow
Cheek Plane

Lateral Plane Shadow
Orbit Shadow

11

Neck

Anatomy of Facial Parts

Working on the facial parts is one of the exciting steps in the figure drawing process. However, to avoid drawing the "lizard" face where every facial part is enlarged on a perfect flat plate of a circle, we need to deconstruct each part and study the anatomy.

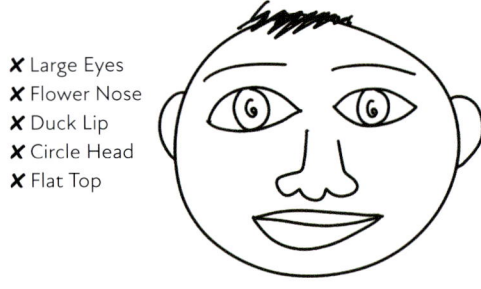

✗ Large Eyes
✗ Flower Nose
✗ Duck Lip
✗ Circle Head
✗ Flat Top

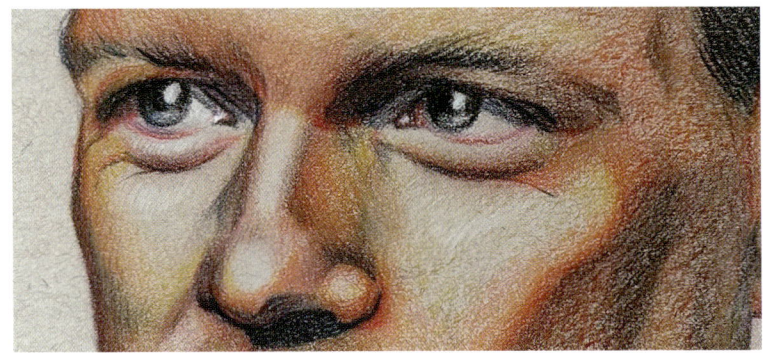

Eyes

Eyeballs

The eye is formed in a spherical shape that we call the eyeball. In the surface anatomy, the eyeball has three main parts: the **Sclera**, the **Iris**, and the **Pupil**. The Sclera is the white surface of the eyeball, the Iris is the colored part of the eye, and the Pupil is the dark center inside the Iris.

The Iris usually has a ring around it that is often slightly darker than the inside tone of the Iris. It also has a unique texture that almost looks like irregular rays coming out of the Pupil.

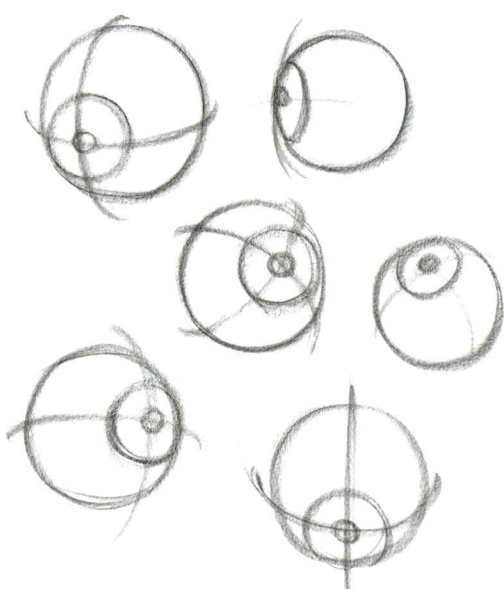

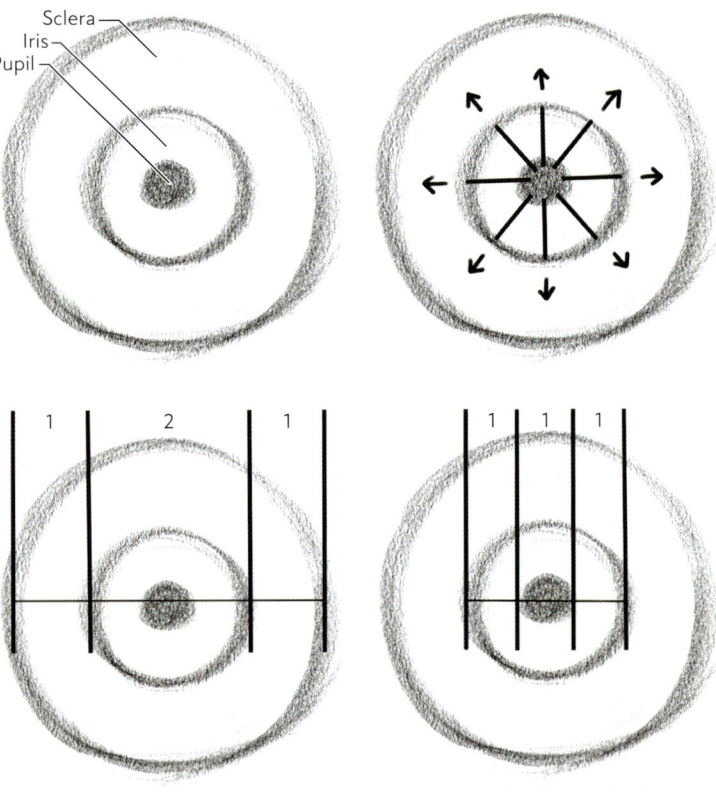

Ratio of Sclera to Iris   Ratio of Iris to Pupil

The Pupil is the center of the Iris. It does not matter what color eyes you have, the pupil will always stay dark in tone. The ratio of the Iris to the Pupil can be 1:1:1, but it varies because the Pupil dilates and shrinks in response to various factors. For example, the Pupil dilates when you walk inside a dark place like a movie theater. The opposite happens when you go outside into bright sunlight—the Pupil would shrink to protect your eye and keep out the bright light.

Orbit

The eyeball sits inside the Orbit cave and is supported by muscles that move it around, allowing you to look up, down, left, and right.

Many people assume that the Orbit is either oval or square in shape, but it is actually more like a slanted soft rectangle. The two Orbits together look like a pair of teardrop sunglasses. The shape of the Orbit can often be spotted on the surface anatomy. In this case, you can see highlights where the bone protrudes around the eyes, and some shadows cast by the Orbit cave.

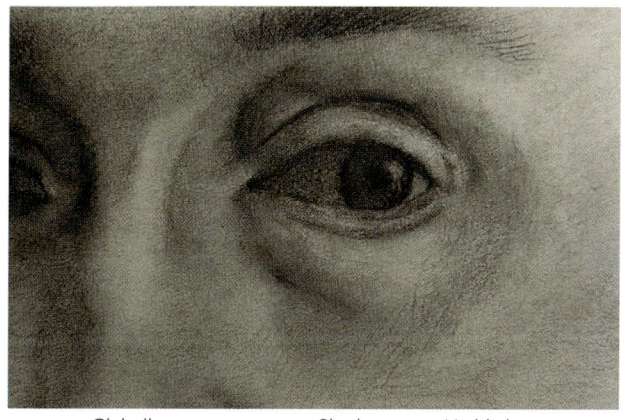

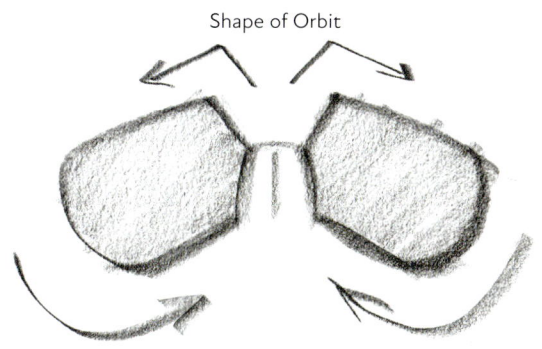

Shape of Orbit

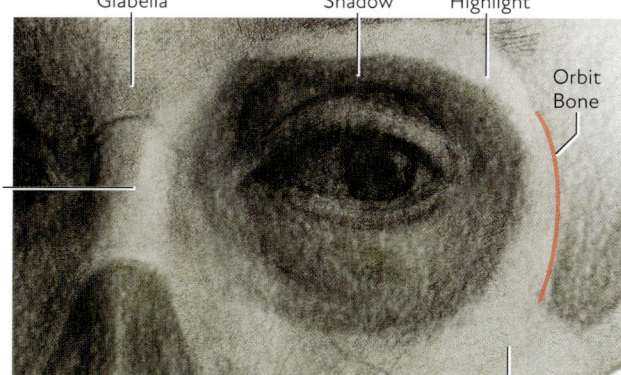

Glabella · Shadow · Highlight · Orbit Bone · Nasal Bone · Zygomatic Bone

Shape of the Eye

The shape of the eye is formed by the upper and lower eyelids. It opens like a window and we see part of the eye sphere's surface.

The open window of the eye looks somewhat almond-shaped, but technically it is more like a **parallelogram** or **hexagon**. The small space right under the tear duct is a bit different. It looks like the skin is pushed up, making the tear duct shape stand out.

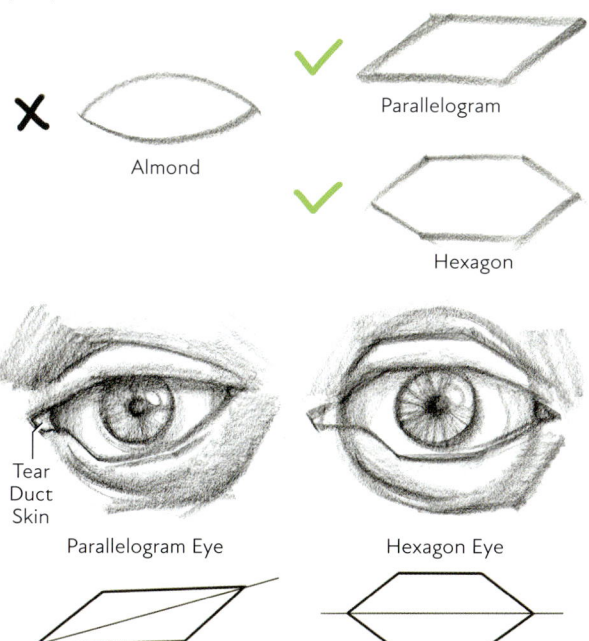

Almond

Parallelogram

Hexagon

Tear Duct Skin

Parallelogram Eye

Hexagon Eye

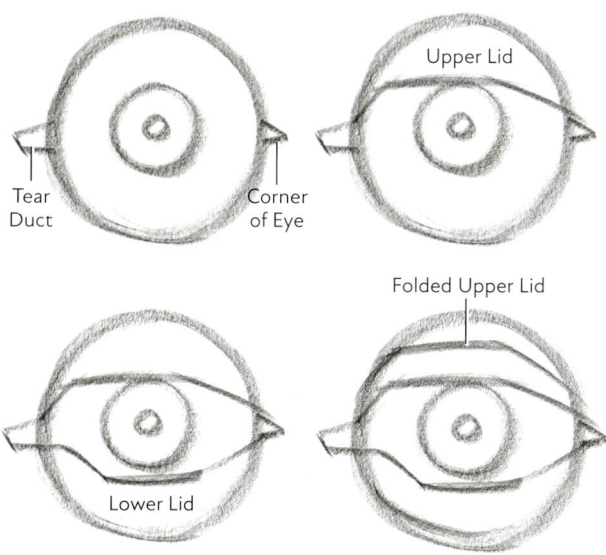

Tear Duct

Corner of Eye

Upper Lid

Folded Upper Lid

Lower Lid

Eyelids

Even though eyeball size is fairly equal among most people, the shape of the eyes is different for everyone. The design of eyelids is diverse, with many characteristics dependent on geography and climate.

A monolid is an eyelid shape that does not have a crease. With this type of eyelid, there is a smooth gradation of tone, just like the light and shadow effect that you would see on a sphere.

On the other hand, a folded, or doubled, eyelid has a crease on the upper lid. With this type of eyelid, imagine that there are two cylinders stacked together. Both cylinders would have a light zone and form shadow. However, cylinder A would drop a cast shadow onto cylinder B. Therefore, for cylinder B, its center becomes the lightest area.

Cylinder B would also drop a cast shadow onto the upper portion of the eyeball. The Sclera is white in color, but don't forget to add some shading on the upper portion of it. This will give your eye drawing depth. It is subtle but makes it look much more realistic.

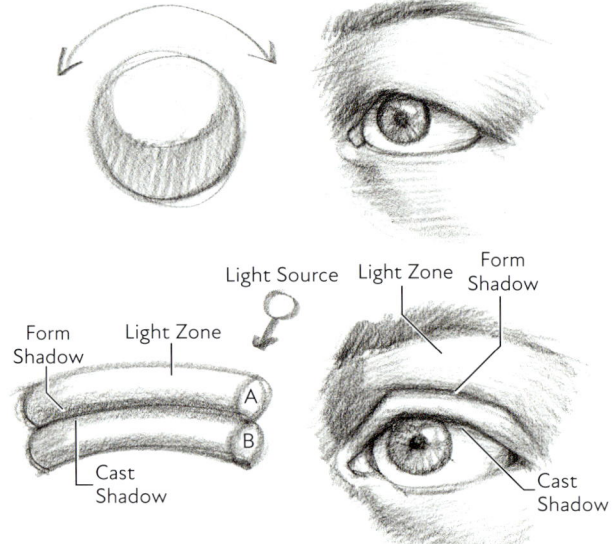

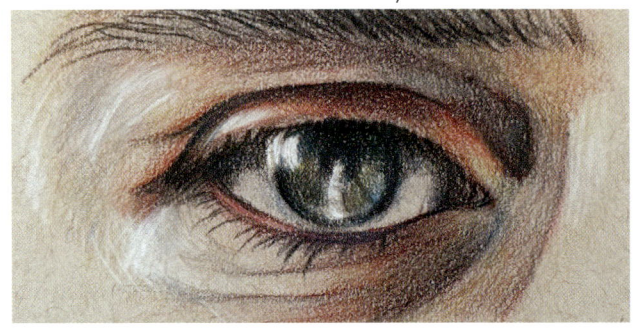

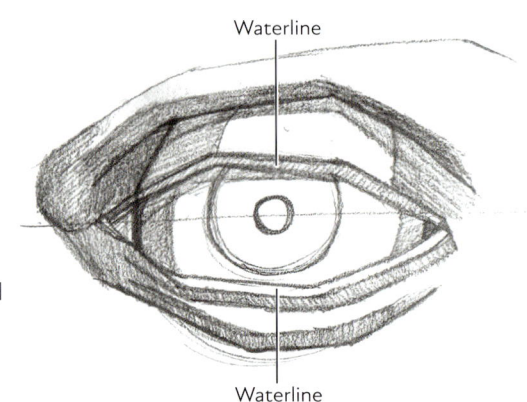

Cast Shadow on the Eyeball

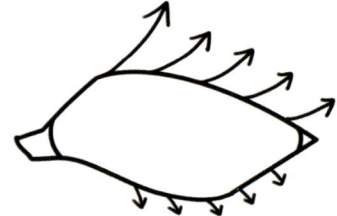

Eyelashes

The lash on the upper lid is fuller and longer than the one on the lower lid. Both lashes grow in order and wing outward. However, from the anterior view, the upper eyelash has a foreshortening effect, and it is difficult to see the full length. The whole shape will not appear unless the person is wearing mascara or fake lashes.

Why Does My Drawing of an Eye Look So Flat?

A common issue in drawings of eyes is that they appear flat with no depth. The key is to focus on the geometry of the sphere and how the light affects the eyelids and eyeball.

The eyelid is only skin, but it has some thickness. The surface that shows the thickness of the lower lid is called the waterline. The waterline is more noticeable on the lower lid than the upper lid because the lower waterline surface usually faces up in the standard environment. Practice breaking down all the parts of the eye into geometric shapes. Paying attention to the different angles and directions of the eye helps to add depth to your drawing.

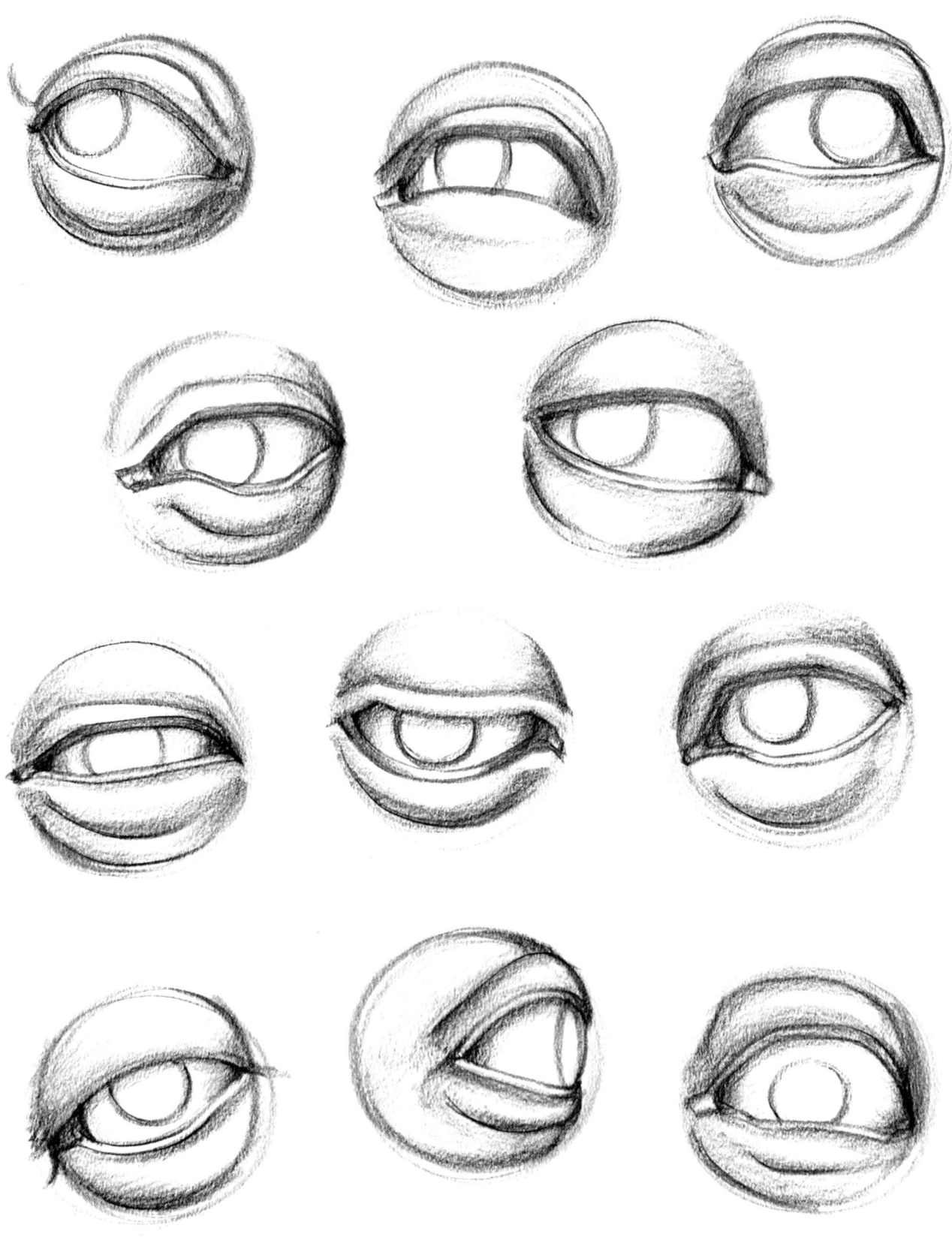

Brows

The brow is the aggregation of hair that sits on the brow ledge. You don't have to work on the individual hair pieces when drawing the brow. Start with a single shape for the whole mass, and then work on the toning.

Start adding the texture to the brow after outlining the volume. The growth of brow hair has an order. The brow hair grows upward from the Glabella, and starts laying down toward the lateral side. After the peak of the brow, you will notice that there is another mass of hair growing downward that meets the hair growing upward to make the shape of an arrow. The hair on the medial side of the brow is thinner and it usually gets thicker toward the middle.

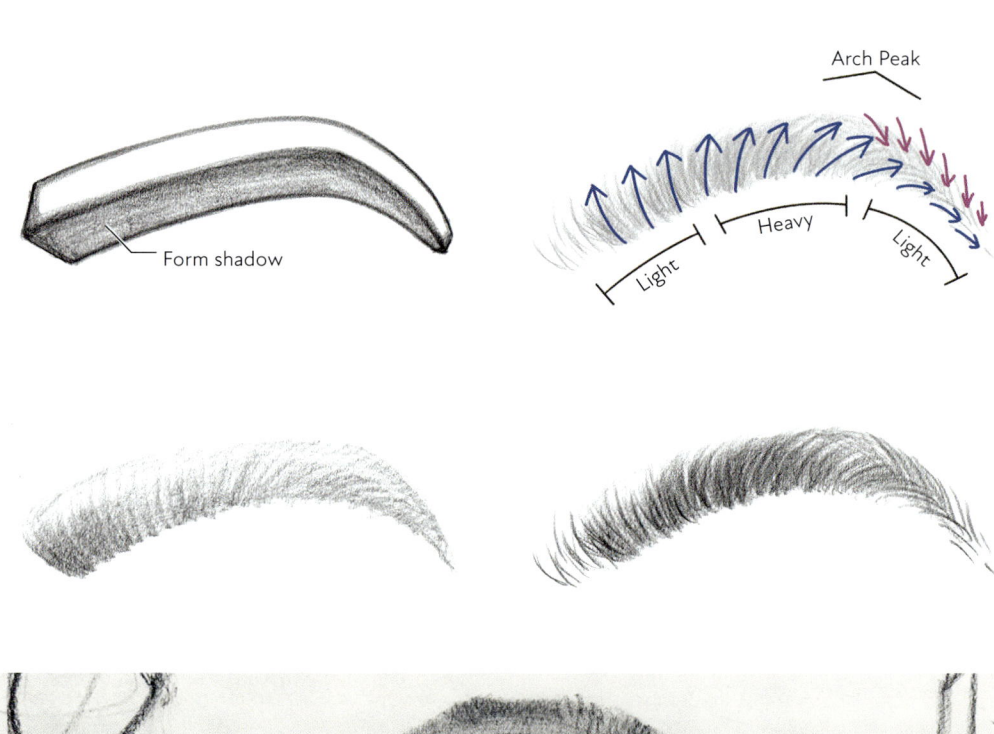

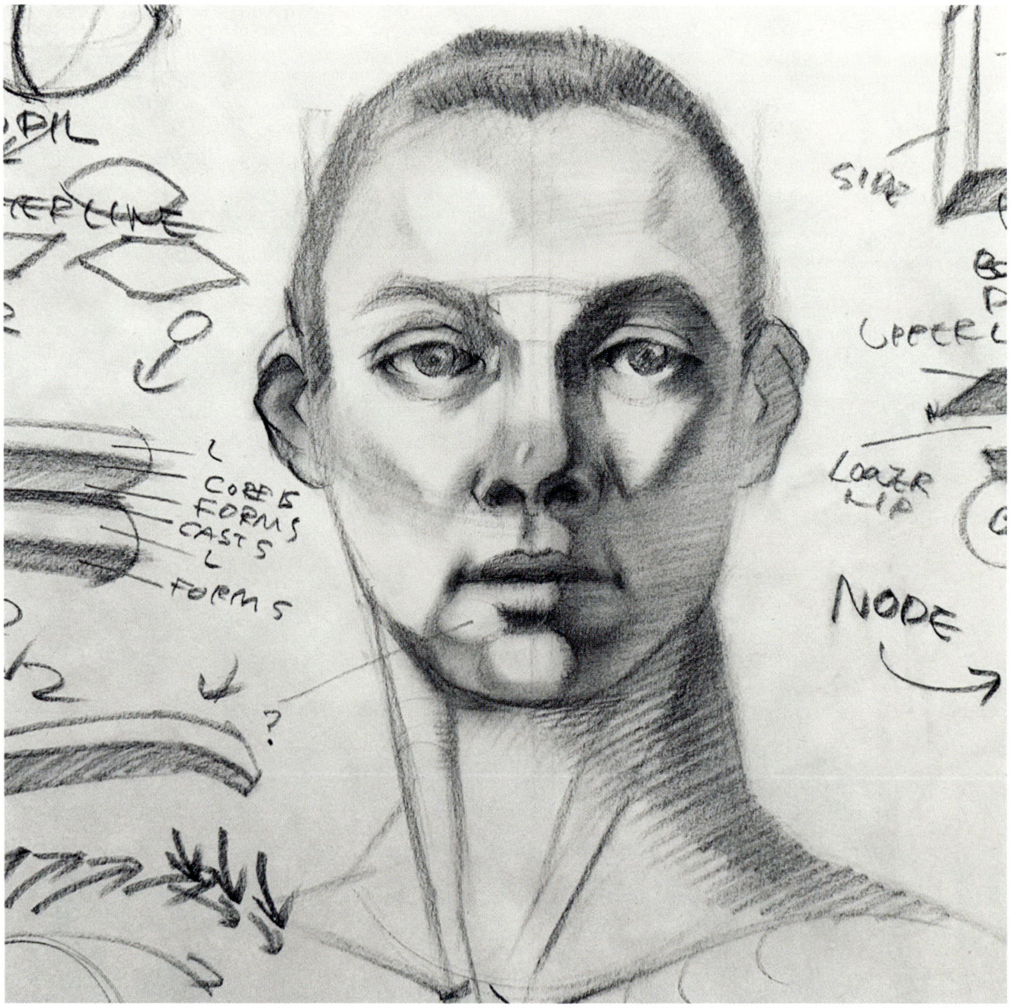

Form shadow

Arch Peak

Light · Heavy · Light

Nose

The nose is formed with bones, cartilages, and some tissues under the skin and muscles. The upper part of the nose right under the Glabella is a pair of bones called the **Nasal bone**. This is the only bony part of the nose; the rest is formed with different pairs of cartilages and tissues.

In between the Nasal bone and the tip of the nose is the **Lateral Cartilage**. This makes a pair of lateral planes in the nose. The tip of the nose is formed with the **Greater Alar Cartilage**. This is also a pair of cartilages, which together make a large round ball shape. The wing of the nose is formed with dense connective tissue. You can also use a ball shape for each wing in the construction drawing process.

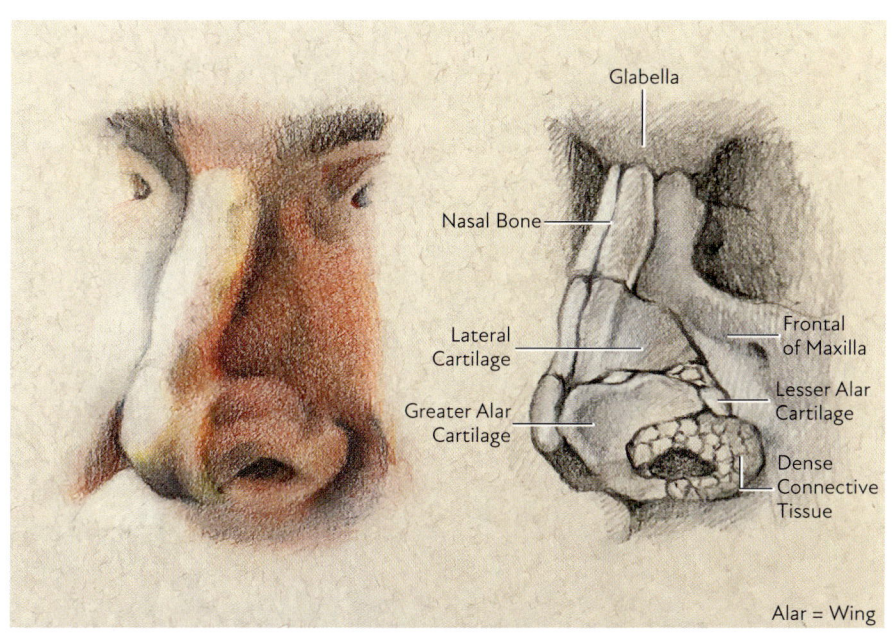

Glabella

Nasal Bone

Lateral Cartilage

Greater Alar Cartilage

Frontal of Maxilla

Lesser Alar Cartilage

Dense Connective Tissue

Alar = Wing

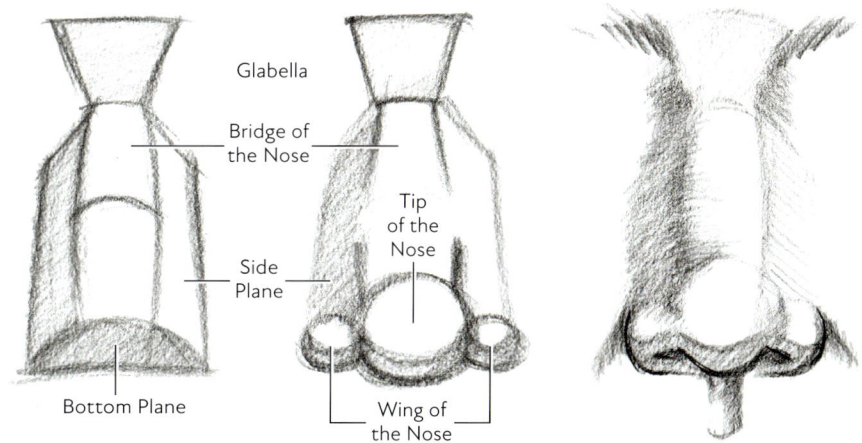

Glabella

Bridge of the Nose

Side Plane

Bottom Plane

Tip of the Nose

Wing of the Nose

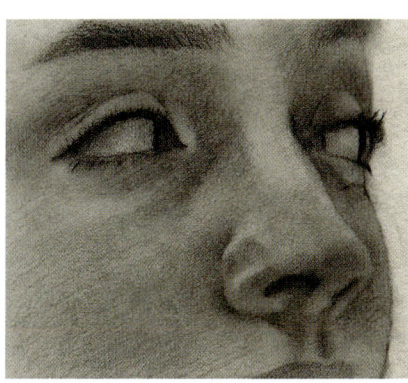

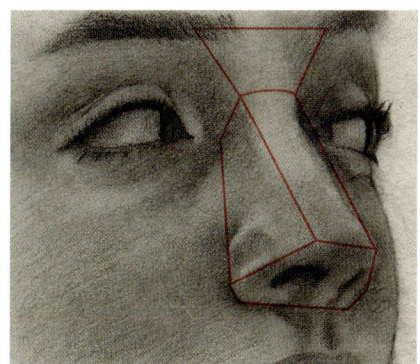

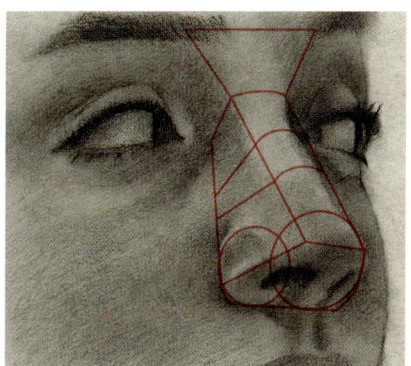

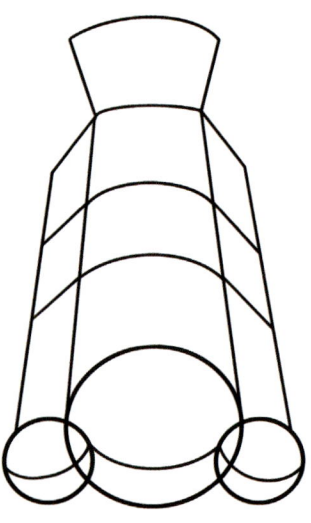

Understanding the Nose Planes

To create an accurate drawing of the nose, understanding how the basic geometric shapes and planes work in light will help. For the lower part of the nose, think about the shading on a sphere. The bottom of the nose usually faces down and the plane becomes a form shadow. But depending on the environment, the shadows on the tip and wing of the nose might be different.

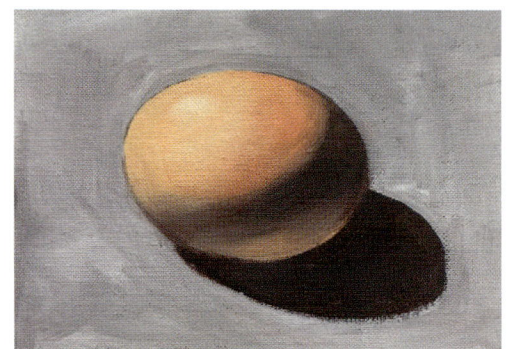

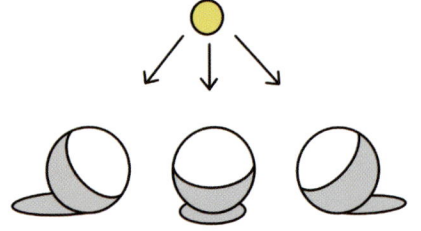

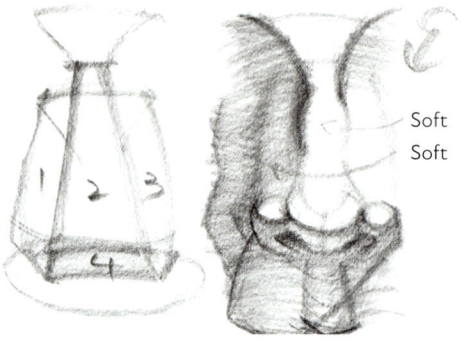

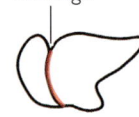

Crease of the Greater Alar Cartilage

Soft
Soft

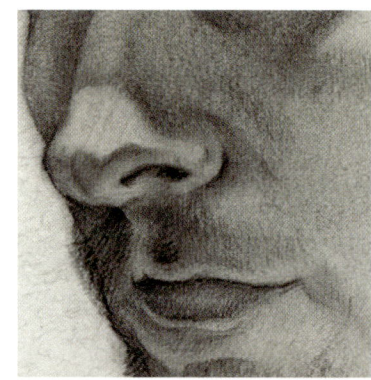

Contouring the Side of the Nose

In the drawing process, it is helpful to deconstruct all the anatomical parts you see in the nose. The shading should be mild, and there should be no firm lines.

The bottom of the nose is the plane that faces down, and it usually does not receive much light. The nostrils are located on this bottom surface, and the tone gets even darker inside the hole.

The line of the wing of the nose should not be connected to the line of the nostril. Make sure to go under the nostrils when working on the wings.

Some people have a vertical crease in the middle of the tip of the nose. This is a midline where the paired Greater Alar Cartilages meet.

The firm, edgy shape of the Nasal bone can be seen on some noses as well.

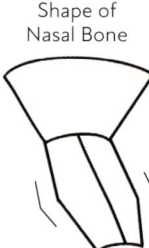

Shape of Nasal Bone

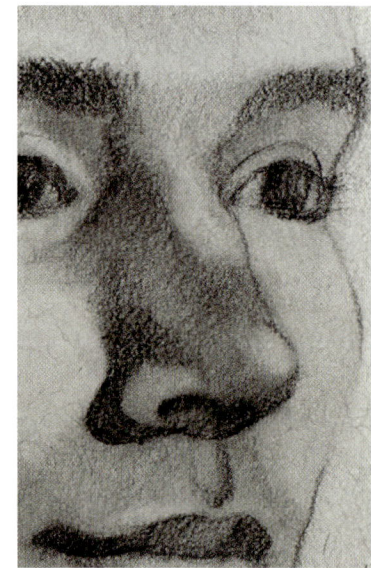

Lips / Mouth

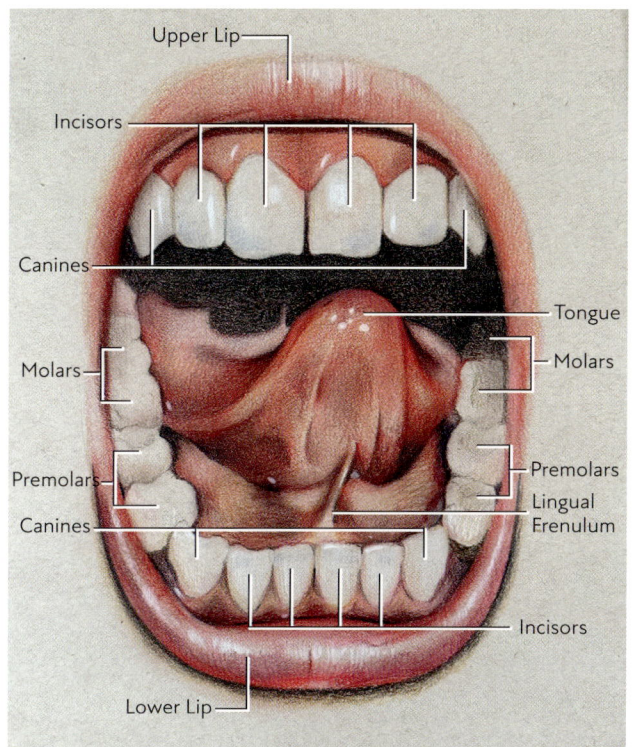

The mouth is located on the surface of the Mandible and Maxilla region in front of the teeth.

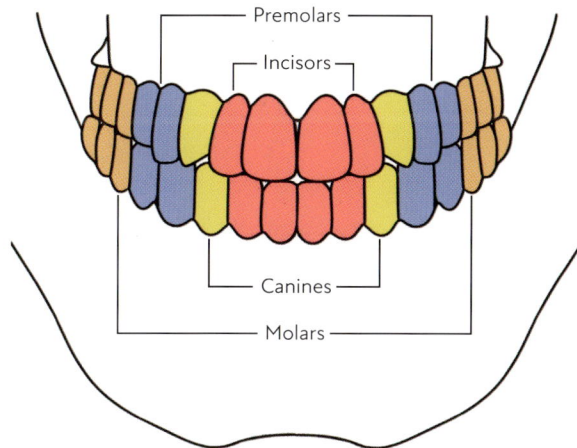

Teeth

Most human adults have thirty-two teeth that are classified into four groups: **Incisors**, **Canines**, **Premolars**, and **Molars**. Most children have twenty teeth (Incisors, Canines, and Molars) that grow in between the age of four months and six years. They eventually fall out and the adult teeth emerge.

Incisors are the frontal teeth that are most visible in the mouth. Canines, also known as "dog teeth," come next. They have a sharp knife-like shape, like a dog's fangs, hence the name. Premolars sit behind the Canines, and Molars are located in the back of the mouth. They work to chew, grind, and crush food.

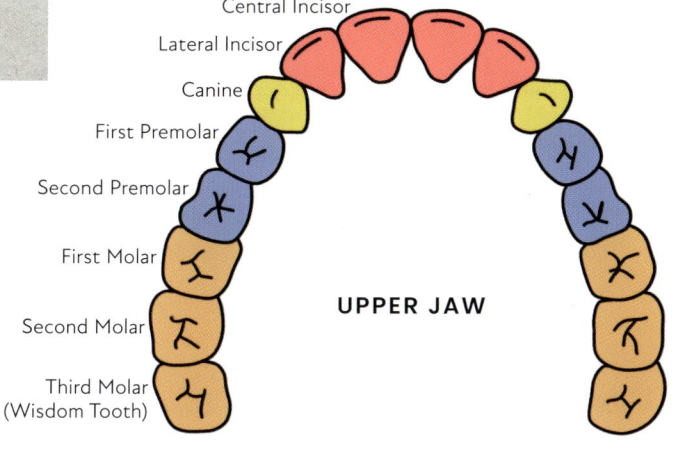

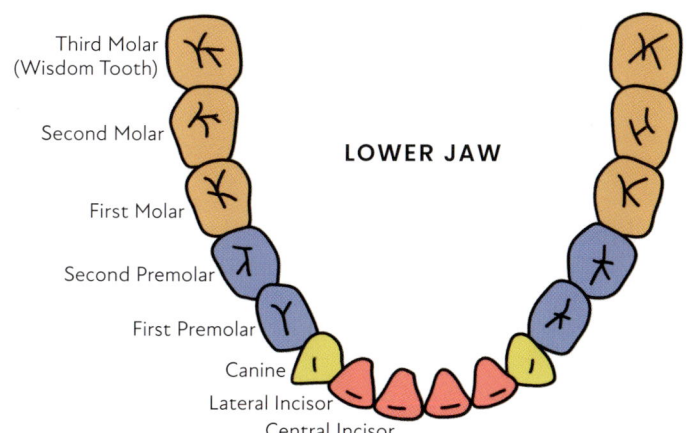

Basic Volume of Lips

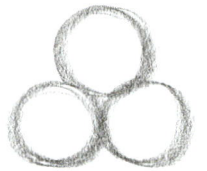

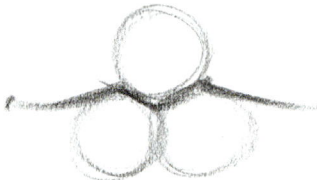

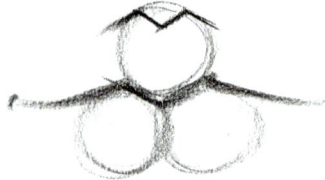

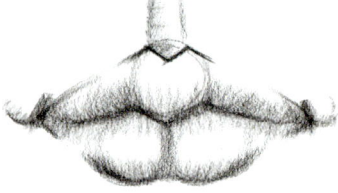

Light Source

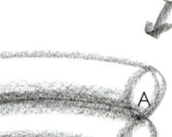

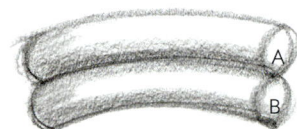

Lips

Inside of the lips, we see three major volumes in the center: one on the upper lip, and two on the lower lip. The two round volumes on the lower lip are pressed against each other. This is the why a vertical crease can be spotted on some people with full lips.

When the three volumes are formed like a pyramid, a wavy horizontal line is traced in between. This line can be used as a line in between the upper and lower lip. Continue the line toward the corner of the lips.

Avoiding the Duck Lip

Many beginning artists outline the lips firmly. This will make the lips appear as a cartoony duck beak. To avoid the firm contour, make sure to start the shading from the line in between the lips.

From the lateral view, you can see that the plane of the upper lip faces down while the plane of lower lip faces upward. In a natural environment where the light source is above the subject's head, the upper lip should be slightly darker than the lower lip.

This technique is often used in the comic book–style portrait. Artists apply a tone on the upper lip and purposely skip toning on the lower lip, then simply drop a cast shadow under the lower lip. This creates an illusion of lips.

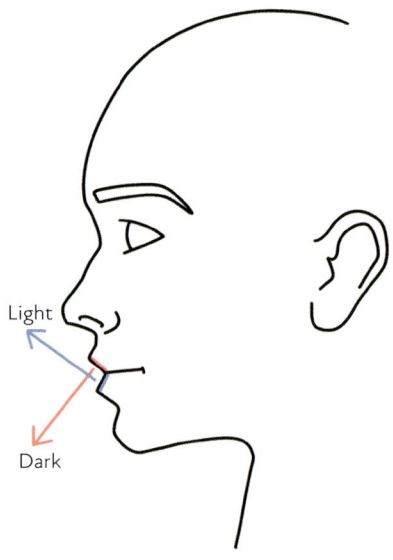

Light

Dark

When shading the lips, think about stacking two cylinders, just like we did with the technique used in the folded eyelid. Cylinder A would drop a cast shadow onto cylinder B. Cylinder B would drop a cast shadow right above the chin. This cast shadow can be emphasized to push the volume of the lower lip.

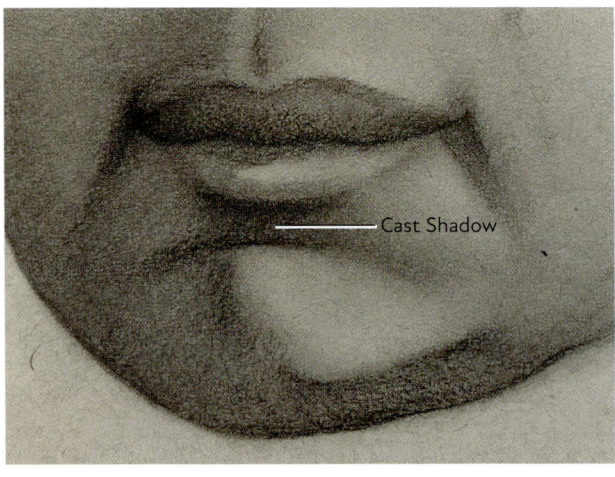

Cast Shadow

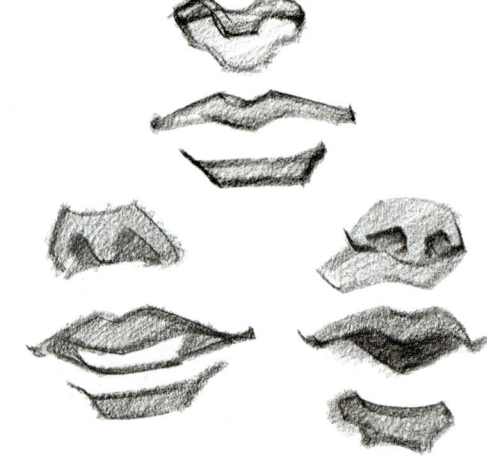

Philtrum, Nasolabial Fold, and Node

We must understand that the lips lay on the mouth region, and the shape cross-contours the arch shape. This means that the lips are not placed on a flat surface, but lie along the U-curve of the mouth.

The **Philtrum** is a small vertical groove located in between the bottom of the nose and the mid-upper lip. This cuts the top of the upper lip into a V shape, creating two peaks in the middle.

From the wing of the nose toward the corner of lips we have the **Nasolabial Fold**, known as a "smile line." The space in between the fold lines above the lips forms the arch. Depending on where the light source is located, you can focus on the gradation of shading on the surface. The exception would be seen on the Philtrum. Because of the groove, the shadow moves into the opposite direction.

In each corner of the mouth, we can see a small bean-like volume called the **Node**. The Node, also known as "modiolus" or "knoten," becomes the attachment of many surrounding muscles. On the surface, the Node could also appear like skin folding over the corner of the mouth.

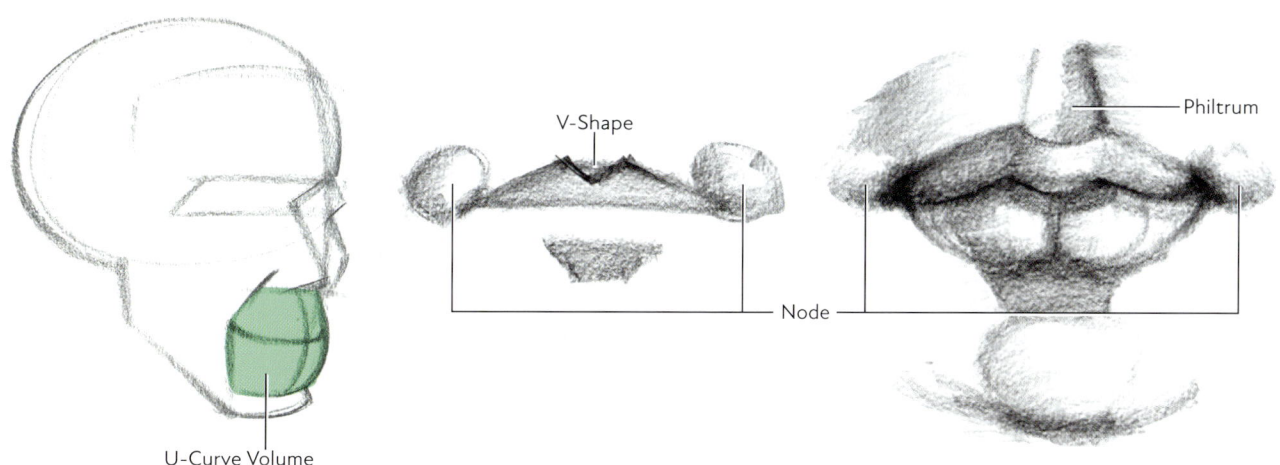

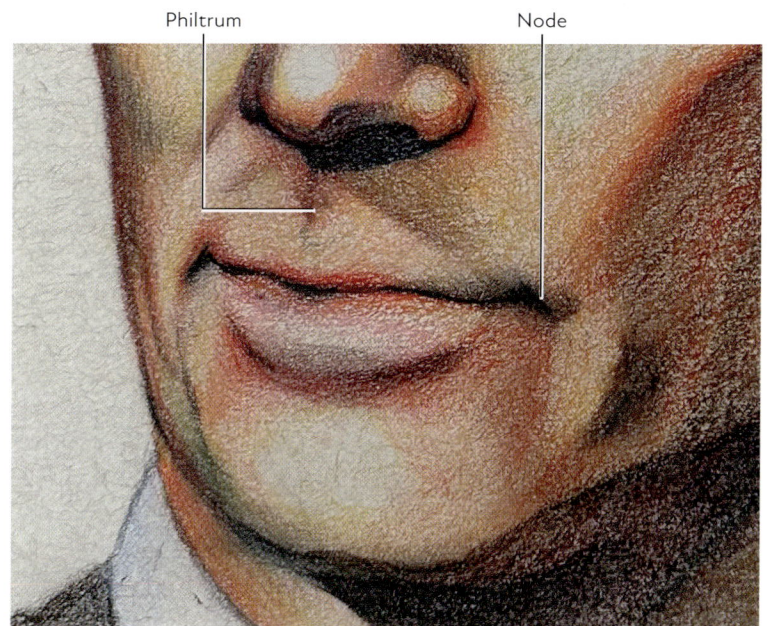

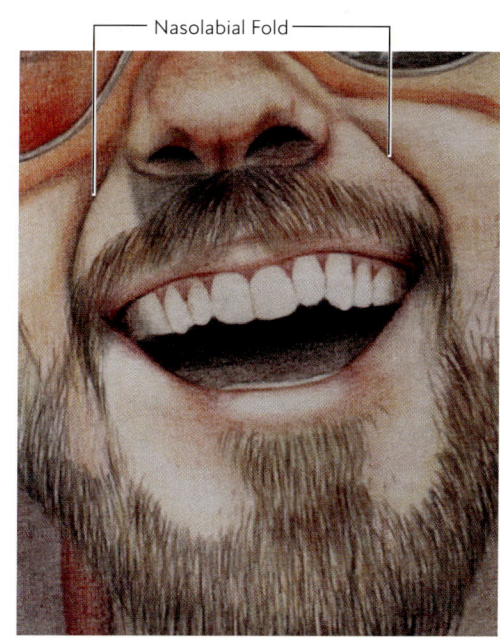

Ears

The ears are located on the lateral side of the head, specifically on the mid-inferior part of the Cranium of the skull where a small hole is above the end of the Mandible. This hole is called the **External Auditory Meatus,** which is your ear hole.

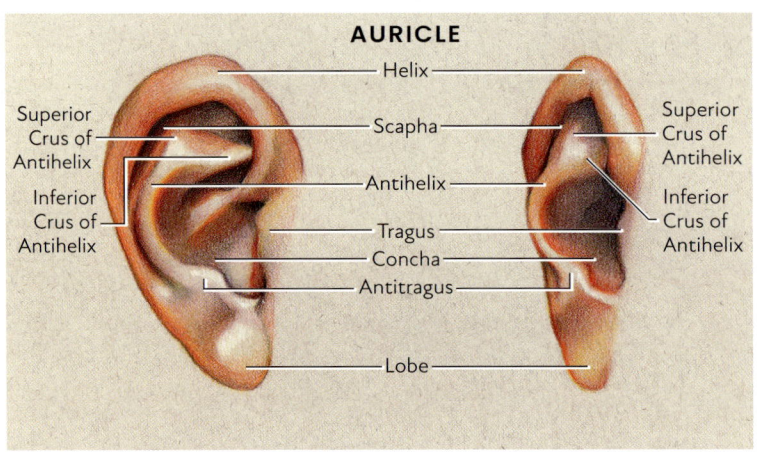

AURICLE

Helix

Superior Crus of Antihelix

Scapha

Antihelix

Inferior Crus of Antihelix

Tragus

Concha

Antitragus

Superior Crus of Antihelix

Inferior Crus of Antihelix

Lobe

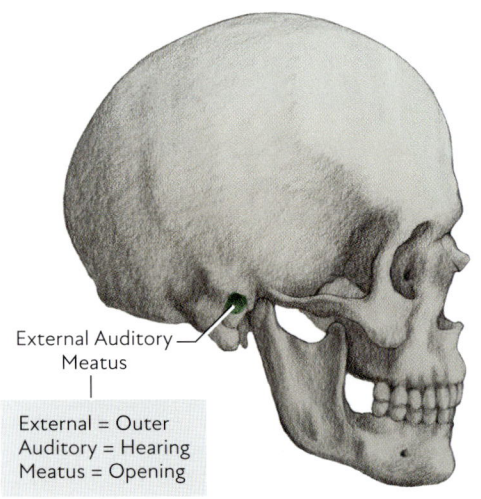

External Auditory Meatus

External = Outer
Auditory = Hearing
Meatus = Opening

External Anatomy of the Ear

The structure of the entire ear is called the **Auricle**, or Pinna ("wing" or "fin" in Latin). It is a cartilage that forms like a small dome, so that we can hear sounds better.

The outer rim of the Auricle is called the **Helix**. This makes the overall shape of the ear, which looks like a question mark. Under the Helix, we see the **Antihelix**. This makes another curved Y-shaped rim inside of the Auricle.

Remember as "Why (Y)?"

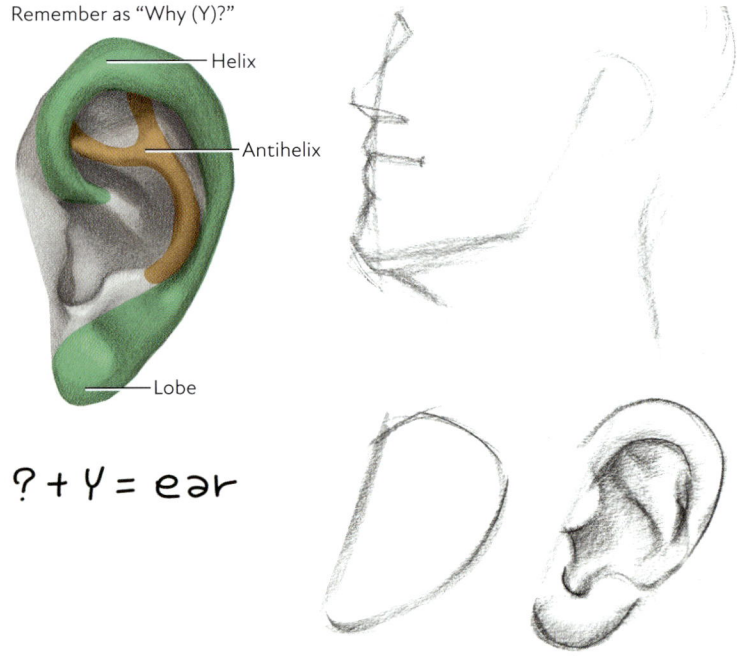

Helix

Antihelix

Lobe

? + Y = ear

The inside surface that creates a dome shape in the auricle is called the **Concha**. The Concha has an opened lid called the **Tragus**, which is a cartilaginous process attached to the facial skin. Another process right next to the Tragus is called the **Antitragus**. It is also located above the **Lobe**, which is made of skin and fat without cartilages.

You see most of the anatomy of the Auricle from both the lateral and anterior view. It seems like the shape of the ear becomes thinner from the anterior view, but the one cartilage that sticks out of the overall shape is the Antihelix. The Helix becomes the rooftop of the ear, meaning that it would drop a shadow on the top of the Antihelix. Both cartilages are tube-like. In shading, more vivid contrast can be seen on them than on the soft texture of the ear lobe.

The Masseter

The Strongest Muscle in the Body

How could we imagine that the strongest muscle of the entire body is located in our head?

The **Masseter** is the muscle that is responsible for closing the mouth. It elevates the Mandible and makes a powerful closure of the mouth. It is one of a group of **mastication muscles** that includes the Temporalis muscle.

The Masseter is located on the lateral side of the jawbone. It starts from the inferior border of the Zygomatic bone and goes to the lateral surface/angle of the Mandible.

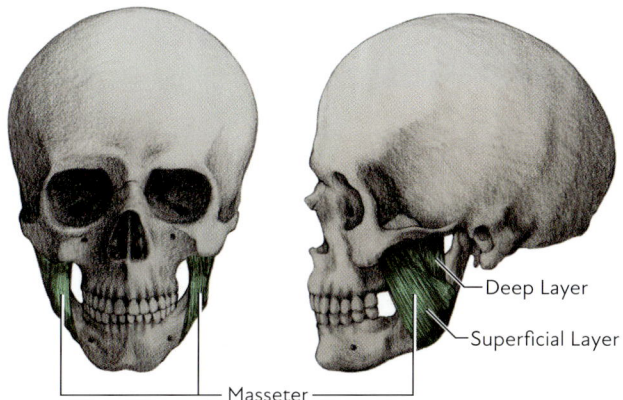

Deep Layer

Superficial Layer

Masseter

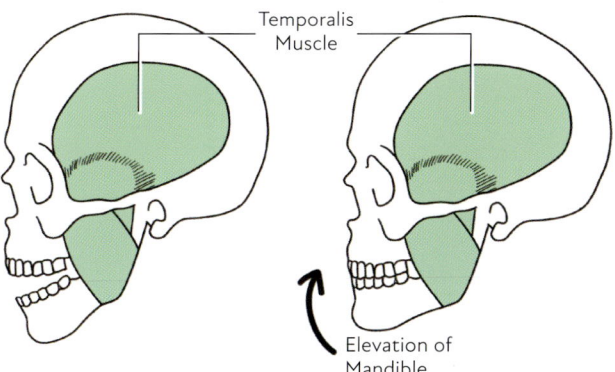

Temporalis Muscle

Elevation of Mandible

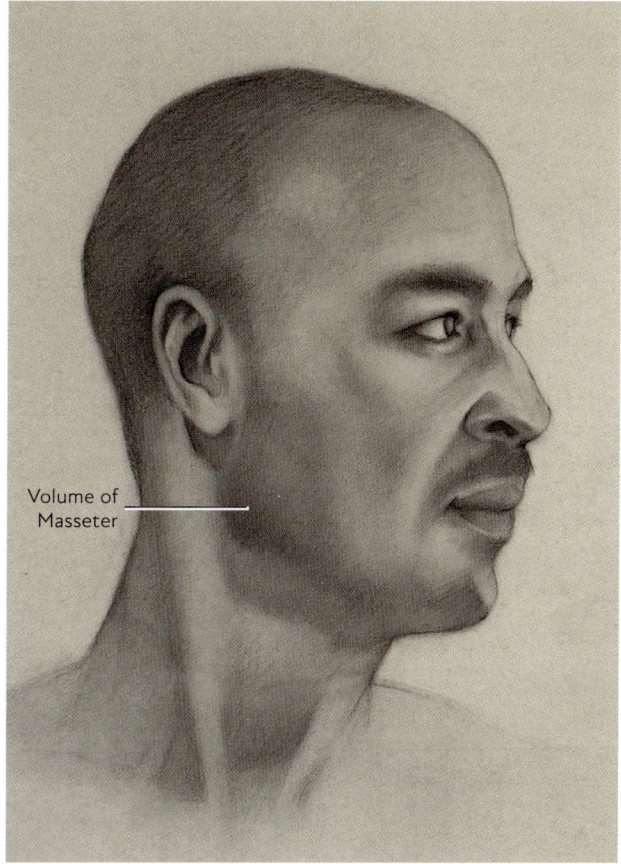

Volume of Masseter

The surface volume of the Masseter can often be spotted on the lower part of the cheek down to the jawline. You can even feel the movement of the muscle when your teeth are compressed tight inside of your mouth.

Sternocleidomastoid   The V-Shaped Neck Muscle

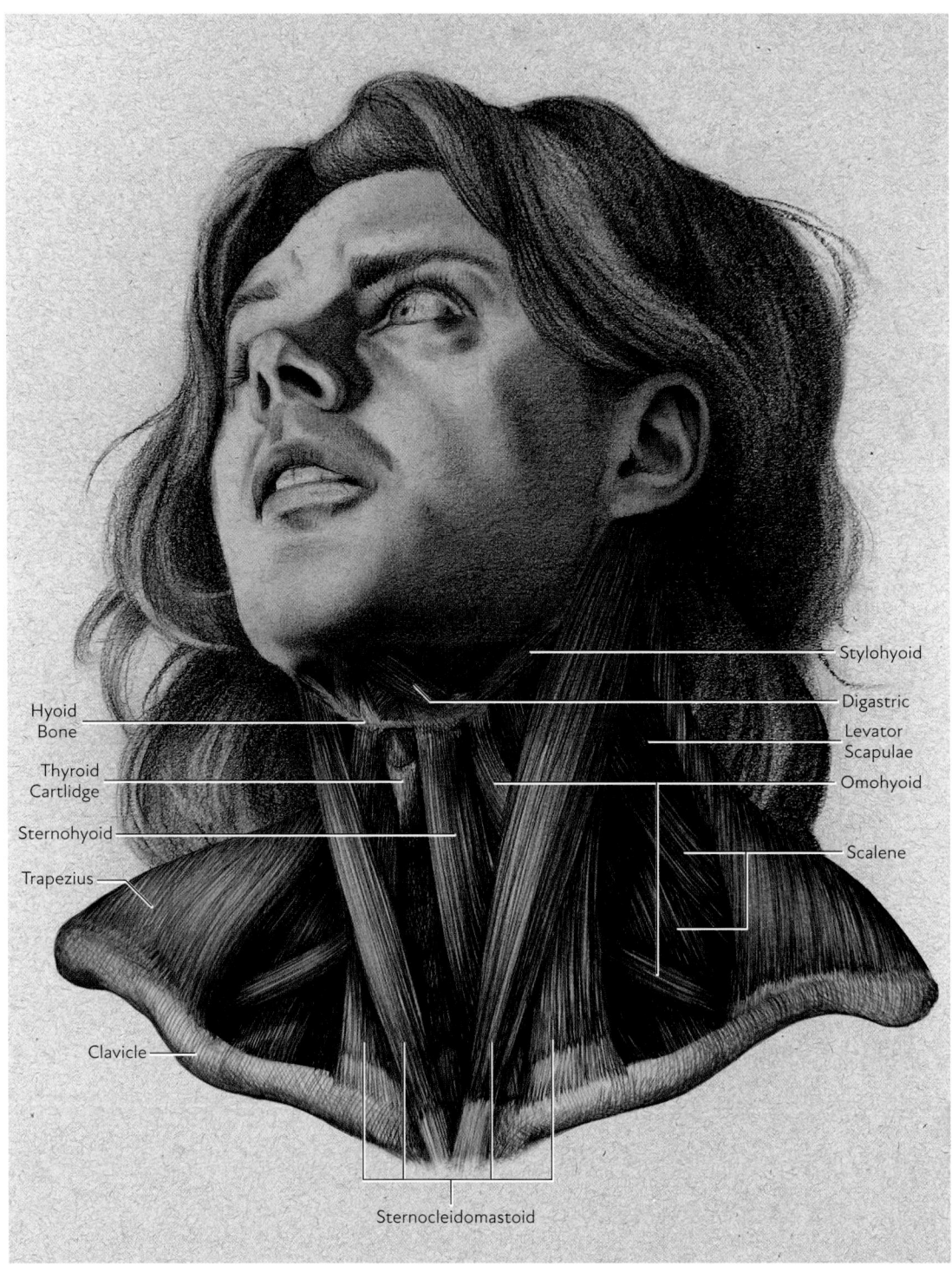

Stylohyoid

Digastric

Hyoid
Bone

Levator
Scapulae

Thyroid
Cartlidge

Omohyoid

Sternohyoid

Scalene

Trapezius

Clavicle

Sternocleidomastoid

The neck can be simplified down to a large cylindrical shape in the construction drawing process. One of the most important muscular structures you can see in the neck is a pair of muscles called the **Sternocleidomastoid**. Its name is quite long, but the term makes perfect sense when you find out the origin and insertion of this muscle.

From the anterior view, you can see this pair of muscles creating a letter M. The origins of the muscle are on the lower side: the **Manubrium of the Sternum** and the **Clavicle**. The insertion of the muscle is on the **Mastoid Process,** located on the Temporal bone in the Cranium. Now you can see the meaning behind this name.

The muscle has a long, tube-like volume in the surface anatomy. The volume is thicker in the superior portion and becomes skinnier toward the Sternum and Clavicle attachments. Because the neck can rotate and flex, the Mastoid attachment will follow the movement of the head. When the head is rotated to the lateral side, the tube of the Sternocleidomastoid appears in a vertical line and becomes perpendicular to the Clavicle.

Sterno (Sternum) – **cleido** (Clavicle) – **mastoid** (Mastoid Process)

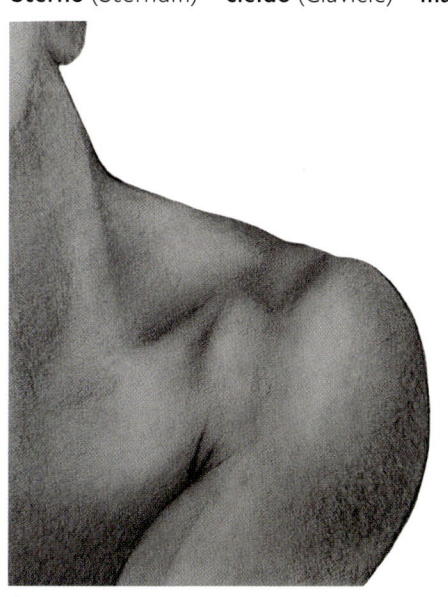
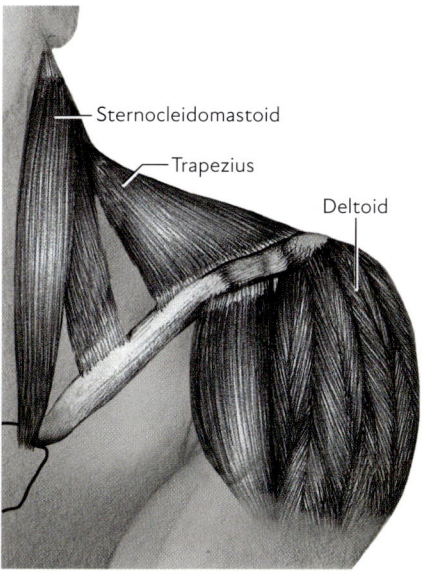

Sternocleidomastoid

Trapezius

Deltoid

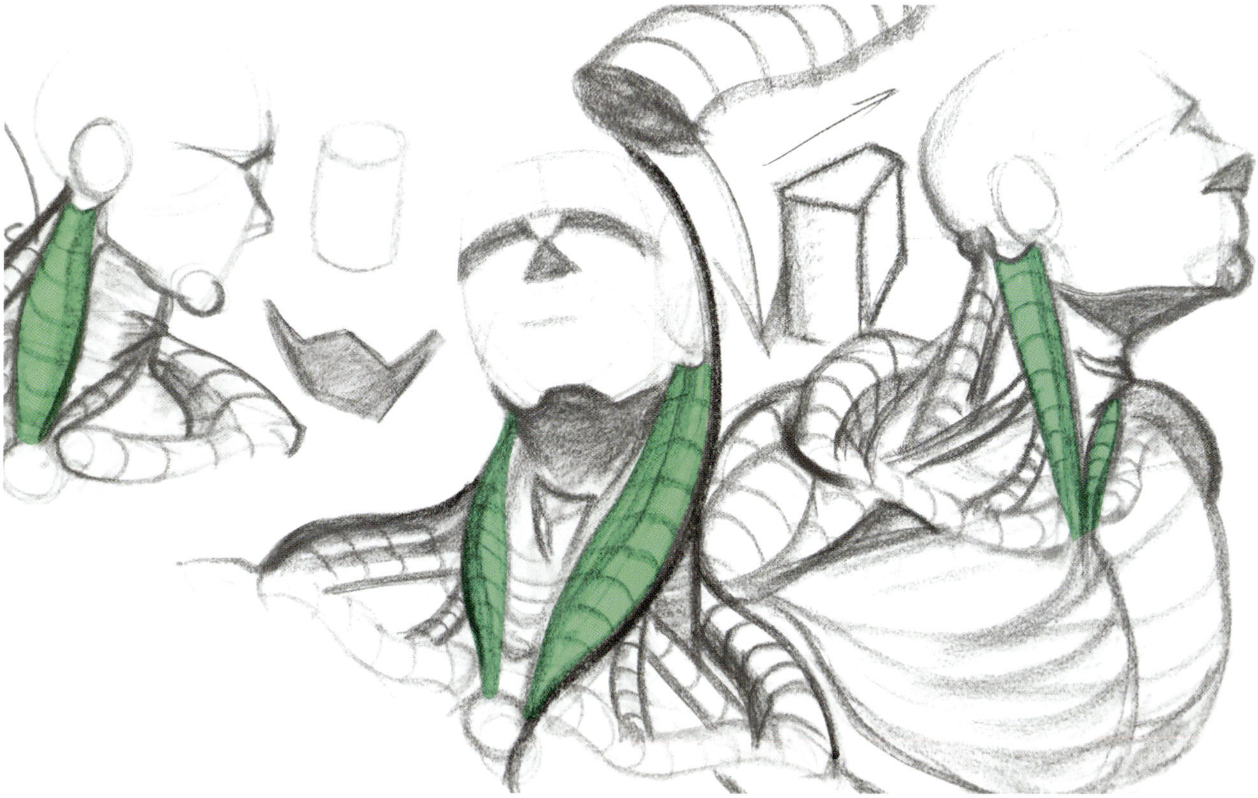

Drawing Under the Chin

Portrait drawing can be pleasing for many artists, until they see the head looking up all of a sudden. What is happening in the space between the chin and the neck? Is there a plate or plane, or is this hollow? Controlling the angle and getting the right shape under the chin can be challenging when the head turns upward.

The bone that creates the jawline is the **Mandible.** The Mandible has two different portions: the **Body** and **Ramus.** You can see a good angle of this bone from the inferior view.

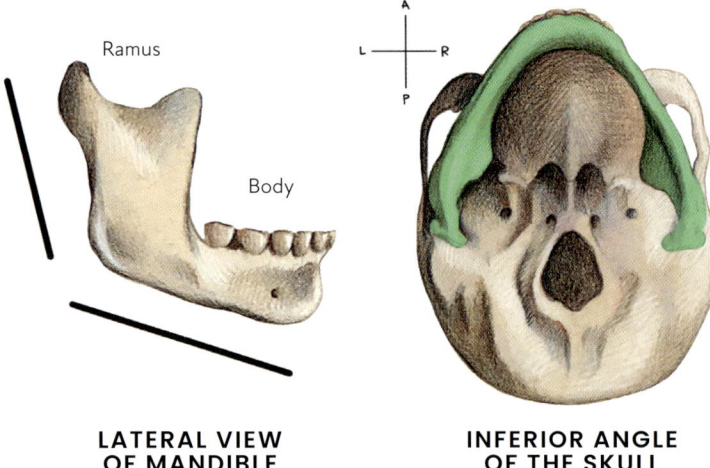

LATERAL VIEW OF MANDIBLE

INFERIOR ANGLE OF THE SKULL

Let's take the simple geometric shapes of a cuboid and a cylinder. Imagine that the cuboid that was used to form the basic shape of the head fits right onto the cylinder that represents the neck. You can see that the bottom plane of the cuboid has a specific shape. This is the basic form of the underside of the jaw.

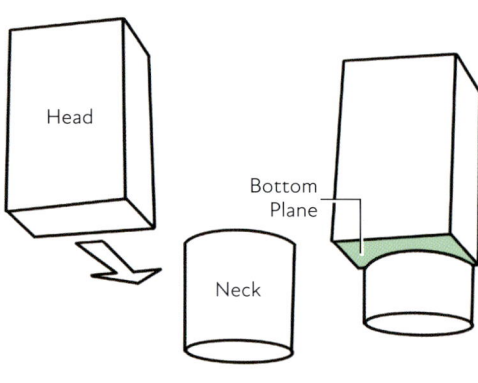

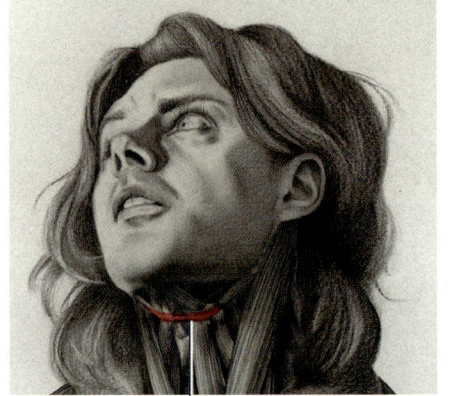

Hyoid Bone

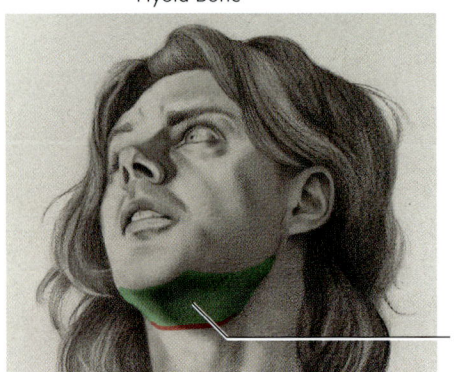

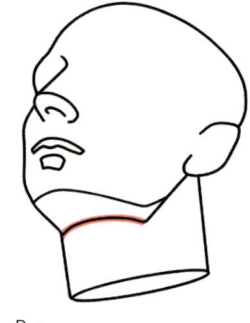

Line of Hyoid Bone

Plane Between Hyoid Bone and Mandible

The line of the attachment has a subtle curve onto the surface of the cylinder neck, and this curve can represent another bone found on the surface of the neck: the **Hyoid bone.** This bone lies horizontally in the anterior neck, and it divides the neck planes into the Mandible line and the anterior surface of the neck. There are several muscles surrounding the throat, and all together, they create a big, tube-like shape on the anterior side of the neck.

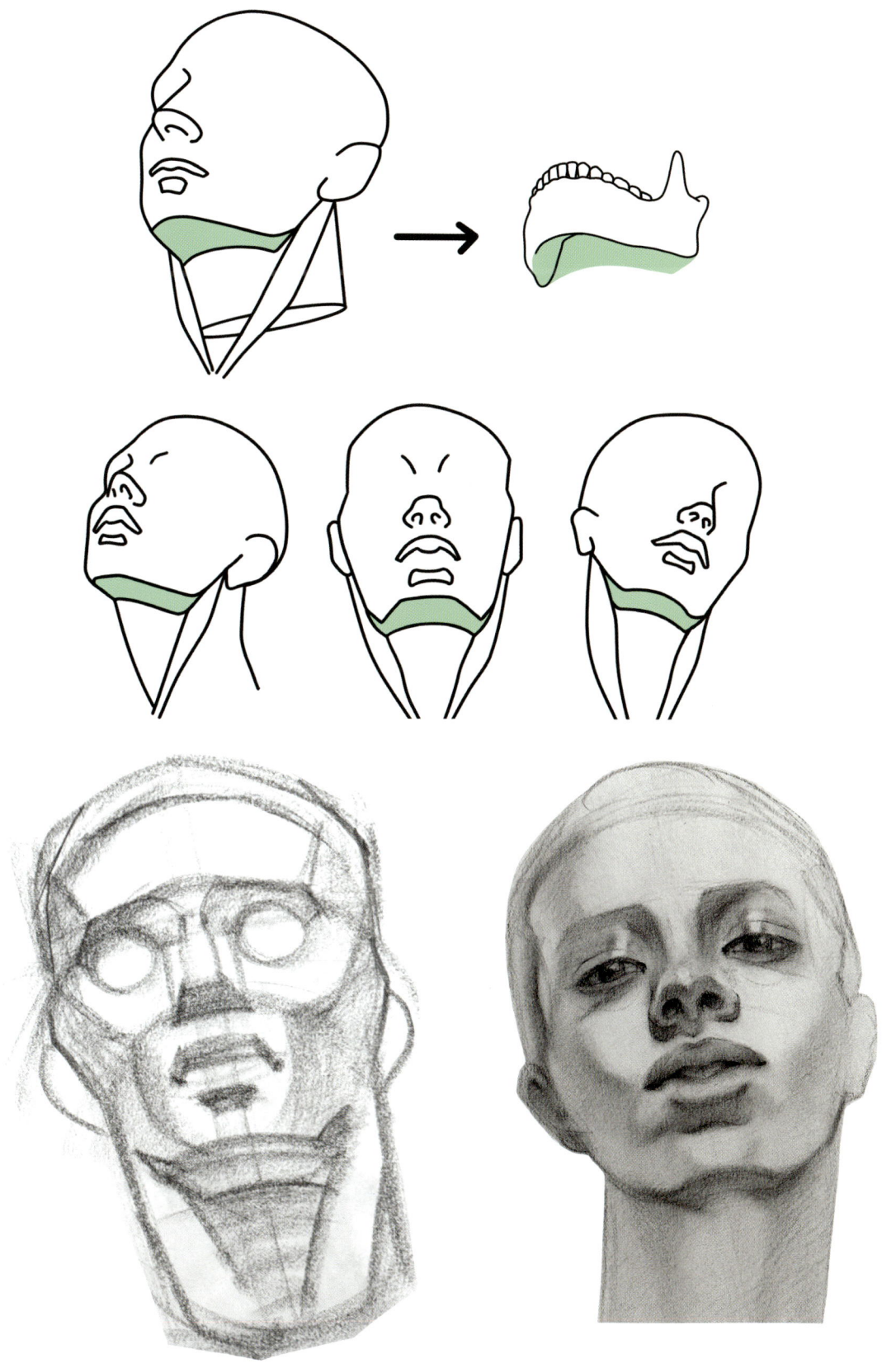

Head Drawing Overview

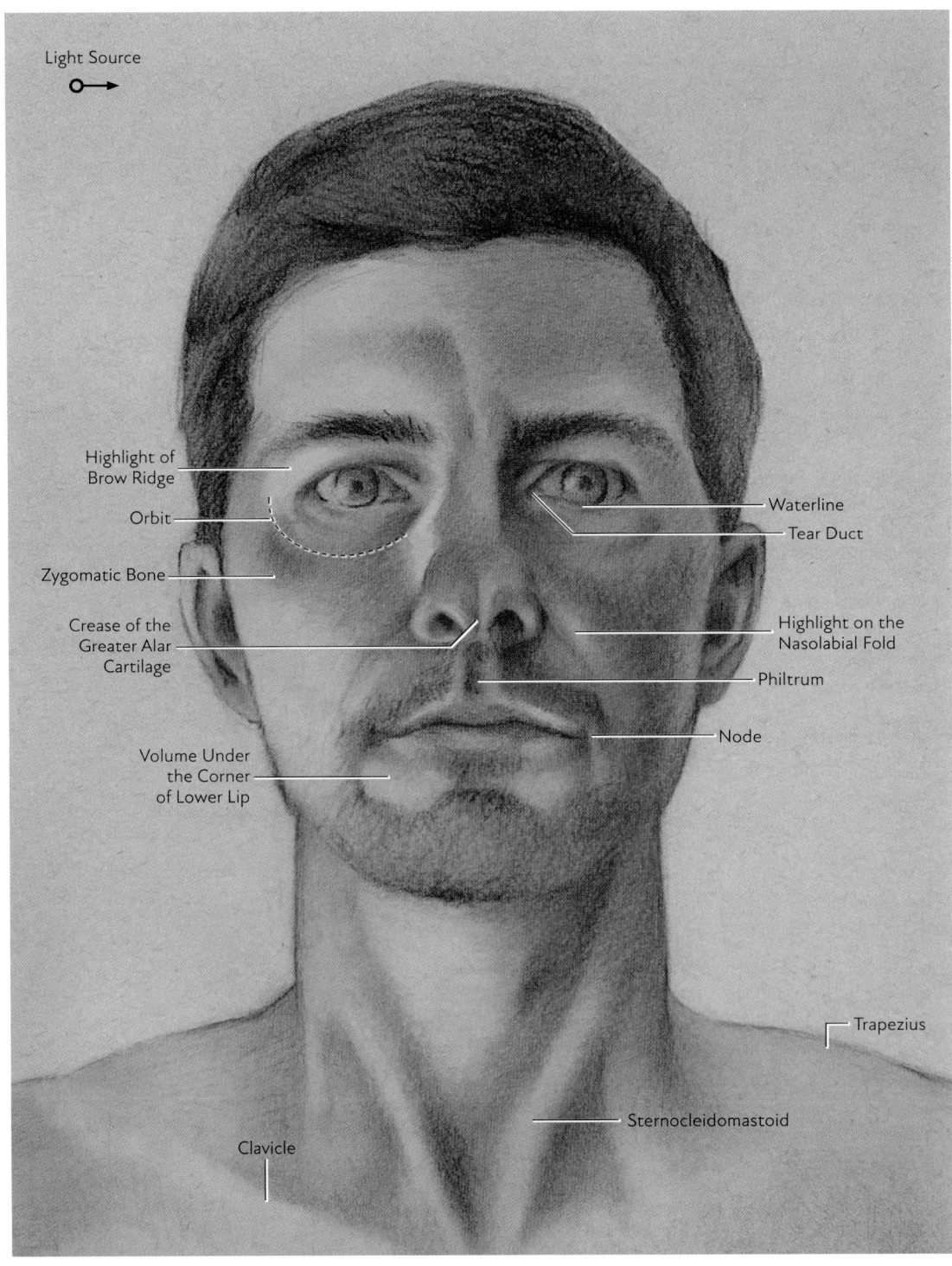

Light Source

Highlight of Brow Ridge

Orbit

Zygomatic Bone

Crease of the Greater Alar Cartilage

Volume Under the Corner of Lower Lip

Waterline

Tear Duct

Highlight on the Nasolabial Fold

Philtrum

Node

Trapezius

Sternocleidomastoid

Clavicle

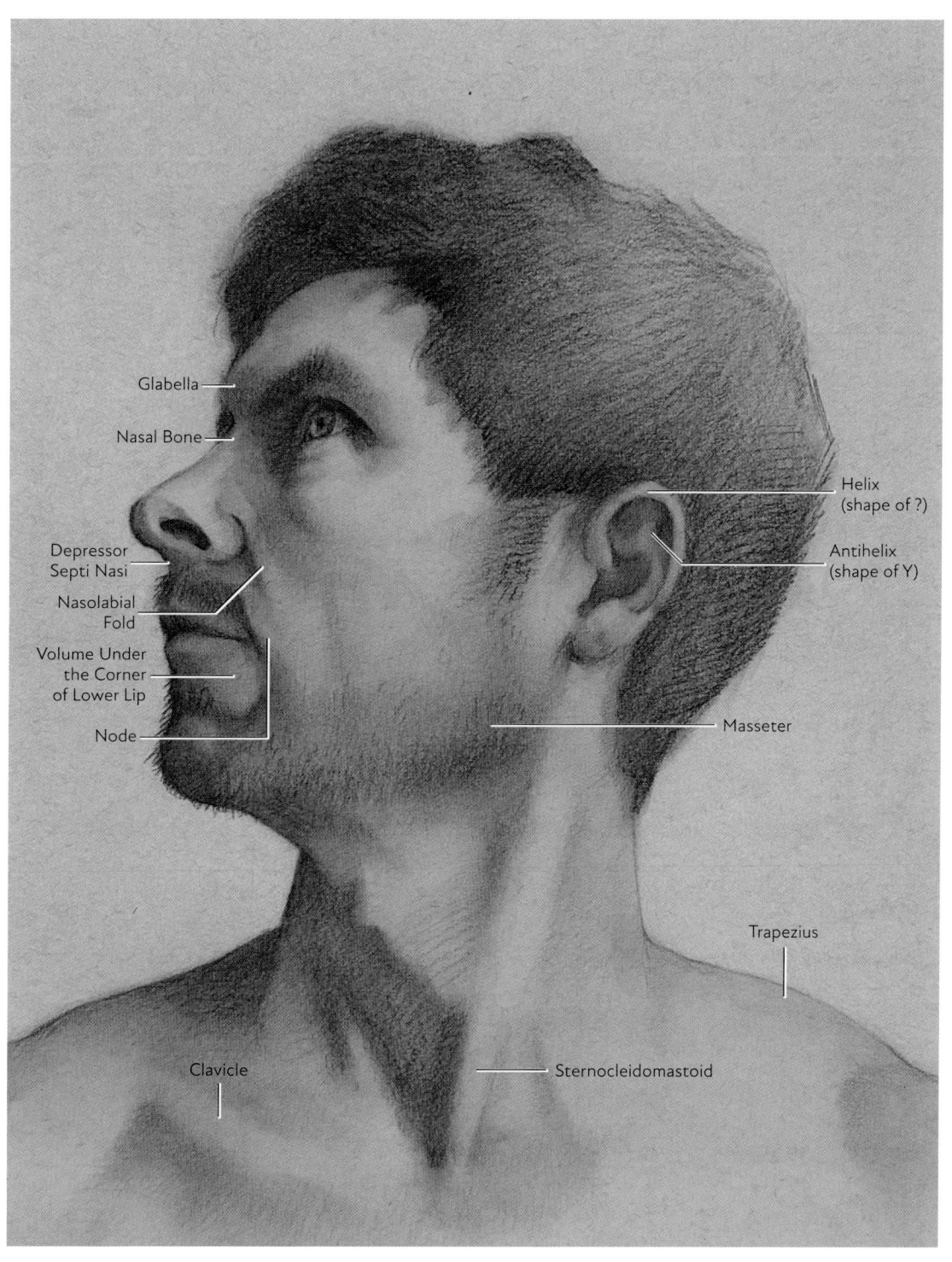

Glabella

Nasal Bone

Depressor
Septi Nasi

Nasolabial
Fold

Volume Under
the Corner
of Lower Lip

Node

Helix
(shape of ?)

Antihelix
(shape of Y)

Masseter

Trapezius

Clavicle

Sternocleidomastoid

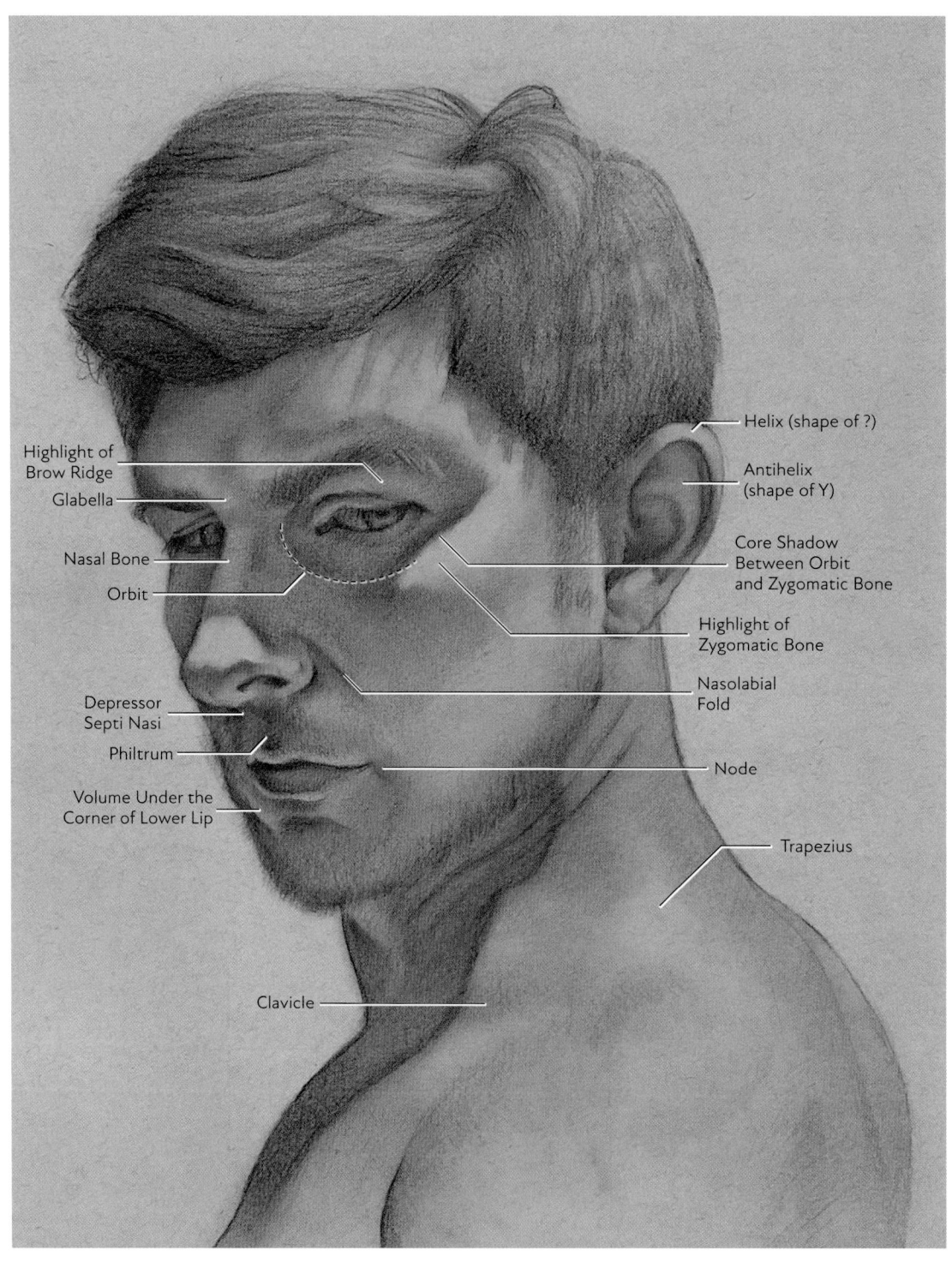

Helix (shape of ?)

Antihelix
(shape of Y)

Highlight of
Brow Ridge

Glabella

Nasal Bone

Orbit

Core Shadow
Between Orbit
and Zygomatic Bone

Highlight of
Zygomatic Bone

Nasolabial
Fold

Depressor
Septi Nasi

Philtrum

Node

Volume Under the
Corner of Lower Lip

Trapezius

Clavicle

It's Disgusting!

The Longest Muscle Name in the Body

We have learned the best of the human anatomy in this book: the biggest bone (the Femur), the strongest muscle (the Masseter), and the largest muscle (the Gluteus Maximus). What about the muscle with the longest name?

The muscle with the longest name is located in the face. It is called the **Levator Labii Superioris Alaeque Nasi**. Is it so long that it disgusts you? Well, that's appropriate, because the muscle contracts when you hold the emotion of disgust.

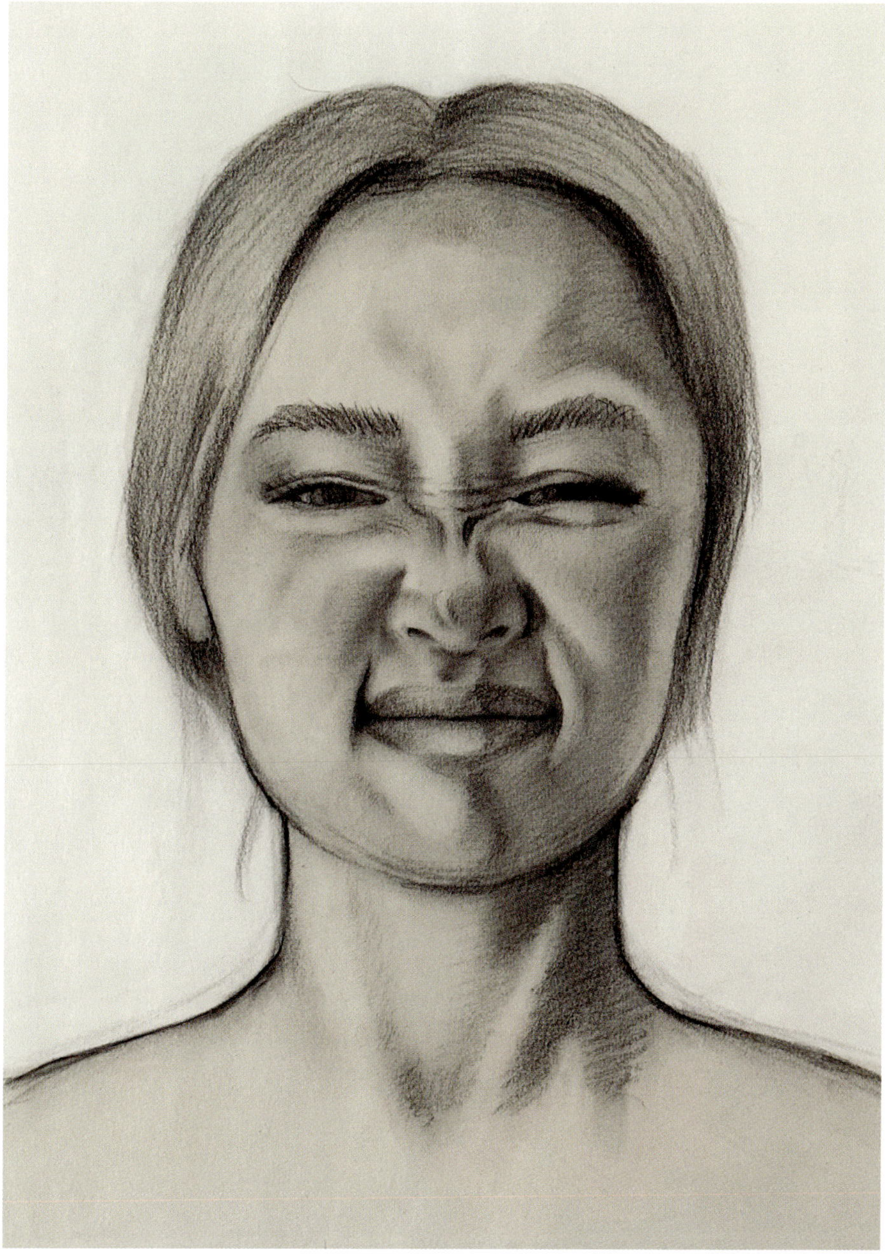

The Levator Labii Superioris Alaeque Nasi is a small, paired, tape-like muscle located on the lateral side of the nose. It widens the nostrils and works to elevate the upper lip. In this movement, you will see some wrinkles forming on the bridge of the nose.

Think about something gross, creepy, or distasteful. You might already be making this facial expression subconsciously.

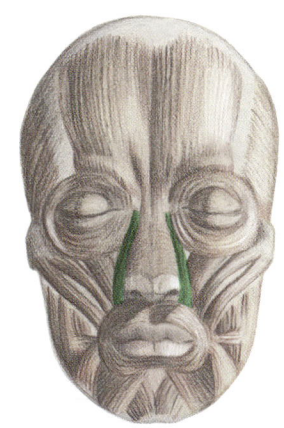

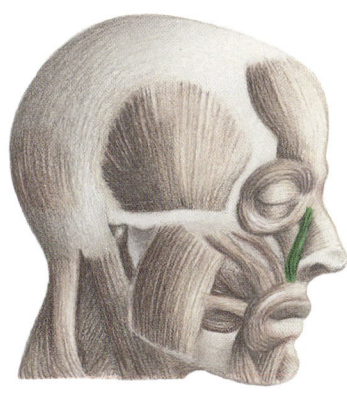

Levator Labii Superioris Alaeque Nasi

Happiness and Sadness Are Right Next to Each Other

Have you ever been in a situation where you can't tell if a person is laughing or crying, or feeling happy or sad by looking at their facial expression? The reason it is confusing is because the smiling muscle and crying muscle lie right next to each other in the face.

The muscle that pulls the corner of the mouth to make a smiley face is called the **Zygomaticus Major**. This muscle is attached from the cheekbone, the Zygomatic bone, to the corner of the mouth. It contracts when we smile, yanking the lips to the side and creating a round hump on the cheek.

On the other hand, the muscle that creates a sad face is called the **Zygomaticus Minor**. This muscle only contracts when we feel sad. Just like the smiling muscle, the Zygomaticus Minor is attached from the cheekbone to the lips. It lies parallel to the Zygomaticus Major, but on the medial side.

The difference is that the Zygomaticus Minor muscle would make the skin under the eyes slightly tighter because of its location. You might squint your eyes when you cry, and it is a different tension than when you make crescent-shaped eyes while relaxing and smiling.

Both of the muscles pull the corner of the lips to the side and create humps on the cheeks. This is why it can be difficult to tell if a person is laughing or crying, or both.

The feeling of sadness usually contains some other negative feeling, too, like anger, anxiety, or pain. The feeling of happiness is pretty much individual. However, "weeping for joy" is an emotion that occurs when the happiness overflows and brings the tears in our eyes. We don't know why it happens exactly, but it is a beautiful thing.

Laughing or Crying?

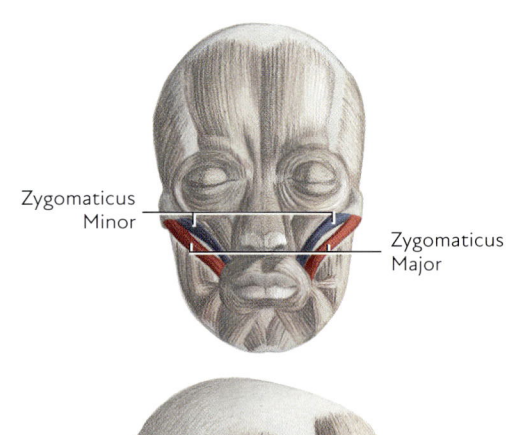

Zygomaticus Minor

Zygomaticus Major

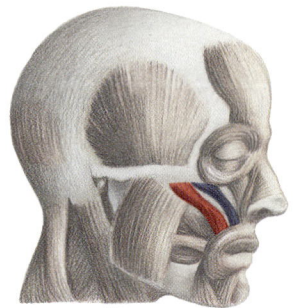

Facial Muscles and Emotions

Let's *face* it together.

In the process of drawing portraits, it's more important to study the skull structure. Some muscles, like the Masseter, will show on the surface anatomy, but most of the facial muscles are for facial expressions. Every muscle in the face has its own role, and it helps to make our expressions look so much more dramatic.

Facial Muscles

We have about forty muscles in our face and they are positioned to surround the facial openings like the eyes, ears, mouth, and nose. They are also responsible for making facial expressions.

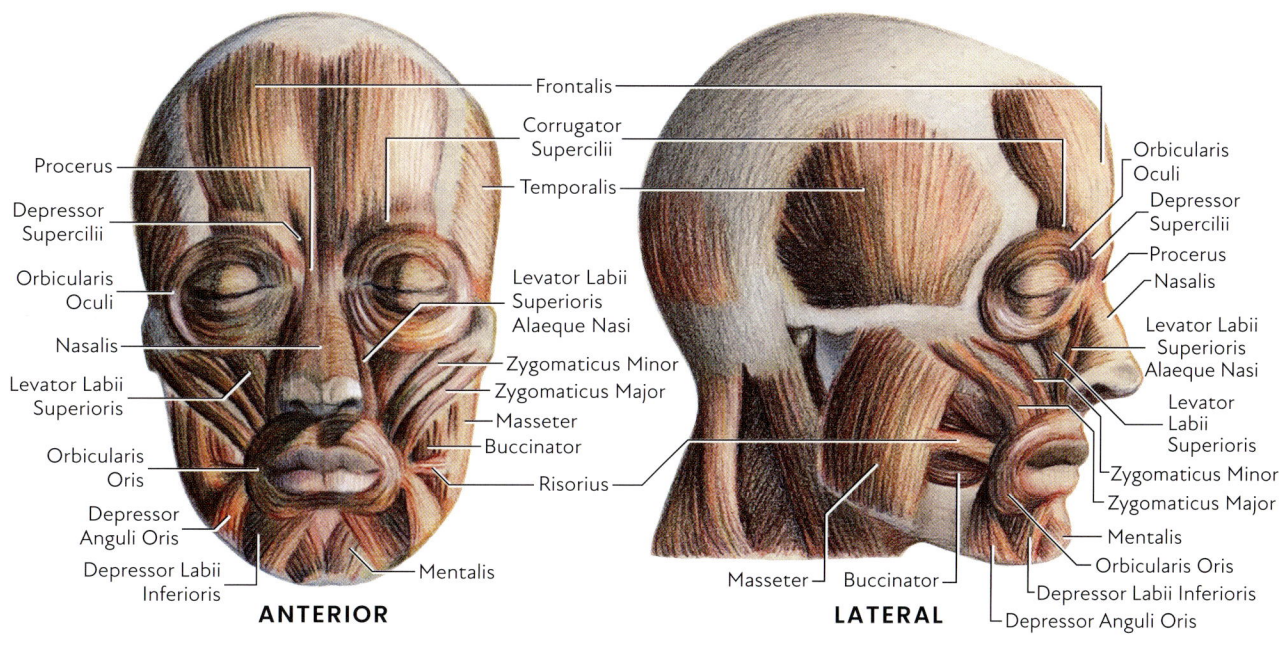

ANTERIOR — Frontalis, Corrugator Supercilii, Temporalis, Procerus, Depressor Supercilii, Orbicularis Oculi, Nasalis, Levator Labii Superioris, Orbicularis Oris, Depressor Anguli Oris, Depressor Labii Inferioris, Levator Labii Superioris Alaeque Nasi, Zygomaticus Minor, Zygomaticus Major, Masseter, Buccinator, Risorius, Mentalis

LATERAL — Orbicularis Oculi, Depressor Supercilii, Procerus, Nasalis, Levator Labii Superioris Alaeque Nasi, Levator Labii Superioris, Zygomaticus Minor, Zygomaticus Major, Mentalis, Orbicularis Oris, Depressor Labii Inferioris, Depressor Anguli Oris, Masseter, Buccinator

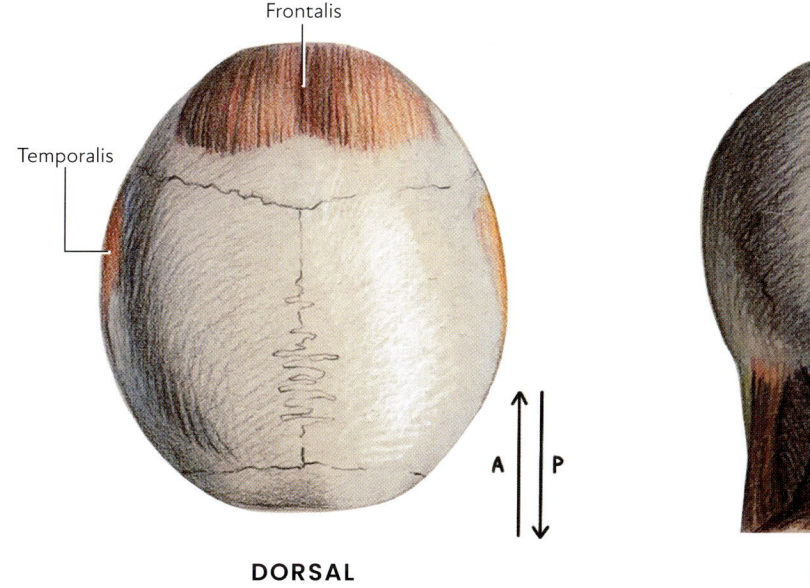

DORSAL — Frontalis, Temporalis, A P

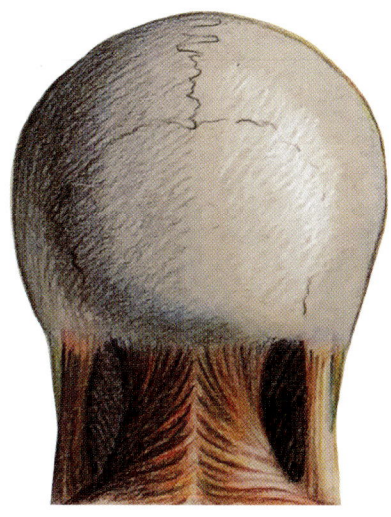

POSTERIOR

Facial Muscles (Paired)

1. **Frontalis**
2. **Temporalis**
3. **Procerus**
4. **Corrugator Supercilii**
5. **Depressor Supercilii**
6. **Orbicularis Oculi**
7. **Nasalis**
8. **Levator Labii Superioris Alaeque Nasi**
9. **Levator Labii Superioris**
10. **Depressor Septi Nasi**
11. **Zygomaticus Major**
12. **Zygomaticus Minor**
13. **Orbicularis Oris**
14. **Depressor Anguli Oris**
15. **Depressor Labii Inferioris**
16. **Mentalis**
17. **Masseter**
18. **Risorius**
19. **Buccinator**
20. **Platysma**
(sheet muscle covering the anterior neck)

Function

1. **Frontalis**
Raises the brows and creates wrinkles on the forehead.

2. **Temporalis**
One of the mastication muscles that helps move the jawbone.

3. **Procerus**
Depresses the medial side of the brows and creates wrinkles on the skin of the Glabella.

4. **Corrugator Supercilii**
Pulls the brows medially and inferiorly and creates wrinkles on the skin of the Glabella.

5. **Depressor Supercilii**
Depresses the brows and creates wrinkles on the skin of the Glabella.

6. **Orbicularis Oculi**
Closes the upper and lower eyelids.

7. **Nasalis**
Creates wrinkles on the nose.

8. **Levator Labii Superioris Alaeque Nasi**
Widens the nostrils and elevates the upper lip.

9. **Levator Labii Superioris**
Elevates the upper lip.

10. **Depressor Septi Nasi**
Depresses the nasal tip and narrows the nostrils.

11. **Zygomaticus Major**
Pulls the mouth to the sides. Known as the "smile muscle."

12. **Zygomaticus Minor**
Pulls the mouth to the sides and elevates the upper lip.

13. **Orbicularis Oris**
Moves the mouth.

14. **Depressor Anguli Oris**
Depresses the corner of the mouth.

15. **Depressor Labii Inferioris**
Depresses the lower lip.

16. **Mentalis**
Elevates the lower lip and creates wrinkles on the chin.

17. **Masseter**
One of the mastication muscles that helps elevate the jawbone.

18. **Risorius**
Pulls the mouth laterally.

19. **Buccinator**
Compresses the cheek against the molar teeth.

20. **Platysma**
Depresses the jawbone.

Origin and Insertion of Facial Muscles

1. Frontalis
Origin: Epicranial Aponeurosis[1]
Insertion: Eyebrow Skin

2. Temporalis
Origin: Temporal Fossa
Insertion: Coronoid Process of Mandible

3. Procerus
Origin: Nasal Bone
Insertion: Glabella, Frontalis

4. Corrugator Supercilii
Origin: Superciliary Arch[2]
Insertion: Eyebrow Skin

5. Depressor Supercilii
Origin: Frontal Process of Maxilla
Insertion: Eyebrow Skin

6. Orbicularis Oculi
Origin: Frontal Process of Maxilla, Frontal Bone, Medial Palpebral Ligament[3], Lacrimal Bone
Insertion: Skin of Orbital Region

7. Nasalis
Origin: Frontal Process of Maxilla
Insertion: Skin of Ala[4]

8. Levator Labii Superioris Alaeque Nasi
Origin: Frontal Process of Maxilla
Insertion: Skin of Ala[4]

9. Levator Labii Superioris
Origin: Zygomatic Process of Maxilla, Zygomatic Bone
Insertion: Muscle of Upper Lip

10. Depressor Septi Nasi
Origin: Incisive Fossa of Maxilla[5]
Insertion: Nasal Septum

11. Zygomaticus Major
Origin: Zygomatic Bone
Insertion: Skin of Angle of Mouth

12. Zygomaticus Minor
Origin: Zygomatic Bone
Insertion: Muscle of Upper Lip

13. Orbicularis Oris
Origin: Medial Part of Maxilla and Mandible
Insertion: Skin and Mucous Membrane[6] of Lips

14. Depressor Anguli Oris
Origin: Base of Mandible
Insertion: Skin of Lower Lip

15. Depressor Labii Inferioris
Origin: Medial part of Mandible
Insertion: Skin and Mucous Membrane[6] of Lips

16. Mentalis
Origin: Incisive Fossa of Mandible
Insertion: Skin of Chin

17. Masseter
Origin: Zygomatic Bone
Insertion: Ramus and Angle of Mandible

18. Risorius
Origin: Parotid Fascia[7]
Insertion: Skin of Angle of Mouth

19. Buccinator
Origin: Maxilla and Mandible
Insertion: Muscle of Upper Lip

20. Platysma
Origin: Skin and Fascia of Lower Neck and Upper Chest
Insertion: Inferior Border of Mandible, Skin of Cheeks and Lower Lip

---

1: Fibrous tissue of the upper part of the skull
2: Brow ridge
3: Ligament near the tear duct
4: Wing of nose
5: Shallow depression above the incisor teeth
6: Moist inner soft tissue
7: Dense connective tissue

Breaking Down the Emotions

There are six basic human emotions: **Happiness**, **Surprise**, **Fear**, **Sadness**, **Anger**, and **Disgust**. Of course, there are different levels of facial expressions for each emotion and some mixed emotions as well. Here are some of the examples of different levels of each emotion.

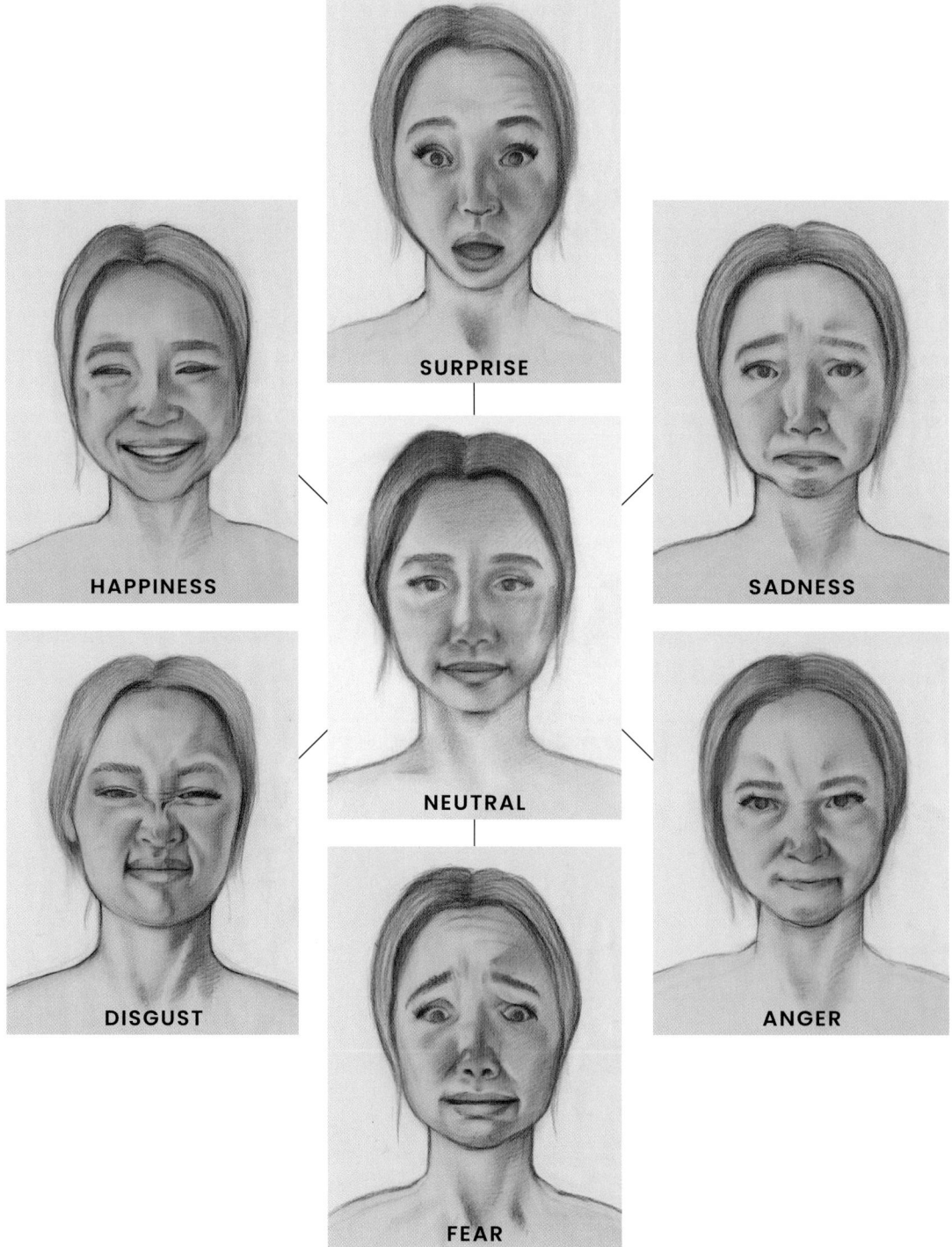

SURPRISE

HAPPINESS

SADNESS

NEUTRAL

DISGUST

ANGER

FEAR

Neutral

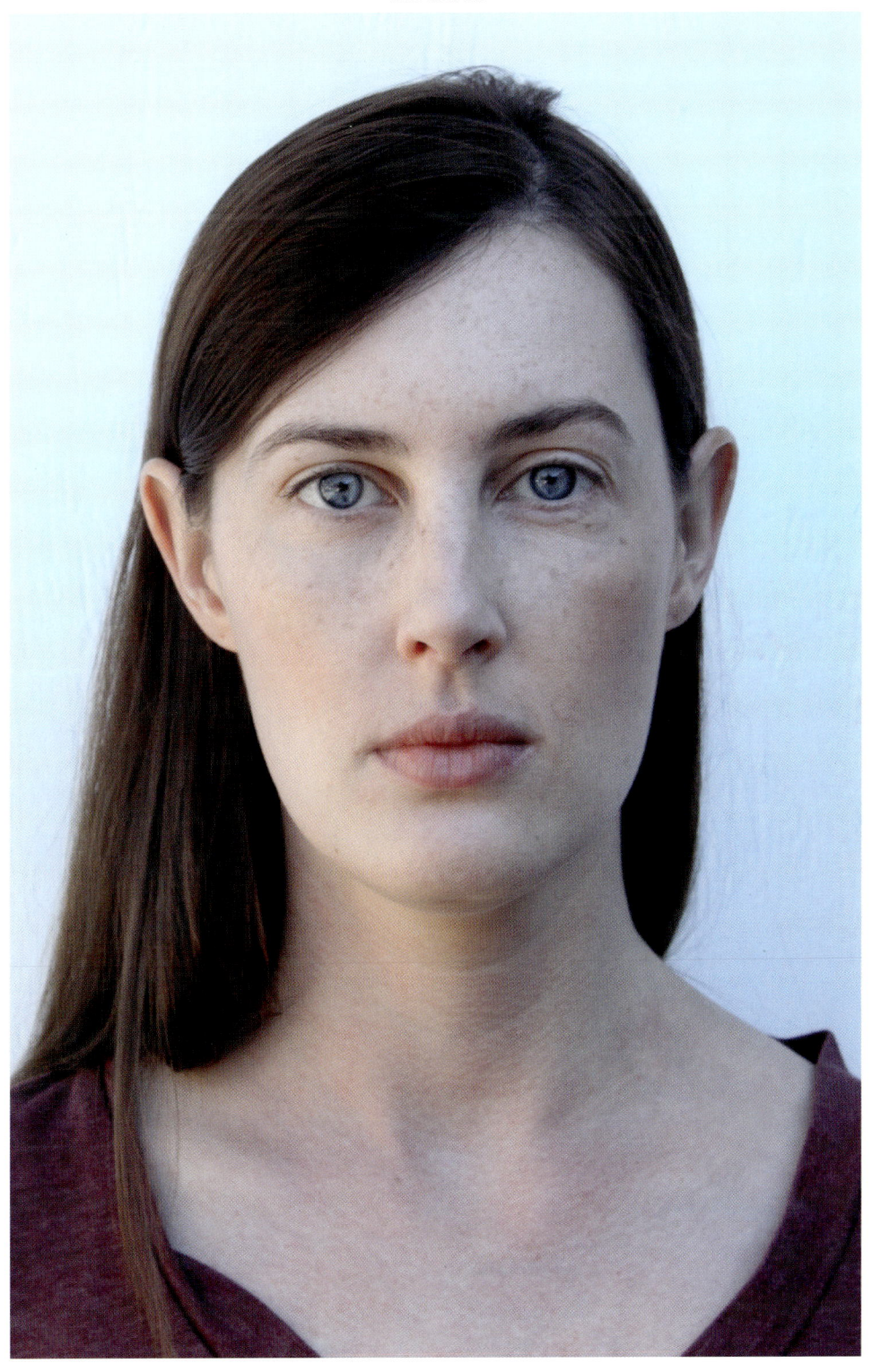

Happiness

The common characteristics in the expression of happiness are the mouth being pulled to the side, raised cheeks, and crescent moon-shaped eyes.

The muscle that plays the major role in making the mouth smile is the **Zygomaticus Major**. The movement of this muscle also helps to create the round cheeks and the Nasolabial folds. The muscle that surrounds the eyes is called the **Orbicularis Oculi**, which contracts to make the crescent moon-shaped eyes. The "happiness" wrinkles around the corners of the eyes are often called "crow's feet" based on their shape.

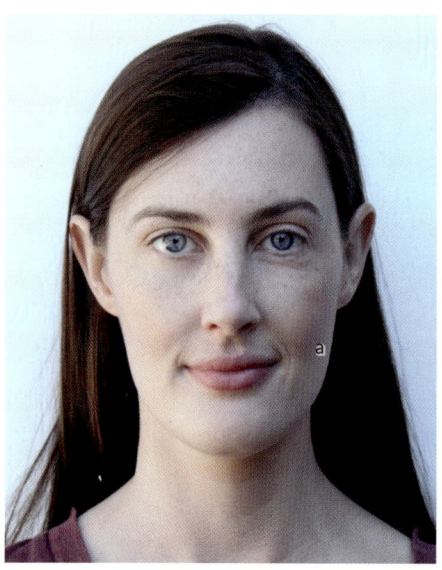

1. Mona Lisa Smile

The corners of the mouth are pulled subtly to the side (a) while the brows and the eyes remain neutral.

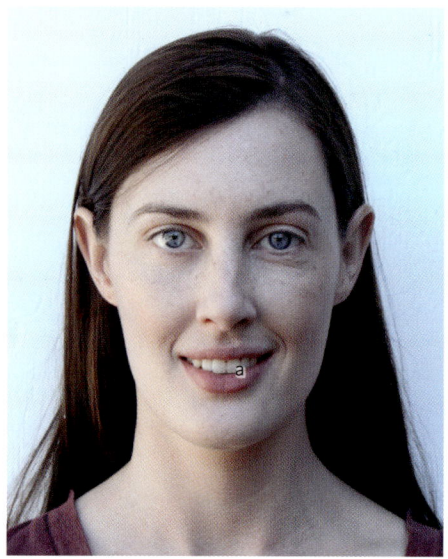

2. Picture Smile

The corners of the mouth are pulled to the side and the upper teeth (a) become visible while the brows and the eyes remain neutral.

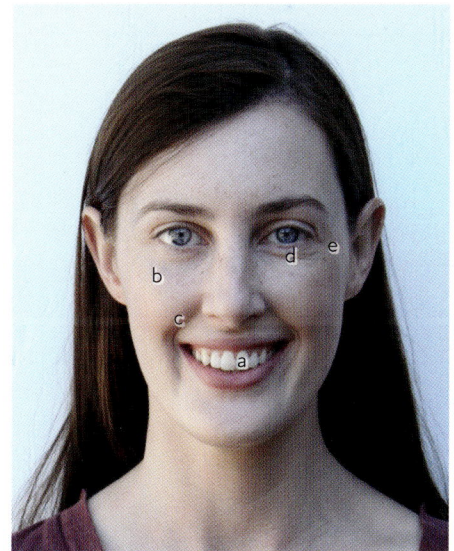

3. True Smile

Both muscles around the mouth and the eyes contract together. The upper teeth (a), round cheeks (b), Nasolabial folds (c), wrinkles on the lower eyelid (d), and wrinkles at the corners of the eyes, called "crow's feet" (e), can be seen.

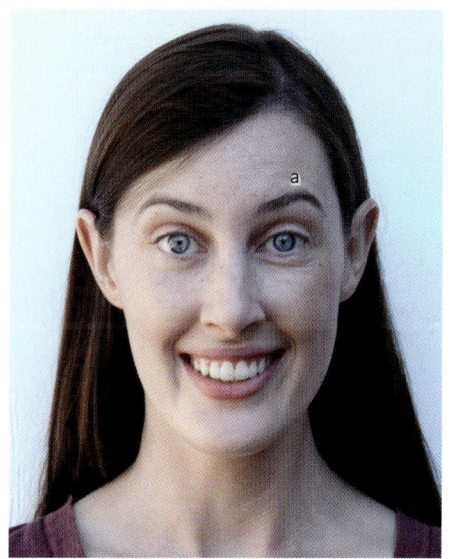

4. Excitement

Similar to the True Smile, but with brows raised (a).

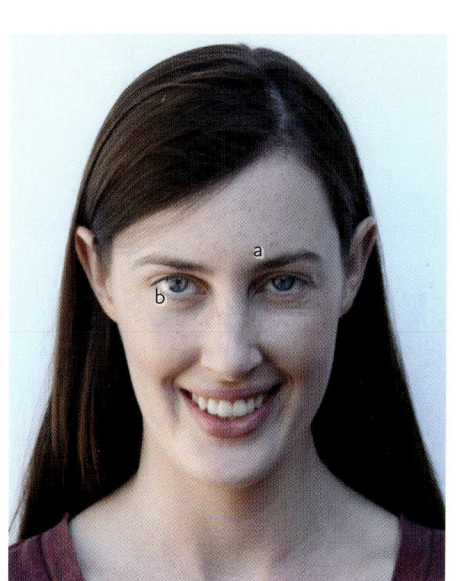

5. Evil Smile

The brows lower down (a) and the surface of the lower Sclera appears (b) while the corners of the mouth are pulled to the side.

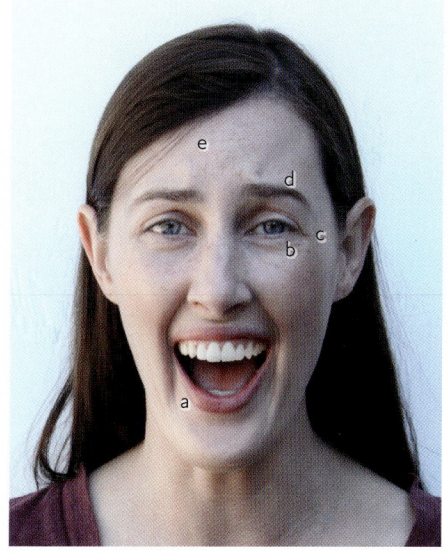

6. Cracking Up

The mouth opens wider (a), the skin of the lower eyelids gets tense and wrinkled (b), deeper wrinkles of the crow's feet appear in the corners of the eyes (c), the brows get warped (d), and some wrinkles and hollows can be found on the forehead (e).

Surprise

The feeling of surprise occurs when something unexpected happens to us. Things that you don't plan for will always shock you, whether they are good or bad. In the expression of surprise, all the facial parts tend to be pulled vertically. The **Frontalis** muscle contracts and raises the brows, and the **Platysma** and other deeper muscles drop the Mandible and open the mouth. One of the biggest characteristics in the surprise expression can be seen in the eyes: The eyelids open up and the surface of the Sclera appears all around the Iris.

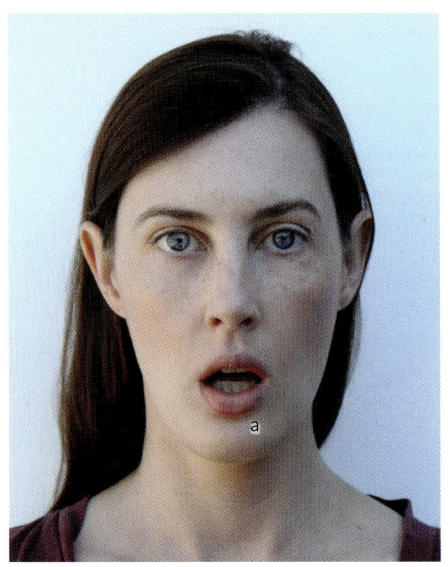

1. Open Mouth

The most subtle expression of surprise. The mandible drops a little (a) while the brows and eyes remain neutral.

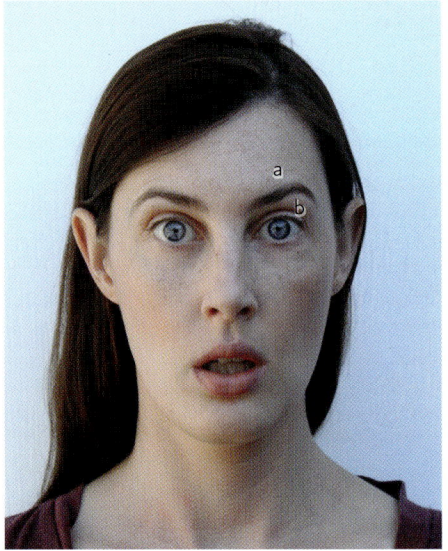

2. Startled

The brows raise (a) and pull up the upper lids a little (b) while the mouth opens.

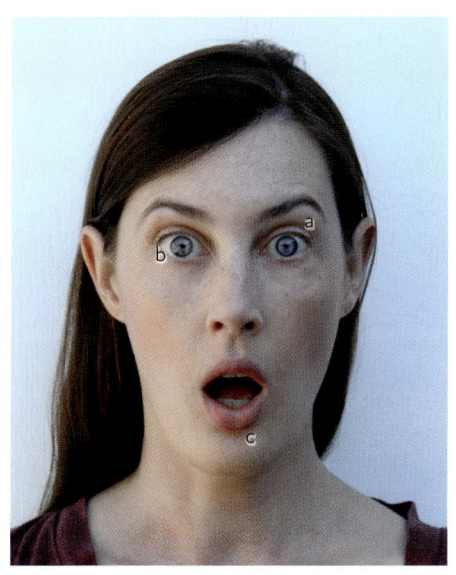

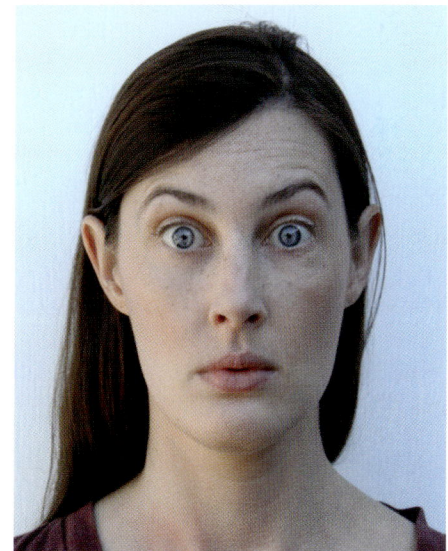

3. Gasp

The brows raise and lift the upper eyelids even more (a), showing the bigger surface of the Sclera around the Iris (b). The Mandible drops lower and the mouth opens wider (c).

4. Doubt (really?)

The brows raise and lift the upper eyelid while the mouth remains closed.

Fear

Compared to the emotion of surprise, the emotion of fear usually contains some kind of negative feelings within, like damage, loss, or distress. From a small worry to a bigger fright, this expression can usually be seen in the area of the brows and eyes. One of the characteristics in the fear expression is the warped brows. When the **Frontalis** pulls up the forehead and raises the brows, the **Corrugator Supercilii** makes the opposite movement and pulls the brows down toward the center. These contractions not only make brows look wavy, but they also raise the medial side of the brows, and a small triangular space can be seen on the medial side of the upper eyelid. In the emotion of fear, the skin of the lower eyelid usually gets more tense than usual, and the surface of the Sclera starts disappearing under the Iris.

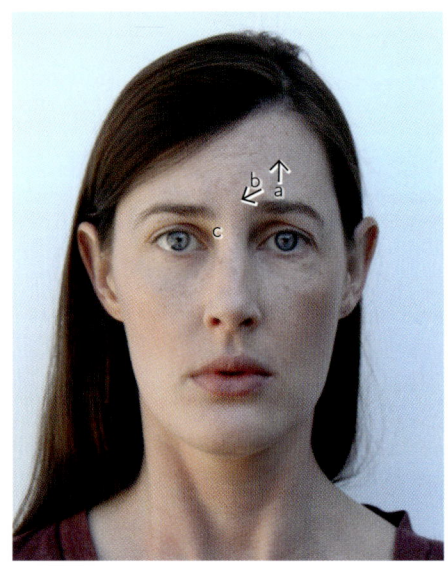

1. Worry

A small movement of the brows raising up (a) and pulling toward the center (b) at the same time. A small triangular space is created in between the medial side of brow and the tear duct (c).

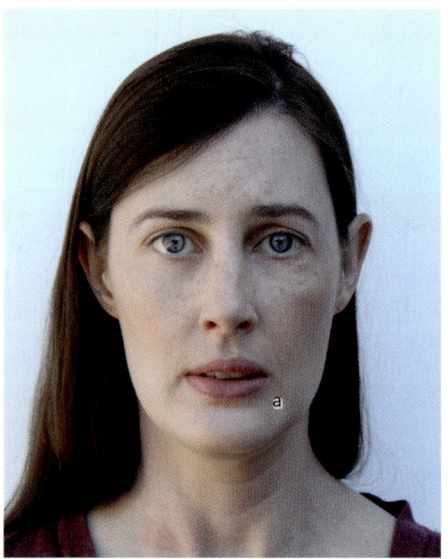

2. Anxiety

The corners of mouth are pulled toward the sides (a).

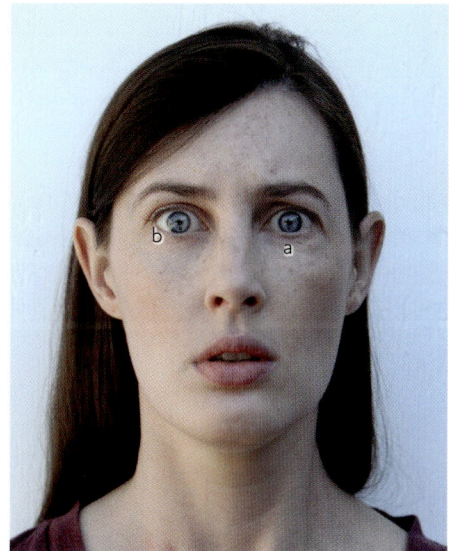

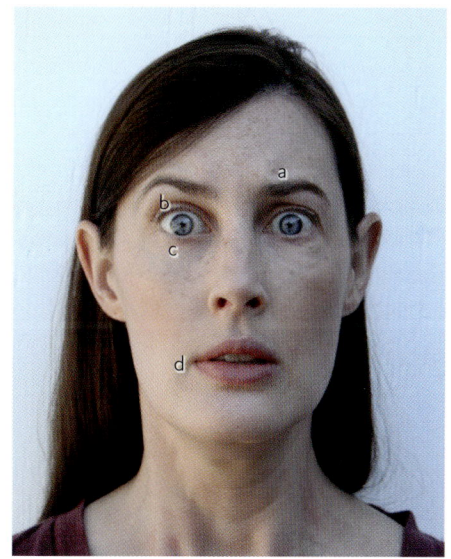

3. Alarm

The skin of the lower eyelids gets tense (a) and touches the lower part of the Iris (b).

4. Panic

The brows warp even more (a) and pull the upper eyelids up, showing the surface of Sclera above the Iris (b). The skin of the lower eyelids gets tense and touches the lower part of the Iris (c). The corners of the mouth are pulled toward the sides (d).

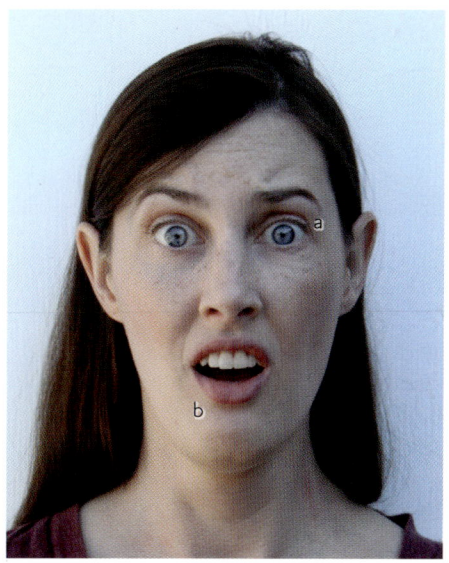

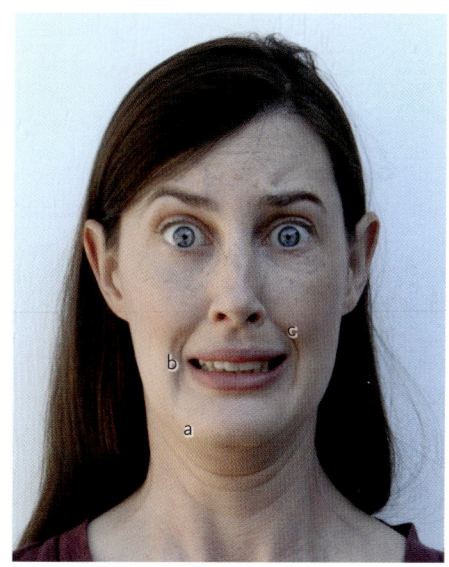

5. Shock

While the basic fear expression of the warped brow and tensity of the eyelid skin is maintained, the basic surprise expression of wide-open eyes (a) and dropped jaw (b) is mixed in.

6. Terror

The chin is pulled back (a) and the corners of the mouth are pulled to the side even more (b), which makes the Nasolabial folds standout (c). All the other characteristics of the fear expression are contained around the brows and eyes.

Sadness

The feeling of sadness usually contains suffering, pain, and distress. The brow movement is similar to the expression of fear, but the pulling force of the **Frontalis** could be slightly stronger than the Corrugator Supercilii. For the area of cheeks and mouth, the **Zygomaticus Minor** muscle starts contracting more in this expression. This is the muscle that sits next to the Zygomaticus Major, which takes a big role in the emotion of happiness. Both muscles usually contract together, changing the angle of the mouth and pumping up the roundness of the cheeks.

However, the Zygomaticus Minor muscle tends to elevate the upper mouth instead of pulling it to the side, so the tensity of the cheek skin in sadness looks different from the apple-like cheeks you see in the happiness expression. For the mouth region, the **Orbicularis Oris** might contract and tighten the mouth. The **Mentalis** might push up the middle of the lower lip and create a pebble-like texture on the chin. The **Depressor Anguli Oris** pulls the corners of the mouth down and creates a typical upside-down U-curve like a sad face emoji.

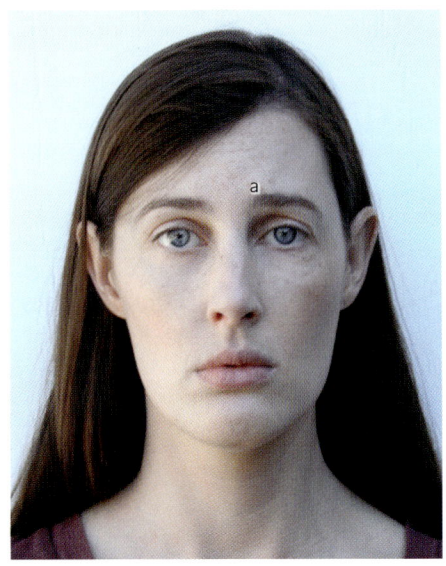

1. Melancholy
The smallest expression in sadness where the brows are slightly raised (a).

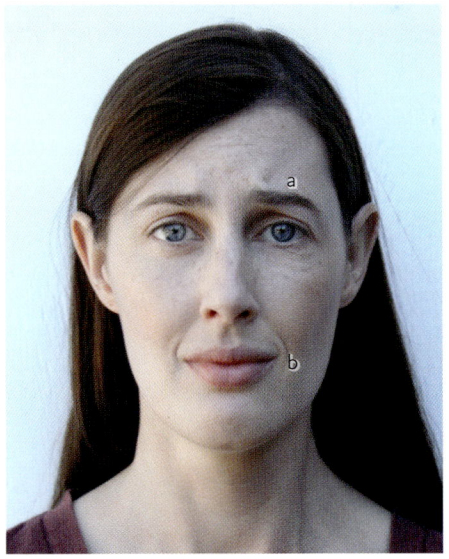

2. Sorrow
The brows are warped (a) and the mouth is pulled slightly to the side and up (b).

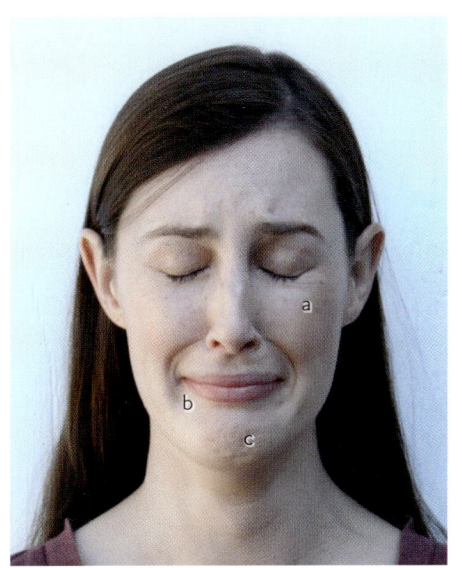

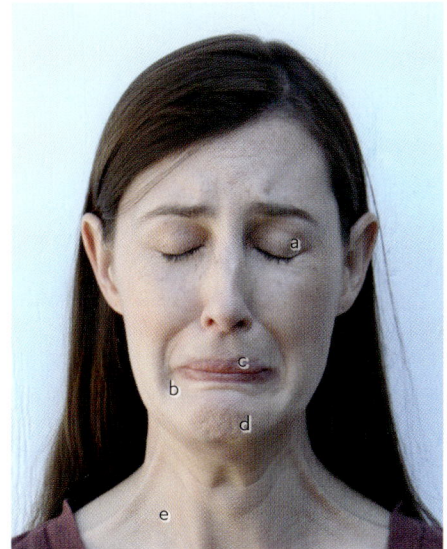

3. Weeping

The cheeks pump up and the skin gets tense (a). The mouth tightens (b). The contraction of the Mentalis muscle causes a pebbled texture with multiple dimples on the chin (c).

4. Sobbing

Eyes can be closed tight (a). The corners of the mouth are pulled down (b) while the mouth gets even firmer (c). A more defined pebbled texture can be seen on the chin (d). Some of the neck muscles can be more defined under the skin when a strong emotion of sadness occurs (e).

Anger

The emotion of anger is aggressive. Not only does the body language communicate anger when a person steps forward and their fists get tighter, but the facial expression also gets dense and firm, and the whole head might start to get red like the blood is boiling.

The expression of anger is very different from what we have been looking at with the previous expressions. In anger, the brows usually go down and are yanked toward the center. This is when the **Corrugator Supercilli** and the **Procerus** work together to lower the brows. The **Orbicularis Oculi** contracts and the eyes will glare like the whole sphere could come out of the Orbit. The shape of the mouth becomes square-like: The **Levator Labii Superioris** lifts the upper lip, and the **Depressor Labii Inferioris** pulls the corners of the mouth lower.

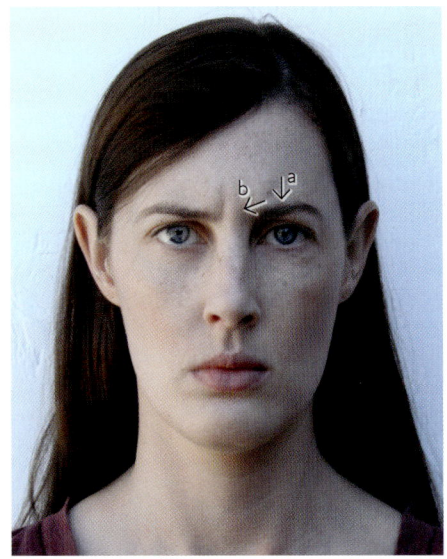

1. Bitter
The brows are pushed down (a) and pulled toward the middle (b).

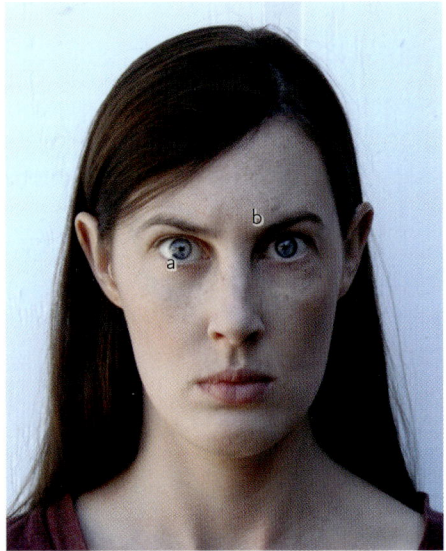

2. Annoyed
The eyes glare and the surface of the Sclera appears under the Iris (a) while the brows are pushed down (b).

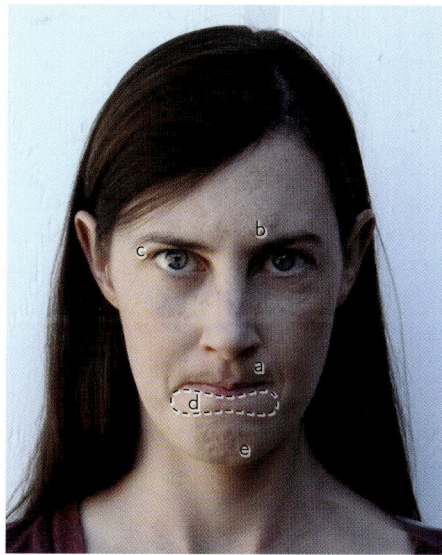

3. Irritated

The mouth is tightened (a) while the brows are pushed down (b) and the eyes glare (c). A sausage-like volume can be noticed under the firm mouth (d) and the pebbled texture appears on the chin (e).

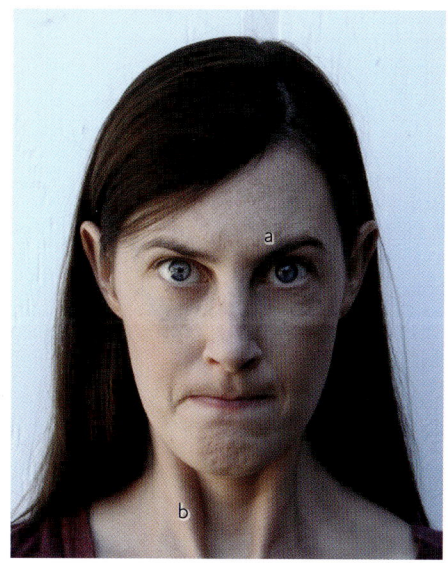

4. Heated

The mouth remains the same, but the angle of the brows becomes more sloped (a). Some muscles on the neck are defined (b).

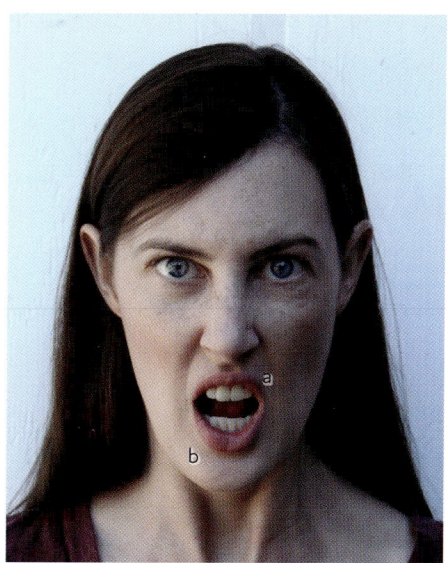

5. Furious

The mouth is opened and becomes a square-like shape: The upper lip is lifted (a) and the sides of the lower lip are pulled down slightly (b).

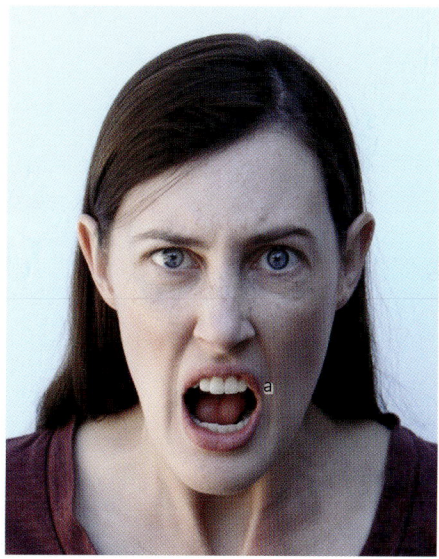

6. Outraged

The head is pushed forward while the expression shows a high level of anger. The mouth becomes even more square-shaped (a).

Disgust

The feeling of disgust tends to create many wrinkles in the face. The facial parts get squished and the facial proportions become warped. Some people might stick their tongue out to show their feeling of rejection.

The brow movement is similar to the expression of anger or fear, where you see the brows being pushed down or warped. The biggest characteristic in the emotion of disgust can be seen in the nose and mouth area. The upper lip will be lifted by the muscle called the **Levator Labii Superioris**, which sometimes allows the teeth to peek out from the mouth. The **Levator Labii Superioris Alaeque Nasi** will help this upper lip movement even further by opening the nostrils and creating many wrinkles on the nose. The **Mentalis** pushes the lower lip in, or pulls it slightly forward and up. The **Depressor Anguli Oris** might contract and pull the corners of mouth down at the same time.

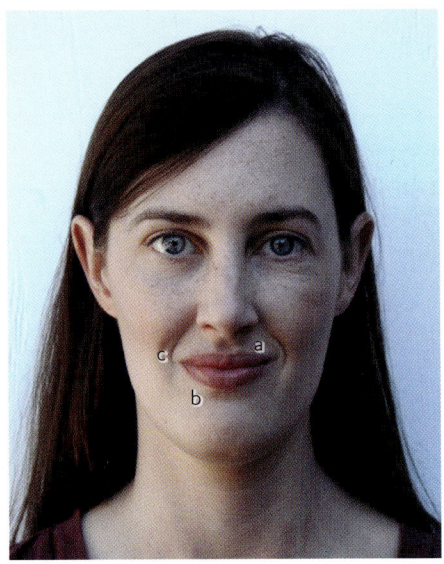

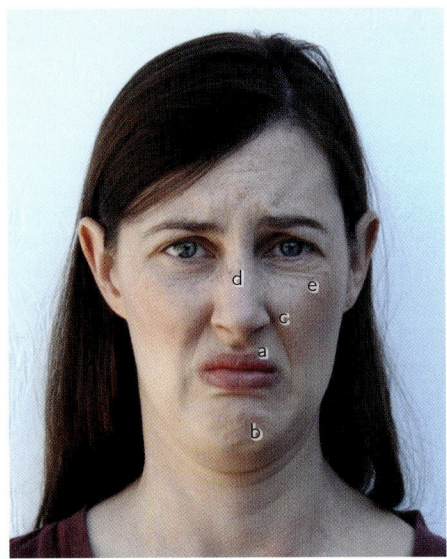

1. Dislike

The upper lip is slightly lifted (a) and the lower lip is pushed up (b). This subtle movement positions the whole mouth higher. A firm wrinkle appears around the corner of the mouth (c). This changes the shape of the nostril and shifts the placement of the nose. This expression often conveys contempt.

2. Ew

The mouth is pursed up: The lower lip is pushed up even more and the mouth gets firm (a). The pebbled texture can be noticed on the chin (b). The wing of the nose is wider/ higher (c) and some wrinkles start appearing around the bridge of the nose (d). Because of this, the cheek and the lower eyelid are slightly pushed up, creating more wrinkles under the eyes (e). This narrows the field of vision.

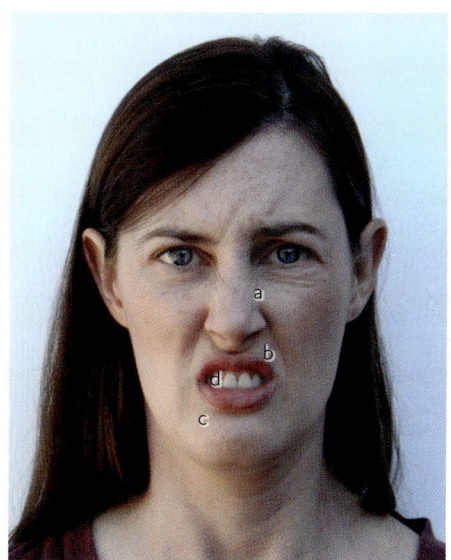

3. Sickened

The wrinkles around the nose and the eyes increase (a).
The upper lip is lifted more (b) and the lower lip is
lowered (c), which allows the teeth to peek out (d).

Eye in Emotion

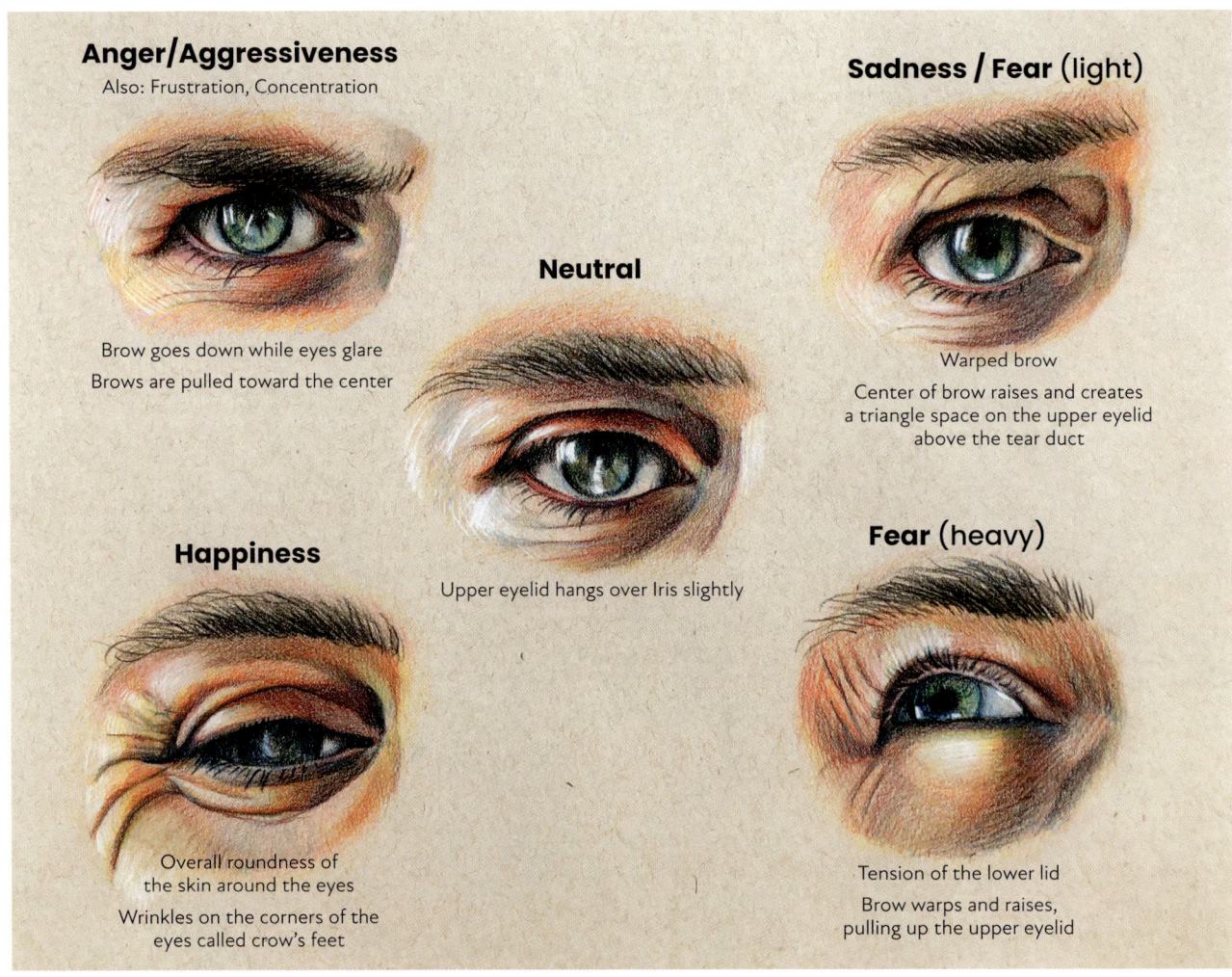

Anger/Aggressiveness

Also: Frustration, Concentration

Brow goes down while eyes glare

Brows are pulled toward the center

Neutral

Upper eyelid hangs over Iris slightly

Sadness / Fear (light)

Warped brow

Center of brow raises and creates
a triangle space on the upper eyelid
above the tear duct

Happiness

Overall roundness of
the skin around the eyes

Wrinkles on the corners of the
eyes called crow's feet

Fear (heavy)

Tension of the lower lid

Brow warps and raises,
pulling up the upper eyelid

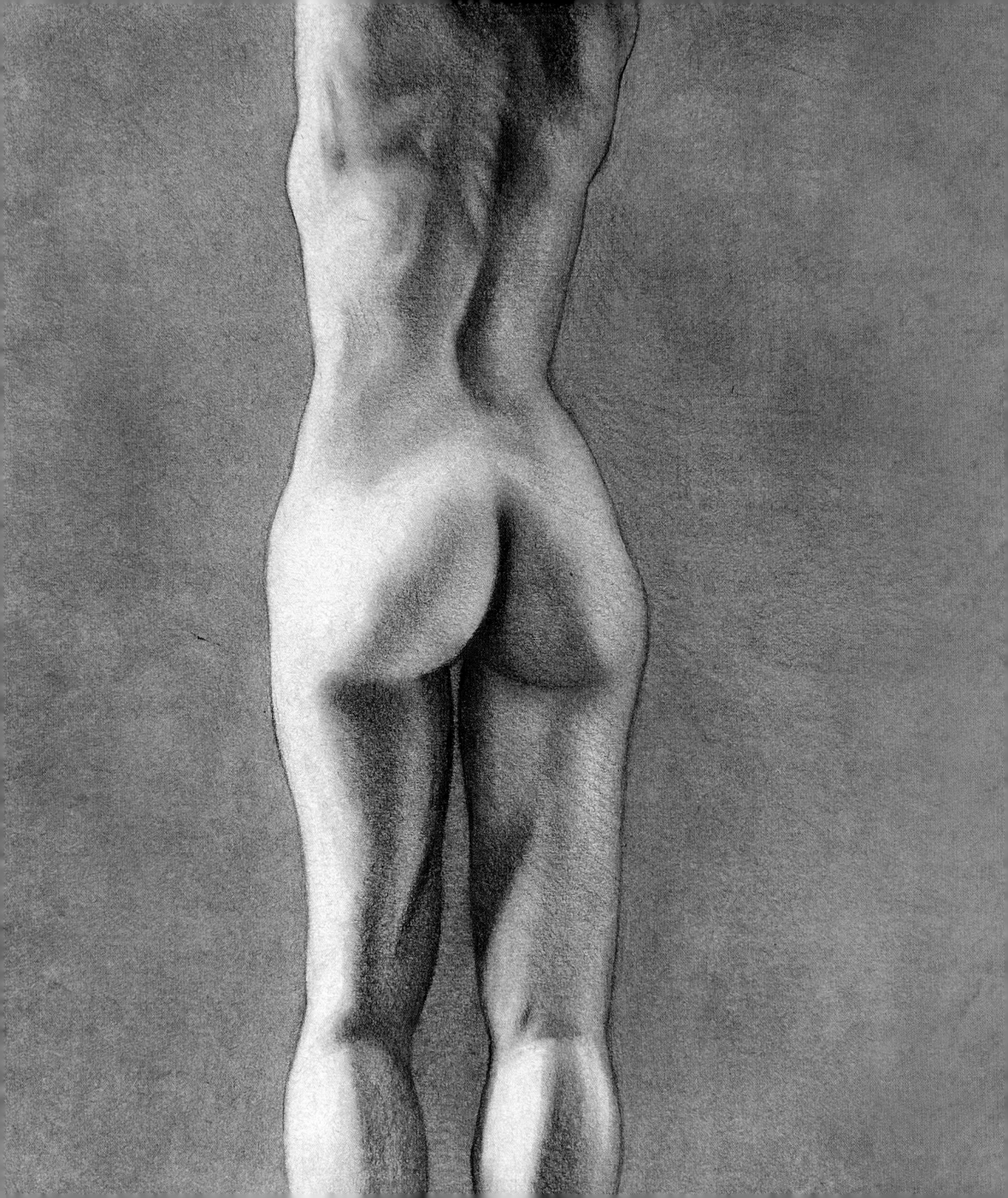

APPENDIX

Full
Figure

Gesture

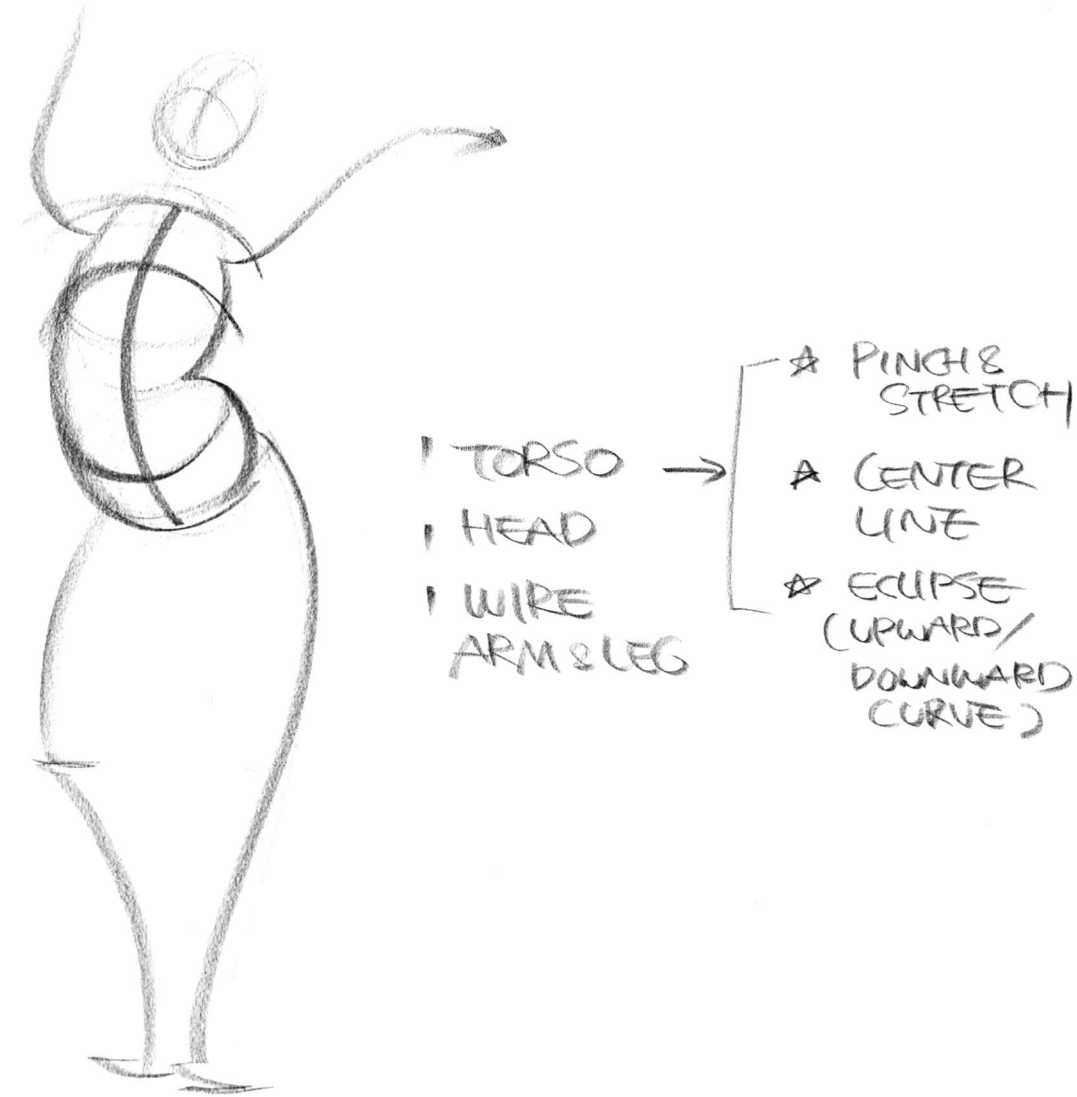

TORSO →
HEAD
WIRE ARM & LEG

☆ PINCH & STRETCH
☆ CENTER LINE
☆ ECLIPSE (UPWARD/ DOWNWARD CURVE)

Mannequin Figures

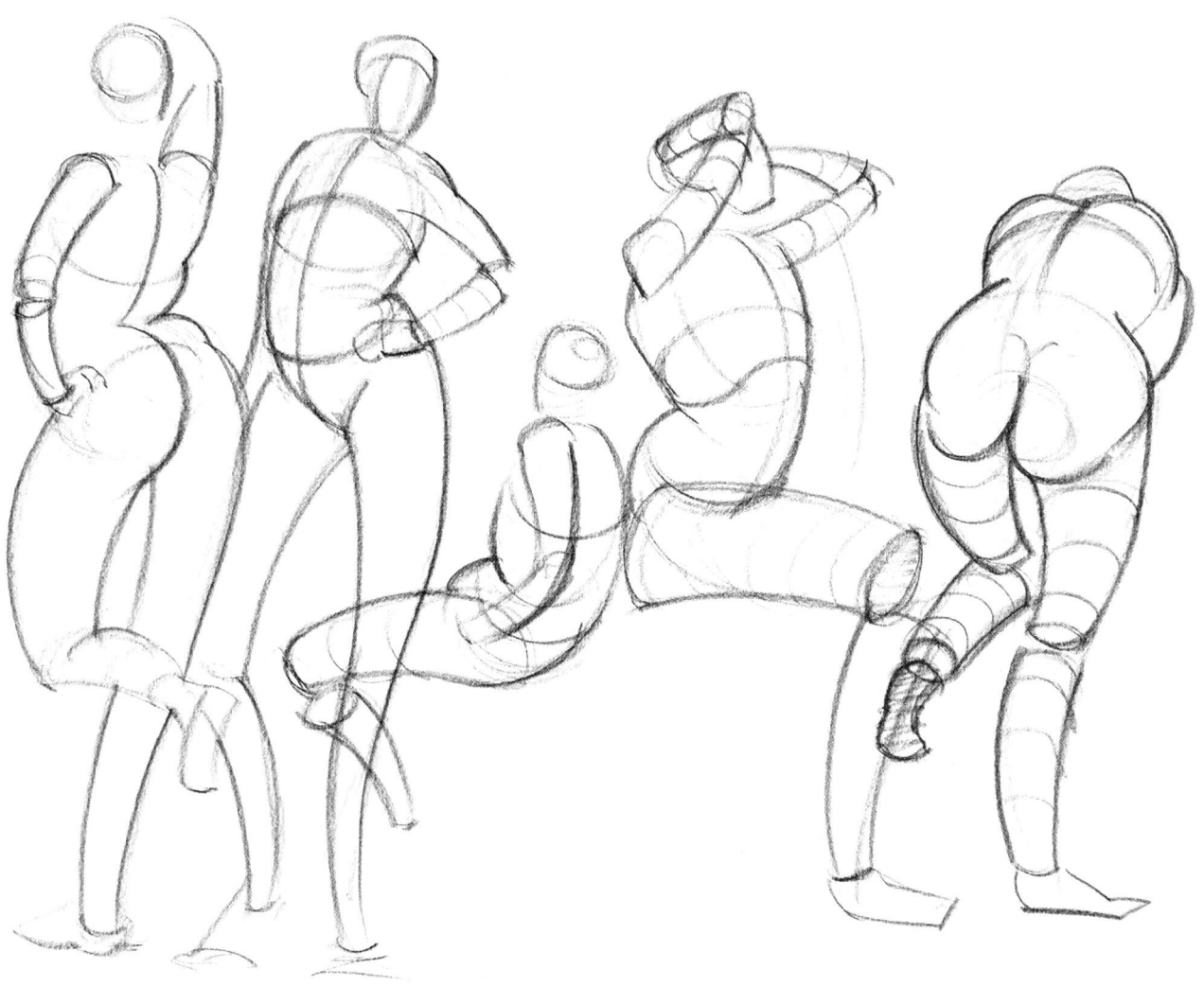

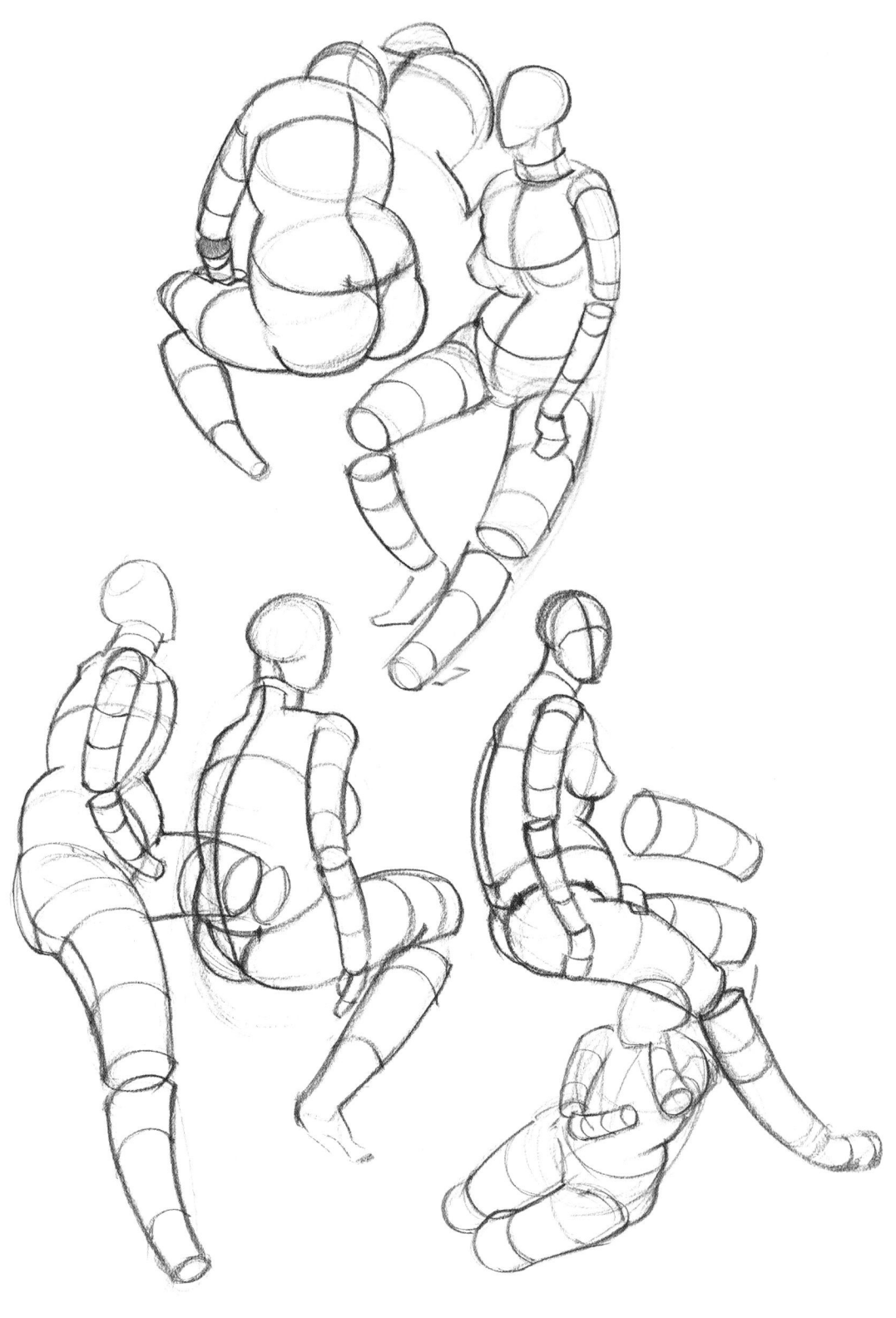

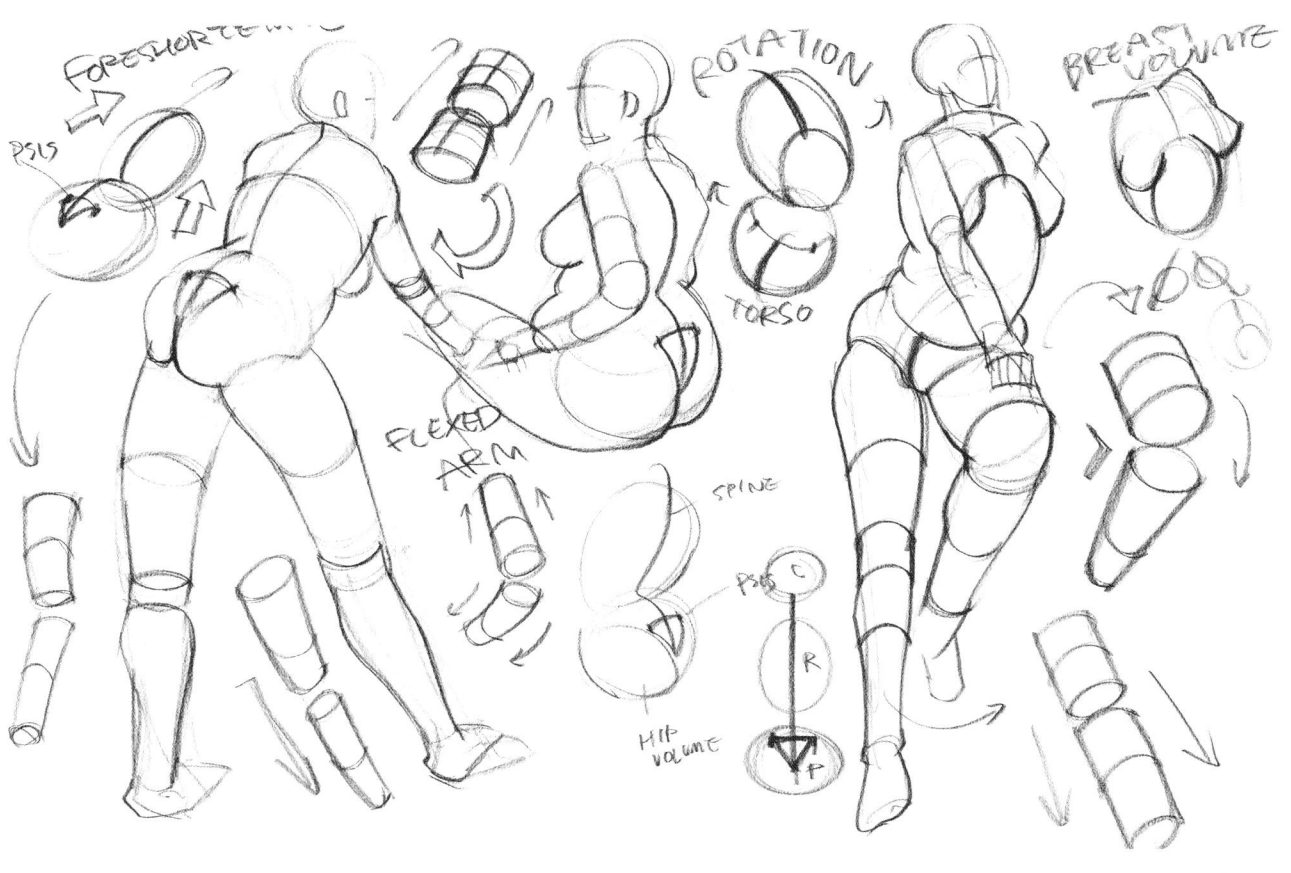

Anatomical Construction Drawing

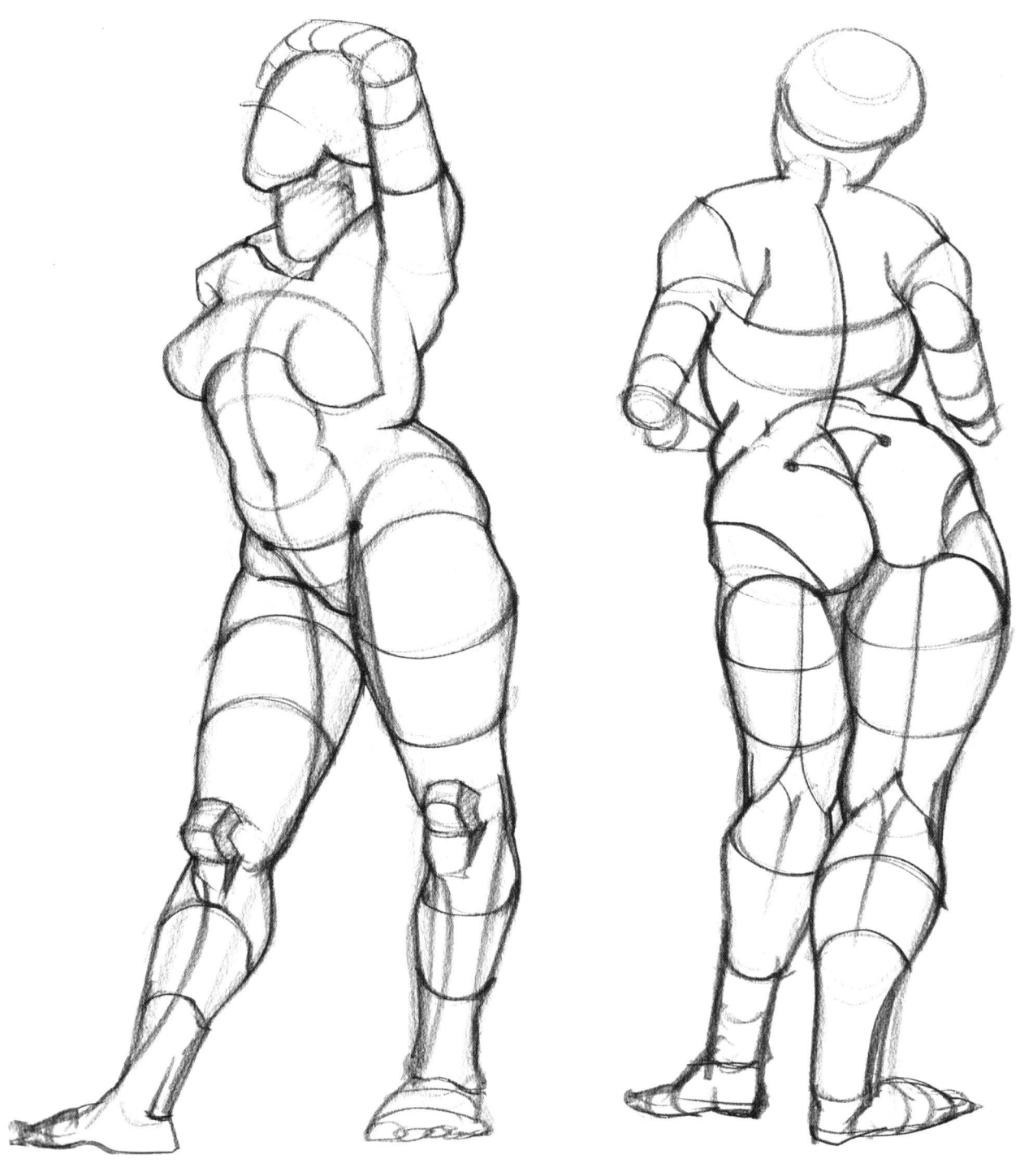

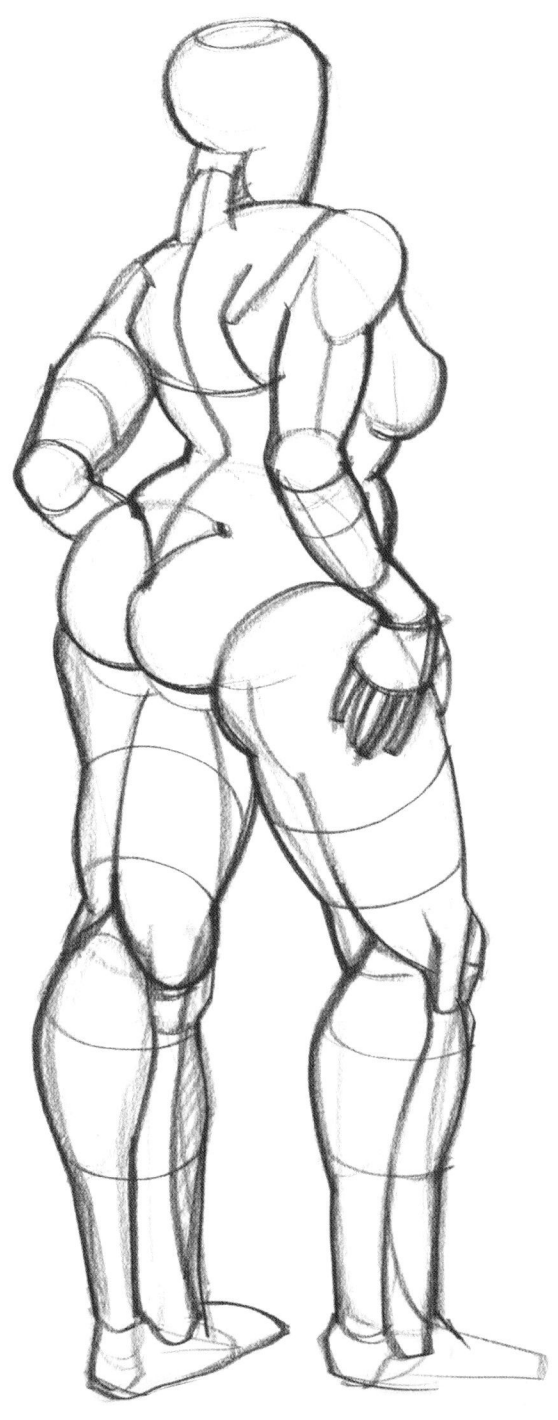

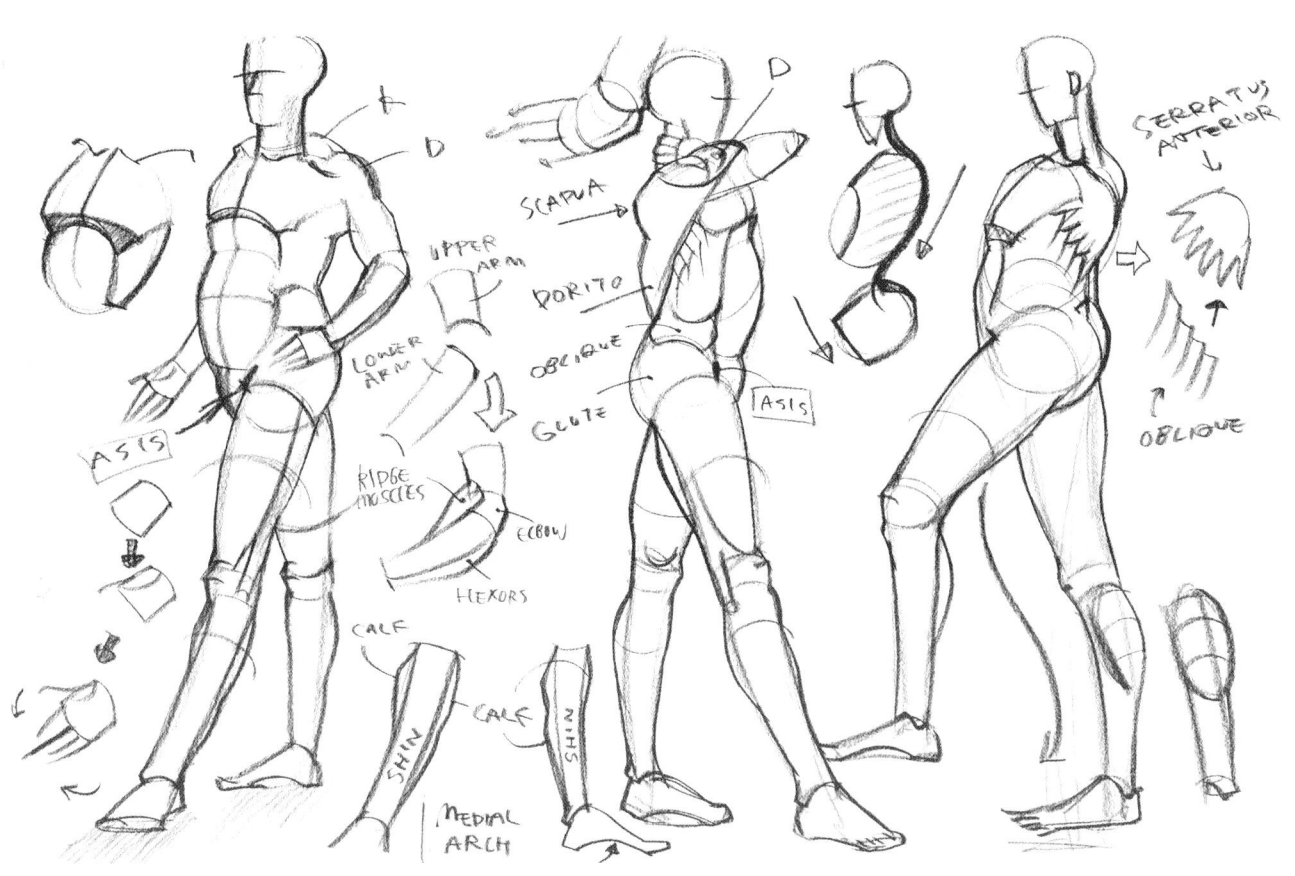

UPPER ARM

LOWER ARM

ASIS

RIDGE MUSCLES

ELBOW

FLEXORS

CALF

CALF

SHIN

SHIN

MEDIAL ARCH

SCAPULA

DORITO

OBLIQUE

GLUTE

ASIS

SERRATUS ANTERIOR

OBLIQUE

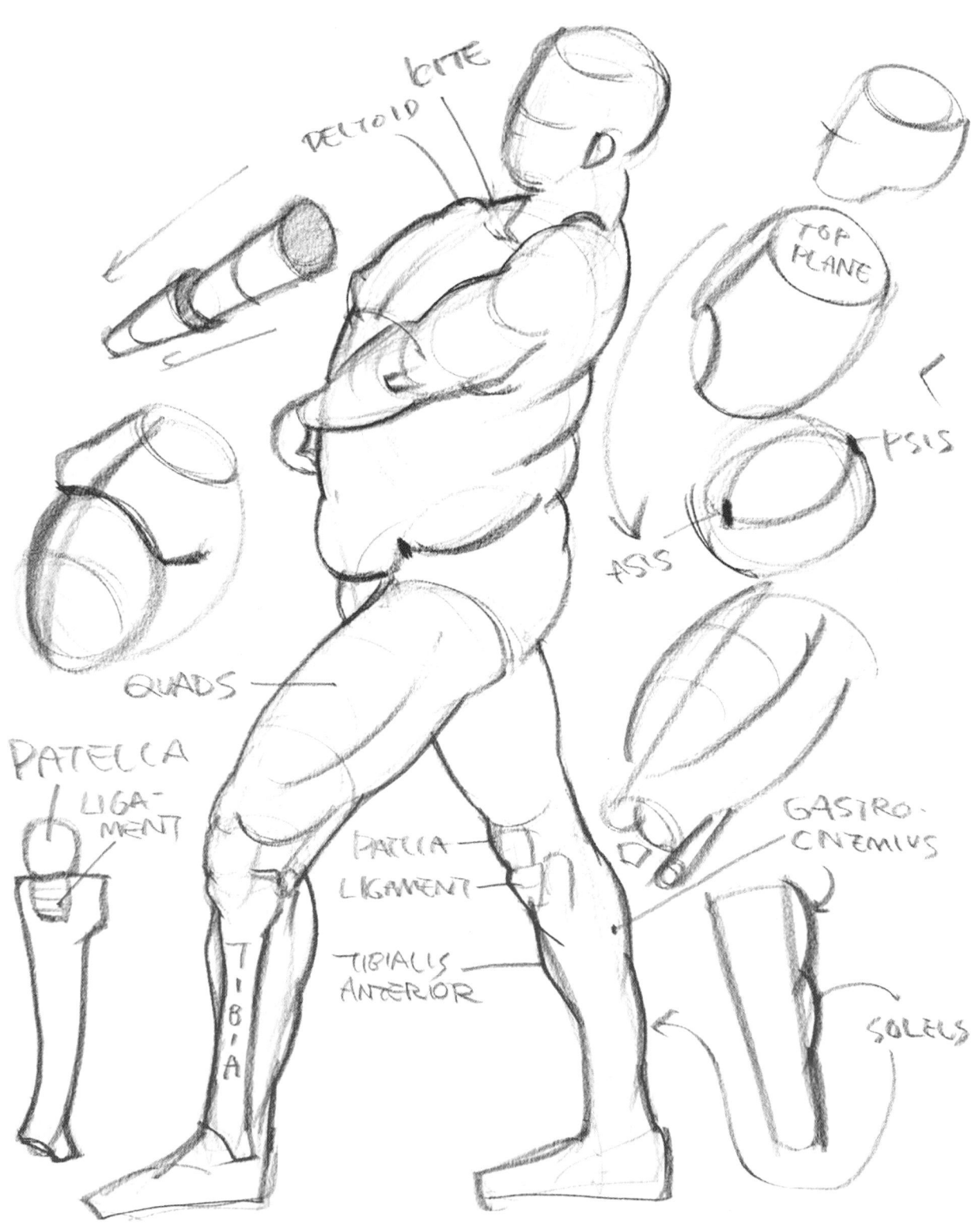

DELTOID

BITE

TOP PLANE

PSIS

ASIS

QUADS

PATELLA

LIGA-
MENT

PATELLA
LIGAMENT

GASTRO-
CNEMIUS

TIBIA

TIBIALIS
ANTERIOR

SOLEUS

Muscular System

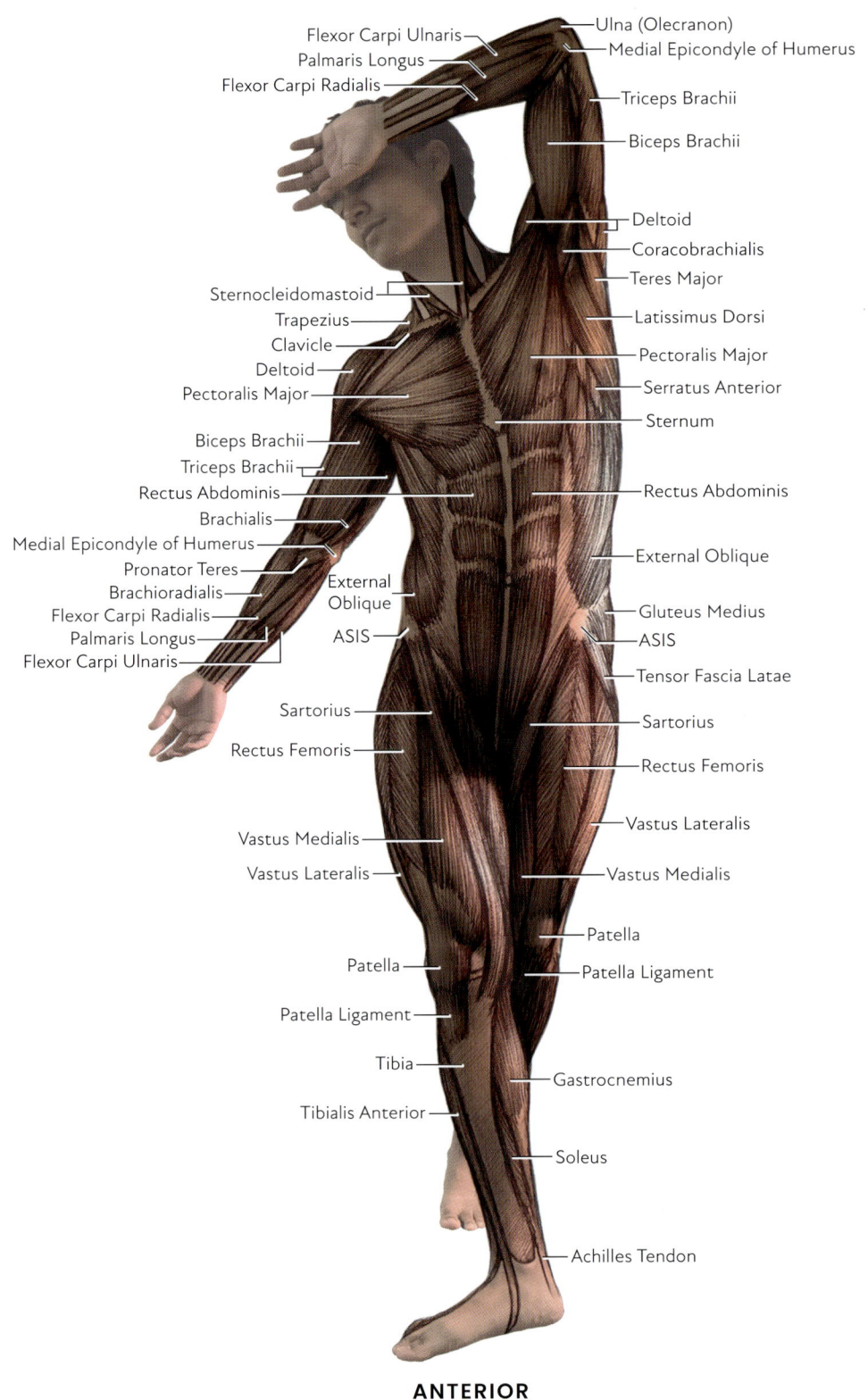

Flexor Carpi Ulnaris
Palmaris Longus
Flexor Carpi Radialis

Ulna (Olecranon)
Medial Epicondyle of Humerus
Triceps Brachii
Biceps Brachii

Deltoid
Coracobrachialis
Teres Major
Latissimus Dorsi
Pectoralis Major
Serratus Anterior
Sternum

Sternocleidomastoid
Trapezius
Clavicle
Deltoid
Pectoralis Major

Rectus Abdominis

Biceps Brachii
Triceps Brachii
Rectus Abdominis
Brachialis
Medial Epicondyle of Humerus
Pronator Teres
Brachioradialis
Flexor Carpi Radialis
Palmaris Longus
Flexor Carpi Ulnaris

External Oblique

External
Oblique

Gluteus Medius

ASIS

ASIS

Tensor Fascia Latae

Sartorius
Rectus Femoris

Sartorius

Rectus Femoris

Vastus Lateralis

Vastus Medialis
Vastus Lateralis

Vastus Medialis

Patella

Patella
Patella Ligament

Patella Ligament

Tibia

Gastrocnemius

Tibialis Anterior

Soleus

Achilles Tendon

ANTERIOR

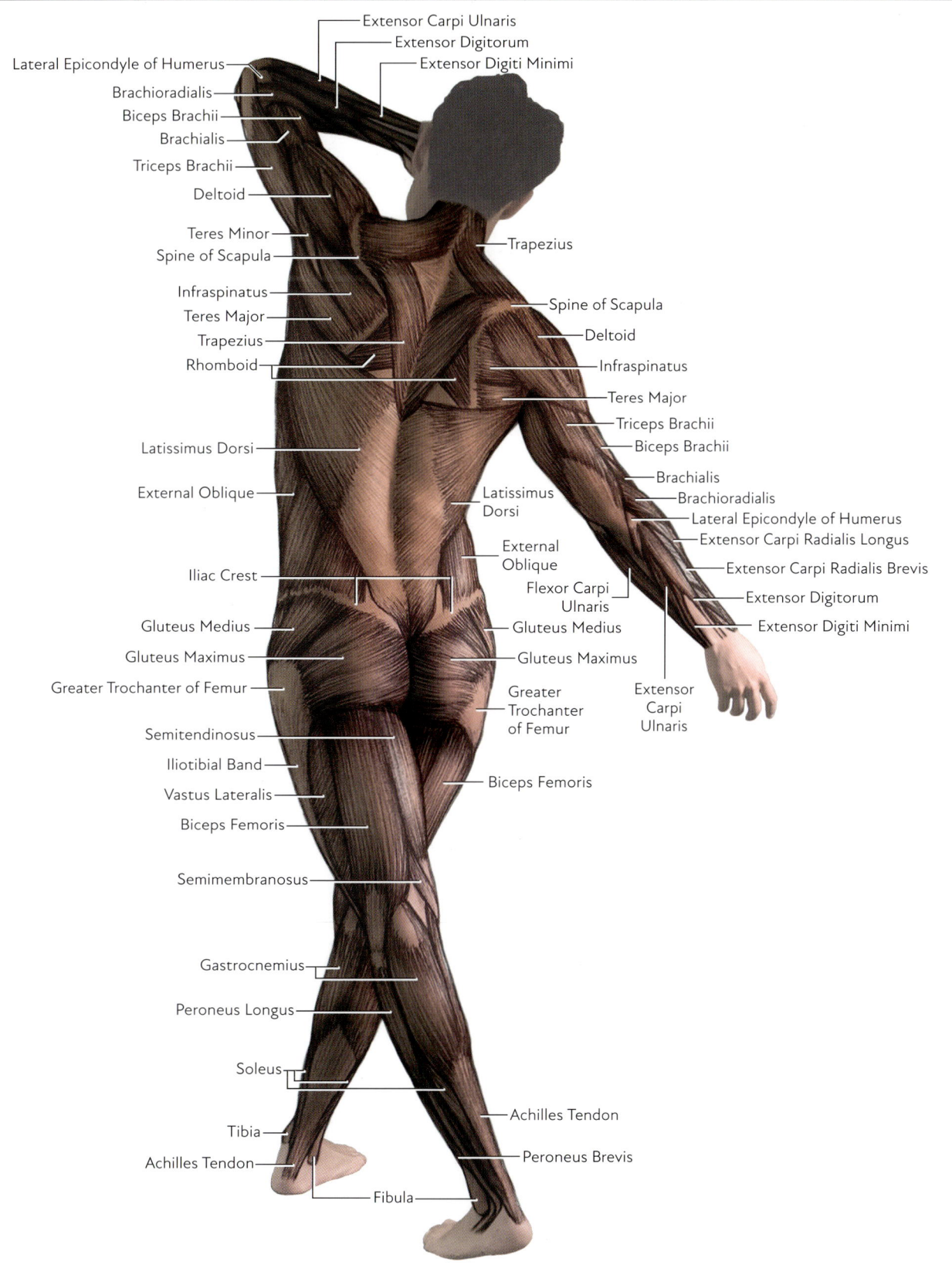

Extensor Carpi Ulnaris

Extensor Digitorum

Extensor Digiti Minimi

Lateral Epicondyle of Humerus

Brachioradialis

Biceps Brachii

Brachialis

Triceps Brachii

Deltoid

Teres Minor

Spine of Scapula

Infraspinatus

Teres Major

Trapezius

Rhomboid

Latissimus Dorsi

External Oblique

Iliac Crest

Gluteus Medius

Gluteus Maximus

Greater Trochanter of Femur

Semitendinosus

Iliotibial Band

Vastus Lateralis

Biceps Femoris

Semimembranosus

Gastrocnemius

Peroneus Longus

Soleus

Tibia

Achilles Tendon

Fibula

Trapezius

Spine of Scapula

Deltoid

Infraspinatus

Teres Major

Triceps Brachii

Biceps Brachii

Brachialis

Brachioradialis

Lateral Epicondyle of Humerus

Extensor Carpi Radialis Longus

Extensor Carpi Radialis Brevis

Extensor Digitorum

Extensor Digiti Minimi

Latissimus Dorsi

External Oblique

Flexor Carpi Ulnaris

Gluteus Medius

Gluteus Maximus

Greater Trochanter of Femur

Extensor Carpi Ulnaris

Biceps Femoris

Achilles Tendon

Peroneus Brevis

POSTERIOR

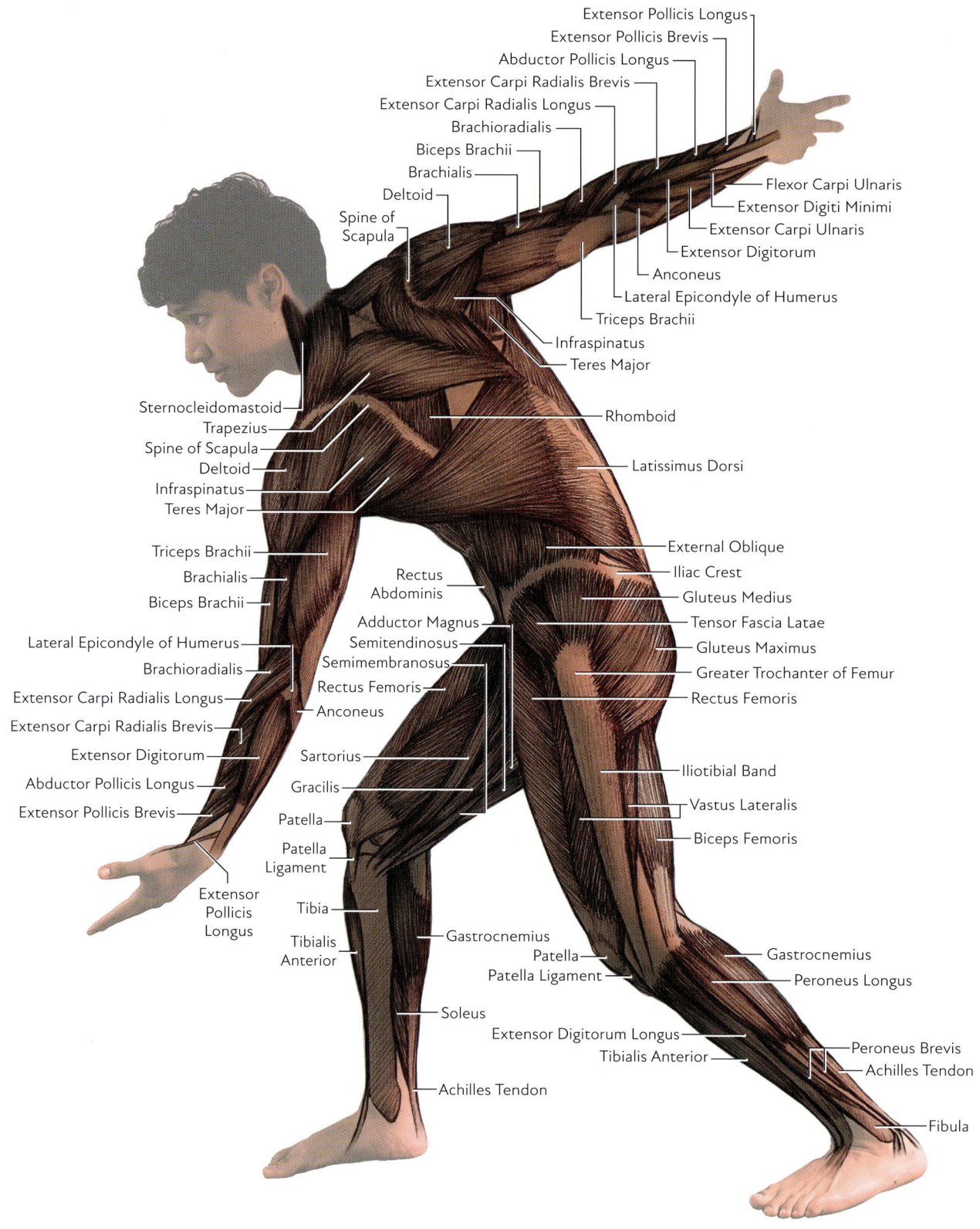

Extensor Pollicis Longus
Extensor Pollicis Brevis
Abductor Pollicis Longus
Extensor Carpi Radialis Brevis
Extensor Carpi Radialis Longus
Brachioradialis
Biceps Brachii
Brachialis
Deltoid
Spine of
Scapula
Sternocleidomastoid
Trapezius
Spine of Scapula
Deltoid
Infraspinatus
Teres Major
Triceps Brachii
Brachialis
Biceps Brachii
Lateral Epicondyle of Humerus
Brachioradialis
Extensor Carpi Radialis Longus
Extensor Carpi Radialis Brevis
Extensor Digitorum
Abductor Pollicis Longus
Extensor Pollicis Brevis
Extensor
Pollicis
Longus

Flexor Carpi Ulnaris
Extensor Digiti Minimi
Extensor Carpi Ulnaris
Extensor Digitorum
Anconeus
Lateral Epicondyle of Humerus
Triceps Brachii
Infraspinatus
Teres Major
Rhomboid
Latissimus Dorsi
External Oblique
Iliac Crest
Gluteus Medius
Tensor Fascia Latae
Gluteus Maximus
Greater Trochanter of Femur
Rectus Femoris
Iliotibial Band
Vastus Lateralis
Biceps Femoris

Rectus
Abdominis
Adductor Magnus
Semitendinosus
Semimembranosus
Rectus Femoris
Anconeus
Sartorius
Gracilis
Patella
Patella
Ligament
Tibia
Tibialis
Anterior

Gastrocnemius
Patella
Patella Ligament
Extensor Digitorum Longus
Tibialis Anterior

Gastrocnemius
Peroneus Longus
Peroneus Brevis
Achilles Tendon
Fibula

Soleus
Achilles Tendon

LATERAL

Full Figure Drawing

Even Tone

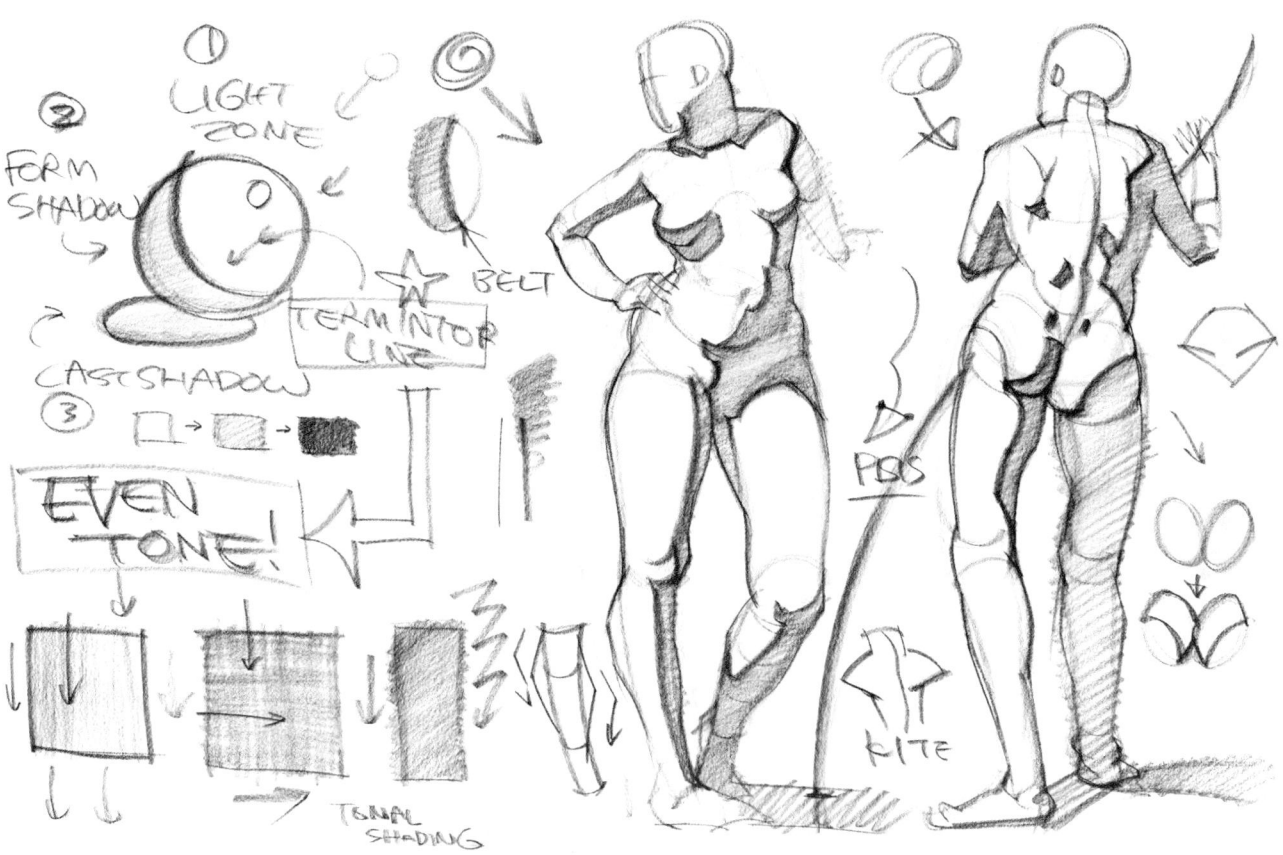

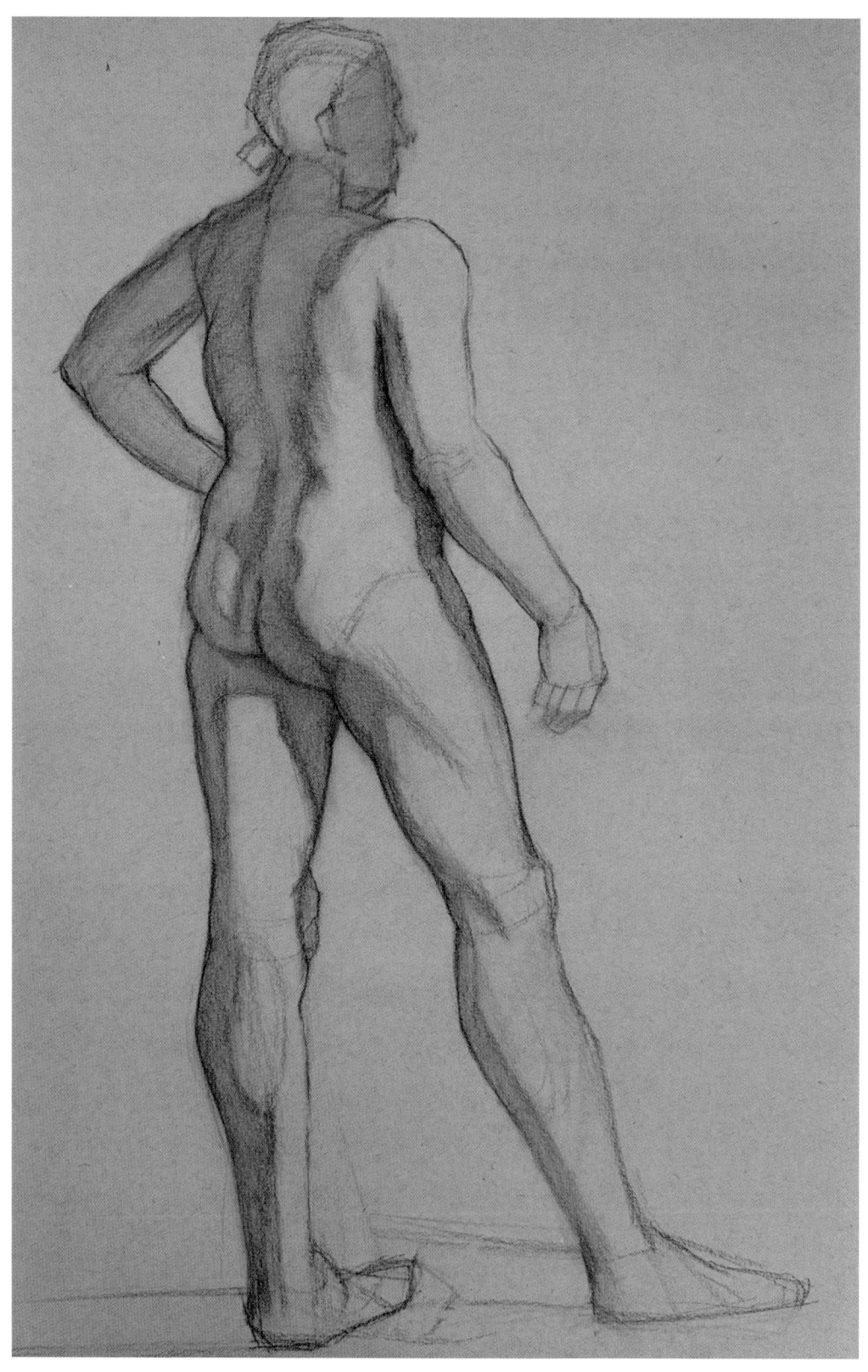

EVEN TONE: TWO-TONE VALUE

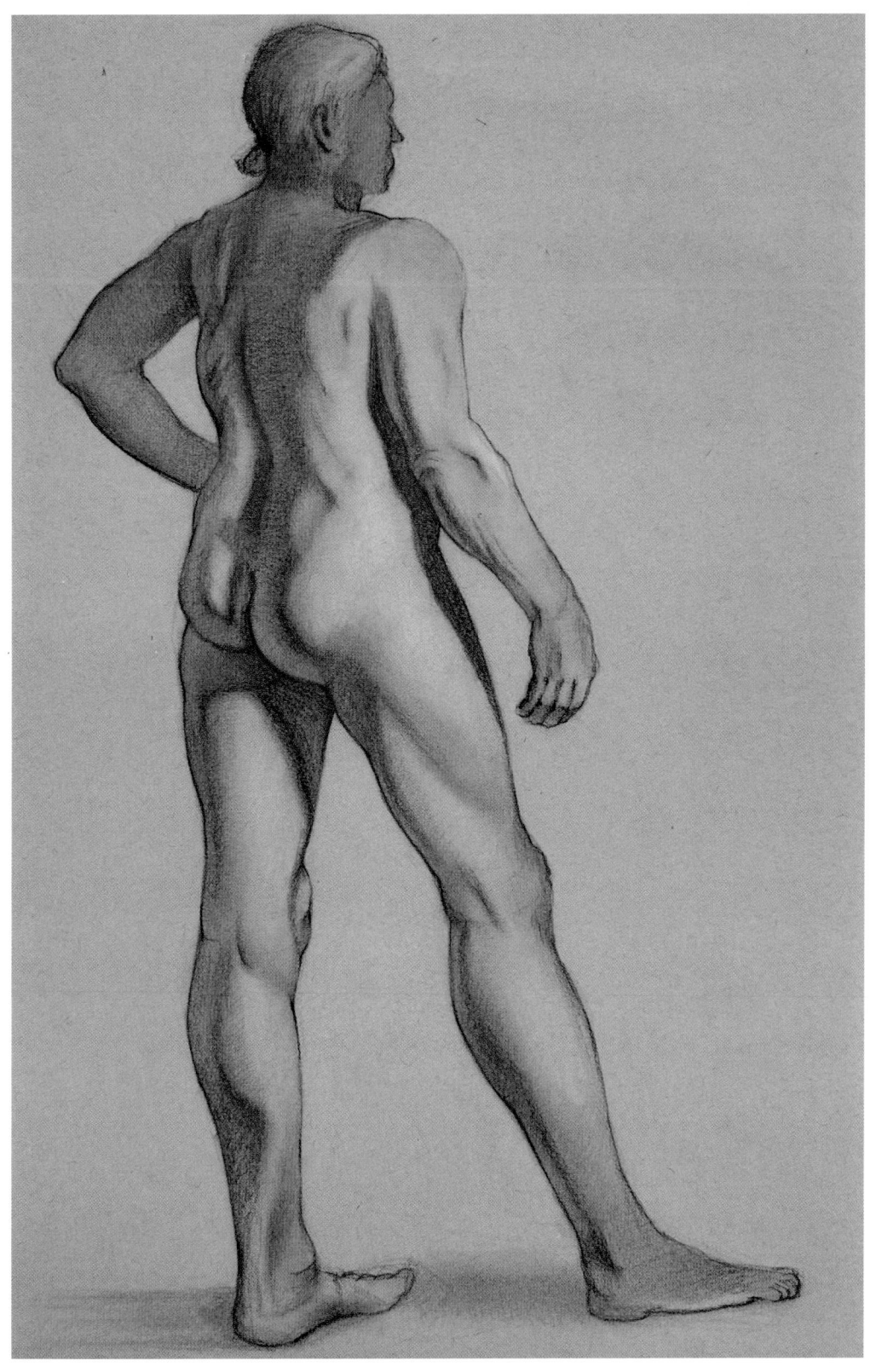

BLENDED: FULL-TONE VALUE

Full Tone

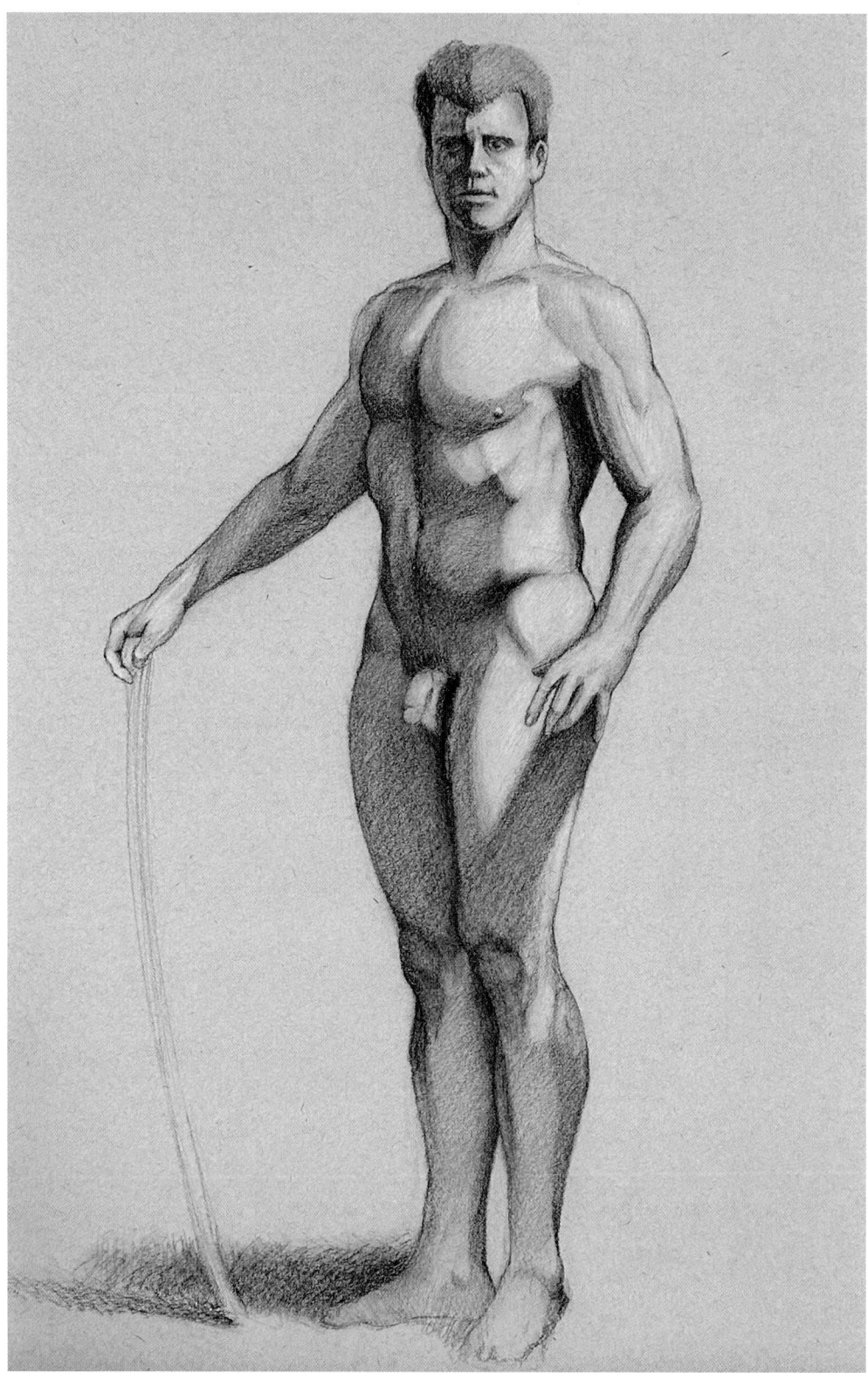

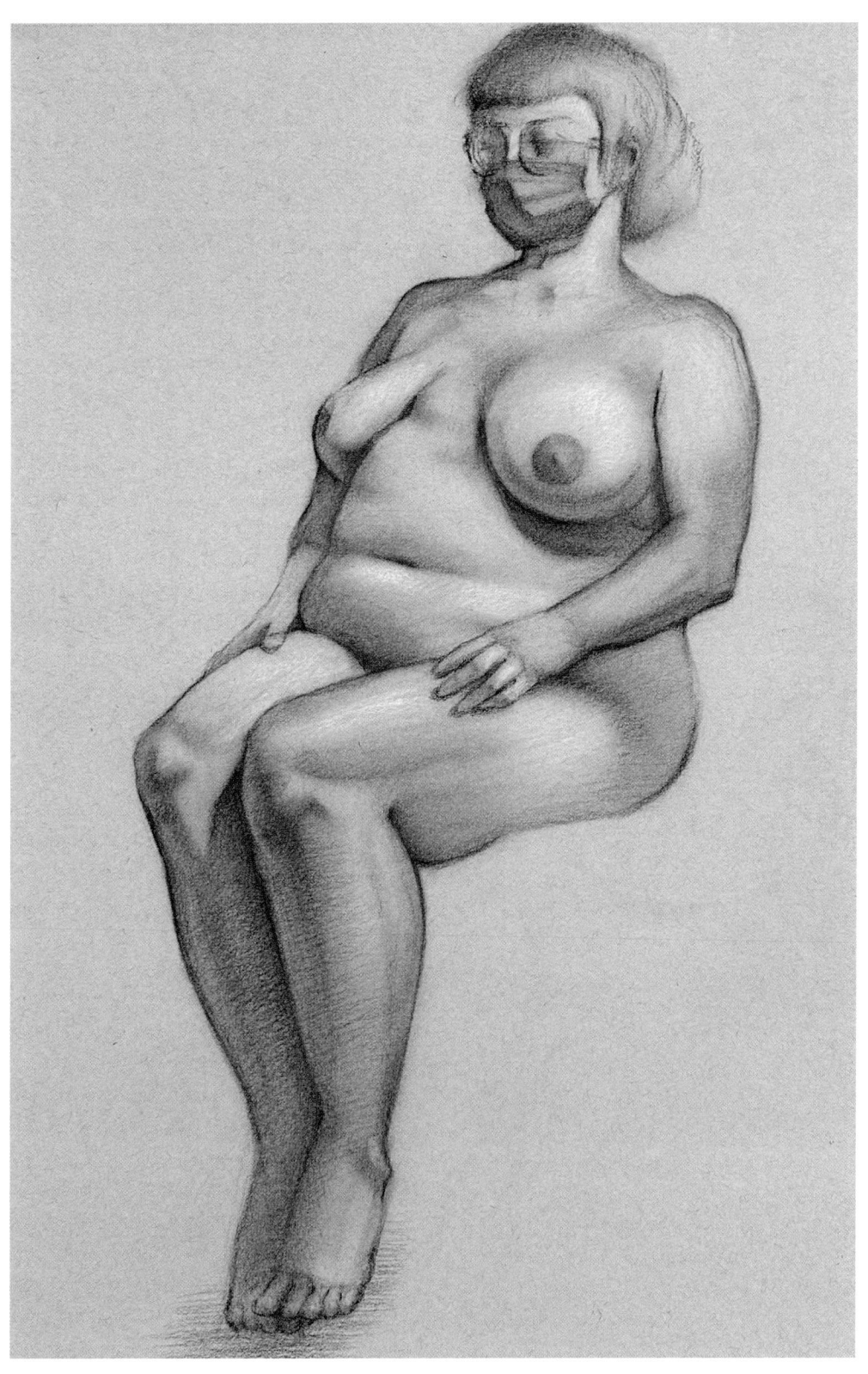

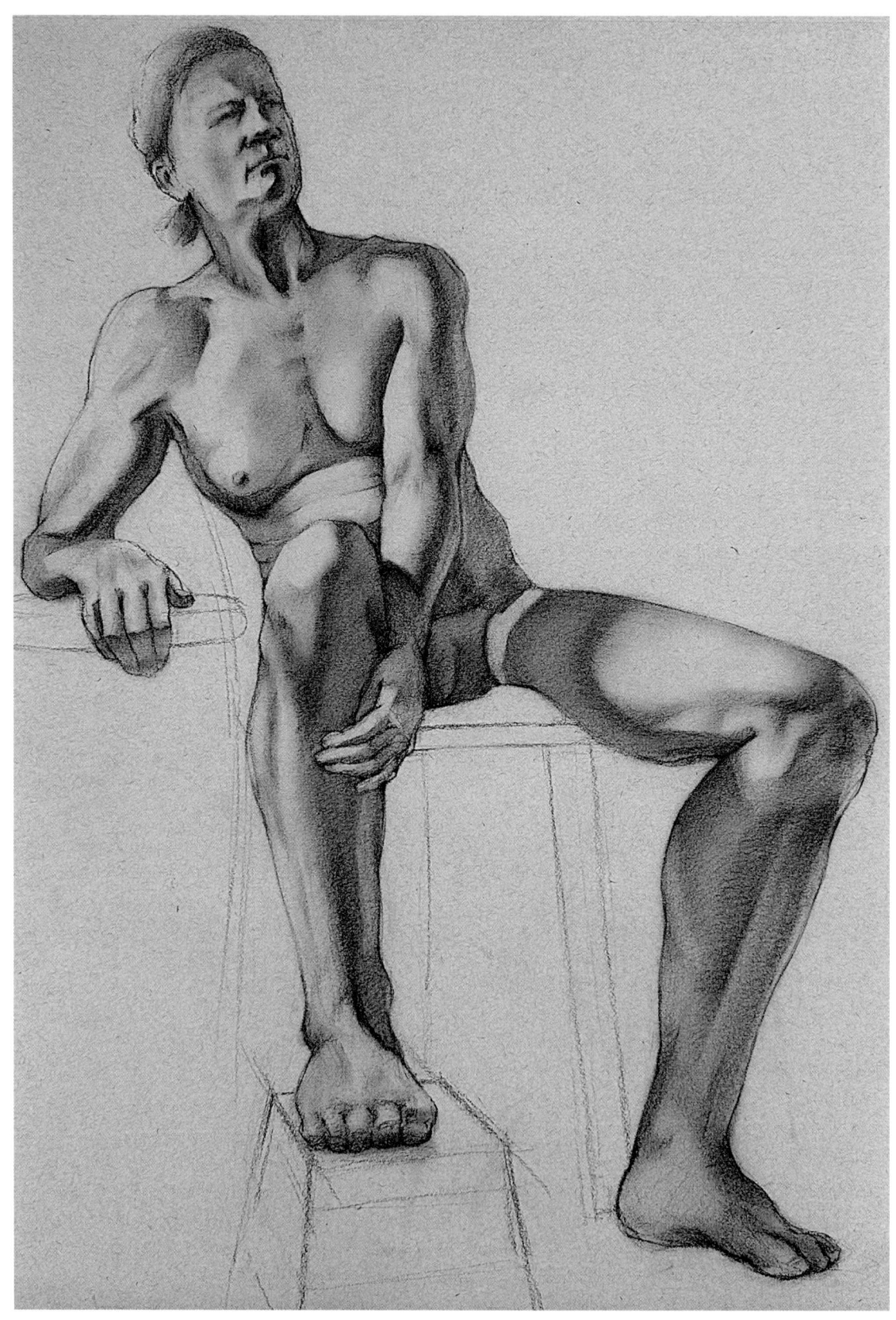

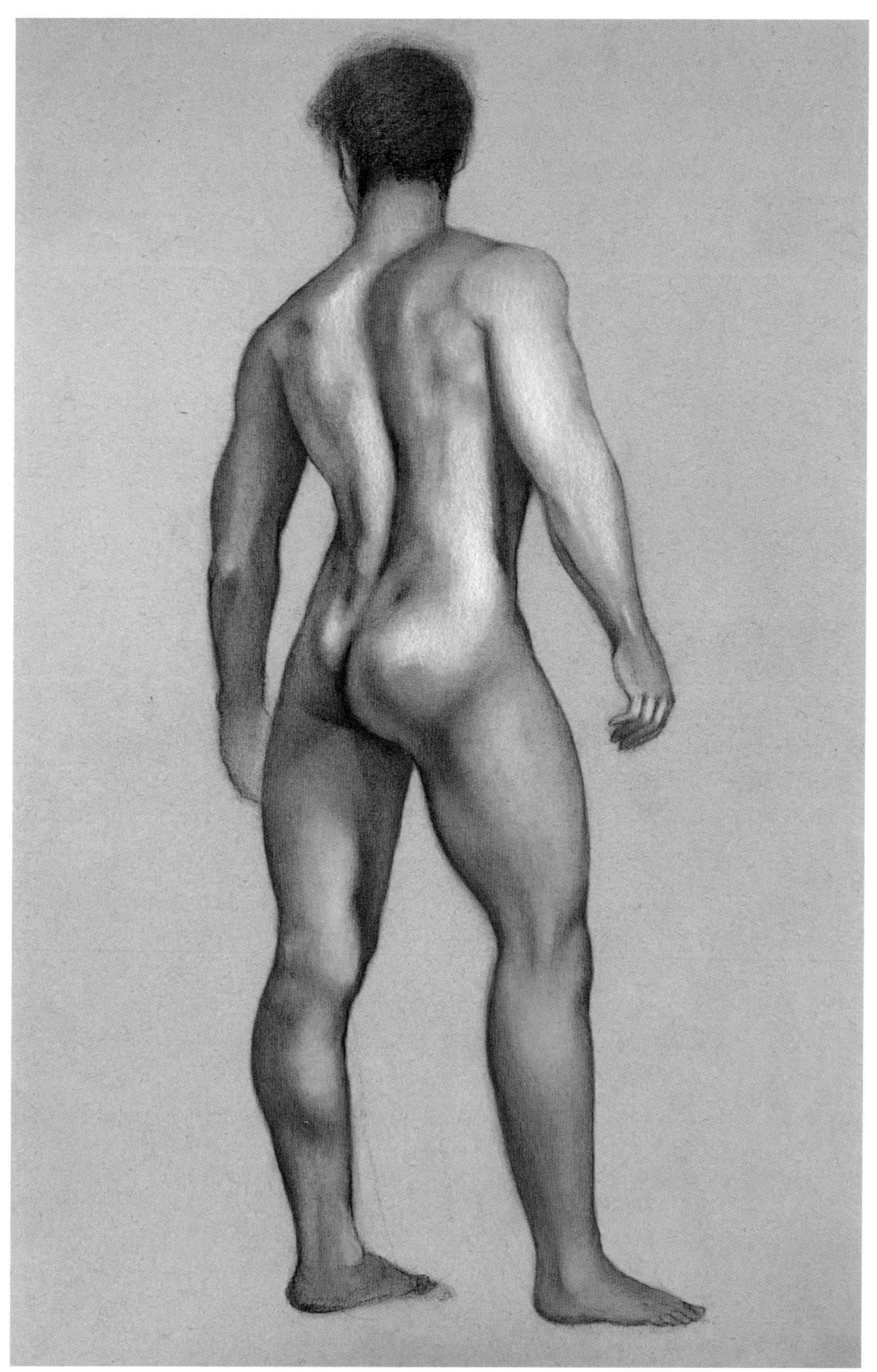

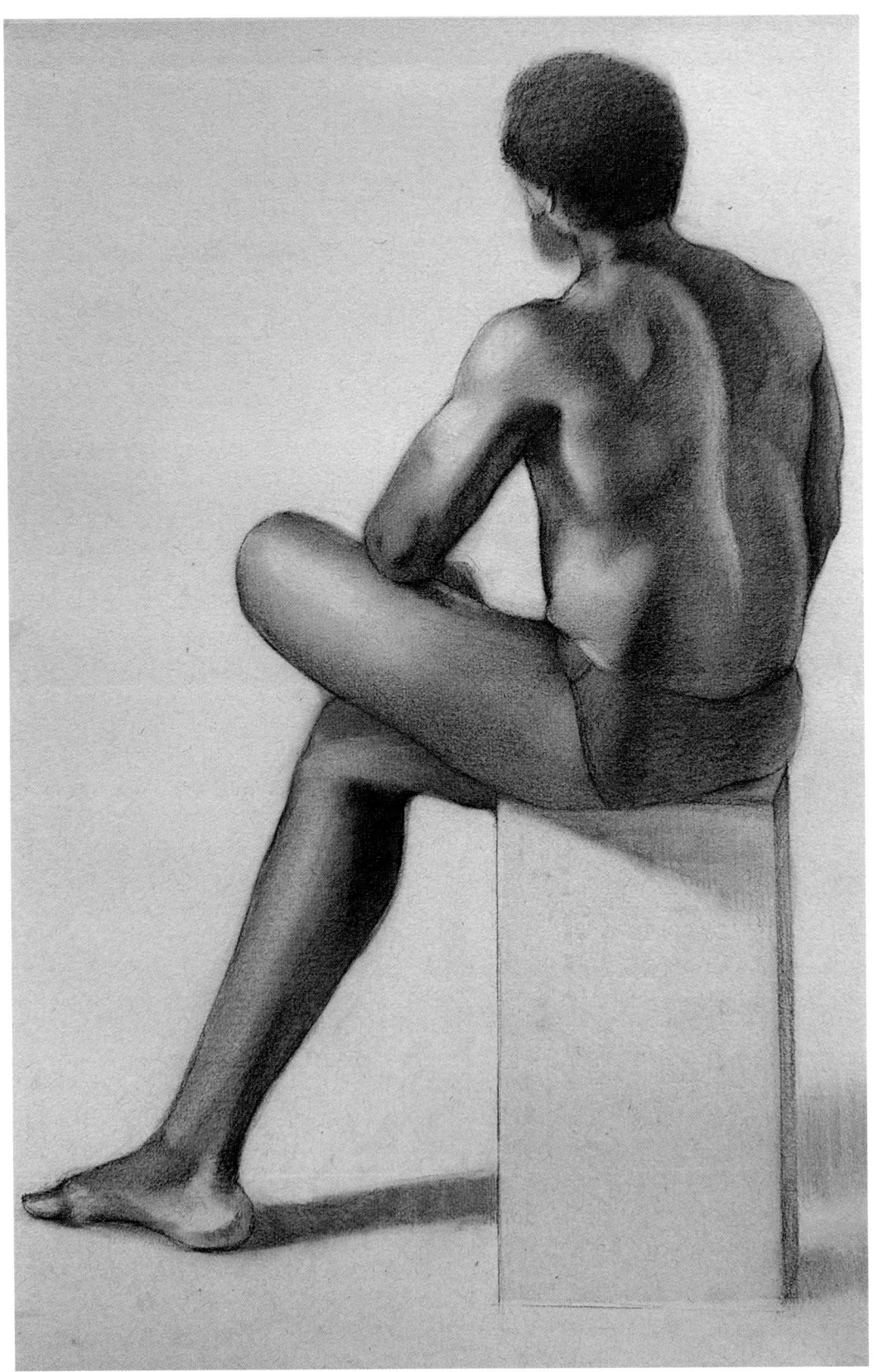

INDEX